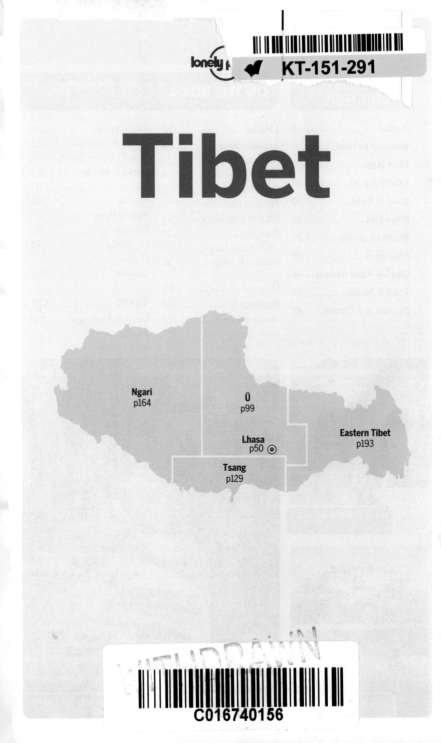

lonely KT-151-291

Tibet

Ngari
p164

Ü
p99

Eastern Tibet
p193

Lhasa
p50 ◉

Tsang
p129

C016740156

PLAN YOUR TRIP

ON THE ROAD

VLADIMIR ZHOGA / SHUTTERSTOCK ©

ASIA TRAVEL / SHUTTERSTOCK ©

DONAVAN / SHUTTERSTOCK ©

YAK AT YAMDROK-TSO P132

POTALA PALACE P64

MARKET STALL AT THE BARKHOR P53

Contents

UNDERSTAND

SURVIVAL GUIDE

SPECIAL FEATURES

Above: Prayer flags at Yamdrok-tso (p132)

Preface

THE DALAI LAMA

The issue of Tibet is not nearly as simple and clear cut as the Chinese government often tries to make out. I believe that there are still widespread misunderstandings about Tibetan culture and misapprehensions about what is happening inside Tibet. Therefore, I welcome every opportunity for open-minded people to discover the reality of Tibet for themselves.

In the context of the growing tourist industry in Tibet, the Lonely Planet travel guide makes an invaluable contribution by providing reliable and authoritative information about places to visit, how to get there, where to stay, where to eat and so forth. Presenting basic facts and observations allows visitors to prepare themselves for what they will encounter and exercise their own choice.

There is a Tibetan saying: 'The more you travel, the more you see and hear.' At a time when many people are not clear about what is actually happening in Tibet, I am very keen to encourage whoever has the interest to go there and see for themselves. Their presence will not only instil a sense of reassurance in the Tibetan people, but will also exercise a restraining influence on the Chinese authorities. What's more, I am confident that once they return home they will be able to report openly on what they have seen and heard.

Great changes have lately taken place in this part of the world. Recent events have made it very clear that all Tibetans harbour the same aspirations and hopes. I remain confident that eventually a mutually agreeable solution will be found to the Tibetan problem. I believe that our strictly non-violent approach, entailing constructive dialogue and negotiation, will ultimately attract effective support and sympathy from within the Chinese community. In the meantime, I am also convinced that as more people visit Tibet, the numbers of those who support the justice of a peaceful solution will grow.

I am grateful to everyone involved in the preparation of this 10th edition of the Lonely Planet guide to Tibet for the care and concern they have put into it. I trust that those who rely on it as a companion to their travels in Tibet will enjoy themselves in what, despite all that has happened, remains for me one of the most beautiful places on earth.

July 2018

Welcome to Tibet

Tibet offers fabulous monasteries, breathtaking high-altitude walks, stunning views of the world's highest mountains and one of the most likeable cultures you will ever encounter.

A Higher Plain

For many visitors, the highlights of Tibet will be of a spiritual nature: magnificent monasteries, prayer halls of chanting monks, and remote cliffside meditation retreats. Tibet's pilgrims – from local grandmothers murmuring mantras in temples heavy with the aromas of juniper incense and yak butter to hard-core professionals walking or prostrating themselves around Mt Kailash – are an essential part of this experience. Tibetans have a level of devotion and faith that seems to belong to an earlier, almost medieval age. It is fascinating, inspiring and endlessly photogenic.

The Roof of the World

Tibet's other big draw is the elemental beauty of the highest plateau on earth. Geography here is on a humbling scale and every view is illuminated with spectacular mountain light. Your trip will take you past glittering turquoise lakes, across huge plains dotted with yaks and nomads' tents, and over high passes draped with colourful prayer flags. Hike past the ruins of remote hermitages, stare open-mouthed at the north face of Everest or make an epic overland trip along some of the world's wildest roads. The scope for adventure is limited only by your ability to get permits.

Politics & Permits

There's no getting away from politics here. Whether you see Tibet as an oppressed, occupied nation or an underdeveloped province of China, the normal rules of Chinese travel simply don't apply. Restrictions require foreign travellers to pre-arrange a tour with a guide and transport for their time in Tibet, making independent travel impossible. On the plus side, new airports, boutique hotels and paved roads offer a level of comfort unheard of just a few years ago, so if the rigours of Tibetan travel have deterred you in the past, now might be the time to reconsider.

The Tibetan People

Whatever your interests, your lasting memories of Tibet are likely to be of the bottle of Lhasa Beer you shared in a teahouse, the yak-butter tea offered by a monk in a remote monastery or the picnic enjoyed with a herding family on the shores of a remote lake. Always ready with a disarming smile, and with great tolerance and openness of heart despite decades of political turmoil and hardship, the people truly make travelling in Tibet a profound joy. Make sure you budget time away from your pre-planned tour itinerary to take advantage of these chance encounters.

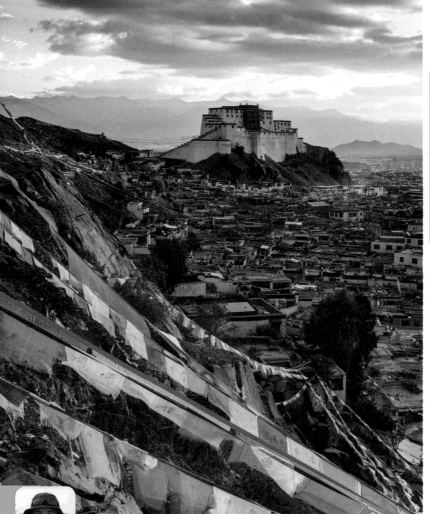

Why I Love Tibet

By Bradley Mayhew, Writer

For me Tibet is a uniquely spiritual place. Those moments of peace, fleeting and precious, when everything seems to be in its proper place, just seem to come more frequently here. Despite the overpowering pace of change and a sobering political situation, underpinning everything for me are the Tibetan people, whose joy and devotion remain deeply inspiring. Tibet is a place that will likely change the way you see the world and remain with you for years to come. And that for me is the definition of the very best kind of travel.

For more about our writers, see p352

Above: Tashilhunpo Monastery (p143), Shigatse

Tibet

Nam-tso
A taste of the Changtang
northern plateau (p104)

CHINA

XINJIANG

Qiemo

Karghilik (Yecheng)

Potala Palace
Spectacular fortress home
of the Dalai Lamas (p64)

Kunlun Shan

Xinjiang–Tibet Hwy

Yutian (Keriya)

Drepung & Sera Monasteries
Great monastic cities
(p84 & p89)

Mt Kailash
Asia's most sacred
mountain (p185)

Sumzhi

Changtang Nature
Preserve

Guge Kingdom & Tsaparang
Lost kingdom of exquisite
Kashmiri-style art (p179)

Rutok
Xian

Dormar

Tsaphuk

**Nganglong Kangri
(6596m)**

CHANGTANG
(NORTHERN
PLATEAU)

Tashigang

Ali

Chaktsakha

Gar Dzong

Gegye

Tsaka

Oma-chu

Dzango
Tsangon

Tsaparang

Namru

Zhungba

Gertse

Zanda
(Tholing)

Ba'er

Lhadrong

INDIA

Moincer

**Mt Kailash
(6714m)**

*Tagste-
tso*

Dongpo

Darchen

Tsochen

Ombu

Zangdo

**Nanda Devi
(7816m)**

Barkha

Hor Qu

Gangtse Range

Tuoya

*Tsari
Najn-tso*

*Dangru-
tso*

*Lake
Manasarovar*

Saipal
(7050m)

Simikot

Paryang

Friendship Highway
Epic Lhasa–Kathmandu
overland trip (p325)

Great Himalaya Range

Zhongba

*Phuntso
Monaste*

Raka

Delhi

NEPAL

Mustang

Saga

Yarlung Tsangpo

Shigatse

Peiku-tso

Dzongkhar

Lhatse

Sakya Monastery
Atmospheric, timeless and
full of sacred relics (p150)

Pokhara

Kyirong

Siling

Gutso

Shegar

Sakya

Rasuwagadhi

Kodari

**Mt Everest
(8848m)**

Lucknow

Kathmandu

**Kanchenjunga
(8598m)**

Yatun

Gangtok

INDIA

Mt Everest
Unsurpassed views of the
north face (p153)

BANGLADES

Gyantse Kumbum
A Tibetan architectural and
artistic masterpiece (p135)

The external boundaries of India on
this map have not been authenticated
and may not be correct.

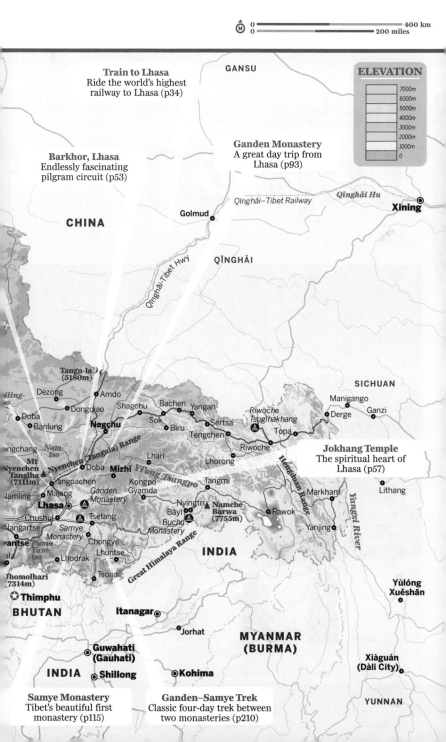

Train to Lhasa
Ride the world's highest railway to Lhasa (p34)

Barkhor, Lhasa
Endlessly fascinating pilgram circuit (p53)

Ganden Monastery
A great day trip from Lhasa (p93)

ELEVATION

7000m
6000m
5000m
4000m
3000m
2000m
1000m
0

GANSU

Qīnghǎi–Tibet Railway

Qīnghǎi Hu

Xining

Golmud

CHINA

Qīnghǎi–Tibet Hwy

QĪNGHǍI

SICHUAN

Manigango

Tangu-la
(5180m)

Dezong

Amdo

Shagchu

Bachen

Yangan

Riwoche Tsuglhakhang

Derge

Ganzi

ling-
o

Doba

Dongqiao

Nagchu

Sok

Biru

Sertsa

Tengchen

Topa

Banlung

Riwoche

ngchang

Nam-tso

Nyenchen (Tangula) Range

Lhari

Lhorong

Mt
Nyenchen
Tanglha
(7111m)

Doba

Mízhí

Yi'ong Tsangpo

Tangmi

Hengduan Range

Markham

Lithang

Jokhang Temple
The spiritual heart of Lhasa (p57)

Yangpachen

Kongpo
Gyamda

Majang

Ganden Monastery

Lhasa

Chushul

Tsetang

Nyingtri

Bayi

Namche Barwa
(7755m)

Buchu Monastery

Rawok

Yangzi River

Yanjing

Nangartse

Samye Monastery

Chongye

Lhuntse

ala

antse

Puma Yum-tso

Lhodrak

Tsona

Great Himalaya Range

INDIA

Yùlóng
Xuěshān

Jhomolhari
(7314m)

Thimphu

BHUTAN

Itanagar

Jorhat

MYANMAR
(BURMA)

Xiàguán
(Dàlǐ City)

Guwahati
(Gauhati)

INDIA

Shillong

Kohima

YUNNAN

Samye Monastery
Tibet's beautiful first monastery (p115)

Ganden–Samye Trek
Classic four-day trek between two monasteries (p210)

0 — 400 km
0 — 200 miles

Tibet's
Top 20

Mt Kailash, Ngari

1 Worshipped by more than a billion Buddhists and Hindus, Asia's most sacred mountain (p185) rises from the Barkha plain like a giant four-sided 6714m chörten (Buddhist stupa). Throw in the stunning nearby Lake Manasarovar and a basin that forms the source of four of Asia's greatest rivers, and who's to say this place really isn't the centre of the world? Travel here to one of the world's most beautiful and remote corners brings an added bonus: the three-day pilgrim path around the mountain erases the sins of a lifetime. Below left: Pilgrims completing the kora around the mountain.

Barkhor Circuit, Lhasa

2 You never know quite what you're going to find when you join the centrifugal tide of Tibetans circling the Jokhang Temple on the Barkhor Circuit (p53). Pilgrims and prostrators from across Tibet, stalls selling prayer wheels and turquoise, Muslim traders, Khampa nomads in shaggy cloaks, women from Amdo sporting 108 braids, thangka (religious painting) artists and Chinese military patrols are all par for the course. It's a fascinating microcosm of Tibet and a place you'll come back to again and again.

YONGYUT KUMSRI / SHUTTERSTOCK ©

DOMINIC BYRNE / AGE FOTOSTOCK ©

Potala Palace, Lhasa

3 There are moments in travel that will long stay with you, and your first view of Lhasa's iconic Potala Palace (p64) is one such moment. A visit to the former home of the Dalai Lamas is a spiralling descent past gold-tombed chapels, opulent reception rooms and huge prayer halls into the bowels of a medieval castle. It's nothing less than the concentrated spiritual and material wealth of a nation. Finish by joining the pilgrims on a walking kora (pilgrim circuit) of the entire grounds.

Jokhang Temple, Lhasa

4 The atmosphere of hushed awe is what hits you first as you inch through the dark, medieval passageways of the Jokhang (p57), Lhasa's most sacred temple. Queues of wide-eyed pilgrims shuffle up and down the stairways, past medieval doorways and millennium-old murals, pausing briefly to stare in awe at golden buddhas or to top up the hundreds of butter lamps that flicker in the gloom. It's the beating spiritual heart of Tibet, despite some damage caused by a fire in 2018. Welcome to the 14th century.

Views of Mt Everest

5 Don't tell the Nepal Tourism Board, but Tibet has easily the best views of the world's most famous mountain from its northern base camp (p153). While two-week trekking routes on the Nepal side offer only fleeting glimpses of the peak, in Tibet you can drive on a paved road right up to unobstructed views of Mt Everest's incredible north face framed in the prayer flags of Rongphu Monastery. Bring a sleeping bag, some headache tablets and a prayer for clear skies.

Samye Monastery

6 Tibet's first monastery (p116) is a heavily symbolic collection of chapels, chörtens and shrines arranged around a medieval Tibetan-, Chinese- and Indian-style temple. The 1200-year-old site is where Guru Rinpoche battled demons to introduce Buddhism to Tibet and where the future course of Tibetan Buddhism was sealed in a great debate. The dreamy location on the desert-like banks of the Yarlung Tsangpo is just superb and there are some fine hiking excursions nearby. It's also the end point of Tibet's most popular trekking route.

SERGIU TURCANU / ALAMY STOCK PHOTO ©

Train Ride to Lhasa

7 For all its faults, China's railway to Tibet (the world's highest) is an engineering wonder and a delightful way to reach the holy city. Pull up a window seat to view huge salt lakes, plains dotted with yaks and herders' tents, and hundreds of miles of desolate nothing, as you inch slowly up onto the high plateau. Peaking at 5072m may send you diving for the piped oxygen, but it's still a classic rail trip (p34). Train-travel addicts can now extend the journey by taking the side spur to Shigatse.

Drepung & Sera Monasteries, Lhasa

8 Lhasa's institutions of Sera (p89) and Drepung (p84; above right) are more than monasteries – they are self-contained towns. A web of alleyways climbs past medieval kitchens, printing presses and colleges to reach giant prayer halls full of chanting, tea-sipping, red-robed monks. Don't miss the afternoon debating, a sport of Buddhist dialectics and hand slapping. Best of all, both monasteries are encircled by pilgrim paths that offer fine views, Buddhist rock paintings and plenty of pilgrims.

Saga Dawa Festival

9 The line between tourist and pilgrim can be a fine one in Tibet, and never more so than during the Saga Dawa Festival (p26), when thousands of pilgrims pour into Lhasa to visit the city and make a ritual procession around the 8km Lingkhor path. Load up on small bills and juniper incense before joining the pilgrims past chapels and prostration points, or travel west to Mt Kailash for the mountain's biggest annual party. There are also monastery festivals around this time in Tsurphu and Gyantse.

Guge Kingdom, Ngari

10 The spectacular lost kingdom of Guge (p179) at Tsaparang is quite unlike anything you'll see in central Tibet; it feels more like Ladakh than Lhasa. As you are lowering yourself down a hidden sandstone staircase or crawling through an interconnected cave complex, there's a moment when you can't help but stop and think: 'This is incredible!' What's really amazing is that you'll likely have the half-forgotten ruins to yourself. Rank this as one of Asia's great travel secrets.

FENG WEI PHOTOGRAPHY / GETTY IMAGES ©

HAKAT / SHUTTERSTOCK ©

Ganden Monastery

11 A 90-minute drive from Lhasa takes you to the stunning location of Ganden (p93), set in a natural bowl high above the braided Kyi-chu Valley. Brought back to life after nearly total destruction during the Cultural Revolution, the collection of restored chapels centres on the tomb of Tsongkhapa (the 14th-century founder of the important Gelugpa school), and boasts two delightful kora paths that offer fabulous views and will soon have you breathing hard from the altitude. If you only make one excursion from Lhasa, let it be to Ganden.

Ganden–Samye Trek

12 Tibet is one of those places you really should experience away from the tour-group circuit, at the pace of one foot in front of the other. This classic four-day trek (p210) between two of Tibet's most important monasteries takes you past herders' camps, high alpine lakes and a Guru Rinpoche hermitage, as well as over two 5000m-plus passes. Hire a horse or yaks for a wonderful wilderness trek, with just the marmots for company. May to October are the best months.

Nam-tso

13 Just a few hours north of Lhasa, spectacular Nam-tso (p105) epitomises the dramatic but harsh scenery of northern Tibet. This deep blue salt lake is fringed by prayer-flag-draped hills, craggy cliffs and nesting migratory birds, all framed by a horizon of snow-capped 7000m peaks. Walking the kora path at dusk with a band of pilgrims is superb. It's cold, increasingly developed and devastatingly beautiful. To see the lake at its best, try to minimise your time in the ugly and poorly planned accommodation centre.

Gyantse Kumbum

14 The giant chörten at Gyantse (p135) ranks as one of Tibet's great artistic treasures and is unique in the Himalayas. As you spiral around and up the snail-shell-shaped building, you pass dozens of dim alcoves full of serene painted buddhas and bloodthirsty Tantric demons. It's an unrivalled collection of early Tibetan art. Finally, you pop out onto the golden eaves, underneath all-seeing eyes, for fabulous views of Gyantse fort and old town. An added bonus is the attached monastery complex.

Adding Your Prayer Flags to a High Pass

15 Crossing a pass to view a horizon of Himalayan peaks is an almost daily experience in Tibet. Join your driver in crying a breathless 'so, so, so' and throwing squares of paper into the air like good-luck confetti, as the prayer flags flap and crackle in the wind. Better still, add your own to a pass's collection for some super-good karma. Our suggestions: try the Khamba-la (p132; bottom) overlooking Yamdrok-tso, or the Gyatso-la, near Lhatse and the highest pass on the Friendship Hwy.

PLAN YOUR TRIP TIBET'S TOP 20

14

15

Koras & Pilgrims

16 All over Tibet you'll see wizened elderly pilgrims twirling prayer wheels, rubbing sacred rocks and walking around temples, monasteries and sometimes even entire mountains. It's a fantastic fusion of the spiritual and the physical, and there are few better ways of spending an hour than joining a merry band of pilgrims on a monastery kora. En route you'll pass rock paintings and sacred spots, and you'll probably be invited to an impromptu picnic. Our favourite? Shigatse's Tashilhunpo Kora (p146; below).

Friendship Highway: Lhasa to Kathmandu

17 A 4WD trip across Tibet is the quintessential travel experience. You'll have to overcome the permit system and brave terrible toilets, but the rewards are ample: stunning vistas such as those around Yamdrok-tso (p132), little-visited monasteries, a sense of journey and a giant slice of adventure. At the end of the trip you drop off the plateau through alpine forests into the oxygen-rich and curry-scented valleys bordering Nepal. Figure on at least a week; the hard-core can cycle the route.

Sakya Monastery

18 A 25km detour off the main Friendship Hwy takes you to this brooding, massive, grey-walled fortress-like building (p150). In a land of magnificent monasteries, Sakya's main prayer halls are among the most impressive, lined with towering buddhas, tree-trunk-sized pillars, sacred relics, a three-storey library that ranks as Tibet's finest, and a fine kora path. Pilgrims come here from across western Tibet, adding to the colour and charm. Give yourself most of the day to explore monastery complexes on both sides of the river.

Peiku-tso & Shishapangma

19 Tibet is not short on spectacular, remote, turquoise-blue lakes. Of these, none boasts a grander backdrop than little-visited Peiku-tso (p169) near Tibet's southern border with Nepal. Rising south of the huge lake is a wall of glaciers and Himalayan peaks crowned by 8027m giant Shishapangma (top right), the tallest mountain wholly inside Tibet. The lake makes a great picnic or camping spot en route to western Tibet or to the new border crossing with Nepal's Langtang region at Kyirong. Tibet doesn't get wilder or more scenic than this hidden corner.

Rawok-tso Lakes

20 In a land of spectacularly remote, turquoise lakes, none surpasses the crystal-clear waters, sandy beaches and snowcapped peaks of Rawok-tso (p202) and nearby Ngan-tso (above right), way out in eastern Tibet, and more reminiscent of the Canadian Rockies than anything on the high plateau. Stay overnight at a hotel on stilts above the lake and explore the nearby Mikdo Glacier during the day. Even better, continue east on the wild overland route from Tibet through the river gorges of Kham to northwestern Yúnnán. Welcome to a completely different kind of Tibet.

Need to Know

For more information, see Survival Guide (p307)

Currency
Rénmínbì, or yuán (¥)

Language
Tibetan, Mandarin Chinese

Visas
A valid Chinese visa is required. A Tibet Tourism Bureau (TTB) permit is also required to enter Tibet.

Money
ATMs are available in Lhasa, Shigatse and a couple of other towns. Credit cards can be used in Lhasa. Otherwise bring cash US dollars and euros.

Mobile Phones
Buy an inexpensive local pay-as-you-go SIM or data card for cheap local calls, but get it before arriving in Tibet. Buying a mobile phone in China is cheap and easy.

Time
China Time (GMT/UTC plus eight hours)

When to Go

Mt Kailash
GO May–Sep

Nagchu
GO Jun–Aug

Lhasa
GO Apr–Oct

Bayi
GO Feb–Nov

Everest Base Camp
GO May–Sep

Desert, dry climate
Warm to hot summers, mild winters
Mild to hot summers, cold winters
Cold climate

High Season (May–mid-Oct)

➡ The warmest weather makes travel, trekking and transport easiest.

➡ Prices are at their highest, peaking in July and August.

➡ Book ahead during the 1 May and 1 October national holidays.

Shoulder (Apr & mid-Oct–Nov)

➡ The slightly colder weather means fewer travellers and a better range of vehicles.

➡ Prices are 20% cheaper than during high season.

Low Season (Dec–Feb)

➡ Very few people visit Tibet in winter, so you'll have key attractions largely to yourself.

➡ Hotel prices and many entry tickets are discounted by up to 50%, but some restaurants close.

➡ Tibet is closed to foreign tourists in March.

Useful Websites

Land of Snows (www.thelandof snows.com) Inspirational and practical travel advice, including on Tibetan areas outside the Tibet Autonomous Region (TAR).

Phayul (www.phayul.com) Good for Tibet-related news.

Central Tibetan Administration (www.tibet.net) The view from Dharamsala.

China Tibet Information Center (http://eng.tibet. cn) News from the Chinese perspective.

Tibetpedia (www.tibetpedia. com) Travel inspiration on Tibet inside and outside the TAR.

Lonely Planet (www.lonely planet.com/tibet) Destination information, hotel bookings, traveller forum and more.

Important Numbers

China's country code	☑86
International access code	☑00
Ambulance	☑120
Fire	☑119
Police	☑110

Exchange Rates

Australia	A$1	¥5
Canada	C$1	¥4.90
Eurozone	€1	¥7.80
Japan	¥100	¥5.90
Nepal	Rs100	¥6
New Zealand	NZ$1	¥4.60
UK	UK£1	¥8.80
US	US$1	¥6.30

For current exchange rates, see www.xe.com.

Daily Costs

Budget: Less than US$75

➡ One-way hard sleeper Xīníng–Lhasa train: US$75

➡ Room without bathroom: US$8–12

➡ Meal in local restaurant: US$5

Midrange: US$75–150

➡ One-way flight to Lhasa from Kathmandu: US$280–400

➡ One-way flight to Lhasa from Chéngdū: US$180–260

➡ Daily shared vehicle rental per person: US$50–60

➡ Double room with bathroom: US$30–60

➡ Potala Palace entry ticket: US$30

Top End: More than US$150

➡ Boutique or four-star hotel in Lhasa: US$90–150

➡ Main course in a top restaurant in Lhasa: US$8–10

Opening Hours

Opening hours listed are for summer; winter hours generally start half an hour later and finish half an hour earlier.

Government Offices & PSB 9.30am to 1pm and 3pm to 6.30pm Monday to Friday, sometimes 10am to 1pm Saturday

Banks 9.30am to 5.30pm Monday to Friday, 10.30am to 4pm Saturday and Sunday

Restaurants 10am to 10pm

Shops 10am to 9pm

Bars May close at 8pm or 2am, depending on their location and clientele

Arriving in Tibet

Gongkar Airport Your tour guide will meet you in your rented vehicle. Taxis are ¥300 to Lhasa.

Lhasa Train Station Your tour guide will pick you up in your rented vehicle. Taxis cost around ¥30 to Lhasa's old town.

China-Nepal Border Kyirong/ Rasuwagadhi Your tour guide and driver will meet you at the China customs post just across the border bridge.

Getting Around

Tibet's transport infrastructure has developed rapidly in recent years. Most of the main highways are now paved. Airports are springing up across the plateau and the railway line is slowly extending beyond Lhasa. In 2011 Tibet's Metok county was the very last of China's 2100 counties to be connected by road.

Car The only way to travel around Tibet at the moment, since foreign travellers have to hire private transport as part of their obligatory tour.

Train Great for getting to and from Tibet but of limited use inside Tibet, unless you are just taking a short trip from Lhasa to Shigatse and back.

Bus Lots of services, but foreigners are currently not allowed to take buses or shared taxis in Tibet.

For much more on **getting around**, see p323

PLAN YOUR TRIP NEED TO KNOW

If You Like...

Off-the-Beaten-Track Monasteries

Beyond Lhasa's famous monastic cities there are hundreds of smaller, lesser-visited places, each holding their own treasures and with more local pilgrims than tour-group hordes.

Phuntsoling Monastery Remote, little visited and with a spectacular location. (p158)

Dorje Drak Monastery A dramatic location and great kora path surrounded by sand dunes and the braided Yarlung Tsangpo river. (p113)

Korjak Monastery Delightful and quirky monastery at the far western end of Tibet, near the border with Nepal. (p191)

Thöling Monastery The unique frescoes hidden in the remote western Guge Kingdom offer a sublime fusion of Kashmiri and Tibetan styles. (p180)

Reting Monastery Historically important monastery with a fine kora, a guesthouse and a charming nearby nunnery. (p107)

Trekking & Hiking

Trekking 'the roof of the world' isn't easy. The altitude, weather and rugged terrain present significant challenges, but the following trails take hardy walkers into some timeless corners of Tibet.

Ganden to Samye A classic four-day mountain walk between two of Tibet's most important monasteries. (p210)

Dode Valley Hike It's hard to imagine a better way to spend half a day in Lhasa, with the best views in the city. (p92)

Tsurphu to Dorje Ling Get a taste of the wild northern plateau on this high three-day trek past herding camps and nomads' tents. (p215)

Samding Monastery The ridge behind Samding reveals 360-degree views of three lakes, and snow-capped Himalayan giants as far away as Bhutan. (p133)

Chiu Monastery Get a taste of the Manasarovar kora trek on half-day lakeshore walks to/from Gossul Monastery or Langbona Monastery. (p189)

Palaces, Forts & Temples

There's more to Tibet than just monasteries. This mix of spectacular buildings represents a millennium of Tibetan history.

Potala Palace Towering home to the Dalai Lamas, full of priceless Tibetan art and jewel-studded tombs. (p64)

Gyantse Dzong Pack your pith helmet and grow your best Younghusband moustache for this ruined fort with views over Gyantse's old town. (p138)

Tsaparang Your inner Indiana Jones will love the caves, tunnels and hidden stairways of this ruined cliff-side city. (p182)

Gyantse Kumbum One of the great repositories of Tibetan art and a masterpiece of Himalayan architecture. (p135)

Jampaling Kumbum The impressive ruins of Tibet's largest stupa stand as a silent testament to the destruction of the Cultural Revolution. (p127)

Incredible Scenery

Whether it's the rolling grasslands of the north, Mars-like deserts of the west, snow-capped Himalayan views to the south or the huge valleys and gigantic lakes of the centre, all of Tibet is blessed with amazing high-altitude colours.

Everest Base Camp Jaw-dropping views of the north face that are so much better than from the Nepal side. (p153)

Northern Route, Ngari Herds of antelope and wild ass graze

by huge saltwater lakes in this empty end of the world. (p172)

Eastern Tibet Sublime Swiss-style pine forests, green valleys and jagged peaks reveal the other face of little-visited Kham (eastern Tibet). (p193)

Sutlej Valley Look out over weird eroded bluffs and former seabeds towards epic views of the Indian Himalaya. (p179)

Tsari Nam-tso Stunning salt lake lined by cliffs on the remote Changtang Plateau of north-western Tibet. (p173)

PLAN YOUR TRIP IF YOU LIKE...

Cultural Encounters

Simple daily pleasures abound in Tibet. Whether it's spinning prayer wheels with a Tibetan granny, breathing in the heady fragrance of juniper incense or wondering at the devotion in a pilgrim's prostrations, the following encounters will show you Tibet through Tibetan eyes.

Tibetan teahouses Kick back with a thermos of sweet, milky tea and the world is instantly a better place. (p79)

Koras Join a happy band of pilgrims for some prayer-wheel turning, prostrations and a sin test. (p88)

Nangma A Tibetan nightclub is a mix of karaoke, line dancing and *American Idol,* but it's also very Tibetan. (p79)

Chang and butter tea Join the locals for a jerrycan of home-brewed barley beer or a never-ending cup of butter tea. (p304)

Festivals Tibetan cultural life finds its best expression through festivals, opera, horse racing and some epic picnics. (p25)

Top: Thöling Monastery (p180), Ngari

Bottom: Horse-racing festival Tsara, near Lhasa

Pilgrim Paths

Tibet's koras (pilgrim routes) are the keys to its soul. From 30m-long paths around an inner sanctum to month-long treks around a holy peak, koras are the ultimate fusion of mind and body, and the easiest way to meet Tibetans on their own terms.

Mt Kailash One of the world's great pilgrimages – a three-day walk around Asia's holiest mountain. (p221)

Ganden Monastery Choose between the high kora with awesome views and the lower route, lined with sacred rocks and shrines. (p93)

Sera Monastery A delightful walk past painted rock carvings with great views over monastery roofs. (p91)

Barkhor Lhasa's most interesting stroll, endlessly fascinating every time. (p53)

Tashilhunpo Monastery A fine hike that connects Shigatse's main monastery, old town and restored fort, revealing the town's best views. (p143)

Overland Trips

From all four directions the overland routes to Lhasa deliver some of the world's most spectacular scenery and one of the plateau's quintessential travelling experiences.

Lhasa to Kathmandu The classic week-long road trip that delivers the highlights of the plateau. (p29)

Qīnghǎi–Tibet Railway Ride the world's highest railroad past rolling grasslands dotted with yaks. (p34)

Ngari The northern route to Kailash offers scenery, wildlife and isolation unparalleled even in Tibet. (p172)

Yarlung Valley Just an hour from Lhasa and yet totally off the beaten track, a trip here takes in sacred caves, Tibet's first monastery and its oldest statues. (p123)

Kyirong Valley Tibet's brand new Himalayan crossing starts with an epic switchbacking descent into Bhutan-like alpine scenery. (p160)

Lakes

There's nothing quite so blue as the deep turquoise of a high-altitude Tibetan lake. Whether sacred or just plain scenic, the following beauties beg you to pitch a tent or unwrap a picnic.

Manasarovar Yin to nearby Kailash's yang, sacred Mapham Yum-tso is utterly surreal in its beauty. (p188)

Nam-tso Huge tidal salt lake lined with caves and a kora route – a traveller favourite. (p105)

Rawok-tso A strong contender for Tibet's prettiest lake, fringed by sandy beaches and snowy peaks, with glaciers around the corner. (p202)

Tagyel-tso Dramatic detour from the road to Kailash and a great place to spot wildlife. (p172)

Yamdrok-tso Central Tibet's dramatic snaking-scorpion lake. Soak in the views on the short hike down from the Kamba-la. (p132)

Outdoor Activities

Current travel restrictions make DIY adventures difficult, but if you arrange things beforehand or join a specialised group, there are plenty of adventures to be had in Tibet.

Mountain biking Certainly a challenge, but ever-improving roads make the trips to Kathmandu or Mt Kailash once-in-a-lifetime adventures. (p323)

Horse riding Add on to an organised trip from Lhasa or hire a horse at Kailash or Manasarovar for a multiday adventure. (p310)

Rafting Day trip on the Kyi-chu or join a river expedition on the Reting Tsangpo. (p310)

Watching wildlife Pack the binoculars and you'll likely spot black-necked cranes, wild asses, antelope and a rich selection of summer birdlife. (p174)

Month by Month

February

The depths of winter are very cold but still sunny, and are not a bad time to visit Lhasa and central Tibet. Lhasa sees few tourists but lots of visiting nomads. Ensure your hotel has heating!

✲ Year End Festival

On the 29th day of the 12th lunar month monks perform spectacular *cham* dances at Tsurphu, Mindroling and Tashilhunpo monasteries to dispel the evil of the old year and auspiciously usher in the new one. A huge thangka is unveiled the following day at Tsurphu Monastery.

✲ Losar (New Year Festival)

The first week of the first lunar month is a particularly colourful time to be in Lhasa, if Tibet is open. During Losar, Tibetan opera is performed and the streets are thronged with Tibetans in their finest cloaks. Prayer ceremonies take place and new prayer flags are hung. (p316)

March

Political tensions mean that permits are generally not issued and historic celebrations such as the Yak Butter and Great Prayer festivals are no longer held. Stay at home.

April

Spring brings pleasant temperatures, few crowds, and discounted hotel and vehicle rates, making this a good month to visit. High-elevation destinations like Nam-tso will still be frozen.

May

The warmer weather of late April and early May ushers in the start of the trekking season. Views are clear across the Himalaya, especially over Everest. Both April and May are good months to visit eastern Tibet.

✲ May Day

The major three-day national holiday starting 1 May is a very popular time for Chinese travellers to come to Tibet, so expect flights and hotels to be booked solid and rates to be higher than usual, especially in Lhasa.

✲ Birthday of Sakyamuni Buddha

The eighth day of the fourth lunar month sees large numbers of pilgrims visiting Lhasa and other sacred areas in Tibet. Festivals are held around this time at Tsurphu, Ganden, Reting and Samye monasteries instead. Can be in June instead.

✲ Tsurphu Festival

Cham dancing (ritual dances performed by costumed monks), colourful processions and the unfurling of a great thangka are the highlights of this festival, held from the ninth to the 11th day of the fourth lunar month. Can be in June instead. (p104)

TIBETAN LUNAR CALENDAR

Most of Tibet's religious and cultural festivals are fixed according to the Tibetan lunar calendar, which usually runs a month or two behind the Gregorian calendar (and differs slightly from the Chinese lunar calendar). Thus, religious festivals can fall in the next or even the previous month from the prior year. For the actual dates check travel-agency websites or download a Tibetan calendar (or app) at www.rabten. eu/iDevCalendar_en.htm.

✨ Saga Dawa (Sakyamuni's Enlightenment)

The full moon (15th day) of the fourth lunar month marks the date of Sakyamuni's enlightenment and entry into nirvana. For Saga Dawa, huge numbers of pilgrims walk Lhasa's Lingkhor circuit and visit Mt Kailash, where the Tarboche prayer pole is raised each year. Can be in June instead. (p316)

June

Tibet's high season starts in earnest in June. Lots of Indian pilgrims head to Kailash at this time and trekking is good. Even summer days can be chilly at higher elevations (above 4000m).

✨ Worship of the Buddha

During the second week of the fifth lunar month, the parks of Lhasa, in particular the Norbulingka, are crowded with picnickers for Worship of the Buddha. (p74)

✨ Tashilhunpo Festival

From the 14th to the 16th day of the fifth lunar month, Shigatse's Tashilhunpo Monastery becomes the scene of three days of festivities. A huge thangka is unveiled at dawn and *cham* dances are performed.

✨ Samye Festival

Held over two or three days from the full moon (15th day) of the fifth lunar month, the elaborate ritual ceremonies and *cham* dancing in front of the Ütse are highlights. The monastery guesthouse is normally booked out, so bring a tent. Can be in July instead.

July

Monsoon-influenced rain and glacial melting from mid-July to September can bring flooding and temporary road blockages to eastern and western Tibet, as well as on the road to Nepal. Lowland Kathmandu and Chéngdū can be very hot.

✨ Chökor Düchen (Drukwa Tsezhi) Festival

The fourth day of the sixth lunar month celebrates Buddha's first sermon at Sarnath near Varanasi in India. During the festival, many pilgrims climb Gephel Ri (Gambo Ütse), the peak behind Drepung Monastery, and also the ridge from Pabonka to the Dode Valley, to burn juniper incense. (p74)

✨ Guru Rinpoche's Birthday

Held on the 10th day of the sixth lunar month, this festival is particularly popular in Nyingmapa monasteries and is held across Tibet, with rituals and *cham* dancing.

✨ Ganden Festival

On the 15th day of the sixth lunar month, Ganden Monastery displays its 25 holiest relics, which are normally locked away. A large offering ceremony accompanies the unveiling.

✨ Drepung Festival

The 30th day of the sixth lunar month is celebrated with the hanging at dawn of a huge thangka at Drepung Monastery. Lamas and monks perform opera in the main courtyard. (p74)

☆ Gyantse's Dhama Festival

This largely secular festival comes to Gyantse in mid-July, featuring such fun and games as line dances, yak races, archery and equestrian events. (p139)

August

The warm weather, combined with some major festivals and horse racing on the northern plateau, makes this one of the most popular times to visit. Tibet sees half of its (minimal) rainfall in July and August.

⭐ Shōtun (Yogurt Festival)

This major festival in the first week of the seventh lunar month starts with the dramatic unveiling of a giant thangka at Drepung Monastery before moving to Sera and then down to the Norbulingka for performances of *lhamo* (Tibetan opera) and some epic picnics. (p74)

☆ Horse-Racing Festival

Thousands of nomads head to summer pastures around Damxung and Nam-tso for a week of horse racing, archery and other traditional nomad sports. A similar and even larger event is held in Nagchu a few weeks earlier.

⭐ Bathing Festival

The end of the seventh and the beginning of the eighth lunar months sees locals washing away the grime of the previous year in an act of purification that coincides with the week-long appearance of the constellation Pleiades in the night sky.

⭐ Onkor

In the first week of the eighth lunar month, Tibetans in central Tibet get together and party in celebration of the upcoming harvest.

⭐ Tashilhunpo

More *cham* dances, from the ninth to the 11th day of the eighth month, at Shigatse's Tashilhunpo Monastery.

October

Clear Himalayan skies and good driving conditions in eastern and western Tibet make this a good off-peak time to visit before the winter cold arrives, as the trekking season comes to a close.

⭐ 1 October

Many Chinese take an entire week off for National Day, so expect flights and hotels to be full and rates higher than normal.

November

Temperatures are still pleasant during the day in Lhasa and Shigatse but cold in the higher elevations of the north and west.

⭐ Lhabab Düchen

Commemorating Buddha's descent from heaven, the 22nd day of the ninth lunar month sees large numbers of pilgrims in Lhasa. Ladders are painted afresh on rocks around many monasteries to symbolise the event.

⭐ Palden Lhamo

The 15th day of the 10th lunar month sees a procession in Lhasa around the Barkhor bearing Palden Lhamo (Shri Devi), the protective deity of the Jokhang. (p74)

December

By December temperatures are starting to get seriously cold everywhere and some high passes start to close, but there's still surprisingly little snow in the Land of Snows.

⭐ Tsongkhapa Festival

The anniversary of the death of Tsongkhapa, the founder of the Gelugpa order, is on the 25th day of the 10th lunar month. Monasteries light fires and carry images of Tsongkhapa in procession. Check for *cham* dances at the monasteries at Ganden, Sera and Drepung.

Itineraries

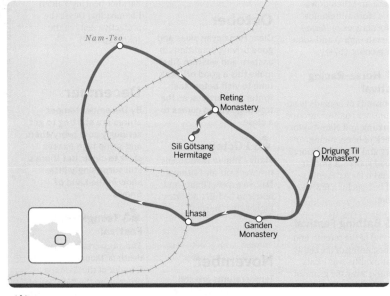

 **Lhasa & Around**

Everyone coming to Tibet visits Lhasa and there's enough to see in and around the city to occupy at least five days. This loop gives a great taste of Tibet without travelling thousands of kilometres.

If you are on a tight budget you can avoid pricey vehicle hire by staying in Lhasa, or maybe taking a side trip by train to Shigatse. Must-sees in **Lhasa** include the Potala Palace (a Unesco World Heritage site), the Jokhang Temple and the Barkhor pilgrimage circuit. The huge monastic institutions of Drepung and Sera lie on the edge of town and both offer worthwhile pilgrim circuits.

Plenty of excursions can be made from Lhasa. An overnight return trip to the stunning salt lake of **Nam-tso** offers a break from peering at Buddhist deities, though allow a few days in Lhasa to acclimatise before heading out here.

If you add three days you can loop back to Lhasa from Nam-tso via the timeless and little-visited **Reting Monastery**, the amazing cliff-side **Sili Götsang Hermitage** and the atmospheric **Drigung Til Monastery**, visiting **Ganden Monastery** en route.

To get way off the beaten track, explore the monasteries between Reting and Drigung Til, or around Nyima Jiangre.

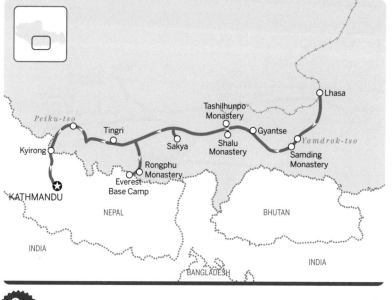

9 DAYS Lhasa to Kathmandu

The 1300km Friendship Hwy between Lhasa and Kathmandu in Nepal is a classic overland journey and easily the most popular travellers' route through Tibet. It allows excellent detours to central Tibet's most important monasteries, plus views of the world's highest peak.

From **Lhasa** you can head straight to the coiling-scorpion-shaped lake of **Yamdrok-tso** and take in the views from **Samding Monastery** before heading over the glacier-draped Karo-la pass to **Gyantse**. This town is well worth a full day: the *kumbum* (literally '100,000 images') chörten is a must-see and the fort is a fun scramble. A 90-minute drive away is Shigatse, with its impressive **Tashilhunpo Monastery**. **Shalu Monastery** is a worthwhile short detour en route, especially if you have an interest in Tibetan art.

A popular side trip on the way to Kathmandu is to brooding **Sakya**, a small monastery town located just 25km off the Friendship Hwy. Overnight here and you'll have time to investigate the northern ruins.

The most popular excursion from the highway is to **Rongphu Monastery** and **Everest Base Camp**, just a few hours from the main highway. An overnight stay at 5000m guarantees both clear views and a pounding headache – it's not a good idea to stay here if you've come straight from Nepal because the altitude gain is simply too rapid to be considered safe.

After Everest most people take the opportunity to stay the night in old **Tingri**, with its wonderful views of Mt Cho Oyu and option to visit vertiginous Shegar Dzong. From here on your route is more uncertain. The old road via misty waterfalls and lush green gorges to Zhāngmù was closed at time of research. The new route via **Kyirong** branches off the Friendship Hwy and passes jaw-dropping views of Mt Shishapangma, the highest mountain inside Tibet, before skirting **Peiku-tso**, a stunning turquoise lake nestled at the base of the Langtang Himal range. From here on is *terra incognita,* as the road drops into the lovely forested Kyirong Valley and descends to the Nepal border at Rasu-wagadhi in the Langtang region. Only a handful of foreigners have taken this road since it opened in 2017.

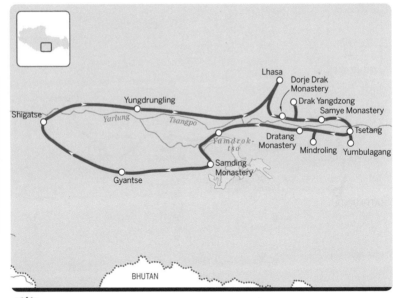

Yarlung Tsangpo Valley loop

8 DAYS

If your time is limited, you can't get much more bang for your buck than a short trip along the Yarlung Tsangpo Valley. The valley is just an hour from Lhasa and yet there are loads of surprisingly off-the-beaten-track destinations here. In just three days you can see the main valley sights.

Spend the first few days in **Lhasa** acclimatising, and then head south to the airport and swing into the northern side of the valley, stopping first at charming **Dorje Drak Monastery**, with its demanding kora path and its dramatic views of sand dunes and the maze-like braids of the river. To get off the beaten track, make the overnight trip up the side Drak valley to the nunnery and caves of **Drak Yangdzong**, where you can join pilgrims as they squeeze themselves up wooden ladders and through narrow tunnels.

Next up is **Samye Monastery**, one of Tibet's great highlights and a fine place to overnight. Take in the morning views from Hepo Ri and then continue to the modern city of **Tsetang** to pick up permits. Budget a full day to visit the Yarlung Valley via Trandruk Monastery, photogenic **Yumbulagang** and the ruins of Rechung-puk.

Headed back towards Lhasa, the first stop is **Mindroling**, one of Tibet's most important Nyingmapa-school *gompas* and home to a simple monastery guesthouse where you can overnight. Nearby **Dratang Monastery** will appeal to art lovers with its important Pala-era wall murals. History buffs will want to make the short hike to the ruins of Jamapaling chörten, a sobering monument to the wanton destruction of the Cultural Revolution.

From here Lhasa's Gongkar airport is less than an hour away. Alternatively, consider heading south to the Khamba-la for a short hike overlooking dramatic **Yamdrok-tso** and then an overnight stay at the guesthouse at **Samding Monastery**, with its fabulous views. The next day, drive over the high Karo-la pass to **Gyantse**. Continue the following day via the ruined Tsechen fort to **Shigatse**, spending a day at Tashilunpo Monastery and its kora, before returning to Lhasa or the airport via the unusual Bön monastery of **Yungdrungling**.

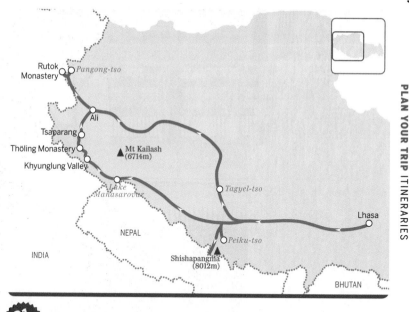

21 DAYS Mount Kailash pilgrimage

Much talked about but little visited, Mt Kailash occupies one of the most remote and sacred corners of Asia. Once a rugged 4WD expedition, the ride is now much less of an ordeal thanks to a new paved road. The scenery remains just as spectacular.

If you just want to visit Mt Kailash and Lake Manasarovar, the most direct route is along the southern road (870km), a four-day drive from **Lhasa** along the spine of the Himalayas. Most people stop en route at Shigatse and Saga, but Drongba, Paryang and Lhatse are also possibilities. We'd recommend extra stops in Gyantse and Sakya, for a minimum 14-day return trip.

A kora (pilgrimage circuit) of the mountain will take three days and you should allow at least half a day afterwards to relax at **Lake Manasarovar**, probably at Chiu Monastery. It's well worth budgeting a day to drive a circuit of the lake, one of the most spectacular in Tibet. After they complete the kora, pilgrims traditionally visit the sacred hot springs at Tirthapuri.

An ambitious but rewarding alternative is to travel to/from Lhasa along the longer (1700km) northern route to **Ali**, making a loop that will take three weeks. The six-day drive is astonishingly scenic, but the towns en route are pretty charmless, so consider camping somewhere beautiful such as **Tagyel-tso** or remote Tsari Nam-tso. From Ali you can make a good day trip to spectacular **Pangong-tso** bordering Ladakh, as well the petroglyphs and old town around **Rutok Monastery**.

You'll need at least three extra days if you want to add the Guge Kingdom sites around Zanda: you need most of a day to explore the other-worldly ruins at **Tsaparang**, plus a few hours in Zanda at **Thöling Monastery**. Adventurers could add an extra day on the way to Kailash, to explore the Bön-school Gurugyam Monastery and the amazing ruins of the ancient Shangshung kingdom in the **Khyunglung Valley**.

Finally, if you are heading to Nepal from Mt Kailash, you can make the short detour to stunning **Peiku-tso**, with its views of Shishapangma, before descending into the Kyirong Valley.

HUNG CHUNG CHIH / SHUTTERSTOCK ©

Top: Drepung Monastery (p84), near Lhasa
Bottom: Pilgrim and prayer wheels near Potala Palace (p64), Lhasa

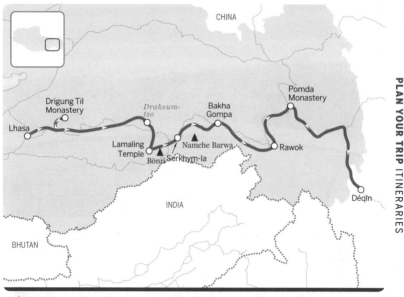

Best of Eastern Tibet

10 DAYS

For a completely different view of Tibet, head out to the lush forested valleys, alpine scenery and wild gorges of the wild east. Unlike the overland route to Sìchuān province, the following route through Kongpo and southern Kham to Yúnnán is open. Check with agents to see if this has changed; if so you'll have to return to Lhasa from Rawok-tso.

From **Lhasa** a logical first step is the detour to **Drigung Til Monastery**, where you can overnight before continuing east over a high pass to the beautiful but touristed lake of **Draksum-tso** at the entrance to the fascinating Kongpo region. The Swiss-style alpine scenery is like nothing you'll see in central or western Tibet. The lovingly restored **Lamaling Temple** is worth a visit, and you could make an adventurous trip to sacred **Bönri mountain**, perhaps even trekking around it.

From here the road climbs to the **Serkhym-la**, for excellent views of 7755m Namche Barwa, before winding down switchbacks into lovely alpine villages and then the mist-drenched gorges north of the Yarlung Tsangpo. Road conditions are always dicey here but are generally best from late March to late April, and late September to early November.

The 800-year-old **Bakha Gompa** is well worth a stop for both its unusual island location and its historical connections to a scandalous 1400-year-old story about Chinese Princess Wencheng and Tibetan minister Gar Tongtsen. From here you reach the incredibly scenic twin lakes of **Rawok**. There's some great accommodation right on scenic lake Ngan-tso, or camp by the shores of turquoise Rawok-tso, from where you can visit nearby glaciers.

Depending on the state of permits in eastern Tibet, you may have to return to Lhasa from Rawok, possibly detouring via the Yarlung Tsangpo Valley and Samye Monastery.

If permits are being issued for southern Chamdo prefecture (confirm with your agency), you can continue east out of the lush mountains of Nyingtri prefecture and into the harsh dry landscapes of the upper Mekong Valley, stopping at small but lively **Pomda Monastery**. Remote roads continue southeast along former salt-and-tea-trade routes, over a series of roller-coaster passes and through gorges to the junction town of Markham. From here branch southeast to reach **Déqīn** in Yúnnán province, for an incredible overland adventure.

XINING RAILWAY STATION

Xīníng Railway Station (p248)

Plan Your Trip
Qīnghǎi–Tibet Railway

The world's highest railway links Lhasa with Xīníng up over the Tibetan plateau. Built at high altitudes on some of the harshest and trickiest terrain on earth, the Qīnghǎi–Tibet Railway is considered an engineering marvel and is a swaying, dreamy trip up to the Roof of the World.

At a Glance

Stations Xīníng's railway station was upgraded in 2015 and has shops selling basic snacks (instant noodles, crisps, drinks) and Chinese fast-food. Stops at through stations aren't long enough to alight for a snack break, so bring everything you need.

Dining There is a restaurant carriage serving Chinese dishes (¥35 to ¥60). Beers are on sale, but be very careful drinking on board due to the altitude.

Toilets These are older train stock and the toilets can range from tolerable to truly grim. The majority are squatters, and there are sink basins at the ends of carriages for general washing up. Bring your own toilet paper.

Showers There are no showers on board.

Electricity There are very few outlets; bring external batteries to keep your devices charged overnight.

Security This is a safe railway journey, but it's still a good idea to watch your bags. Soft sleeper berths have a lockable door, but hard sleepers are open, so keep any valuables close if you move around the train.

Arrive early You'll need to pass a permit/passport/ticket check, and then a luggage scan before entering the station. It's advisable to arrive 45 minutes to one hour before departure. Most trains only stop for a few minutes at Xīníng, so don't dawdle.

What to Bring

Currency Cash (Chinese rénmínbì) to buy meals and drinks on the train.

Food Stock up on fruit, nuts and instant noodles before you board, and bring plenty of bottled water, as the trains tend to be hot and dry. A dispenser at the end of each carriage provides constant boiling water.

Spare battery External batteries to keep your devices charged.

Other essential items Sandals or slippers, plenty of tissues/toilet paper, altitude sickness tablets, earphones, torch (flashlight), toiletries, a mug or thermos, hand lotion, chopsticks or travel cutlery, wet wipes, reading material, loose comfortable clothing, earplugs.

Baggage allowance Though in practice it seems little attention is paid to how much luggage you bring, the official stated limit is 20kg per adult passenger. If you happen to go over the limit, it should be a very negligible fee.

Classes

The Qīnghǎi–Tibet Railway operates much like any other Chinese train: there are hard-seat carriages, as well as hard and soft sleeper berths. Smoking is not allowed. In sleeper berths and not travelling in a group, expect to share with strangers.

Seats

Hard seats (硬座; *yìng zuò*) are the least comfortable way to travel: 98 passengers packed into a single carriage in upright, stiff seats that do not adjust. What you sacrifice in comfort and sleep, you may receive back in unique experiences meeting local travellers.

Hard sleeper

Hard-sleeper (硬卧; *yìng wò*) carriages consist of doorless six-berth compartments with triple-tier bunks. Bedding is provided. Luggage is stored in a shared and not easy-to-reach console over the door and under bottom bunks. Hard sleepers have a nice community atmosphere – your berthmates will likely be friendly, curious and chatty.

Soft sleeper

Four-bed soft-sleeper (软卧; *ruǎn wò*) berths are roomier and come with individual TVs in each bed and a door that closes and locks. Bathrooms in soft-sleeper carriages have western-style (seated) toilets. Luggage is stored in a console over the door, and there is space under the bottom bunks.

Tickets

Book early Tickets can be purchased two months in advance and you should buy your ticket as early as possible, especially for summer travel. In the busiest months of July and August, as well as during China's spring bank holidays, you'll pay a premium.

Securing tickets In general, getting a ticket for a train out of Lhasa is much easier than getting a ticket in, and most travellers opt to use a booking agency to ensure they get their tickets. Reliable ticket booking agencies include **China Highlights** (www.chinahighlights), **China Tibet Train** (www.chinatibettrain.com) and **China DIY Travel** (www.china-diy-travel.com).

Buying your own tickets If you want to secure a ticket independently, you can use **Ctrip** (www.ctrip.com), but be aware that tickets usually sell out almost the instant they go on sale.

Breaking the journey If travelling from further afield in China, for example Běijīng or Chéngdū, it is advisable to break the journey into at least two legs. Xīníng is a pleasant city for a stopover and, at 2500m, is a good midway point at which to spend a couple of days acclimatising slowly to altitude gain. To do this, you'll need to book your journey in two parts: your departure point to Xīníng, and then your rail ticket onward from Xīníng to Lhasa. Many travellers opt to fly to Xīníng.

Permits & Arrival

A Tibet Travel Bureau (TTB) permit is required for all non-Chinese travellers to board a train to Lhasa. Unlike with air travel which requires the original permit, for the train, you may present a copy or printout of the permit, which is obtained by your travel agency and emailed to you. Most travellers use the same agency handling their TTB permits to buy train tickets.

In Xīníng, you will present your passport, ticket and permits before boarding.

USEFUL WEBSITES

China Highlights (www.chinahigh lights.com) Searchable timetables.

China Tibet Train (www.chinatibet-train.com) The official website. Good background information.

China Train & Tours (www.china traintickets.net) You can book tickets up to 60 days in advance on this English-language site.

Railway Customer Service Centre (www.12306.cn) Chinese speakers might be able to reserve train tickets at this site.

Travel China Guide (www.travel chinaguide.com/china-trains) Searchable timetables.

On board, an attendant will provide a health waiver to fill in. The forms are only in Chinese, so ask a fellow passenger for help or a translation app.

Upon arrival in Lhasa, passengers detrain and pass an exit permit check, where a chaotic procedure requires you to be shuffled across the front station plaza to a small outbuilding. Here, passports and TTBs are checked, photocopied and handed back in a scrum of weary foreigners and stressed-out guides.

If travelling in a group, your guide will likely meet you outside the station's exit gate and escort you through this, but be prepared to go it alone in some cases. Don't panic: it is normal procedure for either your guide or an entry official to take your passport and permit away during this process.

Out Your Window

Trains cross the Tibetan plateau during at least some hours of daylight, guaranteeing great views. About an hour outside Xīníng, the train rambles alongside the still, blue waters of vast Qīnghǎi Lake for some time before carving across large swaths of desert flatland and brown canyon country. After Golmud, you climb through desert into the jagged, caramel-coloured mountains of Nánshānkǒu (Southern Pass), passing what feels like a whisper from the imposing glaciers beside Yùzhū Fēng (Jade Pearl Peak; 6178m). The train crosses into Tibet over the 5072m Tanggu-la (Tánggǔlā Shānkǒu) Pass, the line's high point.

Other highlights include the tunnel through frigid 4905m Fēnghuǒshān Pass and trundling alongside Conag Lake (4608m), claimed to be the world's highest freshwater lake. Keep your eyes peeled throughout for antelope, foxes, yaks and wild asses, plus the occasional nomad.

Altitude on Board

Riding the world's highest train, altitude is always going to be a consideration. Though most travellers pass the journey with little-to-no problem, altitude sickness can strike anyone, regardless of fitness or general health, so it's important to come prepared and be careful. It's a common misconception that the relative 'slowness' of train travel will prevent you from suffering AMS upon ar-

Qīnghǎi–Tibet Railway passes over the Lhasa River

rival in Tibet. While the pace of train travel can be a benefit in altitude adjustment, it is not a cure-all, and many travellers will feel gentle altitude sickness on the journey, be it light-headedness or headache.

All passengers have access to piped-in oxygen through a special socket beside each seat or berth.

Be sure to carry altitude sickness tablets, drink more water than usual and alert the train attendant if you are feeling unwell.

Ecology & Culture

There's no doubt the Qīnghǎi–Tibet train line is an engineering marvel. Topping out at 5072m, it is the world's highest railway, snatching the title from a Peruvian line. The statistics speak for themselves: 86% of the line is above 4000m, and half the track lies on permafrost, requiring a cooling system of pipes driven into the ground to keep it frozen year-round to avoid a rail-buckling summer thaw. Construction of the line involved building 160km of bridges and elevated track, seven tunnels (including the world's highest) and 24 hyperbaric chambers, the latter to treat altitude-sick workers.

Aside from environmental concerns, many locals are deeply worried about the cultural and political impact of the train. The trains unload thousands of tourists and immigrants into Lhasa every day.

The authorities stress the economic benefits of the line: highly subsidised, it has decreased transport costs for imports by up to 75%. But Tibetans remain economically marginalised. More than 90% of the 100,000 workers employed to build the line came from other provinces and few, if any, Tibetan staff members work on the trains. The US$4.1 billion cost of building the line is greater than the amount Běijīng has spent on hospitals and schools in Tibet over the past 50 years.

As ambitious as the current line is, connecting Lhasa with the rest of China was only the beginning. An extension to Shigatse opened in 2014, and a new railway line under construction will expand the line east to Tsetang, Nyingtri and Sìchuān province, starting/ending at Chéngdū. While this undoubtedly eases travel and provides a comfortable and romantic method of transport into Tibet, travellers should remain mindful of the impact on the culture and delicate ecology of this special region.

Qīnghǎi–Tibet Railway

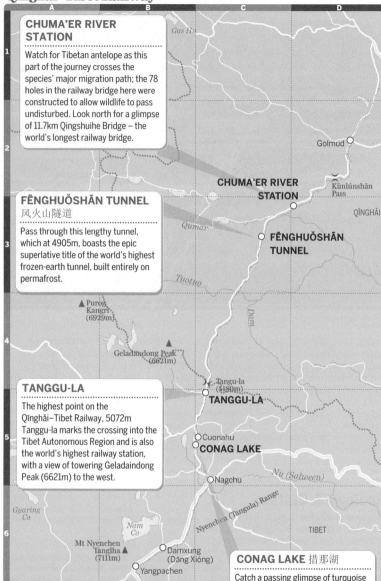

CHUMA'ER RIVER STATION

Watch for Tibetan antelope as this part of the journey crosses the species' major migration path; the 78 holes in the railway bridge here were constructed to allow wildlife to pass undisturbed. Look north for a glimpse of 11.7km Qingshuihe Bridge – the world's longest railway bridge.

FĒNGHUǑSHĀN TUNNEL
风火山隧道

Pass through this lengthy tunnel, which at 4905m, boasts the epic superlative title of the world's highest frozen-earth tunnel, built entirely on permafrost.

TANGGU-LA

The highest point on the Qīnghǎi–Tibet Railway, 5072m Tanggu-la marks the crossing into the Tibet Autonomous Region and is also the world's highest railway station, with a view of towering Geladaindong Peak (6621m) to the west.

CONAG LAKE 措那湖

Catch a passing glimpse of turquoise Conag Lake – the train passes less than 100m from the lakeshore. Conag Lake is among Tibet's holy lakes and is home to migratory birds, including cranes, mandarin ducks and swans.

Gas Hu

Golmud

Kūnlúnshān Pass

QĪNGHǍI

CHUMA'ER RIVER STATION

Qumar

FĒNGHUǑSHĀN TUNNEL

Tuotuo

Puroŋ Kangri (6929m)

Dam

Geladaindong Peak (6621m)

Tangu-la (5180m)

TANGGU-LA

Cuonahu

CONAG LAKE

Nagchu

Nu (Salween)

Gyaring Co

Nam Co

Nyenchen (Tangula) Range

TIBET

Mt Nyenchen Tanglha (7111m)

Damxung (Dāng Xióng)

Yangpachen

Lhasa

Yarlung Tsangpo (Brahmaputra)

Xigaze

Gyangze

Yamzho Yumco

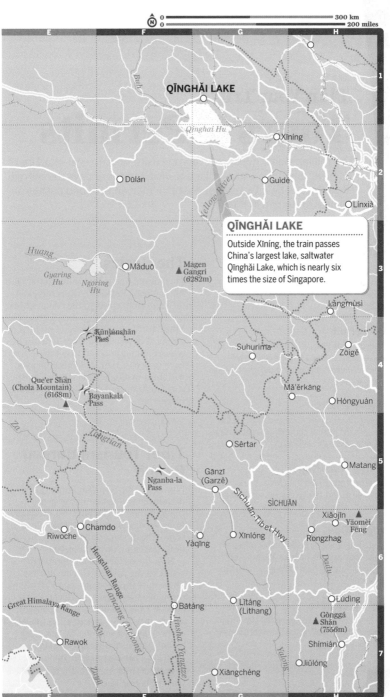

0
N
0

300 km
200 miles

E   F   G   H

QĪNGHǍI LAKE

Qinghai Hu

Xīníng

Dūlán

Guìdé

Línxià

Yellow River

Huang

Gyaring
Hu   Ngoring
Hu

Mǎduō

Mǎgèn
Gangri
(6282m) ▲

QĪNGHǍI LAKE

Outside Xīníng, the train passes China's largest lake, saltwater Qīnghǎi Lake, which is nearly six times the size of Singapore.

Lángmùsì

Kūnlúnshān
Pass

Suhurima

Zöigé

Que'er Shān
(Chola Mountain)
(6168m) ▲

Bayankala
Pass

Mǎ'ěrkāng

Hóngyuán

Za

Tongtian

Sêrtar

Matang

Nganba-la
Pass

Gānzī
(Garzê)

Sìchuān–Tibet Hwy

SÌCHUĀN

Xiǎojīn

Yǎomèi
Fēng ▲

Riwoche   Chamdo

Yǎqīng

Xīnlóng

Rongzhag

Dadu

Hengduan Range

Lancang (Mekong)

Great Himalaya Range

Jinsha (Yangtze)

Bātáng

Lǐtáng
(Lithang)

Lúdìng

Gònggá
Shān
(7556m) ▲

Nu

Rawok

Zayu

Xiāngchéng

Jiŭlóng

Shímián

Yalong

Plan Your Trip
Tours & Permits

The million-dollar question everyone asks: how do I get into Tibet? It's never been the easiest place to visit, but these days the permit situation can be a far greater obstacle than snowbound passes or the lack of oxygen in the air.

Getting into Tibet

Advance Planning
Start your tour planning two months in advance. Agencies need two to four weeks to arrange permits.

TTB Permit
You need a Tibet Tourism Bureau permit to board a train or plane to Lhasa. You will need to pre-arrange an itinerary through a travel agent before arriving in Tibet.

Travel Permits
You need travel permits to travel outside Lhasa prefecture and you can currently only get these by hiring transportation and a guide.

Coming from Nepal
If you plan to enter Tibet from Nepal, you will have to travel on a short-term group visa available in Kathmandu, which is hard to extend.

Budget Tips
In Lhasa you can hire a guide without transport and just take taxis around town. You can also travel to Shigatse by train without the need for vehicle hire.

Stay Up to Date
All of these rules have exceptions and by the time you have finished reading this list, all of them will probably have changed.

The Basics

The bottom line is that travel to the Tibet Autonomous Region (TAR) is radically different from travel to the rest of China; a valid Chinese visa is not enough to visit Tibet. You'll also need several permits, foremost of which is a Tibet Tourism Bureau (TTB) permit, and to get these you have to book a tour. At a minimum you will need to hire a guide for your entire stay and transport for any travel outside Lhasa.

Tibet Tourism Bureau Permit

Without a Tibet Tourism Bureau (TTB) permit you will not be able to board a flight or train to Tibet or cross overland from Nepal and you will not be able to secure the other permits you need to continue travelling throughout Tibet.

How these rules are interpreted depends on the political climate in Tibet. These days you can only get a TTB permit through a tour agency in Tibet (agencies outside Tibet can arrange trips, but ultimately they book through a Tibetan-based agency). Everything must be arranged beforehand, including any trekking.

To get a permit you need to:

➡ work out an itinerary detailing exactly where you want to go in Tibet

➡ pay for a guide for every day of your tour, including arrival and departure days, at a rate of around ¥250 to ¥300 per day

➡ hire a vehicle for all transport outside Lhasa

➡ agree a price and send a deposit, normally through PayPal or a bank transfer (check the transfer charges)

➡ send a scan of your passport information pages and Chinese visa

➡ arrange an address in China (usually that of a hotel, guesthouse or local agency) to receive your posted TTB permit, if flying to Lhasa.

What your tour actually involves depends on the agency. Some offer all-inclusive tours, while others will arrange transport, a guide and permits but leave accommodation, food and entry fees up to you. You can book your own train or air ticket to Lhasa or have the agency arrange this. Some airline offices and online booking agencies will sell flights to Lhasa to foreigners, but others won't unless you can show you have a TTB permit. Some agencies require you to have a prebooked ticket out of Tibet, but most are happy for you to arrange this in Lhasa. Treks fall under the same permit requirements as normal tours.

You need to have the original permit in your hands in order to board a flight to Lhasa, so most agencies arrange to post the permit through an agency or hostel. This can cost anything from ¥25 for normal post (four working days) to ¥180/280/380 for 36-/24-/18-hour express post. A photocopy or scan of an original TTB permit is currently all that is required to board a train to Tibet, which saves on postage fees. The permit is actually free, though most agencies charge a few hundred yuán per person for the bureaucratic runaround.

Agencies can only apply for some permits 15 days before departure, so there is invariably a last-minute rush to get permits posted to you in time. Travel restrictions and closures occur without warning, especially during religiously significant dates, if there is a major political meeting in Běijīng or if there are any political disturbances in Tibet. In 2012 temporary regulations requiring groups to have a minimum of five persons, all of the same nationality, were introduced, though these have since been rescinded. A few months later Tibet was closed to foreigners completely for a short

time, after two cases of self-immolation in Lhasa.

TTB permits are not issued in March due to the anniversary of several politically sensitive dates. Assuming the political situation is calm, permits normally start to be reissued in the last week of March and agencies only know the new season's permit regulations for sure by the end of March. The last-minute nature and uncertainty that comes with this obviously complicates booking train and flight tickets; we recommend booking a fully refundable ticket if possible and taking out trip-cancellation insurance in case your permits fail to materialise.

The Fine Print

➡ Chinese residents of Hong Kong, Macau and Taiwan do not require a TTB permit to enter Tibet, though foreigners residing in China do.

➡ Journalists and embassy staff will find it impossible to get a TTB permit as tourists. Visitors on business, student or resident visas will have to procure a letter of introduction from their school or employer.

➡ A few travellers have managed to sneak into Lhasa without a TTB permit and stay there, but you still need to arrange a permit there in order to travel throughout the rest of Tibet. Most hotels ask to see your TTB permit before checking you in.

➡ TTB permits generally take three days to process and are not available during weekends.

THE IMPERMANENCE OF TRAVEL

Travel regulations to Tibet are constantly in flux, dependent largely on political events in Lhasa and Běijīng. Don't be surprised if the permit system is radically different from how we describe it. In fact, expect it. One of the best places for updated information is the dedicated Tibet page of Lonely Planet's Thorn Tree, at www. lonelyplanet.com/thorntree.

Other good sources of permit information are the websites www. thelandofsnows.com and www. tibetpermit.org. The latter is run by an agency in Sìchuān but is generally reliable on permit matters.

SYBIL SASSOON / ROBERT HARDING / GETTY IMAGES ©

Jokhang Temple (p57), Lhasa

The actual permit is a sheet of paper listing the names and passport numbers of all group members.

➡ If you are planning to arrive in Lhasa on a flight or dates that differ from those of your travel companions, your agency may have to issue a separate TTB permit for the time you are by yourself. When you meet your friends you'll then join the main permit. There doesn't seem to be a problem getting on a flight with one or two group members not present.

➡ You will likely have to wire or transfer a deposit to your travel agency's Bank of China account in Lhasa, though some agencies accept PayPal. You will pay the balance in cash in Lhasa. Check with the agency.

Alien's Travel Permits & Military Permits

Once you have a visa and have managed to wangle a TTB permit, you might think you're home and dry. Think again. Your agency will need to arrange an alien's travel permit for most of your travels outside Lhasa.

Travel permits are *not* needed for Lhasa or places just outside the city such as Ganden Monastery, but most other areas do technically require permits. Permits are most easily arranged in the regional capital, so for Ngari (western Tibet) you'll have to budget an hour in Shigatse, and possibly also Ali or Darchen, for your guide to process the permit. Agencies can only arrange a travel permit for those on a tour with them.

Sensitive border areas – such as Mt Kailash, the road to Kashgar and the Nyingtri region of eastern Tibet – also require a military permit and a foreign-affairs permit. For remote places such as the Yarlung Tsangpo gorges in southeastern Tibet, the roads through Lhoka south of Gyantse or for any border area, you will likely not be able to get permits even if you book a tour. Regions can close at short notice. The entire Chamdo prefecture has been closed since 2010, effectively blocking overland trips from Sìchuān and Yúnnán. You'll have to check to see if this has changed.

You should give your agency a week to 10 days to arrange your permits, and three weeks if military or other permits are required. The authorities generally won't issue permits more than 15 days in advance. Local Public Security Bureau (PSB) officers often make the ultimate decision on whether you can visit a site, so you'll need a certain flexibility if you're headed off the beaten track.

Organising a Tour

Many agencies give a price breakdown for the vehicle, guide, permits, postage fees and transfers, which is very useful. Clarify whether the trip fee includes accommodation and/or entry tickets. It should include food and accommodation for your guide and driver. Airport transfers might be included or you might have to pay an additional ¥300 for airport pick-up. Some agencies allow you to take the airport bus (¥30), but you'll still have to pay for your guide's ticket (both ways). You can normally take public transport around Lhasa.

If you arrange your own tour, expect to pay around US$50 to US$100 per person per day, depending on your itinerary, the amount of time in Lhasa (where vehicle rental is not required) and the number of people in the group.

On top of the costs of this kind of tour, you'll have to figure in the normal travel costs of accommodation, food, entry tickets etc, but these costs you can at least control. About US$40 per person per day is a good ballpark figure. Some agencies will want to book your accommodation and indeed can often get cheaper rates for mid-range or top-end hotels; others will let you arrange your own accommodation, which gives you greater flexibility in changing hotels.

In Lhasa you currently need to visit the major monasteries (the Jokhang, Drepung, Sera and Ganden) with your guide, but beyond that you can generally explore the city yourself, if you don't mind paying for a guide you don't use! The quality of guides varies considerably. Some are great, many are next to useless and a few actually cause more headaches than they solve. Having a Tibetan guide ensures you'll get a Tibetan perspective on monasteries and is highly recommended.

Solo travellers shouldn't be too put off by the official insistence on 'group travel'. For the purposes of getting permits and visas, a 'group' can normally be as small as one person. The Lonely Planet Thorn Tree (www.lonelyplanet.com/thorntree) is full of travellers looking for travel partners. Some agencies (particularly hostels) offer fixed departures and will help you find other travellers to form a small group. A minivan can fit four people (including the guide) comfortably.

Note that the agency that arranges your TTB permit is legally responsible for you in Tibet. Should you be caught talking politics with the wrong person or staying in Tibet after the expiry date on your TTB permit, the agency and guide will likely be questioned by the authorities and perhaps fined. This is one reason that some guides can appear over-cautious.

Fixing Your Itinerary

To arrange a tour you first need to pin down your itinerary. Some agencies offer fixed itineraries, but you can also customise your own. Your itinerary enables your agency to quote a firm price, which depends largely on the kilometres driven, not the time taken. It's a good idea to mention every place you intend to visit at this stage.

Once on the road your driver will probably have been prepaid for all the kilometres and so will be very reluctant to undertake even minor detours. Sensitive regions like Chamdo require to you list every monastery, village or hot springs, especially if it lies off the main highways.

When deciding on an itinerary don't fall into the trap of trying to pack too much in. You'll need some down time to rest or just wash clothes, especially on a longer tour out to western Tibet. It's a good idea to budget time for the occasional hike, if only to get out of your tour vehicle for a couple of hours. Finally, try to include some small, off-the-beaten-track monasteries in your itinerary, as these have a friendliness and authentic charm that many of the big, more touristed monasteries lack.

Tours from Nepal

Arranging a tour to Tibet from Nepal makes sense geographically, but there are several complications to bear in mind, primarily with regard to visas. In general, the same rules of Tibet travel apply – you have to pre-arrange a guide and transport in order to get the requisite permits.

Instead of posting your TTB permit to a city in China, your Tibet travel agency will send the permit details to the Chinese embassy in Kathmandu. You will then need to

---

TRAVEL OUTSIDE TIBET

Note that TTB and Alien Travel Permits are only required for travel in the Tibet Autonomous Region (TAR). You can normally travel through most of the culturally Tibetan areas of Yúnnán, Sìchuān, Gānsù and Qīnghǎi – the former Tibetan provinces of Kham and Amdo – without the need for permits. Certain parts of Sìchuān (notably Aba county, Larung Gar Monastery near Serthar and sometimes parts of Ganzi county) are occasionally closed due to political unrest, but in other areas you are free to travel independently to Tibetan monasteries, Khampa villages and sacred peaks around the region.

pay a Nepali travel agency to obtain your visa. The Nepali or Tibetan travel agency will need at least two weeks to get your TTB permit, and you will then need three or four working days in Kathmandu for the agent to get your China group visa, for which it will need your physical passport.

Note that the Chinese embassy in Kathmandu does not give individual Chinese visas to travellers headed to Tibet; it only provides group visas. If you already have a valid individual Chinese visa (p318) in your passport, it will be cancelled.

A group visa is a separate sheet of paper with all the names and passport numbers of the group members. It's useful to get your own individual 'group' visa (a 'group' can be as small as one person!) because, otherwise, come the end of your tour in Lhasa you will have to exit China with your fellow group members.

Group visas are generally issued for the duration of your tour, though you might be able to get a bit longer if you want to travel through China at the end of your Tibet trip. Note that it is very difficult, sometimes impossible, to extend the duration of a group visa or to split from your group visa, regardless of what agents in Kathmandu may tell you.

Once your trip is arranged and your permits secured, your Tibetan agent will send your Tibetan guide and driver to meet you on the Chinese side of the border. At customs on the Chinese side you will be asked to present your TTB permit.

If you are flying in to Lhasa, you will need to show your group visa and TTB permit at check-in in Kathmandu. Your Tibetan guide will meet you at Lhasa airport.

A simpler option is to join an organised tour from Kathmandu. Travel agents there offer 'budget' tours of Tibet from around US$600 per person for a basic seven-day trip stopping in Kyirong, Tingri, Shigatse, Gyantse and then Lhasa for two days. These trips generally run every Tuesday and Saturday. The main problem with these tours is the dangerously rapid

VEHICLE HIRE

When finalising vehicle hire with a tour agency it's a good idea to look through its contract (if it has one) and see where you stand in the event that things don't go according to plan. Bear the following in mind:

➡ You should agree on the rate for any extra days that may need to be tacked onto an itinerary. For delays caused by bad weather, blocked passes and so on, there should be no extra charge for vehicle hire. At the very least, the cost for extra days should be split 50% between your group and the agency.

➡ For delays caused by vehicle breakdowns, driver illness etc the agency should cover 100% of the costs and provide a back-up vehicle if necessary.

➡ Ask the agency about its policy on refunds for an uncompleted trip. Most agencies refuse any kind of refund, except if they are unable to get permits, while others are more open to negotiation. If you decide to cut a trip short for personal reasons, it's unlikely you'll get a refund.

➡ Establish which vehicle costs are not covered in the price (eg the ¥400 vehicle fee to drive to Everest Base Camp and the ¥60 vehicle fee at Peiku-tso), as well as entry fees for your guides (such as the ¥180 entry ticket for your guide at Everest).

Once you are sorted with the agency, it's a good idea to organise a meeting between your group and the driver a day or two before departure. Make sure the driver is aware of your itinerary (it may be the first time he has seen it!). Ensure that the guide speaks fluent Tibetan, good Chinese and useable English. It's not a bad idea to test the driver and car on a day trip to somewhere like Ganden Monastery before you head off on the big trip.

Unless you are a qualified mechanic, inspecting the soundness of the vehicle may prove to be difficult, but you should at least check that the windows open and close, that the seatbelts are functional and that the handbrake works (ours didn't!). Tyres and spares should be in reasonable condition.

altitude gain, which has you sleeping at 5300m on your second night. In general it's much better to acclimatise for a couple of days in Lhasa and then make your way back to Kathmandu overland.

Prices include transport, permits, shared twin rooms, a fairly useless guide, and admission fees. You'll have to add on visa fee, a flight back from Lhasa to Kathmandu and a single supplement of around $200 if you want your own room.

A nine-day trip that adds a visit to Everest Base Camp costs up to double the seven-day tour and will be harder to find. A two-week overland trip taking in Lhasa, Everest Base Camp and Mt Kailash costs around US$2000 per person.

Travel agents in Kathmandu with experience in Tibet include Tibet International Travels & Tours (p233) and Tashi Delek Nepal Treks & Expeditions (p233).

Bear in mind that most agencies are just subcontractors and normally pool clients, so you could find yourself travelling in a larger group than expected and probably on a bus instead of the promised 4WD. Other potential inconsistencies may include having to share a room when you were told you would be given a single, or paying a double-room supplement and ending up in a dorm. We do get a fair number of complaints about the service of some of these tours; it's best just to view it as the cheapest way to see Tibet.

Alms collecting at Tashilhunpo Monastery (p143), Shigatse

Tour Agencies in Tibet

In general, Tibetan tour agencies are not as professional as agencies in neighbouring Nepal or Bhutan. You'll need to stay on top of the permit process, double check all communications and make sure the places on your itinerary match your permits, especially in eastern or western Tibet.

The following companies in Lhasa are experienced in arranging customised trips.

For good information on responsible tour companies and ecotourism initiatives in Tibet, visit www.tibetecotravel.com.

Explore Tibet (☎0891-630 5152, 158 8909 0408; www.exploretibet.com; 4-5 House, Namsel No 3, Doudi Rd) Contact Sonam Jamphel.

Road to Tibet (☎133 0898 1522; www.roadtotibet.com; Jinzhu Xilu 8-5) Contact Woeser Phel.

Shigatse Travels (☎0891-633 0489; www.shigatsetravels.com; Yak Hotel, 100 Beijing Donglu) Top-end tours from a large agency that uses European trip managers.

Spinn Café (☎139 8908 8152; www.cafespinn.com; 3rd floor, 7-9 Beijing Xilu) Contact Kong/Pazu.

Tibet Highland Tours (☎0891-634 8144, 139 0898 5060; www.tibethighlandtours.com; Danjielin Lu) Contact Tenzin or Dechen.

Tibet Native Tours & Travel (☎139 8909 4160, 0891-682 2349; www.tibetnative.com) This Tibetan-run agency gets great reviews. Contact Sonam Gyatso.

Tibet Roof of World International Travel (☎0891-633 0982; www.tibettraveladventure.com; 25 Sela Nanlu) Offers budget tours, treks and private cultural trips across Tibet. Contact Migmar.

Tibet Songtsan International Travel Company (p207) Run by Tenzin, this up-and-coming outfit is eager to serve new clients.

Tibet Travellers (☎189 0899 0100; www.tibettravelers.com) Owner Tenzin Dondup is experienced at organising custom tours.

Tibet Tsolha Garbo Travel (☑0891-633 3871, 139 0891 5618; www.dmigmar.wix.com/tibet-tsolha-garbo) Contact David Migmar or Sonam Yergye.

Tibet Wind Horse Adventure (p310) Top-end trips, strong on trekking and rafting.

Tibetan Guide (☑136 2898 0074, 0891-635 1657; www.tibetanguide.com) Contact Mima Dhondup.

Visit Tibet Travel and Tours (☑028-8325 7742; www.visittibet.com; Jiaji Lu) Can arrange Nepal add-ons.

Tour Agencies Elsewhere in China

There are several good companies outside the TAR that can arrange tours in Tibet. Many are based in the Tibetan areas of China and operate through local contacts in Lhasa. Depending on your itinerary it can be useful to arrange your tour through one of these outfits; if catching the train from Xīníng, for example, it's handy to use an agency there to help arrange hard-to-find train tickets and permit pickup.

One recommended agency that is particularly knowledgeable when arranging Tibet tours is US-based **Himalaya Journey** (www.himalayajourney.com), which has an office in Lhasa and utilises only local Tibetan guides.

Access Tibet (www.accesstibettour.com) Also with an office in Lhasa.

China Yak (☑135 5126 4372; www.chinayak.com) Part of China International Travel Service (CITS), one of the few agencies able to run tours in eastern Tibet, with an office in Lhasa.

Extravagant Yak (p244) Foreign-owned company that runs tours in both Tibet and Tibetan areas of surrounding provinces.

Gesartour (☑139 0976 9192; www.gesartour.com) Strong on tours to Amdo.

Holly's Hostel (p239) Backpacker hostel in Chéngdū's Tibetan district that arranges tours to Tibet

Kham Voyage (p244) Cultural, trekking and motorbike tours in Kham.

Khampa Caravan (康巴商道探险旅行社; Kāngbā Shāngdào Tànxiǎn Lǚxíngshè; ☑0887 828 8648; www.khampacaravan.com; Jinlong Jie; 金龙街; ☺9am-noon & 2-5.30pm Mon-Fri, 9am-noon Sat) Overland trips from Yúnnán to Lhasa when possible, and strong on Kham, with an emphasis on sustainable tourism and local communities. Contact Dakpa.

Leo Hostel (阿来客栈; Guǎngjùyuán Bīnguǎn; ☑010 6303 1595, 010 6303 3318; www.leohostel.com; 52 Dazhalan Xijie; 大栅栏西街 52号; dm ¥55-90, r ¥240-380; ❇@☎; ⑤Line 2 to Qian-men, exit B or C) Popular backpacker hostel that books tours through an agency in Tibet.

Snow Lion Tours (p248) Contact Wangden Tsering.

Tibet Vista (☑28-855 52138; www.tibetvista.com) The biggest operator arranging tours to Tibet, based in Chéngdū, with an office in Lhasa.

Tibetan Connections (p248) This friendly tour company focuses on remoter parts of Amdo and Kham but can arrange trips into Tibet.

Tibetan Trekking (p244) Contact Gao Liqiang for treks and 4WD trips, especially in Tibetan areas of western Sìchuān.

Wild China (☑010-6465 6602; www.wildchina.com; Room 803, Oriental Place, 9 Dongfang Donglu, North Dongsanhuan Rd; 东三环北路东方东路9号东方国际大厦803室; ☺9am-6pm Mon-Fri; ⑤Line 10 to Liangmaqiao, exit B) Professionally run and top-end private trips.

Windhorse Tour (p244) Chinese agency, not connected to Wind Horse Adventure in Lhasa. Contact Helen.

Regions at a Glance

Tibet is a huge land and you can't see all of it in a single trip. Almost everyone visits Lhasa, Tibet's holy city, which still has a lovely old town despite being at the forefront of modernisation. The nearby valleys of Ü offer great scope for overnight excursions from Lhasa, as well as great trekking. Focus your efforts here if you're short on time.

For most travellers the central region of Tsang means the epic overland route to Kathmandu and the trip to Everest Base Camp. More remote are the outlying regions of Ngari (western Tibet) and eastern Tibet (Kham), each of which require trips of two to three weeks through amazing scenery: one desert and steppe, the other forested valleys and alpine pastures.

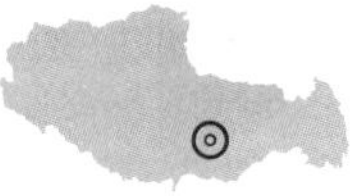

Lhasa

Monasteries
History
Old Town

Great Monastic Cities

The traditional seat of Tibetan power, the great Gelugpa monasteries of Drepung, Sera and Ganden still buzz with monks and pilgrims.

Palaces of the Dalai Lamas

Visit the Potala, the fortress-like home for nine Dalai Lamas; the Norbulingka summer palace, from where the Dalai Lama made his escape in 1959; and the Jokhang Temple, which dates from the arrival of Buddhism in Tibet.

Backstreet Exploration

Lhasa's old town is the one corner of the expanding city that feels truly Tibetan. The backstreets hide teahouses, guesthouses, chapels and craft shops, while the Barkhor Circuit is the spiritual heart of the city.

p50

Ü

Monasteries
Activities
Scenery

Remote Monasteries

Samye is perhaps the loveliest monastery in Ü, while the important hillside centre of Drigung Til is a traveller favourite. Also charming are the rarely visited monasteries of Mindroling, Dorje Drak and Reting.

Tibetan Treks

Trekking is superb in Ü. Ganden–Samye is the classic Tibetan trek, but the Tsurphu–Yangpachen walk has equally outstanding scenery. Ü also offers plenty of day hikes, as well as rafting and horse riding.

Salt Lakes & Sand Dunes

The grandest views are at Namtso, a giant salt lake fringed with the snow-capped Tanglha range. The sand dunes lining the braided Yarlung Tsangpo valley have their own surreal beauty.

p99

Tsang

Monasteries
Mountains
Lakes

Art Treasures

Gyantse's Pelkhor Chöde Monastery boasts the fabulous *kumbum* chörten, but historic Sakya Monastery is an equally worthy destination. Off the beaten track, explore the fine murals of Shalu or the Bön monastery at Yungdrungling.

Everest Highs

Tsang is all about Mt Everest and the awesome views of its north face from Rongphu Monastery or Base Camp. Himalayan views are superb across southern Tsang from Lhasa to Kathmandu.

Turquoise Lakes

Yamdrok-tso is a gorgeous coiling lake and there are great views from just below the Kamba-la. For epic scenery detour to Peiku-tso, just an hour or two off the Friendship Hwy towards Nepal.

p129

Ngari

Lakes
Wildlife
Adventure

Sacred & Salt Lakes

The sight of Mt Kailash or Gurlha Mandata rising from the turquoise waters of Manasarovar is beyond words. The huge salt lakes of the northern Changtang route cry out for a picnic or overnight camp.

The 'Wild' West

Herds of wild ass and antelope grazing the yellow steppe are a regular sight in northern Ngari. Funnier are the marmots sitting on their hind legs or the grunting yaks that haul trekkers' gear.

Lost Cities & Sacred Peaks

Explore the tunnels, caves and mud walls of the ruined cities of Shangshung and Guge. Then shed your sins on a Mt Kailash pilgrimage or set up camp at the base of 8012m Shishapangma.

p164

Eastern Tibet

Monasteries
Scenery
Adventure

Power Places

The east has some real hidden gems: the octagonal temple of Lamaling with its unique architecture; one of Songtsen Gampo's demoness-subduing temples at ancient Buchu Monastery; and Bakha Monastery, in a gorgeous location near a small lake.

Alpine Tibet

Pine forests, lush alpine valleys and turquoise glacial lakes mean that eastern Tibet often feels more like the Canadian Rockies or Swiss Alps than the arid central plateau.

Rough Roads & Pilgrim Paths

Permit hassles make it hard to get off the main routes, but adventurers can trek around the sacred mountain of Bönri or tackle the extremely hairy roads around Tangmi.

p193

On the Road

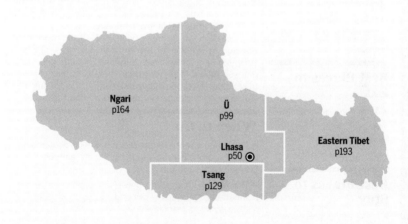

Lhasa

ལྷ་ས་ 拉萨

🎵 0891 / POP 530,000 / ELEV 3650M

Best Places to Eat

➡ Snowland Restaurant (p78)

➡ Woeser Zedroe Tibetan Restaurant (p78)

➡ Lhasa Kitchen (p78)

Best Places to Stay

➡ House of Shambhala (p76)

➡ Kyichu Hotel (p75)

➡ Yak Hotel (p75)

➡ Songtsam Choskyi Linka Lhasa (p76)

Why Go?

The centre of the Tibetan Buddhist world for over a millennium, Lhasa (ལྷ་ས་; 拉萨; Lāsà; literally the 'Place of the Gods') remains largely a city of wonders. Your first view of the red-and-white Potala Palace soaring above the Holy City raises goosebumps and the charming whitewashed old Tibetan quarter continues to preserve the essence of traditional Tibetan life. It is here in the Jokhang, an otherworldly mix of flickering butter lamps, wafting incense and prostrating pilgrims, and the encircling Barkhor pilgrim circuit, that most visitors first fall in love with Tibet.

These days the booming boulevards of the modern city threaten to overwhelm the winding alleyways and back-street temples of the Tibetan old town, but it is in the latter that you should focus your time. If possible, budget a week to acclimatise, see the sights and roam the fascinating back-streets before heading off on a grand overland adventure.

When to Go

➡ Temperatures are comfortable from April to September, with days surprisingly warm and nights pleasantly cool. Sunlight is strong at this altitude, so always wear sunscreen.

➡ The major festival of Saga Dawa (spring) brings huge numbers of pilgrims to the city, and the August Shötun festival is also a major draw.

➡ Accommodation can be tight during the first weeks of May and October and the high-season months of July and August, when Chinese tourists flock to the city.

➡ Consider a winter visit (November to February) for few crowds and big accommodation discounts, but bring warm clothes.

History

Lhasa rose to prominence as an important administrative centre in the 7th century AD, when King Songtsen Gampo (c 618–49) moved his capital from the Yarlung Valley to Lhasa and built a palace on the site now occupied by the Potala. It was at this time that the temples of Ramoche and Jokhang were founded to house the priceless first Buddha statues brought to Tibet as the dowries of Songtsen Gampo's Chinese and Nepali wives.

With the break-up of the Yarlung empire 250 years later, Tibet's centre of power shifted to Sakya, Nedong (Ü) and then Shigatse (Tsang). No longer the capital, Lhasa languished in the backwaters of Tibetan history until the fifth Dalai Lama (1617–82) defeated the Shigatse kings with Mongol support.

The fifth Dalai Lama moved his capital to Lhasa and started construction on his palace, the Potala, on the site of the ruins of Songtsen Gampo's 7th-century palace. Lhasa has remained Tibet's capital since 1642, and most of the city's historical sights date from this second stage of the city's development.

Modern Lhasa in many ways provides the visitor with both the best and the worst of contemporary Tibet. Photographs of the city taken before October 1950 reveal a small town nestled at the foot of the Potala, with a second cluster of residences surrounding the Jokhang, housing a population of between 20,000 and 30,000. Today the prefecture-sized city has a population of around 530,000, and Han Chinese residents outnumber Tibetans.

Shöl, the village at the foot of the Potala, has long since disappeared, and the area in front of the Potala has been made into a Tiān'ānmén-style public square, complete with a 35m-tall monument to what the Chinese administration sees as the liberation of Tibet (under constant guard to prevent vandalism or demonstrations).

Physically the city has at least doubled in size in the last 20 years and it takes 20 minutes to drive through the sprawling Chinese-style western suburbs. The Tibetan quarter is now an isolated enclave at the eastern end of town, comprising only around 4% of the city, and even these lingering remnants of tradition are under threat from the bulldozers, despite official protection. Lhasa has probably changed more in the last 25 years than in the thousand years before.

Permits

Lhasa is currently the only part of Tibet that doesn't require you to hire pricey transport. The only time you will be asked for your Tibet Tourism Bureau (TTB) permit is when you check into a hotel, which your guide will help you with. No other permits are required for the city or surroundings.

At the time of research you had to visit the main monasteries of Drepung, Sera and Ganden and Jokhang Temple and Potala Palace in the company of your guide, but other parts of the city were fine to explore by yourself.

LHASA IN...

Two Days

On arrival in Lhasa you need at least two days to adjust to the altitude; you can expect to be tired and headachey most of the time. We recommend adding an extra day and taking the first day very easy.

Start at Barkhor Square (p53), finding your legs on a relaxed stroll around the Barkhor Circuit (p53) before visiting the Jokhang (p57). Grab lunch at nearby Snowland Restaurant (p78) or Lhasa Kitchen (p78). In the afternoon head to Sera Monastery (p89) to catch the monks debating. If your headache's gone, round off the day with a cold Lhasa Beer at Dunya (p79) or on the roof of Shambhala Palace (p76).

On day two visit the Potala Palace (p64) at your allotted time and then spend the afternoon losing yourself in the fascinating old town (p62).

Four Days

With four days you could leave the Potala until day three, and add on a stroll around the Potala Kora (p68), grabbing some sweet tea en route. On day four leave the city on a day trip out to Ganden Monastery (p93), visiting the hermitage caves of Drak Yerpa (p96) on the way back. Try to budget some time for handicraft shopping at Dropenling (p80) and to explore an off-the-beaten-path chapel such as the Lho Rigsum Lhakhang (p62).

Lhasa Highlights

1 Barkhor Circuit (p53) Following monks, mendicants and pilgrims around this medieval pilgrim path.

2 Jokhang Temple (p57) Joining the lines of awed pilgrims at the glowing shrines of Tibet's holiest sanctum.

3 Potala Palace (p64) Shuffling past murals and stupas in the impressive citadel of the Dalai Lamas.

4 Sera Monastery (p89) Taking in a prayer meeting or some monk-debating at this great monastic centre.

5 Ganden Monastery (p93) Taking a day trip out to this important monastery and its kora (pilgrim path).

6 Dropenling (p80) Visiting this top-notch crafts centre on a walk past the architecture and workshops of Lhasa's old town.

7 Meru Nyingba Monastery (p53) Tracking down one of Lhasa's most delightful off-the-beaten-track temples, located in a hidden courtyard.

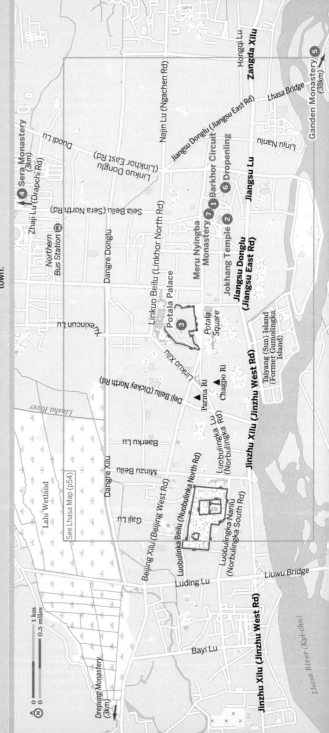

◎ Sights

◎ The Barkhor བར་སྐོར་ 八廓

The first stop for most newcomers to Lhasa is the Jokhang in the heart of the Tibetan old town. But before you even venture into the Jokhang it's worth taking a stroll around the Barkhor, a quadrangle of streets that surrounds the Jokhang complex. It is an area unrivalled in Tibet for its fascinating combination of sacred significance and push-and-shove market economics. This is both the spiritual heart of the Holy City and the main shopping district for Tibetans.

The Barkhor is the one part of Lhasa that has most resisted the invasions of the modern world. Pilgrims from Kham, Amdo and further afield step blithely around a prostrating monk and stop briefly to inspect a jewel-encrusted dagger at a street stall; monks sit cross-legged on the paving stones before their alms bowls muttering mantras; and armed police march by anti-clockwise in strict formation. It's an utterly fascinating place you'll want to come back to time after time.

Barkhor Square   SQUARE
(八角广场, Bājiǎo Guǎngchǎng; Map p56) For your first visit to the Barkhor, enter from Barkhor Sq, a large plaza that was cleared in 1985. The square has been a focus for violent political protest on several occasions, notably in 1998 (when a Dutch tourist was shot in the shoulder) and most recently in 2008. The square is now bordered by metal detectors, riot-squad vehicles, fire-extinguisher teams (to prevent self-immolations) and rooftop surveillance. Despite the stream of selfie-taking tourists, the atmosphere is one of occupation or siege.

Close to the entrance to the Jokhang a constant stream of Tibetans follows the Barkhor circumambulation route in a clockwise direction. Look for the two pot-bellied stone *sangkang* (incense burners) in front of the Jokhang. There are four *sangkang*, marking the four extremities of the Barkhor Circuit; the other two are at the rear of the Jokhang.

Behind the first two *sangkang* are two open enclosures. The northern **stele** atop a turtle is inscribed with the terms of the Sino-Tibetan treaty of 822. The dual-language inscription delimits the Chinese–Tibetan border and guarantees mutual respect of the borders of the two nations, an irony given the political situation over the last 60 years. The southern enclosure harbours an ancient willow tree, known as the hair of the Jowo – according to legend, it was planted by Songtsen Gampo's Chinese wife, Princess Wencheng – and two stele, one of which was erected in 1793 to commemorate the victims of a smallpox epidemic. Over the centuries Tibetans have chiselled out chunks of this stele for its purported protective medicinal properties.

It's impossible not to be swept up in the wondrous tide of humanity that is the **Barkhor** (བར་བསྐོར་, 八廓, Bākuò), a kora (pilgrim circuit) that winds clockwise around the periphery of the Jokhang Temple (p57). You'll swear it possesses some spiritual centrifugal force, as every time you approach within 50m, you somehow get sucked right in and gladly wind up making the whole circuit again! It's the best place to start exploring Lhasa and the last spot you'll want to see before you bid the city farewell.

As you follow the flow of pilgrims past sellers of religious photos, felt cowboy hats and electric blenders (for yak-butter tea), you'll soon see a small building on the right, set off from the main path. This is a charming **mani lhakhang** (Map p56), a small chapel that houses a huge prayer wheel set almost continuously in motion. To the right of the building is the grandiose entrance of the former city jail and dungeons, known as Nangtse Shar.

If you head south from here, after about 10m you will see the entrance to the **Jampa Lhakhang** (Jamkhang, Water Blessing Temple; Map p56) on the right. The ground floor of this small temple has a huge two-storey statue of Miwang Jampa, the Future Buddha, flanked by rows of various protector gods and the meditation cave of the chapel's founder. Join the queue of pilgrims shuffling up to the upper floor to be blessed with a sprinkling of holy water and the touch of a holy *dorje* (thunderbolt).

Continue down the alley following the prayer wheels, then pass through a doorway into the old **Meru Nyingba Monastery** (Map p56). This small but active monastery is a real delight and is invariably crowded with Tibetans thumbing prayer beads or lazily swinging prayer wheels and chanting under their breath. The chapel itself is administered by Nechung Monastery, which accounts for the many images of the Nechung oracle inside. The building, like the adjoining Jokhang, dates back to the 7th century, though most of what you see today is recently constructed.

Lhasa

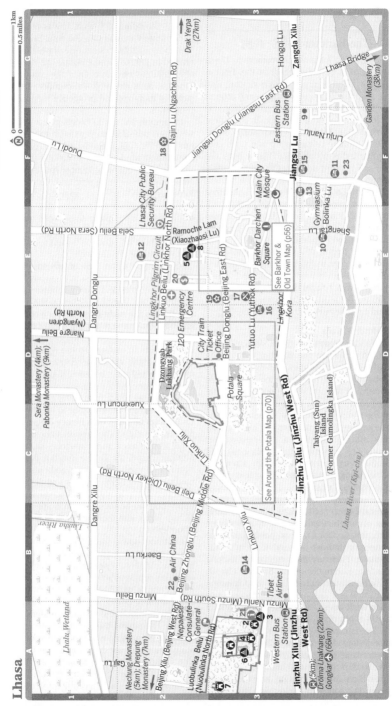

0 ___ 1km
0 ___ 0.5 miles

Najin Lu (Ngachen Rd)

Drak Yerpa (27km)

Duodi Lu

Jiangsu Donglu (Jiangsu East Rd)

Eastern Bus Station

Hongqi Lu

Zangda Xilu

Lhasa Bridge

Ganden Monastery (38km)

18

Lhasa City Public Security Bureau

Sela Beilu (Sera North Rd)

Ramoche Lam (Xiaozhaosi Lu)

Linjiu Nanlu

Jiangsu Lu

15

11

23

Main City Mosque

13

Gymnasium

Bolinka Lu

Shengtai Lu

10

5

8

12

Barkhor Darchen Square

See Barkhor & Old Town Map (p56)

Barkhor & Old Town Map (p56)

Linkhor Pilgrim Circuit

Linkuo Beilu (Linkhor North Rd)

Dangre Donglu

20

120 Emergency Centre

19

17

Beijing Donglu (Beijing East Rd)

Yutuo Lu (Yuthok Rd)

16

Linkhor Kora

Niangre Beilu (Nyangdren North Rd)

Xuexincun Lu

City Train Ticket Office

Dzongyab Lukhang Park

Sera Monastery (4km); Pabonka Monastery (9km)

Dangre Donglu

Potala Square

See Around the Potala Map (p70)

Linkuo Xilu

Deji Beilu (Dickey North Rd)

Taiyang (Sun) Island (Former Gumolingka Island)

Jinzhu Xilu (Jinzhu West Rd)

Lhasa River (Kyi-chu)

Dangre Xilu

Lhasa River

Lhalu Wetland

Baerku Lu

Air China

22

Beijing Zhonglu (Beijing Middle Rd)

14

Minzu Beilu

Minzu Nanlu (Minzu South Rd)

Tibet Airlines

Nechung Monastery (5km); Drepung Monastery (7km)

Beijing Xilu (Beijing West Rd)

Nepalese Consulate General

Luobulinka Beilu (Nuobulinka North Rd)

2 21

1

3

Western Bus Station

6 4

7

Jinzhu Xilu (Jinzhu West Rd)

(5km); Drolma Lhakhang (22km); Gongkar (66km)

LHASA SIGHTS

ancient times...'). Three courtyards make up the one-time residence of the Qing-dynasty Chinese ambans (political representatives), with mock-ups depicting various officials' rooms. Lhasa's original Tromsikhang Market was once just outside.

The eastern side of the circuit has more shops and even a couple of small department stores that specialise in turquoise. In the southeastern corner is a wall shrine and a **darchen** (prayer pole), which mark the spot where Tsongkhapa planted his walking stick in 1409.

On the southern side of the circuit, look out for the **Gendun Choephel Memorial Hall** (根敦群培纪念馆; Gēndūn Qúnpéi Jìniànguǎn; Map p56; www.gdqpzhx.com; ⊙9.30am-6.30pm) FREE, a dull museum on a particularly fascinating character. Choephel (1903–51) was a monk, poet, translator, scientist, travel writer, painter, linguist, medic, sexologist, scholar of Sanskrit and all-round nonconformist. The museum suffers from a dogmatic note in its commentary; you may find your eyes glazing over when text expounds on the 'caesaropapist feudal serf system'. This building, the Garushag, was Choephel's last residence and the place in which he died.

The empty southern square of the Jokhang used to host annual teachings by the Dalai Lama during the Mönlam festival. The circuit finally swings north by a police station back to Barkhor Sq.

On the western side of the courtyard, up some narrow stairs, is the small Sakyapa-school **Gongkar Chöde Chapel** (Map p56). Below is the **Zhambhala Lhakhang** (Map p56), with a central image of Marmedze (Dipamkara), the Past Buddha, and a small inner kora path. Both are dark, moody places that resonate with the sounds of Tantric drumming. From here you can return north or head east to join up with the Barkhor circuit.

A recent addition to the northeast side of the Barkhor Circuit is the **Perdu Ambam Yamen** (清政府驻藏大臣衙门旧址, Qīngzhèngfǔ Zhùzàng Dàchén Yámen Jiùzhǐ; Map p56; ⊙9.30am-6.30pm) FREE, a politicised museum firmly aimed at local Chinese consumption (the text starts off with the phrase 'Tibet has been an inalienable part of China since

⊙ The Old Town

Down the alleys off Beijing Donglu is an active nunnery and five obscure but often charming temples, which can be visited if you prefer the intimacy of local shrines over grandiose temples.

Tsome Ling BUDDHIST TEMPLE
(策门林寺, Cèménlín Sì; Map p56) The small but interesting Tsome Ling is one of the four *ling* temples of Lhasa (along with Kunde Ling (p69) and Tengye Ling (p57)). To the east of the residential courtyard is the Kharpo Podrang (White Palace), built in 1777, and to the west is the more interesting Marpo Podrang (Red Palace), built at the beginning of the 19th century. Both buildings have fine murals and are well frequented by pilgrims.

Shide Tratsang BUDDHIST TEMPLE
(喜德林寺, Xǐdélín Sì; Map p56) Once one of the six principal temples encircling the Jokhang, this partially renovated temple is connected to Reting Monastery. It's in a

Barkhor & Old Town

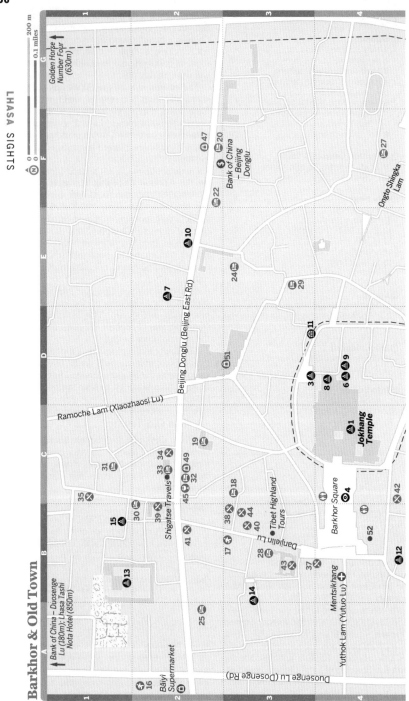

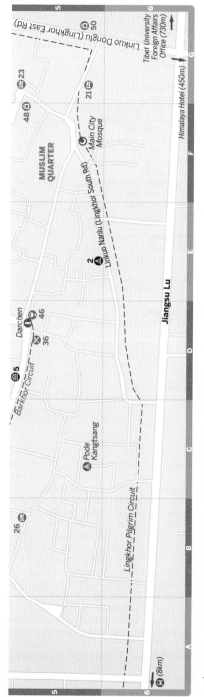

LHASA SIGHTS

housing courtyard, down a back alley near Tashi I restaurant. Look for the brown walls.

Tengye Ling
BUDDHIST TEMPLE

(丹杰林寺, Dānjiélín Sì; Map p56) This obscure and little-visited Nyingmapa-sect temple is dedicated to the central red-faced deity Tseumar, as well as Pehar (a protector linked to Samye) and Tamdrin (Hayagriva). The crates of *báijiǔ* (rice wine) stacked in the corner are there to refill the silver cup in Tseumar's hand; apparently he's in a better mood if constantly plastered. The entire chapel smells like a distillery.

The chapel is hidden in the backstreets west of the Shangbala Hotel and is hard to find; enter through the gateway marked by juniper and *báijiǔ* sellers.

Rigsum Lhakhang
BUDDHIST TEMPLE

(Map p56) One of four chapels surrounding the Jokhang at cardinal points, this recently renovated small chapel southwest of Barkhor Sq is dedicated to the Rigsum Gonpo trinity of Jampelyang, Chenresig and Chana Dorje (Vajrapani). Pilgrims head to the upper floor to receive a water blessing.

Ani Sangkhung Nunnery
BUDDHIST MONASTERY

(仓姑寺, Cānggū Sì; Map p56; 29 Linkuo Nanlu; ¥40; ⊙8am-6pm) This small and politically active nunnery is the only one within the precincts of the old Tibetan quarter. The site of the nunnery probably dates back to the 7th century, but it housed a monastery until at least the 15th century. The principal image, upstairs on the 2nd floor, is a thousand-armed Chenresig. A small alley to the side of the main chapel leads down to the former meditation chamber of Songtsen Gampo, one of the oldest shrines in Lhasa.

◎ The Jokhang ར་ས་ 大昭寺

Also known in Tibetan as the Tsuglhakhang, the **Jokhang** (ར་ས་, 大昭寺, Dàzhāo Sì; Map p56; adult ¥85; ⊙8.15-noon & 3-5.30pm, most chapels closed after noon) is the most revered religious structure in Tibet. Thick with the smell of yak butter, the murmur of mantras and the shuffling of wide-eyed pilgrims spooning yak butter into lamps and bowing their heads to sacred statues, the Jokhang is an unrivalled Tibetan experience. Don't miss it.

The chapels can be very busy, with long queues of pilgrims, so try to view the most popular ones just after the temple opens or just before it closes (around noon). Your guide will often be under pressure to rush you

Barkhor & Old Town

through the chapels; take your time and meet them outside afterwards.

The complex is open in the afternoon via the side entrance (where you buy tickets), but many chapels are closed then, and there are no pilgrims. Once you've left the complex you can't re-enter without buying another ticket. Photos are not allowed inside the chapels.

Estimated dates for the Jokhang's founding range from 639 to 647. Construction was initiated by King Songtsen Gampo to house an image of Mikyöba (Akshobhya) that was brought to Tibet as part of the dowry of his Nepali wife Princess Bhrikuti. The Ramoche Temple was constructed at the same time to house another Buddha image, the Jowo Sakyamuni, brought to Tibet by Songtsen Gampo's Chinese wife Princess Wencheng. It is thought that after the death of Songtsen Gampo, Jowo Sakyamuni was moved from

Ramoche for its protection and hidden in the Jokhang's Chapel of the Hidden Jowo by Princess Wencheng. It has remained in the Jokhang ever since (Jokhang, or Jowokhang, means 'chapel of the Jowo'), and is the most revered Buddha image in all of Tibet.

Over the centuries, the Jokhang has undergone many renovations, but the basic layout is ancient and differs from that of many other Tibetan religious structures. One crucial difference is the building's east–west orientation, said to face towards Nepal to honour Princess Bhrikuti. A few interior carved pillars and entrance arches remain from the original 7th-century work of Newari artisans and architects brought from the Kathmandu Valley in Nepal to work on the construction.

In the early days of the Cultural Revolution, Red Guards desecrated much of the interior of the Jokhang and it is claimed that a section was utilised as a pigsty. Since 1980 the Jokhang has been restored, and without the aid of an expert eye you will see few signs of the misfortunes that have befallen the temple in recent years.

➡ Ground Floor

In front of the entrance to the Jokhang is a forecourt that is perpetually crowded with pilgrims prostrating themselves on the flagstones and polishing grain in brass bowls as a form of meditation.

Just inside the entrance to the Jokhang are statues of the **Four Guardian Kings** (Chökyong), two on either side. Beyond this is the *dukhang* (main assembly hall), a paved courtyard that is open to the elements. Before 1959 the hall was the focus of religious festivals. The throne on the left (north) wall has fine murals and was formerly used by the Dalai Lamas. You'll see a line of pilgrims filing past the main Jokhang entrance as they walk the pilgrim circuit around the temple.

The inner prayer hall of the Jokhang houses the most important images and chapels. Most prominent are six larger-than-life statues that dominate the central prayer hall. In the foreground and to the left is a 6m statue of Guru Rinpoche. The statue to the right is of a seated Jampa (Maitreya), the Future Buddha, with an ornate crown. At the centre of the hall, between and to the rear of these two statues, is a thousand-armed Chenresig (Avalokiteshvara).

Encircling this enclosed area of statues is a collection of chapels, which Tibetan pilgrims visit in a clockwise direction. There are generally long queues for the holiest chapels, particularly the Chapel of Jowo Sakyamuni. Pilgrims rub the doorways and chain-mail curtains, touch their heads to revered statues, throw seeds as offerings and pour molten yak butter into the heat of a thousand prayer lamps. The atmosphere of hushed sanctity is broken only by the occasional mobile-phone ringtone.

The chapels, following a clockwise route, are as follows.

Tsongkhapa was the founder of the Gelugpa order, and you can see him seated in the centre of the **Chapel of Tsongkhapa and His Disciples**, flanked by his eight disciples. Just outside is the large Tagba chörten (stupa). The buddhas in the **Chapel of the Eight Medicine Buddhas** are recent and not of special interest.

The **Chapel of Chenresig** contains the Jokhang's most important image after the

Jowo Sakyamuni. Legend has it that the statue of Chenresig here sprang spontaneously into being and combines aspects of King Songtsen Gampo, his wives and two wrathful protective deities. The doors of the chapel are among the few remnants still visible of the Jokhang's 7th-century origins and were fashioned by Nepali artisans. This and the next four chapels are the most popular with pilgrims and lines can be long.

In the **Chapel of Jampa** are statues of Jampa as well as four smaller bodhisattvas: Jampelyang (Manjushri), Chenresig (to the left), Chana Dorje (Vajrapani) and Drölma (Tara). Öpagme (Amitabha) and Tsongkhapa are also present here, as are two funeral chörtens, one of which holds the remains of the original sculptor.

The image of Tsongkhapa in the **Chapel of Tsongkhapa** was commissioned by the subject himself and is said to be a precise resemblance. It is the central image on top of the steps of the wooden alcove.

The **Chapel of the Buddha of Infinite Light** is the second of the chapels consecrated to Öpagme (Amitabha), the Buddha of Infinite Light. The outer entrance, with its wonderful carved doors, is protected by two fierce deities, red Tamdrin (Hayagriva; right) and blue Chana Dorje (Vajrapani; left). There are also statues of the eight bodhisattvas. Pilgrims generally pray here for the elimination of impediments to viewing the most sacred image of the Jokhang, that of Jowo Sakyamuni, which awaits in the next chapel.

To the right as you leave the chapel are statues of King Songtsen Gampo with his two wives, and of Guru Rinpoche (at the back).

The most important shrine in Tibet, the **Chapel of Jowo Sakyamuni** houses the image of Sakyamuni Buddha at the age of 12, brought to Tibet by Princess Wencheng. You enter via an anteroom containing the Four Guardian Kings, smiling on the left and frowning to the right. Inside are statues of the protectors Miyowa (Achala) and Chana Dorje (Vajrapani, blue). Several large bells hang from the anteroom's Newari-style roof. The carved doorway has been rubbed smooth by generations of pilgrims.

The 1.5m statue of Sakyamuni is embedded with precious stones, covered in silks and jewellery, and surrounded by silver pillars with dragon motifs. The silver canopy above was financed by a Mongolian khan. Pilgrims touch their forehead to the statue's left leg or are blessed with some brocade before being

The Jokhang

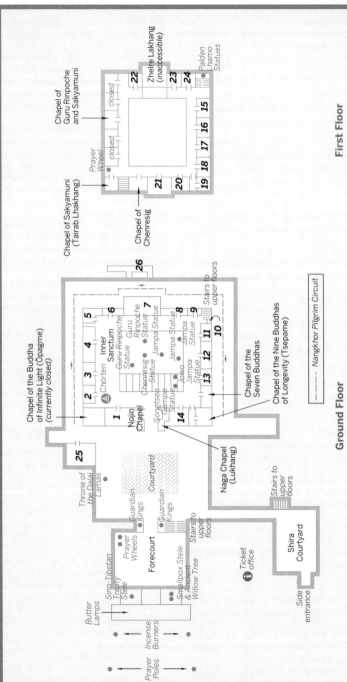

Chapel of the Buddha of Infinite Light (Öpagme) (currently closed)

Chapel of Guru Rinpoche and Sakyamuni

Zhelre Lakhang (inaccessible)

Palden Lhamo Statues

Chapel of Sakyamuni (Tairab Lhakhang)

Chapel of Chenresig

Prayer Wheel

First Floor

Throne of the Dalai Lamas

Guardian Kings

Guardian Kings

Courtyard

Forecourt

Prayer Wheels

Sino-Tibetan Treaty Stele

Smallpox Stele & Ancient Willow Tree

Butter Lamps

Incense Burners

Prayer Poles

Stairs to upper floors

Ticket office

Shira Courtyard

Stairs to upper floors

Side entrance

Inner Sanctum

Nojin Chapel

Guru Rinpoche Statue

Guru Rinpoche Statue

Chenresig Statue

Jampa Statue

Jampa Statue

Jampa Statue

Jowo

Jampa Statue

Songtsen Gampo Statue

Chörten

Naga Chapel (Lukhang)

Chapel of the Seven Buddhas

Chapel of the Nine Buddhas of Longevity (Tsepame)

Stairs to upper floors

Nangkhor Pilgrim Circuit

Ground Floor

tapped on the back by a monk 'bouncer' when it's time to move on.

To the rear of Sakyamuni are statues of the seventh and 13th Dalai Lamas (with a moustache), Tsongkhapa and 12 standing bodhisattvas. A sacred buddha statue hides to the rear of the Sakyamuni statue. Look for the 7th-century pillars on the way out.

From here you can see the other statues that cram the main prayer hall, including two more Jampa statues; to the far rear, facing the main Jowo statue, is a statue of Guru Rinpoche, encased in a cabinet.

The Jampa (Maitreya, or Future Buddha) enshrined in the Chapel of Jampa is a replica of a statue that came to Tibet as part of the dowry of Princess Bhrikuti, King Songtsen Gampo's Nepali wife. Around the statue are eight images of Drölma, a goddess seen as an embodiment of the enlightened mind of buddhahood and who protects against the eight fears – hence the eight statues. There are some fine door carvings here. As you exit the chapel look for the unexpected Tibetan-style statues of the Hindu gods Indra (Yabshen in Tibetan) and Brahma (Tsangba).

In the Chapel of Chenresig Riding a Lion, the statue of Chenresig on the back of a *sengye* (snow lion) is first on the left (it's not the largest of the icons within). Most of the other statues are aspects of Chenresig.

Some pilgrims exit this chapel and then follow a flight of stairs up to the next floor, while others complete the circuit on the ground floor. Unless you're chapelled out (you've seen the important ones already), continue on upstairs, but look out first for a small hole in the wall on the left as you exit the chapel, against which pilgrims place their ear to hear the lapping waters of the Wothang Lake on which the Jokhang was built. The pillar opposite has been rubbed smooth over the centuries.

The Guru Rinpoche Shrine contains two statues of Guru Rinpoche and one of King Trisong Detsen in the corner. Beside the shrine is a self-arisen (not human-made) golden rock painting of the medicine buddha protected by a glass plate.

Inside the Chapel of Tsepame are nine statues of Tsepame (Amitayus), the red Buddha of Longevity, in *yabyum* (sexual and spiritual union) pose.

The Chapel of Jampa holds the Jampa statue that was traditionally borne around the Barkhor on the 25th day of the first lunar month for the Mönlam festival. This yearly

excursion was designed to hasten the arrival of the Future Buddha. Standing statues of Jampelyang and Chenresig flank the Buddha.

The chapel is also named Ramo Gyalmo (Chapel of the Sacred Goat), after the rough 'self-arisen' gold-painted image of the goat emerging from the wall in the first corner, beside the god of wealth Zhambhala.

The Chapel of the Hidden Jowo is where Princess Wencheng is said to have hidden the Jowo Sakyamuni for safekeeping after the death of her husband and the ensuing anti-Buddhism backlash. Inside is a statue of Öpagme (Amitabha) and the eight medicine buddhas with characteristic blue hair. Look for the fabulous stone butter lamp outside the chapel entrance.

The last of the chapels is the Chapel of the Kings, with some original statues of Tibet's earliest kings. The central figure is Songtsen Gampo, flanked by images of King Trisong Detsen and King Ralpachen. Pilgrims touch their head to the central pillar. On the wall outside the chapel on the left-hand side is a fine mural depicting the original construction of the Potala, alongside performances of Tibetan opera, yak dances, wrestling, stone weightlifting and horse racing. Images to the right show the Jokhang being constructed atop Lake Wothang.

➜ First Floor

After visiting the ground-floor chapels, return clockwise to the rear of the ground floor and climb the stairs to the upper floor of the

THE SACRED GOAT

When Princess Wencheng chose the site of the Jokhang, she chose Lake Wothang (perhaps because she was still upset at having to live in barbarian Tibet). The lake was eventually filled in, but it is said that a well in the precincts of the Jokhang still draws its waters from those of the old lake. Over the years, many legends have emerged around the task of filling in Lake Wothang. The most prominent of these is the story of how the lake was filled by a sacred white goat (*ra*, the Tibetan word for goat, is etymologically connected with the original name for Lhasa, Rasa). Look for a small image of the goat peeking out from the Chapel of Jampa on the south wall of the Jokhang's ground-floor inner sanctum.

Jokhang. This floor is also ringed with chapels, though some of them are closed.

As you begin the circuit, the Lamrin Chapel near the southeastern corner features Pabonka Rinpoche, Sakyamuni, Tsongkhapa and Atisha (Jowo-je). You then pass by several newly restored rooms that feature **Sakyamuni** accompanied by his two main disciples, and one featuring the **eight medicine buddhas**. The **Lamrin Chapel** near the southeastern corner features Pabonka Rinpoche, Sakyamuni, Tsongkhapa and Atisha (Jowo-je). The chapel in the southwestern corner is the **Chapel of Five Protectors** and has some fearsome statues of Tamdrin (Hayagriva) and other protector deities, often attended by deep Tantric drumming in the atmospheric anteroom.

Next is the **Chapel of the Three Kings**, dedicated to Songtsen Gampo, flanked by Trisong Detsen and Tri Ralpachen. Also featured in the room are the statues of Songtsen Gampo's two wives, various ministers, and such symbols of royalty as the elephant and horse in either corner.

Also worth a look is the **Chapel of Songtsen Gampo**, the principal Songtsen Gampo chapel in the Jokhang. It is positioned in the centre of the west wall (directly above the entry to the ground-floor inner sanctum). The bejewelled king, with a tiny buddha protruding from his turban, is accompanied by his two consorts, his Nepali wife to the left and his Chinese wife to the right. During the annual Palden Lhamo festival, Tibetan families queue up in front of the royal silver-embossed animal-headed *chang* (barley beer) container here to make an offering of their first batch of home brew.

Most of the other rooms are hidden behind grilles, the main exception being the meditation cell of the **Chapel of Songtsen Gampo** near the floor's northeastern corner, which has an incredible carved doorway smeared with decades' worth of yak butter. Murals outside the doorway depict the Jokhang. As you walk back to the stairs, look at the unusual row of carved beams that look like half-lion, half-monkey creatures.

Back by the stairs, notice the curved door frame of the **Chapel of Guru Rinpoche** and the **Chapel of Samvara**, showing Samvara with Tantric consort, both of which date back to the 7th century.

Before you leave the 1st floor by the stairs in the southeastern corner, ascend half a floor up to two statues of the protectress **Palden Lhamo**, one wrathful ('frog-faced')

🏃 **Walking Tour**
Old Town

START BARKHOR SQ
END BARKHOR SQ
LENGTH 3KM; THREE HOURS

The fragile Tibetan old town shelters the soul of Lhasa. This walk takes in craft workshops, backstreet chapels and pilgrim paths, passing en route some of Lhasa's last remaining traditional architecture.

At the first turn of the ❶ **Barkhor Circuit** (p53) make a left and then a quick right, going past strips of dried yak meat and yellow bags of yak butter to the bustling ❷ **Tromsikhang Market** (p80). After a quick look around the modern market (the original Tibetan-style building was demolished in 1997), head north to the main road, Beijing Donglu, and then right to visit the ❸ **Gyüme Tratsang** (p71), Lhasa's Lower Tantric College. It's easy to miss this working temple; look for an imposing entrance set back from the road. About 50m further down the road are the deceptively long white walls of the small but active ❹ **Meru Sarpa Monastery** (p71).

Cross Beijing Donglu, take the alley into the old town and follow the winding branch to the right, past the yellow walls of the House of Shambhala, which has a nice rooftop restaurant if you need a break. As you continue south you'll pass Tibetan craftspeople making statues, embroidery, cabinets, prayer wheels and Tibetan banners. At the junction take a left at the ❺ **monks' clothing store**.

As you head southeast, past statue-makers, noodle producers and a kindergarten, curve right to the quiet but interesting yellow-walled ❻ **Karmashar Temple**, once the home of the Karmashar, Lhasa's main oracle. Look for the Karmashar statue in the far right corner of the back chapel and for the spooky faded icon painted on a pigskin bag in the main hall, pacified with offerings of *tsampa* (roasted-barley flour) and barley beer. Enter from the right (southwestern) side.

Continue east to a T-junction past outdoor pool tables and furniture shops. At the T-junction, take a left to visit stylish ❼ **Dropenling** (p80), where you can watch local craftsmen from the ❽ **Ancient Art**

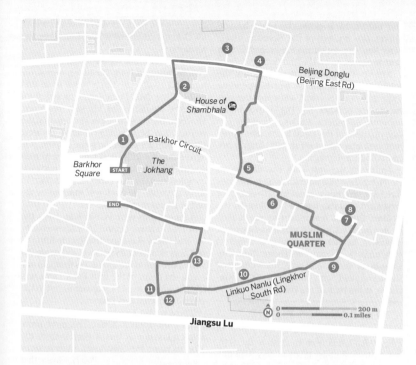

Restoration Centre across the courtyard, as they grind up mineral paints for thangka painting and hammer away at metal sculptures in a corner workshop. Ask to see the interior workshops and the centre's museum, which details the monasteries it has restored (everything from Samye to Ganden). Ask at Dropenling if no one is around. A cafe is planned here.

After loading up with souvenirs, head south towards the ⑨ **Muslim quarter**, the focus of Lhasa's 2000-strong Muslim population. During Friday-lunchtime weekly prayers and at dusk the quarter is full of men with wispy beards and skullcaps (non-Muslims may not enter the mosque itself). At other times the square bustles with wheeling-and-dealing *yartsa gunbu* (caterpillar fungus) traders, alongside a vegetable market and hawkers selling loose tea and Muslim breads. Many women here wear black-velvet headscarfs, characteristic of the Línxià region of China's Gānsù province.

As you face the mosque, turn right and head southwest past Muslim tea stalls and butcher shops, branching along part of the Lingkhor pilgrim circuit to the yellow walls of the ⑩ **Ani Sangkhung Nunnery** (p57), home to one of Lhasa's oldest shrines.

Continue past a second mosque to the charming ⑪ **Lho Rigsum Lhakhang** (signed the 'Temple of South Three Protectors'), one of four chapels surrounding the Jokhang at cardinal points. The lovely chapel, squeezed by modern construction and ignored by tourists, has a central statue of Tsepame (Amitayus) flanked by the four main bodhisattvas and its own inner kora. Monks from Ganden Monastery look after the site.

A ⑫ **prayer-wheel shop** across the road offers the ultimate selection of prayer-wheel accessories – perfect for the pilgrim who has everything. Next door is a prayer-flag shop, should you want to pick up a string to leave at an upcoming pass crossing. If you are in need of refreshment, the pleasant garden restaurant of the Trichang Labrang Hotel is just 100m to the west.

Take a right here, heading north, and then a right, then a left. At the junction you can see the ⑬ **Rabsel Tsenkhang**, a small temple affiliated with Sera Monastery and featuring that monastery's local protector, Tashi Lhamo.

The alley north takes you to the southeastern corner of the Barkhor Circuit, where you can continue clockwise to Barkhor Sq.

and hidden by a cloth, the other benign. There's also a photo of the Nechung oracle here. You can sometimes gain access to a Tantric chapel up on the 2nd floor.

After you've explored the interior of the Jokhang, it's definitely worth spending some time on the roof, with its stunning views over Barkhor Sq. The orange building on the northern side once held the private quarters of the Dalai Lama. The upper roof area was closed off in 2018 after a fire caused minor damage.

Finish off the visit with a walk around the Nangkhor pilgrim path, which encircles the Jokhang's inner sanctum. If you're not exhausted, you can have a brief look at the Drölma Chapel, featuring Drölma flanked by her green and white manifestations and others of her 21 manifestations. Pilgrims sometimes pop into the Guru Rinpoche Chapel, a series of three interconnected shrines stuffed with images of Guru Rinpoche, at the back of the kora.

◎ The Potala རྒྱལ་ 布达拉宫

Lhasa's cardinal landmark and home to every Dalai Lama from the fifth to the 14th, the Potala Palace (Bùdálā Gōng; Map p70; May-Oct ¥200, Nov-Apr ¥100; ⊙9.30am-3pm Nov-Apr, 9am-3.30pm May-Oct, interior chapels close 4.30pm) is one of the great wonders of world architecture. As has been the case with centuries of pilgrims before you, the first sight of the fortress-like structure will be a magical moment that you will remember for years. It's hard to peel your eyes away from the place.

The Potala is a structure of massive proportions, with more than 1000 rooms. It's an awe-inspiring place to visit, but still many visitors come away slightly disappointed. Unlike the Jokhang, which hums with vibrant activity, the Potala lies dormant like a huge museum, and tourists are herded through the chapels in one shuffling line without the chance to truly appreciate the artwork up close. The lifelessness of the highly symbolic building constantly reminds visitors that the government of the Dalai Lama is in exile.

Marpo Ri (Red Hill), the 130m-high eminence that commands a view of all of Lhasa, was the site of King Songtsen Gampo's palace during the mid-7th century, long before the construction of the present-day Potala. There is little to indicate what this palace looked like, but it is clear that royal precedent was a major factor in the fifth Dalai Lama's choice of this site when he decided to move the seat of his Gelugpa government here from Drepung Monastery.

Work began first on the Kharpo Podrang (White Palace) in 1645. The nine-storey structure was completed three years later, and in 1649 the fifth Dalai Lama moved from Drepung Monastery to his new residence. However, the circumstances surrounding the construction of the larger Marpo Podrang (Red Palace) are subject to some dispute. It is agreed that the fifth Dalai Lama died in 1682 and that his death was concealed until the completion of the Red Palace 12 years later. In some accounts, the work was initiated by the regent who governed Tibet from 1679 to 1703, and foundations were laid in 1690 (after the fifth Dalai Lama's death). In other accounts, the Red Palace was conceived by the fifth Dalai Lama as a funerary chörten and work was well under way at the time of his death. In any event, the death of the fifth Dalai Lama was not announced until he was put to rest in the newly completed Red Palace.

There is also some scholarly debate concerning the Potala's name. The most probable explanation is that it derives from the Tibetan name for Chenresig's 'pure land', or paradise, also known as Potala. Given that Songtsen Gampo and the Dalai Lamas are believed to be reincarnations of Chenresig, this connection is compelling.

Since its construction, the Potala has been the home of each of the successive Dalai Lamas, although since construction of the Norbulingka summer palace in the late 18th century it has served as a winter residence only. It was also the seat of the Tibetan government and, with chapels, schools, jails and even tombs for the Dalai Lamas, it was virtually a self-contained world.

The Potala was shelled briefly during the 1959 popular uprising against the Chinese, but the damage was not extensive. The Potala was spared again during the Cultural Revolution, reportedly at the insistence of Zhou Enlai, the Chinese premier, who is said to have deployed his own troops to protect it. The Potala was reopened to the public in 1980 and final touches to the US$4-million renovations were completed in 1995.

Shöl VILLAGE

(Map p70) Nestled at the southern foot of Marpo Ri (Shöl literally means 'at the base'), the former village of Shöl was once Lhasa's red-light district, as well as the location of a prison, a printing press and some ancillary government buildings. Reconstructed buildings include displays on the feudal horrors of Tibetan torture. Most people give the buildings a miss.

Treasures of the Potala Exhibition   MUSEUM

(Map p70) This recently improved exhibition hall in the Potala complex is worth a quick visit for the stunning 15th-century lotus-shaped Vajradhara mandala (just inside the entrance), and some fine thangkas (religious paintings), statues and festival costumes.

Deyang Shar   BUDDHIST SITE

(Map p70) Entry to the Potala is up two steep access ramps that will soon leave you wheezing in the oxygen-depleted air. The stairs lead past the ticket office to the large Deyang Shar, the external courtyard of the White Palace. At the top of the triple stairs leading up to the White Palace, look out for the golden handprints of the fifth Dalai Lama on the wall to the left.

Murals to the north depict Songtsen Gampo's original Potala, the construction of the Jokhang and the transfer of the Jowo Sakyamuni statue there. The beating of two horse-skin drums here once marked the evening closure of the Potala's gates.

Red Palace   PALACE

(Marpo Podrang; Map p70) You start the tour of the main Potala building from the top and descend through the bowels of the building to exit on the ground floor. The gilded buddhas, intricate mandalas and towering funeral stupas you pass en route rank as the highlights of the Potala.

➡ **Third Floor**

On the 3rd floor, the first room is the Chapel of Jampa (Jamkhang), which contains an exquisite image of Jampa (Maitreya, or the Future Buddha) commissioned by the eighth Dalai Lama; it stands opposite the eighth Dalai Lama's throne. To the left of the Jampa statue, in the corner, is a wooden Kalachakra mandala. The walls are stacked with the collected works of Tsongkhapa (founder of the Gelugpa order) and the fifth Dalai Lama. The chapel was damaged in a fire (caused by an electrical fault) in 1984 and many valuable thangkas (religious paintings) were lost.

Next, the **Chapel of Three-Dimensional Mandalas** (Loilang Khang) houses spectacular jewel-encrusted 18th-century mandalas of the three principal *yidam* (Tantric deities) of the Gelugpa order. These are essentially three-dimensional versions of the mandalas you see painted on thangkas everywhere in Tibet and act as meditation maps for the mind.

The **Chapel of the Victory over the Three Worlds** (Sasum Namgyal) houses a library and displays of Manchu texts. The main statue in the corner is a golden thousand-armed Chenresig, while the main central thangka is of the Manchu Chinese emperor Qianlong dressed in monk's robes, with accompanying inscriptions in Tibetan, Chinese, Mongolian and Manchurian.

Next, the **Chapel of Immortal Happiness** (Chimey Dedan Kyil) was once the residence of the sixth Dalai Lama, Tsangyang Gyatso, whose throne remains; it is now dedicated to Tsepame, the Buddha of Longevity, who sits by the window.

In the northwestern corner is the **Lama Lhakhang** and the golden **tomb of the Seventh Dalai Lama** (Serdung Tashi Obar Khang), constructed in 1757 and encased in

---

ℹ THE POTALA ENTRY PROCEDURES

A quota system is in place during high season to cope with the huge numbers of domestic tourists trying to visit the Potala during the summer months. Your guide or travel agency will need to prebook a slot on your intended date and will be allotted a time for your visit. Only 2800 people can visit the palace each day. During peak times you may officially be limited to just one hour inside the Potala, but you really need at least twice this.

Head to the main southern entrance an hour or so before your allotted time and then proceed through the rebuilt village of Shöl up into the palace. Halfway up is the office where you actually buy your ticket (all temples in the Red Palace and White Palace of the Potala are covered by one entry fee). From the roof you wind down into the labyrinthine bowels of the Potala before exiting at the rear of the palace and descending to the Lukhang on the Potala kora. Much of your visit will be in one huge shuffling queue. Water and lighters are not allowed into the Potala.

Photography of the interior of the Potala is forbidden and all rooms are wired with motion sensors and video cameras.

Red Palace of the Potala

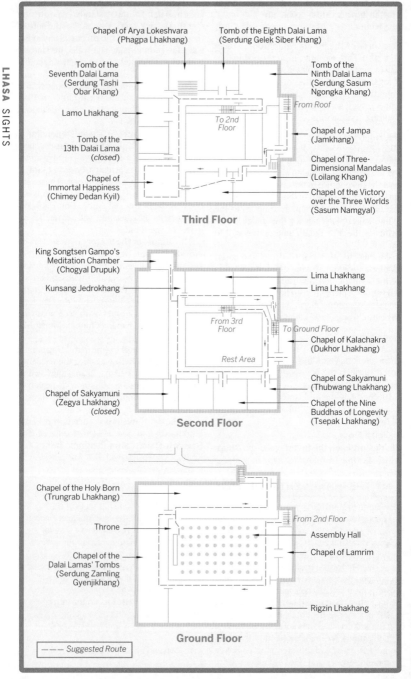

Chapel of Arya Lokeshvara
(Phagpa Lhakhang)

Tomb of the Eighth Dalai Lama
(Serdung Gelek Siber Khang)

Tomb of the
Seventh Dalai Lama
(Serdung Tashi
Obar Khang)

Tomb of the
Ninth Dalai Lama
(Serdung Sasum
Ngongka Khang)

Lamo Lhakhang

From Roof

To 2nd
Floor

Chapel of Jampa
(Jamkhang)

Tomb of the
13th Dalai Lama
(closed)

Chapel of Three-
Dimensional Mandalas
(Loilang Khang)

Chapel of
Immortal Happiness
(Chimey Dedan Kyil)

Chapel of the Victory
over the Three Worlds
(Sasum Namgyal)

Third Floor

King Songtsen Gampo's
Meditation Chamber
(Chogyal Drupuk)

Lima Lhakhang

Kunsang Jedrokhang

Lima Lhakhang

From 3rd
Floor

To Ground Floor

Rest Area

Chapel of Kalachakra
(Dukhor Lhakhang)

Chapel of Sakyamuni
(Thubwang Lhakhang)

Chapel of Sakyamuni
(Zegya Lhakhang)
(closed)

Chapel of the Nine
Buddhas of Longevity
(Tsepak Lhakhang)

Second Floor

Chapel of the Holy Born
(Trungrab Lhakhang)

From 2nd Floor

Throne

Assembly Hall

Chapel of Lamrim

Chapel of the
Dalai Lamas' Tombs
(Serdung Zamling
Gyenjikhang)

Rigzin Lhakhang

Ground Floor

--- Suggested Route

half a tonne of gold. To the right stands a half-hidden statue of Kalsang Gyatso, the seventh Dalai Lama.

Also in the northwestern corner, steps lead up into the small but important **Chapel of Arya Lokeshvara** (Phagpa Lhakhang). It is said that this is one of the few corners of the Potala that dates from the time of Songtsen Gampo's 7th-century palace. It is the most sacred of the Potala's chapels, and the sandalwood image of Arya Lokeshvara inside is the most revered image housed in the Potala. The statue is accompanied on the left by the seventh Dalai Lama and Tsongkhapa, and on the right by the fifth, eighth and ninth Dalai Lamas. Relics include stone footprints of Guru Rinpoche and Tsongkhapa.

The towering, jewel-encrusted **tomb of the Eighth Dalai Lama** dates from 1805 and is more than 9m tall. Pilgrims are blessed here with the hat of the eighth Dalai Lama. The equally impressive **tomb of the Ninth Dalai Lama** was under renovation in 2018.

➡ **Second Floor**

The first of the chapels you come to on the 2nd floor is the **Chapel of Kalachakra** (Dukhor Lhakhang), also known as the Wheel of Time. It is noted for its stunning three-dimensional mandala, which is more than 6m in diameter and finely detailed with more than 170 statues.

In the **Chapel of the Nine Buddhas of Longevity** (Tsepak Lhakhang), look for the murals by the left-hand window if you can get a monk to lift the cloth – the left-hand side depicts Thangtong Gyalpo and his celebrated bridge (now destroyed) over the Yarlung Tsangpo near Chushul. The images of coracle rafts halfway up the wall add an intimate touch. Murals by the right-hand window depict the construction of the Potala. There are also nine statues of Tsepame here, as well as green and white Drölma (Tara, a female bodhisattva).

Passing the closed Chapel of Sakyamuni (Zegya Lhakhang), continue to the northwestern corner, where you'll find a small corridor that leads to **King Songtsen Gampo's Meditation Chamber** (Chogyal Drupuk), which, along with the Chapel of Arya Lokeshvara on the 3rd floor, is one of the oldest rooms in the Potala. The most important statue is of Songtsen Gampo himself, to the left of the pillar. To the left is his minister Tonmi Sambhota (said to have invented the Tibetan script) and to the right are his Chinese and Nepali wives. A statue of the king's Tibetan wife, Mongsa Tricham

(the only one to bear a son), is in a cabinet by the door. The fifth Dalai Lama lurks behind (and also on) the central pillar. Also here is Gar Tsongtsen, the Tibetan prime minister (and Songtsen Gampo's right-hand man), who travelled to the Tang court to escort Princess Wencheng back to Lhasa. Queues for this chapel can be long.

The last three rooms are all linked and are chock-a-block full of 3000 pieces of priceless statuary, many donated by a Khampa businessman in 1995.

The 1st floor has been closed to visitors for years and is unlikely to reopen soon.

➡ **Ground Floor**

As you round the steps on the ground floor, enter the beautiful **assembly hall**, the largest hall in the Potala and its physical centre. Note the fine carved pillar heads. The large throne that dominates the far end of the hall was the throne of the sixth Dalai Lama. Four important chapels frame the hall.

The first chapel on this floor is the **Chapel of Lamrim**. *Lamrim* means 'the graduated path' and refers to the stages that mark the path to enlightenment. The central figure in the chapel is Tsongkhapa, with whom *lamrim* texts are associated. Outside the chapel, to the left, a fine mural depicts the Forbidden City, commemorating the fifth Dalai Lama's visit to the court of Emperor Shunzhi in 1652. Murals depict the tent camps used by the court on its journey across Tibet.

The next chapel, the long **Rigzin Lhakhang**, is dedicated to eight Indian teachers who brought various Tantric practices and rituals to Tibet. The central figure is a silver statue of Guru Rinpoche (one of the eight), who is flanked by his consorts Mandarava and Yeshe Tsogyel (with a turquoise headdress), as well as statues of the eight teachers to the left and further statues on the right of the guru in the eight manifestations known as the Guru Tsengye.

In the west wing of the assembly hall is one of the highlights of the Potala, the awe-inspiring **Chapel of the Dalai Lamas' Tombs** (Serdung Zamling Gyenjikhang). The hall is dominated by the huge 12.6m-high chörten of the great fifth Dalai Lama, gilded with some 3.7 tonnes of gold. Flanking it are two smaller chörtens containing the 10th and 12th Dalai Lamas, who both died as children. Richly embossed, the chörtens represent the concentrated wealth of an entire nation. One of the precious stones is a pearl said to have been discovered in an elephant's brain and thus, in a wonderful piece of understatement, 'considered a rarity'. Eight other chörtens represent the eight major events in the life of the Buddha.

The last chapel is the **Chapel of the Holy Born** (Trungrab Lhakhang). First, in the corner, is the statue and chörten of the 11th Dalai Lama, who died at the age of 17. There are also statues of the eight medicine buddhas with their characteristic blue hair, a central golden Sakyamuni and the fifth Dalai Lama (silver), and then Chenresig, Songtsen Gampo, Dromtönpa (founder of the Kadampa order) and the first four Dalai Lamas.

White Palace   PALACE

(Kharpo Podrang; Map p70) On the roof of the Potala (p64), the private quarters of the 13th and 14th Dalai Lamas are to the right. The Dalai Lamas would have watched festival dances performed in the courtyard below from the hidden balconies of these personal chambers.

The first room you come to is the **throne room** (Simchung Nyiwoi Shar), where the Dalai Lamas would receive official guests. The large picture to the left of the throne is of the 13th Dalai Lama; the matching photo of the present Dalai Lama has been removed, but his throne is marked by a huge pile of silk *khataks* (religious scarves). There are some fine murals here, including those of the Chinese Buddhist mountain Wǔtái Shān and the mythical paradise of Shambhala on either side of of the entry, and a depiction of Bodhgaya (where the Buddha achieved enlightenment) at the far exit.

The trail continues clockwise past a room used for viewing New Year ceremonies in the Deyang Shar (p65) courtyard below into the **reception hall** (Dhaklen Paldseg). Next comes the **meditation room**, where protector gods include Nagpo Chenpo (Mahakala), the Nechung oracle and Palden Lhamo. The final room, the **study** of the Dalai Lama (Chimey Namgyal), has some personal effects of the Dalai Lama on show, such as his bedside clock. The mural above the seat is of Tsongkhapa, the founder of the Gelugpa order of which the Dalai Lama is the head. The locked door leads into the Dalai Lama's bedroom.

☉ Around the Potala

A morning visit to the Potala can easily be combined with a circuit of the Potala kora and an afternoon excursion to some of the temples nearby.

Potala Kora   WALKING

(Map p70) The pilgrim path that encircles the foot of the Potala Palace makes for a nice walk before or after the main event. Budget around half an hour, longer if you stop for tea. The exit from the Potala conveniently deposits you on the northern side of the kora path.

From the large western chörten (formerly the west gate to the city), follow the prayer wheels to the northwestern corner, marked by three large chörtens. There's a particularly nice teahouse (p79) here.

The northeastern corner is home to several rock paintings and the delightful **Sha Rigsum Lhakhang** (Map p70) prayer hall, alive with the murmurs of chanting nuns. Just opposite are stalls selling the best yak's milk yoghurt in Lhasa. Just past here, spin the large prayer wheel of the **Phurbu Chok Hermitage Mani Lhakhang** (Map p70) and then swing past the large square, where pilgrims prostrate themselves in front of the Potala on auspicious dates.

Look out for the three 18th-century *doring* (stele); the two on the northern side of the road commemorate victories over the Central Asian Dzungars (1721) and Nepali Gorkhas (1788 and 1791). King Trisong Detsen is said to have erected the single southern obelisk in the 8th century.

Lukhang Temple   BUDDHIST TEMPLE

(禄康寺, Lùkāng Sì; Map p70; ¥10; ☉9am-5pm) The Lukhang is a little-visited temple on a charming island in a lake, behind the Potala in the pleasant Dzongyab Lukhang Park. The Lukhang is celebrated for its 2nd- and 3rd-floor murals, which date from the 18th century, but frustratingly these are currently not visible.

The lake was created during the construction of the Potala. Earth used for mortar was excavated from here, leaving a depression that was later filled with water. *Lu* (also known as *naga*) are subterranean dragon-like spirits that were thought to inhabit the area, and the Lukhang, or Chapel of the Dragon King, was built by the sixth Dalai Lama to appease them (and also to use as a retreat). You can see Luyi Gyalpo, the *naga* king, at the rear of the ground floor of the Lukhang. The *naga* spirits were finally interred in the nearby Palha Lu-puk.

The 2nd-floor murals tell a story made famous by a Tibetan opera, while the murals on the 3rd floor depict different themes on each of the walls – Indian yogis demonstrating yogic poses (west), 84 *ma-hisaddhas* (masters of Buddhism; east), and the life cycle as perceived by Tibetan Buddhists (north), with the gods of Bardo, the Tibetan underworld, occupying its centre. Look for the wonderful attention to detail, down to the hairy legs of the sadhus and the patterns on the clothes.

The 3rd floor contains a statue of an 11-headed Chenresig and a meditation room used by the Dalai Lamas. To see if the 3rd floor has reopened, walk clockwise around the outside of the building and enter from the back via a flight of stairs. Finish your visit with a kora (pilgrim circuit) of the island.

For a detailed commentary on the murals, check out Ian Baker and Thomas Laird's coffee-table book *The Dalai Lama's Secret Temple: Tantric Wall Paintings from Tibet*.

Drubthub Nunnery BUDDHIST MONASTERY

(Map p70) Southwest of the Potala, a road leads around the eastern side of Chagpo Ri, the hill that faces Marpo Ri, site of the Potala. Take this road past stone carvers and rock paintings to unmarked steps leading up to the Drubthub Nunnery. The small but friendly nunnery is dedicated to Thangtong Gyalpo, the 15th-century bridge maker, medic and inventor of Tibetan opera, who established the original nunnery on the top of Chagpo Ri. Gyelpo's white-haired statue graces the nunnery's main hall.

Palha Lu-puk BUDDHIST TEMPLE

(查拉鲁普寺, Zhālālǔpǔ Sì; Map p70; ¥20; ⊙9am-7pm) Palha Lu-puk (next to Drubthub Nunnery) is an atmospheric cave temple said to have been the 7th-century meditational retreat of King Songtsen Gampo. The main attraction of the cave is its relief rock carvings, some of which are more than a thousand years old, making them the oldest religious images in Lhasa.

Altogether there are more than 70 carvings of bodhisattvas here; the oldest images are generally the ones lowest on the cave walls. Songtsen Gampo is depicted on the western (back) side. The yellow building above the Palha Lu-puk is a chapel that gives access to the less interesting meditation cave *(drub-puk)* of King Songtsen Gampo's Chinese wife, Princess Wencheng.

Gesar Ling BUDDHIST TEMPLE

(关帝格萨尔拉康, Guāndì Gésà'ěr Lākāng; Map p70; Beijing Zhonglu; ⊙9.30am-7.30pm) On the northern side of the small hill Parma Ri is the Gesar Ling, a Chinese construction dating back to 1793. It is the only Chinese-style temple in Lhasa. The main red-walled temple has a statue of Guandi, the Chinese God of War, while a separate yellow chapel holds the Tibetan equivalent, the mythical warrior Gesar, along with statues of Jampelyang, Chana Dorje (Vajrapani) and Chenresig.

Kunde Ling BUDDHIST MONASTERY

(功德林, Gōngdélín; Map p70; Deji Zhonglu; ¥10; ⊙9.30am-7.30pm) At the foot of the hill Parma Ri, close to Beijing Zhonglu, is one of Lhasa's four former royal temples. The *ling* (royal) temples were established by the fifth Dalai Lama, and it was from one of them that regents of Tibet were generally appointed. Only a couple of restored chapels are open, but it's a friendly place with around 60 monks and worth a visit. Upstairs is a 1938 photo of the original Kunde Ling, 80% of which has been destroyed.

Pilgrims come for a water blessing, and there's normally debating between 2pm and 4pm. There's a fine teahouse in the alley leading to the monastery.

★ Chagpo Ri Rock Carvings HISTORIC SITE

(药王山, Yàowáng Shān; Map p70; Deji Zhonglu; ¥10; ⊙dawn-dusk) This hidden corner of Lhasa features more than 5000 painted rock carvings that were created on the back side of Chagpo Ri over the course of a millennium. Throughout the day, pilgrims perform full-body prostrations in front of the images, while stone carvers at the far end of the courtyard contribute to a large chörten built entirely of the carvers' mani stones. The best way to visit the area is as part of the Lingkhor pilgrim route (p73).

◉ Ramoche Temple & Around རམོ ཆེ 小昭寺

The Ramoche Temple was constructed about 1300 years ago, around the same time as the Jokhang Temple. It was originally built to house the Jowo Sakyamuni image brought to Tibet by Princess Wencheng, King Songtsen Gampo's Chinese wife. Sometime in the 8th century the Sakyamuni image was moved to the Jokhang and replaced with the image of Jowo Mikyöba, brought to Tibet in the 7th century by Songtsen Gampo's Nepali wife, Princess Bhrikuti. By the mid-15th century the temple had become Lhasa's Upper Tantric College.

Around the Potala

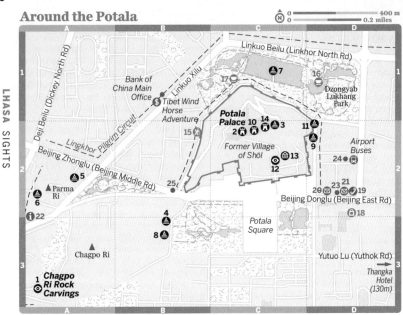

Around the Potala

The pedestrian street **Ramoche Lam** (Xiaozhaosi Lu), which leads from Beijing Donglu to the Ramoche Temple, is one of the more interesting streets in Lhasa, jam-packed with teahouses, restaurants and stalls selling everything from traditional jackets and top-grade *tsampa* (roasted-barley flour) to Tibetan scriptures. It's well worth a stroll.

Ramoche Temple　　　BUDDHIST TEMPLE
(རྭ་མོ་ཆེ, 小昭寺; Xiǎozhāo Sì; Map p54; ¥30; ☉7.30am-8pm) The main image at this temple is the fabulously ornate Jowo Mikyöba (Akshobhya) statue, which represents Sakyamuni

at the age of eight. The statue is in the inner Tsangkhang, protected by the four guardian kings and a curtain of chain mail, which pilgrims rub for good luck. The lower half of the statue was discovered in 1983 in a Lhasa rubbish tip and the head was discovered in Beijīng's Forbidden City and brought back to Lhasa by the 10th Panchen Lama.

As you enter the popular temple, past pilgrims doing full-body prostrations, you'll see a protector chapel to the left, featuring masks on the ancient pillars. On the left-hand side of the chapel is an encased image of the divination deity Dorje Yudronma covered in beads and seated on a horse, while to the right is a statue of the protector Gompo Sedon that was commissioned by the 13th Dalai Lama.

The Ramoche was badly damaged by Red Guards during the Cultural Revolution, but the complex has since been restored with Swiss assistance.

Tsepak Lhakhang BUDDHIST SITE

(Map p54; Ramoche Lam) Just outside the Ramoche Temple, a doorway to the right by a collection of yak-butter and juniper-incense stalls leads to one of Lhasa's hidden gems, the Tsepak Lhakhang. The impressive central image is Tsepame, flanked by Jampa and Sakyamuni, and there's a wonderful kora path. The new protector chapel and assembly hall are testament to the site's growing popularity with pilgrims.

Gyüme Tratsang BUDDHIST TEMPLE

(下密寺, Xiàmì Sì; Map p56; Bejing Donglu) Gyüme was founded in the mid-15th century as one of Tibet's foremost Tantric training colleges, second only in Lhasa to the monasteries of Sera and Drepung. More than 500 monks were once in residence, and students of the college underwent a physically and intellectually gruelling course of study. It's easy to miss the surprisingly impressive temple; look for an imposing entrance set back from Beijing Donglu.

The main *dukhang* (assembly hall) has statues of Tsongkhapa, Chenresig and Sakyamuni and was under renovation in 2018. Look for the monks' alms bowls, encased in crafted leather, hanging from the pillars. Behind are huge two-storey statues of Tsongkhapa and his two main disciples, and next door is a fearsome statue of Dorje Jigje (Yamantaka). Upstairs is a famous speaking rock image of Drölma and views down on the two-story statues below. The college was desecrated during the Cultural Revolution,

but a growing number of monks are now in residence.

Meru Sarpa Monastery BUDDHIST MONASTERY

(Map p56; Beijing Donglu) The wood-block printing press in the middle of this traditional housing compound doesn't welcome visitors, so head instead to the atmospheric chapel in the northwestern corner. Look for the statue of thousand-armed Chenresig, an unusual 'frog-faced' Palden Lhamo and the blackened, preserved jaws of a crocodile-like gharial on the pillar. It's about 50m east of the Gyüme Tratsang.

◎ The Norbulingka ནོར་བུ་གླིང་ཁ་ 罗布林卡

The summer palace of the Dalai Lamas, the **Norbulingka** (ནོར་བུ་གླིང་ཁ་ , 罗布林卡, Luóbùlínkǎ; Map p54; Minzu Nanlu; ¥60; ⊙ 9am-6pm) is in the western part of town. The lifeless temple-like buildings rank well behind the other points of interest in and around Lhasa, since most rooms are closed to the public.

The seventh Dalai Lama founded the first summer palace in the Norbulingka (whose name literally means 'jewel park') in 1755. Rather than use the palace simply as a retreat, he decided to use the wooded environs as a summer base from which to administer the country, a practice that was repeated by each of the succeeding Dalai Lamas. The grand procession of the Dalai Lama's entourage relocating from the Potala to the Norbulingka became one of the highlights of the Lhasa year.

The eighth Dalai Lama (1758–1804) initiated more work on the Norbulingka, expanding the gardens and digging the lake, which can be found south of the New Summer Palace. The 13th Dalai Lama (1876–1933) was responsible for the three palaces in the northwest corner of the park, and the 14th (current) Dalai Lama built the New Summer Palace (p72).

In 1959 the 14th Dalai Lama made his escape from the Norbulingka disguised as a Tibetan soldier. All the palaces of the Norbulingka were damaged by Chinese artillery fire in the popular uprising that followed. At that time, the compound was surrounded by some 30,000 Tibetans determined to defend the life of their spiritual leader. Repairs have been undertaken but have failed to restore the palaces to their former glory.

The **ticket office** (Map p54) is just to the north of the main entrance

As you leave the palace after your visit, pop into the charming yellow-walled **mani lhakhang** (Map p54) to the south of the Norbulingka entrance.

Palace of the Eighth Dalai Lama   PALACE
(Map p54) This palace (also named the Kelsang Podrang, after the seventh Dalai Lama) is the first you come to after entering the Norbulingka (p71) grounds and also the oldest, dating from 1755. Every Dalai Lama from the eighth to the 13th has used it as a summer palace. Only the main audience hall is open; it features 65 hanging thangkas and some lovely painted wooden panels.

New Summer Palace   PALACE
(Takten Migyü Podrang; Map p54) The New Summer Palace in the centre of the Norbulingka's park was built by the present Dalai Lama between 1954 and 1956 and is the most interesting of the Norbulingka palaces. You can only enter the walled complex from its eastern side.

The first of the rooms is the Dalai Lama's audience chamber. Note the wall murals, which depict the history of Tibet in 301 scenes that flow in rows from left to right. As you stand with your back to the window, the murals start on the left wall with Sakyamuni and show the mythical beginnings of the Tibetan people (from the union of a bodhisattva and a monkey in the Sheldrak Cave), as well as the first field in Tibet (representing the introduction of agriculture). The wall in front of you depicts the building of the circular monastery of Samye, as well as Ganden, Drepung and other monasteries to the right. The right wall depicts the construction of the Potala and Norbulingka.

Next come the Dalai Lama's private quarters, which consist of a meditation chamber and a bedroom. The rooms have been maintained almost exactly as they were when the Dalai Lama left them, and apart from the usual Buddhist images they contain the occasional surprise (a Soviet radio, among other things).

The assembly hall, where the Dalai Lama would address heads of state, is home to an extraordinarily ornate gold throne backed by wonderful cartoon-style murals of the Dalai Lama's court (left, at the back). Look out for British representative Hugh Richardson in a trilby hat, and several Mongolian ambassadors. The right wall depicts the Dalai Lamas. The first five lack the Wheel of Law, symbolising their lack of governmental authority.

Last are the suites of the Dalai Lama's mother (other sources state they are meeting rooms), whose bathroom sink overflows with offerings of one-máo notes.

South of the New Summer Palace is an artificial lake commissioned by the eighth Dalai Lama. The only pavilion open here at the time of research was the personal **retreat of the 13th Dalai Lama** (Trudzing Podrang; Map p54) in the southwestern corner, featuring a library, a thousand-armed Chenresig statue, and a stuffed tiger in the corner! Pilgrims walk around the Mongolian-style cairn of stones to the left of the building. The seats overlooking the duck pond offer a wonderful spot for a picnic.

Summer Palace of the
13th Dalai Lama   PALACE
(Map p54) The summer palace of the 13th Dalai Lama (Chensek Podrang) is in the western section of the Norbulingka. The ground-floor assembly hall is stuffed full of various buggies, palanquins, bicycles and a stage coach. The fine murals depicting the life of Sakyamuni are hard to see without a torch.

Nearby, the smaller **Kelsang Dekyi Palace** was also built by the 13th Dalai Lama, in 1926, as a Tantric temple. The fine murals depict Ganden and Potala – not the buildings but the Buddhist paradises of the same name. Note there is an awful zoo inside the complex where animals are kept in poor conditions – steer clear.

🏃 Activities

Lightness Blind Massage Centre   MASSAGE
(光明盲人按摩中心, Guāngmíng Mángrén Ànmó Zhōngxīn; Map p56; ☑ 135 1897 9404; Rm 6501, 5th fl, Lucky Snow Hotel, 9 Zhisenge Lu; massage ¥130-200; ⊙ 11am-9pm) Blind masseur Dawa Tashi offers Tibetan- or Chinese-style massage on the 5th floor of this hotel across from the Times Sq mall.

Tenzin Blind Massage Centre   MASSAGE
(旦增盲人按摩中心, Dànzēng Mángrén Ànmó Zhōngxīn; Map p56; ☑ 135 4901 5532; Danjielin Lu; ⊙ 9.30am-10.30pm) There's no better way to recover from an overland trip than with a massage by these graduates of the Braille Without Borders organisation (www.braillewithoutborders.org). Choose between an hour-long Chinese (¥150) or Tibetan oil massage (¥180), the former clothed, the latter naked. Given prior notice you can have your massage in the privacy of your hotel room.

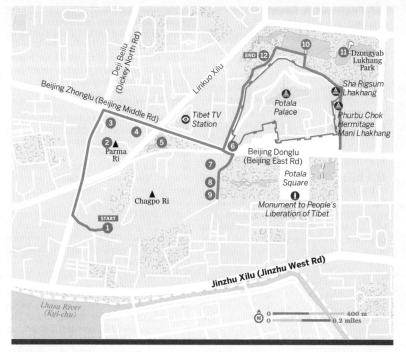

Walking Tour
Lingkhor Kora

START DEJI ZHONGLU (DEKYI LAM)
END POTALA PALACE
LENGTH 3KM TO 4KM; TWO TO THREE HOURS

This walk is best done in the morning, when you'll be joined by hundreds of pilgrims. To start the walk, take a taxi to the Xuefeng Hotel (Xuěfēng Bīnguǎn, 雪峰宾馆; 9 Jinzhu Donglu 金珠东路9号) and walk up the alley to the left. If this is closed, continue to Deji Zhonglu (德吉中路; Dekyi Lam in Tibetan) and take the alley that branches east of here. Both alleys lead to one of the city's real gems: the painted **1 Chagpo Ri rock carvings** (p69), centred on a huge image of Tsepame.

From here, return along the alley back to Deji Zhonglu and head north. Before you hit Beijing Zhonglu (the second crossroads) follow the alleyway to the right to visit the friendly **2 Kunde Ling** (p69). At the intersection with Beijing Zhonglu, watch the pilgrims as they rub their backs, shoulders and hips against a series of polished **3 holy stones**. Head east along Beijing Zhonglu to the yellow walls of the Chinese-style **4 Gesar Ling** (p69).

Continue east to the **5 Golden Yaks statue**, erected for the 40th anniversary of the 'liberation' of Tibet, before reaching the former western **6 city gate** (Daggo Kani), in the shape of a large white chörten. Photos in the Brahmaputra Grand Hotel show British Army troops entering the city through the original gate during the invasion of 1903–04.

Climb up to the **7 viewpoint** just above the white chörten for one of Lhasa's classic photo ops. The hilltop behind you is Chagpo Ri (Iron Mountain), the site of Lhasa's principal Tibetan medical college from 1413 until its destruction in the 1959 uprising.

Head down the nearby alley, past **8 Drubthub Nunnery** (p69), to visit **9 Palha Lupuk** (p69), the site of Lhasa's earliest religious icons. If you have the energy, finish with a quick circuit of the Potala kora, stopping in at the **10 Lukhang Temple** (p68). Finish up with a well-deserved thermos of sweet tea at the **11 eastern teahouse** (p79) or **12 western teahouse** (p79) in the pleasant park.

✽✽ Festivals & Events

If at all possible, try to time your visit to Lhasa with one of the city's main festivals. Thousands of pilgrims walk the city's Lingkhor Circuit during Saga Dawa; Drepung Monastery is the place to be during the Chökor Düchen, Drepung and Shötun festivals. Sera, Drepung and Ganden monasteries are also very active during the Tsongkhapa Festival.

The Tibetan new year festival of Losar (p316) is a fine time to be in the city if you can get permits at this time.

Saga Dawa   RELIGIOUS
(☉May/Jun) The 15th day (full moon) of the fourth lunar month sees huge numbers of pilgrims walking and prostrating along the Lingkhor and Barkhor pilgrim circuits. Follow the locals' cue and change ¥10 into a fat wad of one-máo notes to hand out as alms during the walk.

Worship of the Buddha   RELIGIOUS
(☉Jun) During the second week of the fifth month of the lunar calendar, the parks of Lhasa, in particular the Norbulingka, are crowded with picnickers.

Chökor Düchen   RELIGIOUS
(☉Jul) This festival on the fourth day of the six lunar month commemorates Buddha's first sermon at the Deep Park in Sarnath. Lhasa residents trek up to the summit of Gambo Ütse Ri, the high peak behind Drepung Monastery (p84). In the olden days even the Dalai Lama would ascend the peak, riding atop a white yak.

Drepung Festival   RELIGIOUS
(☉Jul) The 30th day of the sixth lunar month is celebrated with the hanging at dawn of a huge thangka at Drepung Monastery. Lamas and monks perform opera in the main courtyard.

Shötun Festival   RELIGIOUS
(☉Aug) The first week of the seventh lunar month sees the unveiling of a giant thangka at Drepung Monastery; festivities then move down to Sera and to the Norbulingka for performances of *lhamo* (Tibetan opera) and some epic picnics.

Palden Lhamo   RELIGIOUS
(☉Nov) The 15th day of the 10th lunar month (normally November) has a procession around the Barkhor Circuit bearing Palden Lhamo, protective deity of the Jokhang Temple.

Tsongkhapa Festival   RELIGIOUS
(☉Dec) Much respect is shown to Tsongkhapa, the founder of the Gelugpa order, on the anniversary of his death on the 25th day of the 10th lunar month. Check for processions and monk dances at the monasteries at Ganden, Sera and Drepung.

🛏 Sleeping

The Tibetan eastern end of town is easily the most interesting place to be based, with accommodation options in all budgets. There are dozens of shiny, characterless hotels scattered around other parts of town. You might find yourself in one of these if you arrive on a tour or book a hotel online.

Several of Lhasa's stalwart hotels were undergoing major renovations in 2018, including the **Gorkha Hotel**, a historic converted former Nepali consulate, and the **Trichang Labrang Hotel**, a former residence of the Dalai Lama's tutor. Both are hidden in the old town.

Tibet Bike Hostel   HOSTEL $
(风马飞扬旅舍, Fēngmǎ Fēiyáng Lǚshè; Map p56; ☑0891-679 0250; www.tibetbike.com; dm ¥60, d ¥208-298; ☜) This modern courtyard hostel (north of Beijing Donglu behind the Yak Hotel) is a decent option, especially if you speak some Chinese and want to connect with the many overland Chinese cyclists here. The ensuite rooms are bright, modern and good value, varying in size according to price, and the three-bed dorms come with shared hot showers and free washing-machine access.

The excellent top-floor double comes with its own private courtyard.

Dōngcuò International
Youth Hostel   HOSTEL $
(东措国际青年旅社, Dōngcuò Guójì Qīngnián Lǚshè; Map p56; ☑0891-627 3388; yhlhasa@hotmail.com; 10 Beijing Donglu; dm ¥30-55, s/d/tr ¥120/140/180, r without bathroom ¥80-120; @☜) This hostel attracts mainly Chinese backpackers, though a few foreign travellers find their way here. Rooms are smallish but well maintained, with wooden floors and crisp white sheets, but the graffiti-covered walls beloved by Chinese backpackers add to the slightly grim, institutional feel. The hot water is best at night. Prices drop in April and rise in July and August.

★**Kyichu Hotel** HOTEL $$
(吉曲饭店, Jíqǔ Fàndiàn; Map p56; ☑0891-633 1541; www.lhasakyichuhotel.com; 145 Beijing Donglu; r incl breakfast ¥400; ✳@⎈) The renovated Kyichu is a friendly and well-run choice that's very popular with repeat travellers to Tibet. Rooms are comfortable and pleasant, with wooden floors, underfloor heating, Tibetan carpets and private bathrooms, but the real selling points are the location, the excellent service and – that rarest of Lhasa commodities – a peaceful garden courtyard (with espresso coffee). Reservations recommended.

Rates include a fine buffet breakfast in the excellent restaurant. The only grumbles we have are related to occasional issues with hot water. Avoid the cheaper and older roadside rooms above reception. Credit cards accepted.

★**Yak Hotel** HOTEL $$
(亚宾馆, Yà Bīnguǎn; Map p56; ☑0891-630 0008; 100 Beijing Donglu; d ¥200-300, r VIP ¥880; ✳@⎈) The ever-popular Yak has matured in recent years from backpacker hang-out to tour-group favourite, upgrading to a range of comfortable ensuite rooms. The best rates are through an online booking website such as Trip.com. The location is perfect and the 5th-floor breakfast bar offers great views of the Potala.

The cheapest online rates are for smallish doubles with squat toilets. Slightly pricier are the more spacious but noisier deluxe rooms overlooking busy Beijing Donglu. The best options are the colourful Tibetan-style decor of the quiet back block or the plush VIP rooms (guìbīnlóu).

Tashi Choeta Tibetan Folk Hotel HOTEL $$
(扎西曲塔风情酒店, Zhàxī Qūtǎ Fēngqíng Jiǔdiàn; Map p56; ☑139 8998 5865; www.tashichoeta.com; 21 Beijing Donglu, 3rd Alley; d/tr ¥388/528; ✳@⎈) This new hotel has a great location on the edge of the old town, with 58 comfortable and fresh Tibetan-style rooms ranged around a sunny internal atrium of Tibetan-style seating. It's down an alley off Beijing Donglu so is quiet. There's another branch in Shigatse.

Flora Hotel HOTEL $$
(哈达花神旅馆; Hǎdáhuāshén Lǚguǎn; Map p56; ☑0891-632 4491; florahtl@hotmail.com; Hebalin Lu; d incl breakfast ¥280; ⎈) The Flora is a well-run and reliable hotel in the interesting Muslim quarter (it's run by a Nepali Muslim). Nice touches include a laundry service and English-speaking staff. The tiled rooms are clean and spacious, though the bathrooms are a bit crummy. Rooms face inwards so are quiet. Budget tour groups from Kathmandu often stay here.

Gang Gyen Hotel HOTEL $$
(刚坚饭店, Gāngjiān Fàndiàn; Map p56; ☑0891-630 5555; 83 Beijing Donglu; d incl breakfast ¥380-480; ✳⎈) This huge, modern and quiet four-star place is popular with groups for its spacious, plush and clean carpeted rooms. Sure it's bland, but the location is great, and discounted agency or online rates can make this place a steal. There's a clinic and Tibetan massage centre on site.

Dhood Gu Hotel HOTEL $$
(敦固宾馆, Dūngù Bīnguǎn; Map p56; ☑0891-632 2555; tenyang415@hotmail.com; s/d/ste incl breakfast ¥480/530/1050; @⎈) If you're looking for a dash of style, this comfortable Nepali-run three-star place near the Tromsikhang market is a good choice, with ornate Tibetan-style decor, a decent restaurant and a superb location in the old town. Rooms are dark and on the small side, but were recently renovated and come with modern bathrooms. Upper-floor rooms are brighter, but there's no lift.

A room tip: skip the pricier Potala-view rooms and grab a beer or breakfast on the rooftop for even better views.

Lhasa Tashi Nota Hotel HOTEL $$
(拉萨吉祥宝马酒店; Lāsà Jíxiáng Bǎomǎ Jiǔdiàn; Map p54; ☑0891-680 0008; 24 Linkuo Beilu, Tuanjie Xincun; d incl breakfast ¥350-480) This solid Tibetan-run hotel is north of the old town but in an interesting residential district with plenty of restaurants nearby. Rooms are clean and fresh but vary in size. Pluses include sunny courtyard seating and an on-site branch of Summit Café (p79) to serve all your coffee and cheesecake needs.

Tashi Choeta Boutique Hotel HOTEL $$
(扎西曲塔精品酒店; Zhàxī Qūtǎ Jīngpǐn Jiǔdiàn; Map p56; ☑0891-633 3028; No 18, Jirey 1 Lane, Tromsikhang; d/tr ¥217/317; ✳⎈) Travellers from Taiwan and Hong Kong love this reliable old-town choice. The four floors of rooms are set around a pleasant inner courtyard, which means they suffer from a lack of natural light, but the accommodation is clean and fresh, with clean bathrooms. There are great Potala views from the rooftop, and the pleasant ground-floor restaurant offers easy dining options.

Cool Yak Hotel
HOTEL $$

(酷牦牛酒店; Kùmáoniú Jiǔdiàn; Map p56; 0891-685 6777, 139 8999 1204; Danjielin Lu; s ¥180, d ¥300-380; ❄ 🛜) The great old-town location and the giant Tibetan thangka in the central courtyard are the most eye-catching things about this modern place. The carpeted rooms are fresh and comfortable, with good bathrooms, though there's a definite lack of natural light. It's hidden down an alley off Danjielin (Zangyiyuan) Lu. Single rooms are uncomfortably small.

Shangbala Hotel
HOTEL $$

(香巴拉酒店; Xiāngbālā Jiǔdiàn; Map p56; 0891-632 3888; 1 Danjielin Lu; d ¥380-420, ste ¥800; ❄ 🛜) This tour-group blockhouse was recently renovated to include a blindingly golden lobby. Rooms are comfortable and clean, though the glass bathroom partitions can be a bit revealing unless you and your roommate are close. Luxury rooms are worth the extra cost. The central location is unbeatable.

Mandala Hotel
HOTEL $$

(满斋饭店, Mǎnzhāi Fàndiàn; Map p54; 0891-636 7666; Jiangsu Lu; d ¥240-320; ❄ @ 🛜) This newish Tibetan-run three-star place, just south of the old town, is a modern hotel with a few Tibetan design touches and a good Nepali restaurant next door. Rooms are simple, spacious and comfortable, but the old-fashioned bathrooms are small and it's not brilliantly run.

★ Songtsam Choskyi Linka Lhasa
BOUTIQUE HOTEL $$$

(松赞曲吉林卡, Sōngzàn Qūjí Línkǎ; 0891-674 7666; www.songtsam.com; Sicholing; d incl breakfast ¥1380-2250; ❄ 🛜) Lhasa's most stylish accommodation comes thanks to the Songtsam chain, which runs seven boutique

LHASA'S BOUTIQUE HOTELS

A welcome recent trend in the Lhasa hotel scene has been the restoration and conversion of several of the city's crumbling courtyards into stylish, atmospheric luxury lodgings. The following places ooze historic charm and traditional Tibetan decor, though you often pay for this with dark rooms. Several places were undergoing major renovations in 2018, so should boast new and improved rooms when they reopen.

House of Shambhala (卓玛拉宫, Zhuómǎlā Gōng; Map p56; 0891-632 6533; www.shambhalaserai.com; 7 Jiri Erxiang, 吉日二巷7号; d incl breakfast ¥590-1015; ⊙ closed mid-Jan–end Mar; @) Hidden in the old town in a historic Tibetan building, the romantic, boutique-style Shambhala mixes the neighbourhood's earthy charm with buckets of style and a great rooftop lounge, making it perfect for couples who prefer atmosphere over mod cons. The 13 rooms, decorated in natural wood and slate with antique Tibetan furniture, vary only in size. The fabulous rooftop terrace makes up for smallish and dim rooms and is a great place to relax over a Baileys-and-masala-chai cocktail (¥68) or a yak tikka masala. Low-season discounts of 20% are available in April, May, November and December.

Shambhala Palace (香巴拉宫, Xiāngbālā Gōng; Map p56; 0891-630 7779; 16 Taibeng Gang; r incl breakfast ¥450-620; ⊙ closed mid-Jan–end Mar; @ 🛜) This quiet 17-room hotel is hidden deep in the old town, offering stylish rooms, a spacious rooftop and good service. Avoid the smallest rooms, though. Manager Lobsang Jigme is particularly helpful. Low-season discounts of 20% are available in April, May, November and December.

Yabshi Phunkhang (尧西平康, Yáoxī Píngkāng; Map p56; 0891-632 8885; 68 Beijing Donglu; r ¥480-700, ste from ¥880; ❄ 🛜) This mid-19th-century mansion was built for the parents of the 11th Dalai Lama (yabshi is the title given to the parents of a Dalai Lama) and has been well restored. The collection of 21 large but fairly simple rooms linked by traditional courtyards is both stylish and atmospheric, even if the hotel is not particularly well run.

Lingtsang Boutique Hotel (林仓酒店, Líncāng Jiǔdiàn; Map p56; 0891-689 9991; lingtsanghotel@163.com; No 38, No 1 Alley, Lugu; 38鲁固一巷; d incl breakfast ¥600) The eight rooms in this former residence of Nyi Rinpoche, a tutor of the Dalai Lama, make for an interesting choice in the heart of the old town. The hotel has a mix of authentic architecture and modern elements, with open-plan wooden bathrooms and dressed stone floors adding to the designer-monastery feel.

lodges in the Tibetan area of Yúnnán. The 50 rooms here are scattered in nine stone-and-wood villas and are spacious, stylish and very comfortable, with separate living rooms and bedrooms, and private balconies. Upper-floor rooms have distant views of the Potala (¥200 extra).

The free in-room ground coffee and complementary minibar are nice touches, as are the antique Tibetan carpets that decorate the main lodge. One pleasant surprise is the Provençal cuisine and unexpected selection of French wines (the manager is French). The only downside is the location, inconveniently south of the Kyi-chu river, 6km southeast of central Lhasa. The hotel is also known as the Songtsam Retreat.

Shangri-La Hotel   HOTEL $$$
(香格里拉大酒店; Xiānggélǐlā Dàjiǔdiàn; Map p54; ☑0891-655 8888; www.shangri-la.com; 19 Luobulingka Lu; r from ¥1000; @🛜🏊) It was really only a matter of time before the Shangri-La brand opened a hotel in Tibet. The decor is modern and tasteful, and there are fine restaurants, including an excellent buffet and lovely outdoor seating in the Shambhala Bar. Five-star facilities include gym, oxygen lounge and clinic – most likely in that order, considering the altitude –plus a pool and spa.

Dekang Hotel   HOTEL $$$
(德康酒店, Dékāng Jiǔdiàn; Map p54; ☑0891-630 8855; rindolma@foxmail.com; 2 Shengtai Lu; d/tr ¥480/500; ❄@🛜) A well-run, modern Tibetan-run choice, with easy vehicle access but walking distance from the old town, offering fresh and modern Tibetan-style rooms. Rooms were renovated and expanded in 2018.

St Regis Lhasa   HOTEL $$$
(瑞吉度假酒店, Ruìjí Dùjiǎ Jiǔdiàn; Map p54; ☑0891-680 8888; www.stregis.com/lhasa; 22 Jiangsu Lu; r ¥1000-1500; ❄@🛜🏊) Six-star travellers accustomed to uberluxury, 24-hour butler service and, yes, a gold-plated pool can finally consider a trip to the plateau. The fortress-like main building has three restaurants, a spa, a tearoom and a 6th-floor wine bar with the largest selection of wines in Tibet. Proximity to the old town is an unexpected bonus.

Heritage Hotel   HOTEL $$$
(古艺酒店, Gǔyì Jiǔdiàn; Map p56; ☑0891-691 1333; deena_bai1031@hotmail.com; 11 Chaktsalgang Lu; r ¥400-500; ❄🛜) Located inside the artsy courtyard holding the Dropenling craft centre (p80), the friendly Heritage offers 20 stylish rooms featuring stone-walled

showers, wooden floors and Tibetan wall hangings. The huge suites are particularly good value. The old-town location is atmospheric if you don't mind a bit of a hike to most restaurants. Rooms were upgraded in 2018 and a rooftop cafe added.

Himalaya Hotel   HOTEL $$$
(喜玛拉雅饭店; Xǐmǎlāyǎ Fàndiàn; Map p54; ☑0891-632 1111; 6 Linkuo Donglu; d ¥500-700; ❄🛜) Renovated three-star hotel with fresh, clean and slightly dull rooms, though not particularly spacious. Staff are helpful.

Thangka Hotel   HOTEL $$$
(唐卡酒店; Tángkǎ Jiǔdiàn; Map p54; ☑0891-630 8866; 38 Yutuo Lu; d ¥520-560; ❄🛜) A modern, friendly and comfortable four-star giant, with Tibetan design touches and spacious carpeted rooms to compensate for the otherwise bland feel. For an extra ¥160 they'll pipe oxygen into your room to ease your altitude headache.

🍴 Eating

The best Tibetan, Nepali and Western restaurants are in the Tibetan quarter around Barkhor Sq. Almost all places offer decent breakfasts. Most eateries serve lunch and dinner, but you will struggle to find a meal after about 10pm. For the flashiest Chinese restaurants you'll have to head to the western districts.

Seyzhong Nongze
Bösey Restaurant   TIBETAN $
(金藏持宝藏餐, JJīnzàng Chíbǎo Zàngcān; Map p54; Ramoche Lam; dishes ¥15-35) Super-convenient if you're visiting the next-door Ramoche Temple (p70), this pleasant upstairs Amdo Tibetan restaurant offers great views over the street below from the Tibetan-style tables. Try the set meal of *shemdre* (meat, rice and curried potatoes) for ¥27 or choose something more adventurous from the photo menu, such as the sizzling beef and peppers or the tiger-skin chillies (虎皮青椒, *hǔpíqīngjiāo*).

Yaraso   SICHUAN $
(吖啦嗦, Yālāsuō; Map p56; ☑183 0606 0003; 9 Xiao Xiangzi Lu, 小巷子路9号; dishes ¥16-30) Dimly lit, well-appointed modern restaurant offering authentic Sichuan cuisine, such as Chungking spicy noodles (重庆小面, *Chóngqìng xiǎomiàn*, ¥16), as well as Tibetan-Sichuan fusion plates like noodles with spicy braised yak beef (臻品红烧牦牛肉面, *zhēnpǐn hóngshāo máoniúròu miàn*, ¥25). Despite the sign, it isn't a brewery, but they do have Lhasa's best selection of (mostly Chinese) craft beer (¥35).

At the time of our visit, a rooftop terrace was in the works, with amazing views of the Barkhor and city.

Father Vegetarian Restaurant TIBETAN $
(父亲素食厨房, Fùqīn Sùshí Chúfáng; Map p56; mains ¥17-40; ⊘9am-9pm; 🖋) This hole-in-the-wall ('Yebche Gartse Suertob' in Tibetan) is a good place to get an authentic vegetarian lunch. There's no English menu, so consider going with your Tibetan guide. The combo dishes with rice are good value and the Tibetan fried mushrooms (藏式炒蘑菇, *zàngshì chǎomógu*) and dry hotpot (干锅, *gānguō*) dishes are particularly recommended.

Woeser Zedroe
Tibetan Restaurant TIBETAN $
(光明泽缀藏餐馆, Guāngmíng Zézhuì Zàng Cānguǎn; Map p56; Danjielin Lu; mains ¥15-50; ⊘10am-8pm) This is where visiting and local Tibetans come to fill up after a trip to the Jokhang. Add some pleasant traditional seating and a perfect location to the Tibetan vibe and it's a logical lunch stop. The *momos* (dumplings) are recommended, especially the fried-yak-meat or cheese varieties. Skip the boiled yak hooves and the phenomenally expensive dishes made with cordyceps (a medicinal root).

Pentoc Tibetan Restaurant TIBETAN $
(Map p56; ☑135 1890 0942; dishes ¥10-20; ⊘8.30am-9pm) Charming English-speaking Pentoc and her sister opened this simple local restaurant after working in longtime favourite Tashi I for many years. The menu includes breakfasts (yoghurt and honey) and homemade standards such as *momos* (dumplings) and *shemdre* (rice, potato and yak meat), plus butter tea, *chang* (barley beer) and even *dal bhat* (Nepali-style curry, lentils and rice).

Tashi I INTERNATIONAL $
(Map p56; cnr Danjielin Lu & Beijing Donglu; dishes ¥15-40; ⊘9am-10pm; 🖋) Old Lhasa hands like this unpretentious slice of vintage Lhasa for its mellow vibe, cheerful service, cheap prices and great location. The simple food can be hit and miss, but there are plenty of breakfast and vegetarian options. Try the *bobis* (chapati-like unleavened bread), which come with seasoned cream cheese and fried vegetables or meat.

★Lhasa Kitchen NEPALI, INTERNATIONAL $$
(拉萨厨房, Lāsà Chúfáng; Map p56; 3 Danjielin Lu; mains ¥20-45, Nepali sets ¥35; ⊘9am-10pm) With a wide-ranging menu of Nepali, Indian and Tibetan dishes, good breakfast options, decent prices, pleasant seating and a great location, it's no surprise that this is an extremely popular place with tour groups and locals alike. The menu covers everything from vegetable *dopiaza* (onion-based curry) to chicken sizzlers. Service can be brusque.

★Snowland Restaurant INTERNATIONAL $$
(雪域餐厅, Xuěyù Cāntīng; Map p56; ☑0891-633 7323; 8 Danjielin Lu; dishes ¥25-70; ⊘noon-10pm) This old-timer has a new location but is still an extremely popular place that serves a mix of excellent Continental and Nepali food in very civilised surroundings. The Indian dishes are particularly good, especially the tasty chicken butter masala (¥55) and giant naan breads. The cakes are the best in town; give the lemon pie our fond regards.

Kyaka Shak Kitchen TIBETAN $$
(加嘎霞厨房, Jiāgāxiá Chúfáng; Map p56; No 27 Barkhor Circuit South; mains ¥35-60; ⊘8am-10.30pm; 🖀) The atmospheric stone walls and wooden benches of this Tibetan restaurant on the Barkhor give it the feel of a traditional inn, which is fitting as the building was the residence of a Tibetan noble family before 1959. There are tasty Chinese and Tibetan dishes, as well as Nepali-style curry sets, but there's no English menu so come with your guide.

The Barkhor views and sunny rooftop are a bonus. It's near the Makye Amye restaurant (p80).

Old Tibetan Kitchen TIBETAN $$
(藏家老厨房, Zàngjiā Lǎo Chúfáng; Map p56; Danjielin Lu; mains ¥32-48; ⊘10am-10pm; 🖀) A good new Tibetan place down an alley off central Danjielin Lu. Ask the chef for the *ganggo* (¥58 to ¥98), currently not on the menu, but a wonderfully spicy dish of yak meat and vegetables served in an iron pot over a flame. It's perfect for two or three people. There are thoughts of changing the restaurant name to Hello Kitchen.

Tibetan Family Kitchen TIBETAN $$
(Map p56; ☑138 8901 5053; tibetanfamily kitchen@gmail.com; 1 Pozhang Saba Xiang; dishes ¥30-50; ⊘noon-10pm; 🖀) This former mom-and-pop joint has upgraded to a stylish Tibetan building on the southeastern corner of the Barkhor. The homemade recipes such as yak meat in tomato sauce are still good, but you can now add chicken curry, yak burgers and steak. The three floors are also

much nicer, with a particularly charming rooftop offering great views of the Jokhang.

If you are interested in creating, not only eating, dishes from the menu, take the two-hour cooking class (¥250 per person including dinner; 4.30pm to 6.30pm), during which you can learn to make authentic *momos* (dumplings) and Amdo-style noodles.

Tibet Steak House
INTERNATIONAL $$

(西藏牛排餐厅, Xīzàng Niúpái Cāntīng; Map p54; ☑0891-634 3777; Yutuo Lu; dishes ¥30-60; ⊘10am-10pm) This well-run restaurant serves a mix of excellent Continental, Indian and Nepali food in modern and fresh surroundings. The Indian dishes are particularly good and this might be your only chance to try a rib-eye yak steak (¥90). It's run by traveller favourite Snowland Restaurant (p78) but has a more local Tibetan clientele. No breakfast.

Dunya
INTERNATIONAL $$

(Map p56; ☑0891-633 3374; www.dunyarestaurant.com; 100 Beijing Donglu; dishes ¥40-80; ⊘11am-10pm, earlier opening Jul-Sep; 🛜) With calming decor and wide-ranging food, this cosy place is no longer Dutch-owned but it still captures Lhasa's tour-group zeitgeist, and is often packed with Dutch tourists and American school groups. It's pricier than most other places in town, but the food is pretty authentic, from the oregano-flavoured pizza crust to the imported Italian pasta.

The menu ranges from yak burgers to Indonesian noodles. The homemade sandwiches and soups are good for a light lunch, and it's one of the few places on the plateau to get a decent glass of wine or cocktail with dinner, or grab a beer on the balcony overlooking Beijing Donglu.

🍷 Drinking & Nightlife

There's not a great deal when it comes to nightlife in Lhasa. In the evening most travellers head to one of the restaurants in the Tibetan quarter. Rooftop restaurants offer the best views with your beer.

★ Summit Café
CAFE

(顶峰咖啡店, Dǐngfēng Kāfēidiàn; Map p56; ☑173 0899 7943; www.thetibetsummitcafe.com; 1 Danjielin Lu; coffee ¥22-27, mains ¥50-80; ⊘9am-8.30pm; 🛜) With authentic espresso coffee and smoothies, free wi-fi and melt-in-your-mouth cheesecakes, plus salads, paninis, pizza and American-style breakfast waffles and pancakes, this coffeehouse is mocha-flavoured

nirvana. It's in the courtyard of the Shangbala Hotel (p76), a stone's throw from the Jokhang. There are other, less useful branches around town.

Dzongyab Lukhang Park
Teahouse East
TEAHOUSE

(龙王潭风经情茶园, Lóngwángtán Fēngqíng Cháyuán; Map p70; tea ¥5-12) One of two good Tibetan-style teahouse restaurants in pleasant Dzongyab Lukhang Park, perfect for a break after a visit to the Potala or for snapping photos in the charming local park. Don't miss the traditional Tibetan-style line dancing on the stages outside the teahouse every morning until lunchtime.

Grab a thermos of sweet tea or try a cheap lunch of *shemdre* (meat and curried potatoes; mains ¥15 to ¥20). There's a second identical teahouse (龙王潭风情茶园, Lóngwángtán Fēngqíng Cháyuán; Map p70; Dzongyab Lukhang Park; tea ¥5-12) in the northwest corner of the park.

Guangming Teahouse
TEAHOUSE

(光明港琼甜茶馆, Guāngmíng Gǎngqióng Tiáncháguǎn, Woeser Gamchong Chakhang; Map p56; Danjielin Lu; tea ¥1) For an unfiltered Tibetan experience head to this rough and ready (but friendly) Tibetan teahouse in the centre of town. Grab a glass, find a seat and wait for the tea ladies to come around refilling everyone's glass with sweet *cha ngamo* (milk tea). The hall is also popular with Chinese tourists.

Ganglamedo
BAR

(岗拉梅朵, Gǎnglāméiduǒ; Map p56; www.ganglamedo.com; 127 Beijing Donglu; drinks ¥25-40; 🛜) After dark Lhasa's coolest nighttime spot is this stylish 2nd-floor bar and restaurant, full of sleek designer wooden tables, sofas and cool lighting and boasting a fine rooftop terrace. Draft Lhasa Beer, cocktails and Merlot by the glass are available, alongside a menu of steaks, pizza and Nepali set curries (mains ¥35 to ¥70). Bring a date.

Green Cat Restaurant
ROOFTOP BAR

(绿猫观景餐厅, Lûmāo Guānjǐng Cāntīng; Map p56; ☑189 8900 4006; 5th fl, 9 Zhisenge Lu; beer from ¥15; ⊘11am-midnight; 🛜) For the best nighttime views of the Potala Palace nurse a beer at this restaurant on the very top level of the Lucky Snow Hotel. The spotlit views of the Potala are simply mesmerising. There's western and Tibetan food if you get peckish – groups can try the Tibetan hotpot.

Makye Amye BAR
(玛吉阿米餐吧, Mǎjí'āmǐ Cānbā; Map p56; ☑0891-632 8608; Barkhor Circuit; drinks ¥18-36; ☺11.30am-11pm; ☎) If the stories are true, this was a drinking haunt of the licentious sixth Dalai Lama, who met Tibetan beauty Makye Amye here and composed a famous poem about her. Chinese tourists are drawn to the absorbing views of the Barkhor from the corner tables and summer rooftop terrace, but the Tibetan dishes (mains ¥50 to ¥95) are just so-so.

☆ Entertainment

Unfortunately there is little in the way of cultural entertainment in Lhasa. For authentic performances of Tibetan opera and dancing you'll probably have to wait for one of the city's festivals.

Golden Horse Number Four LIVE PERFORMANCE
(金马四号, Jīnmǎ Sìhào; Map p54; Najin Lu; ☺8pm-5am) If you're in the mood for a glitzy Tibetan night out, head to this impressive Tibetan *nangma* place by 9pm, invest in a tableful of beers and wait for the song-and-dance stage show to kick in around 10.30pm. On weekends the two levels can seat 3000 Tibetans, who keep the modern and traditional Tibetan songs and dancing going until dawn.

Gyelpo's Nangma KARAOKE
(雪域杰布, Xuěyù Jiébù; Map p54; Beijing Donglu; ☺7pm-2am) Gyelpo's has long been a local favourite *nangma* (entertainment club), with a good floor show and singers. Gyelpo was a famous dancer on Tibetan TV. It's a good place to meet local Tibetans, but it's losing popularity to glitzier venues.

🔒 Shopping

You can get most things in Lhasa these days, though water-purifying tablets, deodorant and English-language books and magazines are still almost impossible to find.

★Dropenling ARTS & CRAFTS
(卓番林, Zhuófānlín; Map p56; ☑0891-636 0558; www.tibetcraft.com; 11 Chaktsalgang Lam; ☺9am-8pm) ✈ This impressive nonprofit enterprise aims to bolster traditional Tibetan handicrafts in the face of rising Chinese and Nepali imports. Products are unique and of high quality, and they are made using traditional techniques (natural dyes, wool not acrylic etc) updated with contemporary designs. Ask about the two-hour artisan walk-ing tour of Lhasa's old town (¥50 per person, minimum five people).

Artefacts for sale include woolly carpets (¥2250) from the Wangden region of southern Tsang, silver jewellery from Tingri, Tibetan aprons, leather appliqué bags, cuddly toys and impossibly soft yak-cashmere scarves. Prices are fixed, with proceeds going back to artisans in the form of wages and social funds.

They also arrange interesting day classes on thangka painting (¥600 per group, plus ¥100 for materials) and a half-day introduction to mani stone carving (¥50 per person). Book at least the day before.

Foreign currency and credit cards are accepted and it can arrange international shipping with China Post. A smaller **branch** (Map p56; ☑0891-650 6884; Beijing Donglu, Xiasa Erxiang No 16; ☺11am-7pm Apr-Dec) ✈ is conveniently located opposite the Yak Hotel.

Barkhor Supermarket ARTS & CRAFTS
(八廓商城, Bākuò Shāngchéng; Map p56; Beijing Donglu; ☺9.30am-7.30pm) The souvenir stalls that once clogged the Barkhor Circuit were shepherded a couple of years ago into this three-storey concrete building with a Tibetan facade. It's quite charmless and there are no antiques here, but there's a good range of products, from butter lamps and prayer flags to monk's clothes.

Tromsikhang Market MARKET
(冲赛康市场, Chōngsàikāng Shìchǎng; Map p56; ☺7am-7pm) This bazaar-like area in the old town has the widest selection of dried fruit and nuts (imported from Xīnjiāng) and is the place to buy such Tibetan specialities as *tsampa* (roasted-barley flour), *churpi* (dried yak cheese) and yak butter. Khampa-style cowboy hats are for sale in the streets outside.

Norling Supermarket FOOD
(罗林超市, Luólín Chāoshì; Map p56; 20 Linkuo Donglu; ☺9am-7pm) Located near the Muslim quarter, this Tibetan-run Nepali shop sells everything from imported muesli and digestive biscuits to Indian spices, sun cream and dried coconut, though naturally at prices higher than in Nepal.

Bǎiyì Supermarket SUPERMARKET
(百益超市, Bǎiyì Chāoshì; Map p70; Beijing Donglu; ☺10am-10.30pm) Boasts a wide range of foodstuffs from frozen squid to ripe pineapples to a bewildering array of dried yak meat. The upper floor contains one of Lhasa's best collections of outdoor gear.

ℹ Information

ACCESSIBLE TRAVEL

Lhasa is crowded and not friendly to pedestrians, let alone those with limited mobility. High curbs, road barriers and the uneven flagstones of the old town combine to make getting around a potential challenge.

Lhasa has a flourishing blind massage industry, and many of the massage therapists are graduates of the excellent Braille Without Borders (www.braillewithoutborders.org) program and speak good English, offering a fascinating insight into life as a Tibetan with a disability.

DANGERS & ANNOYANCES

If you fly straight into Lhasa, remember to take things easy for your first day or two.

➡ It's not uncommon to feel breathless, suffer from headaches and sleep poorly because of the altitude.

➡ Don't attempt the steps up to the Potala for the first few days and drink lots of fluids.

➡ Armed-police posts and riot-squad teams currently occupy every street corner in the old town. Most Tibetans ignore them, but you should take care not to photograph any military posts or armed patrols.

Take care when reopening things such as tubes of sunscreen after a flight into Lhasa, or even jars of Coffee-mate from a local shop, as the change in pressure can cause messy explosions of volcanic proportions.

EMERGENCY & IMPORTANT NUMBERS

Ambulance	☑ 120
Fire	☑ 119
Police	☑ 11

ENTRY & EXIT FORMALITIES

You or your guide will need to present your TTB permit when checking in to a hotel in Lhasa.

Lhasa City Public Security Bureau (PSB, 拉萨市公安局, Lāsà Shì Gōng'ānjú; Map p54; ☑ 0891-624 8154; 17 Linkuo Beilu; ◷ 9am-12.30pm & 3.30-6pm Mon-Fri) Visa extensions of up to a week are very rarely given; if they are they will only be granted a day or two before your visa expires and only through your tour agency.

Nepalese Consulate-General (尼泊尔领事馆, Níbó'ěr Lǐngshìguǎn; Map p54; ☑ 0891-681 5744; www.nepalembassy.org.cn; 13 Luobulingka Beilu; ◷ 10am-noon Mon-Fri) Issues visas in 24 hours. The current fee for a 15-/30-/90-day visa is ¥175/280/700. Bring a visa photo. Mainland tourists have to get their visas here and these are currently free; foreigners will find it easier to obtain visas on the spot at the Nepalese border at Rasuwagadhi.

INTERNET ACCESS

Most public internet cafes won't accept foreigners without a local identity card. Almost all hotels and some cafes, including the Summit Café (p79), offer free wi-fi to patrons.

LGBT TRAVELLERS

Lhasa is neither a gay-friendly city nor a place of intolerance. There is little visible gay scene and few, if any, gay-oriented venues.

MEDICAL SERVICES

Several hotels and pharmacies around town sell Tibetan herbal medicine recommended by locals for easing symptoms of altitude sickness. The most common medicine is known as *solomano* in Tibetan and *hóngjǐngtiān* (红景天) in Chinese, though locals also recommend *gāoyuánníng* (高原宁) and *gāoyuánkāng* (高原康). A box of vials will cost you ¥35 to ¥50.

120 Emergency Centre (急救中心, Jíjiù Zhōngxīn; Map p54; ☑ 0891-633 2462; 16 Linkuo Beilu) Part of People's Hospital. Consultations cost around ¥150.

Mentsikhang (Traditional Tibetan Hospital, 藏医院, Zàngyīyuàn; Map p56; Yuthok Lam; ◷ 9.30am-12.30pm & 3.30-6pm) The place for a traditional Tibetan medical consultation.

Tibet Military Hospital (西藏军区总医院, Xīzàng Jūnqū Zǒngyīyuàn; Map p85; ☑ 0891-625 3120; Niangre Beilu) Travellers who have received medical attention confirm that this place is the best option (if you have an option).

MONEY

Changing cash and using ATMs is generally easy in Lhasa. Stock up on cash here for the rest of your trip through Tibet.

ℹ **ORIENTATION**

Street names are generally known in Chinese by both locals (including many Tibetans) and taxi drivers. Traditional Tibetan names have been included in brackets.

➡ Beijing Donglu (Beijing Shar Lam)
➡ Beijing Zhonglu (Beijing Kyil Lam)
➡ Danjielin Lu (Tengyeling Lam), also known as Zangyiyuan Lu (Mentsikhang Lam)
➡ Deji Lu (Dekyi Lam)
➡ Jiangsu Lu (Chingdröl Shar Lam)
➡ Linkuo Lu (Linkhor Lam)
➡ Minzu Lu (Mirig Lam)
➡ Niangre Lu (Nyangdren Lam)
➡ Xiaozhaosi Lu (Ramoche Lam)
➡ Yutuo Lu (Yuthok Lam)
➡ Zhisenge/Qingnian Lu (Dosenge Lam)

Bank of China Main Office (中国银行, Zhōng-guó Yínháng; Map p70; Linkuo Xilu; ⊗9am-1pm & 3.30-6pm Mon-Fri, 10.30am-4.30pm Sat & Sun) West of the Potala, this is the only place to arrange a credit-card advance (3% commission) or a bank transfer. The ATMs outside the building are open 24 hours.

Bank of China – Beijing Donglu (中国银行, Zhōngguó Yínháng; Map p56; Beijing Donglu; ⊗24hr) The most conveniently located branch is fully automated, with a currency-exchange machine that converts cash currencies much more quickly than the main bank branch. Bring your cleanest notes, as the machine can be fussy. ATMs dispense cash 24 hours a day. It's just west of the Banak Shol Hotel.

Bank of China – Duosenge Lu (Map p54; Duosenge Lu; ⊗9.30am-5.30pm Mon-Fri, 10.30am-4pm Sat & Sun) If you actually need to talk to a human to change money, this bank branch is the closest to the Tibetan old town.

OPENING HOURS

Opening hours listed are for summer; winter hours generally start half an hour later and finish half an hour earlier.

Banks 9.30am to 5.30pm Monday to Friday, 10.30am to 4pm Saturday & Sunday

Restaurants 10am to 10pm

Shops 10am to 9pm

Bars May close at 8pm or 2am, depending on their location and clientele.

POST

China Post (中国邮政, Zhōngguó Yóuzhèng; Map p70; 33 Beijing Donglu; ⊗9am-6.30pm) Counter three sells packaging for parcels. Express Mail Service (EMS) is also here. Leave parcels unsealed until you get here, as staff will want to check the contents for customs clearance.

Heaven Tibet Post Office (天上西藏邮局; Tiānshang Xīzàng Yóujú; Map p70; Beijing Donglu; ⊗9.30am-6.30pm) This branch of China Post, just east of the main office, is the easiest place to buy stamps for international postcards (¥5) and letters (¥6.5). It sells a wide range of post-

cards. Look for the fun range of Tibet-themed ink stamps you can put on your envelope or postcard for free.

TELEPHONE

China Mobile (中国移动通信, Zhōngguó Yídòng Tōngxìn; Map p70; Beijing Donglu; ⊗9am-7pm Mon-Sat) This is the easiest place to get a local SIM card for your mobile phone. Choose from data, calls or a mixture of both. It's a fairly complicated procedure and you'll likely need a local ID card, so go with your guide. Expect to pay around ¥120 for a month of data.

TRAVEL WITH CHILDREN

Lhasa is not an easy city for travel with children. There are few child-friendly sights and few facilities aimed at parents.

Kids will like the stuffed toys and puppets for sale at Dropenling (p80), and you'll find plenty of child-friendly foods at Lhasa's Nepali restaurants. Apart from that, it's almost all monasteries and yak-butter tea.

❶ Getting There & Away

While there are a number of ways to get to Lhasa, the most popular routes are by air from Chéngdū (in Sìchuān), by train from Xīníng, and overland or by air from Kathmandu.

TO & FROM CHINA

The popularity of the train has pushed sleeper buses into irrelevancy, especially for foreigners, as they are not allowed to take these services. There are still daily sleeper services to Golmud (20 hours), Xīníng (2½ days) and even Chéngdū (three days and four nights), but most people take the train if they can get tickets.

AIR

Modern Gongkar airport is 66km from Lhasa, via a new expressway and Gālá Shān tunnel.

Flying out of Lhasa is considerably easier than flying in. No permits are necessary – just turn up at the **Civil Aviation Authority of China office** (CAAC, 中国民航, Zhōngguó Mínháng; Map p70;

TRAINS FROM LHASA

TRAIN	DESTINATION	DEPARTURE	FREQUENCY	DURATION (HR)
Z22	Běijīng West	4.30pm	daily	40
Z324	Chéngdū	6.30pm	every other day	37
Z224	Chóngqìng	6.30pm	every other day	36
Z266	Guǎngzhōu	1.10pm	daily	55
Z918	Lánzhōu*	9am	every other day	24
Z166	Shànghǎi	11.25am		48
Z2802/Z918	Xīníng*	9am	daily	22

* NB Multiple other trains pass through Xīníng and Lánzhōu

0891-682 5430; 1 Niangre Beilu; ⊙9am-6pm) and buy a ticket. In August and around national holidays, you'd be wise to book your ticket at least a week in advance. At other times you'll generally get a 30% discount off the full fare.

To book a ticket you'll need to complete a form, get a reservation and then pay the cashier (cash only). Sample full fares include ¥1680 to Chéngdū, ¥3310 to Běijīng (check as only some flights are direct), ¥1950 to Xiàhé, ¥1060 to Yúshù and ¥1900 to Xīníng. Booking online is also an option.

Air China (中国国际航, Zhōngguó Guójì Mínháng; Map p54; ☑0891-682 0777; www.airchina.com.cn; Tibet Hotel, 67 Beijing Zhonglu; ⊙9am-7.30pm)

China Southern (中国南方航空, Zhōngguó Nánfāng Hángkōng; Map p70; ☑0891-683 1868; www.csair.com; 33 Beijing Donglu; ⊙9.30am-6pm)

Sichuan Airlines (四川航空, Sìchuān Hángkōng; Map p70; ☑0891-6828222; www.scal.com.cn; 41 Beijing Zhonglu)

Tibet Airlines (西藏航空, Xīzàng Hángkōng; Map p54; ☑0891-683 0088; www.tibetairlines.com.cn; Guójì Dàjiǔdiàn, cnr Jinzhu Xilu & Minzu Nanlu; ⊙10am-6pm)

BUS & MINIBUS

For several years now foreigners have not been allowed to take bus services around Tibet and had to arrange their own transport. In the unlikely event that this changes, the following public transport operates.

Western Bus Station Hourly services to Shigatse, Tsetang and Nagchu (Nàqū), plus a daily service to Gyantse and long-distance services to Chamdo, Markham, Zhōngdiàn, Golmud and Xīníng. Private cars also run from here for about double the cheapest bus fare per seat.

Eastern Bus Station Frequent minibuses to Lhundrub (Línzhōu) and Medro Gongkar (Mòzhú Gōngkǎ), plus daily buses to Drigung Til and Reting Monastery.

Northern Bus Station Sleeper buses to Ali (60 hours) in western Tibet, as well as buses to Markham, Zhōngdiàn and Shigatse.

RENTAL VEHICLES

Rental vehicles are currently the only way to get around Tibet.

TRAIN

It's possible to ride the rails up onto the Tibetan plateau to Lhasa, and even beyond to Shigatse. There are daily trains to/from Běijīng, Xī'ān, Shànghǎi and Guǎngzhōu and four daily to/from Xī'níng or Lánzhōu, and every other day to/from Chéngdū and Chóngqìng. The train station is 4km southwest of town.

Train services were extended from Lhasa to Shigatse in 2014. Fares for the three-hour trip cost around ¥41 for a hard seat or ¥120/176 for a hard/soft sleeper. Trains depart Lhasa at 8.30am (Z8801) and 3.20pm (Z8803), returning from Shigatse at 12.05pm and 6.40pm. If your tour agency can secure tickets you can add Shigatse onto a Lhasa trip without having to fork out for pricey vehicle hire.

It's only a question of time before rail services extend from Lhasa to Tsetang in the Yarlung Valley.

You can buy train tickets up to two months in advance at the Lhasa **train station ticket office** (⊙7am-10pm) or the more centrally located **city ticket office** (火车票代售处, Huǒchēpiào Dàishòuchù; Map p54; Beijing Donglu; commission ¥5; ⊙8am-5.40pm). You'll need your passport. Note that it's generally much easier to get tickets from Lhasa than to Lhasa.

A taxi to/from the train station costs around ¥30.

🛈 Getting Around

For those travellers based in the Tibetan quarter of Lhasa, most of the major inner-city sights are within fairly easy walking distance. For sights such as the Norbulingka over in the west of town, it's better to jump in a taxi (¥10).

TO & FROM THE AIRPORT

Most agencies send a guide and vehicle to pick up their clients from the airport. Most charge around ¥300, either directly or as part of your tour fee.

Airport buses (Map p70; ☑0891-682 7727; Niangre Beilu) leave up to 10 times a day (¥30, 1¼ hours) between 5am and 8pm from beside the CAAC building and are timed to meet flights. From the airport, buses wait for flights outside the terminal building. Some agencies will let their tourists travel by airport bus as long as they buy a return ticket for the guide. Buy tickets on the bus.

A taxi to the airport costs around ¥200.

BICYCLE

Bicycles could be a reasonably good way to get around Lhasa once you have acclimatised to the altitude but there are currently no bike rentals available to foreigners.

BUS

Buses (¥1) are frequent on Beijing Donglu, and if you need to get up to western Lhasa, this is the cheapest way to do it. That said, route maps are in Chinese only, so if you aren't with your guide it's easiest to just take an inexpensive taxi.

PEDICAB

There is no shortage of pedicabs plying the streets of Lhasa, but they require endless haggling and are only really useful for short trips (around ¥7). At least most are Tibetan-owned. Always fix the price before getting in.

TAXI

Taxis charge a standard fare of ¥10 for the first 3km (then ¥2 per subsequent kilometre), resulting in a ¥10 ride within the city centre.

AROUND LHASA

A short taxi or bus ride from Lhasa are the impressive Gelugpa monasteries of Sera and Drepung. Both are must-sees, even if you have only a brief stay in Lhasa. Far less visited are the monastery complex of Pabonka and the hermitage caves at Drak Yerpa, both of which are well worth the effort, especially if you like hiking. Further afield is the impressive monastery of Ganden, set in a picturesque bowl and a must-do day trip from the capital.

Current regulations require foreign tourists to visit Drepung, Sera and Ganden Monasteries in the company of a registered guide.

Foreign visitors can visit sights within Lhasa such as Drepung and Sera by taxi or bus, but they must hire transportation to visit Ganden and other monasteries that lie outside the city.

Drepung Monastery འབྲས་
སྤུངས་ 哲蚌寺

Drepung (Zhébàng Sì; Map p86; ¥60; ⊙9.30am-5.30pm, smaller chapels close at 3pm) was once one of the largest monasteries in the world, and its ancient prayer halls and self-contained college temples are still a highlight of Tibet.

Drepung was founded in 1416 by a charismatic monk and disciple of Tsongkhapa called Jamyang Chöje. Within just a year of completion the monastery had attracted a population of some 2000 monks.

It suffered through the ages with assaults by the kings of Tsang and the Mongols, but it was left relatively unscathed during the Cultural Revolution and much of interest remains intact.

The word Drepung literally translates as 'rice heap', a reference to the huge number of white monastic buildings that once piled up on the hillside. Rebuilding and resettlement continue at a pace unmatched elsewhere in Tibet and the site once again resembles a small monastic village, with around 600 monks resident (as against a former total of around 7000).

Drepung is bigger and more sprawling than Sera Monastery, so budget half a day here, longer if you want to walk the lovely kora (pilgrim circuit).

⊙ Sights & Activities

The best way to visit Drepung's chapels is to follow the pilgrims or, failing that, the yellow signs that lead up from the car park. When allowed, interior photography costs around ¥20 per chapel. Try to visit in the morning, as many chapels close at 3pm or earlier.

As you walk towards the Ganden Palace (p85), you'll see a colourful and photogenic collection of rock paintings west of the main monastery depicting famous lamas and protector deities.

Once you've seen the main chapels, head east of the main central grouping of *lhakhang* (chapels) to a cluster of friendly colleges that the tour groups never reach, including the **Lamba Mitsang** (Map p86), **Lubum Kangtsang** (Map p86) and **Jurche Mitsang** (Map p86), once home to students from Inner Mongolia, and the **Khardung Kangtsang**, the upstairs hallway of which is defaced with Mao slogans and images.

Loseling College   BUDDHIST SITE
(Map p86) Loseling is the largest of Drepung's colleges, and studies here were devoted to logic. If you have time, pop into the small debating courtyard west of the college. Monks sometimes practise their music in the garden here, blowing huge horns and crashing cymbals. Most visitors call it quits after this college.

The **main hall** houses a throne used by the Dalai Lamas, an extensive library, and a long altar decorated with statues of the fifth, seventh and eighth Dalai Lamas, Tsongkhapa and former Drepung abbots. There are three chapels to the rear of the hall. The one to the left houses 16 *arhats* (literally 'worthy ones'). The central chapel has a large statue of Jampa and a self-arisen stone painting of the Nechung oracle on the opposite wall; the chapel to the right has a small but beautiful statue of Sakyamuni. The two chörtens of Loseling's earlier abbots are covered with offerings.

On the 2nd floor you'll enter a small chapel full of angry deities; you'll then pass under the body of a stuffed goat draped with one-máo notes before entering the spooky *gönkhang* (protector chapel). There are more protective deities here, including the main Dorje Jigje

Around Lhasa

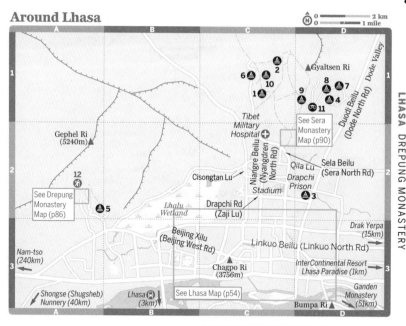

(Yamantaka), plus Nagpo Chenpo (six-armed Mahakala), Dorje Drakden and Dorje Lekpa.

Ganden Palace   PALACE
(Map p86) In 1530 the second Dalai Lama established the Ganden Podrang, the palace that was home to the subsequent Dalai Lamas until the fifth built the Potala. It was from here that the early Dalai Lamas exercised their political as well as religious control over central Tibet, and the second, third and fourth Dalai Lamas are all entombed here.

To reach the palace from the monastery's car park, pass the juniper stalls and follow the kora clockwise around the outside of the monastery until you reach the steps.

The first hall on the left is the **Sanga Tratsang**, a renovated chapel housing statues of the protectors Namtöse (Vaishravana), Nagpo Chenpo (Mahakala), Dorje Jigje (Vajra Bhairavo), bull-headed Chögyel (Dharmaraja), Palden Lhamo (Shri Devi; on a horse) and Dorje Drakden (the Nechung oracle), all arranged around a central statue of the fifth Dalai Lama, with the Wheel of Law characteristically in his hand.

Head up the stairs and across the main courtyard, where performances of *cham* (a ritual dance) are traditionally performed during the Shötun festival. The upper floor of the main building has three chapels that make

Around Lhasa

⦿ Sights

⦿ Activities, Courses & Tours

up the apartments of the early Dalai Lamas. The second of the three chapels is the Nyiwo Tsomchen, the Sunlight Audience Room, with wonderfully detailed murals depicting the life of Atisha and the throne of the fifth Dalai Lama, next to a thousand-armed statue of Chenresig. The third is a simple living room.

From here descend and cross over to an assembly hall whose entrance was defaced by a Cultural Revolution–era political slogan as recently as 2015. Signs lead past a refreshment stand and an easily missed corner rock shrine to Drölma next to the exit to the north, said to have arisen naturally.

Drepung Monastery

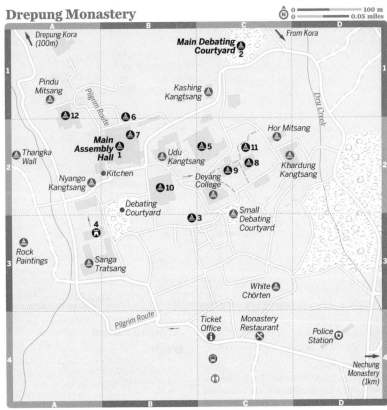

Drepung Monastery

★ **Main Assembly Hall**   BUDDHIST SITE
(Map p86) The main assembly hall, or Tsogchen, is the principal structure in the Drepung complex and is the one chapel you must not miss. The hall is reached through an entrance on the western side, just past a wonderful medieval-looking **kitchen**, whose hot-tub-sized cauldrons and giant ladles look like props from the film *The Name of the Rose*. The butter-tea churner alone is 6ft tall.

The assembly hall's huge interior is very atmospheric, draped with thangkas, covered in monks' robes and yellow hats, and supported by over 180 columns – the ones near the western protector chapel dedicated to goddess Palden Lhamo (no women allowed) are decorated with ancient chain mail and bows.

The back-room chapel features the protector deities Chana Dorje (Vajrapani, blue) and Tamdrin (Hayagriva, red) on either side of the door, and contains statues of Sakyamuni with his two disciples, the Buddhas of the Three Ages, and nine chörtens above. The walls and pillars are lined with statues of eight standing bodhisattvas. To the front centre there is also a youthful-looking statue of Lamrin Ngawang Phuntsok (a former abbot of Drepung, recognisable by his black-rimmed glasses); next to it is his funeral chörten. To the east is Tsongkhapa, the founder of the Gelugpa sect.

Sculptures of interest in the main hall include a two-storey Jampelyang (Manjushri); a small Sakyamuni; a statue of Tsongkhapa that is said to have spoken; the moustached 13th Dalai Lama to the right; the monastery's founder, Jamyang Chöje, in a cabinet to the right; the seventh Dalai Lama; and to the right Sakyamuni, flanked by five of the Dalai Lamas. At the end of the altar you will find a group of eight *arhats* (literally 'worthy ones'). In the back room to the right look for the two-storey statue of Jampa and the tombs of monastery founder Jamyang Chöje and Lama Yeshe Ö, the lama from western Tibet who invited Atisha to Tibet in the 11th century. Back in the main hall the long cabinet on the eastern wall holds a huge building-sized thangka that is unveiled during the Shötun festival (there's a photo of it at one end).

Back by the main entrance, past a great fire-safety mural, steps lead up to the 1st and 2nd floors. At the top of the stairs is the **Hall of the Kings of Tibet**, featuring statues of Tibet's early kings and early Dalai Lamas, including Lobsang Gyatso (the fifth Dalai Lama), and a chapel containing the head of a two-storey **Jampa statue**. Pilgrims prostrate themselves here, throw *kathak* (silk scarves) and drink from a sacred conch shell.

Continue moving clockwise through the Sakyamuni Chapel, stuffed with chörtens, and then descend to the **Miwang Lhakhang**. This chapel contains the assembly hall's most revered image, a massive statue of Jampa, the Future Buddha, at the age of 12. The statue rises through three floors of the building from the ground-floor chapel you saw earlier, and it is flanked by Tsongkhapa to the left and Jamyang Chöje to the right.

Next is the **Drölma Lhakhang**. Drölma is a protective deity, and in this case the three Drölma images in the chapel are responsible for protecting Drepung's drinking water, wealth and authority respectively. There are also some fine examples of gold-inked Tibetan Kangyur scriptures here. The central statue is a form of Sakyamuni, whose amulet encases one of Tsongkhapa's teeth.

Exit the building from the western side of the 2nd floor.

Ngagpa College
BUDDHIST SITE

(Map p86) Ngagpa is one of Drepung's four *tratsang* (colleges) and was devoted to Tantric study. The chapel is dedicated to bull-headed Dorje Jigje (Yamantaka), a Tantric meditational deity who serves as an opponent to the forces of impermanence. The important cartoon-style Dorje Jigje image in the inner sanctum is said to have been fashioned by Tsongkhapa himself.

Walking clockwise, other statues include the Gadong oracle (first clockwise), Nagpo Chenpo (third), Drölma (fourth), Tsongkhapa (fifth), the fifth Dalai Lama (seventh) and, by the door, the Nechung oracle. Look for bull-headed Chögyel to the side, his hand almost thrusting out of the expanded glass cabinet. Pilgrims spin the ancient prayer wheel in the corner of the room.

To get a feel for what Drepung was like before the renovation teams arrived, follow the signs up to the Samlo Kangtsang, unrestored and surrounded by melancholic ruins.

As you follow the pilgrim path (clockwise) around the back of the assembly hall you will pass the small Jampelyang Temple. Just a little further, tucked in on the right of the main building, is the tiny **meditation cave** (Map p86) of Drepung founder Jamyang Chöje, with some fine rock paintings.

Jampelyang Temple
BUDDHIST SITE

(Map p86) Pilgrims pause at this small chapel behind the main assembly hall to pour yak butter on the wall, glimpse holy rock images of Jampelyang and Drölma and then get hit on the back with a holy iron rod.

★ Main Debating Courtyard
BUDDHIST SITE

(Map p86) If you're here in the afternoon, save some time to watch the monk debating (lots of shouting, hand slapping and gesticulation) between 2.30pm and 4pm in the main debating courtyard in the northeastern corner of the monastery (daily except Sunday). Photos here cost ¥15.

Gomang College
BUDDHIST SITE

(Map p86) Gomang is the second-largest of Drepung's colleges. The main hall has a whole row of images, including those of Jampa, Tsepame and the seventh Dalai Lama. Again, there are three chapels to the rear: the most important is the central chapel, chock-a-block with an entire wall of images. There is a single protector chapel on the upper floor. Women are not allowed into this chapel.

★ Drepung Kora WALKING

(Map p85) This lovely kora climbs up to around 3900m and so probably should not be attempted until you've had a couple of days to acclimatise in Lhasa. The path passes several rock paintings, climbs past a high wall used to hang a giant thangka during the Shötun festival, peaks at a valley of prayer flags, and then descends to the east via an encased Drölma (Tara) statue and several more rock carvings. There are excellent views along the way.

The walk takes about an hour at a leisurely pace (it is possible to do it more quickly at hiking speed). Look for the path that continues uphill from the turn-off to the Ganden Podrang palace.

🛏 Sleeping & Eating

Drepung is within Lhasa's city limits, so you can visit from your base in Lhasa. The **Monastery Restaurant** (Map p86; mains ¥7-12; ⊗10am-3pm) near the bus stop serves reviving sweet tea by the glass or thermos (¥7), as well as bowls of *shemdre* (meat and curried potatoes) and vegetable *momos* (dumplings).

❶ Getting There & Away

Located about 8km west of central Lhasa, the easiest way to get out to Drepung is by taxi from the Barkhor for ¥40. To save some pennies, take bus 18, 25 or 16 (¥1), all of which run from Beijing Donglu to a stop at the foot of the Drepung hill. From here minivans (¥2) run up to the monastery bus stop.

Nechung Monastery གནས་ཆུང་ གཙོ 乃琼寺

This **monastery** (Năiqióng Sì; Map p85; ⊗8:30am-5pm), 10 minutes' walk downhill from Drepung Monastery (p84), is worth a visit for its historical role as the seat of the Tibetan State Oracle until 1959.

The Nechung oracle was the medium of Dorje Drakden, an aspect of Pehar, the Gelugpa protector of the Buddhist state, and the Dalai Lamas would make no important decision without first consulting him. The oracle was not infallible, however; in 1904 the oracle resigned in disgrace after failing to predict the invasion of the British under Younghusband. In 1959 the State Oracle fled to India with the Dalai Lama.

Nechung is an eerie place associated with possession, exorcism and other pre-Buddhist

---

TIBET'S GREAT MONASTERIES

The great Gelugpa monasteries of Drepung, Sera and Ganden, collectively known as the *densa chenmo sum*, once operated like self-contained worlds. Drepung alone, the largest of these monasteries, was home to around 10,000 monks at the time of the Chinese takeover in 1951. Like the other major Gelugpa institutions, Drepung operated less as a single unit than as an assembly of colleges, each with its own interests, resources and administration.

The colleges, known as *tratsang* or *dratsang*, were (and still are) in turn made up of residences *(kangtsang)*. A monk joining a monastic college was assigned to a *kangtsang* according to the region in which he was born. For example, it is thought that 60% of monks at Drepung's Loseling College were from Kham, while Gomang college was dominated by monks from Amdo and Mongolia. This gave the monastic colleges a distinctive regional flavour and meant that loyalties were generally grounded much deeper in the colleges than in the monastery itself.

At the head of a college was the *khenpo* (abbot), a position that was filled by contenders who had completed the highest degrees of monastic study. The successful applicant was chosen by the Dalai Lama. Beneath the abbot was a group of religious leaders who supervised prayer meetings and festivals, and a group of economic managers who controlled the various *kangtsang* estates and funds. There was also a squad of huge monks known as *dob-dobs*, who were in charge of discipline and administering punishments.

In the case of the larger colleges, estates and funds were often extensive. Loseling College had more than 180 estates and 20,000 serfs who worked the land and paid taxes to the monastery. Monasteries were involved in many forms of trade. For the most part, these holdings were not used to support monks – who were often forced to do private business to sustain themselves – but to maintain an endless cycle of prayer meetings and festivals that were deemed necessary for the spiritual good of the nation.

rites. The blood-red **doors** at the entrance are painted with flayed human skins, and scenes of torture line the top of the outer courtyard. Tantric drumming booms from the depths of the building like a demonic heartbeat.

For images of Dorje Drakden, the protective spirit manifested in the State Oracle, see the back-room chapel to the left of the main hall. The statue in the left corner shows Dorje Drakden in his wrathful aspect, so terrible that his face must be covered; the version on the right has him in a slightly more conciliatory frame of mind. The *la-shing* (sacred tree) in between the two is the home of Pehar.

The far-right chapel has an amazing **spirit trap** (a collection of coloured threads used to trap evil spirits), some fine painted cabinets and a statue of the Dzogchen deity Ekajati, recognisable by her single fang and eye and representing the power of concentration. On the 1st floor is an audience chamber, whose throne was used by the Dalai Lamas when they consulted with the State Oracle. The 2nd floor features a huge new statue of a wrathful Guru Rinpoche. Don't miss the fine murals in the exterior courtyard (photos are allowed).

Nechung is easily reached on foot after visiting Drepung, on the way to the main road. A path leads past mani stone-carvers to the monastery (10 minutes). En route look for the metal icon moulds that are dipped in streams to act like underwater prayer flags, releasing fleeting fluid icons.

Sera Monastery ས་རྭ་དགོན་པ་
色拉寺

Sera Monastery (Sèlā Sì; Map p90; ¥50; ⊙9am-4pm; 🚌22, 23) was one of Lhasa's two great Gelugpa monasteries, second only to Drepung. Its once-huge population of around 5000 monks has now been reduced by 90% and building repairs are still continuing. Nevertheless, the monastery is worth a visit, particularly in the morning, when the chapels are at their most active, but also between 3pm and 5pm (not Sunday), when debating is usually held in the monastery's debating courtyard. Chapels start to close at 3pm, so it makes sense to see the monastery chapels before heading to the debating.

Sera was founded in 1419 by Sakya Yeshe, a disciple of Tsongkhapa, also known by the honorific title Jamchen Chöje. In its heyday, Sera hosted five colleges of instruction, but at the time of the Chinese invasion in 1959 there were just three: Sera Me specialised in

the fundamental precepts of Buddhism; Sera Je in the instruction of itinerant monks from outside central Tibet; and Sera Ngagpa in Tantric studies.

Sera survived the Cultural Revolution with light damage, although many of the lesser colleges were destroyed.

Interior photography costs ¥15 to ¥30 per chapel; video fees are ¥800.

◉ Sights & Activities

Sera Me College   BUDDHIST SITE
(Map p90) Follow the pilgrims clockwise, past the **Tsangba Kangtsang** (Map p90) and **Tsowa Kangtsang** (Map p90) residential halls and several minor buildings, to Sera Me College. This college dates back to the original founding of the monastery.

The central image of the impressive main hall is a copper Sakyamuni, flanked by Jampa and Jampelyang. To the rear of the hall are four chapels. To the left is a dark chapel dedicated to the dharma protector of the east, Ta-og (in an ornate brass case and wearing a hat), alongside a central Dorje Jigje. Look for the masks, antlers, iron thunderbolts and mirrors hanging from the ceiling. To the left of the entrance is a three-dimensional wooden mandala used to invoke the medicine buddha.

Continue to the central chapel, which contains statues of the Past, Present and Future Buddhas, as well as 16 *arhats* depicted in their mountain grottoes.

The next chapel is home to Dagtse Jowo, a central Sakyamuni statue that dates from the 15th century and is the most sacred of the college's statues. At the back are Tsepame and eight bodhisattvas; all are guarded by the protectors Tamdrin (Hayagriva; red) and Miyowa (Achala; blue). The last chapel is dedicated to Tsongkhapa, and there are also images of several Dalai Lamas, as well as of Sakya Yeshe (in the left corner with a black hat), Sera's founder and first abbot.

There are two chapels on the upper floor. The first, after you mount the stairs, is dedicated to Sakyamuni, depicted in an unusual standing form known as Thuwang. The second is a Drölma chapel with 1000 statues of this protective deity, as well as the Tsela Nam Sum longevity trinity. The third has 1000 statues of Chenresig, as well as a huge brass pot in the corner. All chapels sell amulets and blessed *rilbu* (herbal medicinal pills)

Exit at the back of the compound and jog around a **minor debating courtyard** to reach the Sera Ngagpa College (p90).

LHASA SERA MONASTERY

Sera Monastery

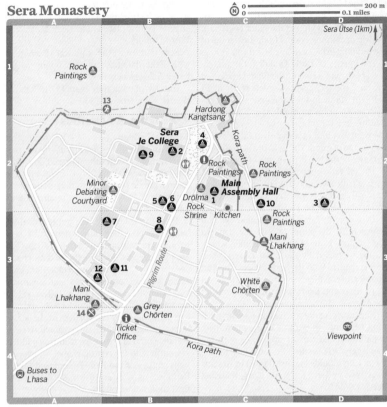

Sera Monastery

Sera Ngagpa College   BUDDHIST SITE
(Map p90) A Tantric college, Ngagpa is also the
oldest structure at Sera. The main hall is dominated by a statue of Sakya Yeshe (wearing a
black hat), behind the throne, surrounded by
other famous Sera lamas.

There are three chapels to the rear of the
hall, the first featuring Jampa and thousand-armed Chenresig, the second with 16

arhats and a Sakyamuni statue, and the
third with a statue of the bull-headed protective deity Dorje Jigje, with an alcove underneath where pilgrims place their head
for a blessing. Also here, to the right, is
Namtöse (Vaishravana), the guardian of the
north, who rides a snow lion and holds a
mongoose that vomits jewels. There is also a
room upstairs featuring Tsepame, the eight

medicine buddhas (Menlha) and the funeral chörtens of several past abbots.

★ Sera Je College   BUDDHIST SITE

(Map p90) This is the largest of Sera's colleges, generally accessed from a western side entrance. It has a breathtaking main hall, hung with thangkas and lit by shafts of light from high windows. Several chörtens hold the remains of Sera's most famous lamas. To the left of the hall is a passage leading, via a chapel dedicated to the Past, Present and Future Buddhas, to the most sacred of Sera Monastery's chapels, the Chapel of Tamdrin.

Tamdrin (Hayagriva) is a wrathful meditational deity whose name means 'horse headed'. He is the chief protective deity of Sera, and there is often a long line of shuffling pilgrims waiting to touch their – and especially their children's – foreheads to his feet in respect. Children get a black mark of butter-lamp soot on their noses as a blessing. Monks sell holy threads, protective amulets and sacred pills here, as well as red slips of inscribed paper called *tsenik*, which pilgrims buy to burn for the recently deceased and newly born. The ornate brass shrine recalls the temples of the Kathmandu Valley. As you queue up to view the shrine, take a look at the weapons, hats and masks hanging from the ceiling. Join the pilgrims in buying a white *khatag* and throwing it up onto the three Buddha statues.

The first chapel to the rear of the hall is devoted to a lovely statue of Sakyamuni, seated below a fine canopy of curling dragons and a ceiling mandala. Pilgrims lean on the steps to the right to touch his left leg. The next two chapels are dedicated to Tsongkhapa, with Sakyamuni and Öpagme (Amitabha), and to Jampelyang, flanked by Jampa and another Jampelyang. From here head to the upstairs chapels, the second of which has a fine embroidered thangka of the fourth Panchen Lama.

To the northeast of Sera Je is Sera's **debating courtyard** (Map p90). Photos are allowed on mobile phones but not actual cameras.

★ Main Assembly Hall   BUDDHIST SITE

(Map p90) The main assembly hall (Tsogchen) is the largest of Sera's buildings and dates to 1710. The central hall is particularly impressive and is noted for its wall-length thangkas and two-storey statue of Jampa. To the left is the large throne of the 13th Dalai Lama, with a figure of Sakya Yeshe to the left of that.

There are some incredibly ornate yak-butter sculptures in this hall.

Of the four chapels to the rear of the hall, the central is the most important, with its 6m-high Jampa statue. The statue rises to the upper floor, where it can also be viewed from a central chapel.

Also on the upper floor (to the far left of the central chapel) is a highly revered statue of a thousand-armed Chenresig. Pilgrims put their forehead to a walking stick that connects them directly and literally to the heart of compassion. The pilgrim path enters the building from the back, so this may be the first chapel you come across before descending to the prayer hall. Also here is a chapel dedicated to Tsongkhapa.

To the west of the assembly hall is an ancient **Drölma rock shrine** that pilgrims circumambulate.

Chöding Hermitage   BUDDHIST SITE

(Map p90) A path branches off the kora (pilgrim circuit) up side steps beside the **thangka wall** (Map p90) to the Chöding hermitage. The hermitage was a retreat of Tsongkhapa's, and predates Sera. There is not a great deal to see, but it's a short walk and the views from the hermitage are worthwhile. A path continues south around the hillside past a holy spring to a **viewpoint** that has fine views of Sera and Lhasa beyond.

Printing Press   BUDDHIST SITE

(Map p90) Before leaving the monastery it's worth having a look at the printing blocks in this new hall. Photos are ¥10. Prints made on site are for sale (¥25 to ¥35). A small building to the side holds three **sand mandalas** (Map p90).

Sera Kora   WALKING

(Map p90) The Sera kora takes less than an hour and is well worth the time. It starts outside the monastery entrance and heads west, following an arc around the western and northern walls. On the eastern descent, look out for several brightly coloured **rock paintings**. The largest ones on the eastern side of the monastery are of Dorje Jigje, Tsongkhapa and others. Next to the rock paintings is a thangka wall used to hang a giant thangka during festivals.

🛏 Sleeping & Eating

Sera is on the fringes of Lhasa's city centre, so it's easily visited as a half-day excursion from the city. The pleasant **monastery restaurant**

DIY: TREKKING THE DODE VALLEY

From the Sera Monastery kora (pilgrim circuit) you can make a great half-day trek up to the Sera Ütse retreat above the monastery and then around the ridge to the little-visited retreats of the Dode Valley. You shouldn't attempt the trek until you are well acclimatised to the altitude.

From Sera the steep, relentless 400m vertical climb up to the yellow-walled **Sera Ütse** (Map p85) retreat takes at least an hour (look up and see it high on the cliff above Sera; if that doesn't put you off, you'll be fine!). Take the path towards the Chöding hermitage and branch off to the left before you get there, climbing the ridge via a switchback path until you reach the yellow building perched high above the valley. Sera Ütse (4140m) was a retreat used by Gelugpa-order founder Tsongkhapa – his *drub-puk* (meditation cave) can be visited – and is currently home to two monks. You can also reach the retreat more easily from Pabonka's Tashi Chöling hermitage, which makes for a stunning day-long hike.

From the Ütse continue east along the new road for 10 minutes to a superb **viewpoint** (Map p85), probably Lhasa's most scenic picnic spot. From here the road continues east down into the Dode Valley, though it's possible for fit climbers to detour straight up the hillside to the summit, a knob of rock covered in prayer flags.

A footpath descends to the small **Rakadrak hermitage** (Map p85), where you can visit three simple caves associated with Tsongkhapa. Five minutes' walk below Rakadrak is the larger **Keutsang Ritrö** (Map p85), a retreat complex that's home to 23 monks. The original hermitage lies in ruins in an incredible location on the side of the sheer cliff face to the east. A painting inside the main chapel (to the right) depicts the original. As you leave the complex a path to the left leads to the dramatic ruins, but the trail is dangerous and ends in a sheer drop. The far section of the ruins can only be reached from the other side of the cliff.

From the Keutsang Ritrö follow the road downhill and after 10 minutes branch left for the short uphill hike to the **Phurbu Chok Monastery** (Map p85) and its hilltop Rigsum Gonpo Lhakhang (an hour's detour in total from the road), dedicated to the popular trinity of deities. You can spot two nunneries from here: Negodong to the east and Mechungri to the southeast. Back at the junction, descend to the main road to flag down bus 14 or 15, both of which terminate at Linkuo Beilu, just north of the Ramoche Temple.

On the ride back it's worth getting off at Zaji (Drapchi) Lu to visit **Drapchi Monastery** (扎基寺; Zājī Sì; Map p85), an active and unusual monastery that is located near Lhasa's most notorious political prison. Huge amounts of rice wine and *chang* (barley beer) are offered continuously to local protectress Drapchi Lhamo and the site has an almost animist feel to it.

(Map p90; dishes ¥3-8; ⊙10am-3pm) is worth a stop.

❶ Getting There & Away

Just 5km north of Lhasa, Sera is a short bus ride on bus 16, 20, 22 or 25 to a stop at the monastery. A taxi (¥20) is the easiest option.

Pabonka Monastery ཕ་བོང་ཁ
དགའ་ལྡན 帕邦喀寺

Built by King Songtsen Gampo in the 7th century, **Pabonka Monastery** (Pàbāngkā Sì; Map p85; ⊙dawn-dusk) **FREE** is one of the most ancient Buddhist sites in the Lhasa region. Though one of the lesser-visited monasteries in the area, it is only a short detour from Sera Monastery (p89). Built on a flat-topped gran-

ite boulder said to resemble a tortoise, Pabonka's timeless chapels may even pre-date the Jokhang and Ramoche.

King Songtsen Gampo and his Chinese wife Princess Wencheng, as well as Tibetan king Trisong Detsen, Guru Rinpoche and Tibet's first seven monks, all meditated here at various times. The original nine-storey tower was destroyed in 841 by the anti-Buddhist King Langdharma but rebuilt in the 11th century. The fifth Dalai Lama added an extra floor to that two-storey building. It suffered damage in the Cultural Revolution and has undergone repairs in recent years.

➡ **Rigsum Gonpo Temple**

This temple is the first you come across when visiting Pabonka Monastery. The most famous relic is the blue and gold carved stone mantra '*Om mani padme hum*' ('Hail to the jewel in the lotus') that faces the entrance on the far side of the hall. It is said to have been carved by Tibetan minister Thonmi Sambhota, who created the Tibetan script here after a visit to India. The central shrine contains a 1300-year-old 'self-arising' stone carving depicting Chenresig, Jampelyang and Chana Dorje (Vajrapani) – the Rigsum Gonpo trinity after which the chapel is named. The stone carvings were buried during the Cultural Revolution and only dug up in 1985.

➡ **Palden Lhamo Cave**

It is said that King Songtsen Gampo once meditated in this cave. Images inside are of Songtsen Gampo (with a turban), his two wives, Guru Rinpoche, Trisong Detsen (in the corner) and a *rangjung* (self-arising) rock carving of the protectress Palden Lhamo.

The cave is located just uphill from the Rigsum Gonpo Temple, on the west side of the Pabonka rock (said to represent a female tortoise).

➡ **Pabonka Podrang**

This temple atop the Pabonka rock is what remains of the original nine-storey palace. The upper floor has an intimate assembly hall with a 'self-arising' Chenresig statue hidden behind a pillar to the right. The inner protector chapel has a statue of red-faced local protector Gonpo Dashey Marpo (second from the right) next to an impressive stag's head. The four-pillared Kashima Lhakhang next door is lined with various lamas, ministers, three kings and their wives. The cosy rooftop quarters of the Dalai Lama have a statue of the meditational deity Demchok (Chakrasamvara). A legend claims that it was here that Songtsen Gampo first hatched the plan of building the Potala Palace on top of Marpo Ri, which is clearly visible from here.

➡ **Gyasa Podrang**

The yellow Gyasa Podrang (Princess Wencheng Temple) sits above the Pabonka Podrang and the remains of 108 chörtens at the top of Pabonka Monastery. The two ground-floor rooms are dedicated to different manifestations of the medicine buddhas and Tsongkhapa, and an upper-floor chapel has a small statue of Wencheng herself in the far right, near an image of Thonmi Sambhota.

Songtsen Gampo's Nepali wife Bhrikuti is also present, as are images of green and white Drölma, of whom the two wives are thought to be emanations. Also present is Gar Tongtsen, the Tibetan minister who travelled to the Tang Chinese court to escort Princess Wencheng back to Tibet.

Just next to the Gyasa Podrang, and next to rows of photogenic white chortens, is a new lhakhang housing the funeral stupa of Tantric teacher Nakchang Rinpoche.

➡ **Getting There**

To get to Pabonka, take bus 20 from Beijing Donglu to the Sera Monastery turn-off on Nangre Beilu. A paved road branches left before the military hospital and leads all the way to Pabonka and Chupsang. You'll soon see Pabonka up ahead to the left, perched on its granite boulder. The 'monastery' to the right is actually Chupsang Nunnery. A ride from the junction in a minivan costs ¥10 per person, or ¥30 for a taxi.

Ganden Monastery ८ग१९ुङ्
甘丹寺

Ganden Monastery (Gāndān Sì; ¥50; ⊘ dawn-dusk) was the first Gelugpa monastery and has been the main seat of this major Buddhist order ever since. If you only have time for one monastery excursion outside Lhasa, Ganden – 60 km from the city – is the best choice. With its stupendous views of the surrounding Kyichu Valley and its fascinating kora (pilgrim circuit), Ganden makes for an experience unlike those at the other major Gelugpa monasteries in the Lhasa area.

Ganden was founded in 1409 by Tsongkhapa, the revered reformer of the Gelugpa order, after the first Mönlam festival was performed here. Images of Tsongkhapa flanked by his first two disciples, Kedrub Je and Gyaltsab Je, are found throughout the monastery. When Tsongkhapa died in 1411, the abbotship of the monastery passed to these disciples. The post came to be known as the Ganden Tripa and was earned through scholarly merit, not reincarnation. It is the Ganden Tripa – not, as one might expect, the Dalai Lama – who is the head of the Gelugpa order. The 104th Ganden Tripa took up his seven-year term in Dharamsala in 2017.

Today Ganden is the scene of extensive rebuilding, but this does not disguise the ruin that surrounds the new structures. In 1959 there were 2000 monks here; today there are just 300. The destruction was caused largely by artillery fire and bombing in 1959 and 1966. New chapels and residences are being opened all the time, so even pilgrims are

Ganden Monastery

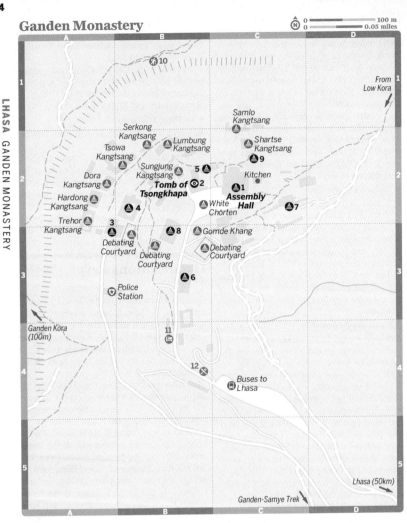

sometimes unsure in which order to visit the chapels.

Ganden was temporarily closed to tourists in 1996 after violent demonstrations against the government's banning of Dalai Lama photos. There were further scuffles in 2006 when monks smashed a statue of the controversial deity Dorje Shugden. A new police station and military barracks were built at the monastery following the riots of 2008.

Ganden means 'joyous' in Tibetan and is the name of the Western Paradise (also known as Tushita) that is home to Jampa, the Future Buddha. There is a certain irony in this

because, of all the great monasteries of Tibet, Ganden suffered most at the hands of the Red Guards, possibly because of its political influence.

Ganden is also the start of the popular wilderness trek to Samye Monastery.

Interior photography fees are ¥20 per chapel; video fees are ¥1500. Make sure you visit the monastery in the morning, as many chapels are closed in the afternoon.

Once you've seen the main sights it's worth climbing the ridge behind to explore one of the little-visited residential colleges such as the Serkong Kangtsang, Tsowa Kangtsang,

Ganden Monastery

Dora Kangtsang, Hardong Kangtsang or Trehor Kangtsang.

⊙ Sights & Activities

Ngam Chö Khang   BUDDHIST SITE
(Map p94) The first chapel you reach from the monastery's parking area is Ngam Chö Khang, one of Ganden's oldest. It is built on the site of Tsongkhapa's original *dukhang* (assembly hall) and has a small shrine with images of Tsongkhapa. On the left is a *gönkhang* (protector chapel) that houses four protective deities, including local deity Genyen.

Shartse Tratsang   BUDDHIST SITE
(Map p94) Shartse Tratsang is one of several renovated *kangtsang* (residences) that offer the opportunity to meet the local monks away from the tourist trail. In the early afternoon (1.30pm to 3pm), listen out for debating in the enclosed **debating courtyard** to the south. Nearby is the interesting **Barkhang** (Map p94), or printing press, where you can watch block printing taking place. Also here is a second **debating courtyard** and the **Changtse Tratsang** (Northern College; Map p94), with its impressive main prayer hall.

★ Tomb of Tsongkhapa   MAUSOLEUM
(Serkhang; Map p94) The red, fortress-like structure of Tsongkhapa's mausoleum is probably the most impressive of the reconstructed buildings at Ganden. It's above a prominent white chörten. Red Guards destroyed both the original tomb and the preserved body of Tsongkhapa inside it. The new silver-and-gold chörten was built to house salvaged fragments of Tsongkhapa's skull.

The main entrance leads to a new prayer hall with an inner Sakyamuni chapel. The protector chapel to the right is the domain of the three main Gelugpa protectors: Chögyel (far right), Dorje Jigje (centre) and Gompo (left). Women are not allowed into this chapel.

Stairs lead to the upper floors and the holy Serdung chapel, which houses Tsongkhapa's funeral chörten. The chapel is sometimes called the Yangpachen Khang, after the stone in the back left, covered in offerings of yak butter that is said to have flown from India. The images seated in front of the chörten are of Tsongkhapa flanked by his two principal disciples. On the wall is a photo of the Ganden Tripa who rebuilt the funeral chörten. Pilgrims line up to buy votive inscriptions written in gold ink by the monks and later recited during prayer dedications. Protective amulets and high-quality incense are sold outside the chapel.

Jampa Lhakhang   BUDDHIST SITE
(Chapel of Jampa; Map p94) This small chapel, located just across from the exit of the Tomb of Tsongkhapa, holds two large images of the Future Buddha, plus the eight bodhisattvas.

★ Assembly Hall   BUDDHIST SITE
(Map p94) The recently renovated *tsogchen* (assembly hall) has statues of the 16 *arhats* and two huge statues of Tsongkhapa (only visible from upstairs). Stairs lead up to the inner sanctum: the Ser Trikhang (Golden Throne Room), which houses the throne of Tsongkhapa. Pilgrims get thumped on the head here with the yellow hat of Tsongkhapa and the shoes of the 13th Dalai Lama.

On exiting the assembly hall there are two entrances on the northern side of the building. The western one gives access to a 2nd-floor view of two Tsongkhapa statues, and the eastern one houses a library (Tengyur Lhakhang). To the east is the main monastery kitchen.

Zimchung Tridok Khang
BUDDHIST SITE

(Residence of the Ganden Tripa; Map p94) To the east of the Assembly Hall's Ser Trikhang (Golden Throne Room) and slightly uphill, this residence contains the living quarters and throne of the Ganden Tripa.

Other rooms include a protector chapel, with statues of Demchok (Samvara), Gonpo Gur (Mahakala) and Dorje Naljorma (Vajrayogini); a Tsongkhapa chapel; and an inner room of living quarters used by the Dalai Lamas when visiting the monastery. To the right is the 'Nirvana Room', which has a shrine to Kurt Cobain (only kidding – it's Tsongkhapa again, who is said to have died in this room). The upper-floor library has a round platform known as a *kyingor*, used for creating sand mandalas.

Nyare Kangtsang
BUDDHIST SITE

(Map p94) Below the main assembly hall, the rather innocuous-looking Nyare Kangtsang houses a controversial statue of the deity Dorje Shugden, worship of which has been outlawed by the Dalai Lama for its alleged dangerous Tantric practices. The statue is in the third chapel, in the far-right corner, with a red face and a third eye, wearing a bronze hat and riding a snow lion. Your guide probably won't want to enter this chapel.

In 2006 monks stormed the building and smashed the Dorje Shugden statue, leading to the arrest of two monks. The statue was replaced in 2007 with the support of the government. The stand-off remains tense and around two dozen soldiers remain barracked in the main chapel.

★ Ganden Kora
WALKING

(Map p94) The Ganden kora is simply stunning and should not be missed. There are superb views over the braided Kyi-chu Valley along the way and there are usually large numbers of pilgrims and monks offering prayers, rubbing holy rocks and prostrating themselves along the path. There are two parts to the walk: the high kora and the low kora. The high kora climbs Angkor Ri south of Ganden and then drops down the ridge to join up with the low kora.

To walk the **high kora**, follow the path southeast of the car park, away from the monastery. After a while the track splits – the left path leads to Hepu village on the Ganden–Samye trek; the right path zigzags up the ridge to a collection of prayer flags. Try to follow other pilgrims up. It's a tough 40-minute climb to the top of the ridge, so don't try this

one unless you're well acclimatised. Here, at two peaks, pilgrims burn juniper incense and give offerings of *tsampa* (roasted-barley flour) before heading west down the ridge in the direction of the monastery, stopping at several other shrines en route.

The **low kora** is an easier walk of around 45 minutes. From the car park the trail heads west up past the new police station and then around the back of the ridge behind the monastery. The trail winds past several isolated shrines and rocks that are rubbed for their healing properties or squeezed through as a karmic test. At one point, pilgrims all peer at a rock through a clenched fist in order to see visions.

Towards the end of the kora, on the eastern side of the ridge, is Tsongkhapa's hermitage, a small building with relief images of Atisha, Sakyamuni, Tsepame and Palden Lhamo. These images are believed to have the power of speech. Above the hermitage is a coloured rock painting that is reached by a narrow, precipitous path. From the hermitage, the kora drops down to rejoin the monastery.

🛏 Sleeping & Eating

Tourists are generally not allowed to stay overnight at Ganden, but there is a **guesthouse** (Map p94; d without bathroom ¥200) here, so check with your tour agency.

Basic food is available at the **monastery restaurant** (Map p94; dishes ¥13-20), and a monastery **shop** (Map p94) sells basic supplies.

❶ Getting There & Away

The road from Lhasa follows a new highway east, from which a paved road switchbacks the steep final 12km to the monastery. Figure on an hour to get here.

Pilgrim buses run to a stop at Ganden in the early morning from a block west of Barkhor Sq, but tourists are currently not allowed to take them.

On the way back to Lhasa, pilgrims traditionally stop for a visit at Sanga Monastery, set at the foot of the ruined Dagtse Dzong (or Dechen Dzong; *dzong* means fort).

Vehicle hire for a day trip to Ganden currently costs around ¥500.

Drak Yerpa
扎叶巴寺
བྲག་ཡེར་པ་

For those with an interest in Tibetan Buddhism, **Drak Yerpa hermitage** (Zhā Yèbā Sì; ¥30), about 30km northeast of Lhasa, is one of the holiest cave retreats in Ü. Among the many ascetics who have sojourned here are Guru Rinpoche and Atisha (Jowo-je). King Songtsen Gampo also meditated in a cave, after his Tibetan wife established the first retreat. The peaceful site (4400m) offers lovely views and is easily combined with Ganden Monastery as a full-day trip.

At one time the hill at the base of the cave-dotted cliffs was home to Yerpa Drubde Monastery, the summer residence of Lhasa's Gyutö College at the Ramoche Temple. The monastery was destroyed in 1959. Monks have begun to return to Yerpa but numbers are strictly controlled by the government, which carries out regular patriotic study sessions.

From the car park, take the left branch of the stairway to visit the caves in clockwise fashion. The first caves are the **Rigsum Gompo Cave** and the **Demdril Drubpuk**, the cave where Atisha (shown in a red hat) meditated as part of his 12 years spent proselytising in Tibet. Look for the stone footprints of Yeshe Tsogyel in the former and the fifth Dalai Lama outside the latter. At one nearby cave pilgrims squeeze through a hole in the rock wall; at another they take a sip of holy water.

The yellow **Jamkhang** has an impressive two-storey statue of Jampa flanked by Chana Dorje (Vajrapani) to the left and Namse (Vairocana) and Tamdrin (Hayagriva) to the right. Other statues are of Atisha (Jowo-je) flanked by the fifth Dalai Lama and Tsongkhapa. The upper cave is the **Drubthub-puk**, offering an upper view of the Jampa statue next to the quarters of the Dalai Lama. Continuing east along the ridge a detour leads up to a chörten that offers fine views of the valley.

Climb to the **Chögyal-puk**, the Cave of Songtsen Gampo. The interior chapel has a central thousand-armed Chenresig (Avalokiteshvara) statue known as Chaktong Chentong. Pilgrims circle the central rock pillar continually. A small cave and statue of Songtsen Gampo are in the right-hand corner.

The next chapel surrounds the **Lhalung-puk**, the cave where the monk Lhalung Pelde meditated after assassinating the anti-Buddhist king Langdharma in 842. A statue of the monk wearing his black hat occupies the back room. Look also for the photo of Drak Yerpa dating from 1937.

The most atmospheric chapel is the **Dawa-puk** (Moon Cave), where Guru Rinpoche (the main statue) is said to have meditated for seven years. Look for the rock carvings of Drölma and Chenresig in the left corner of the

ante-room and the stone footprints (one of his boot, one with his toes) of Guru Rinpoche in the inner room, to the right.

Below the main caves and to the east is the yellow-walled **Neten Lhakhang**, where practice of worshipping the 16 *arhats* was first introduced. Below here is where Atisha is said to have taught. A 15-minute walk takes you around the holy mountain of Yerpa Lhari, topped by prayer flags and encircled by a kora.

There are several caves and retreats higher up the cliff-face and some fine hiking possibilities in the hills if you have time, including a half-day high kora. A pilgrim guesthouse by the car park offers simple food and accommodation.

If you are here in September, specifically the 10th day of the seventh Tibetan lunar month, head here for the Yerpa tsechu festival, during which a large thangka is unveiled and cham dances are performed.

The paved road from Lhasa crosses the prayer-flag-draped 3980m Ngachen-la before turning into the side valley at Yerpa village and passing two ruined *dzong* and a large disused dam en route to the caves, 10km from the main road. The paved side road to Drak Yerpa makes for a good uphill biking destination.

A daily pilgrim bus leaves from Barkhor Sq but foreigners currently can't take it. Drivers often call the site 'Drayab'.

Drölma Lhakhang ষ্ট্র্ম
য়ৣয়ঢ়য় 卓玛拉康

This significant but small **monastery** (Zhuómǎ Lākāng; Netang; ¥30; ⊙ dawn-dusk) is jam-packed with ancient relics and hidden treasures. It's only 30 minutes' drive southwest of Lhasa and is worth a stop en route to or from the airport for those interested in Tibetan Buddhism.

Drölma Lhakhang is associated with the Bengali scholar Atisha (982–1054). Atisha came to Tibet at the age of 53 at the invitation of the king of the Guge kingdom in western Tibet and his teachings were instrumental in the so-called second diffusion of Buddhism in the 11th century. Drölma Lhakhang was established at this time by one of Atisha's foremost disciples, Drömtonpa, who also founded the Kadampa order, to which the monastery belongs. It was here at Netang that Atisha died, aged 72.

The 11th-century monastery was spared desecration by the Red Guards during the

Cultural Revolution after a direct request from Bangladesh (which now encompasses Atisha's homeland). Apparently, Chinese premier Zhou Enlai intervened on its behalf.

The first chapel to the left is a *gönkhang* (protector chapel), decorated with severed stags' heads and arrow holders. As you enter and exit the main monastery building, look for the two ancient guardian deities, which may even date back to the 11th-century founding of the monastery. An inner kora (pilgrim circuit) surrounds the main chapels.

From the entry, pass into the first chapel, the renovated **Namgyel Lhakhang**, which contains a number of chörtens (Buddhist stupas). The black-metal Kadampa-style chörten to the right reputedly holds the staff of Atisha and the skull of Naropa, Atisha's teacher. Statuary includes Atisha and the eight medicine buddhas.

The eponymous middle **Drölma Lhakhang** houses a number of relics associated with Atisha. The statues include an 11th-century statue of Jowo Sakyamuni and at the top, behind a grill, are statues of the 13th Dalai Lama, Green Tara, and Serlingpa (right, with a red hat), another teacher of Atisha. The lower statue to the right behind the grill is an image of Jampa that was reputedly saved from Mongol destruction when it shouted 'Ouch!'. There are also 21 statues of Drölma.

The final **Tsepame Lhakhang** has original statues of Tsepame, cast with the ashes of Atisha, flanked by Marmedze (Dipamkara), the Past Buddha, Jampa (the Future Buddha) and the eight bodhisattvas. The small central statue of Atisha in a glass case is backed by his original clay throne. As you leave the chapel, look out for the great old leather prayer wheel and two sunken white chörtens, which respectively hold the robes of Atisha and his main disciple Dromtonpa. Upstairs is the throne room and, at the far end, the living room of the Dalai Lamas, and to the right is a library.

Just down a side road opposite the monastery is the **Kumbum Lhakhang**, whose two white chörtens enshrine the ashes of Atisha and Lama Dampa Sonam Gyeltsen, a teacher of Gelugpa founder Tsongkhapa.

Drölma Lhakhang is 16km southwest of Lhasa on the old road to Shigatse, but it's bypassed by the main airport expressway that connects the capital to the Yarlung Tsangpo

Valley. En route you'll pass a blue rock carving of Sakyamuni at the base of a cliff about 11km southwest of Lhasa, or 6km north of Drölma Lhakhang (it's easily missed coming from the south). Nyetang village and the monastery are between kilometre markers 4662 and 4663.

Shuksip Nunnery   雄色寺

Hikers and anyone who likes to get well off the beaten track will enjoy this excursion to Tibet's largest **nunnery** (Xióngsè Sì) `FREE`, set in a large natural bowl about 55km south of Lhasa and home to over 160 nuns. The region is a favourite of birdwatchers.

The newly paved road leads right up to the village-like nunnery (4410m). The central **assembly hall** contains statues of Guru Rinpoche and several old lamas of the Nyingma and Dzogchen schools. Stairs to the right lead upstairs to a chapel with a statue of Machik Labdronma (holding a double drum), the famous 11th-century adept who opened up the valley and who is considered an emanation of Yeshe Tsogyel (the consort of Guru Rinpoche). The assembly hall features a B&W photo and wall mural of one of Labdronma's subsequent reincarnations.

You can hike up the hill, following the electric poles, for about 45 minutes to the **Gangri Tokar shrine** (Drubkhang), where Longchenpa, an important 14th-century Dzogchen lama, once meditated. The chapel has a cave shrine and a sacred tree stump in front of a rock image of the Dzogchen deity Rahulla.

From here, fit and acclimatised hikers can climb for a couple of hours up past meditation caves (marked by prayer flags) to the ridgeline behind. The views of the Kyi-chu Valley are fantastic from here and if the weather is clear you'll get views of snowcapped 7191m Nojin Kangtsang and other Himalayan peaks to the south. From the ridgeline you can continue northwest across a boulder field for 15 minutes to a small hill (5160m) topped by a chörten that offers epic views northwards as far as Lhasa. Alternatively you can continue east along the ridge to summit the bowl's main peak.

The road to Shongse branches off the main expressway to Gongkar Airport at Tsena village and diverts 13km up a side valley, passing the picturesque cliffside Samanga Monastery and small Öshang Lhakhang en route.

Ü དབུས་

Best Off the Beaten Track

➡ Chim-puk Hermitage (p120)

➡ Sili Götsang (p111)

➡ Samtenling Nunnery (p107)

Best Places to Stay

➡ Shambhala Source (p113)

➡ Samye Monastery Guesthouse (p119)

➡ Tibetan Source Hotel (p121)

➡ Gāodì Xiāngcūn Jiǔdiàn (p127)

Why Go?

Ü (དབུས་) is Tibet's heartland and contains almost all the landscapes you'll find across the plateau, from sand dunes and meandering rivers to soaring peaks and juniper forests. Due to its proximity to Lhasa, Ü is the first taste of rural Tibet that most visitors experience, and you can get off the beaten track surprisingly easily here. Fine walking opportunities abound, from day hikes and monastery koras (pilgrim circuits) to overnight treks.

Ü is the traditional power centre of Tibet, and home to its oldest buildings and most historic monasteries. The big sights, such as Samye, are unmissable, but consider also heading to lesser-visited places such as the Drigung and Yarlung Valleys, or to smaller monasteries like Dratang and Gongkar Chöde. Make it to these hidden gems and you'll feel as though you have Tibet all to yourself.

When to Go

➡ Nam-tso gets very busy in July and August, so consider visiting in late April or May. The lake remains frozen from November until May.

➡ Pilgrims converge on Tsurphu and Taklung Monasteries in May/June during the Saga Dawa Festival to take part in a festival of *cham* (religious monk dances), the unfurling of a huge thangka and epic bouts of Tibetan-style drinking games.

➡ Festival season at Samye Monastery is in June/July. Time your trek from Ganden to end in the middle of the festivities.

➡ See Tibetan horsemen at their finest during the Dajyur Horse Festival in July/August outside the town of Damxung en route to Nam-tso.

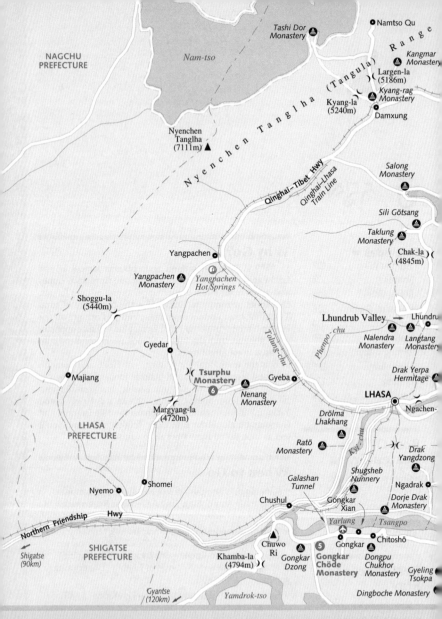

Ü Highlights

1 Samye Monastery
(p115) Exploring the mandala-shaped complex of Tibet's first monastery.

2 Tradruk Monastery
(p123) Stopping at this atmospheric ancient monastery and passing by the ruins of cliffside Rechung-puk.

3 Reting Monastery (p107)
Exploring the juniper-scented kora (pilgrim circuit) and

the meditation retreat of Tsongkhapa before making the lovely walk to Samtenling Nunnery.

4 Drigung Til Monastery
(p112) Admiring the views of

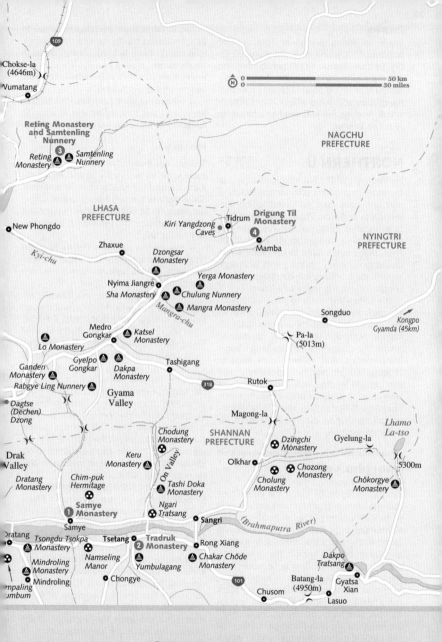

109

Chokse-la
(4646m)
Yumatang

N   0 [====] 50 km
    0 [====] 30 miles

NAGCHU
PREFECTURE

Reting Monastery
and Samtenling
Nunnery

Reting   ❸   Samtenling
Monastery   Nunnery

LHASA
PREFECTURE

Kiri Yangdzong   Tidrum   Drigung Til
Caves   Monastery

● New Phongdo   ❹   NYINGTRI
                         Mamba   PREFECTURE

Kyi-chu   Zhaxue
                        Dzongsar
                        Monastery
                              Yerga Monastery
            Nyima Jiangre
            Sha Monastery ▲ Chulung Nunnery
                        ▲ Mangra Monastery

                        Mangra-chu   Songduo
                                              Kongpo
            Medro   Katsel   Gyamda (45km)
            Gongkar   Monastery
▲ Lo Monastery   Pa-la
                                  (5013m)
         Gyelpo
         Gongkar ▲   Dakpa
Ganden ▲   Monastery Tashigang
Monastery
Rabgye Ling Nunnery ▲   318   Rutok

         Gyama
Dagtse   Valley
(Dechen)   Magong-la
Dzong

                Chodung   SHANNAN   Gyelung-la   Lhamo
Drak   Monastery PREFECTURE   Dzingchi   La-tso
Valley   Keru   Monastery
Dratang   Monastery   Olkhar ●   Chozong   5300m
Monastery   On Valley   Cholung Monastery Chökorgye
      Chim-puk   Tashi Doka   Monastery ▲ Monastery
      Hermitage   Monastery
      ❶ Samye   Ngari
      Monastery   Tratsang
      Samye   Tradruk   ● Sangri
Dratang Tsongdu Tsokpa Tsetang ❷ Monastery Rong Xiang (Brahmaputra River)
         Monastery   Dakpo
      Namseling   Chakar Chöde   Tratsang ▲
Mindroling Manor   Yumbulagang Monastery   Batang-la Gyatsa
Monastery   101   (4950m)   Xian
●mpaling Mindroling ● Chongye   Chusom   Lasuo
umbum

---

the Zhorong-chu Valley from
any of the many courtyards
of this monastic complex
that was spared the brunt
of the Cultural Revolution's
destruction.

❺ **Gongkar Chöde
Monastery** (p128) Searching
the dark interior, heavy with
centuries of butter candle
smoke, for the unusual 16th-
century murals.

❻ **Tsurphu Monastery**
(p102) Seeing the historic
home of the Karmapa school,
still an important monastic
centre.

Permits

Travel in Lhasa prefecture (central and northern Ü) requires only the standard Tibet Tourism Bureau (TTB) permit, but you still need to pre-arrange a guide and transport to receive this. Most of Lhoka prefecture requires an additional Alien's Travel Permit, which your agency will need to arrange in Lhasa or Tsetang.

NORTHERN Ü དབུས་བྱང་

Northern Ü (དབུས་བྱང་) is a wild landscape that has more in common with the grasslands of northern Tibet than the desert valleys further south and west. Physical beauty is here in abundance, from the epic turquoise waters of Nam-tso and the snowy peaks of the Nyenchen Tanglha range to the pretty, fertile Zhorong-chu Valley. There's plenty of history, as well, most notably the birthplace of King Songtsen Gampo in the Gyama Valley.

It's surprisingly easy to get off the beaten track in northern Ü. While hundreds of Chinese day trippers descend daily on fragile Nam-tso you'll find monastery towns like Lhundrub and Taklung almost undiscovered, and sacred sights such as Drigung Til Monastery and Tidrum Hot Springs still bustling with Tibetan pilgrims who visit for religious rather than touristic purposes. Whether you are biking, hiking or just visiting by car, come prepared for some exploration.

Tsurphu Valley

📍 0891 / ELEV 4490M

Tsurphu Valley is the site of the eponymous Tsurphu Monastery, seat of the Karma branch of the Kagyu order of Tibetan Buddhism. The Karma Kagyu (or Karmapa) are also known as the Black Hats, a title referring to a crown given to the fifth Karmapa by the Chinese emperor Yongle in 1407. Said to be made from the hair of 100,000 *dakini*s (celestial beings, known as *khandroma* in Tibetan), the black hat, embellished with gold, is now kept at Rumtek Monastery in Sikkim, India. You'll see images of the 16th Karmapa wearing the hat, holding it down with his hand to stop it flying away.

Most travellers visit Tsurphu as a day trip, but there is a very basic monastery guesthouse here and trekkers might find themselves camping in the upper valley before their trek starts.

About 40km west of Lhasa, the road to Tsurphu crosses the Tolung-chu near the railroad bridge. From here it's another 25km to the monastery, passing Nenung Monastery en route. Most travellers visit Tsurphu as a side trip on the way to Nam-tso.

A pilgrim minibus runs between Lhasa's Barkhor Sq and Tsurphu but was off limits to foreigners at the time of research.

History

Tsurphu was founded in 1187 by Dusum Khyenpa, some 40 years after he established the Karma Kagyu (or Karmapa) order in Kham, his birthplace. It was the third Karma Kagyu monastery to be built and, after the death of the first Karmapa, it became the head monastery for the order.

It was the first Karmapa, Dusum Khyenpa (1110–93), who instigated the concept of reincarnation, and the Karmapa lineage has been maintained this way ever since.

The Karma Kagyu order traditionally enjoyed strong ties with the kings and monasteries of Tsang, a legacy that proved a liability when conflict broke out between the kings of Tsang and the Gelugpa order. When the fifth Dalai Lama invited the Mongolian army of Gushri Khan to do away with his opponents in Tsang, Tsurphu was sacked (in 1642) and the Karmapa's political clout effectively came to an end. Shorn of its political influence, Tsurphu nevertheless bounced back as an important spiritual centre and is one of the few Kagyud institutions still functioning in the Ü region. When Chinese forces invaded in 1950, around 1000 monks were in residence; now there are about 330 monks.

The respected 16th Karmapa fled to Sikkim in 1959 after the popular uprising in Lhasa and founded a new centre at Rumtek. He died in 1981 and his reincarnation, Ogyen Trinley Dorje, an eight-year-old Tibetan boy from Kham, was announced amid great controversy by the Dalai Lama and other religious leaders in 1992. More than 20,000 Tibetans came to Tsurphu to watch the Karmapa's coronation that year. In December 1999, the 17th Karmapa undertook a dramatic escape from Tibet into India via Mustang and the Annapurna region. He currently resides in Dharamsala, India.

🔘 Sights

⭐ **Tsurphu Monastery**   BUDDHIST MONASTERY
(མཚུར་ཕུ་དགོན་པ་, 楚布寺, Chǔbù Sì; ¥50) Tsurphu has four main buildings and you could easily

spend half a day here – longer if you plan to do the excellent outer kora (pilgrim circuit). If you're short on time, concentrate on the large central assembly hall and the upstairs former living quarters of the Karmapa.

Completely destroyed during the Cultural Revolution, the current structures date back from 1982 and reconstruction is ongoing. The monastery is home to 370 monks, with around 50 more living in seclusion in the surrounding mountains.

The large **assembly hall** in the main courtyard houses a funeral chörten (stupa) containing relics of the 16th Karmapa. Statues include the main central image of the first Karmapa, alongside Öpagme (Amitabha), Sakyamuni (Sakya Thukpa), and the eighth and 16th Karmapas. Pilgrims particularly venerate a small speaking statue of Sangye Nyenpa Rinpoche, a 15th-century meditation master and teacher of the eighth Karmapa. Along the right-hand wall of the hall are stacked the monastery's huge festival thangkas.

Scamper up the ladder to the right of the main entrance to visit the private quarters of the Karmapa. First up is the Karmapa's bedroom, complete with a jigsaw puzzle of a Buddhist thangka and the Karmapa's throne. The small Audience Hall contains a footprint of the 14th Karmapa as well as a picture of the 16th Karmapa wearing his holy headgear.

ITINERARIES

Ü is a relatively small region compared to other areas of Tibet, resulting in shorter drives and fewer days on the road. Some sights, including Tsurphu Monastery and Lhundrub, could be visited as day trips from Lhasa, although spending nights out of the city allows for a slower pace and reduces backtracking, particularly on longer itineraries that aim to take in the entire region.

You can combine Ü's main sights with other regions of Tibet. From Nam-tso you can continue to Shigatse directly over the Margyang-la. From Medro Gongkar you can continue east to Draksum-tso and Nyingtri prefecture. From Gongkar (the airport), you can get onto the southern Friendship Hwy and head west to Gyantse or head on to Tsetang and north to Nyingtri via the small town of Rutok.

Ü is usually tackled in three day-long stages, broken up with a stop in Lhasa. If time is short, your priority should be Lhoka prefecture, which houses the highest concentration of historic and religious sites. Head from Lhasa to Samye Monastery (p115) and back, stopping at places like Dorje Drak (p113) and Dratang Monastery (p127).

Day 1 Leave Lhasa towards the Tsurphu Valley (p102), stopping in for a visit at Tsurphu Monastery (p102) before continuing all the way to Nam-tso (p104) to enjoy the lake's tranquillity after the crowds have departed.

Day 2 Circle back to Lhasa via the old eastern route, stopping in along the way in the Reting Valley (p106), Sili Götsang (p111) and Taklung Monastery (p111). If there's still time left in the day, visit the small monasteries of Lhundrub County (p108) on your way back into the capital.

Day 3 Head south along the new airport highway to Lhoka prefecture, detouring to the impressive monasteries near Gongkar (p127) before turning east towards Dratang (p127) and Mindroling (p125), then doubling back across the new bridge to Samye (p114).

Day 4 Samye is easily worth a day itself, particularly if you've got the energy to climb up to the temples of the Chim-puk Hermitage complex (p120) high above. If you can handle more hiking, drive over to Dorje Drak (p113) to walk the steep but impressive kora path above the monastery.

Day 5 Carry on to the Yarlung Valley (p123) and Chongye Valley (p125) to see a bit of Tibet's pre-Buddhist and early Buddhist history, overnighting back in Tsetang (p120).

Day 6 Head north from Tsetang via Rutok (p114) to the Zhorong-chu Valley (p109), visiting the numerous monasteries and nunneries of the area before spending the night at the foot of Drigung Til in the township of Mamba (p111).

Day 7 Return to Lhasa, stopping for a half-day at Ganden Monastery (p93) if it's not included on your itinerary elsewhere.

Across the upper courtyard is the 17th Karmapa's **bedroom**, not always open to visitors, where an attendant monk inside will pat you on the back with a shoe once worn by the man himself. A quick look at the Karmapa's bookshelves reveals an interest in birdwatching and astronomy; unexpected titles include *Peter Pan, The Fantastic Four* and *Star Wars: The Empire Strikes Back.* Other boyhood possessions include a globe and a toy car.

Walking west (clockwise) around the monastery complex, you'll pass a large *darchen* (prayer pole) covered in yak hide and prayer flags before coming to the main **protector chapel** *(gönkhang).* There are five rooms here, all stuffed to the brim with wrathful deities. A row of severed animal heads, including ibex and Marco Polo sheep, lines the entry portico.

The first room is dedicated to Tsurphu's protector deity, an aspect of blue Nagpo Chenpo (Mahakala) called Bernakchen. The third room features Dorje Drolo, a wrathful form of Guru Rinpoche astride a tiger, and the fourth room features a Tantric form of the Kagyud protector Dorje Phurba holding a ritual dagger. The fifth room contains a silver statue of Tseringma, a protectress associated with Mt Everest, riding a snow lion.

The large building behind the *gönkhang* is the **Serdung (Senlung) Lhakhang**, which once served as the residence of the Karmapa. Pilgrims are blessed with sacred scriptures in the upper living room of the Karmapa. The side chapel features new statues of all 16 previous Karmapas. Look for the photos of Tsurphu before and after the Cultural Revolution, and as you approach the building from the left look up to see a golden handprint imprinted by the current Karmapa.

The **Lhachen Lhakhang**, which is to the right of the Serdung Lhakhang, houses a towering 20m-high statue of Sakyamuni that rises through three storeys; this replaced a celebrated 13th-century image destroyed during the Cultural Revolution. Stairs to the right outside the chapel lead to a viewing platform on the upper floor.

Most people call it quits here, but the hardcore can explore several more residences and colleges to the north, as well as the kora path

that runs around the back of the Serdung Lhakhang and Lhachen Lhakhang. The yellow *lhakhang* to the right of the assembly hall houses a small wood-block printing press.

The outer walls of the monastery are marked at four corners by four coloured chörtens.

Nenung Monastery · BUDDHIST MONASTERY

(乃朗寺, Nǎiláng Sì) Rebuilt only in 2016, this hilltop Kagyu school monastery is now home to 30 monks including the 11th Powa Rinpoche, an important Karma Kagyud reincarnation who gives well-known speeches from his seat here.

Tsurphu Festival · RELIGIOUS

(⊙ May/Jun) Tsurphu has an annual festival from the eighth to the 11th days of the fourth Tibetan month during Saga Dawa. There's plenty of free-flowing *chang* (Tibetan barley beer), as well as the raising of the *darchen* (prayer pole; eighth day), ritual *cham* dancing (10th day) and the unfurling of a great thangka (11th day) on the platform across the river from the monastery.

Nam-tso · གནམ་མཚོ 纳木错

📋 0891 / ELEV 4750M

Nam-tso (Nàmùcuò) is the second-largest saltwater lake in China and one of the most beautiful natural sights in Tibet. It is over 70km long, reaches a width of 30km and is 35m at its deepest point. When the ice melts in late April, the lake is a miraculous shade of turquoise and there are magnificent views of the nearby snow-capped mountains.

Nam-tso is the single most popular tourist stop outside of Lhasa, but many visitors come on grueling one-day trips that visit the lake for just a few of the midday hours. Spending a night here provides a far quieter perspective on the lake once the crowds have gone.

◉ Sights & Activities

Almost all travellers head for Tashi Dor (扎西岛, Zhāxīdǎo), a hammerhead of land that juts into the southeastern corner of the lake. Here at the foot of two wedge-shaped hills are a couple of small chapels and several meditation caves with views back across the clear turquoise waters to the huge, snowy Nyenchen Tanglha massif (7111m).

Your initial experience of Tashi Dor is unlikely to inspire visions of Shangri-La. The poorly planned tourist base is an unsightly mess, ringed with barking dogs, litter and overflowing toilets. Food is overpriced and day-tripping tourist crowds taking yak rides can be heavy during summer lunchtimes. Try to ignore all this and push ahead to the monastery and kora (pilgrim circuit). The nicest time to explore the site is between 9am and noon, before day-trip visitors arrive from Lhasa, or during late afternoon and at sunset.

On the eastern edge of the Tashi Dor peninsula is a bird sanctuary populated by migratory birds between April and November. Species to look out for include bar-headed geese and black-necked cranes.

★**Nam-tso**   LAKE

(གནམ་མཚོ, 纳木错, Nàmùcuò; ☏ 0891-611 1111; May-Oct ¥120, Nov-Apr ¥60) The waters of sacred Nam-tso, the second-largest salt lake in China, are an almost transcendent turquoise blue and shimmer in the rarefied air of 4730m. Most people come here for the scenery and for the short but pilgrim-packed kora. Geographically part of the Changtang Plateau, the lake has an incredible location, bordered to the north by the Tǎngǔlā Shān range. The Nyenchen Tanglha (Tangula) range, with peaks of over 7000m, towers over the lake to the south.

It was these mountains – capped by the 7111m Nyenchen Tanglha peak – that Heinrich Harrer and Peter Aufschnaiter crossed on their incredible journey to Lhasa (their expedition is documented in the book *Seven Years in Tibet*). The scenery is breathtaking, but so is the altitude: 1100m higher than Lhasa. Count on a week in Lhasa acclimitising before rushing out here, otherwise you risk symptoms of acute mountain sickness (AMS).

Tashi Dor Monastery   BUDDHIST MONASTERY

(扎西岛寺, Zhāxīdǎo Sì) `FREE` There are two separate monastery buildings near the Tashi Dor camp. The further of the two from the main Tashi Dor tourist compound is the main monastery chapel featuring a central Guru Rinpoche statue and the trinity of Öpagme, Chenresig and Pema Jigme (Guru Rinpoche), known collectively as the Cholong Dusom. Protectors include Nyenchen Tanglha on a horse and the blue-faced Nam-tso, the god of the lake, who rides a water serpent. Both gods are rooted deeply in Bön belief.

Closer to the tourist buildings is the Gar Lotsawa Drub-puk, a smaller but more atmospheric chapel built around a cave and featuring a statue of Luwang Gyelpo, the king of the naga (lake-snake spirits). Pilgrims test their

DON'T MISS

STRETCHING YOUR LEGS

Tightly planned 4WD tours sometimes leave your legs itching for a walk and some exploration. One sure way to shake things up is to embed the following day hikes and koras (pilgrim circuits) into your itinerary.

➡ Chim-puk Hermitage (p120)
➡ Tashi Dor kora
➡ Dorje Drak kora (p113)
➡ Reting Monastery kora (p107)

sin by lifting the heavy stone of Nyenchen Tanglha, the mountain deity who resides in the nearby peak of the same name. Look for the stone footprint of Gar Lotsawa.

Several other chapels and retreats are honeycombed into the surrounding cliffs.

★**Tashi Dor Kora**   WALKING

The short kora takes less than an hour (roughly 4km) and is unmissable. Try to tag along with some pilgrims and do one circuit at dusk, when the light on the lake is magical. If you have enough time, it's well worth also hiking up to the top of the western hill for good views, especially at sunset.

The main kora path leads off west from the accommodation area, past Tashi Dor Monastery to a hermit's cave hidden behind a large splinter of rock. The trail (now a 4WD track) continues round to a rocky promontory of cairns and prayer flags, where pilgrims undertake a ritual washing, and then continues past several caves and a *chaktsal gang* (prostration point). The twin rock towers here look like two hands in the namaste greeting and are connected to the male and female attributes of the meditational deity Demchok (Chakrasamvara). Pilgrims squeeze into the deep slices of the nearby cliff face as a means of sin detection. They also drink water dripping from cave roofs and some swallow 'holy dirt'. It's a great place to explore if you bring a torch.

From here the path curves around the shoreline and eventually passes a group of ancient rock paintings protected by blue railings. Pilgrims test their merit nearby by attempting to place a finger in a small hole with their eyes closed. At the northeastern corner of the hill is the Mani Ringmo, a large mani wall, at the end of which is a chörten with a *chakje* (handprint) of the third Karmapa.

There are several other great hikes around Tashi Dor. If you have time, it's worth walking to the top of the larger and less visited of the two hills to the east (two hours return). There are superb views to the northeast of the Tanglha range, which marks the modern border between Tibet and Qīnghǎi (Amdo). Morning light is best here. You can also walk around the base of this larger hill in about 2½ hours.

For the seriously devout there is a pilgrim route that circles the entire lake. It takes around 18 days to make a full lap, staying occasionally at small chapels and hermitages along the way.

✨ Festivals & Events

Dajyur Horse Festival   CULTURAL
The hippodome (horse-racing stadium) outside the county town of Damxung (འདམ་གཞུང་རྫོང་, 当雄, Dāngxióng) hosts a week-long horse festival at the end of the seventh Tibetan month, generally July or August. Expect horse races, competitive games and even the odd yak race.

🛏 Sleeping & Eating

There are a dozen ugly prefabricated shacks that serve as hotels, restaurants and shops at Tashi Dor, which these days resembles a sort of Wild West mining camp. Bedding is provided at all places, but nights can get cold, so bring plenty of warm clothes. Most accommodation is only available between April and October, with prices peaking in July, August and September.

Between the altitude, the cold and the barking dogs, most people sleep fitfully at best. None of the hotels have indoor toilets or running water – in fact, the whole site is an *E. coli* outbreak waiting to happen, and the lakeside public toilets are particularly grim.

Tashi Dor's many restaurants offer almost identical menus of pricey Sichuanese and Tibetan dishes (¥30 to ¥70 per dish). Several places sell delicious locally made yoghurt for ¥15.

Damxung White Horse Hotel   HOTEL $$
(当雄白马宾馆, Dāngxióng Báimǎ Bīnguǎn; ☑158 8909 6668, 0891-611 2098; 2 Qukahe Donglu; 曲卡河东路2号; r ¥200; ✳🛜) If you need to overnight in Damxung on the way to or from Nam-tso or are visiting for the Dajyur Horse Festival, this standard midrange hotel is the only place in town that is licenced to host foreigners.

God Sheep Hotel   GUESTHOUSE $$
(神羊宾馆, Shényáng Bīnguǎn; ☑139 0890 0990; dm ¥60, r ¥200-260; 🛜) One of the better-run guesthouses at Nam-tso. The metal cabins aren't pretty, but there's a wide range of rooms with proper beds, electric blankets, clean sheets and electrical outlets. The cosy restaurant is warmed by a dung-fuelled stove and the walk to the toilets is shorter than at any other guesthouse. Discounts of 20% are available outside the high season.

Holy Lake Nam-tso Guesthouse   GUESTHOUSE $$
(神湖纳木措客栈, Shénhú Nàmùcuò Kèzhàn; ☑136 1891 1180, 0891-611 0388; dm ¥60-120, r ¥230-360; @🛜) While most places at Nam-tso look like glorified toolsheds, this is an actual structure, decorated with photos taken by the guesthouse owner. The cheapest rooms surround a comfortable sitting area where you can get Chinese or Tibetan meals. The better rooms are in a side building and offer proper mattresses with electric blankets.

You'll need to negotiate for a decent price. On the positive side, it stays open for part of the winter from March through November, when almost all the other guesthouses and restaurants have closed.

ℹ Getting There & Away

Nam-tso is about 240km northwest of Lhasa. En route to the turn-off at Damxung, at Km3778, is a viewpoint of Nyenchen Tanglha (7111m). By road from Damxung (འདམ་གཞུང་རྫོང་, 当雄, Dāng xióng) it's 4.5km to a new visitor centre that was under construction at the time of research, 4.5km further to the checkpost where tickets are checked, a further 16km winding uphill journey to the 5186m Largen-la, 7km to a junction with the road that rings the lake, and then a slow 28km to Tashi Dor.

Around 4km before the checkpost, just past the hippodome (horse-racing stadium) near Najia village, a paved road branches 3km to Kyang-rag (also spelled Jangra or Gyara) Monastery, a possible detour. Another road leads north from the ticket gate for 12km to Kangmar Monastery.

Some domestic tourists visit Nam-tso as an exhausting 480km day trip from Lhasa. It's much better to make this a two- or three-day trip, stopping off at Tsurphu (p102) en route and looping back through Reting (p107), Sili Götsang (p111) and Taklung (p111) monasteries.

Reting Valley   རྭ་སྒྲེང་ 热振沟
☑0891 / ELEV 4200M
The Reting Valley (Rèzhèn Gōu) is the site of the once-influential Reting Monastery.

KYANG-RAG MONASTERY

Though this small **branch** of Lhasa's Sera Monastery may not look like much, home to only three or four monks at a time who are sent for a year to maintain the small temple that was rebuilt in 1984 after nearly complete destruction during the Cultural Revolution, it has a long and storied history in the Gelugpa tradition.

It is said that the sixth Panchen Lama, Palden Yeshe (1738–80), and his retinue once camped along the Kyang-chu. One day a *kyang* (wild ass) wandered into camp and entered the tent used by him in his religious practice. The Panchen Lama tossed a sack containing sacrificial cakes on the back of the wild ass. The *kyang* exited the tent, wandered to the other side of the river and disappeared into a cliff. Curious, Palden Yeshe went in pursuit of the *kyang* and reached the cliff where it was last seen. Here he found an old monk who had covered the spot with his cloak. The Panchen Lama demanded to know what was going on and pulled off the cloak. Immediately his nose began to bleed. Taking this as a mystic sign, he used the blood to paint an image of Palden Lhamo on the rocks. This site became the inner sanctum of Kyang-rag Monastery. As it turned out the *kyang* was no ordinary animal but a local deity and the mount of the great goddess Palden Lhamo. For that reason the place became known as Kyang-rag (Wild Ass Beheld).

North of Damxung look for an unmarked turn-off just north of the Hippodrome, from where the monastery is 2km.

Ü RETING VALLEY

Pre-1950 photographs show Reting Monastery sprawled gracefully across the flank of a juniper-clad hill in the Reting Tsampo Valley. Like many others, it was almost completely destroyed by Red Guards and its remains stand testament to the destruction of the Cultural Revolution.

Still, the juniper groves remain and the monastery has been rebuilt, so the site is one of the most beautiful in the region. The Dalai Lama has stated that should he return to Tibet it is at Reting that he would like to reside. The **Reting Monastery Guesthouse** (r ¥200) operates a small teahouse, while snacks and sundry are available from small shops along the main road through the valley. This is also the only overnight option that accepts international visitors.

◉ Sights & Activities

Reting Monastery dates to 1056. It was initially associated with Atisha (Jowo-je) but in later years it had an important connection with the Gelugpa order and the Dalai Lamas. Two regents – the de facto rulers of Tibet for the interregnum between the death of a Dalai Lama and the majority of his next reincarnation – were chosen from the Reting abbots. The fifth Reting Rinpoche was regent from 1933 to 1947 and played a key role in the search for the current Dalai Lama, serving as his senior tutor. He was later accused of collusion with the Chinese and died in a Tibetan prison.

The sixth Reting Rinpoche (Tenzin Jigne) died in 1997. In January 2001 the Chinese announced that a boy named Sonam Phuntsog had been identified out of 700 candidates as the seventh Reting Rinpoche; the Dalai Lama opposes the choice.

Reting Monastery BUDDHIST MONASTERY
(རྭ་སྒྲེང་དགོན་པ་, 热振寺, Rèzhèn Sì; ¥30) Founded in 1056, Reting Monastery was completely destroyed during the Cultural Revolution. Once the seat of the Reting Rinpoche, several of whom served as regents during the minority of underage Dalai Lamas, the temple retains little of its former political influence but is still an important spiritual centre of the Gelugpa school and is home to 160 monks.

Samtenling Nunnery BUDDHIST SITE
(桑旦林寺, Sāngdànlín Sì) FREE A pleasant hour-long (2.5km) walk or a quick drive northeast of Reting leads to the village-like Samtenling Nunnery, home to more than 140 nuns. The main chapel houses a meditation cave used by Tsongkhapa; to the right is his stone footprint and a hoofprint belonging to the horse of the protector Pelden Lhamo. The trail branches off to the nunnery from the sky burial site to the northeast of the Reting Monastery.

Reting Monastery Kora WALKING
The monastery is still graced by surrounding juniper forest, said to have sprouted from the hairs of its founder Dromtompa. A pleasant 40-minute kora leads up from the

old guesthouse around the monastery ruins, passing several stone carvings, a series of eight chörtens and an active sky burial site.

At the kora's highest point a side trail branches 25 minutes' walk up the hillside to the *drubkhang* (meditation retreat) where Tsongkhapa composed the Lamrim Chenmo (Graduated Path), a key Gelugpa text.

ℹ Getting There & Away

Getting to Reting has been made considerably more difficult by the construction of the huge Phongdo reservoir. Vehicles have to make a massive detour by heading west along the road to Damxung, doubling back at the Rinphu Bridge along the north side of the reservoir and then swinging north 48km into the Reting Valley for an extra 1¼ hours of driving.

From Reting it's 74km to Taklung and 100km to Damxung. A dirt road leads north over the mountains from a signed junction 11km southwest of Reting to join the main Lhasa–Nagchu Hwy near Wumatang (乌玛塘, Wūmǎtáng). Check conditions with locals before attempting this short cut.

Lhundrub County

📞 0891 / ELEV 4050M

Centered on the main town of Lhundrub (ལྷུན་གྲུབ་གཞུང་ ལྷུན་ གྲུབ་, 林周, Línzhōu), peaceful Lhundrub County is dotted with small monasteries and temples that rarely get a foreign visitor despite being only 70km away from Lhasa.

TIBETAN NOMADS

If you get off the beaten track around Nam-tso, you might get a peek at the otherwise inaccessible life of Tibet's *drokpas* (seminomadic herders) who make their home in the Changtang, Tibet's vast and remote northern plateau. In the Changtang the *drokpas* are known as Changpa. You will also get the chance to visit a *drokpa* camp on the trek from Ganden to Samye (p210).

Nomad camps are centred on spider-like brown or black yak-hair tents. Each tent is usually shared by one family, though a smaller subsidiary tent may be used when a son marries and has children of his own. The interior of a nomad tent holds all the family's possessions. There will be a stove for cooking and also a family altar dedicated to buddhist deities and various local protectors, including those of the livestock, tent pole and hearth. The principal diet of nomads is tsampa (roasted-barley flour) and yak butter (mixed together with tea), *churpi* (dried yak cheese) and *sha gambo* (dried yak meat).

Tending the herds of yaks and sheep is carried out by the men during the day. Women and children stay together in the camp, where they are guarded by one of the men and the ferocious Tibetan mastiffs that are the constant companions of Tibet's nomads. The women and children usually spend the day weaving blankets and tanning sheepskins.

With the onset of winter it is time to go to the markets of an urban centre. The farmers of Tibet do the same, and trade between nomads and farmers provides the former with tsampa and the latter with meat and butter. Most nomads these days have a winter home base and only make established moves to distant pastures during the rest of the year.

The nomads of Tibet have also traditionally traded in salt, which for generations was collected from the Changtang and transported south in bricks, often to the border with Nepal, where it was traded for grain (as documented in the film *The Saltmen of Tibet*). These annual caravans are fast dying out. Traditional life suffered its greatest setback during the Cultural Revolution, when nomads were collectivised and forcibly settled by the government. In 1981 the communes were dissolved and the collectivised livestock were divided equally, with everyone getting five yaks, 25 sheep and seven goats.

Until recently *drokpas* numbered around 500,000 across the plateau. Government incentives are forcing the settlement of nomads, further reducing their numbers and grazing grounds. The black 'nomads' tents' you see along the road to Nam-tso are now little more than facades for the nomads' new homes – prefabricated white shacks. The introduction of the motorbike has further transformed nomad life. Pressure also comes in the form of enforced migration dates and winter housing, as well as attitude changes among the *drokpas* themselves, as young people move from the grasslands in search of a 'better life' in urban centres. How far into the 21st century their way of life will persist is a matter for debate among Tibetologists.

The only guesthouse in Lhundrub licenced to accept foreigners is the very basic **Nalendra Monastery Guesthouse** (纳连查寺客栈, Nàliánchá Sì Kèzhàn; dm ¥50), but it's definitely the type of place to stay for the atmosphere rather than the comfort. A small teahouse here sells basic Tibetan favourites, while in Lhundrub town Tibetan and Sichuanese cafes line Gānqū Lù (甘曲路).

⊙ Sights

Nalendra Monastery   BUDDHIST MONASTERY
(纳连查寺, Nàliánchá Sì) FREE Ruins dwarf the rebuilding work at Nalendra, but it's still an impressive monastery. Founded in 1435 by the lama Rongtonpa (1367–1449), a contemporary of Tsongkhapa, it was largely destroyed in 1959. Where there were once 4000 monks now only 30 remain, though around 110 more live in seclusion in the nearby mountains. Nalendra is 12km west of Lhundrub county town.

As you enter Nalendra's main building, the impressive *gönkhang* (protector chapel; women cannot enter) has a central Gompo Gur, a form of Mahakala and protector of the Sakyapa school, as well as statues of Pehar (on an elephant) and Namse (Vairocana, on a snow lion), both in the left corner. Look for the three huge wild yak heads and the stuffed mountain goat, in varying states of decay.

The main hall has a statue of Rongtonpa in a glass case, while the inner sanctum features Rongtonpa in the front centre, flanked by two Sakyapa lamas. The same room contains the silver funeral stupa of Khenpo Tsultrim Gyeltsen, who is credited with rebuilding Nalendra after its destruction during the Cultural Revolution.

The chapel to the left contains hundreds of statues of Buddha Sakyamuni, which pilgrims crawl under to receive a blessing. In the centre is an unusual statue of Nampar Namse (Vairocana) with four faces.

Other chapels worth checking include the Tsar Kangtsang, under renovation at research time, the *shedra* (monastic college), the Jampa Kangtsang (with its interesting statue of skeletons in a *yabyum* pose), and the ruins of the *dzong* outside the monastery gate to the west.

You can get a great overview of the monastery from ascending to the top of the white chörten just below the monastery's main buildings. To get an idea of the original layout, look closely at the mural on the immediate left as you enter the main assembly hall of the monastery.

Langtang Monastery   BUDDHIST MONASTERY
(朗当寺, Lǎngdāng sì) FREE If you have time to spare, this small but pleasant Gelugpa (Yellow Hat) monastery with a bucolic location is worth a quick stop en route to Nalendra Monastery.

❶ Getting There & Away

From the county town of Lhundrub expect a drive of around 1½ hours to Lhasa along the slow highway through small Tibetan villages. It's possible to combine Lhundrub with a visit to Nam-tso (five hours without stops) via Reting, Sili Götsang and Taklung monasteries in one long day on the road.

Medro Gongkar County སམ་ གོ་གུང་དཀར་རྫོང་ 墨竹工卡县

Medro Gongkar County (Mòzhúgōngkǎ Xiàn) is most famously home to Drigung Til Monastery and Tidrum Nunnery, around 120km northeast of Lhasa.

The valley of the Zhorong-chu river (学绒藏布, Xuéróng Zángbù) is home to fortress-like monasteries, sprawling nunneries and central Tibet's holiest sky burial site. Yet, despite being within easy day-trip distance from Lhasa, its bucolic landscapes see very few foreign visitors.

Only a few hours' drive from the capital, the area offers a glimpse into rural life in Tibet. Change is underway in the region: towns are increasingly developed, rivers dammed and hillsides mined. Despite these intrusions of modernity many locals carry on as usual and there are plenty of opportunities to stop off at remote villages as you monastery-hop your way through the region.

When passing through overland between Nyingtri prefecture and Lhasa, it's well worth adding an extra day to your itinerary to explore the region or combining the trip with a visit to Ganden Monastery.

Almost every town in Medro Gongkar County has at least a handful of Tibetan and Sichuanese restaurants along the old highway, so you're never far from a meal in the region.

Medro Gongkar སམ་གྲོ་གུང་དཀར་ 墨竹工卡

🗹 0891 / POP 4100 / ELEV 3830M

On the wide banks of the Kyi-chu, 65km northeast of Lhasa, Medro Gongkar (སམ་གྲོ་གུང་ དཀར་, 墨竹工卡, Mòzhú Gōngkǎ) is a pit stop en route to Drigung Til. If you have time to spare it's worth stopping at Katsel Monastery, which is shrouded in the legend of 7th-century King Songtsen Gampo.

While it is possible to overnight at the **Xiánghé Shāngwù Bīnguǎn** (祥和商务宾馆; ☑0891-613 2888; 2 Nanjing Lu; 南京路2号; s/d/tr ¥150/180/180; ☎) in central Medro Gongkar, visitors looking for an authentic Tibetan experience would do better to overnight at Ganden or Drigung Til instead.

It's an easy hour's drive of around 65km along the Lhasa–Línzhī Hwy from the capital, which continues east to Bāyī in around five hours with minimal sightseeing stops. Continuing up the Drigung Valley through Nyima Jiangre to Drigung Til expect around 1½ hours' driving without stops.

Katsel Monastery   BUDDHIST MONASTERY

(ཀ་ཚལ་དགོན་པ) **FREE** Legend has it that this combined Nyingmapa- and Kagyupa-order monastery was founded by the 7th-century King Songtsen Gampo, who was led here by the Buddha disguised as a doe with antlers. The temple is also significant as one of the original demoness-subduing temples – it pinned the monster's right shoulder. Currently home to 47 monks, the monastery was heavily damaged in 1966 and rebuilt in 1983, with a later reconstruction in 2016.

The yellow house on the hilltop behind the monastery served briefly as the living quarters of the fifth Dalai Lama.

Katsel is several kilometres from the town centre, on the road to Drigung Til.

Nyima Jiangre   འབྲི་གུང་ཆུ   尼玛江热

☑0891 / POP 1900 / ELEV 3880M

The one-yak town of Nyima Jiangre (Drigung Qu, Nímǎ Jiāngrè), halfway between Medro Gongkar and Drigung Til, is a Tibetan Wild West town, with wild-haired traders strolling the streets and rocky escarpments forming the town's backdrop.

It's set at the auspicious confluence of three rivers and Chinese engineers have not overlooked the strategic location; an ugly dam has been stretched across the valley floor, forming a shallow reservoir.

Most travellers blow through in a rush to reach Drigung Til but the intrepid may want to stop off and explore the little-visited monasteries near the town.

A slew of Tibetan restaurants lines the main strip, with the friendly nuns at the **Chulong Nunnery Teahouse** (曲龙寺臧

餐厅, Qūlóngsì Zàng Cāntīng; ☑136 1899 9703; dishes ¥15-20; ⊙8am-9pm; ☎) making it an obvious favourite. There's also a small supermarket where it's possible to buy snacks and drinks. They claim to have the necessary licence to host foreign travellers in the very basic ¥30 shared rooms, with bathrooms on the street outside.

⊙ Sights

Dzongsar Monastery   BUDDHIST MONASTERY

(རྫོང་གསར་དགོན, 德仲寺, Dézhòng Sì) **FREE** About 1km northwest of town is the Drigungpa-school Dzongsar Monastery. A short but steep climb brings you to a monastery located on a jagged slope; its name soon becomes clear – the monastery is a converted *dzong*. Built originally as a five-storey fortress in 1603 to serve as the seat of the highest lama of Drigung Til, the original structure was destroyed in 1959 and rebuilt in 1985 in its present form. It's now home to 29 monks.

Chulong Nunnery   BUDDHIST SITE

(曲龙尼姑寺, Qūlóng Nígūsì) **FREE** Founded by Drignung-Til as a branch of the Drigung Kagyu school in 1253, Chulong's 112 resident nuns are now members of various Red Hat sects. Inside the main assembly hall look for statues of Guru Rinpoche flanked by Shakyamuni and the Buddha of Long Life. In a small chapel beside the main hall is the tomb stupa of the first Dzongsar lama.

Sha Pelma Wangchun Monastery   BUDDHIST MONASTERY

FREE Just 2km southeast of Nyima Jiangre, Sha is dedicated to the Dzogchen suborder. A highlight of the monastery is the pair of 9th-century *doring* (inscribed pillars) that flank the entrance gate. These have inscriptions that detail the estates given to Nyangben Tengzin Zangpo, a boyhood chum of 38th King Tritsug Detsen, who ruled Tibet and much of Central Asia. It was Nyangben Tenzin Zangpo who founded the monastery. Only one of the pillars (to the left when entering) remains intact.

Yerga Monastery   BUDDHIST MONASTERY

(羊日岗寺, Yángrìgǎng Sì) **FREE** This 18th-century monastery, a branch of Drigung Til, is home to 38 monks of the Drigung Kagyu school. On the main altar of the assembly hall look for a photo of Yerga that predates the Cultural Revolution, and a painting of the same inside the entrance of a small chapel to the north of the main hall.

TAKLUNG MONASTERY & SILI GÖTSANG

Off the road between the Reting Valley and Lhundrub County, these two visually spectacular monasteries are worth the quick detour to explore.

Dynamited by Red Guards and with ruins still visible in the green fields of the Pak-chu Valley, the sprawling monastic complex of **Taklung** (Talung, སྟག་ལུང་དགོན་པ་, 达龙寺, Dálóng Sì) is around 120km north of Lhasa. Rebuilding continues but not on the scale of other, more spiritually important, monasteries in the area.

Taklung was founded in 1180 by Tangpa Tashipel as the seat of the Taklung school of the Kagyupa order. At one time it may have housed some 7000 monks (it currently has 115) but was eventually eclipsed in importance and grandeur by its former branch, the Riwoche Tsuglhakhang in Eastern Tibet.

Taklung's most important structure was its **Tsuglhakhang** (Grand Temple), also known as the Red Palace. The building was reduced to rubble but its impressively thick stone walls remain.

To the south of the Tsuglhakhang is the main assembly hall, the **Targyeling Lhakhang**. Look out for the destroyed set of three chörtens behind the building, one of which contained the remains of the monastery's founder.

To the west in the main monastery building, the **Choning (Tsenyi) Lhakhang** is used as a debating hall and has a statue of the bearded Tashipel to the right. The fine *cham* masks are traditionally worn during a festival on the ninth to 11th days of the fourth month during Saga Dawa (the festival clothes are in a metal box in the corner), and in the weeks leading up to the festival it is sometimes possible to see monks practising the elaborate *cham* dances. Snarling stuffed wolves hang from the ceiling of the protector chapel next door.

Just behind here is the **Jagji Lhakhang**. In the small chapel upstairs look for a thankgka depicting a historic representation of Taklung before the destruction of the Cultural Revolution.

Taklung Monastery is 60km north of Lhundrub, over the 4845m Chak-la. It's a 3km detour west of the main road.

A 4km drive north of the turn-off to Taklung brings you to **Sili Götsang**, an amazing eagle's-nest hermitage perched high above the main road, home to 10 resident monks.

Many of the chapels have murals of the main Kagyud teachers – Tiropa, Naropa, Milarepa and Marpa. In the assembly hall ask to see the giant arrow said to have belonged to medieval trader Tsongpon Norbu Tsangpo. Below here is the meditation cave of the site's founder, Tangbu Rinpoche, as well as several sacred rocks. Continue upstairs to see several smaller chapels and a stairway that leads to the rooftop and magnificent views of the surrounding valley.

A road climbing 2km to the base of the hermitage was nearly complete at the time of research, from where it's a 20-minute walk. The village at the base of the hill was moved here in 2013 after old Phondo village was flooded by the dam and reservoir.

Yerga Monastery is around 8km north of Nyima Jiangre, 30km before Drigung Til.

❶ Getting There & Away

From Nyima Jiangre it's 38km (a one-hour drive) to Drigung Til and 24km (30 minutes) to Medro Gongkar.

If you are headed to Reting Monastery, it's possible to take the direct route along the Kyi-chu Valley via New Phongdo (the old town and *dzong* of Phongdo lie at the bottom of the Phongdo reservoir). En route you'll pass the hillside Trakto Monastery, the partially rebuilt Yu Monastery (in Zashu village), the ruined Nyong Dzong and

the impressive Karma Monastery (across the Kyi-chu and accessed by a bridge). Several other monastery ruins line the scenic route, but you'll need to arrange all this well in advance to secure the necessary permits.

Mamba   门巴乡

📞 0891 / POP 2730 / ELEV 4200M

Above the small township of Mamba (Ménbā xiāng) stands Drigung Til Monastery. First established in 1167, it is the head monastery of the Drigungpa school of the Kagyupa order. By 1250 it was already vying with Sakya for political power – as it happened, not a

POWA CHEMNO FESTIVAL

Every 12 years, in the year of the monkey, Drigung Til stages the massive Powa Chemno festival, which brings pilgrims from all over Tibet. The festival was banned by the government in 1959 but was allowed to resume in 1992, 2004 and 2016, when it attracted more than 100,000 people.

particularly good move because the Sakya forces joined with the Mongol army to sack Drigung Til in 1290. Thus chastened, the monastery devoted itself to the instruction of contemplative meditation. There are around 205 monks at Drigung Til today.

Sights

★ **Drigung Til Monastery**   BUDDHIST MONASTERY

(འབྲི་གུང་མཐིལ, 直贡梯寺, Zhígòngtī Sì; ¥35) Drigung Til sprouts from a high, steep ridge overlooking the Zhorong-chu Valley. The 180-degree views from the main courtyard are stunning and it's a joy to hang out in the courtyard by the monastery to take in the view with the monks after their morning prayer or during afternoon debates.

Although it suffered some damage in the Cultural Revolution, the monastery is in better shape than most of the other monastic centres in this part of Ü.

The main **assembly hall** is the most impressive of Drigung's buildings, though the version you see is a complete rebuild dating to only 2016. The left-hand figure inside is Jigten Sumgon, the founder of the monastery, with Sakyamuni in the centre and Guru Rinpoche to the right. Also look for the statue of local protector Abchi on a pillar to the side.

Upstairs on the 1st-floor Serkhang (Golden Chapel) you can see 1000 statues of Sakyamuni. Jigten's footprint is set in a slab of rock to the side of the statue, as is his silver funeral chörten. From the bottom floor you can continue upstairs to a circuit of prayer wheels and a small chapel. Steps lead up to the left from here to the chörtens of the founders of Drigung Til and Tidrum.

Back in the lower courtyard is the monastery's main protector chapel, the **Abchi Lhakhang**, which houses an impressive bronze statue of the protector Abchi Chudu next to the pelt of a snow leopard. Also look out for the pair of yak horns on the pillar,

after which Drigung is said to be named (a *dri* is a female yak and *gung* means 'camp'). The name may also derive from the hillside, which is said to be in the shape of a yak.

In the rear chapel of this building is a photo of Bachung (Agu) Rinpoche, a hermit who lived in the caves above Drigung Til for 65 years. The monks of Drigung Til still praise Bachung Rinpoche for his efforts in helping to rebuild the monastery.

Kora Path   WALKING

Drigung's hour-long monastery kora is worth a stroll for its fine valley views.

Sleeping & Eating

The location of the **Drigung Til Monastery Guesthouse** (直贡梯寺客栈, Zhígòngtī Sì Kèzhàn; dm without bathroom ¥30-40) is hard to beat, right at the foot of the monastery, but more comfortable options exist down in Mamba village. The small teahouse at the zmonastery is better skipped; look instead for the row of Tibetan teahouses and Sichuanese cafes along the main road through the village.

Amdo Homestead Hotel   GUESTHOUSE $

(安达旅馆, Āndá Lǚguǎn; ☑ 139 8908 9930; dm ¥50, d without bathroom ¥200) Run by a local family, this basic guesthouse's Tibetan-style rooms are the cleanest in town. It's in the centre of Mamba village, above a restaurant of the same name.

Drigung Til Monastery Hotel   HOTEL $$

(直贡梯寺旅馆, Zhígòngtī Sì Lǚguǎn; ☑ 158 8907 9071; per person 2-/3-/8-bed dm ¥100/70/40) Conditions are clean but basic at this small hotel run by the monastery. It's at the eastern end of Mamba village.

Getting There & Away

Driving the 62km from Drigung Til Monastery through Mamba to Medro Gongkar takes around 1½ hours without stops for sightseeing, and another hour along the new highway to Lhasa.

Tidrum   德仲

☑ 0891 / POP 170 / ELEV 4440M

The tiny community at Tidrum (Dézhòng) is composed primarily of nuns living in the eponymous nunnery and surrounding hills plus pilgrims who visit to bathe in the medicinal hot springs and worship at sites connected to Yeshe Tsogyal, the wife of King Trisong Detsen and consort of Guru Rinpoche.

The location is spectacularly set in a narrow gorge at the confluence of two streams, backed by a craggy peak and festooned with prayer flags in every direction. Sanitation in the community is underwhelming, so you may want to skip the possibility of overnighting here, but it's a fascinating stop en route to or from Drigung Til.

⊙ Sights

Tidrum Nunnery
BUDDHIST MONASTERY

(གཏེར་སྒྲོམ་བཙུན་དགོན, 德仲寺, Dézhòng Sì; ¥15) The nunnery of 70 nuns has strong connections to Yeshe Tsogyal, the wife of King Trisong Detsen and consort of Guru Rinpoche (who himself is said to have meditated in a cave not far from the settlement). The Kandro-la, the resident spiritual leader of the nunnery, is considered a reincarnation of Yeshe Tsogyal. The **main assembly hall** is worth a visit. A cabinet holds a selection of self-arising rock images found in the hot springs.

Tidrum Hot Springs
HOT SPRINGS

(德仲温泉, Dézhòng Wēnquán; ¥5; ⊙24hr) Strip down and hop into this medicinal natural hot spring said to cure everything from rheumatism to paralysis, separated by sexes into two partially covered natural pools. It's popular with pilgrims and can get quite crowded, but that's all part of the experience at these springs that have been healing visitors for 1400 years or more. The springs are famous for the snakes that sometimes join bathers but locals insist in all those years they've never once been bitten.

At the time of research Tidrum was undergoing major renovation and resembled a shanty town – not really conducive to an enjoyable soak. Far more relaxing is a visit to the lower springs (chu semye) resort of Shambhala Source, which has clean hotel pools and rooms with private tubs.

🛌 Sleeping & Eating

There are two spartan guesthouses near the hot-springs complex if you want to overnight at Tidrum itself, but the better option is the Shambhala Source resort 5km before the settlement.

The nunnery runs a small **teahouse** (德仲寺茶馆, Dézhòngsì Cháguǎn; ☑153 4898 7369; dishes ¥15-30; ⊙8.30am-8pm) just above the hot springs.

Dingjie Temple Limin Hotel
GUESTHOUSE $

(dm ¥30) The guesthouse run by Tengyer Nunnery is probably the nicest place to stay

at Tidrum proper, with conditions clean but basic. Riverside rooms have four beds and are arranged around a sunny glass-roofed atrium. Upper rooms are best. It's on the kora path behind and to the left of the nunnery's main assembly hall.

Shambhala Source
HOTEL $$

(得仲下温泉和宾馆, Dézhòng Xià Wēnquán Hé Bīnguǎn; ☑178 8800 6575; www.shambhalaserai.com; dm ¥50, d with private tub ¥400, d with/without shower ¥360/150; 🐾🏊) Easily the most comfortable place to stay is this chic resort run by Lhasa's Shambhala Serai group. It has its own riverside hot springs, 5km before Tidrum, and the best split-level suites boast their own private hot-water tubs. Simple food is available, but don't expect much in the way of spa service, only towels and flip-flops (thongs) are provided.

If you have trouble getting in touch with the resort directly, try booking through the House of Shambhala (p76) in Lhasa.

ℹ Getting There & Away

Tidrum is along an 8km road that leads up the side valley 3km before the town of Mamba at the foot of Drigung Til.

LHOKA PREFECTURE སློ་ཁ
山南

The serene waters of the braided Yarlung Tsangpo river meander through a swathe of land flanked by dramatic sand dunes and rich in Tibetan history – Lhoka prefecture (སློ་ཁ, 山南, Shānnán). It's only a couple of hours from Lhasa and the numerous attractions are relatively near one another, allowing you to see the main sights in two or three days. Remote monasteries, royal tombs, ruined stupas, meditation retreats and medieval palaces are only some of the highlights you can visit in a three-day itinerary. With more time you could spend days exploring the various side valleys on foot or by mountain bike.

⊙ Sights

Dorje Drak Monastery
BUDDHIST MONASTERY

(རྡོ་རྗེ་བྲག་དགོན་པ, 多吉扎寺, Duōjízhá Sì) **FREE** Along with Mindroling Monastery (p126), Dorje Drak (3520m) is one of the two most important Nyingmapa monasteries in Ü, both considered among the six great Nyingmapa monasteries in Tibet. With a remote and romantic location, historically less accessible than Mindroling, it consequently gets few

RUTOK MONASTERY & SPRINGS

Around three hours' drive from Lhasa is the one-street hot-springs town of Rutok (རུ་ཐོག, 日多, Rìduō), named after the small but pleasant monastery on the hillside north of town. This is nomads' country, and every family takes their herds of 15 to 200 animals up into the mountains from May to September, during which the town is even quieter than normal.

Founded in the 12th century as a Black Hat monastery, **Rutok Monastery** (日多寺, Rìduō Sì) converted to the Yellow Hat sect in 1509 during the reign of the second Dalai Lama. Before destruction in 1959 it was home to 35 monks, though only 12 currently inhabit the 1982 reconstruction. To the right of the main hall is a small protector chapel that houses relics, some of which pre-date the Cultural Revolution, including a large wooden *dorje* (lightning bolt).

Western visitors and the 40 resident monks seem happy to welcome travellers. It was under expansion at the time of research.

Dorje Drak was forcibly relocated to its present site in 1632 by the kings in Tsang. A line of hereditary lamas known as the Rigdzin leads the monastery. The title is named after the first Rigdzin Godemachen, thought to be a reincarnation of Guru Rinpoche. The fourth Rigdzin, Pema Trinley, was responsible for expanding the monastery in the early 18th century, though his efforts were for naught as the Dzungar Mongols sacked the place in 1718; Pema Trinley did not survive the onslaught. The 10th Rigdzin Lama currently resides in Lhasa.

Dorje Drak's **main assembly hall** has statues of the first and second Rigdzins and the fifth Dalai Lama, while the inner room features Pema Trinley, the fourth Rigdzin, next to Sakyamuni; a small side chapel holds the ornate tomb stupa of the ninth Rigdzin lama. The old B&W photo by the entryway shows the extents of the original monastery.

The **Samsum Namgyel Gönkhang** to the right has five butter sculptures representing the chapel's five protectors. A cabinet holds the monastery's treasures, including a fragment of a staff belonging to Milarepa that was smashed in the Cultural Revolution.

To the east of the older structures, a new **assembly hall** was finished in 2015 with murals depicting the life of Shakyamuni. Up on the 2nd and 3rd floors are two smaller chapels, but the real draw here is the excellent vista of the monastic complex and Yarlung Tsangpo Valley beyond.

A demanding 1½-hour **kora** leads around the back of the *dorje*-(thunderbolt-)shaped rock behind the monastery, up to the ruined Sengye Dzong atop the rock. The path overlooks some dramatic sand dunes and the

views from the retreat are simply stunning, but the faint, sandy trail is a hard slog up and a steep scramble down. You need to scale a fence to get to the dzong ruins.

Dorje Drak is on the northern bank of the Yarlung Tsangpo, 18km east of the Gālá Shān tunnel and bridge leading to the airport and a quick 50km west of Samye, along a well-sealed road. Hard-core trekkers can approach Dorje Drak from Lhasa, a trek of around four days.

Samye ·

བསམ་ཡས 桑耶镇

📞 0893 / ELEV 3550M

The monastic town of Samye (Sāngyé Zhèn) is home to the beautiful Samye Monastery (p115), deservedly the most popular destination for travellers in the Ü region. As Tibet's first monastery and the place where Tibetan Buddhism was established, the monastery is also of major historical and religious importance. Surrounded by barren mountains and rolling sand dunes, the monastery has a quiet magic about it that causes many travellers to rate it as the highlight of Ü.

If you are heading to Everest Base Camp or the Nepali border, a trip here will only add one day to your itinerary. You may have to detour briefly to the nearby town of Tsetang (རྩེད་ཐང ; 泽当; Zédāng) for your guide to pick up the required travel permit.

History

Samye was Tibet's very first monastery and has a history that spans more than 1200 years. The monastery was founded during the reign of King Trisong Detsen, who was born close by, though the exact date is subject to some debate – it was probably founded between 765 and 780. Whatever the case, Samye represents the Tibetan state's first efforts to allow the Buddhist faith to set down roots in the country. The Bön majority at court, whose religion prevailed in Tibet prior to Buddhism, were not at all pleased with this development.

The victory of Buddhism over the Bön-dominated establishment was symbolised by Guru Rinpoche's triumph over the massed demons of Tibet at Hepo Ri, just to the east of Samye. It was this act that paved the way for the introduction of Buddhism to Tibet.

Shortly after the founding of the monastery, Tibet's first seven monks (the 'seven examined men') were ordained here by the monastery's first abbot, Indian Shantarakshita (Kenchen Shiwatso in Tibetan), and Indian and Chinese scholars were invited to assist in the translation of Buddhist texts into Tibetan.

Before long, disputes broke out between followers of Indian and Chinese scholarship. The disputes culminated in the Great Debate of Samye, an event regarded by Tibetan historians as a crucial juncture in the course of Tibetan Buddhism. The debate, which probably took place in the early 790s, was essentially an argument between the Indian approach to bodhisattvahood via textual study and scholarship, and the more immediate Chan (Zen) influenced approach of the Chinese masters, who decried scholarly study in favour of contemplation on the absolute nature of buddhahood. The debates came out on the side of the Indian scholars.

Samye has never truly been the preserve of any one of Tibetan Buddhism's different orders. However, the influence of Guru Rinpoche in establishing the monastery has meant that the Nyingmapa order has been most closely associated with Samye. When the Sakyapa order came to power in the 15th century it took control of Samye, and the Nyingmapa influence declined, though it did not disappear completely.

Samye's most common icons are of the Khenlop Chösum – the trinity of Guru Rinpoche, King Trisong Detsen and Shantarakshita.

Samye has been damaged and restored many times over the last 1000 years. The most recent assault on its antiquity was during the Cultural Revolution. Extensive renovation work has been ongoing since the mid-1980s and there are now 200 monks at Samye.

⊙ Sights

★**Samye Monastery**   BUDDHIST MONASTERY
(བསམ་ཡས་དགོན་པ།, 桑耶寺, Sāngyē Sì; Map p117; ⊙dawn-dusk) About 170km southeast of Lhasa, on the north bank of the Yarlung Tsangpo (Brahmaputra River) is Samye Monastery, the first monastery in Tibet. Founded in 775 by King Trisong Detsen, Samye is famed not just for its pivotal history but for its unique mandala design: the Main Hall, known as Ütse (p116), represents Mt Meru, the centre of the universe, while the outer

Ü SAMYE

LHAMO LA-TSO

One of Ü's most important pilgrimage destinations, Lhamo La-tso (ལྷ་མོ་བླ་མཚོ།, 拉姆拉措, Lāmǔ Lācuò) has been revered for centuries as an oracle lake.

The Dalai Lamas have traditionally made pilgrimages to Lhamo La-tso to seek visions that appear on its surface. The Tibetan regent journeyed to the lake in 1933 after the death of the 13th Dalai Lama and had a vision of a monastery in Amdo that led to the discovery of the present Dalai Lama. The lake is considered the home of the protector Palden Lhamo.

The gateway to Lhamo La-tso is the dramatic, but mostly ruined, **Chökorgye Monastery** (4500m; 琼果杰寺, Qióngguǒjié Sì). Founded in 1509 by the second Dalai Lama, Gendun Gyatso (1476–1542), the monastery served later Dalai Lamas and regents as a staging post for visits to the lake. On the nearby slope is a mani wall that consecrates a footprint stone of the second Dalai Lama.

From Chökorgye Monastery, it's a 12km drive (about 40 minutes) up a twisting mountain road to the *shökde*, a ritual throne built for the Dalai Lamas just short of the mountain pass that overlooks Lhamo La-tso. It is now buried under a mound of *kathak* (prayer scarves). It's a further 90-minute walk to get down to the lake (roughly 3.5km in total), which is encircled by a kora.

Though Lhamo La-tso has not been open to international travellers for years, it remains an incredibly important place in Tibetan culture and history. It is always worth asking your travel agency if the area is open during your visit.

temples represent the oceans, continents, subcontinents and other features of the Buddhist cosmology.

As renovation work continues at Samye, the original *ling* (royal) chapels – lesser, outlying chapels that surround the Ütse – are slowly being restored. Wander around and see which are open. Following is a clockwise tour of the major chapels open at the time of research. Aside from the Ütse, none require any entry fees.

Just inside the **East Gate**, the square in front of the **Ütse** has some interesting elements, including the **Jampel Ling** *gönkhang* (protector chapel). The top-floor balcony offers fine views of the Ütse. The ruined seven-storey **Geku** (Tower) that used to display festival thangkas has been rebuilt in recent years, and is once again used to display a large thangka during the **Samye Dhoede** (☉ Jun/Jul) festival.

From the East Gate follow the prayer wheels south to the **Tsengmang Ling** (Map p117), once the monastery printing press, and just beyond the minor **Mela Ling**. Further on is another renovated chapel, the **Ngamba Ling** (Subdued Demon Temple), with modern murals and two 3D mandalas.

Past the yellow-walled residential college of the Shetekhang (p118), the restored Aryapalo Ling (p118), Samye's first building, and **Drayur Gyagar Ling** (Map p117), originally the centre for the translation of texts, are worth extended stops.

Beside the **Sacred Tree** that serves as a popular stop for pilgrims and upon which they place stones and tie threads, the upper floor of the **Vairosana Lakhang** is lined with old paintings and a small chapel to Tantric Buddhist masters. Just north of here is a small **chörten** that pilgrims circumambulate.

The Nugko Jampa Ling (p118) is where Samye's Great Debate was held, and an essential stop. Beyond the modern rebuilds of the relatively minor buildings of the **Samten Ling** and **Jampa Lakhang**, the delightful **Triple Mani Lhakhang** (Map p117) just to the north also has lovely murals.

Rounding the corner of the complex past the large **Tree Shrine**, the first major structure is the **Natsok Ling**. The chapel is a modern rebuild, but the statues of 21 Taras and the Past, Present, and Future Buddhas are worth a look inside.

The green-walled, Chinese-roofed Jangchub Semgye Ling (p119) is well worth a stop before breaking from the kora to walk south

along the concrete path here to the **Dawa Ling** (Map p117), returning after to the kora path.

East of here is the **Kordzo Pehar Ling** (Map p117), the home of the oracle Pehar until he moved to Nechung Monastery outside Lhasa. It was once a highlight of Samye, but only time will tell what it looks like after the ongoing renovation.

Finally, return to the Ütse past the **Namdok Trinang Ling**. Though quite impressive from the outside, this temple is of relatively minor importance and was not open to visitors at the time of research.

It's also possible to enter the four reconstructed concrete **chörtens** (white, red, green and black), though there is little of interest inside.

If you walk for 10 minutes beyond the southern gate, you'll reach the **Khamsum Sankhung Ling**, a smaller version of the Utse that once functioned as Samye's debating centre. It's been under renovation for years, but there are seemingly no plans to reopen it soon.

★ Ütse   BUDDHIST TEMPLE

(Map p117; ¥35; ☉ dawn-dusk) The central building of Samye, the Ütse comprises a unique synthesis of architectural styles. The ground and 1st floors were originally Tibetan in style, the 2nd floor was Chinese and the 3rd floor Khotanese. The corner parapets with green and gold *dorje* (thunderbolt) designs are also unique. There's a lot to see here, so budget a couple of hours and carry a torch (flashlight) for the darker spaces.

Just to the left of the East Gate is a **stele** dating from 779. The elegant Tibetan script carved on its surface proclaims Buddhism as the state religion of Tibet by order of King Trisong Detsen. The entryways are flanked by two snow lions and two ancient stone elephants. Upon entering the building itself, look for photos showing the Ütse before and after the Cultural Revolution.

From here the entrance leads into the first of the ground-floor chambers: the **assembly hall**. As you enter the hall, look for the statue of a chicken that is said to have once saved the monastery by waking up its monks during a fire. Pass statues of Thangtong Gyalpo and the writers Buton Rinchen Drup and Longchen Rabjampa to the left, before a row of figures greets you straight ahead: the translator Vairocana, Shantarakshita, Guru Rinpoche, Trisong Detsen and Songtsen Gampo (with an extra head in his turban). The photo

Samye Monastery

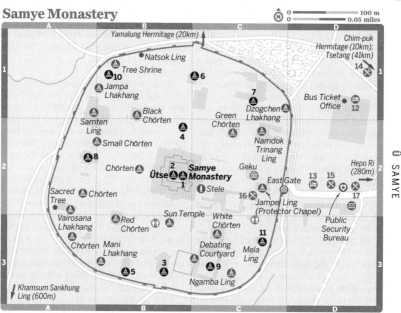

Samye Monastery

◎ Top Sights
1 Samye Monastery	B2
2 Ütse	B2

◎ Sights
3 Aryapalo Ling	B3
4 Dawa Ling	B2
5 Drayur Gyagar Ling	B3
6 Jangchub Semgye Ling	C1
7 Kordzo Pehar Ling	C1
8 Nugko Pema Ling	A2
9 Shetekhang	C3
10 Triple Mani Lhakhang	B1
11 Tsengmang Ling	C3

◎ Sleeping
Friendship Snowland Hotel	(see 15)
12 Samye Monastery Guesthouse	D1
13 Tashi Guesthouse & Restaurant	D2

◎ Eating
14 Dōngběi Xiǎofàndiàn	D1
15 Friendship Snowland Restaurant	D2
16 Monastery Restaurant	C2
17 Snowland Yungdruk Restaurant	D2

below the Guru Rinpoche statue is of the famous original statue (now destroyed), which was a likeness of the guru and allegedly had the power of speech. Come here between 7am and 9am to hear the monks chanting.

To the rear of the assembly hall are steps leading into Samye's most revered chapel, the **Jowo Khang**. You enter the inner chapel via three painted doors – an unusual feature. They symbolise the Three Doors of Liberation: those of emptiness, signlessness and wishlessness. A circumambulation of the inner chapel follows at this point (take a torch).

The centrepiece of the inner chapel is a 4m statue of Sakyamuni said to have appeared miraculously in the stone. Ten bodhisattvas and two protective deities line the heavy side walls of the chapel, which are decorated with ancient murals. Look also for the blackened Tantric mandalas on the ceiling.

Back in the main assembly hall, on the right are two groups of three statues: the first group is associated with the Kadampa order (Dromtompa and Atisha); the second group is multi-denominational and includes lamas from the Nyingmapa, Sakyapa and Gelugpa orders.

To the right of the hall is a *gönkhang* (protector chapel), with statues of deities so terrible they must be masked. A stuffed snake lurks over the blocked exit, while a stag's head adorns the inside entrance.

Before ascending to the 1st floor, take a look at the **Chenresig Chapel**, outside and to the left of the main assembly hall, which features a dramatic 1000-armed statue of Chenresig known as Chaktong Chentong.

As you head up to the 2nd floor, look for the giant troughs used to store the monks' tsampa (roasted-barley flour) and a series of wall paintings depicting the life of Guru Rinpoche. The structure here echoes the inner chapel and features an image of Guru Rinpoche in a semi-wrathful aspect, flanked by Tsepame and Sakyamuni, with Shantarakshita and Trisong Detsen flanking them. Look up to see the Chinese-influenced bracketing on the beams. There is an inner kora (pilgrim circuit) around the hall.

As you leave the inner chapel, look for a hole in the wooden panelling; steps lead up from inside the false wall to a secret room with statues of Vairocana and Trisong Detsen, which was used by King Trisong Detsen to listen to the lamas' teaching without being observed.

Some of the murals outside this hall are very impressive; those on the southern wall depict Guru Rinpoche, while those to the left of the main door show the fifth Dalai Lama with the Mongol Gushri Khan and various ambassadors offering their respects. The Dalai Lama's quarters are just behind you at the southeastern corner of this floor, featuring a fine mural depicting Samye.

The 3rd floor is a modern renovation to the Ütse, the original having been entirely

THE SAMYE MANDALA

Samye's overall design was based on that of the now-vanished Odantapur Temple of Bihar in India, and is a highly symbolic mandalic representation of the universe. The central Ütse temple represents Mt Meru (Sumeru; Rirab in Tibetan), and the temples around it in two concentric circles represent the oceans, continents and subcontinents that ring the mountain in Buddhist cosmology. The complex originally had 108 buildings (an auspicious number to Tibetans). The 1008 chörtens on the circular wall that rings the monastery represent Chakravala, the ring of mountains that surrounds the universe.

destroyed during the Cultural Revolution. It holds statues of four of the five Dhyani Buddhas, with a mandala of the fifth (Namse) on the ceiling, and along the outside of the hall's walls are paintings of Tibetan, Indian and Nepalese masters.

Walk around the back to a ladder leading up to the 4th floor. This chapel holds the sacred core of the temple, as well as an image of Dukhor (Kalachakra), a Tantric deity, but it is generally locked. As you descend from the 3rd floor there is a rare mural of the 14th (current) Dalai Lama at the top of the stairwell to the left. It was left on view for decades, but at the time of research the authorities had blocked the mural with a wooden board.

As you head back downstairs, stop at the 1st-floor relic chamber. Among the sacred objects on display are the staff of Vairocana, the stone skull of Shantarakshita, a *dorje* made from meteorite and a turquoise amulet containing a lock of Guru Rinpoche's hair. A shop in the corner of the hallway sells protective amulets, though it is often unmanned.

Back on the ground floor, you can follow the prayer-wheel circuit of the Ütse, and look at the interesting murals showing the founding of the monastery. You can also ascend to the outer roof for views over the complex. The roof was restored in 2016 using the traditional materials of twigs and packed earth.

Shetekhang   BUDDHIST SITE
(Map p117) If you pass this yellow-walled residential college between 11am and noon, or between 5.30pm and 7pm, listen for the sounds of teachings from the main hall or debating in the attached **courtyard**.

Aryapalo Ling   BUDDHIST SITE
(Map p117) The restored Aryapalo Ling was Samye's first building and retains a lovely ancient feel. The statue of Arya Lokeshvara is similar to one seen in the Potala Palace. A small door allows pilgrims to inch around the base of the protector Tamdrin. There's a sacred tree in the courtyard, a birdsong-filled space that epitomises the tranquility of Samye.

Nugko Jampa Ling   BUDDHIST SITE
(Map p117) The Jampa Ling, on the western side of the Samye complex, is the site of Samye's Great Debate, which determined the course of Tibetan Buddhism. On the right as you go in, look out for the wall mural depicting the original design of Samye, with zigzagging walls. There is an unusual semicircular inner kora (pilgrim circuit) here that is decorated with images of Jampa.

Jangchub Semgye Ling   BUDDHIST SITE

(Map p117) The green-walled, Chinese-roofed Jangchub Semkye Ling houses a host of bodhisattvas around a statue of Marmedze (the Past Buddha) on an ornate lotus plinth, with a 3D wooden mandala to the side. Look for the sacred stone to the left. Take a torch (flashlight) to see the exceptional Central Asian-style murals.

Hepo Ri   VIEWPOINT

(ཧེ་པོ་རི, 海不日神山, Hǎibùrì Shénshān) Hepo Ri is the hill some 400m east of Samye where Guru Rinpoche vanquished the demons of Tibet. A 30-minute climb up the side ridge brings you to an incense burner festooned with prayer flags and superlative views of Samye below. Head south along the ridge and descend along the paved path. Early morning is the best time for photography.

Pilgrims honour Hepo Ri as one of the four sacred hills of Tibet (the others being Gangpo Ri at Tsetang, Chagpo Ri in Lhasa and Chuwo Ri at Chushul). King Trisong Detsen established a palace here. Trails branch off here from the road leading from Samye's East Gate.

🛏 Sleeping & Eating

Outside the monastery's eastern gate is a line of almost identical restaurants that double as budget guesthouses on the 2nd floor or out the back. For something a little nicer, head northeast to the Samye Monastery Guesthouse, which is functionally a standard modern hotel.

Tashi Guesthouse & Restaurant   GUESTHOUSE $

(扎西旅馆, Zhāxī Lǚguǎn; Map p117; ☏189 8993 7883; dm/r without bathroom ¥60/120; 🐕) Pleasant two-, four- and five-bed dorms with clean foam beds above a restaurant by the East Gate. If things are busy, you may have to pay for all beds in a room to keep it private. The nice teahouse restaurant downstairs (8.30am to 10.30pm) has an English menu of Tibetan and Chinese staples from ¥15 to ¥30 per dish.

Friendship Snowland Hotel   GUESTHOUSE $

(雪域同胞旅馆, Xuěyù Tóngbāo Lǚguǎn; Gangjong Pönda Sarkhang; Map p117; ☏136 1893 2819; dm ¥100) Proper mattresses (not just foam ones) are on offer here, in concrete triples out the back or above the cosy restaurant of the same name.

Samye Monastery Guesthouse   HOTEL $$

(桑耶寺宾馆, Sāngyēsì Bīnguǎn; Map p117; ☏0893-783 6666; d ¥240, without bathroom ¥200, tr ¥300; 🐕) This huge modern hotel is the default option for most visitors. Although devoid of monastic charm, the carpeted double rooms are comfortable (check for barking dogs when choosing your room) and have a hot-water shower and the only western toilets in town. The cheaper doubles share a bathroom down the hall (no showers).

Friendship Snowland Restaurant   CHINESE $

(Gangjong Pönda Sarkhang, 雪域同胞藏餐旅馆, Xuěyù Tóngbāo Zàngcān Lǚguǎn; Map p117; ☏136 1893 2819, 136 5958 4773; dishes ¥16-50; ⏱8.30am-11pm; 🐕) The backpacker-inspired menu at this pleasant Tibetan-style restaurant includes banana pancakes, hash browns and omelettes, making this your best breakfast bet. Good Chinese and Tibetan dishes are also available, as well as yak sizzlers.

Monastery Restaurant   TIBETAN $

(Map p117; dishes ¥15-28; ⏱8am-8pm; 🐾) Expect loads of atmosphere, sunny outdoor seating, a vegetarian menu and pilgrims galore at this welcoming place within the monastery compound. Fried Chinese dishes are the best options for food, but you can also just sit around and drink sweet tea like the locals.

Snowland Yungdruk Restaurant   TIBETAN $

(雪域玉龙饭馆, Xuěyù Yùlóng Fànguǎn, Kangchen Yungdruk Sarkhang; Map p117; ☏133 9803 9191; dishes ¥5-20; ⏱8am-11pm) Take tea or simple Tibetan meals in the sunny atrium if it's not full of locals playing dice. There are also a handful of very basic dorms off the back courtyard from ¥30 to ¥60.

Dōngběi Xiǎofàndiàn   DUMPLINGS $

(东北小饭店; Map p117; dishes ¥12-30; ⏱8am-11pm; 🐕🐾) If you need a change from Tibetan and Sichuanese cuisine, these northeast-style dumplings prepared by a friendly transplant from Shāndōng province are delicious. The picture menu makes ordering a breeze for non-Chinese speakers, and a veg-heavy menu will suit vegetarians.

ℹ Getting There & Away

Once only accessible by a charming old ferry across the Yarlung Tsangpo river, the boats have stopped and since 2017 a highway connects Samye to Lhasa in 1½ hours or less, but this will get even shorter when the direct highway between Lhasa and Samye opens within the next few years.

Leaving Samye, Tsetang is around one-hour's drive along the highway, but if you're not interested in heading to the east of Lhoka, it's also possible to take a new bridge across the Yarlung Tsangpo, 17km west of Samye, to head directly

A CAVE SHRINE RETREAT

Chim-puk Hermitage (མཆིམས་ཕུ་སྒྲུབ་གནས་, 青朴修行地, Qīngpǔ Xiūxíngdì) is a collection of cave shrines northeast of Samye that grew up over the centuries around the meditation retreat of Guru Rinpoche. Chim-puk's Tantric practitioners were once famed for their ability to protect fields from hailstorms. It is a popular excursion for travellers overnighting at Samye. Make sure your agency knows in advance that you want to visit or you'll have to haggle over the return 20km trip.

Pop into the impressive new nunnery at the base of the hill to hear the nuns chanting between 8am and noon.

From here trails lead up for about an hour past dozens of cave shrines to the *lhakhang* (subsidiary chapel) built around Guru Rinpoche's original **meditation cave** halfway up the hill and that of Jigme Lingpa in a small cave just behind. Most of the hillside shrines here are still inhabited by practitioners.

Ascending clockwise along the kora that visits all of the hillside's temples, the first is the **Yongdu Lahkong** (Gathering Chapel). Built in 2006, it houses statues of Guru Rinpoche and Samye's former abbots. Continuing up the kora path leads to the **Champung Guru** temple, built atop the entrance to the meditation cave said to have been used by Guru Rinpoche himself, and believed to grant wishes to devout buddhists who visit. From here it's a short climb to the complex's highest temple, the **Samye Changpu** (Victorious Stupa). Originally used as a library, the building now houses another large statue of Guru Rinpoche and three large thangka paintings, plus the views from the courtyard present spectacular views of the rest of the Chim-puk complex and the Yarlung Tsangpo river.

From the parking lot up to the Champung Guru temple expect a 1½-hour walk, and slightly more to the Samye Changpu. The descent, which loops around the east of the complex via another small temple housing statues of the wrathful form of Guru Rinpoche, can be accomplished in around 40 minutes.

If you are feeling fit and acclimatised, it's possible to climb to the top of the peak above Chim-puk. To make this climb from the Guru Rinpoche cave, follow the left-hand valley behind the caves and slog it uphill for 1½ hours to prayer flags at the top of the ridge. From there a path leads for another 1½ hours to the top of the conical peak, where there are a couple of meditation retreats and fine views of the Yarlung Tsangpo Valley. You'll need the whole day to make this hike, and plenty of water.

to Mindroling, Dratang or Gongkar without backtracking.

A pilgrim bus runs daily between Lhasa's Barkhor Sq and Samye, but at the time of research foreigners were not allowed to take it in either direction. If that ever changes, tickets can be purchased from the small **ticket office** (Map p117) in front of the Samye Monastery Guesthouse.

Tsetang ཪྩེ་ཐང་ 泽当

📞 0893 / POP 52,000 / ELEV 3610M

An important Chinese administrative centre and army base, Tsetang (Zédāng) is the fourth-largest city in Tibet and the capital of huge Lhoka prefecture. The centre of town is a thoroughly modern city where you'll find decent restaurants, midrange accommodation and a couple of internet cafes. The more interesting area is the small former Tibetan town, and the monasteries clustered there on the slope of Gangpo Ri, one of Ü's four sacred mountains.

Most travellers use Tsetang as a base to visit outlying sites of the Yarlung and Chongye Valleys.

🅞 Sights

Ngamchö Monastery BUDDHIST MONASTERY
(安曲寺, Ānqū Sì; Map p122) **FREE** Originally founded as a hospital of Tibetan medicine, this site transitioned first to a Kagyupa monastery. In the 14th century the highest lamas here set off to debate with Tsongkhapa, but found themselves so overwhelmed with respect for the great teacher that they couldn't carry through with their plans and converted the monastery to the Gelugpa tradition upon their return.

On the top floor is the bedroom and throne used by the current Dalai Lama. A side chapel is devoted to medicine, with images of the eight medicine buddhas. The protector chapel displays fine festival masks, representing snow lions, stags and demons. It's possible to see ritual *cham* dances with these masks on the 20th day of the 10th month of the Tibetan calendar.

Ganden Chökhorling Monastery
BUDDHIST MONASTERY

(甘丹曲果林寺, Gāndān Qūguǒlín Sì; Map p122) **FREE** This 14th-century monastery was originally a Kagyu institution, but by the 18th century the Gelugpas had overtaken it with the blessing of the seventh Dalai Lama; explaining why the large central statue is of Tsongkhapa. From a height of around 130 monks, the monastery is now home to only 10, partly because during the Cultural Revolution the building was used as an army hospital. At the time of research it was undergoing a complete renovation, expected to finish by the end of 2018.

Sang-ngag Zimchen Nunnery
BUDDHIST SITE

(桑阿赛津尼姑寺, Sāng'ásàijīn Nígūsì; Map p122; ¥10) Inside the main assembly hall the principal image to the left is of a 1000-armed Chenresig dating back to the time of King Songtsen Gampo. According to some accounts, the statue was fashioned in the 7th century by the king himself. There are around 20 resident nuns now, down from a peak of about 50. After visiting the main hall, head upstairs to see two small protector chapels.

Gangpo Ri
MOUNTAIN

(གོང་པོ་རི, 贡布日神山, Gòngbù Rì Shénshān) Gangpo Ri (4130m) is of special significance for Tibetans as the legendary birthplace of the Tibetan people, where Chenresig in the form of a monkey mated with the white demon Sinmo to produce the beginnings of the Tibetan race. The **Monkey Cave**, where all this took place, can be visited near the summit of the mountain. Do it in the spirit of a demanding half-day walk in the hills, as the cave itself is somewhat uninspiring.

The most direct trail leads up from the Sang-ngag Zimche Nunnery, climbing about 550m to the cave. The walk up will take about two hours – bring plenty of water. The walk up Gangpo Ri is part of a long pilgrim route, which local Tibetans make each year on the 15th day of the fourth lunar month.

🛏 Sleeping & Eating

Finding good budget accommodation is a problem in Tsetang. Its cheaper hotels are prevented from accepting foreigners by a strong PSB presence, and those that have a licence for foreigners are on the mid- to high-end of the price spectrum.

Given the size of Tsetang there's a surprisingly lack of culinary diversity, with the same range of Sichuanese cafes and Tibetan teahouses available across most of Ü, though the Aba Home Tibetan Restaurant (p122) is admittedly a nicer than average example of the latter. For a bit of a change, check out Shǎnxī Fēngwèi (p122) for a taste of the flavours of Shǎnxī province in northwestern China.

Yulong Holiday Hotel
HOTEL $$

(裕馨假日大酒店, Yùlóng Jiàrì Dàjiǔdiàn; Map p122; ☎ 0893-783 2888, 0893-782 5558; 30 Naidong Lu; 乃东路30号; r ¥220-300, tr ¥340, incl breakfast; ❋ 🎧) This three-star place offers clean plush rooms, though some streetside rooms are noisy. You can even listen to your favourite Chinese pop tunes in the power shower, if you can figure out how the thing works.

Tibetan Source Hotel
HOTEL $$

(藏之源大酒店, Zàngzhīyuán Dàjiǔdiàn; Map p122; ☎ 131 0232 8810, 0893-782 1588; 12 Naidong Lu; 乃东路12号; d/tr incl breakfast ¥280/320; ❋ 🎧) Standard rooms in the main building are decorated with Tibetan motifs but are quite small. The cheaper rooms in the back are bigger and almost as good.

Ze Soure Theme Hotel
HOTEL $$$

(泽源主题宾馆, Zé yuán zhǔtí bīnguǎn; Map p122; ☎ 0893-766 8585, 0893-766 8686; 10 Sare Lu; 萨热路10号; r/ste ¥520/720; ❋ 🎧) If you're looking for luxury in Tsetang, this is your best bet. We're still not sure what the 'theme' is, but at least rooms are spacious and public

---

TSETANG'S OLD TOWN KORA

The best way to visit the small monasteries in the Tibetan quarter is to join the pilgrims on the clockwise kora (pilgrim circuit).

From Ganden Chökhorling Monastery swing north and then east to Ngamchö Monastery. From here the kora path winds round the base of Gangpo Ri to a holy spring where pilgrims wash their hair. The trail climbs to a bundle of prayer flags and a throne-shaped incense burner before descending to Sang-ngag Zimche Nunnery. A side trail ascends the hill to the Monkey Cave.

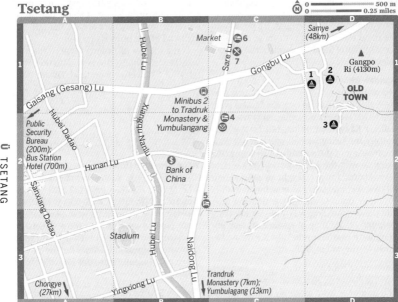

Tsetang

spaces are decked out in a modern, understated decor.

Aba Home Tibetan Restaurant   TIBETAN $
(Map p122; ☑ 139 8993 2031; 8 Sare Lu; 萨热路8号; dishes ¥7-40; ⊙ 7am-late; ☏) Invite your guide to this cosy, friendly and modern Tibetan restaurant, featuring traditional seating, a partial picture menu and lots of local colour. Choose one of the set meals that all the other Tibetans are diving into.

Shǎnxī Fēngwèi   CHINESE $$
(陕西风味; ☑ 177 8916 3209; Sanxiang Dadao; 三湘大道; dishes ¥20-45; ⊙ 10am-11pm; ☏) If you find yourself hungry while waiting for the PSB to open, pop across the street to this fantastic little joint run by a family from Shǎnxī province. There's a picture menu as well, if you're stuck for what to order.

ⓘ Information

The **Public Security Bureau** (公安局, Gōng'ānjú; Sanxiang Dadao; 三湘大道; ⊙ 9am-12.30pm & 3-6pm) has a strong presence here so your guide will probably disappear for a few minutes to register your passport and pick up an alien's travel permit for outlying sights, including Samye Monastery (p115). Try to time your arrival so that you're not waiting around for their lunch break (12.30pm to 3pm) to end.

Bank of China (中国银行, Zhōngguó Yínháng; Map p122; ☑ 95566; 18 Hunan Lu; 湖南路18号; ⊙ 9.30am-6pm Mon-Fri, 10.30am-4.30pm Sat & Sun) Changes cash and travellers cheques and has an ATM.

ⓘ Getting There & Away

Tsetang is 2½ hours from Lhasa along the highway on the north side of the valley, passing by Samye (one hour) and Dorje Drak (1½ hours) en route. Along the old road through the south of the valley expect around 2½ hours to Gongkar via Dratang (1½ hours) and the turn-off for Mindroling (one hour).

At the time of research, a direct highway to Lhasa via Samye was under construction; it will shave up to an hour off the direct trip. Further into the future, Tsetang will be a stop on the Sìchuān–Tibet train line that is expected for completion in 2025.

Locally, **Minibus 2** (Map p122) runs from the centre of Tsetang to Tradruk Monastery and Yumbulangang.

Yarlung Valley   ཡར་ཀླུང་གཞུང་
雅鲁流域

ELEV 3220M

The Yarlung Valley (Yǎlǔ Liúyù) is considered the cradle of Tibetan civilisation. Tibetan creation myths tell of how the first Tibetan people evolved here from the union of a monkey and an ogre, and early histories state that the first kings descended from heaven on a sky cord at Mt Yarlha Shanpo on the western edge of the valley. The early Tibetan kings unified Tibet from their base here in the 7th century and their massive burial mounds still dominate the area around Chongye to the west. Yumbulagang, perched on a crag like a medieval European castle, is the alleged site of Tibet's oldest building, while Tibet's first cultivated field is said to lie nearby.

There are no guesthouses in the Yarlung Valley, so most travellers will visit from Tsetang.

◉ Sights

The major attractions of the Yarlung Valley can be seen in a half-day trip combined with Chongye Valley.

★**Tradruk Monastery**   MONASTERY
(ཁྲ་འབྲུག་དགོན་པ་, 昌珠寺, Chāngzhū Sì; ¥35; ⊙ dawn-dusk) Dating back to the 7th-century reign of Songtsen Gampo, Tradruk is one of the earliest Buddhist temples in Tibet. It was founded at the same time as Lhasa's Jokhang and Ramoche to act as one of Tibet's demoness-subduing temples (Tradruk pins down the demoness's left shoulder). In order to build the monastery here, Songtsen Gampo had first to take the form of a hawk (tra) in order to overcome a local dragon (druk), a miracle that is commemorated in the monastery's name.

Tradruk was significantly enlarged in the 14th century and again under the auspices of the fifth and seventh Dalai Lamas. The monastery was badly desecrated by Red Guards during the Cultural Revolution.

The entrance of the monastery opens into a courtyard area ringed by cloisters. The building to the rear of the courtyard has a ground

plan similar to that of the Jokhang, and shares the same Tibetan name, Tsuglhakhang. Like the Jokhang, there is both an outer and inner kora path.

The principal chapel, to the rear centre, holds a statue of a speaking white Tara known as Drölma Sheshema (under a parasol), in front of the reconstructed remains of five stone Dhyani Buddhas. The statue of Jampelyang (Manjushri) in the corner allegedly swam to the monastery during a flood.

To the left is the Choegyel Lhakhang, with statues of Songtsen Gampo and his wives and ministers, next to original fragments of stone statuary from next door's stone Dhyani Buddhas.

The Tuje Lhakhang to the right has statues of Chenresig, Jampelyang and Chana Dorje, who form the Tibetan trinity known as the Rigsum Gonpo. The stove to the right is said to have belonged to Princess Wencheng (Wencheng Konjo), the Chinese consort of Songtsen Gampo.

Upstairs and to the rear is a central chapel containing a famous 400-year-old thangka of Chenresig (known as Padmapani) made up of 29,000 pearls, as well as an ancient applique thangka depicting Sakyamuni, said to have been presented by Princess Wencheng to Songtsen Gompa. A protector chapel to the side has an unusual statue of the Hindu god Brahma.

Tradruk is around 7km south of the centre of Tsetang, accessible by local bus 2.

Rechung-puk Monastery   BUDDHIST MONASTERY
(རས་ཆུང་ཕུག, 日琼布寺, Riqióngbù Sì) FREE A popular pilgrimage site associated with the illustrious Milarepa (1040–1123), the scenic ruins of Rechung-puk Monastery are set high on a dramatic escarpment that divides the two branches of the Yarlung Valley.

Milarepa, founder of the Kagyupa order, is revered by many as Tibet's greatest songwriter and poet. It was his foremost disciple, Rechungpa (1083–1161), who founded Rechung-puk as a puk (cave) retreat. Later a monastery was established at the site, eventually housing up to 1000 monks. This now lies in ruins. For pilgrims, the draw of the monastery is the atmospheric cave of Black Heruka, draped with hundreds of bracelets; the pilgrims are thumped on the back with Milarepa's walking stick and the stone footprint of Rechungpa.

Yarlung & Chongye Valleys

Samye
(27km)

Yarlung Tsangpo (Brahmaputra River)

Gangpo Ri
(4130m)

Tsetang

Sheldrak
Cave

Tsechu
Bumpa
Chörten

Trandruk Monastery

Lhabab Ri

Rechung-puk
Monastery

Tashi
Chöden
Monastery

Gongtang
Bumpa Chörten

Bhairo-
puk Cave

Yumbulagang

Tangboche
Monastery

Riwo
Dechen
Monastery

Chingwa
Tagtse Dzong

Tomb of
Songtsen
Gampo

Chongye

Tomb of
Trisong Detsen

Mt Mura

Tombs of the Tibetan Kings

Yumbulagang
HISTORIC BUILDING

(ཡུམ་བུ་བླ་སྒང, 雍布拉康, Yōngbùlākāng; chapel ¥60; ☉ 7am-7pm) A fine, tapering finger of a structure that sprouts from a craggy ridge overlooking the patchwork fields of the Yarlung Valley, Yumbulagang is considered the oldest building in Tibet. At least that is the claim for the original structure – most of what can be seen today dates from reconstructions in 1982 and 2018. It is still a remarkably impressive sight, with a lovely setting.

The founding of Yumbulagang stretches back into legend and myth. The standard line is that it was built for King Nyentri Tsenpo, a historic figure who has long since blurred into mythology. Legend has him descending from the heavens and being received as a king by the people of the Yarlung Valley. More than 400 Buddhist holy texts (known collectively as the 'Awesome Secret') are said to have fallen from the heavens at Yumbulagang in the 5th century. Murals at Yumbulagang depict the magical arrival of the texts.

There has been no conclusive dating of the original Yumbulagang, although some accounts indicate that the foundations may have been laid over 2000 years ago. It is more likely that it dates from the 7th century, when Tibet first came under the rule of Songtsen Gampo.

The plan of Yumbulagang indicates that it was originally a fortress and much larger than the present structure. Today it serves as a chapel and is inhabited by around eight monks who double as guards – in 1999 some 30 statues were stolen from the main chapel. Its most impressive feature is its **tower**, and the prominence of Yumbulagang on the Yarlung skyline belies the fact that this tower is only 11m tall.

The ground-floor **chapel** is consecrated to the ancient kings of Tibet. A central buddha image is flanked by Nyentri Tsenpo on the left and Songtsen Gampo on the right. Other kings and ministers line the side walls. There is another chapel on the upper floor with an image of Chenresig, similar to the one found in the Potala. There are some excellent murals by the door that depict, among other things, Nyentri Tsenpo descending from heaven, Tradruk Monastery, and Guru Rinpoche arriving at the Sheldrak meditation cave (in the mountains west of Tsetang).

Perhaps the best part is a walk up along the ridge above the building, if only to get some peace from the syrupy Chinese pop music blasting from the car park below. There are fabulous views from a promontory topped with prayer flags. It's an easy five-minute climb and no entry fee is needed.

Across the valley from Yumbulagang is an incredibly fertile and verdant crop field known as zortang, said to be the first cultivated field in Tibet. Farmers who visit the valley will often scoop up a handful of earth to sprinkle on their own fields when they return home, thereby ensuring a good crop.

Yumbulagang is 6km south of Tradruk Monastery. Local bus 2 from Tsetang passes by Yumbulagang.

ⓘ Getting There & Away

The Yarlung Valley is due south of Tsetang, around 13km from the town centre to Yumbulagang. Bus 2 from Tsetang reaches into the valley, but most visitors with their own drivers will visit along with a trip to the Chongye Valley for a half-day excursion from Tsetang.

Chongye Valley ཕྱོངས་རྒྱས་གཞུང་
琼结山谷
ELEV 3810M

The Chongye Valley (Qióngjié Shāngǔ) holds a special place in the heart of every Tibetan, for it was here that the first great Tibetan monarchs forged an empire on the world's highest plateau and was also the birthplace of the fifth Dalai Lama. The capital eventually moved to Lhasa but the valley remained hallowed ground and the favoured place of burial for Tibetan kings. Rugged cliffs surround the scenic burial ground on all sides.

Most visitors to the Chongye Valley go as a day trip from Tsetang and combine it with attractions in the Yarlung Valley.

◎ Sights

Chongye Burial Mounds   TOMB
(འཕྱོང་རྒྱས་སྲོ་ང་བཙན་བང་ས, 藏王墓, Zàngwáng Mù; ¥30; ⏰8am-7pm) The tombs of the Tibetan kings at Chongye represent one of the few historical sites in the country that give any evidence of a pre-Buddhist culture in Tibet. Accounts of the location and number of the heavily eroded mounds differ – the most common consensus is that 21 exist altogether, though only 16 have so far been pinpointed. All said and done, the faint mounds of earth are somewhat underwhelming, but the views back towards Chongye are impressive.

Most of the kings interred here are now firmly associated with the rise of Buddhism on the high plateau, but the methods of their interment point to the Bön faith. It is thought that the burials were probably officiated by Bön priests and accompanied by sacrificial offerings. Archaeological evidence suggests that earth burial, not sky burial, might have been widespread in the time of the Yarlung kings, and may not have been limited to royalty.

The most revered of the 10 burial mounds, and the closest to the main road, is the 130m-long **Tomb of Songtsen Gampo**. It has a small Nyingmapa temple atop its 13m-high summit, rebuilt in 1985, which is hardly worth the entry fee. The furthest of the group of mounds, high on the slopes of Mt Mura, is the **Tomb of Trisong Detsen**.

Chingwa Tagtse Dzong   FORT
(འཕྱིང་བ་སྟག་རྩེ་རྫོང, 青瓦达孜宫, Qīngwǎ Dázī Gōng)
FREE This *dzong* can be seen clearly from Chongye town and from the burial mounds, its crumbling ramparts straddling a ridge of Mt Chingwa. Once one of the most powerful forts in central Tibet during the 14th century, it dates back to the time of the early Yarlung kings in the 7th century when it originally served as a palace. The *dzong* is also celebrated as the birthplace of the great fifth Dalai Lama.

Riwo Dechen Monastery   BUDDHIST MONASTERY
(ཕྱོགས་ར་རི་བོ་བདེ་ཆེན, 日乌德庆寺, Rìwū Déqìng Sì)
FREE The large, active, Gelugpa-sect Riwo Dechen Monastery sprawls above Chongye's old town across the lower slopes of Mt Chingwa below the fort. The main assembly hall has a statue and throne of the fifth Dalai Lama. Just below the monastery is a grand new chörten.

Tangboche Monastery   BUDDHIST MONASTERY
(བང་པོ་ཆེ, 唐布齐寺, Tángbùqí Sì; ¥10) A minor site thought to date back to 1017, Tangboche Monastery is about 15km southwest of Tsetang on the way to Chongye. Atisha, the renowned Bengali scholar, stayed here in a meditation retreat. The monastery's murals, which for most visitors are the main attraction, were commissioned by the 13th Dalai Lama in 1913. They can be seen in the monastery's main hall – one of the few monastic structures in this region that was not destroyed by Red Guards.

One thing to look out for are the unusual long side chapels lined with protector puppets dressed in monk's robes. The assembly hall is home to local protector Yongsten Gyelpo and a heart-shaped stone made of meteorite.

● Getting There & Away
The Chongye Valley is southwest of Tsetang, 28km from the city centre to the Chongye Burial Mounds – expect the trip to take around 40 minutes without stops. Most travellers will combine a trip here with a visit to the Yarlung Valley to the east, returning to Tsetang after the half-day outing.

Mindroling སྨིན་གྲོལ་གླིང 敏珠林
☎0893 / POP 320 / ELEV 3750M
Home to the largest, most important Nyingmapa monastery in Ü, Mindroling (Mǐnzhūlín) is a worthwhile detour from the Lhasa–Tsetang road. Nice walks lead off the kora around the Tsuglhakhang, west up the surrounding valley through the village to the ruins of a meditation retreat and a nunnery.

Very few tourists overnight at Mindroling, but it is possible, and if you can stomach the

NAMSELING MANOR

One of the only buildings of its type still standing in Tibet, **Namseling Manor** (རྣམ་སྲས་གླིང་ , 襄色林庄园, Nángsèlín Zhuāngyuán; ☑ caretaker 133 9803 5933) is a seven-storey family mansion that dates from the 17th century and was once used as a local lama's summer palace. The interior is typically closed to visitors but it's worth a scramble around if you can track down the caretaker. The moat and bridge are a modern addition.

The building is 3km south of the main highway near Km161, around 13km east of the turn-off for Mindroling and 26km west of Tsetang.

dirty rooms of the **monastery guesthouse** (敏珠林寺宾馆, Mǐnzhūlín Sì Bīnguǎn; ☑ 133 9803 0301; dm ¥50, s/d without bathroom ¥100/120) you'll appreciate having the extra time to explore the village and the ruins surrounding the monastery.

Skip the stuffy monastery restaurant in favour of the Lāsà Cáishén Cáng Cān teahouse on the far side of the parking lot. There's also a small teahouse opposite the Kumbum Tongdrol Chenmo and a small shop just beside the monastery guesthouse.

⊙ Sights

Mindroling Monastery   BUDDHIST MONASTERY
(སྨིན་གྲོལ་གླིང་དགོན་པ་ , 敏珠林寺, Mǐnzhūlín Sì; admission ¥25, photography ¥45) Although a small monastery was founded at the present site of Mindroling as early as the 10th century, the date usually given for the founding of Mindroling is the mid-1670s. The founding lama, Terdak Lingpa (1646–1714), was highly esteemed as a *terton* (treasure finder) and scholar, and counted among his students the fifth Dalai Lama. Subsequent heads of the monastery were given the title Minling Trichen, which passed from father to son

The monastery was razed in the Dzungar Mongol invasion of 1718 and later restored, but is still renown as one of the best educational centres in the Nyingmapa tradition. From a height of around 500, the monastery is now home to 70 monks.

The central **Tsuglhakhang** is an elegant brown stone structure on the western side of the courtyard. The bare main hall itself has a statue of Terdak Lingpa, along with Dorje Chang (the founder of Tantric Buddhsm) and

a row of seven Kadam-style chörtens – the monastery originally belonged to the Kadampa school. The inner chapel has a large Sakyamuni statue. The hands were destroyed by Chinese troops looking for relics, but the rest is original.

Upstairs, the first chapel you'll see is the **Zheye Lhakhang**, with statues of Guru Rinpoche and Terdak Lingpa (with a white beard and an excellent hat). The **Terza Lhakhang** houses several treasures, including a stone hoof print, a mirror that takes away disease and a famed old thangka with the gold footprints and handprints of Terdak Lingpa, which was given to the fifth Dalai Lama.

The top floor holds the central **Lama Lhakhang**, with some fine ancient murals of the Nyingma lineages, plus a central statue of Kuntu Zangpo (Samantabhadri) and two 3D mandalas. The Dalai Lama's quarters remain empty.

The other main building, to the right is the **Sangok Podrang**, used for Tantric practices. To the left of the main entrance is a famous 'speaking' mural of Guru Rinpoche. Flanking the left wall of the assembly hall is a huge thangka that is unfurled once a year on the 18th day of the fourth lunar month. The views from the rooftop here are excellent.

Nice walks lead off from the kora around the Tsuglhakhang, west up the valley through the village to the ruins of what used to be a meditation retreat and a nunnery.

Mindroling has *cham* dancing on the 10th day of the fifth Tibetan lunar month and the fourth day of the fourth lunar month. The latter festival features the creation of four sand mandalas nine days later.

Mindroling Incense Factory   FACTORY
(敏珠林寺藏香厂, Mǐnzhūlín Sì Zàngxiāng Chǎng; ⊙ 7am-1pm & 2-7pm) After a visit to Mindroling Monastery it's worth popping into this traditional factory just off the parking lot. Tibetan workers split fragrant logs and machines pulp, mix and press the juniper and other herbs into incense sticks. Bundles of the incense are available for purchase at a shop beside the parking lot in large (¥40) and small (¥20) boxes.

Kumbum Tongdrol Chenmo   BUDDHIST SHRINE
(白塔, Báitǎ; ¥10) This white chörten outside and below Mindroling Monastery was constructed in 2000 with Taiwanese funds. It replaces a 13-storey chörten destroyed in the Cultural Revolution, though the fantastic paintings along the internal kora appear

much older than they are. It's possible to climb past the ground-floor statue of Jampa to its six upper floors, recommend if for nothing else than the views of the surrounding monastery from the rooftop walkway.

ⓘ Getting There & Away

Mindroling is 8km up the Drachi Valley south of the Gongkar–Tsetang road, 5km east of Dratang. Foreigners are not allowed to take the daily monastery bus to or from Tsetang.

Dratang ग्रॅ་རང་གལེང་ 扎塘

📞 0893 / POP 9500 / ELEV 3600M

The small town of Dratang (Zhātáng) is of outsized importance to scholars and enthusiasts of Tibetan Buddhism, primarily for the rare murals of the Dratang Monastery around which the town has grown. Nearby and worth a visit are the ruins of the Jampaling Kumbum, a 13-storey chörten (Buddhist stupa) built in 1472.

⊙ Sights

Dratang Monastery BUDDHIST MONASTERY
(ग्रॅ་རང་གལེང་, 扎塘寺, Zhātáng Sì; ¥25) This small Sakyapa monastery of 20 monks is of interest mainly to art specialists for its rare murals, which combine Indian (Pala) and inner Asian (Western Xia) styles. Bring a torch to see the murals.

The assembly hall has central statues of Dorje Chang (Vajradhara; with crossed arms) and, to the right, the monastery's founder, Drapa Ngonshe, who helped establish Tibet's earliest medical canon. Look for the interesting seatlike oracle costume and mirror (left of Dorje Chang) in which the oracle would discern his visions – pilgrims receive a blessing from the ancient rope, sword and knife here. The inner sanctum holds all that remains of the murals, the best of which are on the back (western) wall.

A side protector chapel is accessed by steps outside and to the left of the main entrance. The chapel (whose central image is that of a yak's head) has a hidden passage at the back that leads to a rooftop chapel and kora. A rooftop protector chapel features some wooden skeletons.

Jampaling Kumbum BUDDHIST SHRINE
[FREE] The 13-storey chörten, built in 1472, was one of the largest in Tibet, with an attendant monastery of 200 monks, before it was dynamited by the Chinese in 1963.

Rebuilding efforts are limited to a two-storey Jampa chapel. Check out the little brass toe on the throne – all that remains of the original Jampa statue after which the complex was named. Old B&W photos show the chörten in its original glory. Hike up among the ruins for the sobering views.

The ruins of the Jampaling Kumbum are on the hillside a 2km walk or drive southeast of Dratang and can be seen from the monastery there. To get to Jampaling, head south from Dratang Monastery and after a couple of minutes turn left, following a path to the base of the ruins visible on the hillside above.

⏾ Sleeping

There are several sleeping options in Dratang, but most people visit en route between Tsetang/Samye and Gyantse.

Gāodì Xiāngcūn Jiǔdiàn HOTEL $
(高地乡村酒店; 📞 139 0893 0489, 189 8903 7333; d ¥180, tr without bath ¥150; ❉ 🛜) Your best option is this hotel on the main highway by the junction to Dratang. Rooms are clean and modern, with hot showers, and you can watch the traffic from the pleasant teahouse just off the lobby.

Zhūzhōu Hotel HOTEL $$
(株洲宾馆, Zhūzhōu Bīnguǎn; 📞 158 8903 0208; Zhuzhou Lu; 株洲路; d ¥200) A back-up option, this government-run place has doubles with attached squat toilets. It's 100m south of the main highway, tucked inside a small courtyard.

ⓘ Getting There & Away

Dratang is halfway between Gongkar airport and Tsetang, around 50km from each. The eponymous monastery is located about 2km off the main road.

If you're not continuing to Tsetang and points in the east of Lhoka prefecture, a new bridge connecting Dratang and Samye makes what was once a several-hour trip now less than half an hour.

Gongkar

📞 0891 / POP 11,000 / ELEV 3570M

Gongkar's main claim to fame is its airport, but there are also a couple of interesting monasteries west of the town centre and one in the town itself. Note that there are three places called Gongkar: the Lhasa Gongkar Airport (ग्रॅ་ང་གལ་ང་གར་རནམ་ག་ག, 拉萨贡嘎机场, Lāsà Gònggā Jīchǎng), the Gongkar Chöde

SIGHTS IN GONGKAR TOWN

Built in the 14th century as a Sakya monastery with five colleges and 80 monks at its peak, this post–Cultural Revolution rebuild of **Thupten Ramye Monastery** (土旦热麦寺, Tǔdàn Rènmài Sì) is now home to just 20 monks. Inside the assembly hall the main statues are representations of the Past, Present, and Future Buddhas.

The town is also home to Tibet's only public **Chairman Mao statue** (毛主席 雕像, Máozhǔxí Diāoxiàng), erected in 2006.

Monastery 10km to the west and the county town of Gongkar Xian (ষ্ণীশূর্ষ্ণ , 贡嘎县, Gònggǎ Xiàn), about 10km to the east.

⊙ Sights

★ Gongkar Chöde Monastery
BUDDHIST MONASTERY
(র্শ্মশ্মস্কীব্র্শ্বা , 贡嘎曲德寺, Gònggǎ Qūdé Sì; admission ¥20, photography ¥10) Surprisingly large, the Sakyapa-school Gongkar Chöde Monastery, founded in 1464, is famous for its 16th-century Kyenri-style murals. It lies 400m south of the highway, around 10km from the airport, along the road to Gyantse. The monastery has been renovated with the help of the Shalu Foundation (www.asianart. com/shalu).

The **assembly hall** has statues of Sakya Pandita, Drölma, Guru Rinpoche and the monastery founder, Dorje Denpa (1432–96). To the left of the hall is the *gönkhang* (protector chapel), whose outer rooms have black murals depicting a sky burial. The inner hall has a statue of the Sakyapa protector Gonpo Gur (Mahakala Panjaranatha) and some elaborate spirit traps (in a case to the right). The inner sanctum has fine murals of the Sakyapa founders by the entrance, and an inner kora *(nangkhor)*. Art specialists say the Khyenri-style murals show a marked Chinese influence, most noticeable in the cloud and landscape motifs. Bring a powerful torch (flashlight).

The chapel to the right of the assembly hall has particularly fine images of the Past, Present and Future Buddhas. To the left of the main hall is a protector chapel with mandalas made of coloured string and a collection of exquisite offering cakes made of yak butter, tsampa and flour.

The upper floor has more lovely old murals, including some showing the original monastery layout. On either side of the roof is the **Kyedhor Lhakhang**, which has fine protector murals and statues in *yabyum* (Tantric sexual union) pose, and the **Kangyur Lhakhang**.

As you walk clockwise around the main monastery building, look for the *shedra* on the northern side. The monks practise debating here at around 6pm.

Shedruling Monastery
BUDDHIST MONASTERY
(夏珠林寺, Xiàzhūlín Sì) **FREE** The impressive 600-year-old Shedruling Monastery rises from the main road like a miniature Potala, and is home to 31 monks. The monastery is less impressive close up, but the views over the valley are fine in the afternoon light. Just below the monastery are the ruins of Gongkar Dzong, which was bombed by the Chinese military in 1959.

The monastery is around 13km west of Gongkar airport and 3km west of Gongkar Chöde Monastery. A road leads right up to the monastery gates.

ⓘ Information

At the time of research no hotels near the airport were allowed to accept foreigners. You might get special permission from the Public Security Bureau (PSB) office by the main crossroads, but it's easiest to simply drive from Lhasa.

Bank of China (中国银行, Zhōngguó Yínháng; ⊙9.30am-5pm Mon-Fri, 11am-4pm Sat & Sun) This bank is located 300m south of the airport; it changes cash and travellers cheques into yuán and has a 24-hour ATM. Illogically for an international airport bank, though, it cannot change yuán back into foreign currency.

ⓘ Getting There & Away

From the centre of Lhasa to Gongkar airport it's usually one hour by car, slightly more to the monasteries or county town. Continuing along the old road through the south of the valley it's about a one-hour drive to Dratang, 1½ hours to the turn-off for Mindroling and 2½ hours to Tsetang.

Airport buses run frequently between the office of the Civil Aviation Authority of China (CAAC) in Lhasa and Gongkar airport (¥30). Return buses to Lhasa are timed to coincide with the arrival of flights. Taxis to Lhasa cost ¥300 when arranged through a travel agency, ¥200 if organised independently.

Tsang ག་ཙང་

Includes ➡

Best Places to Eat

➡ Wordo Tibetan Courtyard (p147)

➡ Third Eye (p147)

➡ Tashi (p140)

➡ Rindhing Garden (p140)

Best Places to Stay

➡ Yeti Hotel (p139)

➡ Jilong Legend Hotel (p161)

➡ Tashi Choeta Hotel (p147)

➡ Qomolangzong Hotel (p146)

Why Go?

The historical province of Tsang (ག་ཙང་) is either the first or last place that most travellers experience in Tibet, and the setting for two of Asia's great mountain drives: out to far western Tibet and across the Himalaya to Nepal. The great overland trip across Tibet – from Lhasa along the Friendship Hwy to the Nepali border via Gyantse, Shigatse and Mt Everest Base Camp – goes straight through Tsang, linking most of Tibet's highlights on one irresistible route. Along the way is a scattering of atmospheric Tibetan monasteries and historic towns, an adventurous detour to the base of Mt Everest and multitudes of snowy peaks and moonlike landscapes to behold. Dozens of smaller monasteries just off the highway offer plenty of scope to get off the beaten track and experience an older Tibet.

When to Go

➡ The best time of year to visit Tsang is from May to June: views of Mt Everest are usually clear before the monsoon brings cloud cover and this is an excellent time for trekking. Travel along the Friendship Hwy is possible year-round.

➡ A colourful three-day monastery festival at Tashilhunpo takes place in the fifth lunar month (June or July) and culminates in the unrolling of a massive thangka. Also in July, visit Gyantse for the Dhama Festival of horse racing and archery, which also includes traditional games, folk singing, picnics and much swilling of barley beer.

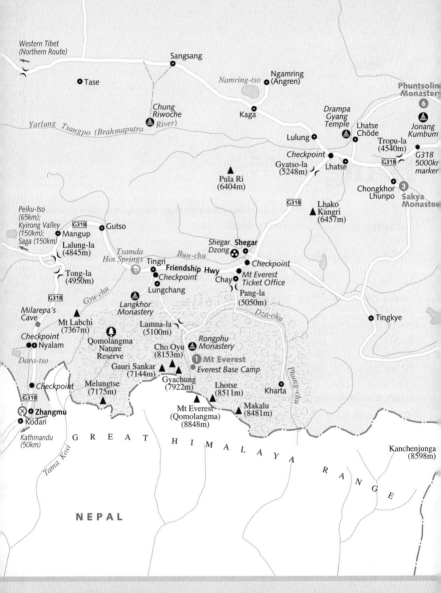

Western Tibet
(Northern Route)

Sangsang

Tase

Namring-tso

Ngamring
(Angren)

Chung
Riwoche
River

Kaga

Yarlung Tsangpo (Brahmaputra River)

Lulung

Drampa
Gyang
Temple

Lhatse
Chöde

**Phuntsolin
Monastery**
6

Jonang
Kumbum

Checkpoint

Gyatso-la
(5248m)

Lhatse

Tropu-la
(4540m)

G318

G318
5000kr
marker

Pula Ri
(6404m)

Chongkhor
Lhunpo

Sakya
Monastery

3

G318

Lhako
Kangri
(6457m)

Peiku-tso
(65km);
Kyirong Valley
(150km);
Saga (150km)

G318

Gutso

Mangup

Lalung-la
(4845m)

Tsamda
Hot Springs

Shegar
Dzong

Shegar

Bun-chu

Tingri

Friendship Hwy

Checkpoint

Checkpoint

Chay

Mt Everest
Ticket Office

Tong-la
(4950m)

Gyu-chu

Lungchang

G318

Milarepa's
Cave

Langkhor
Monastery

Pang-la
(5050m)

Checkpoint

Mt Labchi
(7367m)

Lamna-la
(5100m)

Dza-chu

Tingkye

Nyalam

Qomolangma
Nature
Reserve

Cho Oyu
(8153m)

Rongphu
Monastery

Dara-tso

Gauri Sankar
(7144m)

1 **Mt Everest**

Everest Base Camp

Phung-chu

Checkpoint

G318

Melungtse
(7175m)

Gyachung
(7922m)

Lhotse
(8511m)

Kharta

Zhangmu

Kodari

Mt Everest
(Qomolangma)
(8848m)

Makalu
(8481m)

Kathmandu
(50km)

Tama Koşi

G R E A T

H I M A L A Y A

R A N G E

Kanchenjunga
(8598m)

N E P A L

Tsang Highlights

1 **Mt Everest** (p153) Trying
to catch your breath under the
unparalleled north face of the
world's highest peak.

2 **Tashilhunpo Monastery**
(p143) Exploring the cobbled
laneways and glowering
chapels of one of Tibet's
most important monastic
institutions.

3 **Sakya Monastery**
(p150) Soaking up the sacred
atmosphere and reams of
ancient scriptures inside this
impressive monastery.

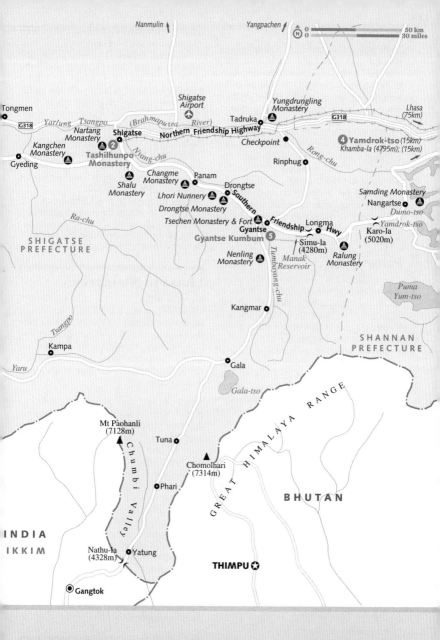

4 Yamdrok-tso (p132)
Taking in the dazzling views of this sparkling turquoise lake from atop dizzying Khamba-la pass.

5 Gyantse Kumbum (p135)
Winding around the multiple storeys and mural-filled chapels of this monumental chörten.

6 Phuntsoling Monastery (p162) Enjoying sweeping vistas of the Yarlung Tsangpo Valley from this quiet monastery in the shadow of a sand dune.

History

Tsang lies to the west of Ü and has shared political dominance and cultural influence over the Tibetan plateau with its neighbour. With the decline of the Lhasa kings in the 10th century, the epicentre of Tibetan power moved to Sakya, under Mongol patronage from the mid-13th to the mid-14th centuries.

After the fall of the Sakya government, the power shifted back to Ü and then again back to Tsang. But until the rise of the Gelugpa order and the Dalai Lamas in the 17th century, neither Tsang nor Ü effectively governed all of central Tibet, and the two provinces were rivals for power. Some commentators see the rivalry between the Panchen Lama and Dalai Lama as a latter-day extension of this provincial wrestling for political dominance.

Permits

As with the rest of Tibet, travellers need permits to visit anywhere in Tsang and this requires travelling on an organised tour with a guide and transport. Your guide will need to register and get an alien's travel permit while in Gyantse or Shigatse.

Special trekking permits are needed to trek in the Everest region beyond Base Camp. Trekking permits for Camp III (also known as Advanced Base Camp or ABC) are issued by the China Tibet Mountain Association. Trekkers will need help from an agency to get the permits.

🍽 Sleeping & Eating

Tsang offers a range of accommodation, though standards drop outside the cities of Gyantse and Shigatse. Accommodation in

---

BEST WALKS IN TSANG

➡ Rongphu (p154) Walk to a charming collection of chörtens in the shadow of Mt Everest.

➡ Tashilhunpo Kora (p146) Follow pilgrims on this lovely path offering great views of one of Tibet's most important monasteries.

➡ Sakya Monastery Kora (p150) Walk the ramparts for stellar views of mountain peaks and glimpses into this monastery's inner workings

➡ Samding Monastery (p133) Climb the ridge here for incredible views as far as the Bhutan Himalaya.

---

the Everest region is very basic, often with pit toilets and shared rooms.

There are Sichuanese and Tibetan restaurants in every town in Tsang, and some international and Nepali dishes in Shigatse and Gyantse. Food is simple further afield, so you may wish to bring some snacks.

❶ Getting There & Around

The Qīnghǎi–Tibet railway extension from Lhasa to Shigatse opened in 2014, making train travel through the region possible.

Shigatse has its own airport with direct flights to Chéngdū, Shànghǎi and Xī'ān.

As with the rest of Tibet, public transport exists but international travellers are not permitted to use it (beyond the train). In Tsang's larger towns, taxis are available, though most places are not big enough to them to be needed.

Lhasa to Nangartse

Khamba-la   VIEWPOINT

(¥40) This pass is one of the highest points on the drive from Lhasa to Gyantse. It climbs from the Yarlung Valley to its 4795m apex, where a parking lot and viewpoint offer incredible vistas over turquoise Yamdrok-tso to the south. Far in the distance is the huge massif of Mt Nojin Kangtsang (7191m).

Yamdrok-tso   LAKE
(ཡར་འབྲོག་གཡུ་མཚོ : 羊卓雍措; Yángzhuó Yōngcuò)
Dazzling Yamdrok-tso is one of Tibet's four holy lakes (the others are Lhamo La-tso, Nam-tso and Manasarovar) and home to wrathful deities. Its turquoise waters are shaped like a coiling scorpion, doubling back on themselves on the western side, effectively creating a large island within its reaches. Most travellers see the lake from the summit of 4795m Khamba-la as they drive en route between Lhasa and Gyantse.

Devout Tibetan pilgrims circumambulate the lake in around seven days but most western travellers are content with views of the lake from the drive. The lake lies several hundred metres below the road at 4440m, and in clear weather is a fabulous shade of deep turquoise.

Nangartse   སྣ་དཀར་རྩེ 浪卡子

📞 0893 / ELEV 4400M

Nangartse (Làngkǎzi) is the largest town on Yamdrok-tso and a popular lunch spot for groups headed to Gyantse. It's not

TSANG IN EIGHT DAYS

Most travellers see Tsang as part of a trip to the Nepali border, or via a loop journey through the province to Mt Everest Base Camp and back to Lhasa. The 835km journey from Lhasa to the Nepali border normally takes six to eight days at a safe pace, with slow altitude climbs each day. It's a nice idea to take your time, scheduling in extra days for deeper exploration in some of Tsang's historic towns, or detouring to several of the important monasteries in the region.

From Lhasa, head out on the Southern Friendship Hwy, which takes you over Khamba-la (p132) pass to Yamdrok-tso (p132), then to Samding Monastery and Gyantse (p134). You'll need a full day in Gyantse before moving on to Shigatse (p141). If you're in a hurry, it's quicker to take the Northern Friendship Hwy when travelling between Lhasa and Shigatse, but this means you'll miss Gyantse, one of Tsang's highlights.

West of Shigatse, most travellers zip down to Shegar overnight before getting a super early start to watch the sun rise on the road to Everest Base Camp (p153). Though Shigatse–Shegar is a long day driving, it's still easy and very worthwhile to add in a detour to Sakya Monastery (p150) on the way.

If you're not moving on over the border into Nepal, making a loop back to Lhasa allows you to explore the uncharted, unpaved road from Everest to Tingri, which feels more like driving across Mars than the top of the world. You could linger a night at Lhatse (p160) and take a scenic side trip to Phuntsoling Monastery (p162) from here.

Any way you go you'll find good facilities and relatively easy drives, because the Friendship Hwy is entirely paved, all the way to Mt Everest itself.

Heading overland into Nepal, the old route via Zhāngmù was closed after Nepal's 2015 earthquake, and a new crossing via Kyirong into Nepal's Langtang region opened in 2016.

TSANG NANGARTSE

particularly attractive but there's a small monastery just south of town, an old Tibetan quarter and a small *dzong* (fort) to the north (famed as the birthplace of the mother of the fifth Dalai Lama). In the summer months birdwatchers will have a field day in the surrounding lake shore and marshlands.

◎ Sights

Samding Monastery   BUDDHIST MONASTERY
(桑丁寺; Sāngdīng Sì; ¥25) Near the shores of Yamdrok-tso, about 10km east of Nangartse, Samding Monastery is situated on a 4550m-high ridge that separates two smaller lakes encircled by the northern and southern arms of Yamdrok-tso. Samding is noted for the unusual fact that it is traditionally headed by a female incarnate lama named Dorje Phagmo (Diamond Sow).

When the Mongolian armies invaded Samding in 1716, Dorje Phagmo changed her nuns into pigs to help them escape. Her current incarnation works for the government in Lhasa but often travels to Samding for the monastery's annual *cham* (ritual dance) festival on the eighth day of the fifth lunar month. There are 50 monks in residence.

It's possible to visit the main *dukhang* (assembly hall), on the right-hand side of the courtyard, which is dominated by an inner statue of Sakyamuni (Sakya Thukpa). There are also photos of the 11th and 12th (the current) Dorje Phagmo, a statue of Dorje Phagmo wearing a turquoise amulet and a gold-painted footprint of the ninth Dorje Phagmo, plus a sacred conch shell and an eerie protector chapel. There are several more chapels upstairs.

The Sangok Phodrang to the left is a Tantric chapel with a central chörten and a fine thangka depicting five manifestations of Jampelyang (Manjushri). Upstairs is a chapel housing a statue of Jampa (the Future Buddha) at the age of eight, and a side room of slate carvings that houses a collection of stone relics and scriptures that survived the Cultural Revolution. The living rooms of Dorje Phagmo are also here.

The compassion chapel to the left of the courtyard houses a gilded stupa made by the seventh Dorje Phagmo.

For dramatic views over the surrounding three lakes of Gongmo-tso, Dumo-tso and Yamdrok-tso, hike for 45 minutes up to the ridge-top cairns behind the monastery. The snowcapped Himalayan giants to the south are Kula Kangri (7538m) and Gangkhar Phuensum (7570m), both bordering Bhutan.

It's possible to stay overnight in the monastery's extremely simple guesthouse.

Samding Monastery Guesthouse
GUESTHOUSE $

(桑丁寺招待所; Sāngdīng Sì Zhāodàisuǒ; dm ¥30) The accommodation at this guesthouse attached to Samding Monastery (p133) is extremely simple, in dorms of four, six or seven beds with a shared, dirty pit toilet (no showers). The reception is warm, though, and the Tibetan-style restaurant (noodles only) is cosy. The real draw here is waking up to the superb views over the valley. Located 10km east of Nangartse.

Karo-la
VIEWPOINT, GLACIER

(¥50) The road from Nangartse to Gyantse crosses the 5020m Karo-la, where a picture-perfect glacier topping out at 7190m spills off side peaks right along the roadside. The pass was the site of the highest battle in British imperial history during the Younghusband invasion of 1903–04.

In May 2018, an admission fee was added for everyone travelling over the pass. There is a viewing platform with a stupa, and lots of touts, but the views are unbeatable.

🛏 Sleeping & Eating

There are no hotels accepting international travellers in Nangartse, so most people opt to overnight in Gyantse. A 15-minute drive from Nangartse brings you to Samding Monastery, a charming place with scenic views of the surrounding plain and lakes from the simple but pleasant monastery guesthouse.

Nangartse is essentially a lunch stop on the road between Gyantse and Lhasa. The Lhasa and Yamdrok Yak restaurants are the usual stops.

There is no nightlife in Nangartse.

OFF THE BEATEN TRACK IN TSANG

➡ Phuntsoling Monastery (p162)

➡ Shegar Dzong (p153)

➡ Tsang Traditional Folk House (p137)

➡ Ralung Monastery (p135)

➡ Lhori Nunnery (p141)

Lhasa Restaurant
CHINESE, INTERNATIONAL $$

(拉萨餐厅; Lāsà Cāntīng; Hunan Lu, 湖南路; buffet ¥40, dishes ¥25-60; ⊙8am-10pm) This well-established restaurant has a colourful dining hall with old photos of Lhasa and is firmly aimed at tour groups, with a lunchtime buffet (11am to 3pm), an à la carte menu in English and big portions. It's a tad overpriced but upstairs is clean and pleasant.

Yamdrok Yak Restaurant
INTERNATIONAL $$

(羊卓亚餐厅; Yángzhuó Yà Cāntīng; ☑156 9262 0077; Duixi Lu, 对西路; buffet with drink ¥45, dishes ¥30-40; ⊙9am-10pm) After years working in a French restaurant in Kathmandu, owner Nudry now serves credible western, Indian and Chinese dishes here, including unexpected treats like bacon sandwiches and yak-liver pâté, as well as a lunch buffet in high season. The red-walled restaurant is located on the road into town, just after you turn off the highway when coming from Lhasa.

ℹ Getting There & Away

The main road from Lhasa climbs from the Yarlung Valley up to Khamba-la (4795m), before dropping to Yamdrok-tso. It's around 150km from Lhasa to Nangartse – the drive takes about three hours.

Heading west from Nangartse, the highway climbs again to a dramatic roadside glacier at the Karo-la pass (5050m). About 60km before Gyantse, there's a viewpoint over scenic Manak Reservoir. It's approximately 100km (two hours) from Nangartse to Gyantse.

Gyantse
རྒྱལ་རྩེ། 江孜

☑0892 / POP 15,000 / ELEV 4000M

Lying on a historic trade route between India and Tibet, Gyantse (Jiāngzī) has long been a crucial link for traders and pilgrims journeying across the Himalaya. It was once considered Tibet's third city, behind Lhasa and Shigatse, but in recent decades has been eclipsed by fast-growing towns such as Bāyī and Tsetang. Perhaps that's a good thing, as Gyantse has managed to hang onto its small-town charm and laid-back atmosphere.

Gyantse's greatest sight is Gyantse Kumbum, the largest chörten remaining in Tibet and one of its architectural wonders, but there's plenty more to see. With good hotels and restaurants, Gyantse is the town in Tibet that most warrants an extra day to explore little-visited nearby monasteries or wander the town's charming back streets.

RALUNG MONASTERY

If you want to get off the beaten track, make an 8km detour south off the Friendship Hwy from the road between Nangartse and Gyantse, across a huge, sweeping plain to **Ralung Monastery** (རྭ་ལུང་དགོན་པ་ 热龙寺, Rèlóng Sì; 4740m). Ralung was founded in 1180 and gets its name from the 'self-arising' image of a *ra* (goat) that spurred the monastery's construction. It was from Ralung that the religious leader Nawang Namgyel (1594–1651) fled Tibet, finally arriving in Bhutan in 1616 to reshape that country's identity as its top religious leader, the Zhabdrung.

The original *tsuglhakhang* (great temple) stands in ruins, as does a multistoried, multichambered chörten (stupa) visible from the roof. As you wander around, look for images of the yellow-hatted founder, Tsanpa Gyare, and the Drukpa Rinpoche (head of the monastery's Drukpa Kagyud school), who resides in India. In the far left corner is the local protector Ralung Gyelpo riding a snow lion, beside the mountain deity Nojin Gangtsang, who rides a blue mule.

The monastery is home to 12 monks. Ask one of them to point out the meaning of the mountains behind the monastery; each one stands for one of the eight auspicious symbols. The dramatic snowcapped peak to the northeast is 7191m high Nojin Gangtsang. There are *cham* (ritual dances) here between the 13th and 15th of the sixth Tibetan month.

At the time of writing, the monastery was undergoing big renovation works expected to finish in October 2018, and was open for free. Post-renovation admission prices had not been decided.

History

Between the 14th and 15th centuries, Gyantse emerged as the centre of a fiefdom with powerful connections to the Sakyapa Buddhist order. By 1440, Gyantse's most impressive architectural achievements – the *kumbum* (100,000 Buddha images) and the *dzong* (fort) – had been completed. Palcho Monastery also dates from this period.

Gyantse's historical importance declined from the end of the 15th century, although the town continued to be a major centre for the trade of wood and wool between India and Tibet. Gyantse carpets, considered the finest in Tibet, were exported by yak cart to Gangtok, Kalimpong and beyond. In 1904 it became the site of a major battle during the British advance on Lhasa.

⊙ Sights

★**Gyantse Kumbum**   BUDDHIST STUPA
(སྐུ་འབུམ་ ; 江孜千佛塔; Jiāngzī Qiānfótǎ; Map p136; incl with Palcho Monastery) Commissioned by a local prince in 1427 and sitting beside Palcho Monastery (p136), Gyantse Kumbum is the town's foremost attraction. This 32m-high chörten, with its white layers trimmed with decorative stripes and crown-like golden dome, is awe-inspiring. But the inside is no less impressive, and in what seems an endless series of tiny chapels you'll

find painting after exquisite painting (*kumbum* means '100,000 images').

It costs a worthwhile ¥10 for photos (not included in the ticket, bring cash).

Gyantse Kumbum has been described as the most important of its kind in Tibet. There are only two contemporaries, both ruined, remote and off limits, in the Buddhist world: Jonang Kumbum, 60km northeast of Lhatse, and the even more remote Chung Riwoche, in the west of Tsang. However, it is commonly held that neither could ever compare with the style and grandeur of the Gyantse Kumbum.

Upon entering, follow a clockwise route marked by red arrows that leads murmuring pilgrims up through the six floors, taking in the dozens of tiny chapels that recede into the walls along the way. Much of the statuary in the chapels was damaged during the Cultural Revolution but the murals have weathered well. They date back to the 14th century, and if they were not created by Newari (Nepali) artisans then they were obviously influenced by Newari forms. Experts also see evidence of Chinese influence and, in the fusion of these Newari and Chinese forms with Tibetan sensibilities, the emergence of a syncretic but distinctly Tibetan style of painting.

The **1st floor** has four main chapels, two storeys high, oriented according to the

Gyantse

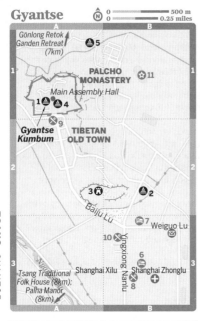

N

0 ——————— 500 m
0 ——————— 0.25 miles

Gönlong Retok
Ganden Retreat
(7km)

🚹 5

PALCHO
MONASTERY

☸11

Main Assembly Hall

1 🚹 🚹 4

Gyantse
Kumbum 🚹 9

TIBETAN
OLD TOWN

3 🏛

🚹 2

Bǎijú Lù

🏠 7 Weiguo Lu

10 🍴

Yingxiong Nanlu

6

Tsang Traditional
Folk House (8km);
Palha Manor
(8km)

Shanghai Xilu Shanghai Zhonglu

8 ✚

Gyantse

◉ **Top Sights**
  1 Gyantse Kumbum A1

◉ **Sights**
  2 Guru Lhakhang Temple.......................B2
  3 Gyantse Dzong A2
  4 Palcho Monastery A1
  5 Rabse Nunnery.....................................A1

🛏 **Sleeping**
  6 Gyantse Hotel B3
  7 Yeti Hotel...B3

🍴 **Eating**
  8 Gyantse Kitchen B3
  9 Rindhing Garden A2
  10 Tashi B3
  Yeti Hotel Restaurant ....(see 7)

☸ **Entertainment**
  11 Gyantse Sound & Light Show..............B1

cardinal points. The four chapels are dedicated to: Sakyamuni (Sakya Thukpa; along with two disciples, medicine buddhas and Guru Rinpoche) in the south; Sukhavati, the 'pure land of the west' and home of red Öpagme (Amitabha) in the west; Marmedze (Dipamkara, the Past Buddha) in the north; and Tushita, another 'pure land' and home of orange-faced Jampa (Maitreya), in the east. In between are some excellent murals depicting minor Tantric and protector deities. Statues of the Four Guardian Kings in the east mark the way to the upper floors.

On the **2nd floor**, the first four chapels in clockwise order from the stairs are dedicated to Jampelyang (known in Sanskrit as Manjushri), Chenresig (Avalokiteshvara), Tsepame (Amitayus) and Drölma (Tara). Most of the other chapels are devoted to wrathful protector deities, including Drölkar (White Tara; 12th chapel from the stairs), Chana Dorje (Vajrapani; 14th chapel) and Mikyöba (Akshobhya; 15th chapel), a blue buddha who holds a *dorje* (thunderbolt). You can only view the chapels on this floor through the doorway windows.

The **3rd floor** is also dominated by a series of two-storey chapels at the cardinal points portraying the four Dhyani Buddhas: red Öpagme (Amitabha) in the south; orange Rinchen Jungne (Ratnasambhava) in the west; green Donyo Drupa (Amoghasiddhi) in the north; and blue Mikyöba (Akshobhya) in the east. There are several other chapels devoted to the fifth Dhyani Buddha, white Namse (Vairocana). Again, most of the other chapels are filled with wrathful deities.

The 11 chapels on the **4th floor** are dedicated to teachers, interpreters and translators of obscure orders of Tibetan Buddhism. Exceptions are the Three Kings of Tibet on the north side (eighth chapel clockwise from the steps) and Guru Rinpoche (10th chapel).

The **5th floor**, which is also known as the Bumpa, has four chapels and a fine mandala gives access to the roof of the *kumbum*. Most people are taken in by the outstanding views, especially looking south over the old town where, in the background, the white-walled Gyantse Dzong is perched atop a colossal outcrop. Hidden steps behind a statue on the eastern side lead to the **6th floor** and take you onto the verandah at the level of the eyes painted on the wall (this floor was closed for renovation in 2018).

The **top floor** of the *kumbum* portrays a Tantric manifestation of Sakyamuni (Sakya Thukpa), but you will likely find the way up locked.

Palcho Monastery BUDDHIST MONASTERY
(白居寺; Báijū Sì, Pelkor Chöde Monastery; Map p136; high/low season ¥60/30; ⊘9.30am-6pm, some chapels closed 1-3pm) The high-walled compound in the far north of Gyantse houses Palcho Monastery, founded in

1418. The main assembly hall is of greatest interest, but there are several other chapels to see. There's a small but visible population of 80 monks and a steady stream of prostrating, praying, donation-offering pilgrims doing the rounds almost any time of the day.

This was once a compound of 15 monasteries that brought together three different orders of Tibetan Buddhism – a rare instance of multi-denominational tolerance. Nine of the monasteries were Gelugpa, three were Sakyapa and three belonged to the obscure Büton suborder whose head monastery was Shalu (p148) near Shigatse.

The **main assembly hall** is straight ahead as you walk into the compound, and is where most people begin their explorations. The entrance is decorated with statues of the Four Guardian Kings, and just inside to the right is a large Wheel of Life mural.

The hall is kept quite dark, though most of the faded wall murals are original, dating to the 15th century. The chapels also contain a staggeringly beautiful selection of carved wooden statues, also dating to the monastery's founding.

To the left as you enter is the Dorjeling Lhakhang, a chapel containing a four-headed Nampa Namse (Vairocana) and the other four Dhyani (or Wisdom) Buddhas in dark, ornate wooden frames. The big thangka wrapped in the yak leather bag is displayed during the Saga Dawa festival on the 18th day of the fourth Tibetan month. Pilgrims put their heads in a hole underneath a set of ancient scriptures that is older than the monastery itself.

The impressive main chapel is located in the centre of the hall. The towering central image is of Sakyamuni (Sakya Thukpa), who is flanked by the Past and Future Buddhas. To the right of the main chapel is a lovely Jampa statue. There is an interior kora route around the chapel, which is lined with fine but dusty murals.

The chapel to the right features the Rigsum Gonpo trinity, along with the three religion-kings of Tibet. A small hall within contains a chörten built by Prince Rabten Kunzang Phok for his mother. Outside the door is a large tent used during *cham* (ritual dance) festivals.

There are a number of chapels on the upper floor that, at the time of writing, were only open to religious pilgrims. If you are able to access them, you will find a three-dimensional mandala, wall paintings

of the Indian-looking *mahasiddhas* (highly accomplished Tantric practitioners) and lacquered images of key figures in the Sakyapa lineage. Each of the 84 *mahasiddhas* is unique and shown contorted in a yogic posture.

Photos cost ¥10 to ¥20 per chapel; pay a monk directly as you go through.

Rabse Nunnery BUDDHIST MONASTERY
(热赛尼姑庙; Rèsài Nígū Miaò; Map p136) FREE
This charming nunnery (*ani gompa* in Tibetan) hidden behind the hill that runs between Palcho Monastery (p136) and the Gyantse Dzong (p138), is home to 44 nuns. It is a delightful place decorated with prayer flags, chörtens, *mani lhakhang* (prayer wheel chapels) and butter lamps. There are also some lovely thangka paintings hanging in the main assembly hall.

The 'correct' way to visit is along the clockwise pilgrim trail lined with prayer wheels that goes around the back of the monastery.

The nunnery was moved to its current location in 1985 after two original monasteries further up in the hills were destroyed during the Cultural Revolution. The reconstructed Gomang chörten is filled with inner murals (though you may not be able to glimpse inside).

A maze of streets leads back to the old town along a path that follows the contours of the hillside and offers superb views of the fort in the distance. Be particularly careful of dogs if walking here alone.

Tsang Traditional Folk House MUSEUM
(后藏民俗风情园, Hòuzàng Mínsú Fēngqíng Yuán; ☑0892-817 7555; Penjor Lhunpo village; ¥30; ⊙9am-6pm, closed winter) This private folk museum opposite Palha Manor (p138) offers an excellent introduction into Tibetan farm life. Alongside mock-ups of a traditional kitchen, mustard-seed oil press and *chang* (barley beer) still, are such treasures as a fish-skin saddle, a barley guillotine, and yak-skin bags used for transporting salt. Upstairs, you can learn traditional Tibetan table games such as *sho* (dice) and *bak* (mahjong), before having snacks and excellent home-brewed tea or *chang*, all included in the ticket.

Opened in 2008, the museum is a labour of love for retired couple Dawa Shilo and Drolma, who give visitors a personalised guided tour (some English signage is also present). Make sure you have at least 40

BAYONETS TO GYANTSE

The early-20th-century British invasion of Tibet, also known as the Younghusband expedition, began, as wars sometimes do, with unreliable intelligence. Newspapers were spreading the claim that Russia had designs on Tibet, and many were lapping it up. The British Raj (rule of the Indian subcontinent) feared losing a buffer state and so sent Major Francis Younghusband, an army officer with rich experience of Central Asia, on a diplomatic mission to the Tibetan border. After six months of waiting, no Chinese or Tibetans had showed up for the meetings and it was felt a stronger message had to be sent. Younghusband was instructed to advance on Lhasa with 3000 troops (plus 7000 servants and 4000 yaks) to force a treaty on the Tibetans.

Despite having had previous brushes with British firepower, it seems the Tibetans had little idea of what they were up against. About halfway between Yatung and Gyantse, a small Tibetan army bearing a motley assortment of arms and lucky charms confronted a British force carrying light artillery, Maxim machine guns and modern rifles. The Tibetans' trump card was a charm marked with the seal of the Dalai Lama, which they were told would protect them from British bullets. It didn't. Firing began after a false alarm and the British slaughtered 700 Tibetans in four minutes.

The British buried the Tibetan dead (the Tibetans dug them up at night and carried them off for traditional sky burial) and set up a field hospital, dumbfounding the wounded Tibetans, who could not understand why the British would try to kill them one day and save them the next. The British then continued their advance to Gyantse, but found the town's defensive fort (Gyantse Dzong) deserted. Curiously, rather than occupy the *dzong*, the British camped on the outskirts of Gyantse and waited for officials from Lhasa to arrive. While they waited, Younghusband sped up the Karo-la with a small contingent of troops to take

minutes and a capable Tibetan guide to translate their enthusiastic explanations.

Palha Manor
MUSEUM

(帕拉庄园; Pàlā Zhuāngyuán; Penjor Lhunpo village; low/high season ¥15/30; ⊙9.30am–6pm) This former merchant's house once belonged to the largest noble family in Tsang (the Palha – one of the five largest in Tibet), but is now a government-run museum thick with political spin on the evils of feudal exploitation and pre-liberation Tibet. Only a few fragments remain to give a picture of upper-class Tibetan life a century ago. Might be worth popping in only if you're going to the Tsang Traditional Folk House (p137) across the street.

Guru Lhakhang Temple
BUDDHIST TEMPLE

(莲花生大士寺; Liánhuāshēng Dàshì Sì; Map p136; Yingxiong Beilu; ⊙dawn–dusk) FREE This hugely atmospheric Red Hat sect temple is located east of Gyantse Dzong. The temple is dedicated to the 8th century Indian master Padmasambhava (aka Guru Rinpoche or Guru Lhakhang in Tibetan), who founded Samye Monastery (p115). It dates to the 1400s and is home to 14 monks. There are two small chapels with large central prayer wheels and beautifully colourful wall murals, as well as a larger main prayer hall.

Gönlong Retok Ganden Retreat
RUINS

(ཞིན་ལོང་རག་ལུ་དགོན་; 热托甘丹寺; Rètūo Gāndān Sì) FREE Hidden in the fold of a valley north of town, this ruined and little-visited monastery is a 7km drive from Gyantse from a turn-off near the Rabse Nunnery (p137). Ruins – including what was once the main Drölma Lhakhang – stretch up the mountainside, connected by a dodgy dirt road. This is a nice place for a secluded walk with fine views down the valley to Gyantse.

Gyantse Dzong
FORT

(江孜宗; Jiāngzī Zōng; Map p136) The main reason to make the 20-minute climb to the top of this 14th-century fort is for the fabulous views of Palcho Monastery (p136) and Gyantse's whitewashed old town below. Most visitors drive up halfway to the top but you can walk via the road leading west out of the old town. Unfortunately, the fort is closed to visitors, but it dominates the view from almost everywhere in Gyantse.

The fort was the epicentre of the British attempt to march on Tibet during the Younghusband expedition in 1904.

on 3000 Tibetans who had dug themselves in at over 5000m. The result was the highest land-based battle in British military history and a fine example of frozen stiff upper lip.

After nearly two months of waiting for Lhasa officials, the British troops received orders to retake Gyantse Dzong (which had been reoccupied by Tibetans) and march on Lhasa. Artillery fire breached the walls of the fort, and when one of the shells destroyed the Tibetan gunpowder supply the Tibetans were reduced to throwing rocks at their attackers. The *dzong* fell in one day, with four British casualties and more than 300 Tibetan dead.

With the fort under their command, the British now controlled the road to Lhasa. Younghusband led 2000 troops to the capital with few incidents. In fact, the greatest challenge he faced was getting all the troops across the Yarlung Tsangpo (Brahmaputra River): it took five days of continual ferrying.

Once in Lhasa, Younghusband discovered that the Dalai Lama had fled to Mongolia. After a month, Younghusband managed to get the Tibetan regent to sign an agreement allowing British trade missions at Gyantse and Gartok, near Mt Kailash. (Ironically, the troops discovered that British goods were already trickling into the bazaars – one British soldier wrote that he found a sausage machine made in Birmingham and two bottles of Bulldog stout in the Barkhor.) But the treaty and others that followed in 1906 were largely meaningless because Tibet simply had no capacity to fulfil them.

As for Younghusband himself, the most significant event of the campaign was yet to come. On the evening before his departure, as he looked out over Lhasa, he felt a great wave of emotion, insight and spiritual peace. Younghusband had always been a religious man, but this moment changed him forever. He later wrote, 'that single hour on leaving Lhasa was worth all the rest of a lifetime'.

⚔️ Festivals & Events

Dhama Festival   CULTURAL
(🕙 noon-5pm mid-Jul) If you happen to be in Tibet in mid-July, you can catch Gyantse's three-day Dhama Festival, featuring 19 local villages trying to outdo each other in horse races, yak races, wrestling and traditional dances. Accommodation is tight in Gyantse during the festival, but you could easily commute from Shigatse, two hours away.

🛏️ Sleeping & Eating

Gyantse is a popular stop for tours and has a small but well-formed range of accommodation accepting international travellers.

There is a surprising selection of decent Tibetan restaurants, in Gyantse, some serving western-style food. There are also several supermarkets (超市; *chāoshì*) and a market on Yingxiong Bei/Nanlu selling produce and meat.

Hard-core night owls might be able to track down some late-night karaoke but most travellers are content with a Lhasa beer at Tashi restaurant (p140). The Yeti Hotel's western-style cafe also serves beer and wine into the evening in quiet surrounds.

★ Yeti Hotel   HOTEL $$
(雅迪花园酒店; Yǎdí Huāyuán Jiǔdiàn; Map p136; ☑ 0892-817 5555; 11 Weiguo Lu; d incl breakfast ¥328; ❀✺@📶) The three-star Yeti is easily the best option in Gyantse, offering 24-hour piping hot water, clean, spacious rooms, quality mattresses and reliable wi-fi, so make sure you reserve in advance. The western-style cafe and excellent lobby Chinese restaurant serve everything from Sìchuān favourites and yak steak to pizza, alongside a decent buffet breakfast.

At the time of writing, the Yeti's owners were constructing a second, larger four-star hotel in Gyantse – the **Manor House Hotel** – due to open in summer 2018. If plans go ahead as promised, the hotel will boast sparkling new facilities, including a swimming pool, restaurants and a bar, all in a good location near the Palcho Monastery (p136) complex. Ask your travel agency for details.

Gyantse Hotel   HOTEL $$
(江孜饭店; Jiāngzī Fàndiàn; Map p136; ☑ 0892-817 2222; 2 Shanghai Zhonglu; d ¥320; ✺📶) The largest hotel in town and popular with groups, this cavernous old-school place was built in the 1980s and it shows. The lobby and restaurant are brightened up by colourful Tibetan-style murals. Rooms are

smallish but carpeted, the furniture is pretty worn (hard beds) and the en-suite bathrooms, which have 24-hour hot water, are clean if not a bit dank.

Rindhing Garden
TIBETAN $$

(江孜日鼎园餐厅, Jiāngzī Rìdǐng Yuán Cāntīng; Map p136; ☏0892-817 3566; off Baiju Lu, 白居寺 30米处) This pleasant courtyard restaurant offers Tibetan specialities such as stir-fried yak with celery (¥28), fried potatoes with lamb (¥45) and a selection of different *momos* (dumplings). There are lots of vegetarian options on offer, and in fine weather, locals often sit in the extensive garden for a picnic. Great location two minutes' walk from Palcho Monastery (p136). Plus, it has clean toilets!

Tashi
NEPALI, INTERNATIONAL $$

(扎西餐厅; Zhāxī Cāntīng; Map p136; Yingxiong Nanlu; mains ¥30-50; ⊗8.30am-9pm; 🗟🖉) This Nepali-run place (a branch of Tashi in Shigatse) whips up tasty and filling curries, pizza, pastas and yak sizzlers. It also has the best range of western breakfasts. The decor is Tibetan but the Indian films and Nepali music give it a head-waggling subcontinental vibe.

Yeti Hotel Restaurant
CHINESE $$

(雅迪花园酒店中餐厅; Yǎdí Huāyuán Jiǔdiàn Zhōng Cāntīng; Map p136; 11 Weiguo Lu; dishes ¥40-60) In addition to its upstairs cafe serving western-style meals, the Yeti Hotel operates a smart Chinese restaurant on its ground floor. Most dishes are Sìchuān style with spicy chillis and peppercorns. No English menu.

Gyantse Kitchen
TIBETAN, INTERNATIONAL $$

(江孜厨房; Jiāngzī Chúfáng; Map p136; 11 Shanghai Zhonglu; dishes ¥25-40; ⊗7.30am-10pm; 🗟) This popular local place serves western, Tibetan and Indian favourites, from sandwiches (¥25 to ¥32) to breakfast pancakes (¥25), plus unique fusion dishes like yak pizza (¥45). Particularly nice are the yak *chǎomiàn* (¥30): Chinese-style noodles stir-fried with yak mince and crunchy carrots and bell peppers.

☆ Entertainment

Gyantse
Sound & Light Show
PERFORMING ARTS

(Map p136; Horse-racing Ground; tickets ¥280-480; ⊗9.30pm Jun-Aug) This glitzy song-and-dance show is aimed squarely at Chinese tour groups but is performed on a grand scale, using the entire old town as its backdrop. Expect plenty of happy, shiny minority dances from the all-Tibetan cast of 300, mixed with a dash of patriotic anti-imperialism.

❶ Information

At the time of research, there were no ATMs in Gyantse accepting foreign cards. Shigatse is the nearest place to access money, but come prepared from Lhasa.

❶ Getting There & Around

The drive from Gyantse to Shigatse takes around two hours, but allow half a day with stops en route.

All of Gyantse's sights can be reached comfortably on foot, though most travellers see the sights in the company of their guide and driver. Should you strike out on your own, there are rickshaws and even taxis if you need them.

Nyang-chu Valley གཉང་ཆུ
尼洋曲

The drive from Gyantse to Shigatse wends through the fertile Nyang-chu Valley (Níyángqū), a wide agricultural plain following the Nyang River, fronted by dried-up glacial flows, where Tibetan farmers plough their fields with colourfully decorated livestock. If you're here in spring, you'll see giant red tassels placed on the horns of *dzomo* (a yak-cattle hybrid common in this area) as a sort of lucky talisman before the serious spring ploughing begins. There are a few sights of note along the way – mainly lesser-visited monasteries.

Locals say that 13 of the hills scattered down the valley are bad luck, and so atop each was built a monastery to ward off evil spirits. Drongtse (p141) and Tsechen are two that are worth visiting.

The drive between Gyantse and Shigatse is only a couple of hours and there's nowhere to stay overnight in between.

Normally travellers have lunch when they arrive in Shigatse, but if you get to dallying in some of the quieter monasteries along the way, there are a few teahouses and restaurants in the tidy town of Panam (白朗, Báilǎng), about halfway.

◉ Sights

Tsechen Monastery
BUDDHIST MONASTERY

(རྩེ་ཆེན་དགོན་པ; 慈青寺; Cíqīng Sì) **FREE** The traditional village of Tsechen is located about 5km northwest of Gyantse en route to Shigatse.

The small Sakyapa-school Tsechen Ge Tub-den Rabgye Ling Monastery – home to 26 monks – sits just above the village. In good weather, you might also be able to climb up to the ruined fortress and wander along its defensive walls, where there are great views of the river valley below.

The fortress is believed to have been built as early as the 14th century and the early kings of Gyantse lived here until the 18th century. The British used the site during their 1904 invasion, although it was already partly ruined by then. The current monastery was rebuilt in 1987.

At the time of writing, a new assembly hall was being completed, due to open in 2018. Look for the central statue of Jowo Sakyamuni (only the lower section from the waist down is original) and also the two 1300-year-old stone carvings of Guru Rinpoche and Chenresig. A displayed black-and-white photo of the site from 1927 shows the extents of the original monastery, when it housed 850 monks.

Drongtse Monastery BUDDHIST MONASTERY
(重孜寺, Zhòngzī Sì) FREE On a *tse* (peak) said to resemble a wild yak, this Yellow Hat monastery was founded in 1442, and later adopted as a branch of Tashilhunpo. In the *gönkhang* (protector chapel) look for the mummified human skull (the servant of the monastery's Rinpoche, Singchen Lobsant Gantsen), and an old embroidery of Namtose. The main statute is of the sixth Rinpoche, whose tomb is on the top floor; to the left is the founder and first Rinpoche Lhajun Rinchen Gyatso.

The 15th-century monastery grounds were destroyed during the Cultural Revolution, and the current buildings date to 1985. The monastery is 19km northwest of Gyantse.

Lhori Nunnery BUDDHIST MONASTERY
(Lhori Ani Gompa) FREE This tiny place, home to just nine nuns, is built around two ancient meditation caves of Guru Rinpoche, one of which has a stone footprint of the guru aged eight. It's an atmospheric place and you can clamber inside the candlelit caves (at the back of the small main assembly hall), which house some priceless antique statues. Most of the main buildings date to the 1980s.

It's signposted 1km up a side road along the route from Gyantse to Shigatse, and was undergoing some renovations at the time of writing.

A couple of kilometres further is **Chenresig Monastery**, thought to have been built by King Songsten Gampo.

Gepeling Water Mill HISTORIC BUILDING
(¥5) This traditional water mill is located halfway between Gyantse and Shigatse. Peek into the back room to see the working water-powered stone mill grinding barley into *tsampa* (roasted-barley flour). A shop sells *tsampa* milled on site, as well as whole seeds as snacks. There's also a public toilet here (¥2).

Changme Monastery BUDDHIST MONASTERY
(Changmejian) FREE About 41km from Gyantse is the county capital of Panam and the 15th-century Changme Monastery. Levelled in the Cultural Revolution, the monastery was rebuilt in 2006 and is home to 18 monks. In the inner chapel look for three lifelike statues: King Trisong Detsen (wearing a white hat), Shantarakshita (wearing a red hat) and Padmasambhava.

According to lore, it was Shantarakshita (at the behest of Trisong Detsen) who invited Padmasambhava to Tibet in order to subdue Tibetan devils and demons.

ℹ Getting There & Away

It's a 90km drive from Gyantse to Shigatse along a modern highway. The drive takes a maximum of two hours, but allow a little longer if you want to visit monasteries and stop for livestock-based photo ops along the way.

Shigatse ༄གཞིས་ཀ་རྩེ 日喀则

☏ 0892 / POP 120,000 / ELEV 3840M

Tibet's second-largest city and the traditional capital of Tsang province, Shigatse (གཞིས་ཀ་རྩེ; 日喀则; Rìkāzé) is a modern, sprawling city, with wide boulevards humming with traffic. As you drive in across the plains, the sight of the Potala-lookalike Shigatse Dzong, high on a hilltop overlooking the town, will probably fire your imagination, but the fort is empty and most of what you see dates from a 2007 reconstruction. It is Tashilhunpo Monastery that is the real draw here. Since the Mongol sponsorship of the Gelugpa order in the 17th century, Tashilhunpo has been the seat of the Panchen Lama, the second most important spiritual figure in Tibetan Buddhism after the Dalai Lama.

Shigatse

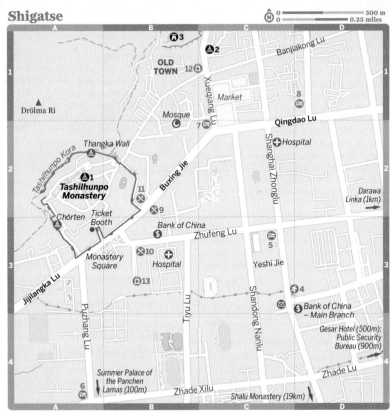

Shigatse

◎ Top Sights
1 Tashilhunpo Monastery A2

◎ Sights
2 Mani Lhakhang C1
3 Shigatse Dzong B1

✈ Activities, Courses & Tours
4 Kunga Dhundup Blind Massage............C3

🛏 Sleeping
5 Qomolangzong Hotel...............................C3
6 Sakya Lhundup Palace Hotel.................A4
7 Tashi Choeta Hotel C2
8 Tibet Zangba Hotel D1

🍴 Eating
9 Songtsen Tibetan Restaurant..............B2
10 Sumptuous Tibetan Restaurant...........B3
Tashi Choeta ....(see 7)
Third Eye ....(see 10)
11 Tibet Family Restaurant B2
Wordo Tibetan Courtyard ....(see 6)

🛍 Shopping
12 Shigatse Tibetan Market B1
13 Tibet Gang Gyen Carpet Factory..........B3

History

The town of Shigatse, formerly known as Samdruptse, has long been an important trading and administrative centre. The Tsang kings exercised their power from the *dzong* (fort) and the fort later became the residence of the governor of Tsang.

Tashilhunpo Monastery is one of the six great Gelugpa (Yellow Hat sect) institutions, along with Drepung, Sera and Ganden Monasteries in Lhasa, and Kumbum (Tǎ'ěr Sì) and Labrang in Amdo (modern Gānsù and Qīnghǎi provinces). It was founded in 1447 by Genden Drup, a disciple of Tsongkhapa, the Yellow Hat sect founder himself. Genden Drup was retroactively named the first Dalai Lama and he is enshrined in a stupa inside Tashilhunpo. Despite this important association, Tashilhunpo Monastery was initially isolated from mainstream Gelugpa affairs, which were centred in the Lhasa region.

The monastery's standing rocketed when the fifth Dalai Lama declared his teacher – then the abbot of Tashilhunpo – to be a manifestation of Öpagme (Amitabha). Thus Tashilhunpo became the seat of an important lineage: the Panchen ('great scholar') Lamas. Unfortunately, with the establishment of this lineage of spiritual and temporal leaders – second only to the Dalai Lamas – rivalry was introduced to the Gelugpa order.

⊙ Sights & Activities

The modern city is divided into a tiny Tibetan old town – a maze of mud houses and dirt streets huddled at the foot of the fort – and a rapidly expanding modern city that has all the charm of, well, every other expanding modern Chinese town.

★ Tashilhunpo Monastery

BUDDHIST MONASTERY

(བཀྲ་ཤིས་ལྷུན་པོ་ ; 扎什伦布寺; Zhāshílúnbù Sì; Map p142; ¥55; ⊙ 9am-6.30pm) One of the few monasteries in Tibet to weather the stormy seas of the Cultural Revolution, Tashilhunpo remains relatively unscathed. It is a pleasure to explore the cobbled lanes twisting around its aged buildings. Covering 70,000 sq metres, the monastery is now the largest functioning religious institution in Tibet – home to around 950 monks – and one of its great monastic sights. The huge golden statue of the Future Buddha is the largest gilded statue in the world.

The ticket booth is located at the monastery's main southern entrance. From the entrance to the monastery, visitors get a grand view. Above the white monastic quarters is a crowd of ochre buildings topped with gold – the tombs of the past Panchen Lamas. To the right, and higher still, is the Festival Thangka Wall, hung with massive, colourful thangkas during festivals. Circumnavigating the exterior of the compound is a one-hour kora that takes you into the hills behind the monastery.

As you start to explore the various buildings, you'll see a lot of photos of the ninth, 10th and 11th Panchen Lamas. The ninth Panchen Lama is recognisable by his little moustache. The 11th Panchen Lama is the disputed Chinese-sponsored lama, now in his early 20s and occasionally resident in the nearby Summer Palace.

Morning is the best time to visit because more of the chapels are open. Monks start to lock chapels up for lunch after 12.30pm. Return around 6pm and you may find monks chanting in the main assembly hall.

Severe restrictions on photography are in place inside the monastic buildings. The going cost for a photograph varies but be prepared for a pricey ¥75 per chapel, and as high as ¥150 in the assembly hall. Video camera fees are an absurd ¥1000 to ¥1800 in some chapels.

Walk through the monastery and bear left for the first and probably most impressive of Tashilhunpo's sights: the Chapel of Jampa (Jamkhang Chenmo). An entire building houses a 26m figure of Jampa (Maitreya), the Future Buddha. The statue was made in 1914 under the auspices of the ninth Panchen Lama and took some 900 artisans and labourers four years to complete. The impressive, finely crafted and serene-looking statue towers high over the viewer. Each of Jampa's fingers is more than 1m long, and in excess of 300kg of gold went into his coating, much of which is also studded with precious stones. On the walls surrounding the image there are 1000 more gold paintings of Jampa set against a red background.

The Victory Chapel (Namgyel Lhakhang) is a centre for philosophy and houses a large statue of Tsongkhapa flanked by his two disciples, and also Jampa and Jampelyang (Manjushri). Look for the photo of the ninth Panchen Lama with his favourite dog.

The tomb of the 10th Panchen Lama (Serdung Sisum Namgyel) is a dazzling gold-plated funeral chörten. A statue of the 10th Panchen Lama, who died in 1989, is displayed atop the tomb. The ceiling of the chapel is painted with a Kalachakra (Dukhor in Tibetan) mandala, with a mural of the deity on the left wall, and the walls are painted with gold buddhas in various *mudras* (hand gestures). From here you can normally follow the pilgrims upstairs to proceed through a line of upper chapels, passing en route an image of the Chinese

TSANG SHIGATSE

Tashilhunpo Monastery

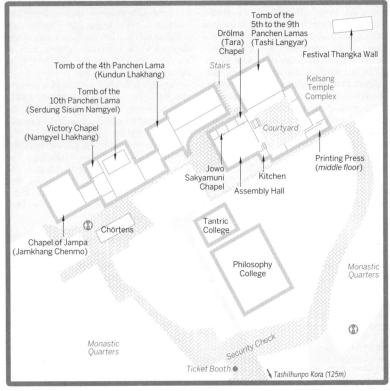

Tomb of the 5th to the 9th Panchen Lamas (Tashi Langyar)

Drölma (Tara) Chapel

Festival Thangka Wall

Tomb of the 4th Panchen Lama (Kundun Lhakhang)

Stairs

Kelsang Temple Complex

Tomb of the 10th Panchen Lama (Serdung Sisum Namgyel)

Victory Chapel (Namgyel Lhakhang)

Courtyard

Jowo Sakyamuni Chapel

Kitchen

Printing Press (*middle floor*)

Assembly Hall

Chörtens

Tantric College

Chapel of Jampa (Jamkhang Chenmo)

Philosophy College

Monastic Quarters

Monastic Quarters

Security Check

Ticket Booth ●

↘ Tashilhunpo Kora (125m)

TSANG SHIGATSE

Emperor Qianlong who was a disciple of the sixth Panchen Lama.

The gold-roofed chapel holds the **tomb of the fourth Panchen Lama (Kundun Lhakhang)**, Lobsang Choekyi Gyeltsen (1567–1662), teacher of the fifth Dalai Lama. This was the only mausoleum at Tashilhunpo to be spared during the Cultural Revolution. The 11m-high funerary chörten is inlaid with semiprecious stones and contains 85kg of gold.

The **Kelsang Temple** is a remarkable collection of buildings, with its centrepiece large courtyard the focus of festival and monastic activities. It's a fascinating place to sit and watch the pilgrims and monks go about their business. Monks congregate here before their lunchtime service in the main assembly hall. A huge prayer pole rears from the centre of the flagged courtyard and the surrounding walls are painted with buddhas. Pilgrims put their ears up to a shrine

of Drölma, who is said to have the power of speech.

The **assembly hall** is one of the oldest buildings in Tashilhunpo, dating from the 15th-century founding of the monastery. The massive throne that dominates the centre of the hall is the throne of the Panchen Lamas. The hall is a dark, moody place, with rows of mounted cushions for monks, and long thangkas, depicting the various incarnations of the Panchen Lama, suspended from the ceiling. The central inner chapel holds a wonderfully ornate statue of Sakyamuni (Sakya Thukpa), while the chapel to the right holds several images of Drölma (Tara). Pilgrims crawl around this chapel underneath shelves of Buddhist scriptures.

You can also visit the huge **Tomb of the Fifth to the Ninth Panchen Lamas (Tashi Langyar)**, built by the 10th Panchen Lama to replace tombs destroyed in the Cultural

Revolution. The central statue is of the ninth Panchen Lama. The 10th Panchen Lama returned to Shigatse from Běijīng to dedicate the tomb in 1989. He fulfilled his prediction that he would die on Tibetan soil just three days after the ceremony.

There are a dozen other chapels in the complex on this floor. Follow the pilgrims on a clockwise circuit, ending up in a tangle of chapels above the assembly hall. Here in the far left (upper) corner chapel you'll find views of the two-storey Jampa statue below and, to the right, the tombs of the first and third Panchen Lamas and first Dalai Lama, with a fine mural of Buddha descending to earth (as celebrated in Tibet's Lhabab Dechen festival). Look for the golden footprint of the first Dalai Lama mounted on the pillar.

Descend to the middle floor and do another clockwise circuit, taking in the interesting corner **printing press**, where monks sell block prints and protective amulets.

As you leave Tashilhunpo, it is also possible to visit the monastery's two remaining colleges, the **Tantric College** and the brown **Philosophy College**. They are on the left-hand side as you walk down towards the main gate. Neither is particularly interesting but you might be lucky and find yourself in time for debating, which is held in the courtyard of the Philosophy College.

Summer Palace of the Panchen Lamas
PALACE

(འདས་ཆེན་སྐལ་བཟང་ཕོ་བྲང་; 德庆格桑颇彰; Déqìng Gésāng Pōzhāng; ¥30; ⊙9.30am-noon & 3.30-6pm) Though it ranks far below Tashilhunpo (p143), if you have extra time in Shigatse, pay a visit to this walled palace complex at the southwestern end of town. The original palace was built in 1844 by the seventh Panchen Lama, Tenpei Nyima and later destroyed, and the current complex was built in 1955 by the 10th Panchen Lama. It's known in Tibetan as the Dechen Kalzang Podrang.

The bottom hall has a pair of massive murals, one of which depicts the 18 levels of Buddhist hell with sadistic ingenuity, complete with humans being boiled, dismembered, speared, hacked and disembowelled.

On the ground floor (opposite the Panchen Lama's stuffed dog) are two rooms, which an attendant monk might open for you. The first room is a *gönkhang* (protector chapel) that features Nyeser Chöda Chenpo, the protector of Tashilhunpo. The second room contains images of the 10th Panchen Lama's two *yunze* (spiritual tutors).

Walk up the grand staircase to the 2nd floor where you will find the 10th Panchen Lama's **sitting rooms**, one of which contains his desk and telephones. This floor also holds his **audience chamber**. Each room contains a *shuegje* (throne), to which pilgrims will bow. The attendant monk may even reveal one of the Panchen Lama's shoes, and proceed to bless you by rubbing the holy shoe on the back of your neck and head.

The palace is about 1km south of Tashilhunpo. Follow the road to the end and turn right into the gated compound. Buy tickets at the gate, then walk or drive further into the compound's main gate.

Shigatse Dzong
FORT

(གཞིས་ཀ་རྩེ་རྫོང་; 日喀则宗; Rìkāzé Zōng; Map p142) Once the residence of the kings of Tsang and later the governor of Tsang, very little remained of this *dzong* (fort) after it was destroyed in the popular uprising of 1959. Rebuilt in the 2000s, Shigatse is now once again graced with an impressive hilltop fort that bears a close resemblance to the Potala, albeit on a smaller scale. The *dzong* was empty and off-limits at the time of research, but is an impressive mark on Shigatse's skyline.

Darawa Linka
PARK

(དྲ་ར་བའི་གླིང་ཁ; 达热瓦林卡, Dárèwǎ Línkǎ; cnr Jilin Lu & Qingdai Lu; ⊙9am-late summer only) **FREE** Locals make merry at this park on the eastern side of Shigatse. Grab a bottle of Lhasa Beer and join them. There are a couple of dozen tents where people kick back, drink and play *sho* (a Tibetan board game) and mahjong. This is also known as the local pick-up spot so you'll see lots of eligible youngsters prowling for potential mates. On weekends it's packed with picnickers.

Kunga Dhundup Blind Massage
MASSAGE

(盲人按摩中心; Mángrén Ànmó Zhōngxīn; Map p142; ✆136 2899 5921; Room 034, Shigatse Hotel, 13 Shanghai Zhonglu; per hour ¥130-150; ⊙11am-11pm) A graduate of the excellent Braille Without Borders training program, English-speaking Kunga offers Tibetan, Chinese and foot massages from a room in the Shigatse Hotel. Ring first or, even better, get your hotel to arrange for him to come to your room.

TASHILHUNPO KORA

The kora around Tashilhunpo Monastery takes an hour or two to complete. From the monastery's main gate, follow the walls in a clockwise direction and look for an alley on the right. The alley curves around the western wall, past *tsatsa* (clay icon) makers, stone carvers and monks reciting scripture for donations, to climb into the hills above, where lines of prayer flags spread over the dry slopes like giant colourful spider limbs. The views of the compound below are wonderful.

After about 20 minutes, you pass the 13-storey white wall used to hang a giant thangka at festival time. The path then splits in two: down the hill to complete the circuit of the monastery, or along the ridge to Shigatse Dzong (p145), a walk of around 20 minutes.

From the *dzong* (fort), head down to the old town Tibetan market (p148), stopping afterwards at the particularly charming and atmospheric roadside **mani lhakhang** (Map p142; Xueqiang Lu; prayer wheel chapel).

★ Festivals & Events

Tashilhunpo Monastery Festival   CULTURAL
During the second week of the fifth lunar month (around June/July), Tashilhunpo Monastery becomes the scene of a three-day festival, featuring masked dances, the creation of a sand mandala and the unveiling of three huge thangkas, one for each day of the festival.

🛏 Sleeping

Shigatse has a good range of decent hotels, most with wi-fi and 24-hour hot water.

Young House Hotel   HOTEL $
(康勋宾馆; Kāngxūn Bīnguǎn; ☑0892-851 5234; 262 Shanghai Nanlu; dm/d ¥100/200; ☎) The rooms at this very budget hotel are surprisingly clean, though lack natural light, and come with en-suite shower-over-toilet bathrooms. Downsides are that it's too far to walk to Tashilhunpo and the common areas are a bit stinky and grotty. There's a Tibetan hotpot restaurant attached. An option only for travellers really penny-pinching. No breakfast.

Sakya Lhundup Palace Hotel   HOTEL $$
(萨迦龙珠宫廷饭店; Sàjiā Lóngzhū Gōngtíng Fàndiàn; Map p142; ☑0892-866 6666; 24 Zhade Xilu, cnr of Puzhang Lu; d/tr/ste ¥260/360/560; ❄☎) This three-star hotel offers modern, fresh and spacious rooms – all very clean – and there's a lovely, sunny atrium bar and restaurant surrounded by interior prayer wheels, where the included breakfast is served. Be aware they don't offer non-smoking rooms. It's right across from the entrance to the Summer Palace of the Panchen Lamas (p145).

Tibet Zangba Hotel   HOTEL $$
(藏巴大酒店; Zàngbā Dàjiǔdiàn; Map p142; ☑0892-866 7888; 9 Renbu Lu; d/tr ¥280/340; ❄☎) This three-star hotel is a good choice with fresh rooms that are modern and carpeted, with fairly modern bathrooms and lots of Tibetan touches. There's a connected Tibetan restaurant. Rooms at the back have stellar views of Tashilhunpo Monastery. No non-smoking rooms.

Qomolangzong Hotel   HOTEL $$$
(乔穆朗宗酒店; Qiáomùlǎngzōng Jiǔdiàn; Map p142; ☑0892-866 6333; cnr Shanghai Zhonglu & Zhufeng Lu; d incl breakfast ¥885; ❄❄☎) This plush 4-star hotel opened in 2014, offering an impressive lobby of stone and wood, and extremely spacious western-style rooms. Some of the upper-floor rooms have views of Tashilhunpo Monastery. There is a top-floor teahouse-restaurant with beautiful views over the city. Surprisingly little English is spoken.

Gesar Hotel   HOTEL $$$
(格萨尔酒店; Gésà'ěr Jiǔdiàn; ☑0892-880 0088; Longjiang Lu; r standard/deluxe incl breakfast ¥380/480; ❄@☎) This four-star giant has clean and modern Tibetan-style rooms, each decorated with its own thangka of Gesar Ling, and a pleasant rooftop teahouse, though the location in the southern suburbs is a bit of a drag. The deluxe rooms are huge and there's 24-hour hot water, but the glass-walled bathrooms won't work unless you and your roommate are close friends.

The large spa complex at the back offers massage and Tibetan herb baths, as well as a dry sauna filled with salt imported from Pakistan.

Tashi Choeta Hotel HOTEL $$$

(扎西曲塔大酒店; Zhāxī Qūtǎ Dàjiǔdiàn; Map p142; ☎0892-883 0111; 2 Xueqiang Lu; d/tr ¥690/800; ❄@🛜) A comfortable four-star place with some Tibetan decor, huge rooms with decently soft beds and a great central location. Bathrooms are modern and spacious but hot water is only available in mornings and evenings. Breakfast is a huge buffet spread of mostly Chinese-style dishes.

✕ Eating & Drinking

Shigatse offers the last options for international food until you get to the Nepali border.

Shigatse has a few karaoke bars hidden in the modern section of town, though most visitors are content to socialise over a post-dinner Lhasa Beer at one of the town's busy restaurants.

Tashi Choeta DUMPLINGS, TIBETAN $

(Map p142; Xueqiang Lu; 8 dumplings ¥20) This bright restaurant offers Amdo-style food, namely steamed yak-meat *momos*. And there's Lhasa Beer to wash them down with. Watch the chefs at work inside a glassed-in kitchen at the entrance. The picture menu (no English) is on the wall above. Point out what you want, pay at the counter and choose any table.

Despite having the same name as Tashi Choeta Hotel and being located right next door, the two establishments are apparently unaffiliated.

Sumptuous Tibetan Restaurant TIBETAN $

(丰盛藏式餐厅; Fēngshèng Zàngshì Cāntīng; Map p142; Zhufeng Lu; mains ¥15-50; ⊙10am-10pm) This centrally located option offers comfy Tibetan-style seats and decor inside and a pleasant back terrace. Prices are reasonable, the food is decent and the staff are eager to please. The menu and management are the same as at the Tibet Family Restaurant.

Tibet Family Restaurant TIBETAN $

(丰盛餐厅; Fēngshèng Cāntīng, Phuntshok Serzikhang; Map p142; Buxing Jie; dishes ¥15-30; ⊙8am-10pm) This teahouse-style Tibetan place is a local favourite for its excellent food, nice outdoor seating and friendly clientele. It also boasts the perfect people-watching location, right at the end of the monastery kora. The food runs from simple and fresh vegetable options to more adventurous yak-meat dishes.

★ Third Eye NEPALI $$

(雪莲餐厅; Xuělián Cāntīng; Map p142; ☎0892-883 8898; Zhufeng Lu; dishes ¥25-50; ⊙9am-10pm) A Nepali-run place that is popular with both locals and tourists. Watch as locals sip *thugpa* (Tibetan noodle soup) while travellers treat their taste buds to the city's best Indian curries and sizzlers. The chicken tikka masala and the yak steak are both excellent. It's upstairs, next to the Gang Gyan Orchard Hotel.

Songtsen Tibetan Restaurant INTERNATIONAL $$

(松赞西藏餐厅; Sōngzàn Xīzàng Cāntīng; Map p142; ☎0892-883 2469; Buxing Jie; dishes ¥30-50; ⊙8.30am-10.30pm) Popular and cosy Nepali-style place that serves hearty breakfasts, yak burgers and curries to tourist groups. It has a great location on the 'pedestrian-only' street, offering good views of the pilgrims ambling past.

★ Wordo Tibetan Courtyard TIBETAN $$$

(吾尔朵大宅院; Wú'ěrduǒ Dà Zháiyuàn; Map p142; ☎0892-882 3994; 10 Zhade Xilu; dishes ¥50-70; ⊙9.30am-11pm) For something a bit special, head out to this stylish Tibetan restaurant near the Summer Palace of the Panchen Lamas (p145). Sit in one of Tibet's loveliest courtyards, bedecked in swirling prayer flags, and enjoy super-fresh Tibetan specialities such as curried potatoes and potato *momos* (dumplings), as well as more ambitious (and pricey) offerings such as roast lamb's leg (¥320).

At the time of writing, the owners were in the process of setting up a small **museum** of antiquities and Tibetan cultural objects adjacent to the courtyard.

🔒 Shopping

The street known as Buxing Jie (Pedestrian Street, though it is not, in fact, pedestrianised) running northeast from the monastery is the best place for Tibetan crafts. The closer you get to the monastery, the more you'll see monks' supply stores selling everything from incense to prayer flags. There is also an outdoor market peddling inexpensive Tibetan jewellery and souvenirs.

Tibet Gang Gyen Carpet Factory HOMEWARES

(西藏刚坚地毯厂; Xīzàng Gāngjiān Dìtǎn Chǎng; Map p142; ☎139 0892 1399; 9 Zhufeng Lu; ⊙9am-1pm & 3-7pm Mon-Sat) This workshop employs local women to weave quality wool carpets.

Upon arrival you'll be directed to the workshop, where you can watch the craftswomen work, singing as they weave, dye, trim and spin; you're free to take photos.

Expect to pay US$920, including shipping, for a carpet measuring 190cm by 90cm. All the wool used is locally sourced and the vegetable and mineral dyes are natural. Credit cards are accepted.

Shigatse Tibetan Market   ARTS & CRAFTS
(Map p142; Bangjiakong Lu; ⊙10am-6pm) In this grimy, open-air market in Shigatse's old town you can pick up low-grade Tibetan crafts and souvenirs, such as prayer wheels, rosaries and jewellery. Bargain hard. The street market just to the east is the best place to get a Tibetan *chuba* (cloak).

ℹ Information

Bank of China The **main branch** (中国银行; Zhōngguó Yínháng; Map p142; Shanghai Zhonglu; ⊙9.30am-6pm Mon-Fri, 11am-4pm Sat & Sun) in the south part of town has a 24-hour ATM. The most useful **branch** (中国银行; Zhōngguó Yínháng; Map p142; Zhufeng Lu; ⊙9.30am-6pm Mon-Sat, from 10am Sun) is a short walk from the monastery square, and also has a 24-hour ATM.

Public Security Bureau (PSB; 公安局; Gōng'ānjú; ☑0892-882 2240; Jilin Nanlu; ⊙9.30am-12.30pm & 3.30-6pm Mon-Fri, 10am-1.30pm Sat & Sun) Your guide will likely have to stop here for half an hour to register and/or pick up an alien's travel permit for the Friendship Hwy or western Tibet. It's in the southern suburbs, near the Gesar Hotel.

ℹ Getting There & Around

AIR
Tibet Airlines has daily flights from Shigatse's Peace Airport, 45km east of town, to Chéngdū (¥1850). China Eastern also runs two flights a week to Shànghǎi Hóngqiáo, stopping in Xī'ān (¥3920).

TRAIN
The 250km train spur line from Lhasa to Shigatse opened in late 2014 and international travellers can now theoretically take these trains as part of their guided tour. Though this option may be a lot faster, travelling by train means you miss many opportunities to visit some of the lesser-known monasteries en route from Lhasa, and also the chance to stand breathless at some of the region's high mountain passes.

TAXI
Central Shigatse can be comfortably explored on foot but many of the hotels are a short drive away. For short trips around town you can use a taxi – anywhere in town costs ¥10.

Around Shigatse

Shalu Monastery   BUDDHIST MONASTERY
(ཞ་ལུ་དགོན་པ; 夏鲁寺; Xiàlǔ Sì; ¥60) It's a treat for the traveller when a sight is both a pleasure to explore and of great artistic importance. Such is Shalu Monastery, which dates back to the 11th century. It's worth a visit for its fine murals and pilgrim crowd, though a ticket is somewhat pricey.

The monastery rose to prominence in the 14th century when its abbot, Büton Rinchen Drup, emerged as the foremost interpreter and compiler of Sanskrit Buddhist texts of the day. (A suborder, the Büton, formed around him.)

It also became a centre for training in skills such as trance walking and *thumo* (generating internal heat to survive in cold weather), feats made famous by the flying monks of Alexandra David-Neel's book *Magic and Mystery in Tibet*.

In the abstract, the design of the monastery represents the paradise of Chenresig (Avalokiteshvara, the Bodhisattva of Compassion), a haven from all worldly suffering. In the concrete, Shalu is the only monastery in Tibet that combines Tibetan and Chinese styles in its design. Much of the original structure was destroyed by an earthquake in the 14th century and, as this was a time of Mongol patronage, many Han artisans were employed in the reconstruction. The green-tiled Chinese-style roof, clearly visible as you approach, is one of the monastery's most easily recognisable features.

What remained of the original 11th-century Tibetan-style monastery was largely destroyed in the Cultural Revolution, but the Chinese-influenced inner Serkhang has survived reasonably well, as it was used as a storeroom and therefore spared. If you enjoy looking at murals, Shalu has some fine ones from the 14th century that fuse Chinese, Mongol and Newari styles. You'll want your phone light or a torch to see them in the darker halls.

The southern Kanjur Lhakhang has particularly lovely Newari-style murals depicting the five Dhyani Buddhas. The main inner **Serkhang** has a black stone statue of Chenresig Kasrapani, the monastery's holiest relic, as well as a vase (in the right corner) from which pilgrims receive a blessing of sacred water. The northern **Gusum Lhakhang**, so named for its three doors, has more fine murals, including one in the left corner depicting the monastery's founder. The walls lining the interior kora path hold some of the finest murals, so ask for a monk to open the gate if it is closed.

There are a couple of upper chapels, including the ancient-feeling **Yum Lhakhang** with its inner kora and other chapels with fine mandala murals. On the way out you can ask the ticket sellers to show you the sacred wood block which confers blessings on anyone who sees it. Monks sell block prints of the now-faded mandala.

Shalu Monastery is 4km off the Shigatse–Gyantse road. En route you can stop off at the 1000-year-old **Gyengong Lhakhang**, a small chapel that actually pre-dates Shalu. Don't miss the sacred mushroom growing on the ground-floor pillar and the upstairs stone basin where Sakya Pandita washed his head before receiving his *gelong* monastic vows. Pilgrims put their heads against the important image of protectress Palden Lhamo, while students hang pens from the cabinet to get a little extra help with their exam results.

From Shalu you can drive for 10 minutes up to **Ri-puk Hermitage**, a former meditation centre and summertime residence for Shalu's monks built around a sacred spring and destroyed chörten. There are lovely views of the Shalu Valley here. A two-day trek to Ngor Monastery starts from here.

Yungdrungling Monastery
BUDDHIST MONASTERY

(雍竹林寺, Yōngzhúlín Sì) FREE Just visible across the river from the road between Lhasa and Shigatse is the Bönpo Yungdrungling Monastery. The monastery, founded in 1834, was once the second-most influential Bön monastic institution in Tibet and home to 700 monks. At first glance, Yungdrungling looks much like a Buddhist monastery, but if you look closely you'll note the swastikas and prayer wheels swirling anticlockwise. You may find your guide and driver are reluctant to enter the monastery grounds.

There are currently around 80 monks here, from all over Tibet. If one of them can find the key, you can visit the large *dukhang* (assembly hall), with its impressive thrones of the monastery's two resident lamas. There are 1300 small iron statues of Tonpa Shenrab (the equivalent of Sakyamuni) along the walls. You may also be able to visit a couple of chapels beside the main hall, including the Namgyel Lhakhang and **Kudung Lhakhang**, the latter featuring the tomb of the monastery founder and Bön protector Gyachen Traksen. Remember to make the rounds in an anticlockwise direction.

The monastery is 80km east of Shigatse, on the road to Lhasa and the north bank of the Yarlung Tsangpo (Brahmaputra River), just east of where the Nangung-chu meets it. Cross the Bailey bridge and follow the dirt road (in the process of being paved at the time of writing) north along the Nangung-chu to a road bridge. The monastery is 7km from the main road.

Nartang Monastery
BUDDHIST MONASTERY

(纳唐寺, Nàtáng Sì) FREE Just a few kilometres outside of Shigatse, this 12th-century Kadampa monastery is famed for woodblock printing the Nartang canon in the 18th century. Treasures in the assembly hall include small statues of Denba Tortumba said to have the power to control lightning; a mantra written in stone by the first Dalai Lama; and the self-arising stone horns and footprints of the wild yak that helped install the monastery's foundation stones.

The chapel to the left is the old *barkhang* (printing press), though printing these days takes place in the room next to the entry gate. Definitely take a peek inside to see local craftsman at work hand-printing scriptures (you can take photos, too).

This makes for an easy stop en route to Lhatse and Shegar.

Sakya
ས་སྐྱ་ 萨迦

☑ 0892 / POP 5000 / ELEV 4320M

A detour to visit the small town of Sakya (Sàjiā) is a treat for any trip down the Friendship Hwy. The draw is Sakya Monastery, which ranks as one of the most atmospheric, impressive and unique monasteries in Tibet. Moreover, Sakya occupies a pivotal place in Tibetan history.

In recent years Sakya has transformed from a village into a town and the area around the monastery has been developed by a private company to include a huge parking lot and a hefty entry fee, but Sakya still feels off the grid.

The town is southwest of Shigatse, about 25km off the Southern Friendship Hwy, accessed via a half-paved road through a pretty farming valley.

◎ Sights

Sakya has two monasteries, on either side of the Trum-chu. The heavy, brooding, fortress-like monastery south of the river is the more impressive main complex, and the only one open to visitors currently. The hillside northern monastery, largely reduced to picturesque ruins (p151), is undergoing restoration work and was closed to visitors at the time of research, but there are fine views of it from the main monastery's upper rampart kora.

One characteristic feature of the Sakya region is the colouring of its buildings. Unlike the standard whitewashing that you see elsewhere in Tibet, Sakya's buildings are dark grey with white-and-red vertical stripes. The colouring symbolises the Rigsum Gonpo (the trinity of bodhisattvas) and stands as a mark of Sakya authority. Sakya literally means 'pale earth'.

★ **Sakya Monastery**   BUDDHIST MONASTERY
(萨迦寺; Sàjiā Sì; ¥60; ⊙9am-6pm) The immense, grey, thick-walled southern monastery is one of Tibet's most impressive constructed sights, and one of the largest monasteries – home to about 200 monks. Established in 1268, it was designed defensively, with watchtowers on each corner of its high walls. Inside, the dimly lit hall exudes a sanctity and is on a scale that few others can rival. Morning is the best time to visit as most chapels are closed over the lunch period.

Directly ahead from the east-wall main entrance is the entry to the inner courtyard and then the main assembly hall (Lhakhang Chenmo or Tsokchen Dukhang), a huge structure with walls 16m high and 3.5m thick.

At first glance the assembly hall may strike you as being like most others in Tibet: a dark interior illuminated with shafts of sunlight and the warm glow of butter lamps; an omnipresent smell of burning butter; and an array of gilded statues representing buddhas, bodhisattvas, Tibetan kings and lamas. But even weary tour groups seem to quickly recognise the age, beauty and sanctity of Sakya. Plan to spend time just soaking up the sacred, medieval atmosphere. You'll find few that are its equal.

A few things to look specifically for in the hall are the huge drum in the far left corner and the massive sacred pillars, some of which are made of entire tree trunks and are famous throughout Tibet. One reputedly was a gift from Kublai Khan.

Another gift from Kublai to the monastery is Sakya's famous white conch shell, which was brought from India and currently sits in a gilded mandala-shaped box in the centre of the hall. Pilgrims queue to hear the soft, low sound of the sacred conch being blown by an attendant monk.

The walls of the assembly hall are lined with towering gilded buddhas, which are unusual in that many also serve as reliquaries for former Sakya abbots. The buddha in the far left corner is said to enshrine a tooth of the Buddha. The large nearby chörten is the funeral stupa of the monastery's 40th abbot; the statue to the right of this houses the tooth of Sangye Wosum, the primordial Buddha. The central Sakyamuni statue enshrines the clothes and relics of Sakya Pandita, though the head monk told us that it also holds the golden turds of Guru Rinpoche that turned into a conch. To the right of the central buddha are statues of Jampelyang (Manjushri), a seated Jampa (Maitreya) and a Dorje Chang (Vajradhara).

Sakya's famous library, long considered the greatest in Tibet, is also accessible from this hall and worth a visit for its floor-to-ceiling collection of around 24,000 texts comprising 8848 reams of scripture. The huge manuscript displayed at the end is written in gold and is 800 years old – the largest and longest scripture in Tibet.

As you exit the assembly hall the chapel to the right (south) is the Phurbu Lhakhang, named for the ancient four-faced metal *phurbu* displayed in a 3D mandala and taken out once a year. Central images are of Sakyamuni (Sakya Thukpa) and Jampelyang (Manjushri), while wall-sized murals behind depict Tsepame (Amitayus) to the left, Drölma (Tara) and white, multi-armed Namgyelma (Vijaya) to the far left, as well as a medicine buddha, two Sakyamunis and Jampa (Maitreya). The giant puppets in the corners are used in annual *cham* (ritual dance) in the 11th Tibetan lunar month.

To the north of the inner courtyard is the Nguldung Lhakhang containing 11 gorgeous silver chörtens, which are also reliquaries for former Sakya abbots. Look to the left corner for the sand mandala inside a dirty glass case. A sometimes-locked door leads into a back chapel with additional amazing chörtens and mandala murals.

Bring a light source as the room is even dimmer than others.

Next door is a **Relic Exhibition** (admission ¥20), which contains several of the monastery's prize statues, including a leaf inscribed with a Tibetan mantra, and the hat, cup and saddle of the monastery's founder.

As you exit the inner courtyard take the entryway left to the **Tsechu Lhakhang**, which houses a speaking statue of Guru Rinpoche and funeral chörtens from the lineage holders of Drölma Phodrang (Sakya had two ruling houses, the Drölma Phodrang and the Phutsok Phodrang).

There are a couple of chapels open outside of this central complex (but still within the walled compound), the most interesting of which is the very spooky protector chapel of the **Lhakhang Lhodrang**. If the thick incense doesn't get you, the terrifying monsters, huge *cham* masks and demonic yaks that wait in the dark recesses just might.

There are several other *gönkhangs* (protector chapels) on the top floor of the monastery, accessed by a long ladder to the side of the main entrance.

It is possible to climb up onto the outer ramparts of the monastery for a stunning **kora** that takes in fine views of the surrounding valley and mountains. Do not miss this.

Northern Monastery Ruins　RUINS
Little is left of the original monastery complex that once sprawled across the hills north of the Trum-chu. The northern monastery predates the main southern monastery complex at Sakya (the oldest temple at

PRIESTS & PATRONS: THE REIGN OF THE SAKYAPAS

The 11th century was a dynamic period in the history of Tibetan Buddhism. Renewed contact with Indian Buddhists brought about a flowering of new orders and schools. During this time, the Kagyupa order was founded by Marpa and his disciple Milarepa, and in Sakya the Khon family established a school that came to be called the Sakyapa. One interesting distinction between this school and others is that the abbotship was hereditary, restricted to the sons of the aristocratic Khon family.

By the early 13th century, the Tsang town of Sakya had emerged as an important centre of scholastic study. The most famous local scholar was the fourth Khon descendent and Sakya abbot, Kunga Gyaltsen (1182–1251), who came to be known as Sakya Pandita, literally 'scholar from Sakya'.

Such was Sakya Pandita's scholastic and spiritual eminence that when the Mongols threatened to invade Tibet in the mid-13th century he represented the Tibetan people to the Mongol prince Godan (descendent of Genghis Khan). Sakya Pandita made a three-year journey to Prince Godan's camp, in modern-day Gānsù, arriving in 1247. Sakya Pandita set about instructing Godan in Buddhist philosophy and respect for human lives. Impressed by his wisdom (and the fact that he cured him of an illness), Godan made Sakya Pandita Viceroy of Tibet.

After Sakya Pandita's death, in 1251, power was transferred to his nephew Phagpa, who became a close advisor to Kublai Khan and even met Marco Polo in Běijīng. Phagpa's greatest legacy was a special script used by Kublai as the official alphabet of the Mongol court. Phagpa was named Imperial Preceptor (the highest religious title in the Mongol empire) and, thus, de facto leader of Tibet. The role of spiritual and temporal head of state became an important precedent for the Tibetan government and had far-reaching effects on the religious life of Mongolia. However, the association between Tibetan lamas and Mongol masters also set a precedent of outside rule over Tibet that the Chinese have used to justify current claims over the high plateau.

As it was, Mongol overlordship and Sakya supremacy were relatively short-lived. Mongol corruption and rivalry between the Sakyapa and Kagyupa orders led to the fall of Sakya in 1354, when power fell into the hands of the Kagyupa and the seat of government moved to Nedong, in Ü.

Sakya was to remain a powerful municipality and, like Shigatse, enjoyed a high degree of autonomy from successive central governments. Even today you can see homes across the plateau painted with the red, white and dark grey stripes associated with Sakya Monastery.

the northern monastery was built in 1073), and it is alleged to have contained 108 buildings, like Ganden (p93). It may once have housed some 3000 monks who concentrated on Tantric studies.

The monastery was undergoing works at the time of writing and visitors were not allowed in. However, there are stellar views of it from the main monastery's (p150) rampart kora route.

🛏 Sleeping & Eating

Most people do not stay overnight in Sakya, as the monastery can be visited en route from Shigatse to Lhatse or Shegar, but there are a couple of hotels if you wish to spend more time.

Sakya has a couple of good English-menu restaurants aimed at tourists, plus many Chinese restaurants set up by Sichuanese migrants.

Sakya Hotel   HOTEL $$
(神湖萨迦宾馆; Shénhú Sàjiā Bīnguǎn; ☑0892-824 2555; 2 Benzhida Zhonglu; d/tr ¥220/280; 🛜) The renovated rooms at this modern hotel are spacious and comfortable, with hot-water bathrooms and electric blankets, making it the best value in town. At the time of research, the owners said it may close due to a threat of the building being demolished. The owners also operate the Yuan Mansion Hotel down the street.

Yuan Mansion Hotel   HOTEL $$$
(元府大酒店; Yuánfǔ Dàjiǔdiàn; ☑0892-824 2222; Gesang Xilu; d ¥480; 🌐🛜) Sakya's best hotel is run by the nearby Sakya Hotel and is similar, but boasts newer bathrooms and better furniture.

Sakya Farmer's Taste Restaurant   TIBETAN $
(萨迦农民美食厅; Sàjiā Nóngmín Měishítīng; ☑0892-824 2221; Benzhida Zhonglu; dishes ¥20-35) Overlooking Sakya's main street, this Tibetan place is located upstairs and has a cosy atmosphere amid Tibetan decor. The waiters are friendly and will help explain the various Tibetan and Chinese dishes available. The food is tasty but portions are small.

It's located across and a few doors down from the Sakya Hotel.

Sakya Hotel Restaurant   INTERNATIONAL $$
(神湖萨迦宾馆餐厅; Shénhú Sàjiā Bīnguǎn Cāntīng; ☑0892-824 2222; 2 Benzhida Zhonglu; dishes ¥25-40) This hotel restaurant is for those craving western food, such as omelettes,

sizzlers and pizza. There are also Tibetan, Nepalese and Indian dishes. The food is OK but the large dining hall lacks a bit of charm.

ℹ Getting There & Away

Sakya is a 25km detour off the Friendship Hwy. En route you'll pass the impressive ridgetop Tonggar Choede Monastery. Just 5km before Sakya at Chonkhor Lhunpo village is the Ogyen Lhakhang, where local farmers go to get blessings from relics said to be able to prevent hailstorms.

Shegar   ཤེལ་དཀར 协格尔

☑0892 / POP 9000 / ELEV 4250M

The last main stop on the way to Everest is the wind-raked truck stop of Shegar (Xiégé'ěr; also known as New Tingri, not to be confused with Tingri), located at Km5133, about 12km before the turn-off to Everest. By the time many travellers arrive from Shigatse, it's already too late to visit Everest, so most spend the night here, heading off to catch the early morning Himalayan views from Pang-la pass en route to Everest. If you have a couple of hours, you can make a short side trip into Shegar's old town a few kilometres west of the hotel-restaurant strip to check out the incredible ruins of Shegar Dzong.

You'll also sometimes hear this place referred to by its historic name, Baber (དཔའ་བེར; 白坝; Báibà).

⊙ Sights

Shegar Chöde
Monastery   BUDDHIST MONASTERY
(协格尔曲德寺; Xiégé'ěr Qūdé Sì; ¥20) This small Gelugpa institution, built in 1269, clings like a limpet to the side of Shegar Mountain. A mural by the entrance depicts the monastery at the height of its power, when it had around 800 monks. These days only 45 remain. As you enter the outer complex look for the Everest expedition oxygen tank that is used as the monastery bell.

The monastery originally followed Nyingma, Sakya, Gelug and Kagyu tradition until the fifth Dalai Lama enforced the Gelugpa doctrine. A chörten in the main assembly hall enshrines the heart, eyes and tongue of a former abbot, while the inner chapel houses a huge Jowo Sakyamuni statue, a kora path and relics that include the monastery founder's hat and a stone conch.

Shegar Dzong   FORT

(ཤེལ་དཀར་རྫོང, Xiégē'ér Zōng) Shegar is dominated by its 'crystal fort' (the word 'Shegar' means 'crystal' in Tibetan), one of Tibet's most fantastical, whose crumbling defensive walls snake up the side of an impossibly steep mountain that looms over town. Some travellers have been able to access trails from the Shegar Chöde Monastery (p152) entrance to the ruined buildings, from where you can see Mt Everest in the distance, though these weren't open at the time of writing.

🛏 Sleeping & Eating

There is limited accommodation on offer here. The vast majority of tourists stay one night and head out early to catch dawn over the Himalaya at the Pang-la.

A number of Chinese restaurants line the main highway, but most people eat in the restaurant at their hotel.

There is no nightlife to speak of in Shegar, and most travellers are feeling the altitude and preparing for arrival at Everest Base Camp, so heading to bed early is a fine proposition.

Tingri Roof of the World
Grand Hotel   HOTEL $$

(定日世界屋脊大酒店, Dìngrì Shìjiè Wūjǐ Dàjiǔdiàn; ☑0892-865 5222; Hwy 318 near fuel station, Baber village; d incl breakfast ¥280; 🛜) Opened in 2017, travellers report that this spiffy place with modern Tibetan design is the nicest option in Shegar, with clean rooms and helpful staff. There's wi-fi throughout but no non-smoking rooms. The on-site restaurant offers western-style meals.

Tingri Bebar Hotel   HOTEL $$

(定日白坝大酒店, Dìngrì Báibà Dàjiǔdiàn; ☑0892 866 2895; drbbjd@163.com; d ¥260; ❄🛜) The rooms at this courtyard hotel were given a real freshen-up in early 2018, with new carpeting, modern bathrooms and double-glazed windows. Though the grounds themselves are not much to look at, the rooms are very cosy and have 24-hour hot water. Prices don't include breakfast (¥35).

It's located on the main road from Lhatse, on the right-hand side as you enter Shegar, before the turn off to the old town.

Qomolangma Hotel Tingri   HOTEL $$

(定日珠峰宾馆; Dìngrì Zhūfēng Bīnguǎn; ☑0892-826 2775; Baber; standard/superior d ¥380/480; 🛜) Though situated in a huge, soulless compound often overrun with Chinese tour groups, this remains one of the best options in Shegar. Rooms are modern and clean, especially the newer and fresher superior rooms, though hot water is only available from 7am to 7pm and heating units can be unreliable. It's on the south side of the river on the way to Shegar.

ℹ Getting There & Away

Shegar is around 80km from Lhatse and 60km from Tingri. The drive to Everest Base Camp takes around three hours.

Everest Region

For most travellers, Everest Base Camp has become the most popular destination in Tibet, offering the chance to gaze on the magnificent north face of the world's tallest peak, Mt Everest (珠穆朗玛峰; Zhūmùlǎngmǎ Fēng; 8848m). The Tibetan approach provides far better vistas than those on the Nepali side, and access is a lot easier as a road runs all the way to base camp.

Everest's Tibetan name is generally rendered as Qomolangma, and some 27,000 sq km of territory around Everest's Tibetan face have been designated as the Qomolangma Nature Reserve.

Most visitors are content with early morning views of the mountain from Rongphu Monastery and Everest Base Camp, though adventurous travellers can add in some explorations on foot to their itinerary, and exiting the region via the little-used dirt road to Tingri offers a lot of wow-factor in the form of Himalaya eye-candy.

⊙ Sights

★ Everest Base Camp   BASE

(ཇོ་མོ་གླང་མའི་གཞམས་དེབ; 珠峰基地營; Zhūfēng Jīdìyíng) Everest Base Camp (5150m) was first used by the 1924 British Everest expedition. Tourists aren't allowed to visit the expedition tents a few hundred metres away, but sometimes (if it's open) you can clamber up the small hill festooned with prayer flags for great views of the star attraction. Most people have their photo taken at the 'Mt Qomolangma Base Camp' marker, which indicates that you are at 5200m above sea level. (Other measurements have it at 5020m or 5150m.)

Note that you can get mobile phone reception at Base Camp, and many of the tent hotels have wi-fi. WhatsApp a friend. They'll be thrilled.

THE ASSAULT ON EVEREST

There had been 13 attempts to climb Everest before Edmund Hillary and Sherpa Tenzing Norgay finally reached the summit as part of John Hunt's major British expedition of 1953. Some of them verged on insanity.

In 1934 Edmund Wilson, an eccentric ex-British army captain, hatched a plan to fly himself from Hendon direct to the Himalaya, crash land his Gypsy Moth halfway up Everest and then climb solo to the summit, despite having no previous mountaineering experience (and marginal flying expertise). Needless to say he failed spectacularly. When his plane was impounded by the British in India he trekked to Rongphu in disguise and made a solo bid for the summit. He disappeared somewhere above Camp III, and his body and diaries were later discovered by the mountaineer Eric Shipton at 6400m. A second solo effort was later attempted by a disguised Canadian from the Tibet side. It was abandoned at 7150m.

From 1921 to 1938, all expeditions to Everest were British and were attempted from the north (Tibetan) side, along a route reconnoitred by John Noel – disguised as a Tibetan – in 1913. The mountain claimed 14 lives in this period. Perhaps the most famous early summit bid was by George Mallory and Andrew Irvine (just 22), who were last seen going strong above 7800m before clouds obscured visibility. Their deaths remained a mystery until May 1999 when an American team led by Conrad Anker found Mallory's body, reigniting theories that the pair may have reached the top two decades before Norgay and Hillary. It was Mallory who, when asked why he wanted to climb Everest, famously quipped 'because it is there'.

With the conclusion of WWII and the collapse of the British Raj, the Himalaya became inaccessible. Tibet closed its doors to outsiders and, in 1951, the Chinese invasion clamped them shut even more tightly. In mountaineering terms, however, the Chinese takeover had the positive effect of shocking the hermit kingdom of Nepal into looking for powerful friends. The great peaks of the Himalaya suddenly became accessible from Nepal.

In 1951, Eric Shipton led a British reconnaissance expedition that explored the Nepali approaches to Everest and came to the conclusion that an assault via Nepal might indeed be met with success. Much to their dismay, the British found that the mountain was no longer theirs alone. In 1952 Nepal issued only one permit to climb Everest – to the Swiss, extremely able climbers who together with the British had virtually invented mountaineering as a sport. British climbers secretly feared that the Swiss might mount a successful ascent on their first attempt, when eight major British expeditions had failed. As it happened, the

Rongphu Monastery BUDDHIST MONASTERY
(绒布寺; Róngbù Sì; ¥25) Although religious centres have existed in the region since around the 8th century, Rongphu Monastery (4980m) is now the main Buddhist centre in the valley. While not of great antiquity, Rongphu can at least lay claim to being the highest monastery in Tibet and, thus, the world. It's worth walking the short kora path around the monastery's exterior walls. The monastery and its large chörten make for a superb photograph with Everest casting its head skyward in the background.

Rongphu was established with the name Dongnga Chöling in 1902 by the Nyingmapa lama Tsedru Ngawan Tenzin. It has traditionally coordinated the activities of around a dozen smaller religious institutions, all of which are now ruined. Renovation work has been ongoing since 1983, and some of the interior murals are superb. Upstairs is a large statue of Guru Rinpoche.

For a great hike, you might be able to follow the walking trail south from the monastery for 30 minutes to the ruins of **Rong Chong**, Rongphu's former meditation retreat. The route passes a ruined nunnery, which is still home to a couple of nuns in retreat. If in doubt about the way, follow the electricity poles. Below the ruins, next to the road, is a set of springs. As this is a sensitive border area, check with your guide (who may check with local officials or insist on accompanying you) before setting off.

🛏 Sleeping & Eating

Sleeping options at Everest essentially boil down to the simple rooms at the Rongphu Monastery Guesthouse (p156) or the noisier and scruffier tourist tent camp 4km closer to the mountain.

Swiss climbed to 8595m on the southeast ridge – higher than any previous expedition – but could not reach the summit.

The next British attempt was assigned for 1953. Preparations were particularly tense. It was generally felt that if this attempt were unsuccessful, any British hopes to be the first to reach the summit would be dashed. There was considerable backroom manoeuvring before the expedition set off, which saw Eric Shipton, leader of three previous expeditions (including one in 1935), dropped as team leader. In his place was John Hunt, an army officer and keen Alpine mountaineer, though relatively unknown among British climbers.

Shipton's 1951 expedition had at the last minute accepted two New Zealand climbers. One was Edmund Hillary, professional bee-keeper and a man of enormous determination. He was invited to join Hunt's 1953 expedition, which was also joined by Tenzing Norgay, a Sherpa who had set out on his first Everest expedition in 1935 at the age of 19.

On 28 May 1953, Hillary and Norgay made a precarious camp at 8370m on a tiny platform on the southeast approach to the summit, while the other anxious members of the expedition waited below at various camps. That night the two men feasted on chicken noodle soup and dates. The pair set off early the next day (29 May) and after a five-hour final push they reached the summit at 11.30am, planting the flag for Britain just a couple of days before the coronation of Queen Elizabeth II.

About 4400 people have now reached the peak of Everest (including George Mallory II, Mallory's grandson), while 282 climbers have died in the attempt. The first woman to reach the summit was Junko Tabei from Japan, on 16 May 1975. The youngest person was 13-year-old Jordan Romero from California, who reached the top in May 2010. The oldest person to make the climb was Yuichiro Miura of Japan, who scaled the peak in 2013 at the age of 80. Over two-thirds of the climbers who summit Everest do so from the Nepali side.

Of all the controversies that Everest generates in the world of mountaineering, its height is not one that should still be an issue. But in May 1999 an American expedition planted a global positioning system (GPS) at the top of Everest and pegged the height at a controversial 8850m – 2m higher than the 8848m accepted since 1954. The Chinese dispute this claim (and even recently lowered the height by 1.5m due to melting of the summit ice cap). Of course, plate tectonics are also at play. It is believed that the summit rises 4mm per year and is shifting 3mm to 6mm per year in a northeasterly direction.

For the latest on Everest, check out www.everestnews.com.

Food options at Everest are limited to small portions of simple Tibetan noodles or dishes cooked by tent hotel owners. It's a good idea to bring snacks, hot drinks and instant soups for the cold evenings, though some of the homemade dishes hit the spot. Given the remote locale, prices tend to be higher than in other places in the region.

EBC Tent Camp
CAMPGROUND $

(dm ¥70; ☺ early Apr–mid-Oct) About 4km beyond Rongphu in the direction of Base Camp is a messy corral of yak-hair tents (5050m), parked Land Cruisers and souvenir stalls. This is the furthest point to which private vehicles can drive; from here you'll have to walk the final 4km to Everest Base Camp or take a minibus (¥25 return). A small post office tent (surely the world's highest?) operates here in high season, offering the chance to send a postcard from Everest.

Don't come expecting an isolated camp of welcoming nomads – Tibetans from nearby Tashi Dzom and other nearby villages run the tents like small hotels. It's a scrappy location for sure but the views towards Everest's north face are amazing.

So that no one tent gets too much business, each tent is allowed a maximum of five tourists. Large groups are divided into different tents, and some groups have reported that they were not even allowed to eat together in the same tent. Some tents have wi-fi and a few have beer for sale if you are in the mood to celebrate, but be very circumspect about drinking at this altitude.

Be careful with your belongings as the tents are open all the time and offer no security. It's best to leave everything in your 4WD if possible. Some tents can get smoky inside. Blankets provided and stoves inside the tents should keep you warm enough, but you may wish to bring along a sub-zero sleeping bag or bag liner for added comfort/hygiene.

Qomo Langma Yak Hotel GUESTHOUSE **$**
(☑136 3892 5910; Tashi Dzom village; dm ¥60, d ¥160; 🖥) If you want to break up the drive to Everest, or want to avoid sleeping at high elevation, this family home in the village of Tashi Dzom has several rooms and a cosy restaurant. At 4200m, it's 1000m lower than Base Camp, which will make a vital difference if you are experiencing symptoms of acute mountain sickness (AMS).

Bathrooms are very basic shared toilets, and there are no showers, but there is wi-fi, rooms are pretty clean, and the welcome is warm.

Rongphu Monastery Guesthouse GUESTHOUSE **$**
(绒布寺招待所; Róngbù Sì Zhāodàisuǒ; ☑136 2892 1359; dm ¥60, tw without bathroom ¥200) The monastery-run guesthouse at Rongphu (p154) has private rooms with proper beds, though the stone walls tend to be a lot colder than the stove-warmed tents at Base Camp. There's certainly more privacy here, though bathrooms are still shared pit-toilet outhouses. Best value are the beds in a four-bed room.

Come the evenings everyone huddles around the yak-dung stove in the cosy restaurant (dishes range from ¥25 to ¥40 for small portions).

ℹ Information

DANGERS & ANNOYANCES
The military maintains a presence at Rongphu Monastery and Everest Base Camp to deal with any potential trouble, which includes attempts

to camp or trek past Base Camp (which is only allowed for those with special trekking permits).

Altitude & Climate
At this elevation of around 5000m it's important that you keep a close eye out for symptoms of acute mountain sickness (AMS, also known as altitude sickness). Typical tours from Lhasa should include several overnights in places such as Gyantse, Shigatse and Shegar to help you acclimatise slowly before reaching the heady heights of Everest.

Travellers coming from the low altitudes of the Kathmandu Valley are particularly susceptible to altitude sickness – even very fit trekkers. Whatever you do, don't attempt any treks or even basic walks directly after arriving in Tingri from Nepal. The altitude gain of over 2600m leaves most people reeling.

It's also important to realise just how high and remote you are, and to carry warm clothing and some kind of rain gear no matter what time of year you visit and no matter how short your walk. Unlike on the Nepali side, there is no rescue service set up here in the shadow of Everest. Get caught wearing shorts and a T-shirt when a sudden rain or snowfall hits and you could be in serious trouble.

Even tourists not planning any treks should come prepared with thermals (even in summer), warm layers, a warm and waterproof coat, hat and gloves. It's also extremely important to wear strong sunscreen or a hat at this altitude.

PERMITS
Apart from a normal Tibet Travel Permit, there is a required entry ticket for the Qomolangma Nature Reserve to visit the Everest region, either at the main turn-off from the Friendship Hwy or in Tingri. The ticket costs ¥400 per vehicle plus ¥180 per passenger. Your guide (but not driver) will also need a ticket. Make sure you are clear with your travel agency about whether this cost is included in your trip (it usually isn't).

WALKS AROUND BASE CAMP
It is a 4km walk from the tourist tent camp to the mountaineering base camp. The way up is gentle and the altitude gain is less than 200m. Along the way you pass scree slopes, jagged ridges, broad glacial valleys and stunning views of Everest. Short-cut paths avoid most of the road, but set off early as eco-buses start rumbling past around 8.30am. The way up is closed or open depending on when you visit; check with your guide before going much past the Mt Qomolangma Base Camp altitude marker. At the time of writing, anywhere past the marker was closed to everyone but those with mountaineering permits.

Less than 10 minutes' walk from the tent camp, near the altitude marker, it's well worth visiting Dza Rongphu retreat on the left, with its photogenic collection of chörtens framed by Mt Everest, and a pit toilet that may boast the world's best loo view. A lone resident monk, or your guide, can show you the trap door that drops to an atmospheric meditation cave used by Guru Rinpoche (Padmasambhava).

WORLD'S WORST TOILETS?

The pit toilets at Everest Base Camp are known as some of the worst toilets in Tibet (and that's saying something), if not the world. Though the local government does empty the toilets semi-regularly, when upwards of 500 people are staying in the tent camp in high season sharing essentially two toilets, you can imagine the results.

Come prepared: the toilets consist of a shed with three doorless squatter slats, very little privacy and a lot of stench. Many people end up taking a wild wee in the middle of the night to avoid having to enter the loos, which is both environmentally unfriendly and very unsanitary and contributes to putting Everest at ecological risk. We strongly urge all travellers intending to sleep at base camp to only use the toilets, and to consider sleeping options carefully. Remember that, in this part of Tibet, difficult toilets are a reality, whether at Everest or elsewhere.

Note also that occasionally a local Tibetan will 'clean' the toilets and then stand outside them asking tourists for money, sometimes rather aggressively. Be sure to carry ¥2 with you every time you go. And scented tissues can help with the stench.

Your passport and Tibet Travel Permit will be checked at a major checkpoint 6km west of Shegar, where you'll have to walk through a security check in person. Queues can be long here, especially after lunch, as even Chinese and local Tibetans need to register to enter the border region.

Tickets are checked again just before Rongphu Monastery. If you are driving in from Tingri, you'll go to the checkpoint at Lungchang. A final checkpost at Rongphu, just before base camp, will also check your permits.

❶ Getting There & Away

There is no public transport to Everest Base Camp. It's either trek in or come with your own vehicle. From Chay it's 91km to Base Camp; from Tingri it's around 70km on an unpaved road.

There are two roads into the Everest region; the main paved road from Shegar via Chay and the 5050m Pang-la, and the more remote, wilder drive from Tingri via the 5100m Lamna-la.

The main paved road to Everest begins around 6km west of the Shegar checkpoint, where you buy your ticket to the region. The 91km drive takes two to three hours. It's a switchbacking initial drive up Pang-la, where the views are stupendous on a clear day, and feature a huge sweep of the Himalayan peaks, including Makalu, Lhotse, Everest, Gyachung and Cho Oyu. Some groups arrange their itinerary to get here at dawn for the clearest views. There are two viewpoints with giant panoramas of Everest and its neighbours, where cars can pull off for photo ops.

The road descends past a couple of photogenic villages and drops into the fertile Dzaka Valley and the villages of Tashi Dzom (also known as Peruche) and Pagsum, both of which offer simple accommodation. The next main village is Chö Dzom and from here the road crosses the river south towards Rongphu (also

Rong-puk or Rongbuk). The first up-close views of Everest appear half an hour before you arrive at Rongphu.

The alternative driving route to or from Tingri is shorter at 70km but the dirt road makes for a wilder, bumpier ride. If you like getting off the beaten track, this route is for you. Keep your eyes peeled for antelope. After a permit check outside Tingri, the dirt road passes a *mani lhakhang* (prayer wheel chapel) at Gandapa village and then branches left at the junction to Cho Oyu Base Camp. You pass the ridgetop monastery at Cholong and then Lonchung village and the ruins of Ngang Tsang Drag Dog Dzong, before climbing slowly to the Lamna-la, 27km from Tingri. The route then descends for 10km to Zombuk village to join the main valley road at Km77 near the ruins of the Chö-puk hermitage across the river. From Zombuk it's 21km to Rongphu.

If you are headed from Lhasa to Nepal via Everest it makes sense to drive into the Everest region from Shegar and then drive out via Tingri, saving you both kilometres and time.

Tingri   རི་ 定日

📋 0892 / POP 520 / ELEV 4330M

The village of Tingri (Dìngrì or Tingri Gankar) comprises a gritty kilometre-long strip of restaurants, guesthouses, loose cattle and truck-repair workshops lining the Friendship Hwy. Generally called Old Tingri, it overlooks a sweeping plain bordered by towering Himalayan peaks (including Everest) and is a common overnight stop for tours heading to or from western Tibet or Nepal, as well as climbing groups coming and going from the nearby peaks. On clear days there are stunning views of Cho Oyu

PHUNTSOLING MONASTERY

If you're travelling down the Friendship Hwy and want to get a taste of what off the beaten track looks like, consider a few hours' scenic diversion along the Yarlung Tsangpo to this monastery (ཕུན་ཚོགས་གླིང་དགོན་སྐུ་འབུམ, 平措林寺, Píngcuòlín Sì; ¥35), situated at the edge of a gargantuan sand dune. The monastery's pre–Cultural Revolution ruined fort, seated high on a rocky crag, just adds to the photogenic atmosphere.

Now home to 50 monks, Phuntsoling was founded in 1615 and was once the central monastery of the Jonangpa. This Kagyu sect is especially known for the examination of the nature of emptiness undertaken at the monastery by its greatest scholar, Dolpopa Sherab Gyaltsen (1292–1361). He was one of the first proponents of the hard-to-grasp notion of *shentong*. Roughly, this is based on the idea that the buddha-mind (which transcends all forms) is not ultimately empty, even though all forms are empty illusions. (No, we don't get it either...)

Shentong has been debated among Buddhist philosophers for seven centuries. The Gelugpa school did not share Dolpopa's view, to the point that, in the 17th century, the fifth Dalai Lama suppressed the Jonangpa school and forcibly converted Phuntsoling into a Gelugpa institution.

The monastery was expanded by the writer and scholar Taranatha (1575–1634), whose next incarnation was the first Bogd Gegeen (spiritual leader) of Mongolia. Thereafter, the monastery was closely associated with the Bogd Gegeens, which is why you will see pictures of the 8th and 9th incarnations in front of the main altar. The ninth Bogd fled to India as a young man but revisited Phuntsoling in 1986 and 1993, helping to reopen the monastery following its closure during the Cultural Revolution.

You can visit the monastery's large assembly hall, which is lined with dusty 17th century murals and dominated by a 2400-year-old statue of Sakyamuni, which was broken apart

from Tingri. Pretty much a one-street town, Hwy 318 juts through town, where you'll find all of the hotels and restaurants.

🏃 Activities

It is possible to trek between Everest Base Camp and Tingri, though the route now follows a dirt road.

Tsamda Hot Springs HOT SPRINGS
(མཚམས་མདའ་ཆུ་ཚན་; outdoor bath/private room ¥20/40) These odourless, iron-rich springs 12km west of Tingri are piped into a tepid outdoor pool with natural-looking rock features surrounded by a dirty, drab courtyard. You can expect to share the water with the locals doing their laundry, but the views from the top of the hill are stunning (note: no views from the pool itself).

Accommodation is available (doubles ¥180 to ¥280), though it's extremely basic and quite overpriced (and your bedding will have been washed in the spring). If you do stay, there are some pleasant easy walks around the nearby hills that offer superb views of Cho Oyu. Just double check with your guide about how far you can roam.

The springs are 1km off the Friendship Hwy near Km5206.

🛏 Sleeping & Eating

Most places in Tingri look like truckers' motels, which fits the mood because Tingri is little more than a truck stop en route to the Nepal border. Expect to see basic double or dorm rooms set around a dusty main courtyard.

The main highway through town is lined with Tibetan and Chinese restaurants.

A beer on the porch of your guesthouse is as close as you'll get to nightlife in Tingri, if the wind doesn't drive you indoors.

Kangar Hotel HOTEL $$
(岗嘎宾馆; Gǎnggǎ Bīnguǎn; ☑ 0892-826 5777; d/tr ¥260/360; 🛜) This option on the east end of Tingri is well-run, with western-style rooms and modernish bathrooms, a sunroof sitting area, a restaurant and great views of the mountains. Water pressure can be iffy upstairs, while rooms on the ends of the corridors can get cold due to the lack of sunlight. Still, your best bet in town.

Hāhū Bīnguǎn HOTEL $$
(哈呼宾馆; ☑ 136 4892 2335; dm ¥50-80, d with bathroom ¥280; 🛜) This large central hotel is one of the better options in Tingri. The ensuite rooms are fairly clean and carpeted, with a western toilet and hot-water shower,

during the Cultural Revolution and repaired several decades later. Other statues include those of the 10th Panchen Lama, Tsongkhapa and the fifth Dalai Lama. The inner sanctum of the hall contains a statue of Mikyöba (Akshobhya), while the murals on the upper floor (also 17th century) tell the story of the life of Sakyamuni (Sakya Thukpa).

If you have extra time, it is a pleasant, steep walk up to the ruined old monastery buildings and fortifications behind the current site, which offer stunning views of the valley. Look for the ruined *dzong* (fort) on a cliff across the Yarlung Tsangpo.

A festival is held at Phuntsoling around the middle of the fourth lunar month (equivalent to June/July) every year, and sees lamas and pilgrims from all over the county gathering in the courtyard for prayers and celebrations.

About 6km south of Phuntsoling are the ruins of the once-spectacular **Jonang Kumbum**. The former 20m-high chörten was built by Dolpopa in the 14th century and was the spiritual centre of the Jonangpas. It was said to be one of the best-preserved monuments in Tibet, resembling the Gyantse Kumbum, before it was wrecked during the Cultural Revolution. Sadly, it's currently off limits to international visitors.

The **monastery restaurant** serves simple potato curries, *shapathu* (yak-meat dumpling noodles served in bone broth with shredded radish and green onion) and the most luxurious sweet tea in Tibet, all made by a resident monk-chef.

Phuntsoling can be visited on the way between Shigatse and Lhatse. Take the road north of the Friendship Hwy at Km4977/8, from which point the monastery is 34km northwest (less than an hour's drive). After visiting the monastery you can continue 61km to rejoin the Friendship Hwy near Lhatse Chöde.

TSANG TINGRI

but are a bit small. The mattresses in the cheaper dorm rooms vary in thickness according to price; these have shared squat toilets but no shared hot showers.

Snow Leopard Guesthouse   HOTEL $$
(雪豹客栈; Xuěbào Kèzhàn; ☑0892-826 2711; d/tr ¥280/320; 🛜) A lot of groups stay in this desolate courtyard hotel on the eastern edge of town. The west-wing rooms are new, with better bathrooms and carpeted floors, but are noticeably colder than the sunny south-facing block. The mountain views are better from here than in the centre of town.

Entry tickets to Qomolangma Nature Reserve are available at an **office** (☑156 9262 6148) within the compound.

Base Camp Restaurant   TIBETAN $$
(大本营餐厅; Dàběnyíng Cāntīng; dishes ¥30-50; ⊙11am-10pm) Probably the best place to eat in Tingri is this pleasant Tibetan-style restaurant attached to Héhū Bīnguǎn (p158), with traditional furniture, helpful staff and decent Chinese and Tibetan dishes. Though it's not listed on the menu, it'll do you a bowl of chips, if that's what you need.

Mt Kailash Coffee House   CAFE
(⊙9am-11pm) This little cafe, which misspells 'coffe' on its sign, serves Tibetan tea and refreshments, as well as a (picture) menu of Indian dishes, soups and rice. You'll have to step past the sheep heads hanging in the doorway, but it's bright inside.

ℹ Information

Newcomers from Kathmandu will likely experience some symptoms of altitude sickness. There is a gleaming new hospital and a very dusty private pharmacy in Tingri. Both can treat all basic ailments, including altitude sickness, and provide staple medicines.

Tingri Hospital (⊙24hr) Opened in 2018, this shiny hospital accepts international visitors and can treat all major ailments, including AMS and other altitude- and mountain-related illness.

Tingri Private Pharmacy (⊙9am-5pm) This extremely dusty pharmacy has a doctor on-call 24/7 who can treat basic ailments, as well as provide simple Tibetan and western medicines. Located in an unmarked shop in a row of Tibetan-style buildings halfway down Tingri's main drag.

ℹ Getting There & Away

Tingri is on the last stretch of the G318 between Lhatse and the Nepal border. Though the previous crossing at Zhāngmù is now closed, a smaller road connects across to the new border further east at Kyirong. The turn-off from the Friendship Hwy is located at Km5265 near Xiàmùdé (夏木德), just before the Lalung-la. This then passes north of Shishapangma base camp and south of Peiku-tso (both stunning) to join the road from Saga before climbing to the high Kongtang-la pass into the Kyirong Valley.

An atmospheric unpaved road leads the 70km between Tingri and Everest Base Camp. Adventurous travellers making a loop back to Lhasa should consider taking this route to really get off the beaten track in truly unspoilt, lunar-like mountainscapes.

Lhatse   왕ಠ 拉孜

☑ 0892 / POP 50,000 / ELEV 3950M

The modern town of Lhatse (Lāzī) is a convenient overnight stop for travellers headed to western Tibet. Lhatse is more or less a one-street town with a small square near the centre. The 3km-long main street runs east–west and used to be part of the Friendship Hwy, but this has now been diverted to the north. Passing traffic will mostly be heading to Everest Base Camp, the Tibet–Nepal border or the turn-off for western Tibet, about 6km out of town past a major checkpoint.

If you have time to kill, you could visit the renovated Changmoche Monastery at the western end of town.

◉ Sights

Lhatse Chöde Monastery   MONASTERY

This small but significant monastery and ruined *dzong* (fort) is just north of Lhatse in the village of Lhatse Chöde. Home to 75 monks, the monastery was built during the 17th century and there are some beautiful original murals lining the main assembly hall, where there is also a statue of the fifth Dalai Lama. Also in the main hall, look out for the black-and-white photo of the monastery and *dzong* taken before it was destroyed during the Cultural Revolution.

To reach the village, head 1km east of Lhatse on the Friendship Hwy to the 5052km mark and then turn north for about 15km. This road continues for 61km to Phuntsoling Monastery, and you'll pass the small Drampa Gyang Temple on your right just after the turn-off.

You need to have the actual monastery name listed on your permits to avoid a run-in with the overly sensitive local PSB. Otherwise it's not worth the inevitable hassle.

Drampa Gyang Temple   BUDDHIST TEMPLE

FREE This tiny one-room temple near the turn-off to Phuntsoling (p162) and Lhatse Chöde Monastery is very special. A larger monastery previously sat on this site, and the small temple you see today was rebuilt by the local people after the Cultural Revolution. There are no resident monks; the temple is tended lovingly by locals. Look out for a small *mani lhakhang* (prayer wheel chapel) on your right as you enter the grounds.

🛏 Sleeping & Eating

Lhatse is a popular lunch stop and the main drag is lined with restaurants. There is no nightlife in Lhatse.

Lhatse Tibetan Farmer's Hotel   HOTEL $$

(拉孜农民旅馆; Lāzī Nóngmín Lǚguǎn; ☑ 0892-832 2333; d ¥280; 🖳) This courtyard guesthouse has long been popular with foreign travellers. There is an older block of basic rooms with shared squat bathrooms, but the back block offers modern en-suite rooms with Tibetan decor and 24-hour hot water (check the water before handing over your cash).

Tibetan Farmer's Hotel Restaurant   INTERNATIONAL $

(mains ¥15-30) The Tibetan-style restaurant at the Lhatse Tibetan Farmer's Hotel is a very cosy place, with simple but decent Tibetan and western food, from pancakes to beef curry, at reasonable prices.

❶ Getting There & Away

Lhatse is located approximately 150km southwest of Shigatse and some 30km west of the Sakya turn-off.

Kyirong Valley

☑ 0892

The Kyirong Valley bordering Nepal has long been known as the 'Valley of Happiness', a *beyul* (hidden land) famed for its warm climate and as the gateway to Nepal. It has historical connections with King Songtsen Gampo and the famous Tibetan yogi Milarepa, and provided a vital corridor for the arrival of Buddhism into Tibet, as well as the advances and retreats of both the Qing and Nepali Gorkha forces.

For decades the valley has been off-limits to international travellers, but this all changed in late 2017 when the border was officially opened to replace Zhāng-mù (Dram) as Tibet's major border crossing with Nepal. Few travellers have had a chance to explore Kyirong yet, so pack an extra day into your itinerary to explore the monasteries, villages and alpine scenery of this beautiful Himalayan valley.

Dzongkhar and Kyirong have a good range of hotels, with half a dozen places to stay in each town.

Both Dzongkhar and Kyirong towns have a good range of restaurants. Kyirong has a couple of Nepali restaurants where you can get your first or last *dal bhat* (curried vegetables, lentils and rice) of your trip.

The Kyirong Valley and its border crossing with Nepal can be accessed from Saga en route from Mt Kailash, or from Tingri en route from Shigatse and Everest Base Camp.

Dzongkhar 宗嘎镇

📞 0892 / ELEV 4135M

The town of Dzongkhar (Zōnggǎ Zhèn), also called Kyirong Xian (吉隆县, Jílóng Xiàn), or sometimes Gyirong County, is set in a wide bowl surrounded by snowcapped peaks. It's a modern, friendly and easygoing Tibetan country town with a good range of accommodation and some minor sights nearby. Most people rush down to lower Kyirong to get an early start on the border crossing the next day, but Dzongkhar is an equally pleasant place to spend a night.

👁 Sights

This most interesting part of town to explore is the southern old town, said to have been the site of the former Mangyul Gungthang kingdom, which once ruled the valley. The small **Choede Monastery** in the south of Dzongkhar was closed for renovation in 2018, but might be worth checking out.

Drölma Lhakhang BUDDHIST TEMPLE
The lovely old pillars and carved wooden snow lions and garudas lend this chapel in Dzongkhar's southern old town an ancient feel. Look for the antique *cham* masks in the left corner, including one hidden by a red cloth depicting local protector Yangtha, a variation of Dorje Jigje.

🛏 Sleeping & Eating

Dzongkhar has a good range of accommodation and there seem to be no restrictions from the PSB on where foreigners can stay.

There are plenty of Sichuanese restaurants, Tibetan teahouses and Chinese Islamic noodle bars in town.

There's not much to do after dark except stare at the stars.

Liángshi Bīnguǎn HOTEL $
(粮食宾馆; 📞 0892-828 2118; Xinfu Lu; d ¥150; 🅿) This unexpectedly welcoming place run by the local Grain Bureau has decent enough standard rooms with good hot water, but it's the epically proportioned corner room (for the same rate) that is the real steal here.

Jilong Legend Hotel HOTEL $$
(吉隆传奇酒店, Jílóng Chuánqí Jiǔdiàn; 📞 0892-891 4777; Xingrong Lu; r ¥350-380; 🅿) Don't be put off by the unassuming entrance, this small guesthouse is the best place in town. The interior decor is surprisingly stylish and the bathrooms are super clean and modern. Not much English is spoken.

Jílóng Bīnguǎn HOTEL $$
(吉隆宾馆; 📞 0892-828 2822; 2 Ping'an Lu; d ¥220-280; 🅿) This central hotel has plain but clean and spacious rooms with modern western bathrooms, making it a friendly, central choice. Also runs a hotel in Kyirong.

ℹ Information

Agricultural Bank of China (中国农业银行, Zhōngguó Nóngyè Yínháng) The ATM here allegedly takes foreign cards but the bank doesn't change foreign currency. For that you need to head to Kyirong.

ℹ Getting There & Away

Dzongkhar is 75km from Kyirong and 115km from Saga. It's about three hours' drive down to the Nepal border.

Roads from Saga and the Friendship Hwy join about 50km before Dzongkhar, not far from Peiku-tso, and climb the dramatic 5236m Kongtang-la pass before descending into the Kyirong Valley on a dramatic series of switchbacks. At road Km95 you pass the ruins of monastery on a spur to the right. Around 6km further, just before a checkpoint, 200m off the road on the right, are the remains of a rock inscription made by a Tang dynasty mission en route to India. Sadly it's often locked and so hard to see.

Kyirong 吉隆

📞 0892 / ELEV 2800M

The pleasant small town of Kyirong (Jílóng), also called Kyirong Gou (吉隆口岸, Jílóng Kǒu'àn), is an unusual border town, surrounded by astounding alpine scenery and

DRIVING FROM DZONGKHAR TO KYIRONG

From Dzongkhar the highway follows the gorge of the Trisuli River, dropping past Oma village to the striking riverside **Mingsinkha Chörten**. Look across the river to make out the hermitage retreat perched on the salmon pink cliffs.

Drakkar Taso Hermitage (Chakar Gompa, 查嘎寺, Chágǎ Sì), high on the cliffs above the road, 34km from Dzongkhar, is the 12th-century Kagyud hermitage complex where Milarepa is said to have spent nine years meditating in two caves. The meditation retreats of around 20 nuns still dot the hillsides. Milarepa's birthplace is not far away in Tsarong (Zalung) village.

A steep climb on concrete steps gains 350m of altitude. Halfway up take the left path to the cave where Milarepa meditated for three years, then continue up to the main cave where he spent a further six years. Inside the small inner cave is his stone staff and footprint. A side trail leads left to two springs or right to the recently renovated assembly hall. A small kora leads behind the assembly hall past several trees to a valley viewpoint. Budget around 2½ hours for the return trip.

Below Chakar Monastery the landscape changes dramatically. Rhododendrons and pine trees start to appear, along with side valleys framed with waterfalls and snow-capped peaks. Before your brain can even register the changes you find yourself in a lush alpine landscape of green pastures thick with the heady aroma of pine needles. It's a landscape more reminiscent of Bhutan than Tibet.

At the new town of Bangxing there is a checkpost with some Nepali restaurants and the Nepali pagoda-style **Chamdrun Tsuglkhahang** beside the road.

At the end of Chongdol village, near kilometre marker 169, a signpost points left for 100m to the **Rigsum Gompo rock carvings**, garish but ancient 3m-high rock images of Chenresig, Chana Dorje and Jampelyang that reputedly date from the 8th century. The Indian-style turbans and dhotis (skirt-like loincloths) point to Nepali craftsmanship. Also nearby is a stone chörten and a collection of cairns said to mark the graves of Qing soldiers killed in 18th-century skirmishes with the Nepali army. From here it's a short drop down to Kyirong town, 4km away.

eye-catching views north towards the impressive peak of 6648m Langbo Kangri, bordering Nepal's Tsum Valley.

Most people are only in transit to or from the Nepal border, 25km to the southeast, but there is plenty of exploring to be done in the lovely surrounding countryside if you have some spare time.

◉ Sights

★**Pakpa Monastery**   BUDDHIST MONASTERY
(帕巴寺, Pàbā Sì) FREE Pride of place in Kyirong's central square is this 1000-year-old, four-tiered Nepali-style pagoda temple, allegedly built by Songtsen Gampo. The main statue here is a copy of the Arya Wati Zangpo, one of three statues of Phakpa Lokeshvara (a form of Chenresig) said to have arisen naturally from a single piece of sandalwood. The original statue resides in the Dalai Lama's private quarters in Dharamsala.

Other things to look for are the mirror of Songtsen Gampo's Nepali wife Bhrikuti Devi hanging on a pillar; the funeral chörten of

previous abbot Ngawang Kunsong; and a stone footprint of Guru Rinpoche in the left corner. Mornings are most active with pilgrims, who circle the courtyard's three tall prayer poles before doing a kora of the building.

Kyipu Canyon   GORGE
(吉普峡谷, Jípǔ Xiágǔ) It's worth making the short (1.5km) drive southwest of town to this canyon, which you can cross on a vertigo-inducing suspension bridge draped in prayer flags. A 10-minute walk up the hill to the right after the bridge leads to a charming collection of Bhutanese-style prayer flags that offers views over Kyirong.

🛏 Sleeping & Eating

Kyirong has a good selection of hotels, and finding a room is rarely a problem.

The road running east from Kyirong's main square is lined with Nepali, Chinese, Tibetan and Hui Muslim restaurants, making it the best place to head for dinner.

A bottle of Lhasa Beer at one of Kyirong's many restaurants is the best way to bid farewell/welcome to Tibet on your last/first night.

Jílóng Fēitiān Bīnguǎn HOTEL $

(吉隆飞天宾馆; ☑0892-828 6858; Jilin Lu; d ¥160; 🛜) The town's best budget choice has fresh and bright rooms with small but modern bathrooms. It's hidden in the north of town, around the corner from the Phuntsok Rabsel Hotel. The English sign calls it the 'Kuala Lumpur Flying Hotel'.

Dà Sìchuān Bīnguǎn HOTEL $

(大四川宾馆; ☑0892-828 6678; d ¥200; 🛜) Rooms at this friendly place are good value, if you don't mind squat toilets, and there's plenty of hot water and a rooftop for drying clothes.

Kyirong Hotel HOTEL $$

(吉隆宾馆, Jílóng Bīnguǎn; ☑0892-828 6558; d ¥260-280; 🛜) This high-profile hotel is well run, with clean and fresh but small rooms, with tiny bathrooms. The suite-like triples are huge, with two bedrooms and a good bathroom, so can be a good deal for small groups.

Phuntsok Rabsel Hotel HOTEL $$

(彭措绕赛酒店, Péngcuò Ràosài Jiǔdiàn; ☑180 8997 2777; r with/without breakfast ¥320/280; 🛜) A Tibetan-run place, popular with guides, with pleasant, modern rooms set around an interior atrium. Some rooms are without windows, so aim for one of the bright corner rooms.

Kerung Nepalese Restaurant NEPALI $$

(吉隆尼泊尔风味餐厅, Jílóng Nípō'ěr Fēngwèi Cāntīng; ☑183 0802 3650; mains ¥15-30; 🛜) Foreign groups often pack out this Nepali-run place, despite having a limited menu of *dal bhat* (rice and curry), chicken curry and breakfast dishes.

ⓘ Getting There & Away

Kyirong is 25km from the China-Nepal border at Rasuwagadhi, and is 75km from Dzongkhar.

CROSSING THE BORDER WITH NEPAL

The China-Nepal border at Rasuwagadhi is a 45-minute drive (25km) from Kyirong. The Chinese side of the border is open 10am to 12.30pm, and 1.30pm to 5pm. To get here your driver and guide will need to obtain a border permit in Kyirong, if they didn't get one in Lhasa. The particularly officious immigration officers at the border will delay you for even the tiniest irregularity in your permits, so make sure your documents are 100% watertight.

After a cursory customs check you walk 100m across a bridge to the Nepal army checkpost, where there is a second equally inefficient customs check. Nepal immigration (open 24 hours) is a further 1.5km downstream. Here you can get a Nepal tourist visa on the spot (US$25/40/100 for 15/30/90 days) but you need cash US dollars and one passport photo. Nepal time is 2¼ hours behind Beijing time.

Private jeeps to Kathmandu wait at the bridge and also at Nepali immigration and charge around Rs 13,000 per vehicle. The road is in terrible shape and is an exhausting ride; expect to spend most of the day bumping around on potholed roads on the side of near vertical slopes. If you are travelling during the monsoon months (May to August) expect potential landslides and delays.

The only formal place to change money on the China side is the **Bank of China** (中国银行, Zhōngguó Yínháng; ⊗9.30am-12.30pm & 3.30-6pm Mon-Fri, 11am-1.30pm Sat) in Kyirong, though Tibetan ladies often hang around hotel lobbies offering to change money out of bank hours. The **Bank of Kathmandu** (Timure; ⊗10am-3pm Sun-Fri) in Timure, just past Rasuwagadhi, changes foreign currency into Nepali rupees. It's also possible to change Chinese yuán into rupees with licensed moneychangers in Kathmandu.

Ngari མངའ་རིས་

Best Places to Eat

➡ Qinghai Salar Noodle Shop (p188)

➡ Uyghur Ashkhana (p177)

➡ Peacock Restaurant (p192)

Best Places to Stay

➡ Himalaya Kailash Hotel (p188)

➡ Thöling Monastery Hotel (p181)

➡ Seralung Monastery Guesthouse (p190)

Why Go?

Vast, thinly populated and with an average altitude of over 4500m, western Tibet (Ngari, མངའ་རིས་) is a rough and ready frontier occupying one of the remotest corners of Asia. For most travellers the main attractions of what is likely to be a two- or three-week overland trip are the almost legendary destinations of Mt Kailash and Lake Manasarovar. Indeed, many of the Tibetan and Indian pilgrims you meet on this road have been planning a visit all their lives.

For those less fussed by the spiritual significance of Mt Kailash, the overland trip across the Changtang plateau, with its endless steppes, huge salt lakes and impossibly high snow-capped peaks, is a sublime attraction in itself. Freshly paved roads, decent hotels and an airport are opening up the region in a way unimaginable a mere decade ago, but this is still one of Asia's great travel frontiers.

When to Go

➡ May to June and mid-September to early October are the best times to head to Ngari, though June and July see huge convoys of Indian pilgrims booking out entire hotels on their way to Mt Kailash.

➡ May to October is best for trekking over the Drölma-la pass on the Kailash kora (pilgrim circuit), as it's normally blocked with snow during other months.

➡ The festival of Saga Dawa in May/June is a particularly popular time to visit Mt Kailash, and hundreds of pilgrims and tourists descend on the mountain. This is also a politically sensitive time due to the government's uneasy control over the area, so the region may be closed to foreign travellers.

History

Most histories of Tibet begin with the kings of the Yarlung Valley region and their unification of central Tibet in the 7th century. But it is thought that the Shangshung (or Zhangzhung) kingdom of western Tibet probably ruled the Tibetan plateau for several centuries before this. According to some scholars, the Bön religion made its way into the rest of Tibet from here. The Shangshung kingdom may also have served as a conduit for Tibet's earliest contacts with Buddhism. There is little material evidence of the Shangshung kingdom in modern Tibet, though the Kyunglung (Garuda) Valley, on the Sutlej River near Tirthapuri hot springs, marks the site of the old kingdom.

The next regional power to emerge in Ngari was the Guge kingdom in the 9th century. After the assassination of the anti-Buddhist Lhasa king Langdharma, one of the king's sons, Namde Wosung, fled to the west and established this kingdom at Tsaparang, west of Lake Manasarovar and Mt Kailash. The Guge kingdom, through its contacts with nearby Ladakh and Kashmir, spearheaded a Buddhist revival on the Tibetan plateau. The great Indian sage Atisha spent three years in the region, and his disciple Rinchen Zangpo brought over 25 artists whose stylistic influences were felt all over Tibet.

In the late 16th century, Jesuit missionaries based in the enclave of Goa took an interest in the remote kingdom of Guge, mistaking it for the long-lost Christian civilisation of Prester John (a legendary Christian priest and king who was believed to have ruled over a kingdom in the Far East). The Jesuits finally reached Tsaparang over the Himalaya from India in 1624 after two failed attempts, but if their leader, Father Antonio de Andrede, had expected to find Christians waiting for him, he was disappointed. Nevertheless, he did meet with surprising tolerance and respect for the Christian faith. The Guge king agreed to allow de Andrede to return and set up a Jesuit mission the following year. The foundation stone of the first Christian church in Tibet was laid by the king himself.

Ironically, the evangelical zeal of the Jesuits led not only to their own demise but also to that of the kingdom they sought to convert. Lamas, outraged by their king's increasing enthusiasm for an alien creed, enlisted the support of Ladakhis in laying siege to Tsaparang. Within a month the city fell, the king was overthrown and the Jesuits were imprisoned. The Guge kingdom never recovered.

At this point, Ngari became so marginalised as to almost disappear from the history books – with one notable exception. In the late Victorian era, a handful of Western explorers began to take an interest in the legend of a holy mountain and a lake from which four of Asia's mightiest rivers flowed. The legend, which had percolated as far afield as Japan and Indonesia, was largely ridiculed by Western cartographers. However, in 1908 the Swedish explorer Sven Hedin returned from a journey that proved there was indeed such a mountain and such a lake, and that the remote part of Tibet they occupied was in fact the source of the Karnali (the northernmost tributary of the Ganges), Brahmaputra (Yarlung Tsangpo), Indus (Sengge Tsangpo) and Sutlej (Langchen Tsangpo) Rivers. The mountain was Kailash and the lake, Manasarovar.

Permits

Foreigners require a fistful of permits: an Alien's Travel Permit, a military permit, a Tibet Tourism Bureau (TTB) permit, a foreign affairs permit... Your travel agency will organise all of these for you, but give it at least a month. You are likely to need to stop in Shigatse to endorse your Alien's Travel Permit and you may need a further stamp in Darchen or Ali, depending on the direction of travel. This is particularly true if you wish to visit off-the-beaten-track places like Gurugyam Monastery. As you travel through the region your guide will need to register you with the Public Security Bureau (PSB) in many towns (such as Tsochen). You will stop and register at literally dozens of checkpoints en route to Kailash or Ali.

Note that Ngari is a politically sensitive area and is periodically closed to foreigners. Reasons for this include political unrest or potential unrest on the Mt Kailash kora (which could simply mean the year is

---

WHAT TO BRING

➡ Sleeping bag – recommended to avoid grubby truck-stop bedding and if you are doing the Kailash kora

➡ Breakfast foods like instant porridge, plus car snacks and picnic foods

➡ Cash rénmínbì – bring enough for your entire trip

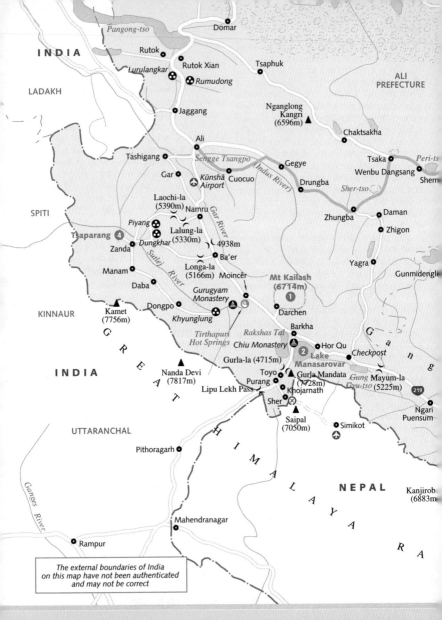

Ngari Highlights

1 Mt Kailash (p185) Joining fellow pilgrims to erase the sins of a lifetime on this three-day trek around the sacred peak.

2 Lake Manasarovar (p188) Hiking the sandy shores of the holy lake or just marvelling at the turquoise waters and snow-capped-mountain backdrop.

3 Tsari Nam-tso (p173) Camping on the shore of this spectacular, otherworldly lake on the northern Changtang; alternatively, try nearby Dawa-tso or Tagyel-tso.

The external boundaries of India on this map have not been authenticated and may not be correct

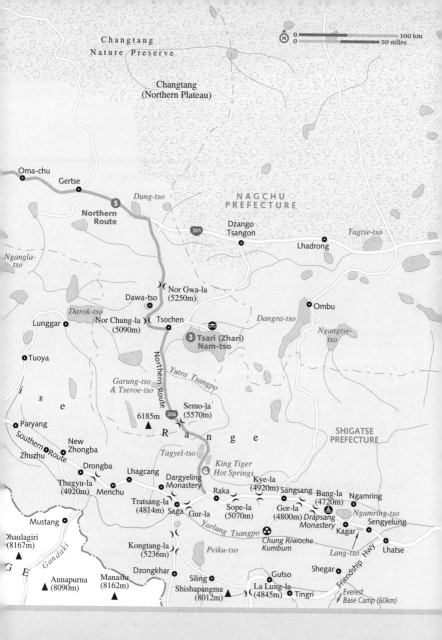

Changtang Nature Preserve

Changtang (Northern Plateau)

NAGCHU PREFECTURE

Oma-chu

Gertse

Dung-tso

5 Northern Route

301

Dzango
Tsangon

Lhadrong

Tagtse-tso

Ngangla-tso

Nor Gwa-la
(5250m)

Dawa-tso

Ombu

Darok-tso

Nor Chung-la
(5090m)

Tsochen

Dangra-tso

Lunggar

3 Tsari (Zhari) Nam-tso

Ngangtse-tso

Tuoya

Northern Route

Yutra Tsangpo

i s e

Garung-tso & Tseroe-tso

Paryang

6185m

206

Semo-la
(5570m)

R a n g e

SHIGATSE PREFECTURE

Southern Route

New Zhongba

Tagyel-tso

Zhuzhu

Drongba

Lhagcang

Dargyeling Monastery

King Tiger Hot Springs

Kye-la
(4920m)

Sangsang

Bang-la
(4720m)

Ngamring

Thugyu-la
(4920m)

Menchu

Tratsang-la
(4814m)

Saga

Raka

Sope-la
(5070m)

Gor-la
(4800m)

Drapsang Monastery

Ngamring-tso

Mustang

Gur-la

Kagar

Sengyelung

Dhaulagiri (8167m)

Gandaki

Kongtang-la
(5236m)

Peiku-tso

Yarlung Tsangpo

Chung Riwoche Kumbum

Lang-tso

Friendship Hwy

Lhatse

G E

Annapurna
(8090m)

Manaslu
(8162m)

Dzongkhar

Siling

Shishapangma
(8012m)

Gutso

La Lung-la
(4845m)

Tingri

Shegar

Everest Base Camp (60km)

100 km

50 miles

4 Tsaparang (p182)
Scrambling through secret passageways and cliff-side tunnels as you explore the Kashmiri-influenced art of one of Asia's lesser-known wonders.

5 Northern route (p172)
Spotting herds of wild asses and gazelles in the untrammelled wilderness of the Changtang, along the northern road to Ali.

a popular one for mountain pilgrimages); military tension along the contested borders of China, India and Pakistan; and other reasons known only to Chinese officialdom.

In short, it's prudent to always be prepared for your trip to be cancelled or changed, even with little to no notice. Do not blame your travel agency when this happens: it has no control over the situation.

The official announcement each year for opening Ngari is made in March or April. If your trip is cancelled, you can expect a full refund from your agency, though it's good to get this in writing beforehand as some agencies require hefty deposits. Airfares are another matter, so consider cancellation insurance.

ⓘ Dangers & Annoyances

If you've acclimatised for a few days in Lhasa, the gradual rate of gain along the southern route to Kailash shouldn't pose any serious problems, though the jump from Lhatse (3950m) to Raka (4925m) or Saga (4610m) involves a potentially dangerous rise in elevation. An overnight at Sakya (4280m) or Rongphu Monastery (4980m) en route will help your body adjust.

If you're coming from Nepal you should be particularly careful as you won't be well acclimatised; an overnight in Kyirong (2800m) or Dzongkhar (4135m) and Drongba (4570m) won't give you enough time to acclimatise unless you've been trekking in Nepal beforehand. Better tours fly to Lhasa for a few days first and then head out to western Tibet via Gyantse, Shigatse and Lhatse.

SOUTHERN NGARI

The tarmacking of the 500km section of road from Saga to Hor Qu means you can now drive from Lhasa to Mt Kailash in as little as three (long) driving days, something unheard of just a decade ago. Resist the temptation to rush, however, and take time to appreciate the scenery and acclimatise.

Saga is the last major town along the southern route and a usual overnight stop, conveniently placed at the junction of roads from Lhasa and Nepal. From here it's a full day's drive to Darchen. If you have a bit of time, consider visits en route to Dargyeling and Tradun monasteries.

If you wish to visit Everest Base Camp en route to Kailash, you can go via the stunning lake views of Peiku-tso before swinging up to Saga.

Most people take two days to drive between Lhatse and Darchen, though three days offers a more leisurely ride. The road is in excellent condition, but most tourist vehicles travel at a near-catatonic 60km/h, which can be frustrating. Expect to stop at over a dozen checkpoints between Lhatse and Darchen.

Foreigners are currently not allowed to take public transport anywhere in Ngari.

Lhatse to Saga

Lhatse is a usual overnight stop on the way from Lhasa to Ngari, though a stay in Sakya is actually preferable as there is little to see or do in Lhatse. From Lhatse or Sakya to Saga, the next main town, is a full day's journey of about eight hours' driving. Just past the Lhatse checkpoint (6km after Lhatse itself), the road leaves the Friendship Hwy and bears northwest. After crossing the Yarlung Tsangpo river the road runs for an hour through barren canyons and green meadowland with scattered Tibetan villages.

About 9km from the checkpoint at Sengyelung village is **Ngonkha Choede Gompa**, built by one of the three main disciples of Sakya master Kunga Ningpo. It's worth a quick visit for its fine thangkas in a side room and a protector chapel with matchlocks and a statue of Sakya protector Ngongkha Gyelpo. Be sure not to miss the nearby **Mani Lhakhang**, covered with carved stone plaques. At over 1000 years old, the chapel predates the monastery and has a powerful, ancient atmosphere.

Another 12km further look right to see a meditation cave high on the hillside above Buma town.

Past the photogenic **Lang-tso** (Ox Lake) the road climbs to the Ngamring-la (4530m), and at Km2085, 60km from Lhatse, through the small town of **Kagar**, which is a decent lunch stop. Nearby is **Ngamring-tso**, whose waters often appear brown because of the nearby mountains reflecting off its surface. On the other side of the lake is the army base of **Ngamring** (Ángrén).

About 10km past Kaga you'll leave behind the last trees for many days, and soon afterwards the last agricultural fields.

Just beyond Km2060, just after crossing a bridge, look right to see Drapsang Monastery (p169), which overlooks the road from a steep fairy tale–like crag.

The road then makes a zigzag ascent past photogenic nomads' camps and their flocks to the Bang-la (4720m), then down and up again to the 4800m Gor-la, before dropping down over one hour to Sangsang.

Sangsang (4590m), 113km and three hours west of Lhatse, is a small, grubby town that offers acceptable accommodation at the **Màoyuán Bīnguǎn** (茂源宾馆; ☑136 1892 6983; Sangsang; dm ¥80, d ¥360, without bathroom ¥150; ☏) and the better-value **Chuān Làzi Bīnguǎn** (川辣子宾馆; ☑139 8990 4607; Sangsang; d ¥240; ☏), the latter above a Sìchuānese restaurant of the same name. A large new tourist hotel is under construction here. If you have time to kill in Sangsang, visit the small Wöseling Nunnery on the northern edge of town.

A side road leads south from Sangsang for 40km to the fascinating but normally off-limits **Chung Riwoche Kumbum**, a large multilevel chörten on the banks of the Yarlung Tsangpo, next to an iron-link bridge attributed to Thangtong Gyalpo. Try to get the site listed on your travel permit in Lhasa to have any chance to visit.

Around 25km from Sangsang look for a particularly photogenic **monastery** atop a crag beside Lhanye village. The main route then climbs to the 4920m Kye-la before entering a huge plain with mountain views to the south. The new villages you see along this stretch were built to house Tibet herders resettled by the government.

The road gradually climbs to the 5070m Sope-la, before dropping down again and passing a checkpoint at **Raka** (4925m, Km1912), a tiny settlement 6km from the junction of the northern and southern routes, 115km from Sangsang. If you're taking the northern route, this is pretty much the last accommodation available (in several rustic guesthouses) for 240km, though a better (but colder) option is to camp at Tagyel-tso. There's decent Sìchuānese food on the main street.

Saga is another 60km away, over the 5090m Gur-la pass and a final checkpoint just before town.

Nepal Border to Saga

The scenic southern route to Saga is used mostly by groups visiting Ngari directly from Nepal, from the border crossing at Kyirong (in Tsang). It's such a scenic route that it's also worth considering if you are headed to Kailash via Everest Base Camp.

WORTH A TRIP

DRAPSANG MONASTERY

Drapsang Monastery (扎桑寺, Zhāsāng Sì) is a dramatically situated, worthy detour off the main highway. Nuns will show you a skull-shaped rock and statues of Guru Rinpoche and his emanations in the main chapel. The guru meditated in a cave 10 minutes' walk away on a cliff-side trail. The path then continues for an hour on a fine kora around the back of the hillside, up to a hilltop chapel and then down past former monastery ruins, making for a fine walk.

Drapsang is a 4km drive off the main road, turning at around Km2062, 15km from Kajar. Pass the lower Nyingma school monastery and then persuade your driver to take the crazy switchback road up to a car park at 4860m. From here it's a 10-minute walk away.

Coming from the east, the southern route to Saga branches west off the Friendship Hwy just before the main highway climbs to Lalung-la (4845m, Km5265–66). From here to Saga it's about 170km, or four hours of driving.

About 24km from the junction is Petse, huddled below a ruined hilltop *dzong* (fort), and then **Siling** (Seylong) village, where travellers must pay for entry to the western section of the **Qomolangma Nature Reserve** (¥40 per person, plus ¥60 per car). Arrange beforehand who will pay this – you or the tour agency.

To the south are views of sand dunes and then massive **Shishapangma** (8012m), known to the Nepalese as Gosainthan, the world's 14th-tallest peak and the only 8000m-plus mountain located completely inside Tibet. The road provides access to the mountain's north base camp before Peiku-tso comes into view.

The beautiful turquoise lake of **Peiku-tso** (4590m) is one of Tibet's magical spots, and it's worth stopping here for a picnic on the pebble shore beside lapping waves with views of snow-capped Shishapangma and the Langtang range bordering Nepal to the south. Camping is an option here, but bring your own drinking water and make sure you are well acclimatised (don't try this if coming straight from Nepal). Try to find a sheltered site, as winds whip up in the afternoon.

NGARI NEPAL BORDER TO SAGA

The bumpy route then climbs to offer a fine overview of the lake before it traverses a side gorge to pass the turn-off to the scenic **Kyirong Valley** and the border crossing with Nepal's Langtang region at Rasuwa. This formerly obscure border crossing in the lovely Kyirong region, nicknamed the 'Valley of Happiness', became the main entryway between Tibet and Nepal in 2016 after the closure of the border at Zhāngmù in the wake of Nepal's 2015 earthquake.

After passing small, salty Drolung-tso you climb to two passes and then drop steeply down to the bridge across the Yarlung Tsangpo river. From here it's 3km to Saga, where you join the southern route.

Saga ས་དགའ 萨嘎

☎ 0892 / ELEV 4500M

The sprawling truck-stop town of Saga (Sàgá), on the banks of the Yarlung Tsangpo river, is the last town of any size on the southern route and a logical overnight stop on the way to Mt Kailash. There's little to see in town – most people use the time to wash, check emails and stock up on supplies.

🛏 Sleeping & Eating

Saga offers some of the best accommodation in western Tibet. Most midrange places are open to negotiation on the room rate.

If your hotel doesn't have hot water, you can get clean at **Sìchuān Shower** (四川淋浴, Sìchuān Línyù; Gesang Lu; shower ¥25; ☺10am-11pm), one of three public shower houses in a row on the main street, Gesang Lu.

There are well-stocked supermarkets and plenty of Sìchuānese restaurants along Gesang Lu. For Tibetan fare, head up the main road north from the Saga Hotel.

Kangjong Gunji Drongkhang GUESTHOUSE $ (雪域贡吉旅馆, Xuěyù Gòngjí Lǚguǎn; ☎157 0808 6048; Lunzhu Lu; dm ¥50, d without bathroom ¥150; ☏) Saga's best budget bet is this Tibetan-run courtyard hotel. The four-bed dorms are chilly but clean and the doubles are fresh, even if the mattresses have the consistency of granite. All share simple squat toilets and hot showers, and guests can use the washing machine. The friendly Tibetan owners live upstairs.

Saga Hotel HOTEL $$ (萨嘎宾馆, Sàgá Bīnguǎn; ☎0892-820 2888; 6 Gesang Lu; d ¥380-420; 🌐☏) After recent renovations this is once again the main tourgroup hotel in town. Bedding is clean and hot water is plentiful in the evenings, making it Saga's most reliable choice. Doubles are discounted to ¥240 in May.

Grand Hotel of Western Post LUXURY HOTEL $$$ (西部驿站大酒店, Xībù Yìzhàn Dàjiǔdiàn; ☎0892-891 3555, 139 8992 3387; Deji Lu; d from ¥360; 🌐☏) The best hotel in town, with plush carpets, lots of space and oxygen machines in the rooms. Rates are discounted as low as ¥280 if things are quiet. Contact English-speaking manager Dorje.

ℹ Getting There & Away

Saga is a full day's drive from Lhatse or Darchen. Closer destinations include Paryang (246km) and Dzongkhar in the Kyirong Valley (115km).

Saga to Drongba

The road northwest of Saga climbs to the 4814m Tratsang-la, 10km from town.

Of the several ruined monasteries along the 145km stretch from Saga to Drongba, **Dargyeling Monastery** (达吉岭寺, Dájílíng Sì) FREE, 42km from Saga (Km1759), is worth the 1.5km detour for its fine views and unusual collection of chörtens.

From Dargyeling you cross a river and, about 12km further along, pass the photogenic ruins of a large **monastery** across the river. The road then passes through Menchu village and climbs to the 4920m **Thugyu-la pass**, marked by hundreds of miniature chörtens, before dropping 23km to Drongba.

With the road from Saga to Darchen now paved, and drivable in a single day, few groups overnight in Drongba or Paryang, but both have food and accommodation if your itinerary doesn't fit neatly between the two towns.

Drongba འབྲོང་པ 仲巴

☎ 0892 / ELEV 4570M

Drongba (Zhòngbā) is split into two: 'Old Drongba' (Drongba Nyingba) is a tiny, dusty town on the main road from Saga to Darchen, with a couple of basic guesthouses and restaurants, and a small but interesting monastery. 'New Zhongba' (Xīn Zhòngbā), 22km northwest, is a modern military town with good restaurants but little else to recommend it.

NGARI SAGA

◉ Sights

Tradun Monastery   BUDDHIST MONASTERY

(扎东寺, Zhādōng Sì) The Sakayapa-school Tradun Gompa just to the north of town is of importance as one of Tibetan King Songtsen Gampo's demoness-subduing temples, in this case pinning down the troublesome demoness' right knee. A picture of the demoness hangs in the entrance way. Don't miss the two unusual side chapels enshrining chörtens dedicated to protectors Chana Dorje and Tamdrin; the inner room of the chapel to the left still has Cultural Revolution–era newspapers defacing the murals.

Two stuffed bears and wolves guard the entrance to the protector chapel, which houses a stone shaped like a dragon's egg and another shaped like a conch shell. The lovely 15-minute kora (pilgrim circuit) around the hill behind the monastery offers fabulous views of the plain below. The severed heads of goats and yaks dangle from a nearby roadside chörten. Watch out for dogs if walking here alone.

🛏 Sleeping & Eating

Apart from the Shishapangma Hotel, there is currently no running water in Drongba and electricity is patchy.

Chóngqìng Zhāodàisuǒ   GUESTHOUSE $

(重庆招待所; ☏187 9892 5327; dm ¥50) Like most guesthouses in Drongba, this place is little more than a mud-walled block of rooms lined up against a central pit toilet, but it's cleaner than most and it has a good Sìchuānese restaurant on-site. It's at the far eastern end of town.

Shishapangma Hotel   HOTEL $$

(希夏邦玛宾馆, Xīxiàbāngmǎ Bīnguǎn; ☏152 0801 7779; tr per bed ¥50-60, d ¥200; 🛜) Opened in 2016, this has the potential to be the most comfortable place in town, with carpeted rooms and en-suite bathrooms surrounding a central tearoom. What you actually get depends on the supply of water and electricity, both of which were patchy in 2018, so check before committing to a room.

ℹ Getting There & Away

Drongba is 145km from Saga and 101km from Paryang. It's possible to drive to Mt Kailash or Kyirong from here in a day.

Drongba to Paryang

The 101km between Drongba and Paryang are the most scenic of the entire drive to Mt Kailash, so budget some extra time for photos – you can often capture steppes, streams, desert dunes and snow-capped mountains in the same shot.

About an hour's drive from Drongba (Km1810), as you cross a small pass, is a fine **viewpoint** of sand dunes, river and Himalayan peaks that is signposted as the source of the Yarlung Tsangpo river (the actual source is up in lakes and glaciers by the border with Nepal). Just past Zhuzhu village are some dramatic **sand dunes** beside the road. Look out for *kyang* (wild ass), *chiru* (antelope) and occasional black-necked cranes along this drive.

About 23km before Paryang you crest a minor 4780m pass and drop into a huge plain, opening up views to the southwest of the impressive peaks, including 6721m **Kubi Kangri**, that border Nepal's Dolpo region.

Paryang   ব্রাཡངা 帕羊

☏ 0892 / ELEV 4600M

Paryang (Pàyáng) is a dusty settlement divided between a paved main drag lined with Chinese businesses and a mud-walled Tibetan village to the south. It's not an inspiring place but there is cheap Tibetan-style accommodation if you are looking to break the drive. The mountain panoramas looking south towards Nepal are particularly impressive.

The town's main street is lined with dozens of Chinese and Tibetan restaurants. From Paryang it's 260km to Darchen and 101km to Drongba.

Paryang Hotel   GUESTHOUSE $

(帕羊宾馆, Pàyáng Bīnguǎn; ☏136 3892 8389; dm ¥60) A typical dusty-courtyard guesthouse in the southeast of Paryang town, with friendly owners, a cosy teahouse and rooms with three to five beds with decent mattresses. It's a big place, so there's always a room. There are pit toilets in the corner of the courtyard but no shower.

Yìzhàn Zhōngxīn Jiǔdiàn   LUXURY HOTEL $$

(驿站中心酒店, ☏0892-865 0666; d ¥300; 🛜) At the eastern edge of town is a huge new top-end government-owned hotel that opened in 2018. It's managed by Shigatse's Gesar Hotel.

Paryang to Hor Qu

This 217km route is a beautiful drive along the spine of the Himalaya, passing through yellow steppes, with craggy, snow-capped peaks looming to the south when the weather is clear.

Around 15km from Paryang is a checkpoint, followed 40km later by a series of plains and wetlands before reaching a series of tent restaurants at **Ngari Puensum**, a village cooperative that offers a good lunch alternative to Paryang. The hill to the side offers fine views over the plains and Nepali peaks to the south. A further 43km is the Mayou Bridge checkpoint, where your passport will be checked.

A further 25km is the **Mayum-la** (5225m), where the road crosses from the drainage basin of the Yarlung Tsangpo to that of the Sutlej, a major watershed moment as you cross from Shigatse to Ngari prefectures. A descent leads to the long **Gung Gyu-tso**, which nomads consider poisoned, even though it drains into Lake Manasarovar. After yet another checkpoint, your first magical views of Mt Kailash come into view approximately 90km after the Mayum-la. The views southwest towards hulking 7728m Gurla Mandata are even more impressive.

Just before the town of **Hor Qu** (ཧོར་ཆུ, 霍尔, Huò'ěr) is a huge new tourist reception centre for Indian pilgrims driving the Manasarovar kora. There are spectacular views here of the lake and Mt Kailash. It's 5km from here to Hor Qu (4620m), a dull place with some stupas and mani walls to explore at the western end of town if you have time.

Hor Qu has a couple of simple hotels, of which the **Sìchuān Dàjiǔdiàn** (四川大酒店; ☏189 8023 3355; Hor Qu; d ¥180, r without bathroom per bed ¥60; ☏) at the main junction is probably the best. The main street, off the highway, is lined with Chinese restaurants.

From Hor Qu, it's 22km to the crossroads settlement and checkpoint of Barkha (巴嘎, Bāgǎ), from where it's 15km south to Chiu Monastery, or 22km west to Darchen.

NORTHERN NGARI

The northern route is the longer of the two routes from Lhasa to Ngari, but there's a reason people put up with the extra travel time. It's the landscapes, the mystical, outsized landscapes, which include huge salt lakes, multicoloured mountains and valleys of semi-nomadic herders. The wildlife is also far richer than along the southern route and you are very likely to see marmots, blue sheep, wild asses, small herds of antelope and lots of yaks.

The entire northern route is now paved and driving conditions are excellent. If you're travelling this route, seriously consider camping at least once or twice, as the towns are dismal. You need to be well acclimatised if you intend to tackle this route before the rest of Ngari as the road from Raka never really drops below 4500m and is often above 5000m.

Northern Ngari is accessed from Raka to the south and from Ali to the west. Either way, the region is seriously remote. It's a three-day drive from Lhasa or an even more remote four-day drive from Kashgar in Xīnjiāng province. Either way, the stunning drive is a central part of the reason to come here.

Raka to Tsochen

Only 21km north of the Raka junction are the Tagyel Chutse, or **King Tiger Hot Springs** (Tagyel Chutse), a collection of Yellowstone-style geysers, bubbling hot springs, puffing steam outlets and smoking holes that seem to lead straight down into the bowels of the earth. Walkways go around the main thermal features, which local Tibetans use to wash themselves and their clothes.

The best time to visit is during the **Tibetan Bathing Festival** (Karma Rikey; early July of the lunar calendar, usually September in the Gregorian), when hundreds of nomad families, with their herds of yak, set up camp around the springs. The festival is associated with the reappearance of Venus in the evening sky.

From the hot springs, the road skirts the western side of beautiful **Tagyemang-tso**, then enters a wide valley. From the 5250m Youlaley-la pass, the route descends to a much larger lake, **Tagyel-tso**, the waters of which are a miraculous shade of the deepest blue imaginable and ringed with snowy peaks. With luck you can spot gazelles, wild asses and even the occasional wolf, hungrily eyeing the valley's many fat marmots. This is a great place to camp but only if you're prepared for the cold and especially the altitude (around 5150m). If you've come from a night or two at Everest Base Camp, you should be

OK; from Lhatse this is too big a jump in altitude to be considered safe.

After Tagyel-tso the road climbs past herding camps to the 5570m Semo-la. About 45km after the pass the road crests a smaller 5115m pass and leads down to the conjoined lakes of Garung-tso and Tseroe-tso. Eventually you pop out into the wide sandy valley of the Yutra Tsangpo.

Not far from Tsochen a collection of prayer flags and mani stones sit on a ledge above the road; 3km later is a major checkpoint where your passport and permit will be checked. The town of Tsochen is just ahead, 5km across the plains.

Tsochen

☑ 0897 / ELEV 4680M

Tsochen (Cuòqín), 235km from the northern turn-off near Raka and 173km south of the northern road proper, is probably the most interesting town on the northern route, full of wild-haired nomads wearing colourful *chubas* (sheepskin coats) and cowboy hats. The eastern end of Guangxi Lu has most of the Tibetan shops. The town is the base for a visit to Tsari Nam-tso, 55km away.

◉ Sights

Tsari Nam-tso   LAKE
(扎日南木错, Zhārì Nánmùcuò) One excellent half-day or overnight excursion from Tsochen is to Tsari (Zhari) Nam-tso, a huge and spectacular salt lake that remains totally undeveloped. Most people head for a **viewpoint** halfway along the northern shore, where several spits of sand frame water so turquoise that it looks almost like the Caribbean. From the viewpoint a road loops back behind a mountain range along the shoreline, past groups of carved mantras to a fine camping spot.

To get to the lake drive 28km northeast of Tsochen on a paved road, then branch right onto a roller-coaster dirt road past several herding communities to a bridge; from here head straight to the viewpoint, and from there turn right to loop around to the campsite and eventually back to the bridge.

You may have to get permission from Tsochen PSB to camp at the lake.

Mendong Monastery   BUDDHIST MONASTERY
At the east end of the 2km-long town, walk through the Tibetan quarter along Guangxi Lu to this small friendly gompa with 18 monks. The atmospheric inner chapel of the main prayer hall holds the funeral chörten of local lama Sherab Rinpoche, plus his stone handprint. The monastery belongs to the Kagyud school, so there are icons of Milarepa, Marpa and the Karmapa here (as well as President Xi Jinping!).

The monastery is headed by a 94-year-old lama who fled to India in 1959 and returned in 1984 to rebuild the ruined monastery. A fine 15-minute kora path climbs the ridge behind the monastery.

🛏 Sleeping & Eating

Tsochen has a decent range of accommodation, so you shouldn't have a problem finding an acceptable place to stay. Alternatively, camp at Tsari Nam-tso, a 1½-hour drive from town.

Guangxi Lu is lined with Chinese restaurants and Tibetan teahouses, but don't expect to find an English menu. There are several supermarkets in town.

Plateau Impression Hotel   HOTEL **$$**
(高原印象宾馆, Gāoyuán Yìnxiàng Bīnguǎn; ☑ 139 8997 9514; cnr Guangxi Lu & Shiquanhe Lu; d ¥300, without bathroom ¥120; 🛜) Rooms with en suite are spacious and clean, have decent hot-water showers and are flanked by a sunny sitting area overlooking the street, but they are still a bit overpriced. Cheaper rooms have hard mattresses and share a sink and a stinky squat toilet.

Tsochen Hotel   HOTEL **$$**
(措勤大酒店, Cuòqín Dàjiǔdiàn; ☑ 0897-266 1111; 30 Guowang Lu; d ¥380-580; 🛜) Hard beds and cramped showers are an inconvenience at this government-run place but rooms are bright and clean, if somewhat overpriced. Upper-floor rooms are more spacious. It's in the south of town.

Lhatse Tashi Restaurant   CHINESE, TIBETAN **$**
(26 Guangxi Lu; mains ¥15-30; ⊙ 8am-11pm; 🛜) Opposite the Lhatse Tashi Dronkhang hotel, this restaurant is owned by the same people and offers cosy Tibetan seating and a good range of food, served by both Chinese and Tibetan cooks.

Tokyeling Teahouse   TIBETAN **$**
(Guangxi Lu; momos ¥20; 🛜) This spacious and cosy teahouse underneath the Plateau Impression Hotel is popular with local Tibetans, primarily for its tasty yak meat momos and milk tea by the mug.

NGARI TSOCHEN

ℹ️ Information

Public Security Bureau (PSB; 公安局;
Gōng'ānjú; cnr Shiquanhe Lu & Guowang Lu)
The local PSB maintain a strong presence and
foreign travellers have to go to the station to
register. They'll be waiting for you.

ℹ️ Getting There & Away

Tsochen is 470km from Lhatse, 290km from
Saga and 257km from Gertse, all on excellent
paved roads.

Tsochen to Gertse

From Tsochen to the junction of the northern road (S301) is a journey of about 180km;
Gertse is another 77km, making a total drive
of four to five hours. If you plan to stay in
Gertse, take your time as the route is far
more interesting and scenic than the town.

About 43km north of Tsochen, the road
passes the 5090m **Nor Chung-la** (Small
Wild Yak Pass) before descending to the
dramatic turquoise waters of **Dawa-tso**
(4680m), a superb camping spot. For the
next 60km the route passes from one attractive valley to another, sometimes connected
by the river and gorge, at other times by minor passes.

After the scenic **Nor Gwa-la** (Wild Yak
Head Pass; 5250m), and for the next 50km,
the road runs alongside a dramatic range
of 6000m-plus glaciated mountains, some
of the most dramatic mountain scenery of
the entire northern route. After the road
meets the northern road proper (linking
Amdo with Ali) it's a 15km drive in an ar-
row-straight line towards **Dung-tso**, with its
purple mountain backdrop and salt marsh
foreground looking like whitecaps on the
water from a distance.

From the junction it's 90km (90 minutes)
west to Gertse through an arid valley dotted
with sheep and prayer flags.

Gertse   ཞེར་རྩེ་ 改则

📞 0897 / ELEV 4440M

Gertse (Gǎizé) is the biggest town you'll
find along the northern route before Ali. The
main street (Luren Lu) begins from the
yak-statue roundabout and runs east
to west for about 1.5km. Dazhong Lu is the
most interesting street, lined with Tibetan
teahouses and pool tables. Several shops sell
colourful *chubas* (Tibetan cloaks) with fake
sheepskin lining.

Budget some time to visit the long wall of
chörtens, mani stones, prayer flags and yak
horns to the south of town.

🛏️ Sleeping & Eating

The Gertse Public Security Bureau restricts
foreigners to just two hotels in town.

Lǔrén Bīnguǎn   HOTEL $
(鲁仁宾馆; 📞189 8997 0523; Luren Zhonglu; d
¥180; 📶) Hot water and wi-fi are a plus but
the bathrooms are poor, with squat toilets,
and rooms face onto the noisy main road.
Acceptable but not much more.

Government Guesthouse   HOTEL $$
(改则县大酒店, Gǎizé Xiàn Dàjiǔdiàn; 📞158 8244
8568; d ¥280-650; 📶) Comfortable, spacious
rooms are set around a pleasant courtyard
of real plants (!) and wicker armchairs; per-
fect for drying clothes or a bit of R&R after a
long day's drive. Full-rate prices are laugha-
bly overpriced so try to haggle.

ℹ️ Getting There & Away

Gertse is 368km from Gegye and 257km from
Tsochen along excellent paved roads.

Gertse to Gegye

It's a seven- to eight-hour drive (368km)
from Gertse to Gegye. The initial landscape
is a dreamy blur of lake and sky, cut by salt
rings and brooding mountains of rust, mus-
tard, turmeric and green barley. Around
Oma-chu, a small village huddled beneath a
small rocky splinter, 54km from Gertse, keep
your eyes open for the round, tomblike build-
ings that are actually *tsampa* (roasted-barley
flour) storage bins.

The road passes some impressive peaks
to the south and then the attractive village
of Sherma, squeezed between the two lakes
of Rali-tso and Loma Gyari-tso. After more
peaks the road drops down to the large and
photogenic aquamarines of **Peri-tso** (a good
picnic spot) and the nearby village of Wenbu
Dangsang, two hours from Gertse.

It's another 50km past a stony plain and
a huge salt lake that looks like it's full of ice-
bergs to ramshackle **Tsaka** (擦咔, Cākā), a
small salt- and sheepskin-processing com-
munity. The centre of town has simple food
and rather overpriced guesthouses should
you need them. The **Qiāngmàicūn Fúpín
Zhāodàisuǒ** (羌麦村扶贫招待所; 📞133 0897
2557; Tsaka; dm ¥50-60) offers the best value,

while the **Qiāngmàicūn Shāngwù Bīn-guǎn** (羌麦村商务宾馆; ☑139 8997 8790; Tsaka; d¥320; ☎) offers the most modern rooms.

From Tsaka one route continues north-west to meet the Ali–Kashgar road just north of Pangong-tso, offering an adventur-ous alternative loop route. The road to Ali branches south and climbs a side valley to the 4895m Namri-la, then descends past no-mads' camps to curve around salty Sher-tso (Bar-tso). After crossing the Drangan Lhan-la (4855m) the road descends to the pas-tures of **Zhungba** (Shungba; 雄巴; Xióngbā; 4590m) via a Gobi-like stony desert. There's food here and accommodation at the sim-ple Tibetan-style **Tashi Guesthouse** (Tashi Namtso Bösey Dromkhang, 扎西纳木措藏餐招待所, Zhāxī Nàmùcuò Zàngcān Zhāodàisuǒ; ☑189 0897 4433; Zhungba; dm¥30-80).

Near Drungba, the road enters a gorge and follows the fledgling Indus River to Gegye. The Indus has its source in the north-ern flanks of Kailash and is known here as the Sengge (or Sengye) Tsangpo (Lion Riv-er). It's astonishing to think that this little stream continues through Ladakh and Paki-stan, crossing the world's highest mountain ranges to become one of the great rivers of Asia.

Gegye   དགེ་རྒྱས་ 革吉

☑0897 / ELEV 4520M

The scruffy little town of Gegye (Géjí), nes-tled below a ridge, is a logical overnight point on the route from Lhatse to Ali, though there's little to actually do except drink beer and play pool with the local nomads. The two main streets (Hebei Lu and Yanhu Lu) join at a T-junction at the east of town.

🛏 Sleeping & Eating

Gegye has a decent selection of hotels, mak-ing it a logical place to overnight.

NGARI   **GEGYE**

ATOP THE WORLD: THE XĪNJIĀNG–TIBET HIGHWAY

With at least two passes above 5400m, the Xīnjiāng–Tibet Hwy is the highest road in the world. Approximately 1350km from Kashgar to Ali, this is an epic journey that can form a wild extension to a trip along the Karakoram Hwy. The route can be bitterly cold, howev-er, and closes down for the winter months from December to February.

The whole trip takes at least four days of travel. There are truck stops along the way, about a day's travel apart, but it's wise to bring food and a sleeping bag. A tent can be useful in emergencies. Coming from Kashgar, you have to be particularly careful about altitude sickness as the initial rate of altitude gain is dramatic.

The Xīnjiāng–Tibet Hwy is off limits without travel permits, but companies such as John's Café (www.johncafe.net) in Kashgar, or any agency in Lhasa can arrange vehicle hire (and permits) along this route.

Leaving Karghilik (Yèchéng in Chinese), the road climbs past Akmeqit village to Kudi Pass (3240m) then follows a narrow gorge to the truck stop and checkpost at Kudi (2960m). From Kudi it's 80km over the Chiragsaldi Pass (4960m) to the village of Mazar (3700m), 240km from Karghilik. The road turns east and climbs over the Kirgizjangal Pass (4930m) to the large village of Xaidulla (Sài Túlā; 3700m), the largest town en route and 363km from Karghilik. The road climbs again over the 4250m Koshbel Pass to the truck stop of Dàhóngliǔtān (4200m), which offers basic food and lodging.

From here the road turns south, and climbs to the Khitai Pass (5150m), past the mil-itary base of Tianshuihai. About 100km from the pass you cross another 5180m pass, 670km from Karghalik, to enter the remote region of Aksai Chin. The construction of the road here, through a triangle of territory that India claimed as part of Ladakh, was a principal cause of the border war between India and China in 1962. The fact that China managed to build this road without India even realising that it was under construction is an indication of the utter isolation of the region!

The road passes Lungma-tso, shortly afterwards entering the Changtang Nature Reserve, and 15km later reaches the small village of Sumzhi (Sōngxī; 5200m). Finally at Km740 you come to the edge of the Aksai Chin region and climb up to the Jieshan Daban pass (5200m). From here, Ali is around 420km away via the village of Domar (4440m), the eastern end of Pangong-tso and Rutok Xian. From here it is 130km south to Ali.

Hebei Lu has several good supermarkets and a number of Tibetan, Sìchuānese and Uyghur restaurants.

Jīntài Bīnguǎn
HOTEL $$

(金泰宾馆; ☑ 0897-266 3123; Yanhu Lu; d ¥260-300) Probably your best choice, in the southern end of town, with gleaming white tiled corridors, regal wallpaper and comfortable rooms, though compact bathrooms. The pricier single-bed rooms are a bit more spacious.

Línyuángé Bīnguǎn
HOTEL $$

(林源阁宾馆; ☑ 0897-273 6688; Hebei Lu; d ¥238-288; 🌐) Hard beds and squat toilets make this a simple option, even with a room humidifier. Water pressure is better in the public showers in the lobby so you can choose to shower there for free. Nonguests can use the showers for ¥30 (10am to midnight).

ℹ️ Information

Agricultural Bank of China ATM (中国农业银行, Zhōngguó Nóngyè Yínháng; Yanhu Lu) There's a chance that you might be able to get cash from this ATM in the south of town.

Public Security Bureau (PSB, 公安局, Gōng'ānjú; ⊘ 10.30am-1.30pm & 3.30-6.30pm Mon-Fri) Your guide may need to register your permits at this office on the eastern edge of town.

ℹ️ Getting There & Away

Gegye is 368km from Gertse and 123km from Ali and the paved road is excellent in both directions.

Gegye to Ali

Ali is just a couple of hours (120km) from Gegye. At first the road follows the meandering infant Indus River, then enters a marshland rich in bird life, including golden ducks and graceful black-necked cranes. After passing through a canyon landscape painted in swirling desert hues of butterscotch, caramel and popcorn, you reach **Cuocuo village** and a dramatic escarpment.

TREKKING FROM NEPAL

Fully organised trekking groups can trek to the Nepal–China border from Humla, a restricted region in the far west of Nepal. You will need a Nepali liaison officer, a specially endorsed Chinese visa and a full trek crew.

Ali gradually emerges like a desert mirage, revealing paved grids of department stores, karaoke bars and taxis. It's a surreal experience to arrive in town after days in the wilds of the northern plateau.

FAR WEST NGARI

Tibet's far wild west has few permanent settlers but is nevertheless a lodestone to a billion pilgrims from three major religions (Buddhism, Hinduism and Jainism). They are drawn to the twin spiritual power places of Mt Kailash and Lake Manasarovar, two of the world's most fabled and far-flung destinations. Also hidden here are the enigmatic ruins of past kingdoms, entire cities consisting of cave dwellings and some of Tibet's most beautiful remaining murals.

This part of Ngari is a huge, expansive realm of salt lakes, Martian-style deserts, grassy steppes and snow-capped mountains. It's a mesmerising landscape, but it's also intensely remote: a few tents and herds of yaks may be all the signs of human existence you'll come across in half a day's drive.

Roads to the far west run from the southern and northern routes, from Xīnjiāng and also from Nepal.

From the Nepali border at Sher, the road makes a long descent to a stream and then follows the Humla Karnali River to the village of Khojarnath, 10km north.

Ali
অ་ལི་ 阿里

☑ 0897 / POP 20,000 / ELEV 4280M

Ali (Ālǐ), also known as Shīquánhé (狮泉河, Lion Spring River) in Chinese and Sengge Khabab (Town of the Lion) in Tibetan, is the capital of the Ngari (Ali) prefecture and the largest town for 1000km in any direction. There's nothing much to see, but it's a good place to clean up, top up supplies and check your email before heading off to the real attractions of Ngari.

Ali is thoroughly Chinese. There are plenty of Tibetans wandering the streets but, like you, they are probably visitors from further afield. The town is expanding rapidly, especially to the south of the river, and there's a big army presence. Fleets of taxis are part of the mirage-in-the-desert shock of arriving in Ali. The town centre is compact enough that you can walk anywhere, though.

Ali

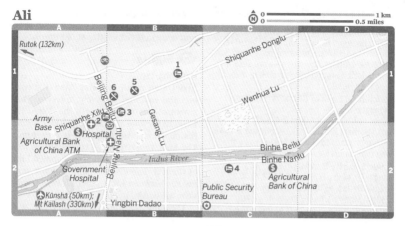

For views of Ali, climb up to the pagoda-topped hill to the north of town. Don't take pictures of the army compound to the west (recognisable by the huge '八一' army symbol painted on the hillside above).

🛏 Sleeping & Eating

Ali has numerous Chinese restaurants south and west of the main junction and, given the town's remote location, they are surprisingly good value for money. There are also a few Tibetan places and a couple of Uyghur restaurants.

Héngyuǎn Bīnguǎn HOTEL $
(恒远宾馆; Map p177; ☑ 0897-282 8996; cnr Beijing Nanlu & Shiquanhe Donglu; d ¥150-160; 🛜) With friendly staff used to dealing with foreigners, the Héngyuǎn has a useful location, a pleasant lobby tearoom and worn rooms with attached bathrooms. First-floor rooms are more spacious than the upper floor and are worth the extra ¥10. Check the room carefully; it took us until the next morning to realise our floor carpet was soaked in water.

Galaxy Grand Hotel HOTEL $$
(银河大酒店, Yínhé Dàjiǔdiàn; Map p177; ☑ 0897-282 8888; 4 Beijing Nanlu; d ¥260-320; ❄🛜) A good three-star choice with heated, comfortable, spacious and carpeted rooms, clean, fresh linens and a rainforest shower. The back block rooms are smaller and ¥60 cheaper, but with similar facilities.

Yíntài Jiǔdiàn HOTEL $$
(银泰酒店; Map p177; ☑ 0897-266 6222; Binhe Nanlu; d ¥288; ❄🛜) An offbeat choice, with bright rooms and small bathrooms but Western toilets and 24-hour hot water, making it a decent option, though the location is far from restaurants or shops.

Ali Hotel HOTEL $$$
(阿里大酒店, Ālǐ Dàjiǔdiàn; Map p177; ☑ 0897-266 6666; 17 Shiquanhe Lu; d with breakfast ¥688; ❄🛜) The revamped Ali Hotel is now the fanciest and most expensive place in town. It's surprisingly stylish and modern, though the occasional fragrant bathroom drain proves that window dressing can only go so far. Still, it's a comfortable choice.

Uyghur Ashkhana UYGHUR $
(新疆羊肉快餐厅, Xīnjiāng Yángròu Kuài Cāntīng; Map p177; Beijing Beilu; kebabs ¥5, noodles ¥25) For a taste of Central Asia head to this popular Uyghur restaurant (*ashkhana* in Turkic), 100m from the main roundabout. A bowl of *suoman* (fried noodle squares) and a couple of kebabs make for a great meal. The smell of grilled mutton is a sure sign that you're close.

Bǎiyì Supermarket SUPERMARKET
(百益超市, Bǎiyì Chāoshì; Map p177; Shiquanhe Donglu; ⏰8am-11pm) To top up supplies try this huge supermarket in the centre of town.

Ali

🛏 Sleeping

1 Ali Hotel	B1
2 Galaxy Grand Hotel	A1
3 Héngyuǎn Bīnguǎn	B1
4 Yíntài Jiǔdiàn	C2

🍴 Eating

5 Bǎiyì Supermarket	B1
6 Uyghur Ashkhana	B1

ⓘ Information

Agricultural Bank of China ATM (中国农业银行, Zhōngguó Nóngyè Yínháng; Map p177; Shiquanhe Xilu) Near the army post, west of the roundabout, though there are several others dotted around town, including below the Hengyuan Hotel.

Agricultural Bank of China (中国农业银行, Zhōngguó Nóngyè Yínháng; Map p177; Binhe Nanlu; ⊙10.30am-1.30pm & 4-6.30pm Mon-Sat) The main branch in the southeast of town is the only place to change foreign cash, though even that is unreliable.

Public Security Bureau (PSB; 公安局; Gōng'ānjú; Map p177; ☑136 4897 7374; 32 Yingbin Dadao; ⊙10.30am-1.30pm & 3.30-6.30pm Mon-Fri) Your guide will need to endorse your travel permits at this office in the southeast of town.

ⓘ Getting There & Away

AIR

Tibet's fourth airport, at Kūnshā (昆莎, Gunsa in Tibetan; 4274m) opened in 2010, 50km south of Ali. There are twice-weekly flights to Lhasa (¥2690) and as of 2018 an interesting twice-weekly connection to Kashgar (¥2040) on Lucky Air. The Lhasa flight in particular is difficult to get tickets.

CAR

From Ali to Darchen, at the base of the Mt Kailash kora, it's a day's drive of around 330km. Headed east, it's a full-day's drive to Gertse, or a half-day's drive to Zhungba or Tsaka.

Rutok

☑0897 / ELEV 4250M

The town of Rutok Xian (Rìtǔ Xiàn), 132km from Ali, is a dull, modern army post, but there are a couple of sights nearby that warrant a visit, including the traditional village of old Rutok. The upgraded road has cut travel time from Ali down to just two hours, making Rutok a comfortable day trip.

The main sight, just north of Rutok Xian, is the huge lake of Pangong-tso (4240m). From here you can return to Ali, continue on the epic and seriously remote Xinjiang–Tibet Hwy, or take an equally remote road southeast to meet the main Northern Route near Tsaka.

Most people visit Rutok as a day trip from Ali, though Rutok Xian offers the **Rìtǔ Yíngbīn Bīnguǎn** (日土迎宾宾馆; r ¥358-458; ☎) and it's possible to camp at Pangong-tso

if you are prepared for stony ground and windy afternoons. There's no accommodation or any other facilities at old Rutok.

⦿ Sights

Pangong-tso   LAKE

About 8km north of Rutok Xian, the road hits the east end of lovely turquoise Pangong-tso (4241m). It's worth the detour for views of the lake and camping is an enticing option (though the lakeshore is very stony). The long, brackish lake extends 110km into Ladakh in India, crossing the disputed Line of Control. There were minor military skirmishes between Indian and Chinese troops near the border in 2017.

The only facilities on the lake are at a dock offering boat rides and log-cabin-style accommodation. Beware the tour boats; several Chinese tourists died here in 2010 when theirs capsized.

Rutok Monastery   BUDDHIST MONASTERY

(Lhundrub Choeding Gompa) The charming, white-painted traditional village of old Rutok huddles at the base of a splinter of rock, atop which is Rutok Monastery, flanked at both ends by the crumbling, but still impressive, ruins of Rutok Dzong. From here, you can see the reservoir below and Pangong-tso in the distance. The surrounding villages are largely deserted in summer, as herders move to higher pastures.

The modern main chapel is centred around a large statue of Jampa (Maitreya). Clearly, at one time the whole eastern face of the hill was covered in monastic buildings. The monastery was destroyed during the Cultural Revolution and rebuilt in 1984, with more construction in 2011; it now has just eight monks of a previous total of 160.

Old Rutok is 10km off the main road, from a junction just before Rutok Xian, and the road is currently being paved. Look for the kitschy Mongolian yurt camp at the junction. A road leads up behind the western side but the eastern approach on foot is much more atmospheric.

Rumudong Petroglyphs   ROCK ART

In 1985 prehistoric rock carvings, or petroglyphs, were found at several sites in Rutok County, the first such carvings found in Tibet. The most impressive carvings are at Rumudong and features four extravagantly antlered deer racing across the rock and looking back at three leopards in hot pursuit. Also depicted are eagles, yaks, camels, goats, tigers, wild boars and human figures. Buddhist images are more recent, some of them carved right over their ancient predecessors.

The fenced collection of carvings at Rumudong is right beside the road, about 36km south of the old Rutok turn-off, or about 96km north of Ali. Travelling north from Ali, look on the east side of the road at Km979, just before the road crosses a bridge over the Maga Zangbu-chu.

There are more rock carvings at Lurulangkar, 12km southwest of Rutok, but rerouting of the highway has made them harder to find.

ⓘ Getting There & Away

Rutok Xian is 125km north of Ali on an excellent paved road. Old Rutok is 10km down a reconstructed side road, with the junction just southwest of Rutok Xian.

Guge Kingdom   གུ་གེ་རྒྱལ་རབ་
古格王国

The barren, eroded landscape around modern Zanda is unlike any in Tibet, and seems an improbable location for a major civilisation to have developed. Yet the ancient Guge kingdom (Gǔgé wángguó) thrived here as an important stop on the trade route between India and Tibet. Today the remains of Thöling Monastery, once a major centre of Tibetan Buddhism, and neighbouring Tsaparang, a 9th-century fortress etched into the very stone of a towering ridge, are two of Ngari's highlights, though few Western tourists manage to make it this far.

History

By the 10th century the Guge kingdom was already a wealthy trade centre supporting several thousand people when the great Guge king Yeshe Ö began to nurture an exchange of ideas between India and Tibet. The young monk Rinchen Zangpo (958–1055) was sent to study in India and returned 17 years later to become one of Tibet's greatest translators of Sanskrit texts and a key figure in the revival of Buddhism across the Tibetan plateau.

Rinchen Zangpo built 108 monasteries throughout western Tibet, Ladakh and Spiti, including the great monasteries of Tabo (Spiti) and Alchi (Ladakh). Two of the most important were those at Tsaparang and Thöling. He also invited Kashmiri artists to paint the murals still visible today. Their influence spread the Kashmiri tradition across Tibet.

It was partly at Rinchen Zangpo's behest that Atisha, a renowned Bengali scholar and another pivotal character in the revival of Tibetan Buddhism, was invited to Tibet. Atisha spent three years in Thöling before travelling on to central Tibet.

The kingdom fell into ruin just 50 years after the first Europeans arrived in Tibet in 1624, after a siege by the Ladakhi army. The centre of Tibet soon became the middle of nowhere.

ⓘ Getting There & Away

There are two main roads to Zanda from the Darchen–Ali road. Both are rough and go over some very high passes. In a 4WD it's possible to make it to Zanda from either Ali or Mt Kailash in a single day.

TO & FROM DARCHEN

It's 243km from Darchen to Zanda on a paved road. It's 65km from Darchen to Moincêr, which is the turn-off needed for Tirthapuri and then another 50km from there to the army base at Ba'er, where the road branches south. The fantastically scenic 122km from Ba'er to Zanda takes you up to the 5166m Longa-la pass with stunning views and then traverses a series of hillsides to pass a turn-off to Dungkar and Piyang. Finally the road descends for 20km through the fantastically eroded gorges and gullies of the Zhada Clay Forest National Geo Park.

TO & FROM ALI

Coming from Ali, the road is equally scenic and will take around five hours of driving to cover the 200km. The first hour climbs to the 4720m Pe-la and then drops down past a scenic viewpoint to the Gar Valley, home to Ali's new airport at Kūnshā. About 74km from Ali the road branches right towards Zanda. The road then climbs up to the 5330m Lalung-la (Laling Gutsa), followed by the 5390m Laochi-la before descending into a remote valley. This section was being paved at the time of research.

At a checkpoint the road branches left onto a plateau from where there are fine 180-degree views of the Indian Himalaya, stretching from Nanda Devi in the south to the Ladakh range in the north. Around 90km from the turn-off (36km from Zanda) look for the turn-off to Dungkhar and Piyang, just before a village surrounded by eroded cliffs with hundreds of tombs carved into the soft rock.

The route then drops down into deep, fantastically eroded wadi-like gullies before finally reaching the Sutlej Valley. The layers of the former sea bed are clearly visible and the scenery is a wonderland of eroded cliff faces and spires that have taken on the most astonishing shapes. You'll swear over and over again that you're seeing the melted ruins of an ancient monastery, or the tall pillars that once held the roof of a mighty palace. It's a cross between Canyonlands National Park and Monument Valley, set high in the Himalalya.

Just before reaching Zanda, 130km from the turn-off, you cross the Sutlej River on a long bridge.

Dungkhar & Piyang Cave Paintings

The most important monastic communities in Guge were at Thöling and Tabo (in Ladakh) but extensive cave paintings discovered in the early 1990s suggest others were of great significance as well. Bring a torch (flashlight) to both these sites.

The 12th-century wall paintings at remote **Dungkhar** (N 31°40.638', E 079°49.471'; ¥50; ⊙dawn-dusk), approximately 40km northeast of Zanda, are possibly the oldest in Ngari. Their Kashmiri–Central Asian style ties them with the Silk Road cave murals of Kizil in China (particularly in their almost-cartoon style, and the flying apsaras, painted on a blue background). There are three main caves in a side valley before the main village, of which the best preserved is the mandala cave. Lovely nearby Dungkhar village (4250m; N 31°40.638', E 079°49.471') also has a ruined **monastery** above the town. A night here at the simple but welcoming homestay-style **Drölma's Family Home** (Drölma Kimsang Dromkhang, 卓玛家庭旅馆, Zhuōmǎ Jiātíng Lǚguǎn; ☑189 0897 2699; Dungkhar; dm ¥25-30) gives you time to explore the village's collection of chörtens, caves and ruins.

A few kilometres west, the village of **Piyang** (N 31°40.962', E 079°47.784'; ¥50) is also worth the small detour. It lies at the foot of a large ridge honeycombed with thousands of caves and topped with a ruined monastery and two caves with fine murals (the caretaker will open three other caves on special request). It's a fabulously atmospheric place to explore. There's a small teahouse in the village (4180m; N 31°40.962', E 079°47.784'). The ruins of the original monastery and its huge central chörten lie just across the river and offer fine views back to warren-like Piyang.

Getting to Dungkhar and Piyang is an attraction in itself. If you come from the Ali–Zanda road, look for the turning east, just north of a village with caves behind it, 35km from Zanda. From here it's 9km on a dirt road past a stunning **Himalayan viewpoint** to Piyang and then another 5km to Dungkhar. From Dungkhar you can continue 8km on a paved road to a junction, then turn right for 16km to join the main Zanda–Moincêr road. From here it's 86km to the main Ali–Darchen road. With an early start you can visit Piyang and Dungkhar en route between Zanda and either Darchen or Ali.

Zanda & Thöling Monastery

☑0897 / ELEV 3760M

Zanda (ཙ་མདའ་, 札达, Zhádá), or Tsamda, is the bland, recently reconstructed town that has been built up alongside Thöling Monastery. The town consists of a few hotels, restaurants, supermarkets and two army bases.

◉ Sights

Allow for a couple of hours to visit Thöling Monastery and an hour to wander the cliffside chörtens at dusk.

If you have more time, the two sets of enigmatic ruins south and southwest of town offer amateur archaeologists plenty of scope to explore crumbling monastery walls, ruined chörtens and elaborate cave complexes.

Thöling Monastery　　BUDDHIST MONASTERY
(མཐོ་ལྡིང་, 托林寺, Tuōlín Sì; ¥35; ⊙dawn-dusk) Founded by Rinchen Zangpo in the 10th century, Thöling Monastery was once Ngari's most important monastic complex. Atisha stayed here for three years during the second diffusion of Buddhism in Tibet. It was still functioning exactly 1000 years later in 1966 when the Red Guards took a sledgehammer to the chapel's magnificent western Tibetan–style interiors. Three main buildings survive within the monastery walls.

Don't miss the lovely series of chörtens, mani walls and open views across the Sutlej Valley just north of the monastery.

Yeshe Ö's Mandala Chapel　　BUDDHIST SITE
(Nampar Nang Lhakhang) Once the main building in the Thöling complex, Yeshe Ö's Mandala Chapel was also known as the Golden Chapel. All the images have been destroyed but the four chörtens remain along with a

few remaining torsos, disembodied heads and limbs, scattered around the chapel like the leftovers from a sky burial. The mood created by the senseless loss of such magnificent art hangs heavy in the air.

Before its destruction in the Cultural Revolution, the square main hall had four secondary chapels at the centre of each wall. Figures of the deities were arrayed around the wall facing towards a central image atop a lotus pedestal, in the form of a huge three-dimensional Tibetan mandala (a representation of the world of a meditational deity).

You enter the Mandala Chapel through the Gyatsa Lhakhang and finish off a visit by walking around an interior kora of chapels. Most are closed and devoid of statues but a few open to reveal broken legs and plinths.

White Chapel   BUDDHIST SITE

(Lhakhang Karpo) The entry to this side chapel is marked by a finely carved deodar (cedar) door frame that originated in India. Inside are vibrant 15th- and 16th-century murals, somewhat affected by water damage though mostly restored with Swiss assistance. Typical elements of Indian-influenced Ngari-style murals include the fine detailing on the Ladakhi-style robes, the images of animals such as elephants and peacocks that don't exist in Tibet, and the slim waists and large breasts of the female figures.

The central statue is an old Sakyamuni Buddha (his hands and ears are new). On either side are niches that once held eight medicine buddhas, while on the right side is a stone footprint attributed to Rinchen Zangpo. Male deities line the left wall; female bodhisattvas the right. The far-right-corner murals depict a sky burial, while nearby is a square stone once used for a checkers-like game that is similar to the Chinese game Go.

Main Assembly Hall   BUDDHIST SITE

(Dukhang) The dimly lit chamber of the *dukhang* has especially fine wall murals, showing strong Kashmiri and Nepali influences; bring a powerful torch (flashlight) to enjoy the rich detail. The Kashmiri influences are noticeable in the shading on the hands and feet, the ornate jewellery and dress, the tight stomach lines and non-Tibetan images of palm trees and *dhotis* (Indian-style loincloths). Scholarly opinion varies on whether the murals date from the 13th and 14th, or 15th and 16th centuries.

SERKHANG CHÖRTEN

A few steps east of the Thöling Monastery compound in Zanda is the recently restored **Serkhang chörten**. A similar chörten stands in total isolation just to the west of the town. To the north, between the monastic compound and the cliff-face that falls away to the Sutlej River below are two long lines of miniature chörtens. The area is superbly photogenic at dusk, when locals do a kora of the complex.

To join the kora look for the trail leading off the road a couple of hundred metres west of the Thöling Monastery main gate.

Sutlej Bridge   HISTORIC BUILDING

If you have time to kill in Zanda, drive 4km east of town to this ancient iron link suspension bridge over the Sutlej River. It's thought to be one of the 58 (some say 108) chain link bridges built across the Himalayas by the Tibetan engineer Tangthong Gyelpo.

🛏 Sleeping

Zanda has two or three good hotels (and a large, modern hotel under construction) and is a comfortable place to fit in an extra day if you have time in your itinerary.

The new **Guge Dynasty Holiday Inn** is set to open in 2019, promising to be the best hotel in the region. A modern annexe of this large Guge Hotel compound was under reconstruction in 2018.

★ Thöling Monastery Hotel   GUESTHOUSE $$

(托林寺宾馆, Tuōlínsì Bīnguǎn; ☑ 0897-266 2688; 33 Tuolinsi Lu; d ¥240; ☎) Easily the best choice in Zanda is this well-run guesthouse across from Thöling Monastery. The six clean and spacious standard rooms come with hot-water bathrooms, while the much simpler Tibetan-style rooms in the old building share grim public toilets outside the hotel (no showers). There's a cosy attached teahouse-restaurant, pleasant upstairs seating and a clothesline out the back to dry laundry.

Xǐmǎlāyǎ Shāngwù Jiǔdiàn   HOTEL $$

(喜玛拉雅商务酒店; ☑ 0897-262 2888; d ¥300; ☎) An acceptable hotel with bright, comfortable rooms but poky bathrooms. It's a decent backup if other options are full.

NGARI GUGE KINGDOM

ℹ️ Information

Agricultural Bank of China (中国农业银行, Zhōngguó Nóngyè Yínháng; ⊘10am-1pm & 4-7pm Mon-Fri) Has a 24-hour ATM but does not change foreign currency.

ℹ️ Getting There & Away

There are two main roads to Zanda, either from Darchen (p179) or Ali (p179). Both are incredibly scenic and go over some very high passes. It's possible to make it to Zanda from either Ali or Mt Kailash in a single day, with a possible stop at Dungkhar and Piyang en route.

Tsaparang ⿰ 古格古城

The citadel of **Tsaparang** (Gǔgé Gǔchéng; Map p183; ¥65), 18km west of Zanda, has been gracefully falling into ruin ever since its slide from prominence in the 17th century. The ruins seem to grow organically out of the hills in tiers and are crowned by a red Summer Palace that sits atop a yellow cockscomb-like outcrop. It's a photogenically surreal landscape that resembles a giant termites' nest.

The site's early Tantric-inspired murals are of particular interest to students of early buddhist art. Even without the magnificent art, it's worth the trip for the views over the Sutlej Valley and to explore the twisting paths and secret tunnels that worm their way through the fortress.

Early morning and evening offers the best light. No photography is allowed inside the chapels and guardians will watch you like a hawk. Bring a strong torch, snacks and water, and expect to spend at least half a day exploring this magnificent site.

There is nowhere to sleep at Tsaparang. The nearest accommodation is at Zanda, 18km away.

🅾️ Sights

★**Lhakhang Marpo**　　　BUDDHIST SITE
(Red Chapel; Map p183) This large building was constructed around 1470. The beautiful murals were repainted around 1630, shortly before the fall of the Guge kingdom. The original chapel door, with its concentric frames and carvings of bodhisattvas, elephants and the syllables of the *'om mani padme hum'* ('hail to the jewel in the lotus') mantra in six panels, has survived and is also worth close inspection.

Inside the chapel, many thin columns support the chapel roof, similar to those of the neighbouring Lhakhang Karpo. By the main door are images of Chenresig (Avalokiteshvara), Green Tara and an angry eight-armed Namgyelma, with white Drölma and orange Jampelyang (Manjushri) to the right.

The statues that once stood in the chapel were placed towards the centre of the hall, not around the edges, and although only the bases and occasional disembodied head remain, the crowded feel to the space, the intense colours and the eerie silence combine to create a powerful atmosphere. The chapel was used as a barley store during the Cultural Revolution.

Although the wall murals have been damaged by vandalism and water leakage, they remain so remarkably brilliant that it's easy to forget they are actually over 350 years old. On the left wall beside the entrance are the famous murals chronicling the construction of the temple: animals haul the building's huge timber beams into place as musicians with long trumpets and dancing snow lions celebrate the completion of the temple. Officials stand in attendance (a Kashmir delegation wears turbans), followed by members of the royal family, the king and queen (under a parasol), Öpagme (Amitabha) and, finally, a line of chanting monks. The royal gifts frame the bottom of the scene.

Murals on the far right (northern) wall depict the life of the Buddha, showing him tempted by demons and finding enlightenment under the bodhi tree, among others. On the eastern wall are murals of eight stylised chörtens, representing the eight events in Buddha's life.

The main deitiy in the chapel has very ornate *toranas,* decorated with birds and crocodiles, and topped with flying apsaras (angels). At the back of the hall, statues of the 35 confessional buddhas once sat on individual shelves; a handful of them still have bodies but all the heads have gone.

As you leave via the entryway, look for the photo of Tsaparang positioned in front of a faint mural map of the site.

★**Lhakhang Karpo**　　　BUDDHIST SITE
(White Chapel; Map p183) The large Lhakhang Karpo holds the oldest paintings at Tsaparang and is probably the most important chapel in all of Ngari. The murals date back to the 15th or 16th century but their influences extend back to 10th-century Kashmiri Buddhist art. Apart from at Tsaparang, very little material evidence of early Kashmiri

art remains (notably at Alchi Monastery in Ladakh). Spot the Kashmiri influence in the slender torsos, thin waists and long fingers of the Hindu-inspired deities.

The ceiling of the chapel is beautifully painted, as are the many thin supporting columns made from composite pieces of wood (trees are scarcer than hen's teeth in Ngari). The carvings and paintings of Sakyamuni that top each column are particularly noteworthy. At one time, 22 life-size statues lined the walls; today only 10 remain and these are severely damaged. Black and white photos of the original statues just underline the sense of cultural loss. In the far left corner are the legs of Jampa; to the right is Yeshe Ö. Originally each statue would have been framed by a *torana* and a Kashmiri-style plinth. Only partial sections of these remain (look in the far left corner and back recess), but you can still see the holes where these structures were once anchored to the walls.

The doors are flanked by two damaged 5m-high guardian figures, red Tamdrin (Hayagriva) and blue Chana Dorje (Vajrapani). Even armless and with straw protruding from their stomachs they hint at the lost marvels of the chapel.

The huge figure of Sakyamuni that once stood in the recess, the Jowo Khang, at the back of the hall was destroyed by Red Guards. On the side walls at the back were once row after row of smaller deities, each perched on its own small shelf.

★ Chapel of the Prefect   BUDDHIST SITE

(Map p183) This small building was a private shrine for Tsaparang's prefect or regent. The caretaker has named it the 'Drölma Lhakhang' after his own sculpture of Drölma (Tara) displayed here. The exuberant wall murals date from the 16th century, by which time the style evinced in other Tsaparang murals was in decline.

The murals include fantastic multi-coloured images of elephants, Garuda-people, hermits and doglike snow lions, among others. The main mural on the back wall shows Sakyamuni flanked by Tsongkhapa and Atisha (Jowe-je). Small figures of the Buddha's disciples stand beside him.

Dorje Jigje Lhakhang   BUDDHIST SITE

(Map p183) The murals in this small chapel are painted red and gold, and are almost solely devoted to wrathful deities in ecstatic yab-yum pose, such as Demchok (Chakrasamvara), Hevajra and the buffalo-headed

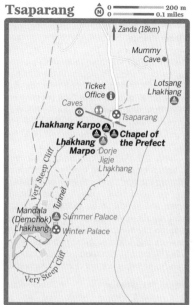

Tsaparang

Dorje Jigje (Yamantaka), to whom this chapel is dedicated. On the left as you look back at the door is Namtöse (Vaishravana), the God of Wealth, who is depicted riding a snow lion and surrounded by mandala-shaped bands of Tibetan warriors. Beside him is a strange dog-faced protector riding a panther.

Like the Chapel of the Prefect, the paintings here are of later origin, central Tibetan in style (rather than Kashmiri-influenced) and less refined; the golden years had passed by this point. All the statues that once stood here were destroyed, including the central Dorje Jigje.

Summer Palace   BUDDHIST SITE

(Map p183) From the four chapels at the base of Tsaparang, the path to the top climbs up through the monastic quarters and then ascends to the palace complex atop the hill via a dramatic tunnel. The Summer Palace, at the northern end of the hilltop, is closed and empty, with a balcony offering wonderful views. The Sutlej Valley is just to the north.

The small but quite well-preserved red-painted Mandala (Demchok) Lhakhang in the centre of the hilltop ridge once housed a wonderful three-dimensional mandala with Tantric murals, only the base of which survived the desecrations of the Cultural Revolution. It is often closed to visitors.

Winter Palace
RUINS

(Map p183) Accessed by a steep and easily missed eroded staircase (now with an iron railing in place), the palace is an amazing ant nest of rooms tunnelled into the clay below the Summer Palace. The rooms were built 12m underground in order to conserve warmth, and the rooms on the left side have windows that open out onto the cliff-face.

There are seven dusty chambers, all empty, linked by a cramped corridor. Branching off from the stairs you will see a dim passage that provided vital access to water during sieges and served as an emergency escape route for the royal family. The easily missed stairs to the Winter Palace lead down from between the Summer Palace and the Mandala (Demchok) Lhakhang. Don't go down if you're prone to vertigo or claustrophobia.

Lotsang Lhakhang
BUDDHIST SITE

This ruined chapel is flanked by an ancient-looking chörten. Only the feet of the main statue remain inside but there are some lovely old thangkas on display.

Mummy Cave
CAVE

North of the main entrance to Tsaparang a trail follows a green river valley down about 700m to a cave on the left that holds the mummified remains of several bodies.

Caves
CAVE

(Map p183) Worth a quick visit are the photogenic caves and chörtens to the west of the main Tsaparang site, near the public toilet.

ⓘ Getting There & Away

From Darchen it's a day's drive to Zanda (札达; Zhádá), the nearest town to Tsaparang (18km away), and home to spectacular Thöling Monastery.

Garuda Valley

Adventurers with a day up their sleeve could explore the Khyunglung (Garuda) region of the upper Sutlej Valley, southwest from Moincêr. Around 16km from Moincêr (8km from Tirthapuri), the Bönpo-school **Gurugyam Monastery** (གུ་རུ་རྒྱམ་དགོན་པ, 故如甲木寺, Gùrújiǎmù Sì) is worth a visit, primarily for exterior views of the dramatic cliff-side retreat of 10th-century Bön master Drenpa Namka (entry closed).

A further 14km down the Sutlej Valley, 3km past Khyunglung (曲龙, Qūlóng) village, is the extensive ruined cave city that archaeologists believe belonged to the early kingdom of **Shangshung**. The road to the site drops past hot-spring terraces to cross the Sutlej over a bridge hung with severed animal heads. Nearby is a riverside hot-springs pool. You could easily spend a fantastic couple of hours exploring the troglodyte caves and buildings of this lost kingdom, but it's dangerous to continue to the upper citadel.

On the way back stop off at **Khyunglung Monastery** (曲龙寺, Qūlóng Sì) a new monastery with a fine location just above the village. The eroded caves and cliff-side ruins visible on the hills behind the monastery are said to be the site of an even earlier Shangshung settlement.

There is a checkpoint just before Khyunglung so make sure the valley is included in your travel permit. From Khyunglung a newly upgraded road continues southwest to seriously remote monasteries at Dongpo, Daba (Danba) and Manam (Malang) en route to Zanda, but also passes near several military bases so you need to bring watertight permissions and be ready for some exploration.

Tirthapuri
ELEV 4360M

On the banks of the Sutlej River, two hours' drive northwest of Darchen, the hot springs at Tirthapuri are the place where pilgrims traditionally bathe after completing their circuit of Mt Kailash.

◉ Sights

Guru Rinpoche
Monastery
BUDDHIST MONASTERY

(Map p185) The monastery *dukhang* (assembly hall) here has the stone footprints of Guru Rinpoche and his consort Yeshe Tsogyel to the right of the altar. Outside the monastery a large circle of mani stones marks the spot where the gods danced in joy when Guru Rinpoche arrived at Tirthapuri.

Tirthapuri Hot Springs
HOT SPRINGS

(ཏི་ར་ཐ་པུ་རི་ཆུ་ཚན, 芝达布日寺, Zhīdá Bùrì Sì; Map p185; ¥60) On the banks of the Sutlej, only a few hours' drive northwest of Darchen, the hot springs at Tirthapuri are where pilgrims traditionally bathe after completing their circuit of Mt Kailash. The one-hour kora route around the site is interesting, though most people can safely give this place a miss if time is tight. Thirteen Tirthapuri koras are considered to bring equal merit to that of one Kailash kora.

🛏 Sleeping & Eating

Accommodation at Tirthapuri is limited to a simple mud-walled guesthouse and a nearby campsite. Nearby Moincêr (门次乡, Méncì Xiāng), 6km north of Tirthapuri, has a better range of accommodation and food.

Tirthapuri Guest House　　GUESTHOUSE $
(Map p185; Tirthapuri; dm ¥30) This simple, mud-walled place is just across from Tirthapuri's main hot springs, at the start of the kora path. The owners can also show you the local camping spot, though you'll have to pay a nominal fee to camp.

Song Sung River Hotel　　GUESTHOUSE $
(象泉河旅馆, Xiàngquánhé Lǚguǎn; ☑136 5897 4055; Moincêr; dm ¥50; 🛜) This welcoming Tibetan-run motel is your best choice in Moincêr, with simple but clean double rooms arranged around compound parking, just beside the turn-off to Tirthapuri and the Khyunglung Valley. The squat toilets are clean, and there's a cosy teahouse on-site. If it's cold, a yak dung fire will be lit in the room's stove.

❶ Getting There & Away

Tirthapuri is 6km south of Moincêr, which in turn is 65km west of Darchen along the main paved road to Ali.

Darchen & Mt Kailash　　དར་ཆེན། 塔钦
☑0897 / ELEV 4670M

Going to Ngari and not attempting a kora around holy Mt Kailash (Kang Rinpoche; Precious Jewel of Snow in Tibetan) is inconceivable. Kailash dominates the region physically and spiritually, with the sheer awesomeness of its surreal four-sided summit and through the combined faith of over one billion people.

The mountain has been a lodestone to pilgrims and travellers for centuries but until recently few had set their eyes on it. Improved road conditions are changing this. Large numbers of Indian pilgrims visit the mountain between July and August and Chinese tourists are starting to discover the region.

Mt Kailash is accessed via the grubby town of Darchen (དར་ཆེན།, 塔钦, Tǎqīn), a rapidly expanding settlement of hotel compounds and pilgrim shops. Almost everyone spends a night here before setting off on the kora, and many spend a second night after the trek to grab a hot shower and check emails.

History

Throughout Asia, stories exist of a great mountain, the navel of the world, from which flow four great rivers that give life to the areas they pass through. The myth originates in the Hindu epics, which speak of Mt Meru – home of the gods – as a vast column 84,000 leagues high, its summit kissing the heavens and its flanks composed of gold, crystal, ruby and lapis lazuli. These Hindu accounts placed Mt Meru somewhere in the

Tirthapuri Hot Springs & Kora

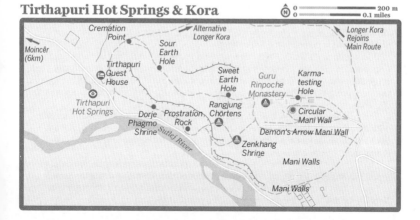

towering Himalaya but, with time, Meru increasingly came to be associated specifically with Mt Kailash. The confluence of the myth and the mountain is no coincidence. No-one has been to the summit to confirm whether the gods reside there (although some have come close), but Mt Kailash does indeed lie at the centre of an area that is the key to the drainage system of the Tibetan plateau. Four of the great rivers of the Indian subcontinent originate here: the Karnali, which feeds into the Ganges (south); Indus (north); Sutlej (west); and Brahmaputra (Yarlung Tsangpo; east).

Mt Kailash, at 6714m, is not the mightiest of the mountains in the region, but with its distinctive shape – like the handle of a millstone, according to Tibetans – and its year-round snow-capped peak, it stands apart from the pack. Its four sheer walls match the cardinal points of the compass, and its southern face is famously marked by a long vertical cleft punctuated halfway down by a horizontal line of rock strata. This scarring resembles a swastika – a Buddhist symbol of spiritual strength – and is a feature that has contributed to Mt Kailash's mythical status. Kailash is actually not part of the Himalaya but rather the Kangri Tise (Gangdise) range.

Mt Kailash has long been an object of worship. For Hindus, it is the domain of Shiva, the Destroyer and Transformer, and his consort Parvati. To the Buddhist faithful, Mt Kailash is the abode of Demchok (Sanskrit: Samvara) and Dorje Phagmo. The Jains of India also revere the mountain as the site where the first of their *tirthankara* (saints) entered nirvana. And in the ancient Bön religion of Tibet, Mt Kailash was the sacred Yungdrung Gutseg (Nine-Stacked-Swastika Mountain) upon which Bönpo founder Shenrab alighted from heaven.

Numerous Western explorers wanted to summit the mountain in the early 20th century but oddly ran out of time on each occasion. Reinhold Messner gained permission to scale the peak in the 1980s, but he abandoned his expedition in deference to the peak's sanctity when he got to the mountain. In May 2001 Spanish climbers reportedly also gained permission to climb the peak, only to abandon their attempt in the

KAILASH & MANASAROVAR BOOKS

The following books about Mt Kailash, Lake Manasarovar and the surrounding area are guaranteed to whet your appetite for adventure.

Charles Allen's *A Mountain in Tibet* chronicles the hunt for the sources of the region's four great rivers and is perhaps the best introduction to the region. Allen's follow-up, *The Search for Shangri-La,* focuses on the region's pre-Buddhist heritage and is also a great read.

The Sacred Mountain by John Snelling reports on early Western explorers, including those who turned up in the early 1980s when the door to China and Tibet first creaked narrowly open.

The Kailash chapters in German-born Lama Anagarika Govinda's *The Way of the White Clouds* (1966) include a classic account of the pilgrimage during a trip to Tibet in 1948.

Sven Hedin's three-volume *Trans-Himalaya: Discoveries & Adventures in Tibet* (1909–13) will keep you company for many a long night on the Changtang plateau. Hedin was the first Westerner to complete the Kailash kora.

Books such as *Kailas: On Pilgrimage to the Sacred Mountain of Tibet* by Kerry Moran (with photos by Russell Johnson) and *Walking to the Mountain* by Wendy Teasdill may make you jealous that you didn't get to the mountain just a decade or two earlier. Both highlight the much greater difficulties (and, in their eyes, rewards) that one could experience on a pilgrimage as recently as the late 1980s.

The more scientifically inclined can turn to Swami Pranavananda's *Kailas Manasarovar,* an account of the author's findings over numerous stays in the region between 1928 and 1947. The book was reprinted in India in 1983 and you should be able to find a copy in a Kathmandu bookshop or online.

Most recent is Manosi Lahiri's *Here Be Yaks,* an unpretentious travelogue that details an Indian pilgrimage to the region, with a special focus on defining the source of the Sutlej.

Finally, Colin Thubron's slender *To a Mountain in Tibet* details his trek from Humla in Nepal to Kailash, under the shadow of loss and personal grief.

face of international protests. Since then the government has maintained that the mountain is off limits to climbers.

⊙ Sights & Activities

The main reason anyone comes to Darchen is to to make the three-day walk around the Mt Kailash kora (p221), but there are also a couple of good acclimatisation hikes around town.

Mt Kailash MOUNTAIN
(གངས་རིན་པོ་ཆེ, Kang Rinpoche, Precious Jewel of Snow in Tibetan, 冈仁波齐峰, Gāngrénbōqí Fēng; ¥150) Sacred Mt Kailash dominates the landscape of western Tibet through both its unique geographical allure and its sacred, metaphysical role as the religious focus of a billion people. Pilgrims show their devotion by walking around the mountain in three days; for nonbelievers it is simply one of Asia's classic treks.

Yak Transport Service Centre TREKKING
(岗仁波齐牛马运输服务中心, Gǎngrén Bōqí Niúmǎ Yùnshū Fúwù Zhōngxīn; ☑133 2257 5733) This central office in the northwest of Darchen is the place to hire a porter, a yak or a horse for the trek around Mt Kailash. All charge for a minimum of three days.

Daily rates are fixed at ¥210 per porter (maximum 15kg), or ¥240 per day per yak (minimum two yaks), plus ¥260 for a yak man. Horses are expensive at ¥310 per day, plus ¥260 for a horse man. A ¥100 service fee is added to every booking.

✵ Festivals & Events

Saga Dawa RELIGIOUS
(☺ May/Jun) The festival of Saga Dawa marks the enlightenment of Sakyamuni, and occurs on the full-moon day of the fourth Tibetan month. In the Kailash region the highlight is the raising of the Tarboche prayer pole in the morning. Monks circumambulate the pole in elaborate costumes, with horns blowing. After the pole has been raised, about 1pm, everyone sets off on their kora.

How the pole stands is of enormous importance. If it stands vertically, all is well; if it leans towards Mt Kailash, things are not good; if it leans away towards Lhasa, things are even worse.

Saga Dawa is a particularly popular time to visit Mt Kailash. There are plenty of stalls, a fair-like atmosphere and a nonstop tidal flow of pilgrims around the prayer pole. Note, though, that you will have to share

WARM-UP HIKES AROUND MT KAILASH

If you've got extra time at Darchen, or you want to spend a day acclimatising before setting out on the Mt Kailash kora (pilgrim circuit), you can hike for an hour up the ridge to the north of the village for fine views of Mt Kailash. To the south you will be able to see the twin lakes of Manasarovar and Rakshas Tal. It gets very windy here in the afternoon

Since 2016 it has not been possible to continue up the dirt road behind Darchen to **Gyangdrak Monastery**, largest of the Mt Kailash monasteries, or to **Selung Monastery**, where a short walk leads to a viewpoint popular with Indian pilgrims for its views of Kailash and Nandi peaks. The secret 'inner kora' of Kailash starts from here but is only open to pilgrims who have completed 13 main koras of the mountain.

the Tarboche camping area with several hundred other foreigners, most of them on group tours. You can also expect that all the hotels in Darchen will be booked solid throughout this time. The presence of so many tourists and their ever-present cameras can change the mood of the trek but the sheer number of pilgrims compensates.

🛏 Sleeping & Eating

Most travellers spend a night in Darchen before the kora. Bigger places can be fully booked with large groups of Indian pilgrims during the summer months of June, July and August.

Supplies on the Mt Kailash kora are limited to instant noodles, beer and the occasional plate of fried vegetables, so stock up on snacks in Darchen's supermarkets before heading off.

★ **Drira-puk**
Monastery Guesthouse GUESTHOUSE $
(☑181 8907 5323; old/new room dm ¥20/80) The quietest and most comfortable accommodation option at Drira-puk is a bed in the monastery guesthouse, which has comfortable new rooms but limited food.

Shénshān Chóngqìng Bīnguǎn HOTEL $
(神山重庆宾馆; ☑180 8405 6366; dm ¥60, d ¥200-280; ❋ ☎) The central heating in this

hostel is a godsend early in the season and there's plenty of hot water in the bathroom. The cheaper four-bed rooms come with a tiny bathroom and no heating.

Zutul-puk

Monastery Guesthouse GUESTHOUSE $
(dm ¥50) The best place to stay at Zutul-puk is at the monastery guesthouse, with five-bed rooms set around a warm greenhouse-style solarium, and tea available at the attached teahouse.

Găngdĭsī

Tuánjié Zōnghé Bīnguǎn GUESTHOUSE $
(岗底斯团结综合宾馆; ☎139 8907 5311; dm ¥80) This simple prefab guesthouse below the Zutul-puk Monastery boasts good mattresses.

Xīngdá Bīnguǎn HOTEL $$
(兴达宾馆; ☎186 0819 4315; d ¥200-300; ☎) An offbeat choice, this place has surprisingly spacious and clean rooms with attached bathrooms. It sees few foreign travellers but it's good value if you can bridge the language gap.

Shénshān Shèngdì Bīnguǎn HOTEL $$
(神山圣地宾馆; ☎136 3897 2997; d ¥200; ☎) One of several simple hotels set in a large compound, this dour place has decent-value rooms with cramped attached bathrooms, making it worth a look.

Himalaya Kailash Hotel HOTEL $$$
(喜马拉雅冈仁波齐酒店, Xǐmǎlāyǎ Gāngrénbōqí Jiǔdiàn; ☎0897-859 500, 139 8997 4987; r ¥580-880; ☎May-Oct) Just what you didn't expect in Darchen: a four-star giant, with 102 rooms spread over half a dozen blocks. The grand lobby is impressive and surprisingly stylish, and the comfortable carpeted rooms come with electric blanket and heater. No competition, if it's in your budget.

Markham Teahouse TIBETAN $
(芒康藏餐; Mángkāng Zàngcān; dishes ¥15-30; ☎8.30am-11.30pm) A cosy Tibetan teahouse whose comfy sofas beckon for sweet tea, breakfast omelettes, noodles and fried dishes, all easy to order on a picture menu. It's on the upper floor, above a shop, on the southwestern corner of Darchen's central crossroad. It goes by several alternative names, including The Four Red Teahouse, or Tunba Phuensey Chakhang in Tibetan.

Qīnghǎi Salar Noodle Shop CHINESE ISLAMIC $
(青海撒拉尔面馆, Qīnghǎi Sālāěr Miànguǎn; mains ¥22-28; ☎) There's a good range of excellent-value and tasty noodle or rice sets at this tiny but super-clean place run by Salar Muslims, an ethnic group from Qīnghǎi. The picture menu on the wall makes ordering a breeze.

Héruìtáng Fàndiàn SICHUAN $$
(和瑞堂饭店; mains ¥20-60) One of many Sìchuānese places on Darchen's main drag, but with a well-translated English menu with photos and even a spiciness rating. The Hunanese dishes are tasty and the owner is friendly.

ℹ Information

Almost all hotels and even restaurants offer free wi-fi. On the kora you can use your mobile phone's 3G connection to go online.

Public Security Bureau (PSB, 公安局, Gōng'ānjú; ☎0897-260 7018; ☎24hr) Travellers need to register and have their travel permit endorsed at this local PSB office. Your guide will arrange this. The office is signposted as the 'Foreigner Service and Management Station of Pulan County'.

Tibetan Medical Clinic (Mentsikhang; ☎9am-5pm)

ℹ Getting There & Away

Darchen is 3km north of the main Ali–Saga road, about 22km from Barkha, 107km north of Purang, 330km southeast of Ali and a lonely 1200km from Lhasa.

Lake Manasarovar
མ་ཕམ་གཡུ་མཚོ་
玛旁雍错

ELEV 4580M

Sacred Lake Manasarovar (Mapham Yumtso, or Victorious Lake, in Tibetan; Mǎpáng Yōngcuò in Chinese) is the most venerated of Tibet's many lakes and perhaps its most beautiful. With its sapphire-blue waters, sandy shoreline and snow-capped-mountain backdrop, Manasarovar is immediately appealing, and a contrast to the often forbidding terrain of Mt Kailash.

Most visitors base themselves at picturesque Chiu village, site of Chiu Monastery, on the northwestern shore of the lake. Indian pilgrims often drive around the lake, immersing themselves in the sacred waters at some point. You'll also see Tibetan pilgrims walking the four-day kora path (p227) around the lake, or inching round on a 40-day prostration.

If you have the time, it's worthwhile travelling around the eastern side of the lake, visiting Seralung and Trugo monasteries en route, and preferably overnighting. It's an easy day slotted in between Hor Qu and Darchen.

History

Manasarovar has been circumambulated by Indian pilgrims since at least 1700 years ago, when the lake was extolled in the Puranas (sacred Sanskrit literature). A Hindu interpretation has it that *manas* refers to the mind of the supreme god Brahma, the lake being its outward manifestation. Accordingly, Indian pilgrims bathe in the waters of the lake and circumambulate its shoreline. Legend has it that the mother of the Buddha, Queen Maya, was bathed at Manasarovar by the gods before giving birth to her son. It is also said that some of Mahatma Gandhi's ashes were sprinkled into the lake.

The Hindi poet Kalidasa once wrote that the waters of Lake Manasarovar are 'like pearls' and that to drink them erases the 'sins of a hundred lifetimes'. Those of a more secular disposition should thoroughly purify Manasarovar's sacred waters before you drink them, as unromantic as that may sound.

⊙ Sights

Of the eight original monasteries built around the lake to represent the spokes of the Wheel of Law, five were reconstructed in the 1980s after being destroyed in the Cultural Revolution.

The lake area has a one-time admission fee of ¥150 per person (the Mt Kailash fee does not cover this).

Chiu Monastery BUDDHIST MONASTERY
(吉吾寺, Jíwú Sì; ¥15) Located 33km south of Darchen, Chiu (Sparrow) Monastery enjoys a fabulous location atop a craggy hill overlooking Lake Manasarovar. The monastery name comes from the story that Guru Rinpoche was guided here by a sparrow before staying for seven days. The main chapel contains the meditation cave and stone footprint of Guru Rinpoche, but most people focus on the lake views and the winding stone staircases of this fairy tale–like structure. On a clear day Mt Kailash looms dramatically to the north.

A short kora (pilgrim circuit) leads to a second chapel with a fine block print in the corner.

Chiu Hot Springs HOT SPRINGS
(吉吾温泉, Jíwú Wēnquán; bath per person ¥60; ⊗10am-sunset Apr-Oct) If you fancy a relaxing post-Kailash soak or just need to get clean after a kora, the small hot springs beside Chiu village are piped into clean, private wooden tubs, making this a fine way to spend an hour.

Seralung Monastery BUDDHIST MONASTERY
(色拉龙寺, Sèlālóng Sì) Seralung was built in 1728 to atone for a war against Ladakh. The most revered image is the central Jowo Katasapani; to the right is a statue of Kunchog Thinley Zangpo, the Drigung master who ordered the construction of the monastery. Pilgrims buy packets of sand, soda and dried Manasarovar fish to take back to their families as blessings. Climb the prayer-flag-lined hill to the south for fabulous views over the lake towards 7728m Gurla Mandata.

Gossul Monastery BUDDHIST MONASTERY
(果珠寺, Guǒzǔ Sì) South of Chiu Monastery on the shore of Manasarovar, this charming 16th-century monastery has long been part of the Manasarovar kora but can now be reached by road. The three resident monks will show you the tiny meditation cave of Götsangpa (the 13th-century ascetic who opened up the Kailash kora) and its sacred stone conch shell. The views of the lake from the short kora path are breathtaking.

Also worth visiting is the upstairs chapel with its painted stone carvings depicting the

RAKSHAS TAL

Manasarovar is linked to a smaller lake, Rakshas Tal (known to Tibetans as Lhanag-tso), by a channel called Ganga-chu. Most Tibetans consider Rakshas Tal to be evil – and in Hindu minds it is home to the demon king Ravanna – though to the secular eye it's every bit as beautiful as Manasarovar. The two bodies of water are associated with the conjoined sun and moon, a powerful symbol of Tantric Buddhism. On rare occasions, water flows through this channel from Lake Manasarovar to Rakshas Tal; this is said to augur well for the Tibetan people and most are pleased that water has indeed been flowing between the two lakes in recent years.

demons of Bardo (the state between death and rebirth), alongside a *rangjung* (self-rising) stone image of Mt Kailash. The monastery was completely destroyed during the Cultural Revolution. Pilgrims stock up on packets of holy Manasarovar sand, incense and natural soap here.

Dirt roads lead to Gossul from both south and north. If you are driving from Purang, an unsigned dirt road branches off the main road 10km north of the Gurla-la (around Km36), crosses a pass and then swings left to follow the lakeshore for 10km. From Chiu it's 6km south on the main paved road and then a further 7km on a dirt road to Gossul.

It's a lovely 12km (four-hour) hike from Gossul to Chiu along the shoreline Manasarovar kora path, or start from the turn-off to Gossul for the second 6km-long section.

Trugo Monastery
BUDDHIST MONASTERY

(竹各寺, Zhúgè Sì) Trugo has a great location on the southern shore of Manasarovar, at a spot where many Indian pilgrims make their ritual immersion in the lake. The main chapel was undergoing reconstruction in 2018 and the major relics, such as a sacred conch that can guide the dead through the Bardo realms, is being housed in a temporary side building.

🛏 Sleeping & Eating

There are over a dozen simple guesthouses at Chiu, between the monastery and the lake, with four- or five-bed rooms all costing around ¥65 per bed per night, and sharing a single set of outdoor pit toilets. There's not much to choose between them except perhaps the availability of food and where the big groups are staying. Most are only open May to October. At the time of writing, a new guesthouse was being built to cater to the many Indian pilgrims who stop here on their *parikrama* (the Hindu equivalent of a pilgrim circuit) of the lake in July and August.

There are simple monastery guesthouses on the lesser-visited eastern side of the lake at **Seralung** (色拉龙招待所, Sèlālóng Zhāodàisuǒ; dm ¥30-50) and **Trugo** (竹各寺招待所, Zhúgè Sì Zhāodàisuǒ; dm ¥70) monasteries, and to the north at **Langbona Monastery** (朗纳寺招待所, Lǎngnà Sì Zhāodàisuǒ; dm ¥30). The guesthouses at Chiu offer basic meals.

Tashi Guesthouse
GUESTHOUSE $

(吉鸟扎西宾馆, Jíniǎo Zhāxī Bīnguǎn; 📞 138 8907 3536; dm ¥60) This is probably the most popular of the half-dozen guesthouses lining the Manasarovar shoreline at Chiu. Rooms are

---

HIKES FROM CHIU

The views of Lake Manasarovar are so spectacular that it's worth budgeting some time to absorb them on foot. Even if you don't have time for the full four-day *tso-kor* (lake kora), it's worth tackling a short section to get a sense of the spectacular scenery.

For a short hour-long hike from Chiu village, walk up to the **ridge** south of the guesthouses for views of Chiu Monastery (p189) and Mt Kailash (p187) rising behind. It's worth continuing south to a second ridge behind the first to get equally fine views south towards Gossul Monastery and snow-capped Gurla Mandata.

For a longer, half-day hike, follow the lake kora northeast from Chiu to the ruined hermit caves and meditation retreats of **Cherkip** (one hour). There are lots of nesting birds along this route, but bring repellent against the shoreline flies. Once you reach the chörten and herders camp (6km) past Cherkip you can return the way you came, or return via the hilltop ridge for fine lake views.

Another option is to continue east on foot for another 6km to **Langbona Monastery**, where you could get picked up and start the drive towards Hor Qu and Saga. The lakeshore trail passes several holy rocks and standing stones before the cliffs recede and the trail swings north away from the shoreline to reach a prayer flag–draped viewpoint above the monastery. There are fine views of Mt Kailash and the surrounding plain from here. Langbona's main chapel still has its original gong and there's a three-room pilgrim guesthouse where foreigners can overnight.

Still another possibility is the lovely 12km (four hours) hike from Gossul Monastery (p189) to Chiu along the shoreline Manasarovar kora path. For a shorter option, concentrate on just the 6km-long northern section by starting from the lakeshore junction turn-off to Gossul, near the ticket office.

simple, with pit toilets outside, but there's a cosy dining room.

ℹ️ Getting There & Away

Chiu, at the northwestern corner of the lake, is 15km south of Barkha junction, from where it is 22km west to Darchen or 22km east to Hor Qu.

The eastern shore of the lake is accessible from Hor Qu, from where a dirt road continues all the way around the lake to Chiu. From Hor Qu it's 8km to Seralung Monastery and a further 24km to Trugo. From Trugo a second dirt road cuts west to join the main paved road south to Purang.

There is some confusion over whether private vehicles are allowed to drive around the lake. So-called 'eco buses' are supposed to take groups from Hor Qu's Tourist Reception Centre onwards around the lake but these are aimed mostly at Indian pilgrims and, at the time of writing, it didn't seem to be a problem for tourists to use their own vehicles. Check with your agency or when you arrive at Hor Qu.

Purang སྤུ་རེང་ 普兰

📞 0897 / ELEV 3890M

Purang (Pǔlán in Chinese, Taklakot in Nepali) is a large trading centre comprising a number of distinct settlements separated by the Humla Karnali River, known in Tibetan as Mabja Tsangpo (Peacock River). Nepali traders come from the Humla and Darchula regions in the extreme west of Nepal to trade a variety of goods, including rice, once carried up from Nepal in huge trains of goods-carrying goats. Indian consumer goods and Nepali rice are traded for Tibetan salt and wool. A huge new modern trading complex is under construction near the original Darchula Bazaar.

Purang is also the arrival point for the annual influx of Hindu pilgrims from India, intent on making a *parikrama* (the Hindu kora) of Mt Kailash, which devout Hindus consider the abode of Shiva. A trickle of foreign trekkers arrives here en route from the Humla region of Nepal.

⊙ Sights

Shepeling Monastery BUDDHIST MONASTERY
(Simbaling Monastery, 贤柏林寺, Xiánbólín Sì) This ruined monastery towers over Purang town from its dramatic hilltop position. In 1949 the Swami Pranavananda described this Kagyud monastery, which housed 170 monks, as the biggest in the region. Soldiers belonging to the fifth Dalai Lama defeated

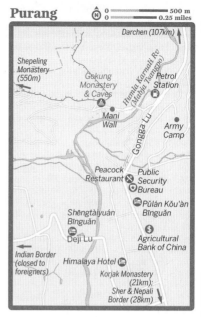

the Zhangzhung army here (ruins of the fortress remain), causing the monastery to be built as a penance. The monastery's treasures allegedly included one testicle of Indian invader Zowar Singh, displayed every four years during a festival.

Gokung Monastery BUDDHIST MONASTERY
(古宫寺, Gǔgōng Sì; Map p191) In the hills north of Purang are many meditation retreat caves formed around the cliff-side Gokung Monastery. A ladder leads up to a couple of upper-floor caves, of which the main one has some excellent murals. Bring a torch (flashlight).

Korjak Monastery BUDDHIST MONASTERY
(འཁོར་ཆགས་, 科迦寺, Kējiā Sì; ¥30) The atmospheric blood-red Korjak Monastery (3790m) has been an important centre for the Sakya order since it was founded by Rinchen Zangpo in 996 as the first monastery of Buddhism's second diffusion in Tibet. It escaped the worst excesses of the Cultural Revolution and the damage sustained has since been repaired. It's an easy stop if heading up from Nepal, and is worth the 20km drive south of Purang.

The atmospheric main hall is entered via an ancient wooden door with particularly fine carvings. The hall itself is presided over by a figure of Jampa (Maitreya). The lhakhang to the left features paintings from the earliest days of the monastery, while the protector chapel to the right has a huge stuffed snake lurking in the corner shadows. The puppet-like figure hanging from the main chapel's pillar is the Sakya protector Jala.

The lovely eight-pillared Jokhang building adjoining the main hall is dominated by the Rigsum Gonpo trinity of Chenresig (Avalokiteshvara), Jampelyang (Manjushri) and Chana Dorje (Vajrapani). To the right of these standing statues is a small *rangjung* (naturally arising) speaking Tara. The revered 2ft-high statue once warned the monastery's abbot how to prevent flooding of the local area. During the Cultural Revolution the statue was buried for safekeeping.

When you finish inside do a final kora around the compound to see the unusual *'om mani padme hum'* ('hail to the jewel in the lotus') mantra painted on the back wall.

The monastery is 130km from Darchen or about 107km from Chiu village on Lake Manasarovar. The drive south from Lake Manasarovar is one of the most scenic in western Tibet and it's easy to visit as a day trip. Travelling north from Nepal, Korjak is the first large village over the border in Tibet.

🛏 Sleeping & Eating

There are several hotels in town, but there are only three or four that the PSB allows foreigners to stay.

Shēngtàiyuán Bīnguǎn   HOTEL $$
(生态园宾馆; Map p191; ☑136 1897 4857; d ¥280; 🛜) A good-value choice if you don't mind being a five-minute drive out of town. Rooms are clean and comfortable and there's pleasant seating in the solarium-style atrium, plus there's a small riverside park next door. It's sometimes signed the 'Grand Hotel Eco Garden'.

Pǔlán Kǒu'àn Bīnguǎn   HOTEL $$
(普兰口岸宾馆; Map p191; ☑0897-260 2222; 13 Gongga Lu; d ¥280-360; 🛜) A decent choice in the town centre, with clean and fresh rooms, though the tiny bathrooms let the side down a bit.

Himalaya Hotel   LUXURY HOTEL $$$
(喜玛拉雅普兰酒店, Xǐmǎlāyǎ Pǔlán Jiǔdiàn; Map p191; ☑0897-260 2888; Shanxi Lu; d ¥580-680, deluxe d ¥980; ❄🛜) This plush-looking branch of Lhasa's Himalaya Hotel chain offers stylish decor, an ATM and that rarest of things in Tibet – a fruit basket, making it Purang's top hotel. The bathrooms are clean and modern but hot water is limited to evenings and mornings.

★Peacock Restaurant   CHINESE $$
(孔雀饭庄, Kǒngquè Fànzhuāng; Map p191; Gongga Lu; dishes ¥25-50; 🛜) This place has a good range of tasty Chinese dishes and friendly service in pleasant surroundings.

ℹ Information

The hill northwest of town is the site of a huge army base said to extend far into the mountain in a series of caves. It's even rumoured there are missiles here. Be careful not to photograph – even inadvertently – this or any of the small compounds in town. It's unlawful and you or your local guide could get in serious trouble for it.

Agricultural Bank of China (中国农业银行, Zhōngguó Nóngyè Yínháng; Map p191; Gongga Lu; ◷10am-1pm & 4-7pm Mon-Fri) Changes cash and has a 24-hour ATM.

Public Security Bureau (PSB; 出入境管理服务中心, Chūrùjìng Guǎnlǐ Fúwù Zhōngxīn; Map p191; ☑133 9804 2111; Gongga Lu; ◷10.30am-6pm) Your guide will most likely need to register your permits at the PSB office before you are allowed to proceed further out of town.

ℹ Getting There & Away

Western trekkers arriving from Nepal usually arrange to be met at the border town of Sher for the 28km drive via Khojarnath to Purang.

From Purang it's 74km north to Chiu Monastery on the shores of Lake Manasarovar and another 33km from there to Darchen, the starting point for the Mt Kailash kora.

The road north from Purang passes some cliff-side caves and then several picturesque villages, one of which has unusual red chörtens on a ledge above town, en route to the Gurla-la (4715m). Though still part of western Tibet, the lush terraced fields and distinct architecture feels connected to Himalayan communities of Nepal and India. Just beyond the pass, Rakshas Tal and (on a clear day) Mt Kailash come into view. Keep looking back south for dramatic views of the Himalayas.

Eastern Tibet

Best Views

➡ Draksum-tso (p196)

➡ Mikdo Glacier (p202)

➡ Rawok-tso (p202)

➡ Rinchen Family
Guesthouse (p201)

Best Temples &
Monasteries

➡ Lamaling Temple (p197)

➡ Dodung Monastery (p202)

➡ Pomda Monastery (p203)

➡ Tsodzong Monastery
(p197)

➡ Demo Monastery (p198)

Why Go?

Overlapping much of the historic Tibetan region of Kham (ཁམས་), eastern Tibet is the face you never knew Tibet had: a land of raging rivers and deep gorges, immense pine forests and azalea-filled meadows, outspoken monks and rebel nomads. It is here that the plateau begins its descent towards the subtropical Sìchuān basin, and the landscapes represent both extremes: you can drive over a scrubby high mountain pass dusted with snow and a few hours later be sliding your way through rainforest on a mud-bath road. Chances are you'll be the only foreigner in sight.

Most of eastern Tibet is off limits these days but fortunately the traditional territory of Kongpo, a cradle of early Tibetan civilisation, is open. In this lush, fairy-tale-like land there are intriguing distinctions in architecture, dress, food, worship (the area has a high number of Bönpo) and quirky legends regarding towering figures of Tibetan history.

When to Go

➡ May and June are the best months to travel in eastern Tibet, followed closely by September and October. Temperatures are at their most comfortable in these periods, while the trade-off for an early-season visit is that heavier rains mean much of the landscape is covered in blankets of bright-yellow rapeseed flowers and, at higher elevations, blooming azaleas.

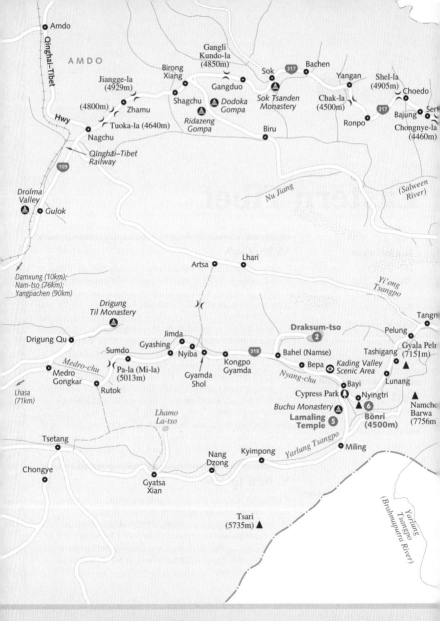

Eastern Tibet Highlights

1 Mikdo Glacier (p202)
Marvelling at this massive glacier in the shadow of a 6385m peak.

2 Draksum-tso (p196)
Exploring the shores of a holy lake and the island monastery therein.

3 Bakha Gompa (p201)
Learning why a monastery was built on the grave of Princess Wenchang's child and enjoying sunset views from the porch of a guesthouse.

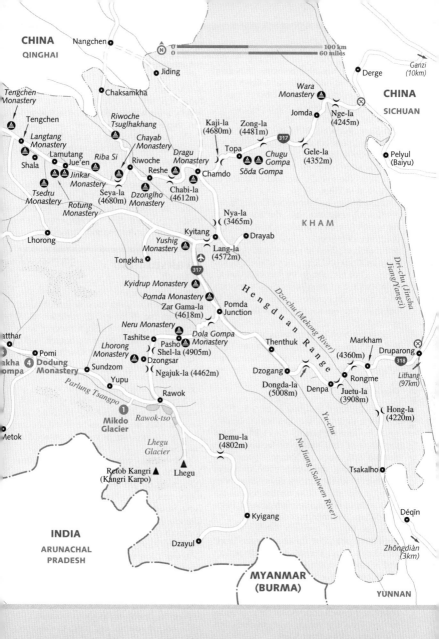

CHINA
QINGHAI

Nangchen

Jiding

Chaksamkha

Tengchen Monastery

Tengchen

Langtang Monastery

Lamutang

Shala Jue'en Jinkar Monastery

Riwoche Tsuglhakhang

Riba Si

Chayab Monastery

Riwoche Reshe

Dragu Monastery

Chabi-la (4612m)

Kaji-la (4680m)

Zong-la (4481m)

Topa

Chamdo

Söda Gompa

Chugu Gompa

Gele-la (4352m)

Wara Monastery

Jomda

Nge-la (4245m)

Derge

Ganzi (10km)

CHINA
SICHUAN

Pelyul (Baiyu)

KHAM

Dri-chu (Jinsha Jiang/Yangzi)

Tsedru Monastery

Rotung Monastery

Seya-la (4680m)

Dzonglho Monastery

Nya-la (3465m)

Drayab

Lhorong

Yushig Monastery

Kyitang

Lang-la (4572m)

Tongkha

317

Kyidrup Monastery

Pomda Monastery

Zar Gama-la (4618m)

Pomda Junction

Neru Monastery

Hengduan Range

Dza-chu (Mekong River)

atthar

Pomi

akha ompa

4 Dodung Monastery

Tashitse

Lhorong Monastery

Sundzom

Pasho Shel-la (4905m)

Dzongsar

Ngajuk-la (4462m)

Dola Gompa Monastery

Thenthuk

Markham (4360m)

Druparong

318

Lithang (97km)

Yupu

Parlung Tsangpo

Rawok

Dzogang

Dongda-la (5008m)

Denpa

Rongme

Juetu-la (3908m)

Hong-la (4220m)

1 Mikdo Glacier

Rawok-tso

Lhegu Glacier

Retob Kangri (Kangri Karpo)

Lhegu

Demu-la (4802m)

Yu-chu

Nu Jiang (Salween River)

Tsakalho

Déqìn

Metok

INDIA
ARUNACHAL PRADESH

Kyigang

Dzayul

MYANMAR (BURMA)

Zhōngdiàn (3km)

YÚNNÁN

4 **Dodung Monastery**
(p202) Seeing traditional wood-block printing at a stunning location atop a forested hillside.

5 **Lamaling Temple** (p197)
Admiring the rare Zangtok Pelri architectural style, unique to the Nyingma order of Tibetan Buddhism.

6 **Bönri kora** (p198)
Emulating the devotional spirit of Bön pilgrims as they circumambulate the religion's holiest mountain.

History

The area around Chamdo was one of the first settled in Tibet, as indicated by the 5000-year-old Neolithic remains at nearby Karo. Fossilised millet hints at a five-millennia-old tradition of agriculture in the region.

Kham was the home of many early lamas, including the founders of the Drigungpa and Karmapa schools. In 1070 many Buddhists fled persecution in central Tibet for Kham, where they set up influential monasteries, later returning to central Tibet to spearhead the so-called second diffusion of Buddhism in Tibet.

Lhasa first gained control of Kham thanks to Mongol assistance, but the majority of the region has traditionally enjoyed de facto political independence. Until recently, much of Kham comprised of many small fiefdoms ruled by kings (in Derge, for instance), lamas (Lithang) or hereditary chieftains (Bathang). Relations with China were mostly restricted to the trade caravans, which brought in bricks of Chinese tea and left with pastoral products.

Today eastern Tibet remains quite heavily Sinicised along the southern Sìchuān–Tibet Hwy. Off the main highways, Khampa life remains culturally strong.

Permits

Military presence is strong in eastern Tibet, and for a long time this has been a heavily restricted area for general travel. Since 2008 the whole of the Chamdo prefecture (except Rawok) and much of Nyingchi prefecture, especially along the border with Arunachel Pradesh (which the Chinese claim), have been closed to foreigners. Be aware that regions can close without notice, especially around Tibetan holidays and important dates.

At the time of research, foreign visitors need three permits to travel in eastern Tibet: an Alien's Travel Permit, a military permit and a Tibet Tourism Bureau (TTB) permit. These permits need to be registered at the Public Security Bureau (PSB), the Foreign Affairs Office and the Military Office. Your travel agency will organise all these permits for you (and the registration process), but give them at least three weeks.

Police in this region are particularly picky about verifying travel permits, so demand that your travel agent lists every single monastery, temple and overnight stay specifically or risk the disappointment of being turned back at the gate.

NYINGTRI PREFECTURE
ཉིང་ཁྲི་གྲོང་ཁྱེར། 林芝

Nyingtri prefecture (ཉིང་ཁྲི་གྲོང་ཁྱེར། , 林芝, Línzhī) is not the Tibet you think you know – it's lush, green and at lower elevations than most of Tibet. Once famous among other Tibetans for wily villagers who would poison guests and offer their souls as sacrifice to the gods, visitors now come for picturesque glaciers, scenic mountain lakes, and quiet sanctuaries of Bön and Tibetan Buddhism hidden up wooded mountain valleys.

Covering much of the area historically known as Kongpo (p199), the region is prime overlanding territory for Chinese road-trippers but only recently came back on the radar for international travellers.

Draksum-tso   བྲག་གསུམ་མཚོ
巴松错

📞 0894 / ELEV 3490M

One of eastern Tibet's most beautiful lakes, **Draksum-tso** (Bāsōng Cuò; admission ¥120, shuttle bus ¥50; ⊙ 8am-9.30pm summer, 9am-6pm winter) is also its most sacred, with strong connections to three towering figures in Tibetan history. It's the soul lake of Gesar of Ling, the semi-mythical king of Tibetan legends and epic poems. Gesar is said to have resided near the lake and spent years in one of the nearby monasteries. Ruins associated with the king can be found on the road up to the lake, as well as around the lake itself.

Draksum-tso was also visited by Guru Rinpoche and, as in many other places, the great sage left signs of his journey on rocks and caves. Finally, the Nyimpgpa lama Sangye Linpa founded the Tsodzong Monastery (p197) on a tiny islet just off the southern shore. Today the monastery is one of Kham's most important pilgrimage sites.

About 12km from the highway junction, the road up to the lake passes tall 12-sided **stone towers** on both sides. No one quite knows for what purpose they were built – they stand empty and entry-less. Locals refer to them as *dudkhang* (demons' houses) and recite legends connecting them to Gesar of Ling.

There's one cluster of inexpensive Sìchuān restaurants in Bahel village at the highway turn-off, and another at the entrance to the Draksum-Tso scenic area.

Draksum-tso is about a six-hour drive east of Lhasa, or two hours west of Bāyī. The road to the lake branches off the Sìchuān–Tibet Hwy 318 at Bahel (also known as Namse). From there it's around 35km to the lake up a gorgeous farming valley dotted with Tibetan villages and intersected with deep-sided canyons.

Tsodzong Monastery   BUDDHIST MONASTERY

The monastery (Fortress on the Lake) is a small Nyingmapa chapel tucked into the forest on a tiny islet off the shore of Draksum-tso. Associated with the 8th-century king Trisong Detsen, it is also the 14th-century birthplace of Sangye Lingpa, a *terton*. *Tertons* are reincarnations of Guru Rinpoche's disciples and are tasked with recovering the great spiritual leader's buried relics and texts. The monastery and surrounding kora are filled with holy relics and attract numerous pilgrims.

Dáqièlā Sightseeing Platform   VIEWPOINT

(达切拉观光台, Dáqièlā Guānguāngtái) Around 500m back to the west from the Mid-lake Island Tourist Service Centre (湖心岛旅游服务中心, Húxīndǎo Lǚyóu Fúwù Zhōngxīn), climb a small hill to a viewing platform with magnificent panoramic views over the lake and Tsodzong Monastery.

Shuba Ancient Fort   ARCHAEOLOGICAL SITE

(秀巴千年古堡, Xiùbà Qiānnián Gǔbǎo; ¥90; ◷9am-6pm) These reconstructed towers, known as the Shuba Ancient Fort, stand off the old highway 7km east of Bahel. They are said to date from the reign of Songtsen Gampo (r 630–49).

Bāyī   བཀྲ་ཤིས། 八一

🖉 0894 / POP 70,000 / ELEV 2990M

Bāyī, a recent Chinese creation close to the older Tibetan town of Nyingtri, is the largest town found along this stretch of Hwy 318 and now the capital of Nyingtri prefecture. It is surrounded by forested hills and the descent into town offers fine views of the valley, though the town itself is nothing remarkable. Locals tend to be coolly curious rather than friendly towards foreigners.

Ask your guide to show you Bayi Pelri mountain, on the east side of town. This holy mountain is associated with the epic battles of Guru Rinpoche against an array of evil forces. The kora (pilgrim circuit) around the mountain takes a few hours to complete, though it is highly unlikely you will be allowed to join.

◉ Sights

★ Lamaling Temple   BUDDHIST TEMPLE

(བླ་མ་གླིང་དགོན་པ་, 喇嘛岭寺, Lǎmalíng Sì; ¥15) The centrepiece of a large walled complex, the colourful Lamaling Temple is a rare example of the Zangtok Pelri style of building. This style, which imitates the 'Glorious Copper Mountain Paradise' of Guru Rinpoche with a three-storey pagoda-like temple, is unique to the Nyingma order. As with all such temples, the ground floor has a statue of Guru Rinpoche, the second Chenresig (Avalokiteshvara), while the top chapel is for Sakyamuni.

The Glorious Copper Mountain is Guru Rinpoche's Pure Land, and has been described as a mountain on an island in the cosmic ocean. The island forms a mandala, which is represented architecturally by the Lamaling complex walls: the temple, with its golden-eaved pagoda structure rising from a square base (itself coloured differently on each side), is the mountain in the centre. Statues of Guru Rinpoche are matched with Chenresig and Öpagme to symbolise his birth legend in which Öpagme imagined a being of perfect enlightenment and compassion, and Chenresig sent a golden *vajra* (thunderbolt) into a lotus bud to give birth to the guru.

The original Lamaling Temple burned down in the 1930s and a new structure was built on the flat below. In the 1960s this, too, was destroyed during the Cultural Revolution. In 1989 work began on the current temple under the supervision of the daughter of Dudjom Rinpoche (1904–87), former head of the Nyingma order, who had his seat at Lamaling. The monastery is home to around 20 monks, 30 nuns and a couple of languid nuns.

Take your shoes off before entering the temple – the floor is polished wood. On the ground floor next to the Guru Rinpoche statue look for a stone footprint of the guru on the altar. A passageway behind the altar leads to a mezzanine level with four protector chapels in each corner. Also note the giant coloured prayer beads festooned on the outer walls.

The complex's other main building, to the right, is the assembly hall, where religious services are held on the 10th, 15th and 25th days of each lunar month. The hall is dominated by a huge statue of Sakyamuni and more images of Dudjom Rinpoche wearing his characteristic sunglasses. Pilgrims circumambulate both this building and the main temple.

Lamaling is about 30km south of Bāyī, around 4km up from the signposted turn-off 1km south of Buchu Temple.

Bāyī

Bāyī

🛏 Sleeping
1 Azalea Hotel..A2
2 Mínshān Grand Hotel...........................A2

🍴 Eating
3 Āmā Chúfáng B2
4 Héngyuán Xiǎochī..................................A2
5 Xiōngdì Xiǎochǎo A2

🛍 Shopping
6 Bǎiyì Supermarket B1

Buchu Temple　　　BUDDHIST TEMPLE

(བུ་ཆུ་དགོན།, 布久寺, Bùjiǔ Sì) **FREE** This small Gelugpa monastery dates from the 7th century, when it was built at the command of King Songtsen Gampo as one of the demoness-subduing temples; it pins the demoness' right elbow. Inside are a number of holy relics, including a footprint of Guru Rinpoche and a *lado* (a 'life supporting' stone) in a glass case. It's home to five monks.

Bönri　　　MOUNTAIN

(བོན་རི།, 苯日神山, Běnrì Shénshān) Bönri is the Bön religion's most sacred mountain, a sprawling massif where Bön founder Tonpa Shenrab fought and defeated his arch rival Khyabpa Lagring, and where legend holds that Guru Rinpoche fought epic battles against an array of evil forces. Bönpo pilgrims come from all over Tibet to circumambulate the mountain in an anticlockwise direction. Foreign travellers are currently not permitted to do the full kora, though it is possible to do a shortened version over the 4500m Bönri-la pass.

Demo Monastery　　　BUDDHIST MONASTERY

(德木寺, Démù Sì; Qunigongga village; 曲尼贡嘎村) **FREE** This small Gelugpa (Yellow Hat) sect monastery with a hilltop location was founded in the 17th century as a branch of Drepung Monastery (p84). It was named after the famous lama Temo, who later became a black sheep and was ostracised from the community after having been accused of trying to harm the 13th Dalai Lama with black magic. The monastery was damaged heavily in a 1949 earthquake and rebuilding started only in 1990; it's now home to 20 monks.

Neche Goshog Monastery　　　MONASTERY

(尼池寺, Níchí Sì; Nyingtri village; 林芝村; Línzhī cūn) **FREE** This small, golden-roofed Bön monastery was rebuilt in 2008 after being gutted in a fire. It's home to eight monks and is famous for a 2000-year-old juniper tree that is sacred to Bönpos (the name Neche Goshog translates roughly to 'Gate of the Juniper Tree'). The modern temple, dating to 1981, is built on the site of a 500-year-old chapel that was destroyed in a fire. It's about 17km east of Bāyī, on your right just before you reach Nyingtri.

Kading Valley Scenic Area　　　FOREST

(卡定沟风景区, Kǎdìnggōu Fēngjǐngqū; ¥50) This small forested park contains a 200m-high waterfall. It's a beautiful, fresh area for an hour-long break. Note that, while the Chinese have built pathways around the forest, lined them with bamboo, and created fresh legends out of the many rocks and land formations in the area, this does not sit right with Tibetans who consider the place sacred to Paldon Lhamo.

Cypress Park　　　FOREST

(世界柏树王园林, Shìjiè Bóshù Wáng Yuánlín; ¥30; ⏰9am-5pm) Two kilometres southeast of Bāyī a stand of ancient cypress trees dot a steep but inviting hillside. The most venerable cypress is a reported 2500 years old, making it the oldest tree in China, and as old as the Buddha himself. This, in addition to the tree being sacred to Bön founder Tonpa Shenrab, makes the site exceptionally holy for Tibetans, and a prime pilgrim spot.

🛏 Sleeping

A full day's drive from Lhasa including stops for sightseeing, Bāyī is an obvious choice for an overnight stay and there are a handful of hotels in town that accept foreigners.

Azalea Hotel HOTEL $$
(杜鹃花酒店; Dùjuānhuā Jiǔdiàn; Map p198; ☑139 8994 0450, 0894-582 3222; azasuoci@168.com; 408 Guangdong Lu; 广东路408号; tw/tr ¥220/340; ❀🛜) The hotel is ageing but is still a good first choice for clean and comfortable rooms in a central location.

Mínshān Grand Hotel HOTEL $$$
(岷山大酒店, Mínshān Dàjiǔdiàn; Map p198; ☑0894-587 2999; www.msanehotel.com; Binhe Dadao Zhongduan; 滨河大道中段; r incl breakfast ¥520; ❀🛜) Clean modern rooms and a riverside location combine to make this the nicest hotel in central Bāyī; discounts of up to 20% make the price a little more palatable as well.

🍴 Eating & Drinking

In northern Bāyī, Xianggang Lu (香港路) and the surrounding alleys make up a small pedestrianised area with the highest concentration of restaurants in town. Outside of there, head to the main roads for Sìchuān noodle shops, and Guangdong Lu (广东路)

for Hui Muslim restaurants. For breakfast, steamed dumplings (包子, *bāozi*) are sold in tiny shops along the main roads.

Āmā Chúfáng TIBETAN $
(阿妈厨房; Map p198; ☑138 8904 8050; dishes ¥10-24; ⊙8.30am-8pm; 🛜) East of the canal area, this small but friendly Tibetan teahouse with a seemingly endless supply of tea does a great job with Tibetan and Chinese dishes.

Héngyuán Xiǎochī CHINESE $
(恒源小吃; Map p198; 109 Fujian Lu; 福建路109号; dishes ¥15-35; ⊙9am-4am) This late-running establishment specialises in pig's trotters (猪蹄, zhūtí; half a trotter ¥15) from the local free-ranging swine. It also serves decent noodles – try the spicy *dàndàn miàn* (担担面; per small/large bowl ¥15/18).

Xiōngdì Xiǎochǎo SICHUAN $$
(兄弟小炒; Map p198; ☑139 8904 6929; 180 Pingan Lu; 平安路180号; dishes ¥28-58; ⊙9am-10pm) Convenient to Bāyī's main cluster of

---

THE KONGPO REGION

Kongpo is a large traditional territory in southwestern Kham. While no longer an official administrative name (though it's more or less the same territory as Nyingtri prefecture), for Tibetans it still spells out an area that is linguistically, culturally and even ecologically distinct. A former kingdom of the early Yarlung kings and a rival to Lhasa, Kongpo has for centuries been vilified by central Tibetan rulers as a land of incest and poison, a land where strangers are drugged so that locals can steal their souls.

The traditional Kongpo costume features a round hat with an upturned rim of golden brocade for men (known as a *gyasha*) and a pretty pillbox hat with winged edges (known as a *dieu*) for women. Men also wear brown woollen tunics, belted around the waist.

Kongpo is a stronghold for Bön, with several of the religion's holiest pilgrim sites found in the forested hills around Bāyī. Locals also revere Princess Wenchang, who is seen as having a special fondness for the region she reputedly passed through on her way to meet King Songtsen Gampo in the 7th century.

Owing to the heavy rainfall, Kongpo houses have slanted roofs, unlike the flat-tops seen in Lhasa. These days sheet metal (often coloured pink or blue) is used, but the open gables allow for ventilation of the attic space (used to store goods).

Barley, potatoes, corn and other staples are farmed all over the region, but several local foods are worth seeking out. Best in our opinion is the red chili mashed into a paste and spread on flat bread. The chili has a sweetness of a jalapeño. You might be able to to eat the adorable free-roaming pigs – they apparently live up to their Chinese name of Zàng xiāng zhū (藏香猪; fragrant Tibetan pig). In the Lunang area check out the stone-pot chicken.

Warmer, wetter and more forested than anywhere else in Tibet, Kongpo has numerous biological niches with large concentrations of rare animals and plants. In the dense forests of the subtropical regions along the southern borderlands are takins, red pandas, long-tailed monkeys, musk deer and abundant bird species. The region is also a botanical powerhouse, and attracted the attention of intrepid 19th- and 20th-century British plant hunters. From May onwards Kongpo is a riot of wildflowers, bursting with 190 species of rhododendron, 110 types of gentians, and rare flowers such as the blue poppy. Pockets of ancient cypresses up to 2500 years old also continue to thrive, and the first week of April brings the bloom of cherry blossom trees.

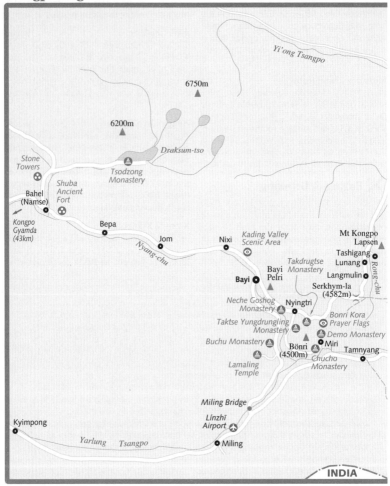

tourist-friendly hotels, this small cafe does excellent Sìchuān dishes.

Bǎiyì Supermarket   MARKET
(百益超市, Bǎiyì Cháoshì; Map p198; 13 Gong-bu Laojie; 工布老街113号; ⊙9.30am-9.30pm) Stock up on snacks for the road and lunches for hikes at Bāyī's best-stocked supermarket.

ⓘ Information

Bank of China (中国银行, Zhōngguó Yínháng; ☑95566; www.boc.cn; 399 Bayi Dajie; 八一大街399号; ⊙9am-6pm Mon-Fri) Two blocks south of Ping'an Lu on the east side of Bayi Dajie. ATM accepts foreign cards.

Bank of China ATM (中国银行取款机, Zhōng-guó Yínháng Qǔkuǎnjī; Map p198; ☑95566; 76 Bayi Dajie Beiduan; 八一大街北段76号; ⊙24hr) Stand-alone ATM near the main roundabout.

Police Station (公安局, Gōng'ānjú; Map p198; ☑0894-524 6185; 88 Pingan Lu; 平安路88号; ⊙9.30am-12.30pm & 3.30-5.30pm)

ⓘ Getting There & Away

Driving from Lhasa to Bāyī directly takes around six hours, more with sightseeing stops. Leaving Bāyī to the east it's around a five-hour drive to Pomi and a further eight hours to Pomda in Chamdo prefecture.

Tsangpo and Rong-chu rivers (coming from different directions) meet here and then continue southeast through a canyon that may be the world's deepest. After Tangmi the valley begins to widen again, the river swells to over a kilometre wide, and stone-house villages with yellow rapeseed fields hemmed in by wattle fences appear on the banks. These achingly beautiful landscapes are backed by towering snow-capped peaks, so be sure you make time for photo breaks.

Travelling east from Tashigang, the Rong-chu river valley narrows and enters a deep canyon where road washouts are common and delays are to be expected: it could take two hours to drive this route, or double that. At Km4036 look for a small bridge south to Bakha Island. Cross and head left 200m to reach Bakha Gompa.

Continuing east from Bakha Island, expect around one hour to reach Pomi.

Bakha Gompa · BUDDHIST MONASTERY

(ঽ'ད, 巴卡寺) On pretty Bakha Island in the middle of the Parlung Tsangpo sits Bakha Gompa, an 800-year-old Nyingma monastery which was previously the seat of power in Powo (the traditional name of the once highly independent region bordering Kongpo). The monastery is home to 11 monks and is reputed to have been built on the grave site of the illegitimate child of Princess Wencheng and Tibetan Minister Gar Tongtsen (who had accompanied her from Chang'an).

★ Rinchen Family Guesthouse · GUESTHOUSE $$

(仁青家庭旅馆, Rénqīng Jiātíng Lǚguǎn; ☑139 0894 0848; r ¥280-380) Set on a slope above the Parlung Tsangpo beside Bakha Gompa, this family-run guesthouse is one of the most scenically placed in all of Kham, overlooking the monastery, the river and snowy peaks beyond. In the handsome pine main lodge you'll find cosy wood-panelled rooms (those on the 2nd floor are best) with large bathrooms, Tibetan details and outstanding balcony views.

Pomi | ষ্ট্রিমন্ম 波密

☑0894 / POP 28,000 / ELEV 2740M

This county capital (Bōmì) has well-stocked shops and plenty of hotels and restaurants, making it a good place to spend the night (though Bakha Island is prettier). The main street sports wide sidewalks, and re-facaded buildings in a fake but still pleasant Tibetan style. High forested mountains provide the

Línzhī Airport (林芝米林机场, Línzhī Mǐlín Jīchǎng), about 50km south of Bāyī near Miling village (米林; Mǐlín), has daily flights to Chéngdū, Chóngqìng and Guǎngzhōu.

Bakha Island ঽ'ད 巴卡岛

☑0891 / ELEV 2680M

The road from Tashigang to Bakha Gompa, situated on idyllic Bakha Island (Bākǎ Dǎo) in the Parlung Tsangpo river, is alternately one of the most dramatic and bucolic in all of Kham.

At the village of Pelung (鲁朗, Lǔlǎng), the water flow changes direction: the Parlung

backdrop, while Dodung Monastery sits on a forested hilltop above town.

On the southeast side of the central square, clean and pleasant rooms at the **Dēngfēng Dàfàndiàn** (登峰大饭店; ☑0894-566 5556; Pomi Sq; 波密广场; r incl breakfast ¥380; ❇️❒️) make it the obvious choice for travellers who aren't on a backpacker budget. The run-down but acceptably clean **Mínzú Bīnguǎn** (民族宾馆; ☑0894-542 8188, 152 8914 5666; Pomi Sq; 新农贸市场; r ¥200; ❇️❒️) caters to lower price points, accessible through an alleyway off the central square to the north of the highway.

Pomi makes a natural stopping point between Bāyī and Pasho, around five hours' drive from each with no stops.

Dodung Monastery
BUDDHIST MONASTERY

(多东寺, Duōdōng Sì) This tranquil 17th-century Nyingma-sect monastery is set on a pine-clad hill overlooking the valley, and is home to 52 monks. The main prayer hall includes the footprint of the seventh Khamtrul Rinpoche, Sangye Tenzin (1909–29). Upstairs are murals depicting the life of two forms of Gesar, as well as Guru Rinpoche and Tsepame (Amitayus). Also look for a traditional wood-block printing room just left of the entrance.

CHAMDO PREFECTURE

Remote and beautiful Chamdo prefecture was for many years the rough overland route from southwestern China into the Tibet Autonomous Region, but most of the area has been closed to foreign visitors since 2010. Rawok, Pasho and Pomda were open at the time of research, accessible either from Nyingtri prefecture or the overland route to Yúnnán via Markham.

Rawok ར་འོག་ 然乌

☑0895 / POP 2900 / ELEV 3910M

Rawok (Ránwū) is a small outpost off Hwy 318 on the northeast corner of the eponymous lake, a decent place to break up the long drive between Pomda and Bāyī and an excellent base for visiting the local glaciers and lakes.

There are camping spots around the lakeshore, but check first that you are allowed to camp; often the authorities don't permit it. In that case, the **Diānzàng Míngzhū Dàjiǔdiàn** (滇藏明珠大酒店; ☑155 9915 8657; Rawok; r¥150; ❇️❒️) is the only show in town.

Rawok is around halfway between Pomi and Pasho, roughly 2½ hours east of the former and two hours west of the latter.

★ Mikdo Glacier
GLACIER

(米堆冰川, Mǐduī Bīngchuān; ¥50) This quiet and picturesque glacier, under a towering 6385m peak, is reached by first driving 7km off the main highway to a car park and a cluster of shops and restaurants at Mǐduī Village (米堆村, Mǐduī Cūn). From here the glacier is a further 1.5km along a wooden pathway ending at a series of viewing platforms overlooking the glacier and a small lake. On the walk back, detour through the village for a glimpse into Tibetan life in the region.

Rawok-tso
LAKE

(然乌湖, Ránwū Hú) Ringed by mountains all around, the two largest of the three connected Rawok lakes are joined by a stream that on the map resembles an infinity symbol. Rawok Lower Lake (然乌下湖, Ránwū Xiàhú) is the first you'll encounter if you approach from Bāyī. Long stretches of sandy beach here call for a leisurely lakeside stroll, while past the town centre Rawok Middle Lake (然乌中湖, Ránwū Zhōnghú) and the craggy hills along the shore call more to climbers and photographers.

Pasho དཔའ་ཤོད་ 八宿

☑0895 / POP 4000 / ELEV 3240M

The pleasant one-street town of Pasho (Bāsù) is worth a few hours' break for the two small monasteries in the vicinity, as well as a convenient overnight from which to visit Pomda as a day trip before returning towards Lhasa.

The local police here are stricter than most, so if you want to visit the nearby monasteries you'll need them specifically listed on your Tibet Tourism (TTB) Permit.

The **Nùjiāngyún Dàjiǔdiàn** (怒江云大酒店; ☑0895-456 6666; Baima Shangjie; 白玛上街; r incl breakfast ¥480; ❇️❒️) is the only place in town that can accommodate foreigners, and standard discounts give it a palatable price.

Pasho's long main street is overwhelmed by Sìchuān joints of various varieties – though if you need a break, there are a handful of midsized markets where it's possible to self-cater something simple.

From Pasho it's three hours east towards Pomda or travelling west it's two hours to Rawok and 10 hours to Bāyī.

DRIVING TOUR: OVERLAND ON THE YÚNNÁN–TIBET HIGHWAY

From Lhasa (p50) to Bāyī is a full-day's drive, so it's best just to include some of the minor stops in Ü region along the route.

On your second day visit temples Lamaling, Buchu and Neche Goshog in Bāyī (p197) before continuing to Bakha Island and overnighting at Rinchen Family Guesthouse; or add a day to your itinerary and spend the afternoon hiking the Bönri kora after a visit to two small monasteries near the trailhead.

Explore Bakha Island (p201) on the morning of your third day before continuing to Pomi (p201) to visit the hilltop Dodung Monastery.

On day four push on to Rawok (p202) and the Rawok-tso lakes (p202) surrounding the settlement, with a stop at the remarkable Mikdo Glacier (p202) about 35km before the town itself. Though it is possible to overnight in Rawok if the day runs short, travellers would be advised to stop in Pasho to prepare for the long trip to Pomda the next morning.

On your fifth day the two small monasteries in Pasho (p202) are worth a look in the morning before hitting the road, along which the landscapes slowly transition to the desertified terrain more typical of Chamdo prefecture. Around three hours after leaving Pasho is Pomda Junction (p203), where hotels and restaurants service road-trippers and overnight travellers looking to spend some serious time at Pomda Monastery.

On days six and seven though the landscapes remain impressive between Pomda and Zhōngdiàn, major tourist sites are scarce. Plan to overnight in the small town of Markham, just north of the Yúnnán border, before finishing in Zhōngdiàn or Lìjiāng (both of which are open to independent travellers and so don't require guides or drivers).

A handful of teahouses lines the main strip, but coffee-starved travellers will want to head to **Wèijìng Coffee** (未境咖啡, Wèijìng Kāfēi; ☑0895-456 5588; 2nd fl, off Baima Shang-lu; ☺9.30am-11pm; 🛜). If you're looking for something a little harder, cafes and markets can rustle up a can of *chang* (barley beer) or sometimes even a bottle of imported beer.

Neru Monastery   BUDDHIST MONASTERY
(呐然寺, Nàrán Sì; ☺dawn-dusk) **FREE** This Ge-lugpa monastery, dating to 1595, is home to 40 monks and nuns and is worth a visit if you have a couple of spare hours in Pasho. There's a daily 7am prayer meeting that's open to visitors and debating is held most days at 6pm, except on the 10th and 25th days of the Tibetan month.

Dola Gompa Monastery   BUDDHIST SITE
(多拉神山, Duōlā Shénshān; Hwy 318; ☺dawn-dusk) **FREE** Today the Nyingmapa school Dola Gompa Monastery is home to 32 monks and nuns. The older lower chapel dates to the 9th century, but was undergoing a complete renovation when we visited. The area is surrounded by chörtens and ancient yak-hide prayer wheels, and is a great place to meet local pilgrims. A popular kora (pilgrim circuit) leads up the mountainside to a plateau and then descends west to Pasho town, with fine views of the arid valley.

Pomda `   ཕོམ་མདའ་ 邦达

☑0895 / POP 150 / ELEV 4120M

Tiny Pomda (Bāngdá) may feel like it's on the edge of the map, but an impressive monastery and arid landscape distinct from west of the region makes for a long, rewarding and offbeat trip.

Pomda junction is a three-point cluster of restaurants, teahouses and guesthouses that makes for a good lunch stop; there are no facilities at the monastery itself.

If you need to overnight here, the **Bāngdá Máogē Dàjiǔdiàn** (邦达毛哥大酒店; ☑136 2895 1738; Pomda junction; r ¥150; 🛜) is the best option. The junction of Hwys 317 and 318 leads west towards Pasho (three hours) and Lhasa (20 hours) or east towards Yúnnán province. Hwy 317 north to Chamdo is closed to foreigners beyond Pomda Monastery, including the next 38km to Qamdo Bamda Airport.

Pomda Monastery   BUDDHIST MONASTERY
(邦达寺, Bāngdá Sì; ☺dawn-dusk) **FREE** The monastery dates back 360 years, but was destroyed in the Cultural Revolution and rebuilt in 1981. It is now home to 53 monks. The main hall has excellent murals and statues of Sakyamuni (Sakya Thukpa) flanked by Jampelyang (Manjushi), Jampa (Maitreya) and Drölma (Tara). The inner sanctum features Tsongkhapa (founder of the Geulgpa sect) and his two disciples.

Tibetan Treks

Best Long Trek

➡ Ganden to Samye (p210)

Best Short Trek

➡ Tsurphu to Dorje Ling
(p215)

Best Cultural Trek

➡ Mt Kailash Kora (p221)

Best Trek to Spot Wildlife

➡ Nyenchen Tanglha
Traverse (p229)

Why Go?

Tibet, the highest land on earth, is a trekker's dream. Its towering mountains, high valleys and sacred landscapes offer unbounded opportunities for walking. On foot the joys of the Tibetan landscape are heightened and immediate, and all other modes of transport pale in comparison. The wonders of Tibet's natural environment are enhanced by the people met along the trail, heirs to an ancient and fascinating way of life.

Treks range from the sacred walk around My Kailash in the festive company of Tibetan pilgrims, to full-on wilderness treks where you'll meet only the occasional herders' camp. Most treks are high but short and are conveniently combined with visits to some of Tibet's great monasteries.

Tibet's landscapes are beautiful but harsh and treks here perhaps best suit experienced trekkers or travellers who know how they react to high altitude.

When to Trek

➡ The best time to trek in Tibet is during the warmer months from May to October.

➡ May and June are excellent months without much rain or snowfall but some high alpine passes may still be closed.

➡ July and August are the warmest months of the year, but they tend to be rainy and this can make walking messy and trails harder to find.

➡ September and October are excellent months for trekking, but in high areas the nights are cold and early snow is always a possibility.

PLANNING YOUR TREK

For all its attractions, Tibet is a formidable environment where even day walks involve survival skills and generous portions of determination. The remoteness of Tibet combined with its extreme climate poses special challenges for walkers – and unique rewards. As it's situated on the highest plateau on earth and crisscrossed by the world's loftiest mountains, nothing comes easily and careful preparation is all important. Even on the most popular treks high passes up to 5600m are crossed.

Trekkers must be prepared for extremes in climate, even in the middle of summer. A hot, sunny day can turn cold and miserable in a matter of minutes, especially at higher elevations. Night temperatures above 4700m routinely fall below freezing, even in July and August. At other times of year it gets even colder. In midwinter in northwestern Tibet, minimum temperatures reach −40°C. Yet Tibet is a study in contrasts, and in summer a scorching sun and hot, blustery winds can make even the hardiest walker scurry for any available shade. Between the two extremes, the Tibetan climate – cool and dry – is ideal for walking, as long as you are prepared for the worst.

It's a good idea to budget an extra day for your trek in case you get on the road more slowly than intended. Your guide might also need additional time hiring local help and beasts of burden.

Before embarking on a trek, make sure you're up to the challenge of high-altitude walking. Test your capabilities on day walks in the hills around Lhasa such as the Dode Valley (p92) or to Bumpa Ri (p205), the prayer-flag-draped peak on the far side of the Kyi-chu from Lhasa.

What to Bring

You need to be prepared for extremes in weather and terrain in Tibet. The time of year and the places where you choose to walk will dictate the equipment you need.

Clothing & Footwear

As a minimum, you will need basic warm clothing, including a hat, gloves, down jacket, thermal underwear, warm absorbent socks, fast-drying base layer and a waterproof and windproof shell, as well as comfortable and well-made pants and shirts. Women may want to add a long skirt to their clothing list. Bring loose-fitting clothes that cover your arms, legs and neck, and a wide-brimmed hat like the ones Tibetans wear.

If you attempt winter trekking, you will certainly need more substantial mountaineering clothing. Many people opt for synthetic clothing, but also consider traditional wool or sheep fleece, which have proven themselves in the mountains of Tibet for centuries. One of your most important assets will be a pair of strong, well-fitting hiking boots. And remember to break them in before starting your trekking!

Equipment

Four essential items are a tent, a sleeping bag, a mattress and a portable stove. There are few settlements in the remote areas of Tibet and provisions are hard to come by, so you and your guide need to be self-sufficient. Only the Kailash kora trek offers accommodation en route – for all others you'll need full camping equipment. Invest in a four-season tent that can handle storms, snow and heavy winds. A warm down sleeping bag rated to −20°C is a must. Manufacturers tend to overrate the effectiveness of their bags, so always buy a warmer one than you think you'll need.

You will also need a strong, comfortable backpack or duffel large enough to carry all of your gear and supplies. When trekking with animal transport a daypack is essential for your immediate daily needs. A bag cover or sack to protect your bag when on the back of a yak or horse is a wise investment.

TREKKING DISCLAIMER

Although the authors and publisher have done their utmost to ensure the accuracy of all information in this guide, they cannot accept any responsibility for any loss, injury or inconvenience sustained by people using this guide. They cannot guarantee that the tracks and routes described here have not become impassable for any reason in the interval between research and publication.

The fact that a trip or area is described in this guidebook does not mean that it is safe for you and your trekking party. You are ultimately responsible for judging your own capabilities in the conditions you encounter.

Your daypack should always contain a water bottle and water purification, snacks, sunglasses, rain gear, a fleece, a head torch (flashlight), map, sun cream, toilet paper, a whistle, Diamox and matches.

Other basic items include a compass, a pocketknife, a first-aid kit, waterproof matches, a sewing kit and walking stick or ski pole. This last item not only acts as a walking aid, but also as a defence against dog attacks. Tibetan dogs can be particularly large and brutal, and they roam at will in nearly every village and herders' camp. Bring your walking stick or pole from home, or purchase trekking poles in Lhasa.

Petrol for camping stoves is very hard to buy these days and you may have to ask your tour driver to siphon fuel for you. Kerosene (煤油; *méiyóu* in Chinese; *sanum* in Tibetan) is equally hard to buy. Butane gas canisters are hard to find in Tibet these days, but your agency should be able to rustle you up a can or two.

Also useful are battery packs to recharge your smartphone, or a solar charger to boost electricity supplies during the day.

Nowadays there are scores of shops in Lhasa selling decent trekking clothes, so you could pick up simple clothes there, with the exception of good quality trek boots. One of the best places to look for outdoor gear is the upper floor of Lhasa's central Bǎiyì Supermarket (p80).

Maps

There are some commercially available maps covering Tibet, but very few of these maps are detailed enough to be more than a general guide for trekkers.

The US-based Defense Mapping Agency Aerospace Center produces a series of charts covering Tibet at scales of 1:1,000,000, 1:500,000 and 1:250,000. The most useful of the American 1:500,000 references for trekking in Tibet:

➡ H-10A (Lhasa region, Ganden to Samye, Tsurphu to Yangpachen)

➡ H-9A (Kailash and Manasarovar)

➡ H-9B (Shigatse region, Shalu to Nartang, Everest region).

Old Soviet 1:200,000 topographic maps can be consulted in many large university library map rooms. Buying them has become easier with commercial outlets in the West stocking them. Punch 'Tibet maps' into your computer search engine to see who carries them in your area.

Google Earth is a fantastic resource and you might find it useful to trace your proposed route on the maps and then save them as screen shot images to view on your mobile phone or tablet.

The Swiss company Gecko Maps (www.geckomaps.com) produces a 1:50,000-scale Mt Kailash trekking map.

Trekking Agencies

The kind of trek you take will depend on your experience and the amount of time you have. Whatever your choice you must go through an officially recognised tour agency and take a guide along with you. In this age of intense government scrutiny the good old days of exploring Tibet independently are over.

One of the main advantages of signing up with an agency is that it takes care of all the red tape and dealings with officials. Most agencies offer a full-package trek, including transport to and from the trailhead, guide, cook, yaks, horses or burros to carry the equipment, mess tent and cooking gear. The package may include sleeping bags and tents if these are required but we recommend bringing all your own personal equipment, as local equipment is not up to international standards. You can negotiate cheaper, less inclusive packages by cooking for yourself along the trail and paying for pack animals and guides directly on the spot. Your driver and vehicle will most likely have to wait for you while you are trekking, meaning you'll have to pay daily rates for both while walking. Trekking in Tibet is hard to do on the cheap.

HEALTHY TREKKING

To maintain your health in such a difficult high-elevation environment you will need to take some special precautions. The golden rules are: bring a well-stocked first-aid kit; never walk alone; and ensure you have adequate health and evacuation insurance. Trekkers are particularly vulnerable to sunburn, hypothermia and acute mountain sickness (AMS), so make sure you're prepared for these.

There is a plethora of private agencies that can arrange treks. Let the buyer beware though, for the standard of service fluctuates wildly and may bear little relation to what you pay.

Make sure the agency spells out exactly what is included in the price it is quoting you, and insist on a written contract detailing all services that are to be provided as well as a money-back guarantee should it fail to deliver what has been agreed. It is prudent to pay one-half of the total cost of a trip up front and the balance after the trek is completed. This is now more or less standard operating procedure in Tibet.

All the Lhasa-based agencies listed here have run many successful treks. Trekkers are particularly at the mercy of those driving them to and from the trailheads. To avoid problems, it is prudent to test the driver and guide on a day trip before heading off into the wilds with them. Always have the phone number of your agency so that you can contact them should something go awry. Mobile (cell) phone coverage has now been extended to all the trailheads and to many places along the trekking routes.

Prices vary according to group size, ranging from US$170 to US$300 per person per day. For treks in remote and border areas, your agency will need up to three weeks to sort out the permits. If you feel you have been cheated by your agent, you may find help with the marketing and promotion department of the **Tibet Tourism Bureau** (Map p70; ☑ 0891-683 4315; 3 Linkuo Xilu, Lhasa) in Lhasa. This government organisation is in charge of training tour guides and monitoring the performance of all trekking and tour companies.

The agencies listed here tend to be tucked away in hard-to-find suburban spots. If you are in Lhasa, call first and ask the staff to meet you at your hotel.

Lhasa Agencies

Higher Ground Treks & Tours (☑ 0891-686 5352; higherground_treks_tours@yahoo.com; 75 Beijing Zhonglu)

Tibet International Sports Travel (Xīzàng Shèngdì Guójì Lǚxíngshè; Map p54; ☑ 0891-633 9151; tist@public.ls.xz.cn; 6 Lingkhor Shar Lam)

Tibet Wind Horse Adventure (Map p70; ☑ 0891-683 3009; www.windhorsetibet.com; B32 Shenzheng Huayuan, Sera Beilu)

Tibet Songtsan International Travel Company (Map p56; ☑ 136 3890 1182, 0891-636 4414; www.songtsantravel.com; 2nd fl, Barkhor Sq)

Tibet Yongdru International Travel Service (☑ 0891-683 5813; info@tibet-yongdru-travel.com; No 5 Bldg, 1st fl, New Shöl Village)

Kathmandu Agencies

Several Kathmandu-based agencies operate treks in Tibet, often bringing their own cooks and sherpas from Nepal. This generally results in higher prices but better food and service than if you use only Tibetan staff. The following are some of the most qualified agencies.

Dharma Adventures (p233)

Mountain Monarch (☑ 01-4373881; www.mountainmonarch.com; Hattigauda)

Sunny Treks and Expeditions (p233)

Tibet International Travels & Tours (p233)

Miteri Nepal International Trekking (☑ 01-4437163; www.miterinepaltrekking.com; Bhagwatisthan 29, Thamel)

Western Agencies

A few Western companies organise fixed-departure treks in Tibet. These tours can be joined in your home country or abroad, usually in Chéngdū or Kathmandu. Prices are

RESPONSIBLE TREKKING

With average temperatures increasing more rapidly than almost any other place on earth, the environment of Tibet is under unprecedented pressure. It is imperative that trekkers make their way lightly and leave nothing behind but their proverbial footprints. Tibet's beautiful but vulnerable landscape deserves the utmost respect. A fire, for instance, can scar the landscape for centuries. Stay off fragile slopes and do not tread on delicate plants or sensitive breeding grounds. Follow the Tibetan ethos, killing not even the smallest of insects. This approach guarantees that later visitors get to enjoy the same pristine environment as you.

Rubbish

➡ Carry out every piece of your rubbish including toilet paper, sanitary napkins, tampons and condoms.

➡ Have a dedicated rubbish bag and minimise packaging materials.

➡ Do not burn plastic and other garbage as this is believed to irritate the Tibetan divinities.

Human Waste Disposal

➡ Where there is a toilet, use it.

➡ Where there is none, human waste should be left on the surface of the ground away from trails, water and habitations to decompose. If you are in a large trekking group, dig a privy pit. Be sure to build it far from any water source or marshy ground and carefully rehabilitate the area when you leave camp. Ensure it's not near shrines or any other sacred structures.

Washing

➡ Don't use detergents or toothpaste in or near watercourses, even if they are biodegradable.

➡ For all washing use biodegradable soap and a lightweight, portable basin at least 50m away from the water source.

➡ Try using a scourer, sand or snow instead of detergent. Widely disperse the waste water to allow the soil to filter it.

Erosion

➡ Hillsides and mountain slopes are prone to erosion, so stick to existing tracks and avoid short cuts.

---

higher than treks arranged directly in Tibet or Kathmandu, but they are more professionally run and save you a lot of effort and time.

A trek organised at home includes a Western leader, a local guide, porters, a cook and often even a kit bag and gear rental. All your practical needs will be taken care of, freeing you up to enjoy the walking.

Companies organising treks to Tibet include **World Expeditions** (www.worldexpeditions.com), the **Mountain Company** (www.themountaincompany.co.uk) and **Mountain Kingdoms** (www.mountainkingdoms.com).

Permits

Individuals are not permitted to trek independently in Tibet and must join an organised group. Trekking, as with all travel in Tibet, requires travel permits, though there are no specific trekking permits in Tibet.

ON THE TREK

Trekking trails in Tibet are not marked and in many places there are no people to ask for directions. Paths regularly merge, divide and peter out, making route-finding inherently difficult. Your guide from Lhasa probably doesn't know the trails any better than you do, so it's always worth hiring a local guide or horseman from the area.

Guides & Pack Animals

The rugged terrain, long distances and high elevations of Tibet make most people think twice about carrying their gear. In villages and

➡ Do not trench around tents.

➡ Never remove the plant life that keeps topsoil in place.

Fires & Low-Impact Cooking

➡ Building fires is not an option. Wood is nonexistent in much of Tibet and where there are trees and bushes they are desperately needed by locals.

➡ Cook on a lightweight kerosene, petrol, alcohol or multifuel stove and avoid those powered by disposable butane gas canisters.

➡ Make sure your guide and porters have stoves.

➡ Ensure that all members are outfitted with adequate clothing so that fires are not needed for warmth.

Good Trekking Partnerships

➡ Monitor all your staff members closely and make it clear that any gratuities will hinge upon good stewardship of the environment.

➡ Stress to your agency that you will not tolerate rubbish being thrown along the trail or at the trailheads.

➡ Explain to your drivers that rubbish should not be thrown out the windows (a common practice in Tibet).

Wildlife Conservation

➡ Do not engage in or encourage illegal hunting.

➡ Don't buy items or medicines made from endangered wild species.

➡ Discourage the presence of wildlife by cleaning up your food scraps.

Camping

➡ Seek permission to camp from local villagers or shepherds. They will usually be happy to grant permission.

nomad camps along the main trekking routes it's often possible to hire yaks or horses to do the heavy work for you.

Your guide will negotiate what you need in the way of pack animals. A mule skinner, horseman or yak driver will also serve as a local guide; they are an important asset on the unmarked trails of Tibet. Local guides can also share their knowledge of the natural history and culture of the place, greatly adding to your experience.

The rates for pack animals vary widely according to the time of the year and location. Horses and yaks are pricey at Mt Kailash, with a fixed price costing upwards of ¥250 per animal. In most other places burros and horses can be had for ¥120 to ¥200 per head. Local guides and livestock handlers usually command ¥150 to ¥200 per day. Remember that your hired help are also paid for the time it takes them to return home.

Food

You should be self-sufficient with food since there isn't much to eat along the trail. Bring anything you can't live without from home, such as high-energy bars and your favourite chocolate. In Lhasa there are thousands of stalls and shops selling a huge variety of foodstuffs, making well-balanced, tasty meals possible on the trail. Even in Shigatse and the smaller cities there are many foods suitable for trekking.

Vacuum-packed yak meat and poultry, as well as packaged dried meat, fish and tofu, are readily found in Lhasa. Varieties of packaged and bulk dried fruits are sold around the city. You can even find almonds and pistachios imported from the USA.

Dairy- and soybean-milk powders can be used with several kinds of prepackaged cereals. Oatmeal and instant barley porridge are widely available in the supermarkets. Our personal favourite Tibetan breakfast is *tsampa* (roasted and ground barley powder) mixed with milk powder, sugar and hot water. For an added touch, Indian pickles and curry powders are available in shops near the Barkhor. Lightweight vegetables such as seaweed, bok choy and dried mushrooms can do wonders for macaroni and instant noodles. Many of China's instant noodles are very spicy so stick with chicken or seafood flavours if you don't want to sweat.

Cooking mediums include butter, margarine, vegetable oil and sesame oil. All kinds of biscuits, sweets and muffins are sold in Lhasa and the larger regional towns.

Drink

As wonderfully cold and clear as much of the water in Tibet is, do not assume that it's safe to drink. Livestock contaminate many of the water sources and Tibetans do not always live up to their cultural ideals.

Follow Tibetan tradition and eliminate the monotony of drinking plain water by downing as much tea as you can. You can buy Chinese green tea and Indian lemon tea in every city and town in Tibet. Instant coffee is widely available, but Coffee Mate is harder to find.

If you're offered Tibetan yak-butter tea, have it served in your own cup as per tradition – this eliminates the risk associated with drinking from used cups. More like a soup than a tea, it helps fortify you against the cold and replenishes the body's salts.

TREKKING ROUTES

A number of popular treks offer fantastic walking and superb scenery; with the exception of Lake Manasarovar and Mt Kailash, they're also close to Lhasa or the main highways. Walking times given are just that: they don't include breaks, nature stops or any other off-your-feet activities. On average, plan to walk five to seven hours per day, interspersed with frequent short rests. You will also need time for setting up camp, cooking and eating, and for the plain enjoyment of being there.

Ganden to Samye

This trek has much to offer: lakes, beautiful alpine landscapes, herders' camps and sacred sites, as well as two of Tibet's greatest centres of religious culture. With so much to offer, its popularity is understandable, but you should not underestimate this walk.

The best time for the trek is from mid-May to mid-October. Summer can be wet, but the mountains are at their greenest and wild flowers spangle the alpine meadows. Barring heavy snow, it's also possible for those with a lot of trekking experience and the right gear to do this trek in the colder months. If you're coming straight from Lhasa, you should spend at least one night at Ganden Monastery (4300m) to acclimatise, or if that's not allowed, at Hepu village (4210m).

If you're fit, acclimatised and have a pack animal to carry your bags, it's not difficult to do the trek in 3½ days, overnighting in Hepu/Yama Do, Tsotup-chu and the herders' camps. If you get an early start from Lhasa on the first day, it's possible to visit Ganden in the morning, start hiking before lunch and continue on to Yama Do. Otherwise you might consider overnighting in Hepu the first night to arrange pack animals and then

---

SOCIAL TREKKING

In most out-of-the-way places trekkers can quickly become the centre of attention, and sometimes just a smile may lead to dinner invitations and offers of a place to stay. If you really detest being the star of the show, don't camp in villages. If you do, don't expect Western notions of privacy to prevail. The spectacle of a few foreigners putting up tents is probably the closest some villagers will ever come to TV.

If you have any religious sentiments, your trek probably qualifies as a pilgrimage, in which case you will generally receive better treatment than if you are 'just going someplace'. Another helpful hint: if all else fails try a song and dance. Even the most amateur of efforts is met with great approval.

Tibetan Treks

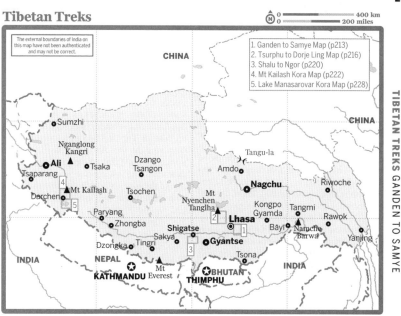

have a short second day to Yama Do before continuing over the Shuga-La on day three.

You'll experience at least three seasons on this trek, probably in the same day! From the wintry feel of the Chitu-la you rapidly descend to the springtime rhododendron blooms of the middle valley until the summer heat hits you on the final approach to Samye. Pack accordingly.

Guides and pack animals can be procured in the villages of Trubshi and Hepu, situated in the Tashi-chu Valley near Ganden. Figure on paying around ¥120 per day for a horse or yak and the same again for a horse/yak handler. Yaks generally won't travel alone, so you'll need a minimum of two. You'll have to pay two days' wages for the animals and handler to return. Single trekkers or pairs could get away with a single horse.

A sealed road now connects Trubshi and Hepu to the Kyi-chu Valley.

Stage 1: Ganden to Yama Do

5-6 HOURS / 17KM / 630M ASCENT/420M DESCENT

The trek begins in the car park at the base of Ganden Monastery (p93). Your driver will most likely transport your packs to Hepu to meet your pack animals there, so you can travel light for the first section of this hike. Some trekkers visit Ganden in the morning, hike to Hepu after lunch and spend the first

night there, meeting their pack animals the next morning.

Leave the car park and look for the well-trodden trail heading south along the side of Angkor Ri, the highest point on the Ganden kora. After 30 minutes the Ganden kora branches off to the right (4360m; N 29°44.891', E 091°28.788'); keep ascending to the south for another 30 minutes. You quickly lose sight of Ganden but gain views of Samadro village below you to the left, before reaching a **saddle**, marked by a large *lapse* (cairn; 4530m; N 29°44.130', E 091°29.729'). (Don't confuse this with a smaller, earlier cairn.) Expect to take around 90 minutes to get here from Ganden.

From the saddle, look south to see the approach to the Shuga-la in the distance. Traversing the western side of the ridge from the saddle, dipping briefly into a side gully, you get views of Trubshi village below and the Kyi-chu Valley to the west. After 45 minutes the trail descends towards Hepu village. About 20 minutes further is a spring and a herders' camp marked by a section of stone wall. From here it's a further 30 minutes to the village, a total of three to four hours' walking from Ganden.

There are around 30 houses in the village of **Hepu** (4240m; N 29°42.387,

E 091°31.442'), also called Lewu or Lepu, and it's often possible for trekkers to find accommodation among the friendly locals. There's good camping to the south and west of the village. Look for a red-and-yellow masonry structure and white incense hearths at the southeastern edge of the village. This is the **shrine** of Hepu's *yul lha* (local protecting deity), the Divine White Yak.

Walk west downhill from the village for 10 minutes towards a bridge crossing the Tashi-chu, near the confluence with another stream, at a tiny settlement called Dekyi Pangka. This is likely where your agency has dropped your bags to be loaded onto pack animals for your arrival. There are several campsites near the confluence. From here, the Shuga-la is at least four hours away.

Follow the dirt road south along the west bank of the side stream for five minutes until it peters out in yak pastures. You are now following the watercourse originating from the Shuga-la.

Twenty minutes from the confluence you reach **Ani Pagong**, a narrow, craggy bottleneck in the valley. A small nunnery used to be above the trail. Across the valley is the seasonal herders' camp of Choden. From Ani Pagong, the trail steadily climbs for another hour through marshy meadows and past stone shelters to cross to the east side of the river just before **Yama Do** (4490m; N 29°40.511', E 091°30.918').

Yama Do offers extensive campsites suitable for larger groups. It's best to spend the night here as it's still a long climb to the pass and there are few other camping places along the way. If you have time on your hands, you could visit the herders' camps on the western side of the valley, though be careful of dogs on the approach.

Stage 2: Yama Do to Tsotup-chu Valley

5-7 HOURS / 10KM / 1000M ASCENT/450M DESCENT

Above Yama Do the valley's watercourse splits into three branches. Follow the central (southern) branch, not the southeastern or southwestern branches. The route leaves the flank of the valley and follows the valley bottom. The trail becomes indistinct, but it's a straight shot up to the pass. About 30 minutes from Yama Do are two single-tent campsites, the last good ones until the other side of the pass, at least five hours away. One hour past Yama Do, leave the valley floor and ascend a shelf on the eastern side of the valley to avoid a steep gully that forms around the stream. If in doubt follow the cairns. In another 45 minutes you enter a wet alpine basin studded with tussock grass.

The **Shuga-la** is at least 1¼ hours from the basin and three hours from Yama Do. Remain on the eastern side of the valley as it bends to the left. You have to negotiate snowfields and boulders along the final steep climb to the pass. The Shuga-la (5250m; N 29°38.472', E 091°32.015') cannot be seen until you're virtually on top of it. It's marked by a large cairn covered in prayer flags and yak horns, and is the highest point of the trek. If you have some spare energy you can scramble up the hill to the west for superb views.

The route continues over the Shuga-la and then descends sharply through a boulder field. Be on the lookout for a clear trail marked by cairns on the left side of the

---

GANDEN TO SAMYE AT A GLANCE

Duration Four days

Distance 80km

Difficulty Medium to difficult

Start Ganden Monastery

Finish Yamalung Hermitage

Highest Point Shuga-la (5250m)

Nearest Large Towns Lhasa and Tsetang

Accommodation Camping

Best Time to Trek Mid-May to mid-October

Summary This demanding trek crosses two passes over 5000m, connects two of Tibet's most important monasteries and begins less than 50km from Lhasa. It has emerged as the most popular trek in the Ü region.

boulder field. Pack animals sometimes have difficulty on this steep, muddy section. This trail traverses the ridge in a southeasterly direction, paralleling the valley below. Do not head directly down to the valley floor from the pass unless you have good reason. It's a long, steep descent and once at the bottom you have to go back up the valley to complete the trek. In case of emergency, retreat down the valley for a bolt back to the Lhasa–Ganden Hwy near Dagtse, a long day of walking away.

The trail gradually descends to the valley floor, 1½ hours from the pass and 200m below it. The views of the valley and the lake at its head are among the highlights of the trek. Cross the large **Tsotup-chu** (4980m; N 29°37.366′, E 091°33.288′), which flows through the valley, and keep an eye out for the herders' dogs. During heavy summer rains take special care to find a safe ford. The pastures in the area support large herds of yaks, goats and sheep, and during the trekking season herders are normally camped here, either in tents or in new plastic cabins. Known as Tsogo Numa, this is an ideal place to meet the herders, but dry, flat campsites are hard to find.

An alternative route to Samye via the **Gampa-la** (5050m) follows the main branch of the Tsotup-chu past a couple of lakes to the pass. South of the Gampa-la the trail plunges into a gorge, criss-crossing the stream that flows down from it. These fords may pose problems during summer rains or when completely frozen. See Gary McCue's *Trekking in Tibet – A Traveler's Guide* for details of this route.

Stage 3: Tsotup-chu Valley to Herders' Camps

5 HOURS / 14KM / 300M ASCENT/400M DESCENT

From the Tsotup-chu ford, the main watercourse flows from the southeast and a minor tributary enters from the southwest. Follow this tributary (which quickly disappears underground) steeply up for about 30 minutes until you reach a large basin and a cairn that offers fine views down onto **Palang Tsodü lake**. You may hear the distant sounds of a mining operation in the valley behind.

Stay on the western side of the basin and turn into the first side valley opening on the right. A couple of minutes into the valley (and 45 minutes from the Tsotup-chu) you'll pass a flat, walled group **campsite** (5079m; N 29°36.604′, E 091°33.544′). This is a nicer alternative campsite to the Tsotup-chu, but

Ganden to Samye

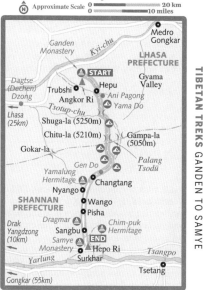

only consider it if you're well acclimatised, as it's 100m higher.

Follow this broad valley, which soon arcs south to the Chitu-la, about two hours away. The pass can be seen in the distance, a low rampart at the head of the valley that is a considerably easier goal than yesterday's pass. The faint main trail stays on the western side of the valley before switching to the eastern side of the valley as you approach the pass. If you lose the trail just look for the easiest route up: the terrain is marshy and hillocky in early summer but not particularly difficult to navigate.

The **Chitu-la** (5210m; N 29°34.810′, E 091°33.160′) is topped by several cairns and a small glacial tarn. Climb onto the stone ledges just above the pass to savour the views over a snack before moving to the western side of the pass to find the trail down and to circumvent a sheer rock wall on its southern flank. A short descent will bring you into a basin with three small lakes. The trail skirts the western side of the first lake and then crosses to the eastern shores of the second two. It takes 45 minutes to reach the southern end of the basin, where you might be lucky enough to spot blue sheep.

Drop down from the basin on the western side of the stream and in 15 minutes

PASS HEIGHTS

Elevations in Tibet, especially for passes, are notoriously inconsistent, with maps and road signs rarely agreeing over the correct elevation. In this guide we have tried to use composite measurements, incorporating the most accurate maps, the most consistently agreed figures and on-the-spot GPS readings (which have their own inconsistencies and inaccuracies). Most figures should be accurate within 50m or so, but use the elevations here as a guide only.

you'll pass a collection of cairns (5077m; N 29°33.924', E 091°32.790') to the right. A further 10 minutes brings you to the stone walls of a camp where herders have carved out level places for their tents.

Below the herders' highest camp, the valley is squeezed in by vertical rock walls, forcing you to pick your way along the rock-strewn valley floor. Pass a side stream after 15 minutes and then cross over to the western side of the widening valley to recover the trail. In 20 more minutes you will come to a flat and a seasonal herders' camp on the eastern side of the valley, which is good place to stop for yak-butter tea. At the lower end of the flat, return to the western side of the valley. The trail again disappears as it enters a scrub-willow and rosebush forest, but there is only one way to go to get to Samye and that is downstream.

In 20 minutes, when a tributary valley enters from the right, cross to the eastern side of the valley to reach another seasonal herders' camp, inhabited for only a short time each year. Another 20 minutes beyond this camp, hop back to the west bank to avoid a cliff hugging the opposite side of the stream. Pass through a large meadow and cross the bridge back to the east bank. From this point the trail remains on the eastern side of the valley for several hours.

Campsites are numerous here. After 20 minutes you'll pass herders' tents near the spot where the side valley coming from the Gampa-la joins the main valley. A bridge crosses the side stream here. There are several possible campsites on the finger of land formed by the river junction, but the area can be busy in early summer with motorbike-riding Tibetan youth heading to the highlands in search of yartsa gunbu (p273),

a valuable medicinal fungus that is almost worth its weight in gold. If so continue on to the Diwaka Zampa bridge.

Stages 4 & 5: Herders' Camps to Samye Monastery

3 HOURS / 11KM / 550M DESCENT

The trail is now wide and easy to follow as it traces a course down the eastern side of the valley. Walk through the thickening scrub forest for 45 minutes and you will come to another stream entering from the eastern side of the main valley. Look for the wood-and-stone Diwaka Zampa bridge (4335m; N 29°30.439', E 091°33.165') 50m above the confluence.

The valley now bends to the right (west) and the trail enters the thickest and tallest part of the scrub forest. The right combination of elevation, moisture and aspect create a verdant environment, while just a few kilometres away desert conditions prevail. Several grassy campsites along this section make for a good alternative end to stage 3.

The next two-hour stretch of the trail is among the most delightful of the entire trek. According to local woodcutters more than 15 types of tree and shrub are found here, some growing as high as 6m. Fragrant junipers grow on exposed south-facing slopes, while rhododendrons prefer the shadier slopes. The rhododendrons start to bloom in early May.

The trail winds through a series of meadows. After 40 minutes the stony floodplain of a tributary joins the river from the north. In another 30 minutes look for a mass of prayer flags, stone shrines and an ancient juniper tree at a place known as Gen Do. This is a shrine (4165m; N 29°29.525', E 091°31.805') to the protector of the area, the goddess Dorje Yudronma. Just past the shrine, cross a small tributary stream beside another potential camping spot. In 45 minutes the forest rapidly thins and Changtang, the first permanent village since Hepu, pops up with its oddly jarring modern street lights. There's good camping just before the village. From Changtang the walking trail becomes a full-fledged motorable road.

Look south to the distant mountains; this is the range on the far side of the Yarlung Tsangpo Valley. About 45 minutes down the valley at a prominent bend in it is the turn-off for the Yamalung Hermitage (ཡ་མ་ལུང་, 聂玛隆圣洞, Nièmǎlóng Shèngdòng), visible on the cliff face high above the valley. A small teahouse run by the nuns of Yamalung sells soft drinks, beer and instant noodles. There's fine camping across the bridge; the path to Yamalung also leads up from here. It's a 45-minute steep climb to the hermitage. Yamalung (also called Emalung) is where the Tibetan wonder-worker Guru Rinpoche is said to have meditated and received empowerment from the long-life deity Tsepame (Amitayus).

Most trekkers end their trek after a visit to Yamalung. On the 20-minute drive to Samye look for a ridge spur called **Dragmar**. On the ridge is the partially rebuilt palace where King Trisong Detsen is said to have been born. Formerly a lavish temple, it now stands forlorn. Below, just off the road, is a small red-and-white **temple** (3687m; N 29°22.802', E 091°30.399'), which is often locked and enshrines the stump of an ancient tree. Legend has it that a red-and-white sandalwood tree grew here, nourished by the buried placenta of Trisong Detsen. During the Cultural Revolution the tree was chopped down.

Tsurphu to Dorje Ling

Beginning at Tsurphu Monastery (p102), this rugged walk crosses several high valleys before emerging into the broad and wind-swept Yangpachen Valley. Combining alpine tundra and sweeping mountain panoramas with visits to monasteries, this trek offers a nice balance of culture and wilderness.

The best time for this walk is from mid-April to mid-October. Summer can be rainy but be prepared for snow at any time. As you will be in nomad country, beware of vicious dogs, some of which take a sadistic pride in chasing hapless foreigners. Fuel and food are not available, so come prepared. There are few permanent settlements along the way and the inhabitants are often away from home. Your only option on this trek is to be fully self-sufficient.

Tsurphu Monastery (4500m) is a good place to spend a night acclimatising. You can overnight at the monastery guesthouse or camp at the area around the Karmapa's former *lingka* (garden), 10 minutes' walk upstream from the monastery. This is the place where you'll likely meet your yaks and yak handler the next morning. Villagers in Tsurphu ask around ¥1500 for a guide and two yaks for a five-day return trip to Yangpachen. Horses are generally not available. Two yaks are the minimum.

It's essential to be properly acclimatised before attempting this trek. It's not enough to just spend a couple of days in Lhasa (3650m), you really need to have spent a night or two at around 4500m before heading to Tsurphu.

The Chinese People's Liberation Army use the plains around Dorje Ling Nunnery for military training and the area can be closed for manoeuvres in late summer. Check with your agency and yak handler before setting off and be sure to get local advice.

Stage 1: Tsurphu Monastery to Leten
3½ HOURS / 11KM / 500M ASCENT

The first day is a short one so consider spending the morning visiting Tsurphu Monastery or walking the monastery kora.

The trek begins by heading west up the valley. Follow the kora trail 10 minutes west

TSURPHU TO DORJE LING AT A GLANCE

Duration Three days

Distance 45km

Difficulty Medium to difficult

Start Tsurphu Monastery

Finish Dorje Ling Nunnery

Highest Point Lasar-la (5400m)

Nearest Large Town Lhasa

Accommodation Camping

Best Time to Trek Mid-April to mid-October

Summary An excellent choice for those who want to get a close look at the lifestyle of the *drokpas* (herders). You need to be well acclimatised for this high-elevation trek, which never dips below 4400m.

Tsurphu to Dorje Ling

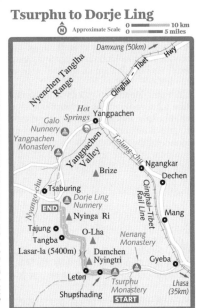

About two hours from the lingka, by a ruined **mani wall** (N 29°43.373', E 90°30.855'), the road climbs up over a high saddle to the left while the trail splits off and follows the valley floor. From the mani wall Leten is about an hour away: the trail passes to the right of a large cliff, past the remains of winter ice, before swinging to the left up into the natural bowl of Leten.

Half a dozen families live year-round in the *drokpa* settlement of **Leten** (5090m; N 29°43.493', E 090°30.237'), braving the severe climate with their livestock. Leten is the last chance to find yaks. Camping spots are limited by the lumpy terrain and places already staked out by the nomads. If you value your peace and quiet, consider camping in the valley below Leten.

Spend at least one night in Leten acclimatising.

Stage 2: Leten to Bartso

5-6 HOURS / 15KM / 300M ASCENT/600M DESCENT

It's about a three-hour walk from Leten to the Lasar-la. Head for the northern half of the settlement (assuming you aren't already there). The route climbs steeply up a short ridge, reaching the highest house. Bear northwest into a steep side valley. As you ascend, a reddish knob of rock looms up ahead. Angle to the north, or right, of this formation, past a mani wall in the centre of the bowl, and leave the valley by swinging right to the top of the minor Damchen-la pass marked by three **cairns** (5270m; N 29°43.936', E 090°29.862'). It's a 45-minute walk to here from Leten. The peak attached to this spur is called **Damchen Nyingtri** and is holy to the god ruling the environs.

As per Buddhist tradition, stay to the left of the three cairns and descend sharply to yak corrals. As you look into the curved valley ahead you'll notice a round, bald, red peak called Tamdrim Dora; the main trail you'll be following for the next hour or so keeps to the right of that.

Once on the valley bottom, stay on the west (true right) side of the stream and strike out north (up the valley). In 15 minutes a side-stream enters from the west: keep following the main north branch as the valley swings to the right. In another 10 minutes you'll see the Mt Kailash-shaped O-Lha peak, the prominent jagged mountain to the northeast. Walk up the widening valley through arctic-like mounds of tundra for 40 minutes, following a minor trail. Then, as the valley floor veers west, look for a **cairn**

to the **lingka** (4550m), a walled copse of old trees with a brook. This garden-like wood has been established as a trekkers' camp free of charge by the monks of Tsurphu. The trees here are the last you will see until after finishing the trek. You'll probably meet your yaks and yak handler here so will need to budget some time to load the yaks.

Just above the copse by the *tarboche* (prayer pole), the valley splits: follow the right (northwest) branch and remain on the north side of the stream. There is now a dirt road and electricity pole all the way to Leten.

Walking through a rocky gorge along a well-graded trail for 45 minutes brings you to **Shupshading** (4700m), a seasonal herders' camp on an easily missed shelf above the trail. After 40 minutes look for a line of ruined red chörtens to your right, known as the Suru Bompa. After a further 15 minutes the valley looks like it splits; follow the main river valley (to the left) and cross the stream on a small concrete **bridge** in another 15 minutes (4890m). Above the north side of the bridge is the six-house village of Sercha Sumdo, but the trail now continues on the south side of the valley. In another 20 minutes you'll pass a popular camping spot. Look out for small herds of *na* (blue sheep) on the slopes to the north.

(5310m; N 29°45.634', E 090°29.812') on the opposite bank of the stream.

Using this cairn as a marker, bear northwest over an inclined plain. Continue ascending as the plain opens wider in the direction of the pass. The **Lasar-la** (5400m; N 29°46.167', E 090°29.602') is a broad gap at the highest point in the plain, and is only heralded by small cairns and few prayer flags. (A separate pass to the northwest, the Tigu-la, also descends towards Yangpachen, but this is not the route described here.)

From the Lasar-la the descent is gradual. A faint trail can be found on the east side of the stream that forms below the pass. About 30 minutes from the pass the trail passes a decent campsite, just before descending into a short gully. A side valley joins from the right, offering fine views of the back side of O-Lha. When this side-stream joins the main stream, cross over to the west side of the main watercourse. The way to the valley bottom is now much steeper but the broad slopes make walking relatively easy. In 20 minutes you'll reach the valley floor. There are many possible campsites along this next stretch, as well as views of the snowcapped Nyenchen Tanglha range to the north. Gravitate to the west side of the valley.

The valley is covered with hummocks, but a trail avoids the ups and downs of these mounds of turf and earth. About 60 minutes along the valley bottom, just past a large corral, you meet a large westward bend in the valley. If water levels are high, you should ford the river here and continue on the north side of the valley. In early summer, when water levels are lower, you can simply follow the valley as it bends to the west and ford the river further downstream.

As you now head westwards, along the north side of the river, there are superb views of the surrounding mountains. In the north is Brize, which is a heavily glaciated peak enclosing the south side of the Yangpachen Valley, and towards the west is a distinctive pinnacle named Tarze. Brize, the 'female-yak herder', and Tarze, the 'horse keeper', are just two of many topographical features in a mythical society ruled by the great mountain god Nyenchen Tanglha. These two mountains make convenient landmarks for trekkers further along the route as you go against the grain by heading north over a series of drainage systems that run from east to west.

Around 40 minutes after the big bend the trail hits the herders' camp of **Tangba** (4950m; N 29°48.955', E 090°28.186'). This *drokpa* village is now devoid of permanent dwellings but is still used as a summer camp. There are decent places to camp in the vicinity. The surrounding hills are still dotted with juniper. In the 1960s and '70s huge amounts of this valuable bush were extracted from the region and trucked to Lhasa to feed the hearths of the new provincial city.

Stage 3: Bartso to Dorje Ling Nunnery
4-5 HOURS / 15KM / 150M ASCENT/150M DESCENT

Look northwest from Tangba to the far end of the valley. A clearly visible trail traverses the ridge from the valley to the top of the ridge. Make for this trail, 25 minutes' walk over marshy ground from Tangba, following the fence line. It's another half-hour to the summit of the ridge. A trail leads up to a saddle north of the valley for fine views of Nyenchen Tanglha. However, the more straightforward main path continues down into a gully heading westward past a fenced-off pasture. As you exit the gully you'll see the village of **Tajung** in the distance. Tajung is a decent alternative spot to end the second stage, though the insatiably curious villagers can be demanding of your time and supplies.

Bear right (north-northeast-wards) in the direction of Brize, keeping Tajung villlage on your left, straight towards a hill topped by solar panels and a mobile phone mast. As you get close to the hill, bear left to join the electricity poles and cross a small yak pasture.

One excellent possible side trip from here is the 20-minute climb to the top of the aforementioned hill, known as **Ani Nyinga Ri** (4800m; N 29°51.683', E 90°25.972'). Views of the Nyenchen Tanglha Range, and the distinctive flat-topped 7111m massif that gives its name to the entire range, are fantastic from here. Nyenchen Tanglha is the holiest mountain in central Tibet, the haunt of a divine white warrior on a white horse. The range is part of the trans-Himalaya, which circumscribes the plateau, dividing southern Tibet from the Changtang. Don't climb to the top if there are military exercises going on nearby.

A descent north from the saddle of Nyinga Ri brings you to a stream at the base of a ridge, aligned east to west. Bear left down the valley to cross the stream at a bridge

TREKKING TIBETAN STYLE

Given the chance, many Tibetans would rather ride or drive than go on foot, but there are also great trekkers among them. The ubiquitous shepherds traipse around on a daily basis searching out pasture for their sheep and goats. Typically they set out early in the morning and cover up to 40km before returning to camp in the evening with their herds.

Then there are the many pilgrims who visit temples, monasteries and holy mountains on foot. Pilgrimages can last two or three years and stretch from one end of the vast Tibetan Plateau to the other.

The greatest Tibetan trekkers though are the 'swift foot', mystic athletes reputed to move many leagues in a single day. Imagine leaving London in the morning and arriving in Edinburgh in the evening without ever taking your feet off the ground! It is said that years of special physical training and esoteric initiation are required to accomplish the amazing feats of the swift foot.

While few trekkers visiting Tibet are likely to attain swift foot status, there is still much to be gained by emulating the native people. When walking long distances they breathe slowly and deeply, filling their lungs completely. Tibetan walkers inhale and exhale exclusively through the nose, conditioning the cold, dry air before it reaches the lungs. Like the proverbial turtle they tread slowly and steadily, avoiding excess rest stops. Being immersed in prayer is also traditionally thought to aid trekkers. At the very least it helps keep the mind off the minor discomforts that inevitably come from moving a long time under one's own steam. For a bit of a challenge try imitating the rolling gait of Tibetans, but be forewarned: you may need to spend a few years on horseback before perfecting this technique!

next to two whitewashed buildings and climb the small ridge on the opposite bank in just a few minutes. From the top of the ridge the terrain gradually falls away to the north. Here you have good views of the village just upstream of Dorje Ling Nunnery. The nunnery, which is out of view, sits at the bottom of a rock outcrop visible from the ridge top.

Strike out directly across the plain in a northwesterly direction for the village, taking in the awesome views of the glaciers tumbling off Brize and the fertile flood plain below. The plain here is criss-crossed by tank tracks and pockmarked with bunkers used by the Chinese army in their training exercises. After dipping briefly into a dry gully you crest a small ridge and see **Dorje Ling** (4460m; N 29°53.615', E 090°24.791'); the nunnery is less than one hour away.

The centrepiece of this friendly place of 60 nuns is the red *dukhang* (assembly hall). A high and low kora offer opportunity for more climbing if the day's walk hasn't been enough for you. A teahouse across the stream to the southwest of the nunnery offers sweet tea and *thugba*, a single-roomed guesthouse (¥50 per bed) and a cramped campsite. Cleaner camps can be found upstream of Dorje Ling.

Most treks now end at Dorje Ling. Roads head northeast from here to Yangpachen Monastery, while a short road cuts northwest to Gyadar to join the paved road to Shigatse over the Margyang-la pass.

Perched on top of a ridge, the 15th-century **Yangpachen Monastery** overlooks a broad sweep of trans-Himalaya peaks and is worth visiting at the end of your trek. The monastery was once home to 115 monks, but many of them have fled to Rumtek Monastery in Sikkim, and less than half remain behind. Yangpachen is headed by Shamar Rinpoche (also known as the Sharmapa), a leading lama of the Kagyupa order, whose 14th incarnation is based in India. You'll see images here of the important fourth Sharmapa (wearing a red hat), the 16th Karmapa (a black hat) and the 'alternative' rival Karmapa, who is supported by the Sharmapa in India.

From Yangpachen Monastery it's an 18km road journey to Yangpachen town. About halfway there look out for **Galo Nunnery**, nestled in the hills to the left after about 7km. From Yangpachen town it's 7km west to the swimming-pool-sized **Yangpachen Hot Springs** (羊八井温泉; Yángbājǐng Wēnchuán; ¥128; ☉7am-9pm) complex, great for easing your aching limbs.

Shalu to Ngor

This mini-trek follows the old trade route between the great Buddhist centres of Shalu and Ngor, marking a glorious chapter in Tibetan history. Treading the ancient trail you can almost feel the caravans laden with scriptures and treasures that once passed this way.

The trek begins at the historic Shalu Monastery (p148) and traverses west over two minor ranges to Ngor Monastery. The scenery is unlike other treks in Tibet, through dry, eroded canyons and gulches that feel more like Texas than Tibet. There are no big mountain views or high-altitude herders' camps here, but the walk is bookended by two fabulous monasteries and the overnight campsite is one of Tibet's finest. The two hikes are not long, so you can spend the morning of day one visiting Shalu Monastery and Ri-puk Hermitage and the afternoon of day two visiting Ngor and Nartang (p149) monasteries.

Logistically the trek is unusual because it essentially consists of two half-day hikes connected by an overnight car camp. Your vehicle can drive to the first night's campsite, so you don't need to worry about hiring pack animals to carry your gear or supplies. You'll still need to be self-sufficient with camping supplies and food and it's a good idea to bring water with you in the car. Your driver and guide will also need camping equipment and food.

Much of the walk is through heavily eroded, waterless ravines and slopes, so bring plenty of drinking water from the trailhead.

Having a local guide from Shalu and Lungsang is a good idea as routefinding is often difficult in the maze of canyons, eroded defiles and side channels. It would be easy to slip and twist and ankle here. Strong-soled shoes are essential on the rocky terrain.

The optimal walking season is from the beginning of April to the end of October. In summer the trail can be sizzling hot, and in other months cold and windy, so be prepared.

Stage 1: Shalu Monastery to Upper Lungsang

4-5 HOURS / 13KM / 420M ASCENT/240M DESCENT

After visiting wonderful **Shalu Monastery** (3980m) drive south from the village, possibly detouring to visit nearby **Ri-puk Hermitage**, set on a hillside on the west side of the valley.

Start the walk at the covered chorten in **Phunup** village, 6km south of Shalu. Head northwest past a stone sheep's pen to a collection of white cairns atop a small ridge. After 15 minutes you'll arrive at a large cairn and can see the path ahead of you in the red rock. The pass is the obvious low point in the range, at least one hour away.

The trail descends through a landscape that varies in colour from white to caramel, rust, magenta and purple to enter the stream bed coming from the Showa-la. The trail soon climbs back up the right side of the valley only to drop back in and out of the purple stream bed in quick succession. After about 30 minutes you pass four white-topped cairns. As the stream narrows to a gulch climb to the right, beside a cairn, passing more cairns as you ascend to the

TIBETAN TREKS SHALU TO NGOR

SHALU TO NGOR AT A GLANCE

Duration Two days

Distance 27km

Difficulty Medium

Start Shalu Monastery

Finish Ngor Monastery

Highest Point Char-la (4440m)

Nearest Large Town Shigatse

Accommodation Camping

Best Time to Trek Early April to late October

Summary This short walk gives you a taste of trekking in Tibet without any of the logistical complications. The trail and passes are not high or difficult and the trailheads are easily accessible from Shigatse.

Shalu to Ngor

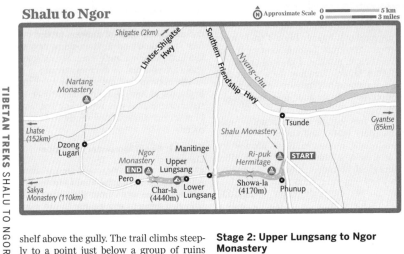

shelf above the gully. The trail climbs steeply to a point just below a group of ruins and then curves left to the pass, about 90 minutes from Phunup. The top is marked by white cairns.

From the **Showa-la** (4170m; N 29°06.371', E 088°56.939'), the second pass, the Char-la, can be seen in the range of hills west of an intervening valley. It is the dip in the crest of the range. The easy-to-follow trail descends from the pass along the south side of a ravine. In one hour you will reach the valley floor. Leave the trail just before it crosses a small rise marked with cairns and continue west towards a distant group of trees. Cross over the sandy north–south valley until you hit the road, where you could meet your vehicle, making today's walk less than three hours. You could then detour south 3.5km in your vehicle to visit the nearby Dropde Monastery.

If you want to continue walking, head northwest along a connecting road to enter the side valley, soon reaching the roadside village of **Manitinge**, where the few copses of trees are protected behind stone enclosures. The road continues up through the village of **Siphu**, past a small reservoir and on to the village of **Lower Lungsang** (4060m; N 29°06.265', E 088°51.824'). Continue on a few minutes to the lovely walled grove that surrounds the abandoned buildings of **Upper Lungsang**. There are plenty of flat, shady campsites here, though there is no water early in the summer. Your vehicle can park nearby. Be wary of dogs from the village during the night.

Stage 2: Upper Lungsang to Ngor Monastery

2-3 HOURS / 6KM / 340M ASCENT/270M DESCENT

From Upper Lungsang the trail cuts across the valley floor, gradually making its way back to the northern side of the valley. The cart track does not extend past the village and the trail up to the pass may be difficult to find in places. It is less than two hours from Upper Lungsang to the Char-la. At first, the trail skirts the edge of a gravel wash. However, in 15 minutes a series of livestock tracks climbs out of the stream bed and onto an eroded shelf that forms above it. Observe the old agricultural fields here, many of which have been long abandoned due to a lack of water.

The terrain becomes more rugged and a gorge forms below the trail. There is a small white building and **reservoir** (4190m; N 29°06.619', E 088°50.763') 45 minutes above Upper Lungsang. This is the last convenient place to collect water until over the pass. From the reservoir, the trail continues along the side valley, crossing two small gullies and a water pipe, sticking to the north side of the main gully.

After 45 minutes from Lungsang the stream splits; head up the central spur, veering towards the right, climbing up the left side of the right-hand valley. Paths also follow the southern side of the valley, joining the main trail at the pass. At one time these trails were well maintained and formed a main trade link between Shalu and Sakya Monasteries, but they have fallen into disrepair.

The trail becomes increasingly exposed, switchbacking steeply to avoid a landslide, before reaching the top of the ridge. Continue along the shelf, dipping one last time into a gully before curving left to the white chörtens of the pass, an obvious notch in the ridge line. From the **Char-la** (4440m; N 29°07.000', E 088°49.850'), mountain ranges stretch to the west across the horizon and Ngor Monastery is visible directly below.

Ngor is a 45-minute steep descent from the pass. The route from the Char-la descends the south side of a ravine that forms below it. It's hard to follow the main path; essentially keep to the south side, eventually dipping into the ravine and climbing to the northern side, to meet the monastery road beside a toilet and rubbish dump, a rather unceremonious end to the hike! Head to the monastery restaurant for a reviving milk tea and bowl of noodles.

Sakya master Ngorchen Kunga Sangpo founded **Ngor Monastery** in 1429, giving rise to the Ngorpa suborder, a distinctive school of Buddhist thought. Once an important centre of learning, Ngor used to boast four monastic estates and 18 residential units inhabited by 340 monks (there are currently 260). Several large buildings have been rebuilt, including the *shedra* (monastic school) and debating courtyard next to the parking lot (there is debating here at 11.30am and 6.30pm). The largest structure is the assembly hall, called the Gonshung. Head upstairs to see the monastery's treasures – a tooth of the primordial buddha, the boot of the fifth Dalai Lama and the horn of a rhino. The outer walls of its gallery are painted in vertical red, white and blue stripes, a characteristic decorative technique used by the Sakya order. The three colours represent the Rigsum Gonpo, the three most important bodhisattvas. The present head of Ngor, Luding Khenpo, resides in northern India.

Most trekkers end their walk at Ngor. A new improved road now connects Ngor to **Nartang Monastery**, 19km away.

Mt Kailash Kora

The age-old path around Mt Kailash is one of the world's great pilgrimage routes and completely encircles Asia's holiest mountain. With a 5650m pass to conquer, this kora is a test of both the mind and the spirit.

There's some gorgeous mountain scenery along this trek, including close-ups of the majestic pyramidal Mt Kailash, but just as rewarding is the chance to see and meet your fellow pilgrims, many of whom have travelled hundreds of kilometres on foot to get here. Apart from local Tibetans, there are normally dozens of Hindus on the kora during the main pilgrim season (June to September). Most ride horses, with yak teams carrying their supplies. There are also plenty of Chinese tourists.

The route around Mt Kailash is a simple one: you start by crossing a plain, then head up a wide river valley, climb up and over the 5650m Drölma-la, head down another river valley, and finally cross the original plain to the starting point. It's so straightforward and so perfect a natural circuit that it's easy to see how it has been a pilgrim favourite for thousands of years.

TIBETAN TREKS MT KAILASH KORA

MT KAILASH KORA AT A GLANCE

Duration Three days

Distance 52km

Difficulty Medium to difficult

Start/Finish Darchen

Highest Point Drölma-la (5650m)

Nearest Large Town Ali

Accommodation Camping or monastery guesthouses

Best Time to Trek May to mid-October

Summary The circuit, or kora, of Mt Kailash (6714m) is one of the most important pilgrimages in Asia. It's been a religious sanctuary since pre-Buddhist times, and a trek here wonderfully integrates the spiritual, cultural and physical dimensions of a trip to Tibet. Being able to meet pilgrims from across Tibet and other countries adds to the appeal.

Mt Kailash Kora

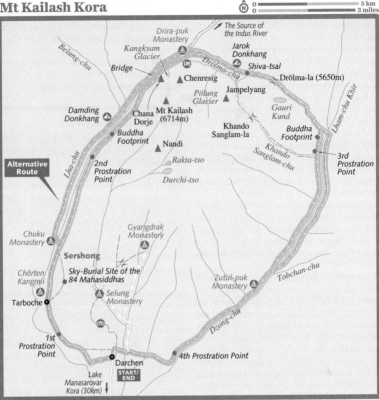

The Mt Kailash trekking season runs from mid-May until mid-October, but trekkers should always be prepared for changeable weather. Snow may be encountered on the Drölma-la at any time of year and the temperature will often drop well below freezing at night. The pass tends to be snowed in from early November to early April.

The kora is becoming more and more popular. A tent and your own food are always a nice luxury, but there is now accommodation and simple food at Drira-puk and Zutul-puk. Guides can even book you a room here in advance. Bottled water, beer, instant noodles and tea are available every few hours at teahouse tents. Natural water sources abound, but you should bring the means of water purification. A dirt road now encircles two-thirds of the kora, but traffic is light and it's fairly easy to avoid.

Horses, yaks and porters are all available for hire in Darchen, the gateway town

to the kora. Big groups often hire yaks to carry their supplies, but yaks will only travel in pairs or herds, so you have to hire at least two. Horses are an easier option but are surprisingly expensive because they are in great demand by Indian pilgrims. Most hikers carry their own gear or get by with the services of a local porter (¥210 per day for a minimum of three days). All guides and pack animals have to be arranged through a central office (p187) in Darchen.

Stage 1: Darchen to Dira-puk Monastery

5-6 HOURS / 20KM / 200M ASCENT

The kora path begins unceremoniously at a checkpoint on the western edge of Darchen, where you will show your Kailash entry ticket. Quickly leaving all traces of the village behind, you head westward across the Barkha plain, a sandy expanse speckled with greenery like a massive camouflage jacket. To the north, the east–west ridge blocks your view of Mt Kailash, but to the southeast are clear views of huge Gurla Mandata (7728m). Api (7132m) and other peaks in Nepal are visible to the south; look to the southwest for the sharp twin humps of Kamet (7756m) in India.

Only 4km from Darchen the trail climbs up over the southwestern end of the ridge to reach a **cairn** at 4790m. The cairn is bedecked with prayer flags and marks the first views of Mt Kailash's southern or lapis lazuli face and a *chaktsal gang,* the first of the kora's four prostration points.

Very quickly the trail bends round to the north and enters the barren Lha-chu Valley. From here on, the narrow Lha-chu River provides a steady supply of water all the way to Drira-puk Monastery. For the best water, however, look for the occasional side stream flowing down from the cliffs.

The valley is so open at this point you can see ahead to the tall **Tarboche** flagpole (4750m) in the distance. The Tarboche area is one of the most significant sites for Tibet's most important festival, Saga Dawa, when hundreds of pilgrims clamour to watch the annual raising of the flagpole. The pole was first erected in 1681 during the reign of the fifth Dalai Lama to commemorate a military victory over Ladakh.

Just west of Tarboche is the 'two-legged' **Chörten Kangnyi**. It's an auspicious act for pilgrims to walk through the small chörten's archway, which is decorated with hanging yak heads.

A short climb above Tarboche to the east is the sky-burial site of the 84 *mahasiddhas* (Tantric practitioners who reached a high level of awareness). The site is revered, as it was once reserved for monks and lamas, but is no longer used and is now off-limits to foreigners: steer well clear as wild dogs guard the site (a Chinese hiker was attacked here in 2015). The first of the kora's three Buddha footprints is here, but it's hard to find.

Beyond Tarboche the valley narrows dramatically at an area called Sershong. You now begin to get clear views of Mt Kailash, standing to attention above the eastern ridge. After passing a series of ruined chörtens and a number of long mani walls, the trail reaches a collection of teahouse tents beside a small bridge across the Lha-chu. The bridge is 40 minutes' walk from Tarboche, about 2½ hours from Darchen, and is directly below Chuku Monastery. Most Indian pilgrims begin their kora here.

Chuku Monastery (4820m), founded in the 13th century by Götsangpa Gompo Pel, a Kagyupa-order master, is perched high on the hillside, a steep 15-minute hike above the valley. It blends so perfectly into its rocky background that you may not even notice it's there. All Mt Kailash monasteries were wrecked during the Cultural Revolution and Chuku was the first to be rebuilt. Inside, look for a glass case over the altar: it contains a highly revered marble statue called Chuku Opame (originally from India and reputed to talk) and a conch shell inlaid with

ESSENTIAL CONSIDERATIONS FOR WALKING AROUND MT KAILASH

There are several important questions to consider when planning to walk the 52km Mt Kailash circuit. First, will you be walking the mountain in a clockwise or anticlockwise direction? Hindus, Jains and Buddhists go clockwise, but followers of Bön go anticlockwise.

If you're Tibetan, you'll probably plan to complete the circuit in one hard day's slog. Achieving this feat requires a predawn start and a late-afternoon return to Darchen. Otherwise, plan on a comfortable three days around the holy mountain. Some very devout Tibetans make the round much more difficult by prostrating themselves the entire way. Count on around three weeks to complete a kora in this manner and be sure to wear knee padding and thick gloves.

It is said by Tibetans that circling the mountain once will wipe out the sins of a lifetime, while completing 108 circuits guarantees instant nirvana. Those with an eye to economy should note that koras completed during a full moon or in the Tibetan Year of the Horse are more beneficial than ordinary ones.

If you're not a Buddhist, Bönpo or Hindu, the promise of liberation may not grab you no matter how caught up in the moment you are. And yet many foreigners go truly expecting to experience something holy or profound. This is a little like trying to fall in love. But why not?

silver. Beside the altar there's a copper pot and elephant tusks, the latter a leftover from when Bhutan exerted religious control over the monasteries around Kailash.

From the Chuku bridge the main pilgrimage trail follows the eastern bank for about three hours to Drira-puk Monastery. Take your time here as this stretch has some of the best scenery of the entire kora. High sedimentary faces, wonderfully puckered and dented, and chiselled into shapes that seem alive, hem you in on both sides. When the weather is warmer there's even the occasional ribbon of water tumbling down the slopes from hundreds of metres above.

Many of the formations along the way have mythical connections, with a number of them related to Tibet's legendary hero Gesar of Ling – but you're unlikely to find them without a guide. One easy one to find is Gesar's saddle, a stone shaped with a central dip like a saddle. Easier to find is the **second prostration point** (N 31°04.430′, E 081°16.942′), with its prayer flags and clear view of the west side of Mt Kailash. Around 30 minutes later, just past a collection of tea tents selling the usual drinks and snacks, look for a second Buddha footprint, and the **Tamdrin Dronkhang** (N 31°05.126′, E 081°17.264′), a carving depicting the protector Tamdrin, a wrathful horse-headed deity, on a black stone smeared with aeons of yak butter.

If you are planning to camp, you could consider taking the west-bank trail from Chuku Monastery, as there are some fine grassy campsites on this side (4890m), across the river from the tent teahouses near the Tamdrin carving, and about an hour before Drira-puk. The west or ruby face of Mt Kailash makes a dramatic backdrop to this campsite and in the early morning Tibetan pilgrims can be seen striding past on the other side of the river, already well into their one-day circuit. Be aware, though, that walking on the western side may require wading across side streams, especially in July and August. Wear socks or trekking sandals when you cross; it helps on the slippery rocks.

From the Tamdrin rock, the trail starts to climb and heads northeast toward Drira-puk Monastery. Cross the large bridge to head directly to the monastery on the west bank or continue straight ahead for the main trail. After 15 minutes you'll spot a couple of buildings. To the right are the rudimentary plastic cabins of the **Snowland Brothers Restaurant & Hotel** (雪域兄弟 欢聚宾馆, Xuěyù Xiōngdì Huānjù Bīnguǎn; ☐ 188 8907 8118; dm ¥60-80), with a friendly restaurant (mains ¥25 to ¥50). Next door is a huge new government **guesthouse**, scheduled for completion in 2019. Below and to the left is the large **Shishapangma Guesthouse** (西夏邦马宾馆, Xīxiàbāngmǎ Bīnguǎn; dm ¥100-150), a two-storey concrete guesthouse boasting Nepali food and real beds for up to 200 guests – but hardly a single working toilet! The quietest and most comfortable option is a bed in the Drira-puk Monastery Guesthouse (p187), which has comfortable new rooms but limited food.

If you're camping, head for the northern valley (leading to the source of the Indus River) 10 minutes' walk east of the monastery.

Drira-puk (Lhalung Drira) Monastery (5080m) sits in a superb location on the hillside north of the Lha-chu across from the Shishapangma Guesthouse. It directly faces the astonishing north face of Mt Kailash, which from this angle appears as a massive,

MILAREPA VERSUS NARO BÖNCHUNG

All around Mt Kailash there are signs of a legendary contest for control that involved Milarepa, the Buddhist poet-saint, and Naro Bönchung, the Bön master. According to the Buddhists, Milarepa was the victor in all the various challenges, but despite this Naro Bönchung still argued for a final, winner-takes-all duel: a straightforward race to the top of the mountain.

Mounting his magic drum, Naro Bönchung immediately set out to fly to the summit. Unperturbed by the progress made by his rival, Milarepa rose from his bed at dawn and was carried by a ray of light directly to the summit. Shocked by this feat, Naro Bönchung tumbled off his drum, which skittered down the south face of the mountain, gouging the long slash marking Mt Kailash to this day. Gracious in victory, Milarepa decreed that Bön followers could continue to make their customary anticlockwise circuits of Mt Kailash, and awarded them Bönri as their own holy mountain.

jet-black slab of granite ornamented with alabaster-white stripes of snow. Three lesser mountains are arrayed in front of Mt Kailash: Chana Dorje (Vajrapani) to the west, Jampelyang (Manjushri) to the east and Chenresig (Avalokiteshvara) in the centre, but there's no doubting who is the superstar in this band.

Drira-puk Monastery takes its name from the words *drira* (meaning 'female yak horn') and *puk* ('cave') – this is where the Bön warrior-god-king Gekho tossed boulders around with his horns. The great saint Götsangpa, who opened up the kora route around Mt Kailash, was led this far by a yak that turned out to be the snow-lion-faced goddess Dakini (Khandroma), who guards the Khando Sanglam-la. Colourful murals mark the entry to Götsangpa's atmospheric meditation cave, one of which depicts Dakini. Head to the top floor to see the unusual meditation niches set around a central shrine. The monastery was rebuilt in 1985 and is currently undergoing expansion. Don't miss the views of Kailash's north face framed in the line of white chörtens outside the monastery.

To get to the monastery from the main collection of guesthouses, cross two footbridges from the Shishapangma Guesthouse.

If you have the time and the energy, consider walking up to the **Kangkyam Glacier** that descends from the sheer north face of Mt Kailash. It takes about two hours there and back and you'll feel you're getting so close to the peak that you could touch it. You'll get great photos part of the way up from a series of prayer flags, or continue almost to the foot of the glacier for the closest neck-craning views.

Stage 2: Dira-puk Monastery to Zutul-puk Monastery

7-8 HOURS / 18KM / 550M ASCENT/600M DESCENT

No doubt when you wake in the morning and step outside you'll want to revel in the glory of your surroundings. Mt Kailash's dramatic black face dominates the skyline, while the middle slopes echo with the moans of yak teams complaining as drivers load them with the day's supplies.

The main kora path heads off to the east, crossing the Lha-chu by bridge, and then climbs on to a moraine to meet the trail on the east bank. The long ascent up the Drölma-chu Valley that will eventually lead to the Drölma-la has begun. Bring water to last a few hours.

Less than an hour along is the meadow at **Jarok Donkhang** (5210m), where some trekking groups set up camp. It's not wise to camp any higher up than here because of the risks associated with altitude.

Near Jarok Donkhang a trail branches off to the southeast, leading over the snow-covered Khando Sanglam-la. This shortcut to the eastern side of Mt Kailash bypasses the normal route over the Drölma-la, but only those on their auspicious 13th kora may use it. The lion-faced goddess Dakini, who led Götsangpa to Drira-puk, makes sure of that. The last teahouse tent before the pass is located near here.

Also accessed from Jarok Donkhang is the **glacier** that descends from the east ridge off the north face of Mt Kailash, down through the Pölung Valley between Chenresig (Avalokiteshvara) and Jampelyang (Manjushri). This glacier can be reached in a return trip of a couple of hours from Jarok Donkhang. You can follow the glacial stream that runs down the middle of the valley to merge with the Drölma-chu, or you can avoid losing altitude from Jarok Donkhang by terracing around the side of Jampelyang.

Only a short distance above Jarok Donkhang, just past a seasonal teahouse tent and about 90 minutes from the day's starting point, is the rocky expanse of **Shiva-tsal** (5330m). Pilgrims are supposed to undergo a symbolic death at this point, entering into the realm of the Lord of the Dead, until they reach the top of the Drölma-la and are reborn. It is customary to leave something behind at Shiva-tsal – an item of clothing, a drop of blood or a lock of hair – to represent the act of leaving this life behind.

After Shiva-tsal the trail mercifully flattens for a time and proceeds along a glacial ridge. There are a number of interesting sights ahead, such as the sin-testing stone of **Bardo Trang** – a flat boulder that pilgrims are supposed to squeeze under to measure their sinfulness.

About 30 minutes from Shiva-tsal the trail swings eastward for the final ascent. The saddle is fairly dull looking, just a long slope of boulders and scree, but there are some stark, jagged peaks to the right. Look south for your last glimpse of the north face of Mt Kailash, since there are no views of the mountain from the pass.

Allow around 45 minutes for the final 200m climb to the top of the **Drölma-la**

(5650m; N 31°05.711', E 081°22.216'). The trail disappears at times, merging with glacial streams in summer, but the way up, up, up is obvious. Take your time. There's no shame in letting children and elderly folks pass you. If you can't go more than a few metres at a time, then don't.

After a few false summits, the rocky pass is reached. The great cubic **Drölma Do** (Drölma's Rock) that marks the top is barely visible behind an enormous number of prayer flags. Pilgrims paste money onto the rock with yak butter, and stoop to pass under the lines of prayer flags and add a new string or two to the collection. They also chant the Tibetan pass-crossing mantra, *'ki ki so so, lha gyalo'* (*ki ki so so* being the empowerment and happiness invocation, *lha gyalo* meaning 'the gods are victorious'). They have now been reborn, and, by the mercy and compassion of Drölma, their sins have been forgiven.

The tale associated with the revered Drölma Do is worth telling. When Götsangpa pioneered the kora and wandered into the valley of Dakini (Khandroma), he was led back to the correct route by 21 wolves that were, of course, merely 21 emanations of Drölma (Tara), the goddess of mercy and protector of the pass. Reaching the pass, the 21 wolves merged into one and then merged again into the great boulder. To this day Drölma helps worthy pilgrims on the difficult ascent.

Weather permitting, most pilgrims and trekkers pause at the pass for a rest and refreshments before starting the steep descent. This section can be very slippery when there is packed snow. Almost immediately,

Gauri Kund (5608m; the Tibetan name, Tukje Chenpo, translates as 'Lake of Compassion') comes into view below. Hindu pilgrims are supposed to immerse themselves in the lake's green waters, breaking the ice if necessary, but few actually do.

It takes approximately an hour to make the long and steep 400m descent to the grassy banks of the Lham-chu Khir. You may have to cross snowfields at first, sometimes leaping across streams that have cut through the valley floor, but later the trail turns dry and rocky. Walking sticks are useful here as the last section is particularly steep.

En route there is a much-revered footprint of Milarepa, though, again, spotting it on your own is difficult. When the trail reaches the valley floor, you can recover over a sweet tea at a collection of teahouse tents. There's a public toilet here. A huge rock topped by the kora's third **Buddha footprint** (*shabje drakdo*) stands just above (5245m). Figure on between 3½ and five hours to get here from Drira-puk.

As with the Lha-chu Valley on the western side of Mt Kailash, there are routes that follow both sides of the river. The main east-bank trail now follows an unpaved road and electricity lines, so consider sticking to the western side for some peace and quiet.

About 30 minutes south, a valley comes down from the Khando Sanglam-la to join the western trail. This valley provides only the briefest glimpse of Mt Kailash's eastern or crystal face. The kora's third prostration point is at the valley mouth, but it's easily missed.

THE FACES & RIVERS OF MT KAILASH

On a mystical level, Tibetans identify Mt Kailash with the mythical world mountain known as Meru, which reaches from the lowest hell to the highest heaven. According to ancient tradition, four rivers flow down the flanks of Kailash. While no major river really issues from this mountain, four do begin within just 100km of it.

Direction	Face	Mythical River	Real River
south	lapis lazuli	Mabja Kambab (Peacock Fountain)	Karnali
west	ruby	Langchen Kambab (Elephant Fountain)	Sutlej
north	gold	Sengge Kambab (Lion Fountain)	Indus
east	crystal	Tamchog Kambab (Horse Fountain)	Yarlung Tsangpo (Brahmaputra)

Grassy fields start to appear alongside the river, affording those with tents endless spots to set up camp. In the meantime the road crosses to the western side of the valley, passing a teahouse and derelict accommodation at Sangye Menlong. A side valley enters from the left. From here on the river changes name to the Dzong-chu (Fortress River). You then pass a teahouse and simple accommodation run by an elderly Tibetan couple, which makes for a quiet alternative to Zutul-puk.

Zutul-puk Monastery (4820m) is a further 30 minutes' walk, a wearisome two hours' walk from the Buddha footprint teahouses. The *zutul puk* (miracle cave) that gives the monastery its name is at the back of the main hall. As the story goes, Milarepa and Naro Bönchung were looking for shelter from the rain. They decided to build a cave together, but Milarepa put the roof in place without waiting for Naro Bönchung to make the walls (thus once again showing the supremacy of Buddhism). Milarepa then made a couple of adjustments to the cave, which left a headprint and a handprint that can both still be seen today, alongside the stone walking stick of Milarepa. A cabinet to the side holds the stone hoofprint of King Gesar of Ling's horse. Look also for the statue of Achi, the main protector of the Kagyud Drigung school to which the monastery belongs. A short but pleasant kora path encircles the outside of the monastery.

The best place to stay is the Zutul-puk Monastery Guesthouse (p188), with five-bed rooms set around a warm greenhouse-style solarium. Other places include the simple prefab Găngdǐsī Tuánjié Zōnghé Bīnguǎn (p188), which boasts good mattresses. A large new **government guesthouse** is under construction.

It's less than three hours from here to Darchen, so some groups opt to push on and finish the trek in two days.

Stage 3: Zutul-puk Monastery to Darchen
3 HOURS / 14KM / 150M DESCENT
From the monastery the trail follows the river closely for an hour or so, then climbs above the river and enters the striking Gold and Red Cliffs, a narrow canyon whose walls are stained purple, cobalt and rust. Just before here are several natural rock footprints at the **Kandrö Tora**, or Place of the Dancing Dakinis.

When the canyon narrows, look for holes gouged into the cliff walls. These are not natural but were made by pilgrims looking for holy stones. Also look for prayer flags lavishly strung across the river, and in the far distance the blue waters of the lake Rakshas Tal (Langa-tso in Tibetan).

Where the trail emerges onto the Barkha plain, close to the fourth prostration point (4700m) at **Dzongdoe**, Gurla Mandata is again visible in the distance. A well-placed teahouse allows you one last chance to savour the scene. It's now an easy one-hour walk back to Darchen along a dirt road. While this is not a very scenic stretch of the kora, the steady ground below does allow you to drift off and reflect on the past three days.

MORE TREKS

Lake Manasarovar Kora
Although there is now a dirt road all the way around Lake Manasarovar (4575m), this is still a very lovely walk. Fortunately, traffic is very light and the road can be avoided for some of the mostly level 110km route. Lake Manasarovar reflects the most lucid shades of blue imaginable. It represents the female or wisdom aspect of enlightenment and is a symbol of good fortune and fertility, explaining why Tibetans are always very eager to circumambulate it. The five Buddhist monasteries around the lake add an extra cultural dimension. Horses and guides (both cost at least ¥180 per day) can be hired in Hor Qu, the town on the northeastern side of the lake, and at Chiu Monastery.

Due to the elevation (averaging 4600m) this is a moderately difficult trek. May, June and September are the best months for the four- or five-day trek; July and August are also good, save for the hordes of gnats that infest the shores. The lake is generally still frozen in April but this can be a lovely time to walk if you are prepared for the cold. You should be prepared for any kind of weather at any time.

There is simple accommodation at Chiu (p190) and at monastery guesthouses at Langbona (p190), Seralung (p190) and Trugo (p190) Monasteries, so you could technically make the walk without a tent or

Lake Manasarovar Kora

stove, though you would miss the pleasure of camping in your own private corner of the lake.

The best place to start the walk is at **Chiu Monastery** on the northwest corner of the lake. Go in either a clockwise or counter-clockwise direction, depending on whether you more closely relate to the Buddhists and Hindus or the Bönpos. If walking in a clockwise direction, you will reach **Langbona Monastery** in about four hours. From Langbona, the pilgrims trail cuts inland to avoid lagoons that form along the north shore of Manasarovar. Look for cairns, prayer flags and other signs of pilgrim activity that herald the way. Do not make the mistake of hugging the lakeshore unless you are up for an icy-cold swim or have a raft in tow. It's about four hours from Langbona to Hor Qu (p172) town, which has hotel accommodation.

Seralung Monastery, on the east side of Lake Manasarovar, is approximately three hours beyond Hor Qu and a good place to stay and experience Tibetan religious life. Three hours' walk (15km) from Seralung is a pair of **teahouses**, 2km apart, where you can get a reviving tea and bowl of noodles. The ruins of Yerngo Monastery are a further 4km away.

Four or five hours' walk from Seralung brings you to **Trugo Monastery** on the southern flank of the lake. Accommodation is available at the monastery guesthouse and also at a new guesthouse built to accommodate the large numbers of Indian pilgrims who drive around the lake in July and August. You can make it back to Chiu Monastery via Gossul Monastery in nine to 10 hours of walking from Trugo Monastery. On either side of Gossul Monastery are caves where one can shelter and get a feel for the meditator's way of life that once ruled in Tibet.

Everest Advance Base Camps

Walking in the shadow of iconic Mt Everest is mentally exhilarating and physically challenging. By following in the footsteps of great explorers one also gets a feeling for the history of the region. Underlying this more recent history is the mountain's primordial aspect, a holy land sheltering the powerful long-life goddess, Miyo Langsangma. Now that the track to Tingri has become a major traffic artery, the focus of trekking in the region has switched to the advance base camps of Mt Everest.

The trekking season in the Everest region extends from April to late October. The trek up from Everest Base Camp to more advanced camps at the foot of the mountain requires much time for acclimatisation. This is a very difficult high-elevation region with altitudes ranging between 5400m and 6400m. Subfreezing temperatures occur all year round in this rarified world of ice and hoar.

For properly prepared groups, with the right permits from Lhasa, it's possible to trek beyond Base Camp as far as **Camp III**. Including time for acclimatising, you would need to allow at least one week for this trek. The route skirts Rongphu Glacier until **Camp I** and then meets East Rongphu Glacier at **Camp II**. This glacier must be crossed in order to reach Camp III (6340m). Those reaching Camp III stand before the north face of Mt Everest, a close encounter between the stupendous and the seemingly insignificant. For detailed information on reaching the advanced base camps, see Gary McCue's *Trekking in Tibet*.

Everest East Face

Following a river conduit breaching the Himalaya, this trek leads to the spectacular forested east flank of Mt Everest. Small lakes and fantastic camping in alpine meadows make this the best trek in the Everest region. Budget at least 10 days for the trek.

NYENCHEN TANGLHA TRAVERSE

Rarely travelled even among trekkers in Tibet, a three-day traverse of the Nyenchen Tanglha range near Nam-tso lake is logistically and physically challenging. Most tour agencies have no experience with it, so shop around and confirm the precise details if this is high on your list of priorities in Tibet.

This is a fabulous trek for those who want to see the ecological mosaic of northern Tibet in all its splendour. Close encounters with the *drokpa,* the seminomadic shepherds of the region with their ancient customs and traditions, enliven the trail. Herds of blue sheep live in the crags, and in the woodlands the endangered musk deer makes its home.

The trek begins at Kyang-rag Monastery (p107) just off the main road to the Nam-tso, 7km beyond the Damxung–Lhasa Hwy turn-off. The trail cuts across the mighty Nyenchen Tanglha range and heads directly for Tashi Dor, the celebrated headland on the southeast shore of Nam-tso (p104).

The route leaves the Damxung Valley and wends its way through a rocky defile, the gateway to a high-elevation forest in which dwarf willow and rhododendron are dominant species. A number of stream crossings await you. A tundra-filled upper valley gradually climbs to the Kyang-la (Onager pass), followed by a steep descent onto the Changtang plains. Fantastic views of sparkling Nam-tso and Tashi Dor are visible from many vantage points on the trail, and colourful *drokpa* camps dot the way.

The best time to make the Nyenchen Tanglha traverse is from May to October. A winter crossing is also sometimes possible but don't attempt one unless you have the green light from local residents. This is a very high elevation trek with a 5350m pass and minimum elevations of 4320m, so factor in plenty of time for acclimatising. It's prudent to spend two nights in Damxung before setting out. You will have to be fully equipped with a tent and a stove and enough food to reach Tashi Dor, three days away. Temperatures regularly dip below freezing, even in summer, and gale force winds are common.

Horses and guides should be available in the villages near the trailhead for ¥150 to ¥200 apiece per day. In June when locals are out collecting caterpillar fungus, horses may be hard to get. If you're not successful in the nearby villages of Nakya or Baga Ara, try Nya Do, Largen Do or Tren Do, which are a little further afield but larger in size.

The first step is to drive to **Kharta**, with its alpine hamlets, some 90km from Shegar on the Friendship Hwy. There are two main passes accessing the east or Kangshung side of Everest. Most groups cross from the Kharta to the Karma valley via Lhundrubling over the **Shao-la** (5030m). The route then heads up the Karma valley to Doksum, Pethang Meadow and Khangsung Valley Base Camp, offering fabulous views of Everest, Lhotse and the huge Kangchung glacier, before returning over the **Langma-la** (5330m). The valley was explored by the 1921 Mt Everest reconnaissance expedition, of whom George Mallory was a member.

For detailed information, see *Trekking in Tibet,* by Gary McCue.

Gateway Cities

Best Places to Stay Kathmandu

➡ Kathmandu Guest House (p234)

➡ Hotel Ganesh Himal (p234)

➡ Kantipur Temple House (p234)

➡ Zostel (p234)

Best Places to Stay Chéngdū

➡ The Temple House (p239)

➡ XiShu Garden Inn (p239)

➡ BuddhaZen Hotel (p240)

➡ Cloud Atlas Hostel (p239)

Best Places to Stay Xīníng

➡ Sofitel Xīníng (p247)

➡ San Want Hotel (p247)

➡ Héhuáng Memory Youth Hostel (p245)

Which City?

Given the complicated logistics of getting into Tibet, it's advisable to at least stay overnight in a gateway city en route to Lhasa, either to pick up your Tibet Tourism Bureau (TTB) permit, meet up with your fellow travellers or to buffer potential delays in your international flights. Most travellers reach Lhasa from Chéngdū or Kathmandu, though it's equally feasible to fly or train in from a half-dozen other Chinese cities.

Kathmandu

Crowded, colourful and chaotic Kathmandu has been a popular destination for travellers since the Hippy Trail in the 1960s and '70s, but there are drawbacks to entering Tibet from here. Prime among these is the time needed to get a Chinese visa (group visas only) and the hassle that this group visa brings if you plan to travel further inside China. However, if you want to get a taste of both sides of the Himalaya and plan to return to Nepal, it's an interesting choice.

Chéngdū

Sìchuān's huge capital city has long been the main logistical gateway to Tibet. With plenty of international air connections and excellent hostels that are very much used to helping travellers headed to Tibet, it's still a logical choice (unless you want to travel by train, then Xīníng is better). It's also a great starting point for exploring the ethnically Tibetan areas of western Sìchuān.

Xīníng

Popular as a gateway to Tibet for travellers entering the Tibet Autonomous Region on the Qīnghǎi–Tibet Railway, Xīníng is also a great place to explore the province's melange of Muslim (Huí, Salar and Uyghur), Tibetan and Han Chinese – especially the rich culinary mix that these groups bring together.

KATHMANDU

📓 01 / POP 1.5 MILLION / ELEV 1300M

For many, stepping off a plane into Kathmandu is a pupil-dilating experience, a riot of sights, sounds and smells that can quickly lead to sensory overload. Whether you're barrelling through the traffic-jammed alleyways of the old town in a rickshaw, marvelling at the medieval temples or dodging trekking touts in the backpacker district of Thamel, Kathmandu can be an intoxicating, amazing and exhausting place.

The 2015 earthquake destroyed several temples in Kathmandu's Unesco-listed Durbar Sq, but most areas emerged unscathed. Stroll through the backstreets and Kathmandu's timeless cultural and artistic heritage still reveals itself in hidden temples overflowing with marigolds, courtyards full of drying chillies and rice, and tiny workshops.

This endlessly fascinating, sometimes infuriating city has enough sights to keep you busy for a week, but be sure to leave its backpacker comforts and explore the 'real Nepal' before your time runs out.

⊙ Sights

Most of the interesting things to see in Kathmandu are clustered in the old part of town, focused on the majestic Durbar Sq and its surrounding backstreets.

Durbar Square   HISTORIC SITE
(Map p232; foreigner/SAARC Rs 1000/150, no student tickets) Kathmandu's Durbar Sq was where the city's kings were once crowned and legitimised, and from where they ruled (*durbar* means palace). As such, the square remains the traditional heart of the old town and Kathmandu's most spectacular legacy of traditional architecture. The square bore the brunt of Kathmandu's 2015 earthquake damage. Half a dozen temples collapsed, as did several towers in the Hanuman Dhoka palace complex, but it's still a fabulous complex. Reconstruction will continue for years.

Although most of the square dates from the 17th and 18th centuries (many of the original buildings are much older), a great deal of rebuilding happened after the great earthquake of 1934. The entire square was designated a Unesco World Heritage Site in 1979.

The Durbar Sq area is actually made up of three loosely linked squares. To the south is the open **Basantapur Sq area**, a former royal elephant stables that now houses souvenir stalls and off which runs Freak St. The main **Durbar Sq area** is to the west. Running northeast is a **second part of Durbar Sq**, which contains the entrance to the Hanuman Dhoka and an assortment of temples. From this open area Makhan Tole, at one time the main road in Kathmandu and still the most interesting street to walk down, continues northeast.

★**Hanuman Dhoka**   PALACE
(Map p232; Durbar Sq; admission free with Durbar Sq ticket; ⊙10.30am-4pm Tue-Sat Feb-Oct, to 3pm Tue-Sat Nov-Jan, to 2pm Sun) Kathmandu's royal palace, known as the Hanuman Dhoka, was originally founded during the Licchavi period (4th to 8th centuries AD), but the compound was expanded considerably by King Pratap Malla in the 17th century. Sadly, the sprawling palace was hit hard by the 2015 earthquake and damage was extensive. At the time of research, the main Nasal Chowk courtyard was open and the Tribhuvan Museum was close to reopening, with other buildings closed for reconstruction.

★**Garden of Dreams**   GARDENS
(Swapna Bagaicha; Map p232; 📞01-4425340; www.gardenofdreams.org.np; Tridevi Marg; adult/child Rs 200/100; ⊙9am-10pm, last entry 9pm; 🛜) The beautifully restored Swapna Bagaicha (Garden of Dreams) remains one of the most serene and beautiful enclaves in Kathmandu. It's two minutes' walk and a million miles from central Thamel.

★**Boudhanath Stupa**   BUDDHIST STUPA
(foreigner/SAARC Rs 400/100) The first stupa at Boudhanath was built after AD 600, when the Tibetan king, Songtsen Gampo, converted to Buddhism. In terms of grace and purity of line, no stupa in Nepal comes close to Boudhanath. From its whitewashed dome to its gilded tower painted with the all-seeing eyes of the Buddha, the monument is perfectly proportioned. Join the Tibetan pilgrims on their morning and evening koras (circumambulations) for the best atmosphere.

★**Swayambhunath Stupa**   BUDDHIST STUPA
(foreigner/SAARC Rs 200/50; ⊙dawn-dusk) The Swayambhunath Stupa is one of the crowning glories of Kathmandu Valley architecture. This perfectly proportioned monument rises through a whitewashed dome to a gilded spire, from where four iconic faces of the Buddha stare out across the valley in the cardinal directions. The site was shaken severely by the 2015 earthquake, but the main stupa sustained only superficial damage.

Central Kathmandu

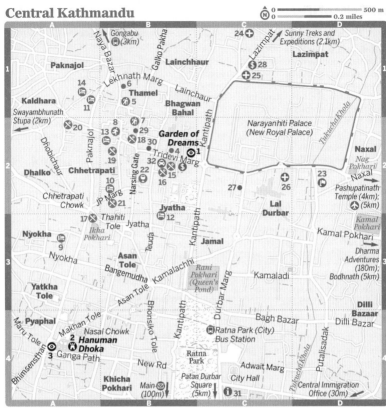

The entire structure of the stupa is deeply symbolic: the white dome represents the earth, while the 13-tiered, tower-like structure at the top symbolises the 13 stages to nirvana. The nose-like squiggle below the piercing eyes is actually the Nepali number *ek* (one), signifying unity, and above is a third eye signifying the all-seeing insight of the Buddha.

The base of the central stupa is ringed by prayer wheels embossed with the sacred mantra *om mani padme hum* ('hail to the jewel in the lotus'). Pilgrims circuiting the stupa spin each one as they pass by. Fluttering above the stupa are thousands of prayer flags, with similar mantras, which are said to be carried to heaven by the Wind Horse. Set in ornate plinths around the base of the stupa are statues representing the five Dhyani Buddhas – Vairocana, Ratnasambhava, Amitabha, Amoghasiddhi and Aksobhya – and their consorts. These deities represent the five qualities of Buddhist wisdom.

Pashupatinath Temple HINDU TEMPLE
(foreigner/SAARC Rs 1000/free, child under 10yr free; ⊙24hr) Undiminished by the earthquake, the pagoda-style Pashupatinath Temple was constructed in 1696, but has been a site of Hindu and Buddhist worship for far longer. Only Hindus are allowed to enter the compound of the famous main temple, but you can catch tantalising glimpses of what is going on inside from several points around the perimeter wall. The nearby riverside steps are Nepal's most holy cremation site.

Durbar Square (Patan) HISTORIC SITE
(Royal Square; foreigner/SAARC Rs 1000/250; ⊙ticket office 7am-6pm) The ancient royal palace of Patan faces on to magnificent Durbar Sq. This mass of temples is perhaps the most visually stunning display of Newari architecture to be seen in Nepal. Temple construction in the square went into overdrive during the Malla period (14th to 18th centuries), particularly during the reign of King Siddhinarsingh

Central Kathmandu

GATEWAY CITIES KATHMANDU

Malla (1619–60). It's well worth at least a half-day trip from Kathmandu.

⟁ Tours

Several agencies in Thamel offer fixed departure tours to Tibet, though these days they aren't much cheaper than arranging a tour yourself through an agency in Lhasa. The following agencies offer tours to Tibet, including fly-in and fly-out tours to Lhasa.

Dharma Adventures TOUR
(☑01-4430499; www.dharmaadventures.com; 38/18 Lhotse Marg, Kamal Pokhari) This reliable agency has experience running treks in Tibet, including interesting short treks around Drigung Til Monastery.

Earthbound Expeditions TREKKING
(Map p232; ☑01-4701041; www.enepaltrekking. com; Thamel) Helpful agency that can arrange guides and porters for teahouse treks and has experience arranging treks into Tibet. Contact Rajan.

Himalayan Offroad TOURS
(Map p232; ☑01-4700770; www.himalayanoffroad. com; Chaksibari Marg, Thamel) Motorbike tours of Nepal and Tibet; based in Kathmandu, sharing office space with High Mountain Wave Trekking and Mountain River Rafting.

Royal Mountain Trekking TRAVEL AGENCY
(Map p232; ☑01-4241452; www.royalmountain trekking.com; Durbar Marg) A centrally located agency that has experience arranging group and private trips from Nepal to Tibet.

Sunny Treks and Expeditions TREKKING
(☑01-4432190; www.sunnytreks.com; Bhakta Marg, Baluwatar) Runs tours and treks in Tibet, among other locations.

**Tashi Delek Nepal Treks &
Expeditions** TRAVEL AGENCY
(Map p232; ☑9841221409, 01-4410746; www.ti-bettour.travel; Narsingh Gate, Thamel) Organises a range of treks and tours in Tibet and operates fixed-departure budget overland tours to Tibet from Kathmandu every Saturday. The office is above Gillingche Restaurant.

**Tibet International
Travels & Tours** TRAVEL AGENCY
(Map p232; ☑9851025110, 01-4444314; www.tibet tours.travel; Thabahi Marg, Thamel) Operates a range of tours to Tibet, including fixed-departure eight-day overland trips every Saturday.

⟐ Sleeping

Kathmandu has a huge range of places to stay, from luxurious international-style hotels to cheap and cheerful lodges. Most budget and some midrange options are found in the bustling Thamel district. Midrange and top-end places are widely scattered around Kathmandu, some quite a way from the centre.

Zostel HOSTEL **$**
(Map p232; ☑ 01-4383579; www.zostel.com; Pipalbot Marg, Kaldhara; dm Rs 750-950, r Rs 3000-3400; 🛜) Part of an Indian chain of hostels, Zostel is a clean, comfortable and well-run place a stone's throw from Thamel. The comfortable mattresses, well-thought-out design (individual bed lights and electrical outlets) and services like bag storage and bus ticketing have made it the most popular hostel in the city.

Hotel Khangsar HOTEL **$**
(Map p232; ☑ 01-4260788; www.hotelkhangsar.com; JP Marg, Thamel; r/tr Rs 1500/2000; 🛜) This friendly and central backpacker option enjoyed a renovation in 2017 and rooms, though simple, have been freshened up. Rooms come with a narrow but clean bathroom and there's a pleasant garden rooftop bar for cold beers under the stars. The upper-floor rooms are best, especially the sunny corner ones away from the road.

★ Hotel Ganesh Himal HOTEL **$$**
(Map p232; ☑ 01-4263598; www.hotelganeshhimal.com; old building US$20-35, deluxe r US$30-60; 🌬🛜) Our pick for midrange comfort on a budget is this well-run and super-friendly place. The rooms are among the best value in Kathmandu, with endless

---

KATHMANDU PRICES
....
For Kathmandu we have used the following price indicators:

Sleeping
The following price ranges refer to a double room with bathroom in the high season. Rates generally do not include taxes, unless otherwise noted.

$ less than US$25 (Rs 2500)

$$ US$25–80 (Rs 2500–8000)

$$$ more than US$80 (Rs 8000)

Eating
Price ranges given for restaurants are defined as the price of a main course, without side dishes, drinks or tax.

$ less than Rs 250

$$ Rs 250–500

$$$ more than Rs 500

---

hot water and lots of balcony and relaxing garden seating. Throw in free airport pick-up and this place is hard to beat.

★ Kathmandu Guest House HOTEL **$$**
(Map p232; ☑ 01-4700632; www.ktmgh.com; Thamel; s/d standard US$45/55, garden facing US$65/75, deluxe US$90/100; 🌬@🛜) The KGH is an institution. A former Rana palace, it was the first hotel to open in Thamel in the late 1960s and still serves as the central landmark. Everyone from Jeremy Irons to Ricky Martin has stayed here. Despite losing a couple of buildings in the 2015 earthquake, the relaxing garden is still Kathmandu's social hub, so book rooms well in advance.

Hotel Moonlight HOTEL **$$**
(Map p232; ☑ 01-4380452; www.hotelmoonlight.com; Paknajol; s/d incl breakfast US$65/70; 🌬🛜) The modern and professional Moonlight is a good midrange choice, with a calming interior garden courtyard, a lobby cafe and a spa, all punctuated with nice design touches. The 67 rooms vary in size; our favourites are the rooms with a balcony in the 'boutique' block. The rooftop bar should boast great views when finished.

★ Kantipur Temple House BOUTIQUE HOTEL **$$$**
(Map p232; ☑ 01-4250131; www.kantipurtemplehouse.com; s/d US$90/100, deluxe US$120/130) 🏊 Hidden down an alley on the southern edge of Thamel, this Newari temple–style hotel has been built with meticulous attention to detail. The spacious rooms are tastefully decorated, with traditional carved wood, terracotta floor tiles, window seats and fairtrade *dhaka* (hand-woven cotton cloth) bedspreads. Due to the traditional nature of the building, rooms tend to be a little dark.

🍴 Eating & Drinking

Kathmandu has an astounding array of restaurants. Indeed, with the possible exception of the canteen at the UN building, there are few places where you can have the choice of Indian, Chinese, Japanese, Mexican, Korean, Middle Eastern, Italian or Irish cuisines, all within a five-minute walk. After weeks trekking in the mountains, Kathmandu feels like a culinary paradise.

Yangling Restaurant TIBETAN **$**
(Map p232; ☑ 01-4260562; JP Marg; momos Rs 150-260; ⏰8am-9pm) Locals and tourists flock to this unpretentious family-run place for possibly the best *momos* (dumplings) in town (try the chicken ones). It also sells Sherpa Beer,

Nepal's best craft brew. The main location is on the southern edge of Thamel, signposted down an alley, but there's a **branch** (Map p232; Kaldhara; momos Rs 150-260; ☺noon-9pm Sun-Fri; 🕾) just west of Thamel.

Gupta Bhojanalaya   INDIAN $
(Map p232; Chhetrapti Chowk; mains Rs 75-250; ☺7am-10pm; 🖉) This hole-in-the-wall restaurant is a refreshing antidote to Thamel's gentrifying eating scene and rising rates. The vegetarian-only food is tasty and authentic, and it's a great place to try a range of curries, South Indian *dosas, momos* (dumplings) and nan breads. The *chola bhatura* (chickpeas and fried puri bread) is a great snack.

New Orleans Cafe   INTERNATIONAL $$
(Map p232; 🖉 01-4700736; www.neworleanscafe ktm.com; mains Rs 400-570; ☺8am-10.30pm; 🕾🖉) Hidden down an alley near Kathmandu Guest House, New Orleans boasts an intimate candlelit vibe, a classy blues and jazz soundtrack and live music on Wednesdays and Saturdays. It's a popular spot for a cocktail, but the menu also ranges far and wide, from Thai curries to Creole jambalaya and oven-roasted veggies. You need to book a table in the high season.

Or2k   MIDDLE EASTERN $$
(Map p232; 🖉 01-4422097; www.or2k.net; Mandala St; mains Rs 300-500; ☺9am-11pm; 🕾🖉) This bright, buzzy and ever-popular Israeli vegetarian restaurant is a favourite for fresh and light Middle Eastern dishes, with plenty of vegan and gluten-free options. The menu spreads to fatoush salad, zucchini and mushroom pie and *ziva* (pastry fingers filled with cheese), as well as a great meze sampler of hummus, felafel and *labane* (sour cream cheese) served in neat little brass bowls.

★Gaia Restaurant   INTERNATIONAL $$$
(Map p232; Jyatha; mains Rs 500-740; ☺7am-9.30pm; 🕾) This popular, dependable place combines good breakfasts, salads, sandwiches and organic coffee in a pleasant garden courtyard with global music, reasonable prices (tax included) and good service. The Thai red curry is good and the chicken *choiyla* (spicy barbecued meat) packs a punch; you're bound to find something good with a menu that ranges from daal bhaat to carrot cake.

★Fire & Ice Pizzeria   PIZZA $$$
(Map p232; 🖉 01-4250210; www.fireandicepizzeria. com; 219 Sanchaya Kosh Bhawan, Tridevi Marg; pizzas Rs 580-760; ☺8am-11pm; 🕾) This excellent and informal Italian place serves the best pizzas in Kathmandu (wholewheat crusts available, as well as combo pizzas), alongside breakfasts, smoothies, crespelle (savoury crêpes) and good espresso, all to a cool soundtrack of Cuban son or Italian opera. The ingredients are top-notch, from the imported anchovies to the house-made tomato sauce.

★Third Eye   INDIAN $$$
(Map p232; 🖉 01-4260160; www.thirdeye.com.np; Chaksibari Marg; mains Rs 500-650; ☺11am-10pm) This long-running favourite is popular with well-heeled tourists. Indian food is the speciality and the tandoori dishes are especially good, even if the portions are a bit small. Spice levels are set at 'tourist' so let the suited waiters know if you'd like extra heat.

Yin Yang Restaurant   THAI $$$
(Map p232; 🖉 01-4425510; www.yinyang.com.np; curries Rs 600, rice Rs 125; ☺10am-10pm) Yin Yang is one of Thamel's most highly regarded restaurants, serving authentic Thai food that is a definite cut above the imitation Thai food found elsewhere. The green curry is authentically spicy; for something sweeter try the massaman curry (with onion, peanut and potato). There's a good range of vegetable choices, as well as Western alternatives.

Yeti Tap Room   CRAFT BEER
(Map p232; www.yetitaproomandbeergarden.com; Chibahal; ☺closes 10pm) The epicenter of Kathmandu's nascent craft-beer scene, this beer garden at the Thamel Eco Resort offers dozens of brews by the can alongside five taps offering an IPA, a pale ale and a saison, with two rotators. The beer mostly comes from Colorado but there are also brews from Vietnam and beyond, with local offerings in the pipeline.

The owners are the force behind the annual Nepal Beer Festival, held every late October/early November.

ℹ Information

DANGERS & ANNOYANCES

Kathmandu is a fairly safe city, but what it lacks in dangers it more than makes up for in annoyances:

➡ The combination of ancient vehicles, low-quality fuel and lack of emission controls makes the streets of Kathmandu particularly polluted, noisy and unpleasant.

➡ Avoid seedy dance bars and street-corner hashish sellers – although variably enforced, the penalties for possession can be severe.

Other annoyances in Thamel are the crazy motorcyclists, and the barrage of irritating flute sellers, Tiger balm hawkers, chess-set sellers, musical-instrument vendors, travel-agency touts, hashish suppliers, freelance trekking guides and rickshaw drivers.

Note that the colourful sadhus (itinerant holy men) who frequent Durbar Sq and Pashupatinath will expect baksheesh (a tip) if you take a photo, as will the Thamel 'holy men' who anoint you with a *tika* on your forehead.

Kathmandu has in the past been the focus of political demonstrations and *bandhs* (strikes), which close shops and shut down transport.

EMERGENCY & IMPORTANT NUMBERS

Country code	☑ 977
International access code	☑ 00
Police	☑ 100
Tourist Police	☑ 01-4247041
Ambulance	☑ 102

HEALTH

Dozens of pharmacies on the fringes of Thamel offer all the cheap antibiotics you can pronounce.

CIWEC Clinic Travel Medicine Center (Map p232; ☑ 01-4424111, 01-4435232; www. ciwec-clinic.com; Kapurdhara Marg, Lazimpat; ⊙ emergency 24hr, clinic 9am-noon & 1-4pm Mon-Fri) In operation since 1982 and has an international reputation for research into travellers' medical problems. Staff are mostly foreigners and a doctor is on call round the clock. Credit cards are accepted and the centre is used to dealing with insurance claims.

Healthy Smiles (Map p232; ☑ 01-4420800; www.smilenepal.com.np; Lazimpat; ⊙ 10am-5pm Sun-Fri) UK-trained dentist, opposite the Hotel Ambassador, with a branch in Patan.

Nepal International Clinic (Map p232; ☑ 01-4434642, 01-4435357; www.nepalinternationalclinic.com; Lal Durbar; ⊙ 9am-1pm & 2-5pm) Just south of the New Royal Palace, east of Thamel. It has an excellent reputation and is slightly cheaper than the CIWEC Clinic. Credit cards accepted.

LAUNDRY

Several laundries across Thamel will machine wash laundry for Rs 80 to Rs 100 per kilo. Get it back the next day or pay double for a three-hour service. Amazingly, it all comes back relatively clean, even after a three-week trek.

MONEY

There are dozens of licensed moneychangers in Thamel. Their hours are longer than those of the banks (generally until 8pm or so) and rates are similar, perhaps even slightly higher if you don't need a receipt.

There are ATMs everywhere in Thamel. Useful locations include beside Yin Yang Restaurant (p235) and Ganesh Man Singh Building.

Himalayan Bank (Map p232; ☑ 01-4250208; www.himalayanbank.com; Tridevi Marg; ⊙ 10am-7pm Sun-Fri, 9am-noon Sat) The most convenient bank for travellers in Thamel, this kiosk on Tridevi Marg changes cash without commission; on Saturdays or if its closed head to the main branch in the basement of the nearby Sanchaya Kosh Bhawan shopping centre. There's a useful ATM next to the kiosk.

Standard Chartered Bank (Map p232; ☑ 01-4418456; Lazimpat; ⊙ 9.45am-7pm Sun-Thu, 9.45am-4.30pm Fri, 9.30am-12.30pm Sat & holidays) Well-located ATM in the compound of the Kathmandu Guest House gives up to Rs 35,000 per transaction but charges a Rs 500 commission. The main branch charges Rs 200 per transaction for cash.

TOURIST INFORMATION

Tourist Service Centre (Map p232; ☑ 01-4256909 ext 223; www.welcomenepal.com; Bhrikuti Mandap; ⊙ 10am-1pm & 2-5pm Sun-Fri, TIMS card 10am-5.30pm, national park tickets 9am-2pm Sun-Fri) On the eastern side of the Tundikhel parade ground; has an inconvenient location but is the place for trekkers to get a TIMS card, and pay national park fees.

There are a number of noticeboards in Thamel that are worth checking for information on apartments, travel and trekking partners, courses and cultural events. Check at the Kathmandu Guest House (p234) and Fire & Ice Pizzeria (p235).

VISAS

Tourist visas (15/30/90 days) are available on arrival for US$25/40/100; fill in your details online beforehand or on the spot, and bring US dollars cash.

For Nepal

All foreigners, except Indians, must have a visa. Nepali embassies and consulates overseas issue visas with no fuss but most people get one on the spot on arrival in Nepal, either at Kathmandu's Tribhuvan International Airport or at road borders at Nepalganj, Birganj/Raxaul Bazaar, Sunauli, Kakarbhitta, Mahendranagar, Dhangadhi and even the Rasuwagadhi checkpoint at the China/Tibetan border.

A Nepali visa is valid for entry for three to six months from the date of issue. Children aged under 10 require a visa but are not charged a visa fee. Citizens of South Asian countries (except India) and China need visas, but if you're only entering once in a calendar year, these are free.

To obtain a visa upon arrival by air in Nepal you must fill in an application form at one of the automatic registration machines, which will also take your digital photo. You can save some time by filling in the form beforehand online at www.online.nepalimmigration.gov.np/tourist-visa and uploading a digital photo, but you must do this less than 15 days before your arrival date.

A single-entry visa valid for 15/30/90 days costs US$25/40/100. At Kathmandu's Tribhuvan Airport the fee is payable in any major currency, but at land borders officials require payment in cash (US dollars); bring small bills.

SAARC countries can get a 30-day visa for free on arrival. Indian passport holders do not need a visa to enter Nepal.

Multiple-entry visas are useful if you are planning a side trip to Tibet, Bhutan or India and cost US$20 extra. You can change your single-entry visa to a multiple-entry visa at Kathmandu's Central Immigration Office for the same US$20 fee.

Don't overstay your visa. You can pay a fine of US$3 per day at the airport if you have overstayed less than 30 days (plus a US$2 per day visa extension fee), but it's far better to get it all sorted out in advance at Kathmandu's **Central Immigration Office** (☏ 01-4429659; www.nepalimmigration. gov.np; Kalikasthan, Dilli Bazaar; ⊗10am-4pm Sun-Thu, 10am-3pm Fri, 11am-1pm Sat), as a delay could cause you to miss your flight.

It's a good idea to keep a number of passport photos with your passport so they are immediately handy for trekking permits, visa applications and other official documents.

For Tibet

The Chinese embassy in Kathmandu only issues Tibet visas to travellers who have paper group visas (not a stamp in your passport). For more visa information, see p318.

❶ Getting There & Away

The ageing **Tribhuvan International Airport** (☏ 01-4472256; www.tiairport.com.np), about 6km east of the centre, is the main international hub in Nepal. The chaotic terminal is regularly voted one of the worst in Asia and you can expect to wait some time for your luggage to arrive. Be sure to check the piles of luggage next to the belt as staff often unload luggage there to minimise congestion.

TO/FROM TIBET

Officially only organised 'groups' are allowed into Tibet from Nepal. The good news is that travel agencies in Kathmandu are experienced in both arranging private tours and assembling overland groups. In general, travellers face fewer restrictions entering Tibet through China, so it makes more sense to visit Nepal after a trip through Tibet, not before. The rules are in constant flux, so allow two weeks for your agency or tour operator to arrange the necessary visa invitation via their Lhasa contacts and plan to physically be in Kathmandu for at least four working days in order to get your visa.

Travelling overland to Tibet from Nepal is a stunning drive, but altitude sickness is a real danger. The maximum altitude along the road is 5140m and most overland tours from Kathmandu do not allow sufficient time to acclimatise safely, sleeping at 4330m on only the second night from Kathmandu (1300m). If you have the option, fly to Lhasa, acclimatise for a few days and then drive overland back to Kathmandu, rather than in the opposite direction.

The former border crossing at Kodari/Zhangmu was severely damaged by the 2015 earthquake, and is currently closed. The new border point is at Rasuwagadhi, due north of Kathmandu on the Langtang road, which only opened to foreigners in August 2017; the Tibetan side is Kyirong. The border is open from 10am to 12.30pm and 1.30pm to 5pm China time (Nepal time plus 2¼ hours).

Landslides are likely on this route during the monsoon months (May to August), particularly on the Nepal side, and there are often additional restrictions on travel at times of political tension. Other road connections, including the road from Tibet to Mustang and Tsum, are not open to foreigners, although organised groups can trek from Simikot through far-western Nepal to Mt Kailash.

❶ Getting Around

TO/FROM THE AIRPORT

Getting into town from Tribhuvan International Airport is quite straightforward. Both the international and domestic terminals offer a fixed-price prepaid taxi service, currently Rs 750 to Thamel. There is a moneychanger next to the taxi counter.

Once outside the international terminal you will be confronted by hotel touts, who are often taxi drivers making commission on taking you to a particular hotel. Many hold up a signboard of the particular hotel they are connected with and, if the one you want is there, you can get a free lift. The drawback with the taxis is that the hotel is then much less likely to offer you a discount, as it will be paying a hefty commission to the taxi driver.

If you book a room in advance for more than one night, many hotels will pick you up for free.

Public buses leave from the main road – about 300m from the terminal – but they're only really practical if you have very little luggage and know exactly how to get to where you want to go.

From Kathmandu to the airport you should be able to get a taxi for Rs 500, or a bit more for a late or early flight.

BICYCLE

Cycling is a good way to explore parts of the Kathmandu Valley and many companies offer bike rentals and tours. You need to be selective about your routes to avoid heavy traffic.

Mountain bikes cost from Rs 800 per day for simple models. For longer trips around the valley, major mountain-bike companies such as **Dawn**

Till Dusk (Map p232; www.nepalbiking.com; Tridevi Marg) and **Nepal Mountain Bike Tours** (Map p232; ☑ 01-4701701; www.nepalmountainbiketours.com; 321 Chaksibari Marg) hire out high-quality bikes with front suspension and disc brakes for around US$10 to US$15 per day.

If you want to make an early start, most places are happy to give you the bike the evening before. For all bikes, negotiate discounts for rentals of more than a day. You should get a helmet, a lock and a repair kit. Check the brakes and be certain to lock the bike whenever you leave it.

CYCLE-RICKSHAW

Cycle-rickshaws cost around Rs 80 for short rides around Thamel or the old town, but you can expect to haggle hard. It's essential to agree on a price before you start.

TAXI

Taxis are quite reasonably priced, though few taxi drivers use the meters in these days of rising fuel prices. Shorter rides around town (including to the bus station) cost around Rs 200. Night-time rates (between 10pm and 6am) cost 50% more.

The closest **taxi stand** (Map p232; Tridevi Marg) to Thamel is close to the junction with Jyatha Rd. Taxis can be booked in advance on 01-4420987; at night call 01-4224374.

Approximate taxi fares from Thamel:

Bhaktapur Rs 700

Bodhnath Rs 600

Pashupatinath Rs 500

Patan Rs 500

Swayambhunath Rs 300

CHÉNGDŪ 成都

☑ 028 / POP 14.42 MILLION / ELEV 500M

Chéngdū is no great draw when it comes to tourist sites – pandas excepted, of course – but many visitors find its laid-back pace and diversity of cultural scenes unexpectedly engaging. It could be its relaxing teahouse culture, with favourite local institutions serving the same brews across generations. Maybe it's the lively nightlife, with a strong showing of local partiers bolstered by large student and expat populations that gather at craft beer bars and super-hip clubs. It might be the food: famous for heat, history and variety even in the cuisine-rich cultures of China; and very much a point of pride. It is, after all, Unesco's first-ever City of Gastronomy.

◉ Sights

★ Giant Panda

Breeding Research Base WILDLIFE RESERVE
(大熊猫繁育基地, Dàxióngmāo Fányù Jīdì; ☑ 028 8351 0033; www.panda.org.cn; 1375 Xiongmao Dadao; 熊猫大道1375号; adult/student ¥58/29; ⊙ 8am-5.30pm; M Panda Avenue) One of Chéngdū's most popular attractions, this reserve 18km north of the city centre is the easiest way to glimpse Sìchuān's most famous residents outside of a zoo. The enclosures here are generally large and well maintained. Home to nearly 120 giant and 76 red pandas, the base focuses on getting these shy creatures to breed.

March to May is the 'falling in love period' (wink wink). If you visit during autumn or winter, you may see tiny newborns in the nursery.

Try to visit in the morning, when the pandas are most active. Feeding takes place around opening time at 8am, although you'll see them eating in the late afternoon too. Pandas spend most of their afternoons sleeping, particularly during the height of midsummer, when they sometimes disappear into their (air-conditioned) living quarters.

From exit A of the Panda Avenue (熊猫大道) station on metro line 3 , a free D025 bus transfer is available from 8.30am to 4pm. A taxi from the city centre costs about ¥50, or hostels run trips here.

★ Wénshū Monastery BUDDHIST TEMPLE
(文殊院; Wénshū Yuàn; Map p240; 66 Wenshuyuan Lu; 文殊院路66号; ⊙ 7am-9pm; M Wenshu Monastery) FREE This Tang dynasty monastery is dedicated to Wénshū (Manjushri), the Bodhisattva of Wisdom, and is Chéngdū's largest and best-preserved Buddhist temple. The air is heavy with incense and the low murmur of chanting; despite frequent crowds of worshippers, there's still a sense of serenity.

★ Chéngdū Museum MUSEUM
(成都博物馆, Chéngdū Bówùguǎn; Map p240; ☑ 028 6291 5593; www.cdmuseum.com; west side of Tiānfǔ Sq; 天府广场西侧; ⊙ 9am-8pm Tue-Sun; M Tianfu Square) FREE Spanning ancient Shu and pre-Qin to the Revolutionary era and modern Chéngdū, this five-storey museum (completed in 2016) is packed with historical and cultural relics of the city's past. Don't miss the two 'Puppetry and Shadow Plays of China' galleries on the top floor, with excellent examples of the art from across the country.

People's Park PARK
(人民公园; Rénmín Gōngyuán; Map p240; 9 Citang Jie; 祠堂街9号; ⊙ 6.30am-10pm; M People's Park) FREE On weekends, locals fill this park with dancing, song and t'ai chi. There's a small, willow-tree-lined boating lake and a number of teahouses: Hè Míng Teahouse (p242) is the most popular and atmospheric.

Qīngyáng Temple
TAOIST TEMPLE

(青羊宫; Qīngyáng Gōng; Map p240; 9 Huanlu Xi Er Duan; 一环路西二段9号; ¥10; ⊙8am-6pm; 🚌11, 27, 45) Located alongside **Culture Park** (文化公园, Wénhuà Gōngyuán; Map p240; 9 Huanlu Xi Er Duan; 一环路西二段9号; ⊙6am-10pm; 🚌11, 27, 45) **FREE**, this is Chéngdū's oldest and most extensive Taoist temple. Qīngyáng (Green Ram) Temple dates from the Zhou dynasty, although most of what you see is Qing. A highlight is the unusually squat, eight-sided pagoda, built without bolts or pegs. There's also a popular teahouse (tea from ¥10) inside towards the back.

Wǔhóu Temple
BUDDHIST TEMPLE

(武侯祠; Wǔhóu Cí; Map p240; ☎028 8555 9027; 231 Wuhouci Dajie; 武侯祠大街231号; adult/student ¥60/30; ⊙8am-8pm; 🚌1, 21, 26) Located adjacent to Nánjiāo Park and surrounded by mossy cypresses, this temple (rebuilt in 1672) honours several figures from the Three Kingdoms period, namely legendary military strategist Zhuge Liang and Emperor Liu Bei (his tomb is here). Both were immortalised in the Chinese literature classic, *Romance of the Three Kingdoms (Sān Guó Yǎnyì)*.

Jīnshā Site Museum
MUSEUM

(金沙遗址博物馆; Jīnshā Yízhǐ Bówùguǎn; ☎028 8730 3522; www.jinshasitemuseum.com; 227 Qingyang Dadao; 青羊大道227号; ¥80; ⊙8am-8pm; 🚇Jinsha Site Museum) In 2001 archaeologists made a historic discovery in Chéngdū's western suburbs: they unearthed a site containing ruins of the 3000-year-old Shu kingdom. This excellent, expansive museum includes the excavation site and beautiful displays of many of the uncovered objects, which were created between 1200 and 600 BC.

🛏 Sleeping

Cloud Atlas Hostel
HOSTEL $

(云图国际青年旅舍; Yúntú Guójì Qīngnián Lǚshè; Map p240; ☎028 8334 6767; cloudatlashostel@163.com; 288 Shuncheng Jie; 顺城街288号; dm ¥49-69, s/d ¥169/189; ⊙🌐🛜; 🚇Luomashi) Excellent facilities, great coffee, lots of common space – this artsy hostel has it all. It's large enough to feel a bit institutional on the dorm floors, but that just means there are tonnes of new friends to be made. Look for it inside the entrance to the Zhūfēng Jiǔdiàn (珠峰酒店).

Holly's Hostel
HOSTEL $

(九龙鼎青年客栈; Jiǔlóngdǐng Qīngnián Kèzhàn; Map p240; ☎028 8555 7349, 028 8554 8131; hollyhostelcn@yahoo.com; 246 Wuhouci Dajie; 武侯祠大街246号; 4-/6-bed dm ¥50/40, r ¥178; 🌐@🛜; 🚌27, 45) Prepare for trips out west by plugging yourself in to Chéngdū's small Tibetan district, which surrounds this welcoming hostel. Holly's has clean, basic rooms plus wi-fi, bike rentals (¥20) and a nice rooftop cafe (western and Chinese mains ¥10 to ¥50). Staff can also help with permits to Lhasa. Discounted doubles go for as low as ¥120 in low season.

Chéngdū Dreams Travel Hostel
HOSTEL $

(梦之旅国际青年旅舍; Mèngzhīlǚ Guójì Qīngnián Lǚshè; Map p240; ☎028 8557 0315; www.dreams-travel.com/youthhostel; 242 Wuhouci Dajie; 武侯祠大街242号; dm ¥50-75, r ¥178-328; ❄🛜; 🚇Gaoshengqiao) Across the street from Wǔhóu Temple, this backpacker joint has loads of common space and friendly, helpful staff. There are no elevators.

Mrs Panda Hostel
HOSTEL $

(熊猫夫人青年旅舍; Xióngmāo Fūrén Qīngnián Lǚshè; Map p240; ☎028 8705 5315; www.nihaosichuan.com; 6 Linjiang Zhonglu; 临江中路6号; dm ¥50, r ¥170-210, without bathroom ¥108; ❄🛜; 🚇Xinnanmen) This friendly hostel attached to the Traffic Hotel comes with an extremely helpful, friendly staff in addition to the standard hostel facilities. Rooms with shared bathrooms remain the best value thanks to the spotless showers and toilets. Close to Xīnnánmén tourist bus station and metro, this is extremely convenient for day trips to the countryside surrounding Chéngdū.

★ Xishu Garden Inn
HOSTEL $$

(探索西部青年旅舍; Tànsuǒ Xībù Qīngnián Lǚshè; Map p240; ☎028 6210 5818; www.hiwestchina.com; Suite 5, 19 Dongcheng Gennanjie; 东城根南街19号附5号; dm ¥50, s/d/tw from ¥138/200/240; ❄🛜; 🚇People's Park) Super-friendly staff, an unbeatable location beside People's Park and big bright rooms make this one of our favourite hostels in the city; not to mention the great rooftop terrace that caps it all off.

★ The Temple House
LUXURY HOTEL $$$

(博舍酒店; Bóshè Jiǔdiàn; Map p240; ☎028 6636 9999; www.thetemplehousehotel.com; 81 Bitieshi Jie; 笔帖式街81号; r/ste from ¥2100/3100; ❄🛜🏊; 🚇Chunxi Rd) Cool to its core, every room from the basic Studio 60 to the luxurious Deluxe Temple Suite is hip and understated with elegant stylings and modern amenities that come together perfectly around a traditional courtyard. Discounts of 25% are available outside of high season when booking directly.

Even if you're not staying, it's worth dropping by the on-site Jing Bar (4pm to 1am) for locally inspired twists on your favourite

Chéngdū

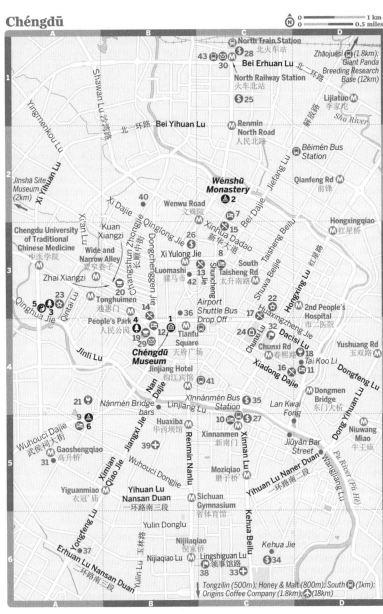

0 ___ 1 km
0 ___ 0.5 miles

GATEWAY CITIES CHÉNGDŪ

North Train Station
北火车站
28
30 43
Bei Erhuan Lu 北二环路

Zhāojuésì (1.8km);
Giant Panda
Breeding Research
Base (12km)

North Railway Station
火车北站

25

Lijiatuo
李家沱

Sha River
沙河

Bei Yihuan Lu 北一环路

Renmin
North Road
人民北路

Bĕimén Bus
Station

Jinshā Site
Museum
(2km)

Qianfeng Rd
前锋

Wénshū
Monastery
文殊院 2

Hongxingqiao
红星桥

Chengdu University
of Traditional
Chinese Medicine
中医学院

Xi Dajie 西大街

Wenwu Road
文殊院

40

Xinhua Dadao
新华大道

Kuan
Xiangzi
宽巷子

Wide and
Narrow Alley
宽窄巷子

Xi Yulong Jie 西玉龙街

26

8

South
Taisheng Rd
太升南路

2nd People's
Hospital
市二医院

Zhai Xiangzi
窄巷子

Luomashi
骡马市

13 Jie
栓橙

42

Shuncheng
Dajie

Airport
Shuttle Bus
Drop Off

17

Tonghuimen
通惠门

20

14

Yushuang Rd
玉双路

23
5 3

People's Park
人民公园

4
19
12
29

1

36

Tianfu
Square
天府广场

24

32
Dacisi Lu

18
Tai Koo Li
太古里

11

Chunxi Rd
春熙路

Chéngdū
Museum
成都博物馆

Jinli Lu

Jinjiang Hotel
锦江宾馆

41

16
Xiadong Dajie

Dongmen
Bridge
东门大桥

21

Nánmén Bridge
bars

Linjiang Lu

Xinnánmén Bus
Station

35

Lan Kwai
Fong

Dong Yihuan Lu

9
6

Huaxiba
华西坝馆

39

10

27

Xinnanmen
新南门

Jiŭyăn Bar
Street

Niuwang
Miao
牛王庙

Gaoshengqiao
高升桥

31

Moziqiao
磨子桥

Fu River (Fŭ Hé)

Yiguanmiao
衣冠庙

Yihuan Lu
Nansan Duan
一环路南三段

Sichuan
Gymnasium
省体育馆

Yulin Donglu

Nijiaqiao
倪家桥

Lingshiguan Lu

Kehua Jie

34

Erhuan Lu Nansan Duan
二环路南三段

Nijiaqiao Lu

38 33

Kehua Beilu

Tongzilin (500m); Honey & Malt (800m); South (1km);
Origins Coffee Company (1.8km); (18km)

---

cocktails – we're fond of the Sìchuān Mule, laced with Sìchuān peppercorn syrup.

BuddhaZen Hotel
HOTEL $$$

(圆和圆佛禅客栈; Yuánhéyuán Fóchán Kèzhàn, 0和0; Map p240; ☎028 8692 9898; www.bud dhazenhotel.com; B6-6 Wenshufang; 青羊区文殊 坊B6-6号; s/d from ¥468/568, ste from ¥788, incl breakfast; ❀@🌐; Ⓜ Wenshu Monastery) Set in a tranquil courtyard building, this boutique hotel near Wénshū Monastery blends traditional decor with modern comforts and a taste of buddhist philosophy. You can ponder

Chéngdū

GATEWAY CITIES CHÉNGDŪ

life while sipping tea on your private balcony, circling the sand garden or soaking in a wooden tub at the spa. It's lovely here.

🍴 Eating

With reportedly the highest density of restaurants and teahouses of any city in the world, and the first city in Asia to be named a Unesco City of Gastronomy, in Chéngdū your most memorable moments are likely to involve food.

Dōngchéng Dàndàn Tiánshuǐmiàn   SICHUAN $
(东城担担甜水面; Map p240; ☑ 028 8625 8168; 13 Dongchenggen Shangjie; 东城根上街13号; mains ¥6-16; ⊙ 7.30am-10pm; Ⓜ People's Park) There's plenty to recommend this neighborhood place just up from People's Park, but the simple flavourful bowls of local classic *dàndàn* noodles (担担面; ¥6.5) are among our favourites.

Táng Sòng Food Street   STREET FOOD $
(春熙坊唐宋美食街; Chūnxīfāng Tángsòng Měishí Jiē; Map p240; 29 Zongfu Lu; 总府路29号; mains from ¥12; ⊙ 10am-10.30pm; Ⓜ Chunxi Rd) This reconstructed ancient alleyway is jam-packed with tourists and Chéngdū favourites like *chāoshǒu* (抄手; wontons; ¥12) and *chuàn-chuàn xiāng* (串串香; the skewer version of the Chóngqìng hotpot; ¥2 to ¥4). Musical performances reverberate in the indoor space in the evening. Look for the wooden sign and doors near Lotte KTV.

If you want to try traditional Sìchuān favourite *tùtóu* (兔头; rabbit head), head for Bāshǔ Shānhuò (巴蜀山货).

Chén Mápó Dòufu   SICHUAN $$
(陈麻婆豆腐; Map p240; ☑ 028 8674 3889; 197 Xi Yulong Jie; 西玉龙街197号; mains ¥22-58; ⊙ 11.30am-2.30pm & 5.30-9pm; 🅟; Ⓜ Luomashi) The plush flagship of this famous chain is a

great place to experience *mápó dòufu* (麻婆豆腐; small/large ¥12/20) – soft, house bean curd with a fiery sauce of garlic, minced beef, fermented soybean, chilli oil and Sìchuān pepper. It's one of Sìchuān's most famous dishes and is this restaurant's speciality. Non-spicy choices are available, too.

Wénshū Monastery Restaurant VEGETARIAN $$
(文殊院素宴厅; Wénshūyuàn Sùyàn Tīng; Map p240; southeast cnr of Wénshū Temple, Wenshuyuan Lu; 文殊院路; dishes ¥12-48, tea from ¥68; ⊙9.30am-11pm; ⌁; M Wenshu Monastery) This excellent volunteer-staffed vegetarian restaurant and the atmospheric teahouse that surrounds it are on the Wénshū Monastery's grounds. There's also a coffee shop in a separate pavilion in the first courtyard.

Arè Tibetan Restaurant #1 TIBETAN $$
(阿热藏餐老店; Arè Zàngcān Lǎodiàn; Map p240; ✆028 8551 0112; 3 Wuhouci Dongjie; 武侯祠东街3号; mains ¥18-118; ⊙8.30am-10pm; ☎⌁; M Gaoshengqiao) Choose from a delicious array of Tibetan staples, from *tsampa* (roasted barley flour; ¥20) to *thugpa* (noodles in soup; ¥18), momo (dumplings; ¥20) and yak butter tea (¥18 to ¥25). The newer, less quaint **branch** (阿热藏餐新店; Arè Zàngcān Xīndiàn; Map p240; ✆028 8557 0877; 234 Wuhouci Dajie; 武侯祠大街234号; mains ¥18-68; ⊙9am-10pm; M Gaoshengqiao), just across from Wǔhóu Temple, has fast counter service and a dining room upstairs. English picture menus.

Lǎo Mā Rabbit Head SICHUAN $$
(老妈兔头; Lǎomā Tùtóu; Map p240; ✆132 1902 5349; 22 Jinsi Jie; 金丝街22号; rabbit head ¥10, mains ¥10-68; ⊙8.30am-10pm; M Wenshu Monastery) The menu has the full range of Sìchuān dishes, but it's mostly worth the trip for the namesake: rabbit head (兔头; *tùtóu*). Order

by the piece, kinda spicy (五香; *wǔxiāng*) or pretty spicy (麻辣; *málà*). Break open the jaw, split open the skull, and don't miss the best bits down in the cranial cavity.

⭐**Mǎ Wàng Zi** SICHUAN $$$
(马旺子; Map p240; ✆028 6423 1923; 1 Dongkang Shijie; 东糠市街1号; mains ¥13-89; ⊙11.30am-2pm & 5.30-8.30pm Mon-Fri, 11.30am-2.15pm & 5.30-8.45pm Sat & Sun; ⌁⌁; M Chunxi Rd) This high-end Sìchuān joint does everything right, from service and cuisine to ambience, but it's decidedly popular so you'd do well to make reservations beforehand.

🍷 Drinking & Nightlife

Sìchuān does teahouses better than anywhere else in China, and an afternoon in a leafy park's teahouse is a quintessential experience. Chéngdū has plenty of options for the harder stuff too, including raucous bar strips but also craft beer joints, refined cocktail bars and upmarket clubs.

For the latest on Chéngdū's nightlife, check out More Chengdu (www.morechengdu.com) or GoChengdoo (www.gochengdoo.com).

⭐**Kǎi Lú Lǎo Zhái Cháyuán** TEAHOUSE
(恺庐老宅茶园; Map p240; ✆180 3041 6632; 11 Kuan Xiangzi; 宽巷子11号; ⊙10am-10pm; ☎; M Wide & Narrow Alley) For 200 years one of the city's most venerable teahouses has been tucked away in a peaceful courtyard behind a stone archway off frenetic Kuan Alley, the distant hum of which is more than countered by the sound of zither music that plays in the background. These days there's wi-fi, but that seems to be about all that has changed. Tea from ¥38; snacks ¥12.

⭐**Honey & Malt** CRAFT BEER
(蜜和麦; Mìhémài; ✆185 1847 5006; 20 Tongzilin Donglu; 桐梓林东路20号; ⊙5pm-late; M Tongzilin) Throw back craft beers from China and abroad – a wide selection will have hop heads coming back night after night. Stock runs low at times, but pull up to the bar and check out the high-tech LCD menu to see what's available at the friendliest beer bar in Chéngdū.

Hè Míng Teahouse TEAHOUSE
(鹤鸣茶馆; Hèmíng Cháguǎn; Map p240; People's Park, 人民公园; ⊙6am-9pm; M People's Park) Always lively, this century-old spot is most pleasant for whiling away an afternoon with a bottomless cup of tea (¥13 to ¥30). Neat tea-pouring performances happen on Saturdays from 2pm to 3pm. Ear cleanings (¥20) available daily.

Origins Coffee Company COFFEE
(奥蕊心咖啡; Àoruǐxīn Kāfēi; ☑028 6842 5782; www.originschengdu.com; 14 Zijingdong Lu; 紫荆东路14号; ☺9am-7pm Tue-Sat; ☎; Ⓜ Tongzilin) A range of internationally sourced beans, ground to order for each cup, and a tempting selection of baked goods. This is your favourite coffee shop from home, dropped into the centre of the busy Tóngzǐlín neighbourhood.

Foam Ranger Taproom CRAFT BEER
(泡沫游侠精酿啤酒馆; Pàomò Yóuxiá Jīngniàng Píjiǔguǎn; Map p240; ☑028 8319 8199; L2-L3, 2316 Tai Koo Li; 太古里二至三层商业2316号; ☺10.30am-1am Sun-Thu, to 2am Fri & Sat; ☎; Ⓜ Chunxi Rd) Stop in for a decent selection of US, European and Chinese craft brews, including from Chéngdū's Wild West Taproom (p243), and a top-floor terrace removed from the crowds of Tai Koo Li. The generous day-long happy hour (10.30am to 8pm) is 'Buy One, Get One' on all beers marked with a star on the menu.

Wild West Taproom CRAFT BEER
(美西啤酒; Měixī Píjiǔ; Map p240; ☑028 8557 8927; 30 Zhangwu Jie; 章武街30号; ☺9am-midnight; ☐1, 21, 26) Sample this Chéngdū-based brewer's wares at its taproom off Jǐnlǐ Gǔjiē. The four- to 10-glass samplers are particularly good value.

☆ Entertainment

Chéngdū is the birthplace of Sìchuān opera, which dates back more than 250 years. Besides glass-shattering songs, performances feature slapstick, martial arts, men singing as women, acrobatics and even fire breathing. An undoubted highlight is *biànliǎn* (变脸; face changing), where performers change character in a blink by swapping masks, manipulating face paint and other conjuring tricks performed as entertainment.

★ Shǔfēng Yǎyùn CHINESE OPERA
(蜀风雅韵; Shǔfēng Yǎyùn; Map p240; ☑028 8776 4530; www.cdsfyy.com; inside Culture Park; 文化公园内面; tickets ¥140-320; ☺ticket office 3-9.30pm, nightly shows 8-9.30pm; Ⓜ Tonghuimen) This famous century-old theatre and teahouse puts on excellent 1½-hour shows that include music, puppetry and Sìchuān opera's famed fire breathing and face changing. Come at around 7.15pm to watch performers putting on their elaborate make-up and costumes. For ¥50 to ¥100, kids (and adults) can try on garb and have a costume artist paint their face.

Jǐnjiāng Theatre CHINESE OPERA
(锦江剧场; Jǐnjiāng Jùchǎng; Map p240; ☑028 8662 0019; www.scopera.com.cn; 54 Huaxingzheng Jie; 华兴正街54号; tickets ¥150-380; ☺8-9pm, ticket office 9am-8pm; Ⓜ Chunxi Rd) Mixed-performance shows with modern stagecraft are held daily at this renowned opera theatre. The adjoining **Yuèlái Teahouse** (悦来茶馆; Yuèlái Cháguǎn; Map p240; ☑028 8609 4909; 54 Huaxingzheng Jie; 华兴正街54号; ☺8.30am-5pm; Ⓜ Chunxi Rd), a local favourite, holds wonderfully informal performances on its small stage on Saturdays from 2pm to 4.30pm. Drop in an hour before performances start for a free tea before your ticketed entry.

ℹ Information

The best sources for restaurant, bar and entertainment listings are the websites GoChengdoo (www.gochengdoo.com), Chéngdū Living (www.chengduliving.com) and Chengdu Places (www.chengduplaces.com).

ACCESSIBLE TRAVEL

China is slowly becoming friendlier to travellers with disabilities, and Chéngdū has followed this trend. Metro stations all include at least one accessible entrance, and government-run sights do as well.

MEDICAL SERVICES

Global Doctor Chéngdū Clinic (环球医生; Huánqiú Yīshēng; Map p240; ☑028 8528 3660, 24hr emergency 139 8225 6966; www.globaldoctor.com.au; 2nd fl, 9-11 Lippo Tower, 62 Kehua Beilu; 科华北路62号力宝大厦2层9-11号; ☺9am-6pm Mon-Sat; Ⓜ Nijiaqiao) English- and Chinese-speaking doctors and a 24-hour emergency line, and can even make house visits.

West China Hospital SCU (四川大学华西医院; Sìchuān Dàxué Huáxī Yīyuàn; Map p240; ☑24hr emergency assistance in Chinese & English 028 8542 2761, for appointment 028 8542 2408; www.eng.cd120.com; 37 Guoxue Xiang; 国学巷37号; Ⓜ Huaxiba) This hospital complex is China's largest and is among the most well regarded. Foreigners should head for the International Hospital here, where doctors and some staff speak English. Note that some treatments without qualifying insurance may require a deposit.

MONEY

ATMs abound throughout the city, and you're never very far from a bank branch either. These are the most useful options for travellers:

Bank of China (中国银行; Zhōngguó Yínháng; Map p240; www.boc.cn; 35 Renmin Zhonglu, 2nd Section; 人民中路二段35号; ☺9am-5pm Mon-Fri, to 4.30pm Sat & Sun; Ⓜ Luomashi)

ICBC (中国工商银行; Zhōngguó Gōngshāng Yínháng; Map p240; ☑ 95588; www.icbc.com. cn; 9 Hongli Lu Siduan; 红星路四段9号; ⊙ 9am-5pm, ATM 24hr; Ⓜ Xinnanmen)

SHOPPING

Fancy-pants shopping centres dot the city, with the highest concentration around the **Chūnxī Lù shopping district** (春熙路步行街; Chūnxīlù Bùxíngjiē; Map p240; Ⓜ Chunxi Rd) east of Tianfu Sq. For traditional Tibetan shopping options, try the shops in the Tibetan neighbourhood southeast of Wǔhóu Temple. Outdoor enthusiasts gearing up for mountain trips should head to **Sanfo Outdoors** (三夫户外; Sānfū Hùwài; Map p240; ☑ 028 8507 9586; www.sanfo.com; 243 Wuhouci Dajie; 武侯词大街243号; ⊙ 10am-8pm; Ⓜ Gaoshengqiao) or **Decathlon** (迪卡侬 运动超市; Díkǎnóng Yùndòng Chāoshì; ☑ 028 8531 0388; www.decathlon.com.cn; 199 Duhui Lu; 都会路199号; ⊙ 10am-10pm; Ⓜ South Train Station).

TRAVEL AGENCIES

Skip the gazillion Chinese travel agencies around town and head to the travel desks at one of Chéngdū's many excellent hostels, or try the following:

Extravagant Yak (Map p240; ☑ 028-8510 8093; www.extravagantyak.com; 11th fl, Rome Plaza Gaosheng Center 1117, 2 Gaoshengqiao Donglu; 高升桥东路2号罗马假日广场 高盛中心1117室; ⊙ 9am-6pm Mon-Fri; Ⓜ Gaoshengqiao)

Kham Voyage (☑ 183 8218 6668; www.kham voyage.com)

Tibetan Trekking (Map p240; ☑ 028 8597 6083; www.tibetantrekking.com; Room 35, 10th fl, Yulin Fengshang, 47 Yongfeng Lu; 47永丰路丰尚玉林 商务港5楼; ⊙ 9am-noon & 2.30-5pm Mon-Fri; Ⓜ Yiguanmiao)

Windhorse Tour (风马旅游; Fēngmǎ Lǚyóu; Map p240; ☑ 028 8559 3923; www.windhorsetour. com; Suite 2103, 21st fl, Bldg C, 1 Babao Lu; 八 宝街1号万和苑C座2103室; ⊙ 9am-6pm; Ⓜ Lu-omashi)

VISAS

PSB Entry & Exit Service Centre (成都市出 入境接待中心; Chéngdūshì Chūrùjìng Jiēdài Zhōngxīn; Map p240; ☑ 028 8640 7067; www. chengdu.gov.cn; 2 Renmin Xilu; 人民西路2号; ⊙ 9am-noon & 1-5pm Mon-Fri; Ⓜ Tianfu Square) Visa extensions (in seven working days), residence permits and paperwork for lost passports are on the 3rd floor. It's in the building behind the Mao statue's right hand, to the left of the Sìchuān Science & Technology Museum.

❶ Getting There & Away

You can fly directly to **Chéngdū Shuāngliú International Airport** (成都双流国际机场; Chéngdū Shuāngliú Guójì Jīchǎng; ☑ 028 8520 5555; www.cdairport.com; Shuangliuqu Jichang Donglu; 双流区机场东路; Ⓜ Shuangliu International Airport), 18km west of the city, from nearly any other major Chinese city in less than three hours. There are also direct international flights from Amsterdam, Bangkok, Doha, Frankfurt, Kathmandu, Kuala Lumpur, London, Melbourne, San Francisco, Seoul, Singapore, Tokyo and many more destinations.

Many travellers fly from here to Lhasa (¥892 to ¥1286; prepare for palpable oxygen deprivation upon arrival). Flights to destinations within Sìchuān include Kāngdìng (¥470 to ¥923), Jiǔzhàigōu (¥830 to ¥1239) and Dàochéng-Yàdīng (¥701 to ¥1468), with Gānzī airport originally scheduled to open in mid-2017 but still under construction at the time of research.

❶ Getting Around

TO/FROM THE AIRPORT

From Chéngdū Shuāngliú International Airport, airport shuttle buses cover five routes, reaching all corners of the city. **Buses for route 2** (机场班 车; Jīchǎng Bānchē; Map p240; Tianfu Square; 天府广场; ¥12; ⊙ 6am-10pm; Ⓜ Tianfu Square) reach the South train station (which also has a metro connection), and then stops frequently along Renmin Lu to the North train station. Route 5 connects with Chádiànzi bus station for western Sìchuān departures.

To return by bus to the airport the easiest bus **pickup** (机场班车; Jīchǎng Bānchē; Map p240; ☑ 028 8507 6868; ¥12; ⊙ 6am-10pm; Ⓜ Jinjiang Binguan) is north of Mínshān Hotel outside Jǐn-jiāng Hotel metro station.

A taxi costs ¥70 to ¥100. Most guesthouses offer airport pick-up services for slightly more.

From the airport, metro line 10 connects to line 3 at Taipingyuan, but it involves a bit of schlepping if you're travelling with luggage.

BICYCLE

Chéngdū is nice and flat, with designated biking lanes, although the traffic can be a strain for cyclists. Youth hostels rent out bikes for around ¥20 per day. Always lock up your bike.

BUS

You can get almost anywhere in Chéngdū by bus, as long as you can decipher the labyrinthine routes. Stops are marked in Chinese and English and some post route maps. Fares within the city are usually ¥2.

Useful routes:

Bus 1 Wǔhóu Temple–City centre–Běimén bus station–Zhāojuésì bus station

Bus 16 Chéngdū North train station–Renmin Lu–Chéngdū South train station

Bus 28 Sichuan University–Xīnnánmén bus station–Chūnxī Rd–Chéngdū North train station

METRO

If you'll be using the metro extensively, it's worth buying a Tiānfǔ Tōng Kǎ (天府通卡) rechargeable payment card (¥25), which also works for local buses. Rides cost ¥2 to ¥10 depending on the distance covered. Stations have bilingual signs, maps and ticket machines.

Line 1 links Chéngdū North and South Railway Stations, running the length of Renmin Lu and beyond.

Line 2 links Chéngdū East Railway Station with the city centre on an east–west route via Chunxi Rd, meeting line 1 at Tianfu Square before continuing west to Chádiànzi bus station.

Line 3 runs to nearby the Giant Panda Breeding Research Base and Xīnnánmén bus station, ending at Taipingyuan for the connection to Line 10 and the airport.

Line 7 rings the city, stopping in at Chéngdū's main railway stations as well as the Jīnshā Site Museum.

TAXI

Taxis are ¥8 (¥9 from 11pm to 6am) for the first 2km, then ¥1.90 (¥2.20 at night) per kilometre.

XĪNÍNG 西宁

☑ 0971 / POP 2.3 MILLION / ELEV 2275M

Situated on the eastern edge of the Tibetan Plateau, this lively provincial capital makes a good base from which to dive into the surrounding sights and on to the more remote regions of Qīnghǎi and beyond. Though many travellers use Xīníng as a jumping-off or landing point from the Qīnghǎi–Tibet Railway, it's also a wonderful place to explore the province's varied cultures – Muslim (Huí, Salar and Uyghur), Tibetan and Han Chinese – especially the rich culinary mix that these groups bring together.

⊙ Sights

★ Tibetan Culture & Medicine Museum
MUSEUM
(藏文化博物馆; Zàng Wénhuà Bówùguǎn; ☑ 0971 531 7881; www.tibetanculturemuseum.org; 36 Jing'er Rd; 经二路36号; ¥60; ⊙ 9am-6pm May-Sep, to 5pm Oct-Apr; ☑ 1, 34, 65, 66, 84) Exhibitions at this museum focus on Tibetan medicine, astronomy and science. The highlight is a 618m-long thangka scroll – the world's longest – which charts most of Tibetan history. Completed in 1997, it's not an ancient relic, but it is unbelievably long. It took 400 artists four years to complete and is displayed in a maze-like exhibition hall.

There's a decent amount of signage in English. The museum is located on the far north-west side of Xīníng. Bus 1 (¥1, 50 minutes) goes here from Dong Dajie (get off at 新乐花园). A taxi costs about ¥20 from the city.

Nánshān
PARK
(南山; Map p246; Nanshan Lu; 南山路; ⊙ temples 9am-5pm; ☑ 16, 103) FREE This park, which is also known as Fènghuáng Shān (凤凰山), rises above Xīníng south of town. The grounds are home to two Buddhist temples: **Nánchán Sì** (Nánchán Sì, 南禅寺; Map p246; 93 Nanshan Lu; 南山路93号; ⊙ 9am-5pm) FREE and **Fǎchuáng Sì** (法幢寺). In between them is a path that leads up to the hill where you'll find more walking paths and panoramic views of the city.

Buses 16 and 103 come from the train station (alight at Nánchán Sì Zhàn, 南禅寺站), but it's an easy walk from the centre of town.

Qīnghǎi Provincial Museum
MUSEUM
(青海省博物馆; Qīnghǎi Shěng Bówùguǎn; ☑ 0971 611 1164; www.qhmuseum.cn; Xinning Sq, 58 Xiguan Dajie; 新宁广场西关大街58号; ⊙ 9.30am-4pm Tue-Sun; ☑ 22, 41) FREE At the east end of Xīníng Square (Xīníng Guǎngchǎng), the provincial museum looks like an ominous government building from afar. Once inside, galleries range from fairly dull provincial economics to historical photos of Xīníng, and an excellent ground-floor exhibit on Tibetan arts, including some beautiful Qing-dynasty thangka and Buddhist statues. English signage is limited. You'll be asked to show a passport and sign in before entering.

If taking the bus, alight at Xīníng Guǎngchǎng Nán (新宁广场南).

🛏 Sleeping

Xīníng has sleeping options aplenty, most of which are located downtown near Zhongxin Guangchang (中心广场) or off Xi and Dong Dajie. There is almost no recommendable accommodation near the main railway station, so you're better off getting a taxi to/from the station and staying in the central part of town. As a fallback, there are several branches of the Jīnjiāng Inn chain around town.

Héhuáng Memory Youth Hostel
HOSTEL $
(河湟记忆青年旅舍; Héhuáng Jìyì Qīngnián Lǚshè; ☑ 189 9722 3551; Longhua Jiayuan, 295 Kunlun Donglu, 昆仑东路295号龙华佳园; dm ¥58; ❋ 🐱; ☑ 83) This cheerful hostel has clean dorms and friendly, English-speaking staff, but the real draw is the communal lounge lined with bookshelves and offering a decent beer selection. In high season, western and Chinese food is available. Pros: great

Xīníng

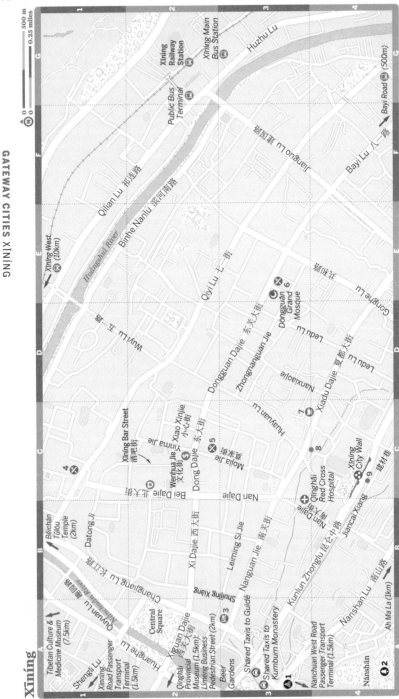

Xīníng

atmosphere and cheap prices. Cons: it's a bit far away from everything. BYO toilet paper.

The bus stop is around the corner on Huangzhong Lu.

Sofitel Xīníng　　　　　　LUXURY HOTEL $$$
(索菲特大酒店, Suǒfēitè Dàjiǔdiàn; ☑ 0971 766 6666; http://sofitel.accorhotels.com; d/ste ¥802/1117; ⊖ ✳ @ 🛪; 🚌 9, 31, 106) Xīníng's first foreign five-star hotel, the Sofitel opened on the city's burgeoning west side in 2015. The plushest rooms in town have soft beds and large bathrooms with bathtubs and giant showers.

San Want Hotel　　　　　　HOTEL $$$
(西宁神旺大酒店; Xīníng Shénwàng Dà Jiǔdiàn; Map p246; ☑ 0971 820 1111; www.sanwant.com.cn/en; 79 Changjiang Lu; 长江路79号; s/d ¥680/780; ✳ @ 🛪) If you're looking to splash out, this hotel does the trick, with clean rooms, English-speaking staff and a tour desk that can arrange excursions in the area. Rooms are of an international standard, with private bathrooms (and tubs), though like many hotels in this part of China, the decor is a bit dated. Breakfast included.

✗ Eating & Drinking

Xīníng is a good place to sample Tibetan and Hui (Chinese Islamic) cuisines. For Chinese Islamic food, head to Dongguan Dajie, near Dōngguān Grand Mosque, or the northern stretch of Nanxiaojie. **Mojia Jie** is a traditional snack street with lots of point-and-go options and local dives. **Lìméng Business Pedestrian Street** has western fast food, chain restaurants and bars.

A **beer garden** operates on the east side of the Nánchuān River between Kunlun Zhonglu and Xiguan Jie. A few cafes and pubs line Xiadu Dajie near Greenhouse. And there are bars and hotpot restaurants in the streets around the Sofitel Xīníng, as well as the hotel's swish lobby bar.

Mǎzhōng Snack Centre　　　　HAWKER $
(马忠美食城; Mǎzhōng Měishíchéng; Map p246; 11-16 Mojia Jie; 莫家街11-16号; noodles ¥10-18, dishes from ¥25) Stalls selling local and regional specialities line this indoor food court. *Miànpiàn* (面片; flat noodle pieces) and *chǎodāo xiāomiàn* (炒刀削面; stir-fried spicy noodles) are popular choices. This is an easy option for a cheap, fresh fill-up, especially for those with limited Mandarin skills, as pointing or grab-and-go are the order of the day.

Before you order, approach the counter in the middle of the hall, hand over some cash and get a refillable card to use at the stalls. Return the card for a refund of the leftover money when you leave.

Zhènyà Niúròu Miàn　　　　NOODLES $
(震亚牛肉面; Map p246; 24 Dongguan Dajie; 东关大街24号; noodles ¥9-13; ⊙ 10am-10pm) Join the local Muslim population for their noodle fix at this busy place by Dōngguān Grand Mosque. There's no menu, but the order of the day is *gān bànmiàn* (干拌面; mince beef noodles; ¥13 for a large plate), which is served swiftly with a side of *suān tāng* (酸汤; black pepper soup) and eaten with a liberal dose of the house chilli oil.

Elite's Bar & Grill　　　　INTERNATIONAL $$
(Map p246; ☑ 138 9747 2199; Qiyi Lu; 七一路; dishes ¥30-80, drinks from ¥20; ⊙ noon-midnight) If you have a hankering for western food, Elite's extensive menu should do the job. Massive burgers, pulled pork, steaks, salads...Elite's serves it all. There's a good wine and beer list (including home-brewed takeaway jugs of amber and hefeweizen on our visit) at decent prices, too. Located 150m east of Xīníng Bīnguǎn (西宁宾馆).

Greenhouse　　　　　　　　CAFE
(古林坊咖啡; Gǔlínfáng Kāfēi; Map p246; ☑ 0971 820 2710; 222-22 Xiadu Dajie; 夏都大街222-22号; ⊙ 9.30am-10.30pm; 🛪) Rustic split-level wood

interior with some of the best coffee in town (from ¥25). You can also munch on pizzas, burgers and sandwiches (¥33 to ¥80) to a mellow music selection. Plenty of plugs and free wi-fi, and mercifully non-smoking.

ℹ Information

MONEY

Bank of China (中国银行; Zhōngguó Yínháng; Map p246; 22 Dong Dajie; 东大街22号; ⊗9am-5pm Mon-Fri, 10am-4pm Sat & Sun) Has a number of large branches around town that exchange cash and have foreign-friendly ATMs.

TRAVEL AGENCIES

Mystic Tibet Tours (☑182 0971 5464; www.mystictibettours.com; 902, 7/2 Bandao Xinjiayuan, Bayi Lu, 城东区八一路半岛新家园7/2号楼 902室) One of the better agencies in town, run by English-speaking Tibetan guide, Gonkho. Arranges tours/treks around Tibet, particularly Amdo and Amnye Machen.

Snow Lion Tours (Map p246; ☑0971 816 3350; www.snowliontours.com; Office 408, Xiadu Dasha Bldg, Xiadu Dajie; 夏都大厦，夏都大街; ⊗9am-6pm) Run by a knowledgeable English-speaking Tibetan guy, Wangden; arranges treks, camping with nomads and Tibet permits.

Tibetan Connections (Map p246; ☑189 9720 0974; www.tibetanconnections.com; 18th fl, Bldg 5, International Village Apts, 2-32 Jiancai Xiang; 建材巷国际村公寓5号楼18层) This tour company focuses on more remote parts of Amdo and Kham but can arrange trips into Tibet.

VISAS

Public Security Bureau (PSB, 公安局, Gōng'ānjú; Map p246; 35 Bei Dajie; 北大街35号; ⊗8.30-11.30am & 2.30-5.30pm Mon-Fri) Can extend visas.

ℹ Getting There & Away

AIR

Xīníng Cáojiābǎo Airport (XNN) is 27km east of the city. There are daily flights to Běijīng (¥1250), Chéngdū (¥990), Dūnhuáng (¥650), Shànghǎi (¥1520), Yùshù (¥1335), Golmud (¥1200), Tiānjīn (¥1175) and Xī'ān (¥590).

Six shuttle bus routes (¥25 to ¥40, 35 minutes) connect the airport to the city. Route 1 goes to the railway station (7am to 6pm) and Bayi Road Bus Station (5.30am to 8pm). Route 2 (8am to 6pm) goes via Zhongxin Guangchang and the Yile Hotel, and Route 3 (8am to 6pm) goes to and from the Sofitel.

A taxi from the airport to central Xīníng costs ¥110 or ¥150 to the Sofitel.

BUS

Xīníng has way too many bus stations for a city of its size. Most leave from the **Xīníng Main Bus Station** (西宁客运车站; Xīníng Kèyùn Chēzhàn; Map p246; 200m east of the main train station) near the main railway station, but some buses leave from one of the three (!) other stations.

Services from Xīníng Main Bus Station:

Kumbum Monastery ¥6, 45 minutes, every 20 minutes from 7am to 6.30pm

Lánzhōu ¥65, three hours, hourly from 7.20am to 6.30pm

Qīnghǎi Lake ¥34, three hours, hourly from 8am to 6pm

Bayi Road Bus Station (八一路汽车站; Bāyī Lù Qìchē Zhàn; cnr Bayi Lu & Huangzhong Lu; 八一路和湟中路路口) runs buses to Tóngrén (¥35, four hours, every 30 minutes from 7.30am to 5pm) and Yòuníng Monastery (¥12, 70 minutes, 10.30am).

Public Bus Terminal (公交车站; Gōngjiāo Chēzhàn; Map p246) has a bus to Píngān (¥5, two hours, every five minutes) and also connects with terminal station for local buses.

TRAIN

Xīníng Railway Station (火车站; Huǒchē Zhàn) is on the high-speed rail line between Lánzhōu in Gānsù province and Ürümqi in Xīnjiāng. Regional trains also start/stop at Xīníng West Railway Station (西火车站; Xī Huǒchē Zhàn), about 10km west of the city centre.

Lhasa-bound trains pass through or start/terminate at Xīníng (hard/soft sleeper ¥520/808, 22 hours) on their way along the Qīnghǎi–Tibet Railway. Be sure to have all your Tibet papers in order and get tickets well in advance.

Other destinations from Xīníng:

Běijīng Hard/soft sleeper ¥377/582, 18 to 24 hours

Chéngdū Hard/soft sleeper ¥247/377, 14½ to 17 hours

Lánzhōu Seat ¥58, 1½ hours

Xī'ān Seat ¥232, 4½ hours

Zhāngyē Seat ¥91.5, two hours

ℹ Getting Around

City buses cost ¥1 to ¥2 per ride. A handy route is bus 1, which runs from Bayi Road Bus Station (p248) along Dongguan Dajie before heading north to the nearby Tibetan Culture Museum, a 45-minute ride.

Taxis are easy to flag and cost ¥8 for the first 3km and ¥1.40 per kilometre thereafter. Ignore the touts at stations.

While it's best to catch official buses from the stations, some travellers prefer to take a shared taxi/minibus to Guìdé or Kumbum Monastery; for both destinations you can find drivers near or in the parking space under the bridge at the corner of Kunlun Zhonglu and Changjiang Lu.

Understand
Tibet

Tibet Today

Change is afoot in Tibet. The economy is booming at the fastest rate in China; extended train, air and road links are revolutionising life across the plateau, and Tibet's urban areas are modernising and expanding at an unprecedented rate. Though economic growth has undoubtedly brought many benefits to the plateau, many Tibetans express feelings of marginalisation in their own land. With every show of Tibetan discontent, Běijīng appears to tighten its political and religious controls.

Best in Print

The Secret Lives of the Dalai Lama (Alexander Norman; 2008) Engaging overview of Tibetan history, full of unexpectedly juicy detail.

Fire Under the Snow (Palden Gyatso; 1997) A moving autobiography of a Buddhist monk imprisoned in Tibet for 33 years.

Tibet, Tibet (Patrick French; 2003) A nuanced look beyond the propaganda and myth surrounding Tibet.

Trespassers on the Roof of the World (Peter Hopkirk; 1982) Chronicles European explorers' early attempts to enter forbidden Tibet. Superbly readable.

Best on Film

Kundun (1997) Martin Scorsese's beautifully shot depiction of the life of the Dalai Lama.

Vajra Sky Over Tibet (2006) John Bush's Buddhist-inspired cinematic pilgrimage to the principal sites of central Tibet.

Seven Years in Tibet (1997) Yes, it's a bit silly, and, no, it's not the greatest film but it's still fine inspiration before a trip to Tibet.

Modernisation, But At What Cost?

As part of its 'great leap west' and 'Belt and Road' initiatives, the Chinese government has poured an astonishing US$90 billion into Tibet's infrastructure in recent years. It has resettled 1.3 million Tibetans in new housing and created a domestic tourist boom that is spurring hotel and restaurant construction across the plateau. The speed of modernisation in Tibet is breathtaking.

In most parts of the world this would all be good news, but herein lies Tibet and China's conundrum. Alongside the short-term tourists has come a flood of Chinese immigrants, whom Tibetans claim are the real beneficiaries of Tibet's economic boom.

As the Tibetan people bristle under a lack of control over their own communities and religion, China reminds the Tibetans that it has brought in education, health and infrastructure to the plateau, and spent millions renovating monasteries. Tibetan groups maintain that it is mostly Chinese immigrants who run Tibet's businesses, and that monasteries remain under tight political control and exist largely for tourism. The Chinese counter that they are just trying to bring economic prosperity to one of its most backward provinces, at a large financial loss. (At this point, everyone storms out of the room.)

Environmental Challenges & International Tensions

Perhaps the greatest loser in Tibet's race towards economic development has been its once-pristine environment. Urbanisation projects, hydroelectric dams, mining projects and seemingly unregulated urban expansion are rapidly changing the face of Tibet. In the last few years hundreds of thousands of Tibetan nomads have been resettled into modern housing communities, effectively bringing an end to a centuries-old traditional way of life. China says it is protecting the grasslands from overgrazing, protesters (often jailed) say it is a cynical move by the government to gain access to mining and drilling rights. In the environment of economic free-for-all, short-term economic gains are starting to leave long-term environmental scars on the high plateau.

Summer 2017 saw border skirmishes with Indian troops on the Tibet border at Doklam (bordering Bhutan) and Pangong-tso (bordering Ladakh), while the issue of Arunachal Pradesh (an Indian state which China regards as part of Tibet) is a festering sore point between the two Asian giants. Border issues will doubtless grow in importance as China increasingly flexes its economic might.

Dark Days

Tibet's long-simmering tensions boiled over on 10 March 2008, the anniversary of the Dalai Lama's flight into exile, kicking off days of protests by monks from Lhasa's big monasteries. At least 19 people, mostly Han Chinese, were killed and disturbances quickly spread to Tibetan towns in Gānsù, western Sìchuān and Qīnghǎi, marking the worst political unrest in Tibet for 20 years.

A decade after the riots Tibet remains a tightly controlled place, with armed riot police posted on every street corner in Lhasa's old town. Basic religious and political freedoms are lacking and political propaganda campaigns and surveillance programs are pervasive. Monastery populations are tightly limited by the government, which forces monks to undergo frequent 'patriotic education' and 'civilising atheism' campaigns. In recent years political management teams and security personnel have set up barracks in hundreds of monasteries. To show support for the Dalai Lama continues to result in long jail sentences.

Cosmetic changes and tightened political controls are unlikely to solve the frustration and resentment that runs deep in Tibet. As Tibetans increasingly feel their culture is under threat and lack channels to air their grievances, their frustration and despair is tangible. The horrific series of recent Tibetan self-immolations (more than 150 at the time of writing) demonstrates the hopelessness felt by many Tibetans. While the root causes remain unaddressed, the longer-lasting result of Tibet's economic boom is clear: the ties that bind China and Tibet are stronger than ever.

POPULATION: **3.2 MILLION**

AREA: **1.23 MILLION SQ KM**

GDP: **US$20 BILLION (2017)**

GDP GROWTH: **12% (2016)**

PER CAPITA DISPOSABLE INCOME: **RURAL/URBAN US$1471/4400 (2016)**

if Tibetans were 100 people

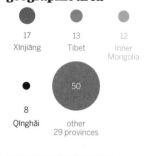

46 would live in the Tibet Autonomous Region (TAR)
22 would live in Qīnghǎi
20 would live in Sìchuān
9 would live in Gānsù
2 would live in Yúnnán
1 would live elsewhere

Province's % of China's geographic area

17 Xīnjiāng
13 Tibet
12 Inner Mongolia

8 Qīnghǎi
50 other 29 provinces

population per sq km

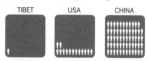

TIBET   USA   CHINA

♀ ≈ 2 people

History

Tibet's history has been a heady mixture of invasion and intrigue, of soaring religious debate and of reincarnation, miracles and murders, all taking place under the backdrop of one of the world's most extreme environments. If one event has defined Tibet, it has been the nation's remarkable transformation from warring expansionist empire to non-violent Buddhist nation. Running alongside Tibet's history has been its knotty, intertwined relationship with its giant neighbour China.

Tibetan Origins

The origins of the Tibetan people are not clearly known. Today Chinese historians claim the Tibetan people originally migrated from the present-day areas of the Qīnghǎi–Gānsù plains and were descended from people known as Qiang. Although there is evidence of westward migration, it is not possible to trace a single origin of the Tibetan people.

The Tibetan people have their own mythic stories explaining their origins. According to legend, the earth was covered in a vast sea; eventually the water receded and land appeared in the present-day Tsetang area in central Tibet. In a curious paralleling of evolution theory, the first humans were descendants of the union between a monkey and ogress (later identified as the emanations of Chenresig, the Bodhisattva of Compassion, and the goddess Drolma). The half-simian offspring eventually evolved into six families known as Se, Mu, Dong, Tong, Wra and Dru, who became the six clans of the Tibetan people.

Kings, Warriors & the Tibetan Empire

The definitive (but weighty) account of Tibetan history since 1947 is *The Dragon in the Land of Snows* by Tsering Shakya.

As early myths of the origin of the Tibetan people suggest, the Yarlung Valley was the cradle of central Tibetan civilisation. The early Yarlung kings, although glorified in legend, were probably no more than chieftains whose domains extended not much further than the Yarlung Valley itself. A reconstruction of Tibet's first fortress, Yumbulagang, can still be seen in the Yarlung Valley, and it is here that the 28th king of Tibet is said to have received Tibet's first Buddhist scriptures in the 5th century AD, when they fell from heaven onto the roof of Yumbulagang.

TIMELINE	28,000 BC	300 BC	c 600
	The Tibetan plateau is covered in ice. It's cold. Very cold. But there are people living there. Tools, stone blades and hunting instruments are in use in Chupsang, 85km from Lhasa.	Throughout the plateau people are building stone dwellings and producing fine pottery; petroglyphs indicate that Buddhism may have started to spread by this time.	Nyatri Tsenpo, the first king of Tibet, founds the Yarlung dynasty and unifies the people and the land; according to legend he is responsible for the first building in Tibet.

By the 6th century the Yarlung kings, through conquest and alliances, had made significant headway in unifying much of central Tibet. Namri Songtsen (c 570–619), the 32nd Tibetan king, continued this trend and extended Tibetan influence into inner Asia, defeating the Qiang tribes on China's borders. But the true flowering of Tibet as an important regional power came about with the accession to rule of Namri Songtsen's son, Songtsen Gampo (r 629–49).

Under Songtsen Gampo the armies of Tibet ranged as far afield as northern India and threatened even the great Tang dynasty in China. Both Nepal and China reacted to the Tibetan incursions by reluctantly agreeing to alliances through marriage. Princess Wencheng, Songtsen Gampo's Chinese bride, and Princess Bhrikuti, his Nepali bride, became important historical figures, as it was through their influence that Buddhism first gained royal patronage and a foothold on the Tibetan plateau.

Contact with the Chinese led to the introduction of astronomy and medicine, while a delegation sent to India brought back the basis for a Tibetan script. It was used in the first translations of Buddhist scriptures, in drafting a code of law and in writing the first histories of Tibet.

For two centuries after the reign of Songtsen Gampo, Tibet continued to grow in power and influence. By the time of King Trisong Detsen's reign (r 755–97), Tibetan influence extended over Turkestan (modern-day Xīnjiāng), northern Pakistan, Nepal and India. In China, Tibetan armies

> Songtsen Gampo went as far as passing a law making it illegal *not* to be a Buddhist.

SHANGRI-LA

The slippery notion of Shangri-la has been captivating foreigners for over 80 years now, but mention the phrase to a Tibetan and you'll likely get little more than a blank stare. The origins of Shangri-la lie in James Hilton's novel *Lost Horizon*, a post-WWI fable of a lost Himalayan utopia, where people live in harmony and never age. Hilton's inspiration may well have been *National Geographic* articles on the remote kingdom of Muli in Kham, and may have even adapted the idea from Tibetan tradition.

Tibetan texts talk of Shambhala, a hidden land to the north whose king will eventually intervene to stop the world destroying itself. The notion of Shangri-la also bears strong similarities to the Tibetan tradition of *baeyul*, hidden lands visible only to the pure of heart that act as refuges in times of great crisis. Tibetan Buddhism also refers directly to various heavenly lands, from the Western Paradise of Ganden to Guru Rinpoche's paradise of Zangtok Pelri.

Whatever the origins, Shangri-la is firmly lodged in the Western psyche. The name has been adopted as a hotel chain and even as a US presidential retreat. In 2001 the Chinese county of Zhōngdiàn upped the ante by renaming itself 'Shanggelila' to boost local tourism. Shangri-la is probably best filed under 'M' for the mythologising of Tibet, on the shelf in between levitating monks and yetis.

608	629	640s	7th century
The first mission is sent to the court of Chinese Emperor Yangdi. This brings Tibet in direct contact with China and sees increasing Tibetan interest in the frontier of China.	Namri Songtsen is assassinated and his son, Songtsen Gampo, aged 13, inherits the throne. He will be regarded as the founder of the Tibetan empire and a cultural hero for the Tibetan people.	Songtsen Gampo marries Chinese Princess Wencheng and Nepalese Princess Bhrikuti. They are credited with bringing Buddhism, silk weaving and new methods of agriculture to Tibet.	The Tibetan empire stretches to include north Pakistan and the Silk Road cities of Khotan and Dūnhuáng.

conquered Gānsù and Sìchuān and gained brief control over the Silk Road, including the great Buddhist cave complex of Dūnhuáng.

Introduction of Buddhism

By the time Buddhism arrived in Tibet during the reign of Songtsen Gampo, it had already flourished for around 1100 years and had become the principal faith of all Tibet's neighbouring countries. But it was slow to take hold in Tibet.

Early Indian missionaries, such as the famous Shantarakshita, faced great hostility from the Bön-dominated court. The influence of Songtsen Gampo's Buddhist Chinese and Nepali wives was almost certainly limited to the royal court, and priests of the time were probably Indian and Chinese, not Tibetan.

It was not until King Trisong Detsen's reign that Buddhism began to take root. Trisong Detsen was responsible for founding Samye Monastery, the first institution to carry out the crucial systematic translation of Buddhist scriptures and the training of Tibetan monks.

Contention over the path that Buddhism was to take in Tibet culminated in the Great Debate of Samye, in which King Trisong Detsen is said to have adjudicated in favour of Indian teachers over the Chan (Zen) approach of Chinese advocates. There was, however, considerable opposition to this institutionalised, clerical form of Buddhism, largely from supporters of the Bön faith. The next Tibetan king, Tritsug Detsen Ralpachen, was assassinated by his brother, Langdharma, who launched an attack on Buddhism. In 842 Langdharma was himself assassinated – by a Buddhist monk – and the Tibetan state soon collapsed into a number of warring principalities. In the confusion that followed, support for Buddhism dwindled and clerical monastic Buddhism experienced a 150-year hiatus.

Second Diffusion of Buddhism

Overwhelmed initially by local power struggles, Buddhism gradually began to exert its influence again. As the tide of Buddhist faith receded in India, Nepal and China, Tibet slowly emerged as the most devoutly Buddhist nation in the world. Never again was Tibet to rise to arms.

The so-called second diffusion of Buddhism corresponded with two developments. First, Tibetan teachers who had taken refuge in Kham, to the east, returned to central Tibet in the late 10th century and established new monasteries. The second great catalyst was the arrival of two figures in far western Tibet: the Bengali Buddhist scholar Atisha (Jowo-je in Tibetan; 982–1054), whom the kings of Guge in far western Tibet invited to Tibet in the mid-11th century; and the great translator Rinchen Zangpo (958–1055), who after travelling to India brought back Buddhist texts and founded dozens of monasteries in the far west. Travellers can still get a sense of the

---

Traces of the Yarlung Kings

Yumbulagang (Yarlung Valley), the first building in Tibet

Tombs of the early Tibetan kings, Chongye

Zortang (Yarlung Valley), the first field in Tibet

The Snow Lion and the Dragon by Melvyn C Goldstein is worth wading through if you want an unsentimental analysis of the historically complex issue of China's claims to Tibet, and the Dalai Lama's options in dealing with the current Chinese leadership.

763	790s	822	842
Trisong Detsen attacks the Chinese capital Chang'an (Xī'ān) after a Chinese tribute of 50,000 bolts of silk is late.	Samye's Great Debate takes place, as Tibet chooses between the Indian and Chinese schools of Buddhist teachings.	The Sino-Tibetan treaty is signed, defining China's and Tibet's boundaries on largely Tibetan terms. The bilingual inscription of the treaty is erected on a stele outside the Jokhang.	Monk Lhalung Palgye Dorje assassinates anti-Buddhist king Langdharma in disguise. The event is still commemorated by the Black Hat Dance performed during monastic festivals.

glory years of the kingdom of Guge at the spectacular site of Tsaparang (p182) and at Thöling Monastery (p180).

Back in central Tibet disciples of Atisha, chiefly Dromtönpa, were instrumental in establishing the Kadampa order and such early monasteries as Reting.

The Sakyas & the Mongols

With the assassination of Tritsug Detsen Ralpachen and the collapse of a central Tibetan state, Tibet's contacts with China withered. By the time the Tang dynasty collapsed in 907, China had already recovered almost all the territory it had previously lost to the Tibetans. Throughout the Song dynasty (960–1276) the two nations had virtually no contact with each other, and Tibet's sole foreign contacts were with its southern Buddhist neighbours.

This was all to change when Chinggis (Genghis) Khaan launched a series of conquests in 1206 that led to a vast Mongol empire that straddled Central Asia and China. By 1239 the Mongols started to send raiding parties onto the Tibetan plateau. Numerous monasteries were razed and the Mongols almost reached Lhasa, before turning back.

Tibetan accounts have it that returning Mongol troops related the spiritual eminence of the Tibetan lamas to Godan Khan, grandson of Chinggis Khaan and ruler of the Kokonor region (which means 'Blue Sea' in Mongolian) in modern-day Qīnghǎi. In response Godan summoned Sakya Pandita, the head of Sakya Monastery, to his court. The outcome of this meeting was the beginning of a blurry priest-patron (*cho-yon*) relationship that has come to dog the definitions of Tibetan independence and its relationship to China. Tibetan Buddhism became the state religion of the Mongol empire in east Asia, and the head Sakya lama became its spiritual leader, a position that also entailed temporal authority over Tibet. The Sakyapa ascendancy lasted less than 100 years but its ties to the Mongol Yuan dynasty was to have profound effects on Tibet's future.

The process of reincarnation has been likened to a flame that passes from candle to candle, yet remains the same flame.

WRITTEN IN STONE

A Sino-Tibetan treaty was signed in 822 during the reign of King Tritsug Detsen Ralpachen (r 817–35), heralding an era in which 'Tibetans shall be happy in Tibet and Chinese shall be happy in China'. It was immortalised in stone on three steles: one in Lhasa, outside the Jokhang; one in the Chinese capital of Chang'an; and one on the border of Tibet and China. Only the Lhasa stele still stands, in Barkhor Square (p53).

Signatories to the treaty swore that '...the whole region to the east...being the country of Great China and the whole region to the west being assuredly that of the country of Great Tibet, from either side of that frontier there shall be no warfare, no hostile invasions, and no seizure of territory...'.

996	1073	1110–1193	1201
Thöling Monastery is founded in far western Tibet and becomes the main centre of Buddhist activities in Tibet, translating large numbers of Buddhist texts from Kashmir.	The Khon family, which traces its lineage from the nobility of the Yarlung dynasty, founds the Sakya school of Tibetan Buddhism. The family remains the hereditary head of Sakya tradition to this day.	The first Karmapa introduces the concept of reincarnation, which eventually spreads to other schools of Tibetan Buddhism and to the institution of the Dalai Lamas.	Sakya Pandita (1182–1251) travels to India, studying under Indian gurus. He becomes a great religious and cultural figure, creating a Tibetan literary tradition inspired by Sanskrit poetry.

Tibetan Independence (Part I)

The best single-volume introduction to Tibetan history is Sam van Schaik's *Tibet: A History*. It's even-handed, engrossing and highly recommended as a key to understanding the region.

Certain Chinese claims on Tibet have looked to the Mongol Yuan dynasty overlordship of the high plateau, and the priest-patron relationship existing at the time, as setting a precedent for Chinese sovereignty over Tibet. The Yuan dynasty may have claimed sovereignty over Tibet, yet this 'Chinese' dynasty was itself governed by the invading Mongols and their ruler Kublai Khan. Pro-independence supporters state that this is like India claiming sovereignty over Myanmar (Burma) because both were ruled by the British.

In reality, Tibetan submission was offered to the Mongols before they conquered China and it ended when the Mongols fell from power in that country. When the Mongol empire disintegrated, both China and Tibet regained their independence. Due to the initial weakness of the Ming dynasty, Sino-Tibetan relations effectively took on the form of exchanges of diplomatic courtesies by two independent governments.

The Tibetans undertook to remove all traces of the Mongol administration, drawing on the traditions of the former Yarlung kings. Officials were required to dress in the manner of the former royal court, a revised version of King Songtsen Gampo's code of law was enacted, a new taxation system was enforced, and scrolls depicting the glories of the Yarlung dynasty were commissioned. The movement was a declaration of Tibet's independence from foreign interference and a search for national identity.

Rise of the Gelugpa & the Dalai Lamas

In 1374 a young man named Lobsang, later known as Tsongkhapa, set out from his home near Kokonor in Amdo to central Tibet, where he undertook training with all the major schools of Tibetan Buddhism. By the time he was 25 he had already gained a reputation as a teacher and a writer.

Tsongkhapa established a monastery at Ganden, near Lhasa, where he refined his thinking, steering clear of political intrigue, and espousing doctrinal purity and monastic discipline. Although it seems unlikely that Tsongkhapa intended to found another school of Buddhism, his teachings attracted many disciples, who found his return to the original teachings of Atisha an exciting alternative to the politically tainted Sakyapa and Kagyupa orders. Tsongkhapa's movement became known as the Gelugpa (Virtuous) order, which today remains the dominant school in Tibet.

By the time of the third reincarnated head of the Gelugpa, Sonam Gyatso (1543–88), the Mongols began to take a renewed interest in Tibet's new and increasingly powerful order. In a move that mirrored the 13th-century Sakyapa entrance into the political arena, Sonam Gyatso accepted an invitation to meet with Altyn Khan near Kokonor in 1578. At the meeting, Sonam Gyatso received the title of *dalai,* meaning 'ocean', and implying 'ocean of wisdom'. The title was retrospectively bestowed on his previous two reincarnations, and so Sonam Gyatso became the third Dalai Lama.

1249	1260	1268	1290
Sakya Pandita becomes the spiritual advisor to Godon Khan and converts the Mongols to Buddhism. Godon invests Sakya Pandita as the secular ruler of Tibet.	Kublai Khan appoints Phagpa as an imperial preceptor. This ushers in what the Tibetans call the priest–patron relationship between Mongol khans, later Chinese emperors and Tibetan lamas.	The first census of central Tibet counts some 40,000 households. Basic taxation and a new administrative system is established in Tibet.	Kublai Khan's army supports the Sakya and destroys the main centres of the Kagyud school. With the death of Kublai Khan in 1294, the power of the Sakya school begins to wane.

Their relationship with the Mongols marked the Gelugpa's entry into the turbulent waters of worldly affairs. It is no surprise that the Tsang kings and the Karmapa of Tsurphu Monastery saw this Gelugpa-Mongol alliance as a direct threat to their power. Bickering ensued, and in 1611 the Tsang king attacked Drepung and Sera Monasteries as the country slid into civil war. The fourth (Mongolian) Dalai Lama fled central Tibet and died at the age of 25 in 1616.

The Great Fifth Dalai Lama

A successor to the fourth Dalai Lama was soon discovered, and the boy was brought to Lhasa, again under Mongol escort. In the meantime, Mongol intervention in Tibetan affairs continued in the guise of support for the embattled Gelugpa order.

Unlike the Sakya-Mongol domination of Tibet, under which the head Sakya lama was required to reside in the Mongol court, the fifth Dalai Lama was able to rule from within Tibet. With the backing of the Mongol Gushri Khan, all of Tibet was pacified by 1656, and the Dalai Lama's control ranged from Mt Kailash in the west to Kham in the east. Ngawang Lobsang Gyatso, the fifth Dalai Lama, had become both the spiritual and temporal sovereign of a unified Tibet.

The fifth Dalai Lama is remembered as having ushered in a great new age for Tibet. He made a tour of Tibet's monasteries, and although he stripped most Kadampa monasteries – his chief rivals for power – of their riches, he allowed them to re-establish. A new flurry of monastic construction began, the major achievement being Labrang Monastery (in what is now Gānsù province). In Lhasa, work began on a fitting residence for the head of the Tibetan state: the Potala.

The fifth Dalai Lama wrote a detailed history of Tibet and his autobiography is regarded as a literary treasure of Tibet.

Manchus, Mongols & Murder

With the death of the fifth Dalai Lama in 1682, the weakness of reincarnation as a system of succession became apparent. The Tibetan government was confronted with the prospect of finding his reincarnation and then

THANGTONG GYALPO

Thangtong Gyalpo (1385–1464) was Tibet's Renaissance man *par excellence*. Nyingmapa yogi, treasure finder, engineer, medic and inventor of Tibetan opera, Thangtong formed a song-and-dance troupe of seven sisters to raise money for his other passion, bridge building. He eventually built 108 bridges in Tibet, the most famous of which was over the Yarlung Tsangpo near modern-day Chushul. Thangtong is often depicted in monastery murals with long white hair and a beard, and is usually holding a section of chain links from one of his bridges.

1357–1419	1368	1565	1578
Tsongkhapa establishes himself as a reformer, founds the reformist Gelugpa school, writes the influential Lamrin Chenpo and introduces the popular Mönlam festival.	The Mongol Yuan dynasty in China ends, and the Ming dynasty begins. This coincides with the final demise of Sakya rule in Tibet.	The kings of Tsang became secular rulers of Tibet from Shigatse. Spiritual authority at this time is vested in the Karmapa, head of a Kagyupa suborder at Tsurphu Monastery.	Mongolian Altyn (Altan) Khan converts to Buddhism and bestows the title 'Dalai Lama' to Sonam Gyatso, who becomes the third Dalai Lama (the first two are honoured retroactively).

waiting 18 years until the boy came of age. The great personal prestige and authority of the fifth Dalai Lama had played no small part in holding together a newly unified Tibet. The Dalai Lama's regent decided to shroud the Dalai Lama's death in secrecy, announcing that the fifth lama had entered a long period of meditation (over 10 years!).

In 1695 the secret was leaked and the regent was forced to hastily enthrone the sixth Dalai Lama, a boy of his own choosing. The choice was an unfortunate one and could not have come at a worse time.

Tibet's dealings with the new Qing government went awry from the start. Kangxi, the second Qing emperor, took offence when the death of the fifth Dalai Lama was concealed from him. At the same time, an ambitious Mongol prince named Lhabzang Khan came to the conclusion that

REINCARNATION LINEAGES

There are thought to be several thousand *trulku* (also spelt *tulku;* 'incarnate lamas') in Tibet. The abbots of many monasteries are *trulku,* and thus abbotship can be traced back through a lineage of rebirths to the original founder of a monastery. The honorific *rinpoche,* meaning 'very precious', is a mark of respect and does not necessarily imply that the holder is a *trulku*. The Chinese use the confused translation 'Living Buddha' for *trulku*.

A *trulku* can also be a manifestation of a bodhisattva that repeatedly expresses itself through a series of rebirths. The most famous manifestation of a deity is, of course, the Dalai Lama lineage. The Dalai Lamas are manifestations of Chenresig (Avalokiteshvara), the Bodhisattva of Compassion. The Panchen Lama is a manifestation of Jampelyang (Manjushri), the Bodhisattva of Insight. There is no exclusivity in such a manifestation: Tsongkhapa, founder of the Gelugpa order, was also a manifestation of Jampelyang (Manjushri), as traditionally were the abbots of Sakya Monastery.

Lamas approaching death often leave behind clues pointing to the location of their reincarnation. Potential reincarnations are often further tested by being required to pick out the former lama's possessions from a collection of objects. Disputes over *trulku* status are not uncommon. A family's fortunes are likely to drastically improve if an incarnate lama is discovered among the children; this creates an incentive for fraud.

It is possible to see in the *trulku* system a substitute for the system of hereditary power (as in Western royal lineages) in a society where, historically, many of the major players were celibate and unable to produce their own heirs. Not that celibacy was exclusively the case. The abbots of Sakya took wives to produce their own *trulku* reincarnations, and it is not uncommon for rural *trulkus* to do the same.

The major flaw in the system is the time needed for the reincarnation to reach adulthood. Regents have traditionally been appointed to run the country during the minority of a Dalai Lama but this tradition takes on an added dimension under modern political circumstances. The current Dalai Lama has made it clear that he will not be reincarnated in Chinese-occupied Tibet and may even be the last Dalai Lama.

1601	1624	1640–42	1652
The Mongolian great-grandson of Altyn Khan is recognised by the Panchen Lama as the fourth Dalai Lama. This establishes the tradition of the Dalai Lamas being recognised by the Panchen.	Jesuits open their first mission at Tsaparang in far western Tibet after an epic journey across the Himalaya from bases in Goa.	Mongolian Gushri Khan executes the King of Tsang and hands over religious and secular power to the fifth Dalai Lama. Lhasa becomes the capital and construction begins on the Potala.	The Manchu Emperor Shunzhi invites the fifth Dalai Lama to China; to mark the occasion the Yellow Temple is built on the outskirts of Běijīng.

earlier Mongol leaders had taken too much of a back-seat position in their relations with the Tibetans and appealed to Emperor Kangxi for support. It was granted and, in 1705, Mongol forces descended on Lhasa, deposing the sixth Dalai Lama. Depending on your source, he either died at Lithang (where he was probably murdered), or he lived to a ripe old age in Amdo. The seventh Dalai Lama was subsequently found in Lithang, fulfilling a famous poem written by the sixth.

In 1717 the Dzungar Mongols from Central Asia attacked and occupied Lhasa for three years, killing Lhabzang Khan and deposing the seventh Dalai Lama. The resulting confusion in Tibet was the opportunity for which Emperor Kangxi had been waiting. He responded by sending a military expedition to Lhasa. The Chinese troops drove out the Dzungar Mongols and were received by the Tibetans as liberators. They were unlikely to have been received any other way: with them, they brought the seventh Dalai Lama, who had been languishing in Kumbum Monastery under Chinese 'protection'.

Emperor Kangxi wasted no time in declaring Tibet a protectorate of China. Two Chinese representatives, known as *ambans* (a Manchurian word), were installed at Lhasa, along with a garrison of Chinese troops. It was just a beginning, leading to two centuries of Manchu overlordship and serving as a historical precedent for the communist takeover nearly 250 years later.

Manchu Overlordship

The seventh Dalai Lama ruled until his death in 1757. However, at this point it became clear that another ruler would have to be appointed until the next Dalai Lama reached adulthood. The post of regent *(gyeltshab)* was created.

It is perhaps a poor reflection on the spiritual attainment of the lamas appointed as regents that few were willing to relinquish the reins once they were in the saddle. In the 120 years between the death of the seventh Dalai Lama and the adulthood of the 13th, actual power was wielded by the Dalai Lamas for only seven years. Three of them died very young and under suspicious circumstances. Only the eighth Dalai Lama survived into his adulthood, living a quiet, contemplative life until the age of 45.

Barbarians at the Doorstep

Early contact between Britain and Tibet commenced with a mission to Shigatse headed by a Scotsman, George Bogle, in 1774. Bogle soon ingratiated himself with the Panchen Lama – to the extent of marrying one of his sisters. With the death of the third Panchen Lama in 1780 and the ban on foreign contact that came after the Gurkha invasion of Tibet in 1788, Britain lost all official contact with Tibet.

Meanwhile, Britain watched nervously as the Russian empire swallowed up Central Asia, pushing its borders 1000km further towards India. The

The Dalai Lamas are depicted in wall paintings holding the Wheel of Law (Wheel of Dharma) as a symbol of the political power gained under the great fifth Dalai Lama.

HISTORY BARBARIANS AT THE DOORSTEP

Marco Polo and Alexandra David-Neel both wrote about the magical powers of Tibetan monks, including the ability to move cups with their minds, travel cross-country while levitating or keep warm in subzero temperatures simply through the power of their minds.

1695	1706	1716–21	1724
Completion of Potala Palace. The death of the fifth Dalai Lama is announced the following year, though in reality he had died 15 years previously.	Lhabzang Khan's army marches into Lhasa, deposes (and likely poisons) the sixth Dalai Lama and installs Yeshi Gyatso, who is not accepted by Tibetans as a Dalai Lama.	Italian priest Ippolito Desideri travels to the Guge kingdom and Lhasa, where he lives for five years, trying to convert Tibetans to Catholicism. He is the first Westerner to see Mt Kailash.	The Manchu Qing dynasty appoints a resident Chinese *amban* (official) to run Tibet.

The Tibetan Lama Phagpa, nephew of Kunga Gyetsen, enjoyed a close relationship with the Mongol leader Kublai Khan, likely met Marco Polo in Běijīng and even helped create a new Mongol script.

reported arrival of Russian 'adviser' Agvan Dorjieff in Lhasa exacerbated fears that Russia had military designs on British India, the 'jewel in the crown' of the empire.

When Dorjieff led an envoy from the Dalai Lama to Tsar Nicholas II in 1898, 1900 and 1901, and when British intelligence confirmed that Lhasa had received Russian missions (while similar British advances had been refused), the Raj broke into a cold sweat. There was even wild conjecture that the tsar was poised to convert to Buddhism.

It was against this background that Russophobe Lord Curzon, viceroy of India, decided to nip Russian designs in the bud. In late 1903, a British military expedition led by Colonel Francis Younghusband entered Tibet via Sikkim. After several months waiting for a Tibetan delegation, the British moved on to Lhasa, where it was discovered that the Dalai Lama had fled to Mongolia with Dorjieff. However, an Anglo-Tibetan convention was signed following negotiations with Tri Rinpoche, the abbot of Ganden whom the Dalai Lama had appointed as regent in his absence. British forces withdrew after spending just two months in Lhasa.

The missing link in the Anglo-Tibetan accord was a Manchu signature. In effect, the accord implied that Tibet was a sovereign power and therefore had the right to make treaties of its own. The Manchus objected and, in 1906, the British signed a second accord with the Manchus, one that recognised China's suzerainty over Tibet. In 1910, with the Manchu Qing dynasty teetering on collapse, the Manchus made good on the accord and invaded Tibet, forcing the Dalai Lama once again into flight – this time into the arms of the British in India.

Tibetan Independence Revisited

In 1911 a revolution finally toppled the decadent Qing dynasty in China, and by the end of 1912 the last of the occupying Manchu forces were escorted out of Tibet. In January 1913 the 13th Dalai Lama returned to Lhasa from Sikkim.

THE PLAYBOY LAMA

Tsangyang Gyatso (1683–1706), the young man from Tawang (in modern-day India) chosen as the sixth Dalai Lama, was, shall we say, unconventional. A sensual youth with long hair and a penchant for erotic verse, he soon proved himself to be far more interested in wine and women than meditation and study. He refused to take his final vows as a monk and he would often sneak out of the Potala at night to raise hell in the inns and brothels of Lhasa, under the pseudonym Norsang Wangpo. A resident Jesuit monk described him as a 'dissolute youth' and 'quite depraved', noting that 'no good-looking person of either sex was safe from his unbridled licentiousness'.

1774	1788	1879	1893
Scotsman George Bogle, aged 27, travels to Tibet to investigate the opening of trade and spends the winter at Tashilhunpo Monastery in Shigatse.	Chinese troops expel Nepali invaders from Tibet. Three years later the Nepali troops return and are beaten back again.	The 13th Dalai Lama is enthroned. In 1895 he takes his final ordination and becomes the secular and spiritual ruler of Tibet.	Tibet cedes Sikkim and opens the Chumbi Valley to trade with British India.

In reply to overtures from the government of the new Chinese republic, the Dalai Lama replied that he was uninterested in ranks bestowed by the Chinese and that he was assuming temporal and spiritual leadership of his country.

Tibetans have since read this reply as a formal declaration of independence. As for the Chinese, they chose to ignore it, reporting that the Dalai Lama had responded with a letter expressing his great love for the motherland. Whatever the case, Tibet was to enjoy 30 years free of interference from China. What is more, Tibet was suddenly presented with an opportunity to create a state that was ready to rise to the challenge of the modern world. The opportunity foundered on Tibet's entrenched theocratic institutions, and Tibetan independence was a short-lived affair.

Visit The Tibet Album (http://tibet.prm.ox.ac.uk/) to browse over 6000 period photographs taken in Tibet between 1920 and 1950 by British officers such as Charles Bell and Hugh Richardson.

Attempts to Modernise

During the period of his flight to India, the 13th Dalai Lama had become friends with Sir Charles Bell, a Tibetan scholar and political officer in Sikkim. The relationship was to initiate a warming in Anglo-Tibetan affairs and to see the British playing an increasingly important role as mediators between Tibet and China.

In 1920 Bell was dispatched on a mission to Lhasa, where he renewed his friendship with the Dalai Lama. It was agreed that the British would supply the Tibetans with modern arms, providing they agreed to use them only for self-defence. Tibetan military officers were trained in Gyantse and India, and a telegraph line was set up linking Lhasa and Shigatse. Other developments included the construction of a small hydroelectric station near Lhasa and the establishment of an English school at Gyantse. Four Tibetan boys were even sent to public school at Rugby in England. At the invitation of the Dalai Lama, British experts conducted geological surveys of parts of Tibet with a view to gauging mining potential.

It is highly likely that the 13th Dalai Lama's trips away from his country had made him realise that it was imperative that Tibet begin to modernise. At the same time he must also have been aware that the road to modernisation was fraught with obstacles, foremost of which was the entrenched Tibetan social order.

Since the rise of the Gelugpa order, Tibet had been ruled as a (some would say feudal) theocracy. Monks, particularly those in the huge monastic complexes of Drepung and Sera in Lhasa, were accustomed to a high degree of influence in the Tibetan government. And the attempts to modernise were met with intense opposition.

Before too long, the 13th Dalai Lama's innovations fell victim to a conservative backlash. Newly trained Tibetan officers were reassigned to nonmilitary jobs, causing a rapid deterioration of military discipline; a newly established police force was left to its own devices and soon

Kate Teltscher's *The High Road to China* details the 1774–45 journey of 27-year-old George Bogle to Shigatse and his fascinating relationship with the Panchen Lama.

1904	1907	1909	1910
The British mobilise over 8000 soldiers and launch an invasion of Tibet from the Sikkim frontier. The ill-equipped Tibetan army is no match. The 13th Dalai Lama escapes to Mongolia.	Britain and Russia acknowledge Chinese suzerainty over Tibet in a resolution of Great Game tensions.	The 13th Dalai Lama returns to Lhasa after an absence of five years.	Chinese resident in Tibet Zhao Erfeng attempts to re-establish Qing authority and storms Lhasa. The Dalai Lama escapes again, this time to India. On his return he declares Tibet independent.

became ineffective; the English school at Gyantse was closed down; and a mail service set up by the British was stopped.

However, Tibet's brief period of independence was troubled by more than just an inability to modernise. Conflict sprang up between the Panchen Lama and the Dalai Lama over the autonomy of Tashilhunpo Monastery and its estates. The Panchen Lama, after appealing to the British to mediate, fled to China, where he stayed for 14 years until his death.

In 1933 the 13th Dalai Lama died, leaving the running of the country to the regent of Reting. The present (14th) Dalai Lama was discovered in Amdo but was brought to Lhasa only after the local Chinese commander had been paid off with a huge 'fee' of 300,000 Chinese dollars. The boy was renamed Tenzin Gyatso and he was installed as the Dalai Lama on 22 February 1940, aged 4½.

In 1947 an attempted coup d'état, known as the Reting Conspiracy, rocked Lhasa. Lhasa came close to civil war, with 200 monks killed in gunfights at Sera Monastery. Reting Rinpoche was thrown into jail for his part in the rebellion and was later found dead in his cell, though it remains unclear whether he was set up or not.

It was not a good time for Tibet to be weakened by internal disputes. By 1949 the Chinese Nationalist government had fled to Taiwan and Mao Zedong and his Red Army had taken control of China. Big changes were looming.

Liberation

Unknown to the Tibetans, the communist takeover of China was to open what is probably the saddest chapter in Tibetan history. The ensuing Chinese 'liberation' of Tibet eventually led to the deaths of hundreds of thousands of Tibetans, an assault on the Tibetan traditional way of life, the flight of the Dalai Lama to India and the destruction of almost every historical structure on the plateau. The chief culprits were Chinese ethnic chauvinism and an epidemic of social anarchy known as the Cultural Revolution.

On 7 October 1950, just a year after the communist takeover of China, 40,000 battle-hardened Chinese troops attacked central Tibet from six different directions. The Tibetan army, a poorly equipped force of around 4000 men, stood little chance of resisting, and any attempt at defence soon collapsed. In Lhasa, the Tibetan government reacted by enthroning the 15-year-old 14th Dalai Lama, an action that brought jubilation and dancing on the streets but did little to protect Tibet from advancing Chinese troops.

Presented with a seemingly hopeless situation, the Dalai Lama dispatched a mission to Běijīng with orders that it refer all decisions to Lhasa. As it turned out, there were no decisions to be made. The Chinese had already drafted an agreement. The Tibetans had two choices: sign on the dotted line or face further military action.

Fans of Great Game history can visit Gyantse Dzong and nearby Tsechen Dzong, both of which were taken by Younghusband in 1904, as well as the Karo-la, scene of the highest battle in British Imperial history.

Scott Berry's *A Stranger in Tibet* tells the fascinating story of Ekai Kawaguchi, a young Japanese monk, who was one of the first foreigners to reach Lhasa in 1900; he stayed over a year in the capital before his identity was discovered and he was forced to flee the country.

1913	1923	1933	1935
The Simla Convention between Britain, China and Tibet is held in India. The main agenda for the conference is to delimit and define the boundary between Tibet and China.	A clash with Lhasa sends the Panchen Lama into exile in China. This is to have disastrous consequences for Tibet: he comes under Chinese influence and never returns.	The 13th Dalai Lama dies, and secular authority is passed to Reting Rinpoche, who rules as regent until 1947. He is an eminent Gelugpa Lama, but young and inexperienced in state affairs.	Birth of the present and 14th Dalai Lama in Taktser village, Amdo, just outside Xīníng in present Qīnghǎi; his younger and older brothers are also *trulkus* (reincarnated lamas).

The 17-point *Agreement on Measures for the Peaceful Liberation of Tibet* promised a one-country-two-systems structure much like that offered later to Hong Kong and Macau, but provided little in the way of guarantees. The Tibetan delegates protested that they were unauthorised to sign such an agreement but were strongarmed and the agreement was ratified.

Initially, the Chinese occupation of central Tibet was carried out in an orderly way, with few obvious changes or reforms, but tensions inevitably mounted. The presence of 8000 Chinese troops in Lhasa (doubling the city's population) soon affected food stores and gave rise to high inflation. Rumours of political indoctrination, massacres and attacks on monasteries in Kham (far eastern Tibet) slowly began to filter back to Lhasa.

In 1956 uprisings broke out in eastern Tibet in reaction to enforced land reform, and in 1957 and 1958 protests and armed guerrilla revolt spread to central Tibet (with covert CIA assistance). With a heavy heart, the Dalai Lama returned to Lhasa in March 1957 from a trip to India to celebrate the 2500th anniversary of the birth of the Buddha. It seemed inevitable that Tibet would explode in revolt and equally inevitable that it would be suppressed by China.

Uprising & Bloodshed

The Tibetan New Year of 1959, like all the New Year celebrations before it, attracted huge crowds to Lhasa, doubling the city's population. In addition to the standard festival activities, the Chinese had added a highlight of their own – a performance by a Chinese dance group at the Lhasa military base. The invitation to the Dalai Lama came in the form of a thinly veiled command. The Dalai Lama, wishing to avoid offence, accepted.

As preparations for the performance drew near, however, the Dalai Lama's security chief was surprised to hear that the Dalai Lama was expected to attend in secrecy and without his customary contingent of 25 bodyguards. Despite the Dalai Lama's agreement to these conditions, news of them soon leaked, and in no time simmering frustration at Chinese rule came to the boil among the crowds on the streets. It seemed obvious to the Tibetans that the Chinese were about to kidnap the Dalai Lama. A huge crowd (witnesses claim 30,000 people) gathered around the Norbulingka (the Dalai Lama's summer palace) and swore to protect him with their lives.

The Dalai Lama had no choice but to cancel his appointment at the military base. In the meantime, the crowds on the streets were swollen by Tibetan soldiers, who changed out of their People's Liberation Army (PLA) uniforms and started to hand out weapons. A group of government ministers announced that the 17-point agreement was null and void, and that Tibet renounced the authority of China.

The Dalai Lama was powerless to intervene, managing only to pen some conciliatory letters to the Chinese as his people prepared for battle

The Younghusband invasion of Tibet included 10,091 porters, 7096 mules, 2668 ponies, 4466 yaks and six camels in a train that stretched for 7km!

HISTORY UPRISING & BLOODSHED

Over the centuries Tibet has suffered from ill-defined borders and a lack of internal unity, with large parts of Amdo, Kham and Ngari and independent tribes like the Goloks only nominally ruled by Lhasa.

1950	1950	1951	1954
China attacks Chamdo; the Tibetan army is greatly outnumbered and defeat is swift. The Tibetan government in Lhasa reacts by enthroning the 15-year-old 14th Dalai Lama. There is jubilation in the streets.	El Salvador sponsors a UN motion to condemn Chinese aggression in Tibet. Britain and India, traditional friends of Tibet, convince the UN not to debate the issue.	The 17-point agreement is signed by the Governor of Kham, acknowledging Tibet's autonomy as a part of the People's Republic of China. Chairman Mao's first remark is 'Welcome back to the motherland'.	In 1954 the Dalai Lama spends almost a year in Běijīng, where, amid cordial discussions with Mao Zedong, he is told that 'religion is poison'.

on Lhasa's streets. In a last-ditch effort to prevent bloodshed, the Dalai Lama even offered himself to the Chinese. The reply came in the sound of two mortar shells exploding in the gardens of the Norbulingka. The attack made it obvious that the only option remaining to the Dalai Lama was flight (a measure the Nechung oracle agreed with). On 17 March he left the Norbulingka disguised as a soldier and surrounded by Khampa bodyguards; 14 days later he was in India. The Dalai Lama was 24 years old.

With both the Chinese and the Tibetans unaware of the Dalai Lama's departure, tensions continued to mount in Lhasa. On 20 March Chinese troops began to shell the Norbulingka and the crowds surrounding it, killing hundreds of people. Artillery bombed the Potala, Sera Monastery and the medical college on Chagpo Ri. Tibetans armed with petrol bombs were picked off by Chinese snipers, and when a crowd of 10,000 Tibetans retreated into the sacred precincts of the Jokhang, that too was bombed. It is

THE FALL OF CHAMDO

In spring 1950, Chamdo in eastern Tibet was in real trouble. Although pockets of resistance remained at Derge and Markham, the communist Chinese had taken control of most of Kham without a fight. Chinese armies were quickly tightening the noose around Tibet, moving in from Xīnjiāng and Xikang (now Sìchuān) provinces in a pincer movement masterminded by, among others, Deng Xiaoping.

The first skirmish between Chinese and Tibetan troops took place in May 1950 when the People's Liberation Army (PLA) attacked Dengo on the Dri-chu (Yangzi River). Then on 7 October 1950 the PLA moved in earnest, as 40,000 troops crossed the Dri-chu and attacked Chamdo from three directions: Jyekundo to the north, Derge to the east and Markham to the south.

As panic swept through Chamdo, the city responded to the military threat in characteristic Tibetan fashion – with a frenzy of prayer and religious ritual. When the local Tibetan leader radioed the Tibetan government in Lhasa to warn of the Chinese invasion, he was coolly told that the government members couldn't be disturbed because they were 'on a picnic'. To this the Chamdo radio operator is said to have replied 'skyag pa'i gling kha!', or 'shit on your picnic!'. It was to be an inauspicious last ever communication between the Chamdo and Lhasa branches of the Tibetan government.

The city was evacuated but the PLA was one step ahead. Chinese leaders knew that speed was of the essence (the Chinese described the military operation as 'like a tiger trying to catch a fly') and had already cut the Tibetans off by taking Riwoche. The Tibetans surrendered without a shot on 19 October. The Tibetan troops were disarmed, given lectures on the benefits of socialism, then given money and sent home. The British radio operator Robert Ford, who was based in Chamdo, was less lucky. He was arrested, subjected to thought reform and held in jail for five years. It was the beginning of the end of an independent Tibet.

1955	1956	late 1950s	1962
Xikang province is absorbed into Sìchuān province, eating up a large chunk of the traditional Tibetan province of Kham.	Rebellions break out in monasteries in Kham (modern-day western Sìchuān). The siege of Lithang rebellion lasts 67 days and ends in aerial bombardment of the monastery.	The Khampas found the resistance group Four Rivers, Six Ranges. The Tibetan exile groups in India make contact with the CIA; Tibetans are sent for training to the Pacific island of Saipan.	The Indo-Chinese war ends in defeat for India, but territorial disputes over Arunachal Pradesh and Aksai Chin continue to this day between the two rising giants.

thought that after three days of violence, hundreds of Tibetans lay dead in Lhasa's streets. Some estimates put the numbers of those killed far higher.

Socialist Paradise on the Roof of the World

The Chinese quickly consolidated their quelling of the Lhasa uprising by taking control of all the high passes between Tibet and India and disarming the Khampa guerrillas. As the Chinese themselves put it, they were liberating Tibet from reactionary forces, freeing serfs from the yoke of monastic oppression and ushering in a new equitable socialist society, whether the Tibetans liked it or not.

The Chinese abolished the Tibetan government and set about reordering Tibetan society in accordance with their Marxist principles. The monks and the aristocrats were put to work on menial jobs and subjected to violent ideological struggle sessions, known as *thamzing,* which sometimes resulted in death. A ferment of class struggle was whipped up and former feudal exploiters – towards some of whom Tibet's poor may have harboured genuine resentment – were subjected to cruel punishments.

The Chinese also turned their attention to Tibet's several thousand 'feudal' monasteries, *lhakhangs* (chapels) and shrines. Tibetans were refused permission to donate food to the monasteries, and monks were compelled to join struggle sessions, discard their robes and marry. Monasteries were stripped of their riches, Buddhist scriptures were burnt and used as toilet paper. The wholesale destruction of Tibet's monastic heritage began in earnest.

Notable in this litany of disasters was the Chinese decision to alter Tibetan farming practices, as part of an economic 'Great Leap Forward'. Instead of barley, the Tibetan staple, farmers were instructed to grow wheat and rice. Tibetans protested that these crops were unsuited to Tibet's high altitude. They were right, and mass starvation resulted. It is estimated that by late 1961, 70,000 Tibetans had died or were dying of starvation. Across China it is estimated that up to 35 million people died.

By September 1961 even the Chinese-groomed Panchen Lama began to have a change of heart. He presented Mao Zedong with a 70,000-character report on the hardships his people were suffering and also requested, among other things, religious freedom and an end to the sacking of Tibetan monasteries. Four years later he was to disappear into a high-security prison for a 14-year stay. Many more would soon join him.

The Cultural Revolution

Among the writings of Mao Zedong is a piece entitled 'On Going Too Far'. It is a subject on which he was particularly well qualified to write. What started as a power struggle between Mao and Liu Shaoqi in 1965 had morphed by August 1966 into the Great Proletarian Cultural Revolution, an anarchic

HISTORY SOCIALIST PARADISE ON THE ROOF OF THE WORLD

Neither Mao Zedong nor Deng Xiaoping ever visited Tibet.

While laying in state the head of the 13th Dalai Lama's corpse allegedly turned repeatedly towards the northeast, indicating that the 14th Dalai Lama would be born in Amdo.

1964	1965	1967–76	1975
Three years after writing a 70,000-character petition, accusing China of committing genocide, the Panchen Lama is arrested and charged with instigating rebellion.	The Tibetan Autonomous Region (TAR) is formally brought into being on 1 September with much fanfare and Chinese talk of happy Tibetans fighting back tears of gratitude at becoming one with the great motherland.	The Cultural Revolution sweeps China and Tibet. Ideological frenzy results in the destruction of monasteries, shrines and libraries and the imprisonment of thousands of Tibetans.	The last CIA-funded Tibetan guerrilla bases in Mustang, northern Nepal, are closed down, bringing an end to armed rebellion and CIA involvement in the Tibetan resistance movement.

Education was once under the exclusive control of the monasteries, and the introduction of a secular education system has been a major goal of the communist government. These days most education is in the Chinese language.

movement that was to shake China to its core, trample its traditions underfoot, cause countless deaths and turn the running of the country over to rival mobs of Red Guards. All of China suffered in Mao's bold experiment in creating a new socialist paradise, but Tibet suffered more than most.

The first Red Guards arrived in Lhasa in July 1966. Two months later, the first rally was organised and Chinese-educated Tibetan youths raided the Jokhang, smashing statues and burning thangkas. It was the beginning of the large-scale destruction of virtually every religious monument in Tibet, and was carried out in the spirit of destroying the 'Four Olds': old thinking, old culture, old habits and old customs. Images of Chairman Mao were plastered over those of Buddha, as Buddhist mantras were replaced by communist slogans. The Buddha himself was accused of being a 'reactionary'.

Tibetan farmers were forced to collectivise into communes and were told what to grow and when to grow it. Anyone who objected was arrested and subjected to struggle sessions, during which Tibetans were forced to denounce the Dalai Lama as a parasite and traitor.

The Dust Settles

By the time of Mao's death in 1976 even the Chinese had begun to realise that their rule in Tibet had taken a wrong turn. Mao's chosen successor, Hua Guofeng, decided to soften the government's line on Tibet and called for a revival of Tibetan customs. In mid-1977 China announced that it would welcome the return of the Dalai Lama and other Tibetan refugees, and shortly afterwards the Panchen Lama was released from 14 years of imprisonment.

The Tibetan government-in-exile received cautiously the invitation to return to Tibet, and the Dalai Lama suggested that he be allowed to send a fact-finding mission to Tibet first. To the surprise of all involved, the Chinese agreed. As the Dalai Lama remarked in his autobiography, *Freedom in Exile,* it seemed that the Chinese were of the opinion that the mission members would find such happiness in their homeland that 'they would see no point in remaining in exile'. In fact, the results of the mission were so damning that the Dalai Lama decided not to publish them. Nevertheless, two more missions followed. They claimed up to 1.2 million deaths (one in six Tibetans, according to the disputed report), the destruction of 6254 monasteries and nunneries (also disputed), the absorption of two-thirds of Tibet into China, 100,000 Tibetans in labour camps and extensive deforestation.

In China, Hua Guofeng's short-lived political ascendancy had been eclipsed by Deng Xiaoping's rise to power. In 1980 Deng sent Hu Yaobang on a Chinese fact-finding mission that coincided with the visits of those sent by the Tibetan government-in-exile. Hu's conclusions, while not as damning as those of the Tibetans, painted a grim picture of life on the roof

Around 2500 monasteries existed in Tibet in 1959. By 1962 only 70 remained.

1979–85	1982	1987–89	1989
China enters a period of liberalisation and reform and limited religious freedoms are restored in Tibet. Out of a pre-1950 total of around 2000 monasteries, only 45 are reopened.	A three-person team sent to Běijīng from Dharamsala is told Tibet is part of China and that the Dalai Lama would be given a desk job in Běijīng on his return. By 1983 talks had broken down.	Pro-independence demonstrations take place in Lhasa; the response is violent, several tourists are injured and martial law is declared.	The Dalai Lama's efforts to achieve peace and freedom for his people are recognised when he is awarded the Nobel Peace Prize.

of the world. A six-point plan to improve the living conditions and freedoms of the Tibetans was drawn up, taxes were dropped for two years and limited private enterprise was allowed. The Jokhang was reopened for two days a month in 1978; the Potala opened in 1980. As in the rest of China, the government embarked on a program of extended personal and economic freedoms in concert with authoritarian one-party rule.

Reforms & Riots

The early 1980s saw the return of limited religious freedoms. Monasteries that had not been reduced to piles of rubble began to reopen and some religious artefacts were returned to Tibet from China.

Importantly, there was also a relaxation of the Chinese proscription on pilgrimage. Pictures of the Dalai Lama began to reappear on the streets of Lhasa. Talks aimed at bringing the Dalai Lama back into the ambit of Chinese influence continued, but with little result. Tibet, according to the Chinese government, became the 'front line of the struggle against splittism', a line that continues to be the official government position to this day.

In 1986 a new influx of foreigners arrived in Tibet, with the Chinese beginning to loosen restrictions on tourism. The trickle of tour groups and individual travellers soon became a flood. For the first time since the Chinese takeover, visitors from the West were given the opportunity to see the results of Chinese rule in Tibet.

When in September 1987 a group of 30 monks from Sera Monastery began circumambulating the Jokhang and crying out 'Independence for Tibet' and 'Long live his Holiness the Dalai Lama', their ranks were swollen by bystanders and arrests followed. Four days later, another group of monks repeated their actions, this time brandishing Tibetan flags. The monks were beaten and arrested. With Western tourists looking on, a crowd of 2000 to 3000 angry Tibetans gathered. Police vehicles were overturned and Chinese police began firing on the crowd.

The Chinese response was swift. Communications with the outside world were broken but this failed to prevent further protests in the following months. The Mönlam festival of March 1988 saw shooting in the streets of Lhasa, and that December a Dutch traveller was shot in the shoulder; 18 Tibetans died and 150 were wounded in the disturbances.

The Dalai Lama & the Search for Settlement

By the mid-1970s the Dalai Lama had become a prominent international figure, working tirelessly from his government-in-exile in Dharamsala to make the world more aware of his people's plight. In 1987 he addressed the US Congress and outlined a five-point peace plan.

Cultural Revolution-Era Ruins

Jampaling Chorten, Tsangpo Valley

Thöling Monastery, Zanda

HISTORY REFORMS & RIOTS

An illuminating glimpse of the Tibetan experience is provided by *Freedom in Exile: The Autobiography of the Dalai Lama*. With great humility the Dalai Lama outlines his personal philosophy, his hope to be reunited with his homeland and the story of his life.

2006	2006	2007	2008
Western climbers on Mt Cho Oyu film Chinese border guards shooting unarmed nuns as they flee China over the Nangpa-la to Nepal.	The 4310m Nathu-la pass with Sikkim opens to local traders for the first time in 44 years, hinting at warmer ties between India and China.	The Chinese government passes a new law requiring all incarnate lamas to be approved by the government, part of an attempt to increase political control over Tibet's religious hierarchy.	In the run-up to the Olympic Games in Běijīng, the worst riots for 20 years hit Lhasa, southern Gānsù and western Sìchuān; 19 people are killed and thousands are arrested.

The plan called for Tibet to be established as a 'zone of peace'; for the policy of Han immigration to Tibet to be abandoned; for a return to basic human rights and democratic freedoms; for the protection of Tibet's natural heritage and an end to the dumping of nuclear waste on the high plateau; and for joint discussions between the Chinese and the Tibetans on the future of Tibet. The Chinese denounced the plan as an example of 'splittism'. They gave the same response when, a year later, the Dalai Lama elaborated on the speech before the European Parliament in Strasbourg, France, dropping demands for full independence in favour of a form of autonomy and offering the Chinese the right to govern Tibet's foreign and military affairs.

John Avedon's *In Exile from the Land of Snows* is largely an account of the Tibetan community in Dharamsala, and is an excellent and informative read.

On 5 March 1989, three months before the student demonstrations in Běijīng's Tiān'ānmén Square, Lhasa erupted in the largest anti-Chinese demonstration since 1959. Běijīng reacted strongly, declaring martial law in Tibet, which lasted for more than a year. Despairing elements in the exiled Tibetan community began to talk of the need to take up arms. It was an option that the Dalai Lama had consistently opposed. His efforts to achieve peace and freedom for his people were recognised on 4 October 1989, when he was awarded the Nobel Peace Prize.

In January 1989, after denouncing the Communist Party's policies in Tibet and while visiting Tashilhunpo, the traditional seat of all the Panchen Lamas, the 10th Panchen Lama died, triggering a succession crisis that remains unresolved. The Dalai Lama identified the 11th Panchen Lama in 1995, whereupon the Chinese authorities detained the boy and his family (who have not been seen since) and orchestrated the choice of their own preferred candidate. The Chinese began to toughen their policy towards the Dalai Lama and launched the anti–Dalai Lama campaign inside Tibet, compelling all government officials and monks to denounce the Dalai Lama.

The Chinese authorities believe that one of the reasons for continuing separatist sentiments and opposition is Tibet's lack of integration with China. The solution since the mid-1980s has been to encourage Han immigration to the high plateau, a policy already successfully carried out in Xīnjiāng, Inner Mongolia and Qīnghǎi. As Běijīng attempts to shift the economic gains of the east coast to its underdeveloped hinterland, hundreds of thousands of Han Chinese have taken advantage of attractive salaries and interest-free loans to 'modernise' the backward province of Tibet. By the end of the millennium Tibetans were facing the fastest and deepest-reaching changes in their history.

2008	2010	2011	2012
The British government recognises China's direct rule over Tibet for the first time, shifting the language from 'suzerainty' to 'sovereignty'.	A huge 6.9-scale earthquake devastates the Tibetan town of Jyekundo (Yùshù) in Amdo (southeast Qīnghǎi), killing over 1700 people and leaving tens of thousands homeless.	Dalai Lama cedes political control as head of the Tibetan government-in-exile to former Harvard academic and lawyer Lobsang Sangay.	Two Tibetans set themselves on fire in the Barkhor Circuit, joining the more than 150 Tibetans who have committed self-immolation since 2011 in protest against Chinese rule.

Tibetan Landscapes

It's hard to overstate the global significance of the Tibetan plateau. Not only is it the earth's highest ecosystem and one of its last remaining great wildernesses, but it also contains the headwaters of Asia's greatest rivers; rivers that deliver water to half the world's population! How the Chinese government harnesses these resources, particularly Tibet's water, without harming their long-term sustainability will shape the future of half the planet.

The Roof of the World

The Tibetan plateau is one of the most isolated regions in the world, bound to the south by the 2500km-long Himalayan arc, to the west by the Karakoram and to the north by the Kunlun and Altyn Tagh ranges, two of the least explored ranges on earth. The northwest in particular is bound by the most remote wilderness left on earth, outside the polar regions. Four of the world's 10 highest mountains straddle Tibet's southern border with Nepal.

The plateau is also home to the world's highest number of glaciers outside the poles, making it the source of Asia's greatest rivers. Furthermore, it is thought that the high plateau affects global jet streams and even influences the Indian monsoon. With an average altitude of 4000m and large swaths of the country well above 5000m, the Tibetan plateau aptly deserves the title the 'roof of the world'.

Much of Tibet is a harsh and uncompromising landscape, best described as a high-altitude desert. Little of the Indian monsoon makes it over the Himalayan watershed, which is one reason why there is surprisingly little snow in the Land of Snows! Shifting sand dunes are a common sight along the Samye Valley and the road to Mt Kailash.

The plateau's regions are surprisingly diverse and can be loosely divided into four major regions.

Two of the best places to go birdwatching are Yamdrok-tso and Nam-tso; a section of the latter has been designated a bird preserve, at least on paper. April and November are the best times.

Ütsang

Made up of the combined regions of Ü and Tsang, which constitute central Tibet, Ütsang is the political, historical and agricultural heartland of Tibet. Its relatively fertile valleys enjoy a mild climate and are irrigated by wide rivers such as the Yarlung Tsangpo and the Kyi-chu.

Changtang

Towards the north of Ütsang are the harsh, high-altitude plains of the Changtang (northern plateau), the highest and largest plateau in the world, occupying an area of more than one million sq km (think France, the UK and Germany). The dead lakes of the Changtang are the brackish remnants of the Tethys Sea that found no run-off when the plateau started its skyward ascent.

Ngari

Ngari, or western Tibet, is similarly barren, although here river valleys provide grassy tracts that support nomads and their grazing animals.

The Chinese province commonly referred to as Tibet is officially called the Tibetan Autonomous Region (TAR) and has an area of 1.23 million sq km; bigger than the combined area of France, Spain and Portugal.

Indeed, the Kailash range in the far west of Tibet is the source of the subcontinent's four greatest rivers: the Ganges, Indus, Sutlej and Brahmaputra. The Ganges, Indus and Sutlej Rivers all cascade out of Tibet in its far west. The Brahmaputra (known in Tibet as Yarlung Tsangpo) meanders along the northern spine of the Himalaya for 2000km, searching for a way south, before draining into India not far from the Myanmar border.

Kham

Eastern Tibet marks a tempestuous drop in elevation down to the Sìchuān plain. The concertina landscape produces some of the most spectacular roller-coaster roads in Asia, as Himalayan extensions such as the Héngduàn Mountains are sliced by the deep gorges of the Yangzi (Dri-chu in Tibetan; Jīnshā Jiāng in Chinese), Salween (Gyalmo Ngulchu in Tibetan; Nù Jiāng in Chinese) and Mekong (Dza-chu in Tibetan; Láncáng Jiāng in Chinese) headwaters.

The Yarlung Tsangpo crashes through an incredible 5km-deep gorge here (often described as the world's deepest) as it swings violently around 7756m Namche Barwa. Many parts of this alpine region are lushly forested and support abundant wildlife, largely thanks to the lower altitudes and effects of the Indian monsoon.

The Struggle for Life

The vast differences in altitude in Tibet give rise to a spread of ecosystems from alpine to subtropical, but generally speaking life on the Tibetan Plateau is a harsh one and travellers are unlikely to encounter too much in the way of wildlife. Nevertheless, for those that have the time to get off the beaten track – particularly in western Tibet – or to go trekking in more remote areas, there are some unusual and understandably hardened species out there.

THE IMPORTANCE OF YAKS

Only 50 years ago an estimated one million wild yaks roamed the Tibetan plateau. Now it is a rare treat to catch a glimpse of one of these huge creatures, which weigh up to a tonne and can reach 1.8m at the shoulder. Wild yaks have diminished in number to 15,000 as a result of the increased demand for yak meat and a rise in illegal hunting.

Few, if any, of the yaks that travellers see are *drong* (wild yaks). In fact, most are not even yaks at all but rather dzo, a cross between a yak and a cow. A domestic yak rarely exceeds 1.5m in height. Unlike its wild relative, which is almost always black, the dzo varies in shade from black to grey and, primarily around Kokonor in Qīnghǎi, white.

With three times more red blood cells than the average cow, the yak thrives in the oxygen-depleted high altitudes. Its curious lung formation, surrounded by 14 or 15 pairs of ribs rather than the 13 typical of cattle, allows a large capacity for inhaling and expelling air (one reason why its Latin name *Bos grunniens* means 'grunting ox'). In fact, a descent below 3000m may impair the reproductive cycle and expose the yak to parasites and disease.

Tibetans rely on yak milk for cheese, as well as for butter for the ubiquitous butter tea and offerings to butter lamps in monasteries. The outer hair of the yak is woven into tent fabric and rope, and the soft inner wool is spun into *chara* (a type of felt) and used to make bags, blankets and tents. Tails are used in both Buddhist and Hindu religious practices. Yak hide is used for the soles of boots and the yak's heart is used in Tibetan medicine. In the nomadic tradition, no part of the animal is wasted and even yak dung is required as a fundamental fuel, left to dry in little cakes on the walls of most Tibetan houses. In fact, so important are yaks to the Tibetans that the animals are individually named, like children.

FROM SEABED TO SNOW CAPS: THE RISE OF TIBET

Some 50 million years ago, the Indian and Eurasian plates collided. What happened next in the long development of the Tibetan plateau is the subject of much debate.

Geologists have several different ideas about how the landscape here developed. One theory is that big pieces of Eurasia were pushed away towards what is now southeast Asia. Another is that the crust of Eurasia piled up in thick faults next to India. Another theory is that, rather than a collision, the lower part of the Indian crust was shoved underneath the Eurasian crust and kept moving northwards, meaning there could be pieces of India laying below central Tibet today. In all likelihood, it was a combination of these geological events that led to the plateau's formation, but scientists are still searching the evidence.

The plateau is anything but settled. India moves toward the rest of Asia at a rate of about 4cm each year; the region is actually spreading out rather than getting higher, and devastating earthquakes, such as the one that rocked Yùshù (Jyekundo) in Amdo in 2010 killing 2700 people, testify to the powerful tectonic forces still at play.

For those interested in the geological history of Tibet, the boundary between India and Eurasia can still be seen in the geology around the Yarlung Tsangpo River. Rocks here surfaced from below the floor of the ocean that once separated the two plates. A clear day at Everest Base Camp reveals horizontal layering on the very top of Mount Everest. The peak is comprised of limestone (once the ocean floor), which was thrust on top of the rocks above and then lifted all the way up to the top of the world.

Indeed, visitors to Shegar may well find locals selling ancient fossils of marine animals – at 4000m above sea level.

What Will I See?

On the road out to Mt Kailash, it is not unusual to see herds of fleet-footed Tibetan gazelles *(gowa)*, antelope *(tso)* and wild asses *(kyang)*, particularly along the northern route. During the breeding season antelope converge in groups numbering several hundred.

Trekkers might conceivably see the Himalayan black bear or, if they're exceeding lucky, the giant Tibetan blue bear searching for food in the alpine meadows. Herds of blue sheep, also known as bharal *(nawa na)*, are frequently spied on rocky slopes and outcrops (although the dwarf bharal is much rarer), but the argali, the largest species of wild sheep in the world, now only survives in the most remote mountain fastnesses of western Tibet.

Wolves of various colours can be seen all over the Tibetan plateau. Much rarer than the all-black wolf is the white wolf, one of the sacred animals of Tibet. Smaller carnivores include the lynx, marten and fox.

Marmots *(chiwa* or *piya)* are very common and can often be seen perched up on their hind legs sniffing the air curiously outside their burrows – they make a strange birdlike sound when distressed. The pika *(chipi)*, or Himalayan mouse-hare, a relative of the rabbit, is also common. Pikas have been observed at 5250m on Mt Everest, thus earning the distinction of having the highest habitat of any mammal.

A surprising number of migratory birds make their way up to the lakes of the Tibetan plateau through spring and summer. Tibet has over 30 endemic birds, and 480 species have been recorded on the plateau. Birds include the black-necked crane (whose food supply is being affected by changes in farming practices on the plateau), bar-headed goose and lammergeier (bearded vultures), as well as grebes, pheasants, snowcocks and partridges. Watching a pair of black-necked cranes, loyal mates for life, is one of the joys of travelling the wetlands of northern and western Tibet between April and October. Flocks of huge vultures can often be seen circling monasteries looking for a sky burial.

Geographically speaking, the Tibetan plateau makes up almost 25% of China's total landmass, spread over five provinces.

TIBETAN LANDSCAPES THE STRUGGLE FOR LIFE

Tibet in Bloom

Juniper trees and willows are common in the valleys of central Tibet and it is possible to come across wildflowers such as the pansy and the oleander, as well as unique indigenous flowers such as the *tsi-tog* (a light-pink, high-altitude bloom).

Eastern Tibet, which sees higher rainfall, has an amazing range of flora, from oak, elm and birch forests to bamboo, subtropical plants and flowers, including rhododendrons, azaleas and magnolias. It was from here that intrepid 19th-century plant hunters FM Bailey, Frank Kingdon-Ward and Frank Ludlow took the seeds and cuttings of species that would eventually become staples in English gardening.

On the Brink

About 80 species of animal that are threatened with extinction have been listed as protected by the Chinese government. These include the almost-mythical snow leopard *(gang-zig)* as well as the wild yak *(drong)*.

The Tibetan red deer was recently 'discovered' only 75km from Lhasa after a 50-year hiatus, as was a hitherto unknown breed of ancient wild horse in the Riwoche region of eastern Tibet.

Wild yaks are mostly encountered in the far northern region of the Changtang. The biggest bull yaks are reputed to be as large as a 4WD. Even rarer is the divine giant white yak, thought by Tibetans to inhabit the higher reaches of sacred mountains.

The *chiru*, a rare breed of antelope, has made an encouraging comeback in recent years. Numbers in Tibet dropped from over a million *chiru* in the 1960s to around 70,000 by the mid-1990s, largely because of the illegal market for its fine *shatoosh* wool, used in Indian cashmere shawls. After several high-profile campaigns in India, numbers of *chiru* have recently rebounded to as many as 150,000.

The illegal trade in antelope cashmere, musk, bear paws and gall bladders, deer antlers, and other body parts and bones remains a problem. You can often see Tibetan traders huddled on street corners in major Chinese cities selling these and other medicinal cures.

In the arid climate of much of Tibet, water takes on a special significance. The *lu* (or *naga*; water spirits) guard the wellbeing of the community and are thought to be very dangerous if angered.

TIBET'S ENDANGERED SPECIES

SPECIES	ESTIMATED WORLD POPULATION	ESTIMATED TIBETAN POPULATION	CURRENT STATUS
snow leopard *(gang-zig)*	6500	2000	endangered
Tibetan antelope *(chiru)*	75,000–150,000	75,000–150,000	endangered
white-lipped deer *(sha-wa chukar)*	7000	5000	endangered
dwarf blue sheep, or dwarf bharal *(nawa na)*	7000	7000	endangered
Tibetan blue bear *(dom gyamuk)*	a few hundred	a few hundred	endangered
wild yak *(drong)*	22,000	10,000	vulnerable
black-necked crane	11,000	7000	vulnerable
Tibetan gazelle *(gowa)*	100,000	100,000	near threatened
argali, or wild sheep	150,000	7000	near threatened
Tibetan wild ass *(kyang)*	60,000-70,000	50,000	least concern

FLORA OR FAUNA?

In early summer (May and June) you will see nomads and entrepreneurs camped in the high passes of eastern Tibet, digging for a strange root known as *yartsa gunbu (Cordiceps sinensis)* that locals say is half vegetable, half caterpillar. It is actually a fusion of a caterpillar and the parasitic fungus that mummifies it and then grows *Alien*-like out of the dead caterpillar's head. The Chinese name for the root is *dōngchóng xiàcǎo* (冬虫夏草; 'winter-worm, summer-grass'), a direct translation of the Tibetan name. Used by long-distance Chinese runners, it's also nicknamed 'Himalayan Viagra', and is highly prized in Tibetan and Chinese medicine as an aphrodisiac and tonic similar to ginseng.

Fetching around ¥20,000 (US$3200) per kilo, it's one of the most expensive commodities in Tibet and is fast being harvested to extinction. The business is most lucrative in Tengchen county, where amazingly it accounts for more than 60% of the local GDP. Entire tent villages spring up on the grasslands during harvest time, equipped with restaurants and shops, causing great environmental damage, and it's not unusual for literal turf wars to erupt between local communities and outside speculators. The economic boom in Tibet and China has caused *yartsa gunbu* fever to spread over the Himalayas, with the Himalayan gold rush revolutionising local economies as far away as Bhutan, Dolpo and Ladakh.

A Fragile Ecosystem

Tibet has an abundance of natural resources: many types of minerals, strong sunlight, fierce winds and raging rivers that supply water to the more than one billion people who live downstream.

The Tibetan Buddhist view of the environment has long stressed the intricate and interconnected relationship between the natural world and human beings. Buddhist practice in general stands for moderation and is against overconsumption, and tries to avoid wherever possible hunting, fishing and the taking of animal life. Tibetan nomads, in particular, have traditionally lived in a fine balance with their harsh environment.

Modern communist experiments, such as collectivisation and the changing of century-old farming patterns (for example, from barley to wheat and rice), upset the fragile balance in Tibet and resulted in a series of great disasters and famines in the 1960s (as, indeed, they did in the rest of China). By the mid-1970s, the failure of collectivisation was widely recognised and Tibetans have since been allowed to return to traditional methods of working the land.

The Tibetan plateau has rich deposits of gold, zinc, chromium, silver, boron, uranium and other metals. The plateau is home to most of China's huge copper reserves. A single mine in northern Tibet is said to hold over half the world's total deposits of lithium, while the Changtang holds five billion tonnes of oil and gas. Reports indicate mining now accounts for one-third of Tibet's industrial output. The Gyama Valley alone holds five million tons of copper, 135 tons of gold and 580,000 tons of zinc and lead. Mining has long been traditionally inimical to Tibetans, who believe it disturbs the sacred essence of the soil. The Chinese name for Tibet, Xīzàng – the Western Treasure House – now has a ring of prophetic irony.

Rapid modernisation threatens to bring industrial pollution, a hitherto almost unknown problem, onto the high plateau. Mass domestic tourism is also beginning to take its toll, with litter and unsustainable waste management a major problem in areas like Nam-tso and the Everest region.

Sustainable Energy

Tibet has abundant supplies of geothermal energy thanks to its turbulent geological history. The Yangpachen Geothermal Plant already supplies Lhasa with much of its electricity. Portable solar panelling has also

Sacred Animals

The mythical *sengye*, or snow lion, is one of Tibet's four sacred animals and acts as a mount for many Tibetan protector deities. The other three animals are the garuda (*khyung*), dragon (*druk*) and tiger (*dak*).

PROTECTING THE PLATEAU

Nature reserves officially protect over 20% of the Tibetan Autonomous Region (TAR), although many exist on paper only. The reserve with the highest profile is the Qomolangma National Park, a 34,000-sq-km protected area straddling the 'third pole' of the Everest region. The park promotes the involvement of the local population, which is essential as around 67,000 people live within the park.

Tibet's newest reserve is the Changtang Nature Reserve, set up in 1993 with the assistance of famous animal behaviourist George Schaller. At 247,120 sq km (larger than Arizona), this is the largest nature reserve in the world after Greenland National Park. Endangered species in the park include bharal, argali sheep, wolves, lynxes, gazelles, snow leopards, wild yaks, antelopes, brown bears and wild asses. In 2006 Chinese officials announced that since the formation of the reserve the number of antelopes had grown from 50,000 to 150,000, wild yaks had increased from 7000 to 10,000, and the number of *khyang* (wild ass) had risen from 30,000 to 50,000

Other protected areas include the Nam-tso National Park, the Great Canyon of the Yarlung Tsangpo Nature Reserve (formerly the Metok reserve) to the south of Namche Barwa, the Dzayul (Zayu) Reserve along the far southeast border with Assam, and the Kyirong and Nyalam Reserves near the Nepali border. Unfortunately, these reserves enjoy little protection or policing.

enjoyed some success; the plateau enjoys some of the longest and strongest sunlight outside the Saharan region. And experimental wind-power stations have been set up in northern Tibet.

But, much to the dismay of worried environmental groups worldwide, it's Tibet's enormous potential for hydroelectricity that has been the focus of the Chinese government in recent years. The undisputed heavyweight champion of dam building, China has 24 dams up and running on the Tibetan plateau and a further 76 in the pipeline. One particularly sensitive hydroelectric project has been draining water from sacred Yamdrok-tso for years now.

Plans to construct a so-called 'super-dam' (which could generate twice as much electricity as the Three Gorges Dam) on the Yarlung Tsangpo (Brahmaputra) in the remote southeast of Tibet still seem to be on the table, and have the Indians and Bangladeshis downstream deeply concerned. Five dams are currently under construction on the Yarlung Tsangpo further upstream near Gyatsa.

The Future

In the long term, climate change is expected to affect Tibet as much as the earth's low-lying regions. The rate of temperature rise in Tibet is around double the average global level. Of 680 glaciers monitored by Chinese scientists, 95% of them are shrinking, particularly in the south and east of the plateau. Chinese scientists believe that 40% of the plateau's glaciers could disappear by 2050 if current trends hold. Considering that the Tibetan plateau is the source of Asia's greatest rivers, and that more than one billion people live downstream, this is of profound importance to China and the Indian subcontinent.

For a damning look at the state of Tibet's environment, and China's epic plans for hydroelectricity projects on the plateau, read Michael Buckley's *Meltdown in Tibet* (2014).

In 2016 two glaciers in western Tibet collapsed within months of each other, creating a 320km/h avalanche of snow and ice that killed several villagers. The collapse has been blamed squarely on climate change.

The results of glacial melting are likely to include initial flooding and erosion, followed by a long-term drought that may turn Tibet into a desert wasteland and the rest of Asia into a region desperately searching for new supplies of water.

The People of Tibet

Tibetans have a unique identity that mixes influences from their Himalayan neighbours, extreme mountain environment and war-like past. In terms of language, script, food, temperament and above all religion, they are poles apart from their Han Chinese neighbours. Where the Chinese drink their tea green, Tibetans take theirs with yak butter; when the rest of China eats rice and drinks rice wine, Tibetans eat _tsampa_ (roasted-barley flour) washed down with barley beer.

Traditional Lifestyle

Tibetans are such a deeply religious people that a basic knowledge of Buddhism is essential in understanding their world view. Buddhism permeates most facets of Tibetan daily life and shapes aspirations in ways that are often quite alien to the Western frame of mind. The ideas of accumulating merit, of sending sons to be monks, of undertaking pilgrimages, and of devotion to the sanctity and power of natural places are all elements of the unique fusion between Buddhism and the older shamanistic Bön faith.

Traditionally there have been at least three distinct segments of Tibetan society: the _drokpa_ (nomads); _rongpa_ (farmers); and _sangha_ (communities of monks and nuns). All lead very different lives but share a deep faith in Buddhism.

These communities have traditionally shared a remarkable resistance to change. Until the early 20th century Tibet was a land in which virtually the only use for the wheel was as a device for activating mantras. Tibet has changed more in the past 50 years than in the previous 500, although many traditional social structures have endured Chinese attempts at iconoclasm.

Nomads' marriage customs differ from those of farming communities. When a child reaches a marriageable age, enquiries are made, and when a suitable match is found the two people meet and exchange gifts. If they like each other, these informal meetings may go on for some time. The date for a marriage is decided by an astrologer, and when the date arrives the family of the son rides to the camp of the prospective daughter-in-law to collect her. On arrival there is a custom of feigned mutual abuse that appears to verge on giving way to violence at any moment. This may continue for several days before the son's family finally carry off the daughter to their camp and she enters a new life.

Older country folk may stick out their tongue when they meet you, a very traditional form of respect that greeted the very first travellers to Tibet centuries ago.

GOOD GENES

In case you're wondering why your Tibetan guide can run up the side of a 4500m hill with ease, while you collapse gasping in the thin air after less than one minute, recent DNA research has shown that the Tibetan people are genetically adapted to living at high altitudes. In fact the 3000 years it took Tibetans to change their genes is considered the fastest genetic change ever observed in humans. You never stood a chance.

PILGRIM MAGNETS

In Tibet there are countless sacred destinations, ranging from lakes and mountains to monasteries and caves that once served as meditation retreats for important yogis. Specific pilgrimages are often prescribed for specific ills; certain mountains, for example, expiate certain sins. A circumambulation of Mt Kailash offers the possibility of liberation within three lifetimes, while a circuit of Lake Manasarovar can result in spontaneous buddhahood. Pilgrimage is also more powerful in certain auspicious months and years.

Pilgrims often organise themselves into large groups, hire a truck and travel around the country visiting all the major sacred places in one go. Pilgrim guidebooks have existed for centuries to help travellers interpret the 24 'power places' of Tibet. Such guides even specify locations where you can urinate or fart without offending local spirits (and probably your fellow pilgrims).

Making a pilgrimage is not just a matter of walking to a sacred place and then going home. There are a number of activities that help focus the concentration of the pilgrim. The act of kora (circumambulating the object of devotion) is chief among these. Circuits of three, 13 or 108 koras are especially auspicious, with sunrise and sunset the most auspicious hours. The particularly devout prostrate their way along entire pilgrimages, stepping forward the length of their body after each prostration and starting all over again. The hardcore even do their koras sideways, advancing one side-step at a time!

Most pilgrims make offerings during the course of a pilgrimage. *Kathaks* (white ceremonial scarves) are offered to lamas or holy statues as a token of respect (and then often returned by the lama as a blessing). Offerings of yak butter or oil, fruit, *tsampa*, seeds and money are all left at altars, and bottles of *chang* (barley beer) and rice wine are donated to protector chapels.

Outside chapels, at holy mountain peaks, passes and bridges, you will see pilgrims throwing offerings of *tsampa* or printed prayers into the air. Pilgrims also collect sacred rocks, herbs, earth and water from a holy site to take back home to those who couldn't make the pilgrimage, and leave behind personal items as a break from the past, often leaving them hanging in a tree. Other activities in this spiritual assault course include adding stones to cairns, rubbing special healing rocks, and squeezing through narrow gaps in rocks as a method of sin detection.

Koras usually include stops that are of particular spiritual significance, such as rock-carved syllables or painted buddha images. Many of these carvings are said to be *rangjung* ('self-rising'), meaning that they haven't been carved by a human hand. The Mt Kailash kora is a treasure trove of these, encompassing sky-burial sites, stones that have 'flown' from India, monasteries, bodhisattva footprints and even a *lingham* (phallic image).

Other pilgrimages are carried out to visit a renowned holy man or teacher. Blessings or *tsering rilbu* (long-life pills) from holy men, *trulkus* (reincarnated lamas) or *rinpoche*s (highly esteemed lamas) are particularly valued, as are the possessions of famous holy men. According to Keith Dowman in his book *The Sacred Life of Tibet,* the underpants of one revered lama were cut up and then distributed amongst his eager followers!

Pilgrimage sites:

Mountains	Lakes	Caves
Mt Kailash, western Tibet	Manasarovar, western Tibet	Drak Yerpa, outside Lhasa
Bönri, eastern Tibet	Nam-tso, northern Ü	Chim-puk, near Samye
Tsari, southern Tibet	Yamdrok-tso, Tsang	Sheldrak, Yarlung Valley
Mt Labchi, east of Nyalam	Lhamo La-tso, eastern Ü	Drakyul, Yarlung Tsangpo Valley

Tibet's traditional nomadic lifestyle is particularly under threat. According to some estimates, over one million nomads or herders across the Tibetan plateau have been moved off their land by local government, often under the guise of environmental protection. Critics accuse the government of making a massive land grab in order to gain access to rare minerals for mining. Either way, the result is a serious blow to an ancient lifestyle that has thrived in harmony with the environment for generations.

As in most societies, there is some generational divide among Tibetans. The younger generation (in Lhasa and the main towns at least) is as enamoured with pop music, karaoke, mobile phones and the internet as most young people around the world and most know little about 'old' Tibet, having often grown up in a Chinese-language environment. That said, young Tibetans still have a remarkably strong sense of Tibetan identity and you'll still see many young Tibetans visiting monasteries, wearing traditional dress and making pilgrimages to holy sites.

Farming & Trading

Farming communities in Tibet usually comprise a cluster of homes surrounded by agricultural lands that were once owned by the nearest large monastery and protected by a *dzong* (fort). The farming itself is carried out with the assistance of a dzo, a breed of cattle where bulls have been crossbred with yaks. Some wealthier farmers own a small 'walking tractor' (a very simple tractor engine that can pull a plough or a trailer). Harvested grain is carried by donkeys to a threshing ground where it is trampled by cattle or threshed with poles. The grain is then cast into the air from a basket and the task of winnowing carried out by the breeze. Animal husbandry is still extremely important in Tibet, and there are around 21 million head of livestock in the country.

Until recently these communities were effectively self-sufficient in their needs and, although theirs was a hard life, it could not be described as abject poverty. Plots of land were usually graded in terms of quality and then distributed so that the land of any one family included both better- and poorer-quality land. This is changing rapidly as many regions become more economically developed.

Imports such as tea, porcelain, copper and iron from China were traditionally exchanged for exports of wool and skins. Trading was usually carried out by nomads or in combination with pilgrimage. Most villages now have at least one entrepreneur who has set up a shop and begun to ship in Chinese goods from the nearest urban centre.

One significant change to rural life has been the government-sponsored construction of over 230,000 new houses across Tibet, providing new housing for some 1.3 million Tibetan farmers and herders. Families are given around ¥10,000 to ¥15,000 as a base subsidy to construct a home. A typical house might cost around ¥33,000 to ¥44,000 so farmers usually take out a loan (interest-free for three years) to cover the remaining costs. Critics of the scheme claim that many of the new homeowners then have to rent out their farmland to Chinese immigrants in order to pay off the loans.

Individual households normally have a shrine in the home and some religious texts, held in a place of honour, which are reserved for occasions when a monk or holy man visits the village. Ceremonies for blessing yaks and other livestock to ensure a productive year are still held. One of the highlights of the year for rural Tibetans is visiting nearby monasteries at festival times or making a pilgrimage to a holy site.

As traditional life reasserts itself after 60 years of communist dogma and the disastrous Cultural Revolution, many of these traditions are slowly making a comeback.

Torma (or *towa*) are small offerings made of yak butter and *tsampa* adorned with coloured medallions of butter. They probably developed as a Buddhist substitute for animal sacrifice. Most are made during the Shōtun festival and remain on display throughout the year.

Pilgrimage

Pilgrimage is practised throughout the world, although as a devotional exercise it has been raised to a level of particular importance in Tibet. This may be because of the nomadic element in Tibetan society; it may also be that in a mountainous country with no roads and no wheeled vehicles, walking long distances became a fact of life, and by visiting sacred places en route pilgrims could combine walking with accumulating merit. To most Tibetans their natural landscape is imbued with a series of sacred visions and holy 'power places': mountains can be perceived as mandala images, rocks assume spiritual dimensions and the earth is imbued with healing powers.

The motivations for pilgrimage are many, but for the ordinary Tibetan it amounts to a means of accumulating *sonam* (merit) or *tashi* (good fortune). The lay practitioner might go on pilgrimage in the hope of winning a better rebirth, to cure an illness, end a spate of bad luck or as thanks for an answered prayer.

Death

Although the early kings of Tibet were buried in tomb mounds with complex funerary rites (the tombs are still visible in Chongye), ordinary Tibetans have not traditionally been buried. The dead bodies of the very poor were usually dumped in a river and the bodies of the very holy were cremated and their ashes enshrined in a chörten (or their bodies dried in salt). But in a land where soil is at a premium and wood for cremation is scarcer still, most bodies were, and still are, disposed of by sky burial.

After death, the body is kept for 24 hours in a sitting position while a lama recites prayers from *The Tibetan Book of the Dead* to help the soul on its journey through the 49 levels of Bardo, the state between death and rebirth. Three days after death, the body is blessed and early-morning prayers and offerings are made to the monastery. The body is folded up (the spine is broken and the body itself is folded into a surprisingly small package) and carried on the back of a close friend to the *dürtro* (burial site). Here, special body-breakers known as *rogyapas* cut off the deceased's hair, chop up the body and pound the bones together with *tsampa* for vultures to eat.

There is little overt sadness at a sky burial: the soul is considered to have already departed and the burial itself is considered to be mere disposal, or rather a final act of compassion to the birds. Sky burial is, however, very much a time to reflect on the impermanence of life. Death is seen as a powerful agent of transformation and spiritual progress. Tibetans are encouraged to witness the disposal of the body and to confront death openly and without fear. This is one reason that Tantric ritual objects such as trumpets and bowls are often made from human bone.

Dress

Traditional dress is still the norm among TIbetans in the countryside. The Tibetan national dress is a *chuba* (long-sleeved sheepskin cloak), tied around the waist with a sash and worn off the shoulder with great bravado by nomads and Khampas (people from Kham). An inner pouch is often used to store money belts, amulets, lunch and even small livestock. Most women wear a long dress, topped with a colourful striped

> Tibetan babies are considered to be one year old at the time of birth, since reincarnation took place nine months previously upon conception.

TOURISTS & SKY BURIAL

Sky burials are funeral services and, naturally, Tibetans are often very unhappy about camera-toting foreigners heading up to sky-burial sites. The Chinese authorities do not like it either and may fine foreigners who attend a burial. You should never pay to see a sky burial and you should *never* take photos. Even if Tibetans offer to take you up to a sky-burial site, it is unlikely that other Tibetans present will be very happy about it. As tempting as it may be, if nobody has invited you, don't go.

Ethnic Tibetan Regions of China (Greater Tibet)

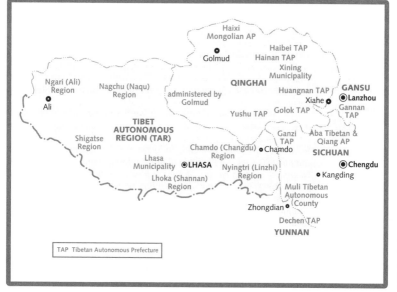

apron known as a *pangden*. Traditional Tibetan boots have turned-up toes, so as to kill fewer bugs when walking (or so it is said).

Women generally set great store in jewellery and invest their personal wealth and dowry in it. Coral is particularly valued (as Tibet is so far from the sea), as are Baltic amber, Indian ivory, Afghan turquoise and silver of all kinds. The Tibetan *zee,* a unique elongated agate stone with black and white markings, is highly prized for its protective qualities and can fetch tens of thousands of US dollars. Earrings are common in both men and women and they are normally tied on with a piece of cord. You'll see Tibetans shopping for all these goodies around the Barkhor in Lhasa.

Tibetan women, especially those from Amdo (northeastern Tibet and Qīnghǎi), wear their hair in 108 braids, an auspicious number in Buddhism. Khampa men plait their hair with red or black tassels and wind the lot around their head. Cowboy hats are popular in summer and fur hats are common in winter. Most pilgrims carry a *thogcha* (good luck charm) or *gau* (amulet), with perhaps a picture of the owner's personal deity or the Dalai Lama inside.

The Politics of People

Modern political boundaries and history have led to the fracture of the Tibetan nation. Large areas of historical and ethnic Tibet are now incorporated into the Chinese provinces of Qīnghǎi and Gānsù (traditionally known as Amdo), and Sìchuān and Yúnnán (traditionally known as Kham). More Tibetans now live outside the Tibetan Autonomous Region (TAR) than inside it.

Population Control

Population control is a cornerstone of Chinese government policy, but the regulations are generally less strictly enforced in Tibet. 'Minority nationalities' such as the Tibetans are allowed two children before they

Tibetans are often named after the day of week they were born on; thus you'll meet Nyima (Sunday), Dawa (Monday), Mingmar (Tuesday), Lhakpa (Wednesday), Phurba (Thursday), Pasang (Friday) and Pemba (Saturday). Popular names such as Sonam (merit) and Tashi (good fortune) carry religious connotations.

lose certain stipends and housing allowances. Ironically, the most effective form of birth control in modern Tibet still seems to be to join a monastery.

Ethnic Groups

There are considerable variations between regional groups of Tibetans. The most recognisable are the Khampas of eastern Tibet, who are generally larger and a bit more rough-and-ready than other Tibetans and who wear red or black tassels in their long hair. Women from Amdo are especially conspicuous because of their elaborate braided hairstyles and jewellery.

From Ütsang (central Tibet) comes the best religion, from Amdo the best horses, from Kham the best men.

Traditional Tibetan Saying

The people of Kongpo in eastern Tibet have a distinctive traditional dress that features a round hat with an upturned rim of golden brocade for men (known as a *gyasha*) and a pretty pillbox hat with winged edges for women. Men and women wear brown woollen tunics, belted around the waist. The former kingdom of Kongpo has for centuries been vilified by central Tibetan rulers as a land of incest and poison, whose inhabitants would routinely drug unsuspecting strangers to steal their souls.

There are pockets of other minority groups, such as the Lhopa (Lhoba) and Monpa in the southeast of Tibet, but these make up less than 1% of the total population and only very remote pockets remain. A more visible ethnic group are the Hui Muslims. Tibet's original Muslim inhabitants were largely traders or butchers (a profession that most Buddhists abhor), although the majority of recent migrants are traders and restaurant owners from southern Gānsù province. Tibetans are also closely related

RESPONSIBLE TOURISM

Tourism has already affected many areas in Tibet. Most children will automatically stick their hand out for a sweet, a pen or anything. In some regions, locals have become frustrated at seeing a stream of rich tourist groups but few tangible economic results. Please try to bear the following in mind as you travel through Tibet:

➡ Try to patronise as many small local Tibetan businesses (including your tour agent), restaurants and guesthouses as possible. Revenues created by organised group tourism go largely into the pockets of the Chinese authorities.

➡ Doling out medicines can encourage people not to seek proper medical advice, while handing out sweets or pens to children encourages begging. If you wish to contribute something constructive, it's better to give pens directly to schools and medicines to rural clinics, or make a donation to an established charity.

➡ Monastery admission fees go largely to local authorities, so if you want to donate to the monastery, leave your offering on the altar.

➡ Don't buy skins or hats made from endangered animals such as snow leopards.

➡ Don't pay to take a photograph of someone, and don't photograph someone if they don't want you to. If you agree to send a photograph of someone, ensure you follow through on this.

➡ If you have any pro-Tibetan sympathies, be very careful with whom you discuss them. Don't put Tibetans in a politically difficult or even potentially dangerous situation. This includes handing out photos of the Dalai Lama (these are illegal in Tibet) and politically sensitive materials.

➡ Try to buy locally made souvenirs and handicrafts, especially authentic and traditionally made products whose profits go directly to artisans, such as Dropenling (p80).

➡ If you have a guide, try to ensure that he or she is a Tibetan, as Chinese guides invariably know little about Tibetan Buddhism or monastery history.

to the Qiang people of northern Sìchuān, the Sherpas of Nepal and the
Ladakhis of India.

Han Migration

Official statistics claim 93% of the TAR's population is Tibetan, a figure
that is hotly contested by almost everyone except the government. Chinese figures for the population of Lhasa, for example, suggest it is just
over 87% Tibetan and just under 12% Han Chinese, a ratio that stretches
the credulity of anyone who has visited the city in recent years. It is more
likely that well over 50% of Lhasa's population is Han Chinese.

The current flood of Chinese immigrants into Tibet has been termed
China's 'second invasion'. The Chinese government is very coy about releasing figures that would make it clear just how many Chinese there
are in Tibet, but for visitors who have made repeated trips to Tibet the
increased numbers of Han Chinese are undeniable.

Perhaps unsurprisingly, there's an endemic mistrust between the Tibetans and Chinese and ethnic tensions bubble just under the surface.
Many Tibetans see the Han Chinese as land-hungry outsiders, while
the Chinese often complain that the Tibetans are ungrateful and slow
to adjust to economic opportunities. Actual violence between the two
communities is rare, but it's quickly apparent to visitors that most towns
have quite separate Chinese and Tibetan (and in some cases also Hui
Muslim) quarters.

Women in Tibet

Women have traditionally occupied a strong position in Tibetan society,
often holding the family purse strings and running businesses like shops
and guesthouses. Several of Tibet's most famous Buddhist practitioners,
such as Yeshe Tsogyel and Machik Labdronma, were women, and Tibet's
nuns remain at the vanguard of political dissent. Most of the road workers you see across the plateau are women!

Up until the Chinese invasion many Tibetan farming villages practised
polyandry. When a woman married the eldest son of a family she also
married his younger brothers (providing they did not become monks).
The children of such marriages referred to all the brothers as their father. The practice was aimed at easing the inheritance of family property
(mainly the farming land) and avoiding the break-up of small plots.

Tibetans often
gesture with their
lips to indicate
a direction, so
if a member of
the opposite sex
pouts at you, they
are just showing
you where to go.
If a road worker
starts blowing
you kisses, he
probably just
wants a cigarette.
Or maybe he's
just blowing you
kisses...

THE PEOPLE OF TIBET WOMEN IN TIBET

Tibetan Buddhism

A basic understanding of Buddhism is essential to getting beneath the skin of things in Tibet. Exploring the monasteries and temples of Tibet and mixing with its people, yet knowing nothing of Buddhism, is like visiting the Vatican and knowing nothing of Roman Catholicism. To be sure, it's an awe-inspiring experience, but much will remain hidden and indecipherable. A little studying here will give you a far deeper connection to Tibet and its people.

The Roots of Religion in Tibet

For those who already know something of Zen Buddhism, Tibet can seem baffling. The grandeur of the temples, the worship of images and the bloodthirsty protective deities that stand in doorways all seem to belie the basic tenets of an ascetic faith that is basically about renouncing the self and following a path of moderation.

One reason for this is that in Tibet the establishment of Buddhism was heavily marked by its interaction with the native religion Bön. This animist or shamanistic faith – which encompassed gods and spirits, exorcism, spells, talismans, ritual drumming, sacrifices and the cult of dead kings, among other things – had a major influence on the direction Buddhism took in Tibet. Many popular Buddhist symbols and practices, such as prayer flags, sky burial, the rubbing of holy rocks, the tying of bits of cloth to trees and the construction of spirit traps, all have their roots deep in Bön tradition.

Tibetan Buddhism's interaction with both Bön spirit worship and the Hindu pantheon, as well as Tibet's affinity for the Tantric side of Buddhist thought, has resulted in a huge range of deities, both wrathful and benign. Grafted onto these have been the scholastic tradition of the Indian Buddhist universities and the ascetic, meditative traditions of the Himalayan religion. Yet for all its confusing iconography and philosophy, the basic tenets of Buddhism are very much rooted in daily experience. Even high lamas and monks come across as surprisingly down-to-earth.

FOLK RELIGION

Closely linked to both Bön and Buddhism is the folk religion of Tibet, known as *mi chös* (the dharma of man), which is primarily concerned with the appeasement of spirits. These spirits include *nyen,* which reside in rocks and trees; *lu* or *naga,* snake-bodied spirits, which live at the bottom of lakes, rivers and wells; *sadok,* lords of the earth, which are connected with agriculture; *tsen,* air or mountain spirits, which shoot arrows of illness and death at humans; and *dud,* demons linked to the Buddhist demon Mara. Into this stew are thrown the spirits of the hearth, roof and kitchen that inhabit every Tibetan house, and a collection of local deities, border gods and pilgrimage site protectors. Like most Himalayan people, the religious beliefs of the average Tibetan are a fascinating melange of Buddhism, Bön and folk religion.

WHEEL OF LIFE

The Wheel of Life (Sipa Khorlo in Tibetan), depicted in the entryway to most monasteries, is an aid to realising the delusion of the mind. It's a complex pictorial representation of how desire chains us to samsara, the endless cycle of birth, death and rebirth.

The wheel is held in the mouth of Yama, the Lord of Death. The inner circle of interdependent desire shows a cockerel (representing desire or attachment) biting a pig (ignorance or delusion) biting a snake (hatred or anger). A second ring is divided into figures ascending through the realms on the left and descending on the right.

The six inner sectors of the wheel symbolise the six realms of rebirth: gods, battling demigods and humans (the upper realms); and hungry ghosts, hell and animals (the lower realms). All beings are reborn through this cycle dependent upon their karma. The Buddha is depicted outside the wheel, symbolising his release into a state of nirvana.

At the bottom of the wheel are hot and cold hells, where Yama holds a mirror that reflects one's lifetime. A demon to the side holds a scale with black and white pebbles, weighing up the good and bad deeds of one's lifetime.

The *pretas,* or hungry spirits, are recognisable by their huge stomachs, thin needle-like necks and tiny mouths, which cause them insatiable hunger and thirst. In each realm the Buddha attempts to convey his teachings (the dharma), offering hope to each realm.

The 12 outer segments depict the so-called '12 links of dependent origination', and the 12 interlinked, codependent and causal experiences of life that perpetuate the cycle of samsara. The 12 images (whose order may vary) are of a blind woman (representing ignorance), a potter (unconscious will), a monkey (consciousness), men in a boat (self-consciousness), a house (the five senses), lovers (contact), a man with an arrow in his eye (feeling), a drinking scene (desire), a figure grasping fruit from a tree (attachment), pregnancy, birth and death (a man carrying a corpse to a sky burial).

The Buddha

Buddhism originated in the northeast of India around the 5th century BC, at a time when the local religion was Brahmanism. Some Brahman, in preparation for presiding over offerings to their gods, partook of an asceticism that transported them to remote places where they fasted, meditated and practised yogic techniques.

Many of the fundamental concepts of Buddhism find their origin in the Brahman society of this time. The Buddha (c 480–400 BC), born Siddhartha Gautama, was one of many wandering ascetics whose teachings led to the establishment of rival religious schools. Jainism was one of these schools; Buddhism was another.

Little is known about the life of Siddhartha. It was probably not until some 200 years after his death that biographies were compiled, and by that time many of the circumstances of his life had merged with legend. It is known that he was born in Lumbini (modern-day Nepal) of a noble family and that he married and had a son before renouncing a life of privilege and embarking on a quest to make sense of the suffering in the world.

After studying with many of the masters of his day he embarked on a course of intense asceticism, before concluding that such a path was too extreme. Finally, in the place that is now known as Bodhgaya in India, Siddhartha meditated beneath a *bo* (pipal) tree. At the break of dawn at the end of his third night of meditation he became a buddha (awakened one).

You'll see many famous stories from Buddha's life painted on monastery murals, from his birth (his mother Maya is depicted holding on to a tree) and his first seven steps (lotus flowers sprouted from the ground) to his skeletal ascetic phase and temptation by the demon Mara.

Whether hand-held or building-sized, prayer wheels are always filled with prayers which are 'activated' with each revolution of the wheel. Pilgrims spin the wheels to gain merit and to concentrate the mind on the mantras they are reciting.

Buddhist Concepts

Buddhism's early teachings are based on the insights of the Buddha, known in Mahayana tradition as Sakyamuni (Sakya Thukpa in Tibetan), and form the basis of all further Buddhist thought. Buddhism is not based on any revealed prophecy or divine revelation but rather is firmly rooted in human experience. The later Mahayana school (to which Tibetan Buddhism belongs) diverged from these early teachings in some respects, but not in its fundamentals.

The Buddha commenced his teachings by explaining that there was a Middle Way that steered a course between sensual indulgence and ascetic self-torment – a way of moderation rather than renunciation. This Middle Way could be pursued by following the Noble Eightfold Path. The philosophical underpinnings of this path were the Four Noble Truths, which addressed the problems of karma and rebirth. These basic concepts are the kernel of early Buddhist thought.

In modern terms, Buddhist thought stresses nonviolence, compassion, equanimity (evenness of mind), mindfulness (awareness of the present moment) and non-attachment.

The Dharma Wheel (chokyi khorlo) symbolises the Buddha's first sermon at Sarnath. The eight spokes recall the Eightfold Path. The wheel was the earliest symbol of Buddhism, used for centuries before images of the Buddha became popular.

Rebirth

Life is a cycle of endless rebirths. The Sanskrit word 'samsara' (Tibetan: khorwa), literally 'wandering on', is used to describe this cycle, and life is seen as wandering on limitlessly through time, and through the birth, extinction and rebirth of galaxies and worlds. There are six levels of rebirth or realms of existence, as depicted in the Wheel of Life. It is important to accumulate enough merit to avoid the three lower realms, although in the long cycle of rebirth, all beings pass through them at some point. All beings are fated to tread this wheel continuously until they make a commitment to enlightenment.

RELIGIOUS FREEDOM IN TIBET

Religious freedoms in Tibet have certainly increased since the 1980s, though any form of nationalist or political protest is still quickly crushed. Monks and nuns, who have traditionally been at the vanguard of protests and Tibetan aspirations for independence, are regarded with particular suspicion by the authorities. The demonstrations of 2008 were initially led by monks from Sera, Drepung and Ramoche Monasteries and turned to riots after police beat a line of monks from the Ramoche Temple. Nuns, in particular, considering their small numbers, have been very politically active, accounting for 55 of the 126 independence protests in the mid-1990s. Regulations make it impossible for nuns, once arrested and imprisoned, to return to their nunneries.

Political indoctrination or 'patriotic education' teams are frequent visitors to (or residents in) most monasteries, as are the recurring campaigns to denounce the Dalai Lama. Images of the current Dalai Lama are illegal, which is why you'll see pictures of the 13th Dalai Lama on most monastery thrones, as a symbolic stand-in. Since 2008 most monasteries now have a police station or army post on site and the numbers of resident monks are strictly controlled. The friendly orange-clad Chinese fire prevention teams you may see in larger monasteries are actually there to keep an eye on the monks, not potential arsonists. While many monasteries now gleam after million-dollar renovations and are bustling with monks and tourists, the authorities are also there in the background, keeping an eye open for the first sign of dissent.

According to the US government's 2016 International Religious Freedom Report, across Tibet 'there were reports of forced disappearance, physical abuse, prolonged detention, and arbitrary arrest of people due to their religious practice, as well as forced expulsions from monasteries, restrictions on religious gatherings, and destruction of monastery related dwellings.'

Karma

All beings pass through the same cycle of rebirths. Their enemy may once have been their mother, and like all beings they have lived as an insect and as a god, and suffered in one of the hell realms. Movement within this cycle, though, is not haphazard. It is governed by karma.

Karma (Tibetan: *las*) is a slippery concept. It is sometimes translated simply as 'action', but it also implies the consequences of action. Karma might be thought of as an overarching condition of life. Every action in life leaves a psychic trace that carries over into the next rebirth. It should not be thought of as a reward or punishment, but simply as a result. In Buddhist thought karma is frequently likened to a seed that ripens into a fruit: thus a human reborn as an insect is harvesting the fruits of a previous immoral existence.

Merit

Given that karma is a kind of accumulated psychic baggage that we must lug through countless rebirths, it is the aim of all practising Buddhists to try to accumulate as much 'good karma' – merit – as possible. Merit is best achieved through the act of rejoicing in giving. The giving of alms to the needy and to monks, the relinquishing of a son to monkhood, and acts of compassion and understanding are all meritorious and have a positive karmic outcome.

The Four Noble Truths

If belief in rebirth, karma and merit are the basis of lay-followers' faith in Buddhism, the Four Noble Truths (Tibetan: *phakpay denpa shi*) might be thought of as its philosophical underpinning.

Dukkha (Suffering)

The first of the Four Noble Truths, *dukkha*, is that life is suffering. This suffering extends through all the countless rebirths of beings, and finds its origin in the imperfection of life. Every rebirth brings with it the pain of birth, the pain of ageing, the pain of death, the pain of association with unpleasant things, the loss of things we are attached to and the failure to achieve the things we desire.

Tanha (Desire)

The reason for this suffering is the second Noble Truth, *tanha*, and lies in our dissatisfaction with imperfection, in our desire for things to be other than they are. What is more, this dissatisfaction leads to actions and karmic consequences that prolong the cycle of rebirths and may lead to even more suffering, much like a mouse running endlessly in a wheel.

Nibbana (Cessation of Desire)

Known in English as nirvana, *nibbana* (Tibetan: *namtrol*) is the cessation of all desire; an end to attachment. With the cessation of desire comes an end to suffering, the achievement of complete nonattachment and an end to the cycle of rebirth. Nirvana is the ultimate goal of Buddhism. Nitpickers might point out that the will to achieve nirvana is a desire in itself. Buddhists answer that this desire is tolerated as a useful means to an end, but it is only when this desire, too, is extinguished that nirvana is truly achieved.

Noble Eightfold Path

The fourth of the Noble Truths prescribes a course that for the lay practitioner will lead to the accumulation of merit, and for the serious devotee may lead to nirvana. The components of this path are (1) right

If you see a collection of spider-web-like coloured threads woven around a wooden frame, this a *dzoe*, or spirit-trap, designed to catch and then get rid of troublesome evil spirits.

The Ten Meritorious Deeds in Buddhism are to refrain from killing, stealing, inappropriate sexual activity, lying, gossiping, cursing, sowing discord, envy, malice and opinionatedness.

Prayer flags are strung up to purify the air and pacify the mountain gods. All feature a *longta*, or windhorse, which carries the prayers up into the heavens. The colours are highly symbolic – red, green, yellow, blue and white represent fire, wood, earth, water and iron.

TIBETAN BUDDHISM BUDDHIST CONCEPTS

understanding, (2) right thought, (3) right speech, (4) right action, (5) right livelihood, (6) right effort, (7) right mindfulness and (8) right concentration. Needless to say, each of these has a 'wrong' corollary.

Schools of Buddhism

Not long after the death of Sakyamuni, disagreements began to arise among his followers – as they tend to do in all religious movements – over whose interpretations best captured the true spirit of his teachings. The result was the development of numerous schools of thought and, eventually, a schism that saw the emergence of two principal schools: Hinayana and Mahayana.

Hinayana, also known as Theravada, encouraged scholasticism and close attention to what were considered the original teachings of Sakyamuni. Mahayana, on the other hand, with its elevation of compassion *(nyingje)* as an all-important idea, took Buddhism in a new direction. It was the Mahayana school that made its way up to the high plateau and took root there, at the same time travelling to China, Korea and Japan. Hinayana retreated into southern India and took root in Sri Lanka and Thailand.

Buddhism is perhaps the most tolerant of the world's religions. Wherever it has gone it has adapted to local conditions, like a dividing cell, creating countless new schools of thought. Its basic tenets have remained very much the same and all schools are bound together in their faith in the original teachings of Sakyamuni (Sakya Thukpa), the Historical Buddha. The Chinese invasion has ironically caused a flowering of Tibetan Buddhism abroad and you can now find Tibetan monasteries around the world.

Mahayana

The claims that Mahayanists made for their faith were many, but the central issue was a change in orientation from individual pursuit of enlightenment to bodhisattvahood. Rather than striving for complete non-attachment, the bodhisattva aims, through compassion and self-sacrifice, to achieve enlightenment for the sake of all beings.

In the meantime, Sakyamuni slowly began to change shape. Mahayanists maintained that Sakyamuni had already attained buddhahood many aeons ago and that there were now many such transcendent beings living in heavens or 'pure lands'. The revolutionary concept had the effect of producing a pantheon of bodhisattvas, a feature that made Mahayana more palatable to cultures that already had gods of their own. In Tibet, China, Korea and Japan, the Mahayana pantheon came to be identified with local gods as their Mahayana equivalents replaced them.

Tantrism (Vajrayana)

A further Mahayana development that is particularly relevant to Tibet is Tantrism. The words of Sakyamuni were recorded in sutras and studied by students of both Hinayana and Mahayana, but according to the followers of Tantrism, a school that emerged from around AD 600, Sakyamuni left a corpus of esoteric instructions to a select few of his disciples. These were known as Tantra *(Gyü).*

Tantric adepts claimed that through the use of unconventional techniques they could jolt themselves towards enlightenment, and shorten the long road to bodhisattvahood. The process involved identification with a tutelary deity invoked through deep meditation and recitation of the deity's mantra. The most famous of these mantras is the *'Om mani padme hum'* ('hail to the jewel in the lotus') mantra of Chenresig (Avalokiteshvara). Tantric practice also employs Indian yogic techniques to channel energy towards the transformation to enlightenment. Such yogic techniques might even include sexual practices. Tantric techniques are rarely written down, but rather are passed down verbally from tutor to student, increasing their secret allure.

From ritual thigh bones and skull cups to images of deities in *yab-yum* sexual union, many of the ritual objects and images in Tibetan monasteries are Tantric in nature. Together they show the many facets of enlightenment – at times kindly, at times wrathful.

Buddhism in Tibet

The story of the introduction of Buddhism to Tibet is attended by legends of the taming of local gods and spirits and their conversion to Buddhism as protective deities. This magnificent array of buddhas, bodhisattvas and sages occupies a mythical world in the Tibetan imagination. Chenresig is perhaps chief among them, manifesting himself in the early Tibetan kings and later the Dalai Lamas. Guru Rinpoche, the Indian sage and Tantric magician who bound the native spirits and gods of Tibet into the service of Buddhism, is another, and there are countless others, including saints and protector gods. While the clerical side of Buddhism concerns itself largely with textual study and analysis, the Tantric shamanistic-based side seeks revelation through identification with these deified beings and through their *terma* ('revealed' words or writings).

It is useful to consider the various schools of Tibetan Buddhism as revealing something of a struggle between these two orientations: shamanism and clericalism. Each school finds its own resolution to the problem. In the case of the last major school to arise, the Gelugpa order, there was a search for a return to the doctrinal purity of clerical Buddhism. But even here, the Tantric forms were not completely discarded; it was merely felt that many years of scholarly work and preparation should precede the more esoteric Tantric practices.

The clerical and shamanistic traditions can also be explained as the difference between state-sponsored and popular Buddhism, respectively. There was always a tendency for the state to emphasise monastic Buddhism, with its communities of rule-abiding monks. Popular Buddhism, on the other hand, with its long-haired, wild-eyed ascetic recluses capable of performing great feats of magic, had a great appeal to the ordinary people of Tibet, for whom ghosts, demons and sorcerers were a daily reality.

Nyingmapa Order

➡ **Main Monasteries** Mindroling (p126), Dorje Drak (p113)

➡ **Also known as** Red Hats

The Nyingmapa order is the Old School, and traces its origins back to the teachings and practices of the 8th- or 9th-century Indian master Guru Rinpoche. Over the centuries the Nyingmapa failed to develop as a powerful, centralised school, and for the most part prospered in villages throughout rural Tibet, where it was administered by local shamanlike figures.

The Nyingma school was revitalised through the 'discovery' of hidden texts in the 'power places' of Tibet visited by Guru Rinpoche. In many cases these *terma* (revealed texts) were discovered through yogic-inspired visions by spiritually advanced Nyingmapa practitioners, rather than found under a pile of rocks or in a cave. Out of these *terma* arose the Dzogchen (Great Perfection) teachings, an appealing Tantric short cut to nirvana that teaches that enlightenment can come in a single lifetime. Today the Nyingmapa have a particularly strong presence in western Sìchuān.

The Buddhist parable of the Four Harmonious Brothers is painted on walls at the entrance to many monasteries. The image is of a bird picking a tree-top fruit, while standing atop a hare, who is atop a monkey, who is atop an elephant, symbolising cooperation and harmony with the environment.

The *dorje* (thunderbolt) and *drilbu* (bell) are ritual objects symbolising male and female aspects used in Tantric rites. They are held in the right and left hands respectively. The indestructible thunderbolt cuts through ignorance.

EIGHT AUSPICIOUS SYMBOLS

The Eight Auspicious Symbols *(tashi targyel)* are associated with gifts made to Sakyamuni (Sakya Thukpa) upon his enlightenment and appear as protective motifs across Tibet.

Knot of eternity Representing the entwined, never-ending passage of time, harmony and love and the unity of all things, the knot of eternity is commonly seen on embroidery and tents.

Lotus flower The lotus flower, or *padma*, stands for the purity and compassion of Sakyamuni and has become a symbol of Buddhism.

Pair of golden fishes Shown leaping from the waters of captivity, they represent liberation from the Wheel of Life (for years they were the logo of Lhasa Beer!).

Precious umbrella Usually placed over buddha images to protect them from evil influences, the precious umbrella is a common Buddhist motif also seen in Thailand and Japan.

Vase of treasure The vase is a sacred repository of the jewels of enlightenment or the water of eternity.

Victory banner Heralding the triumph of Buddhist wisdom over ignorance.

Wheel of Law Representing the Noble Eightfold Path to salvation, the wheel is also referred to as the Wheel of Dharma. The wheel turns 12 times, three times for each of the Four Noble Truths.

White conch shell Blown in celebration of the enlightenment of Sakyamuni and the potential of all beings to be awakened by the sound of dharma, the shell is often used to signal prayer time.

Knot of eternity

Lotus flower

Pair of golden fishes

Kagyupa Order

➡ **Main Monastery** Tsurphu (p102)

➡ **Sub-schools** Drigungpa, Drigung Til Monastery (p112); Taglungpa, Taklung (p111); Drukpa, Ralung (p135); Karma Kagyu, Tsurphu (p102)

➡ **Founder** Milarepa

➡ **Also known as** Black Hats

This resurgence of Buddhist influence in the 11th century led many Tibetans to India to study. The new ideas they brought back with them had a revitalising effect on Tibetan thought and produced other new schools of Tibetan Buddhism. Among them was the Kagyupa order, established by Milarepa (1040–1123), who was the disciple of Marpa the translator (1012–93).

The establishment of monasteries eventually overshadowed the ascetic-yogi origins of the Kagyupa. The yogi tradition did not die out completely, however, and Kagyupa monasteries also became important centres for synthesising the clerical and shamanistic orientations of Tibetan Buddhism.

In time, several suborders of the Kagyupa sprang up, the most prominent of which was the Karma Kagyupa, also known as the Karmapa. The practice of reincarnation originated with this suborder, when the abbot of Tsurphu Monastery, Dusum Khyenpa (1110–93), announced that he would be reincarnated as his own successor. The 16th Karmapa died in 1981, and his disputed successor fled to India in 1999.

Sakyapa Order

➡ **Main Monasteries** Sakya (p150)

➡ **Sub-schools** Tsarpa, Ngorpa

➡ **Founder** Kongchog Gyelpo

From the 11th century many Tibetan monasteries became centres for the textual study and translation of Indian Buddhist texts. One of the earliest major figures in this movement was Kunga Gyaltsen (1182–1251), known as Sakya Pandita (literally 'scholar from Sakya').

Sakya Pandita's renown as a scholar led to him, and subsequent abbots of Sakya, being recognised as a manifestation of Jampelyang (Manjushri), the Bodhisattva of Insight. Sakya Pandita travelled to the Mongolian court in China, with the result that his heir became the spiritual tutor of Kublai Khan. In the 13th and 14th centuries, the Sakyapa order became embroiled in politics and implicated in the Mongol overlordship of Tibet.

Precious umbrella

Many Sakyapa monasteries contain images of the Sakyapa protector deity Gompo Gur and photographs of the school's four head lamas: the Sakya Trizin (in exile in the US), Ngawang Kunga (head of the Sakyapa order), Chogye Trichen Rinpoche (head of the Tsarpa subschool) and Luding Khenpo Rinpoche (head of the Ngorpa subschool). You can easily recognise Sakyapa monasteries from the three stripes painted on the generally grey walls.

Gelugpa Order

➡ **Main Monasteries** Ganden (p93), Sera (p89), Drepung (p84), Tashilhunpo (p143)

➡ **Founder** Tsongkhapa

➡ **Also known as** Yellow Hats

Vase of treasure

It may not have been his intention, but Tsongkhapa (1357–1419), a monk who left his home in Amdo (Qīnghǎi) at the age of 17 to study in central Tibet, is regarded as the founder of the Gelugpa (Virtuous School) order, which came to dominate political and religious affairs in Tibet.

Tsongkhapa studied with all the major schools of his day, but was particularly influenced by the Sakyapa and the Kadampa orders, the latter based on the teachings of 11th-century Bengali sage Atisha. After experiencing a vision of Atisha, Tsongkhapa elaborated on the Bengali sage's clerical-Tantric synthesis in a doctrine that is known as *lamrim* (the graduated path). The Gelugpa school eventually subsumed the Kadampa school.

Victory banner

Tsongkhapa basically advocated a return to doctrinal purity and stressed the structure of the monastic body and monastic discipline as prerequisites to advanced Tantric studies. Tsongkhapa established Ganden Monastery, which became the head of the Gelugpa order. The Ganden Tripa is actually the titular head of the order, but it was the Dalai Lamas who came to be increasingly identified with the order's growing political and spiritual prestige.

Bön

➡ **Main Monasteries**: Yungdrungling (p149), Gurugyam (p184)

➡ **Founder** Shenrab Miwoche

Wheel of Law

The word 'Bön' today has three main connotations. The first relates to the pre-Buddhist religion of Tibet, suppressed and supplanted by Buddhism in the 8th and 9th centuries. The second is the form of 'organised' Bön (Gyur Bön) systematised along Buddhist lines, which arose in the 11th century. Third, and linked to this, is a body of popular beliefs that involves the worship of local deities and spirit protectors.

The earliest form of Bön, sometimes referred to as Black Bön, also Dud Bön (the Bön of Devils) or Tsan Bön (the Bön of Spirits), was concerned with counteracting the effects of evil spirits through magical practices. Bönpo priests were entrusted with the wellbeing and fertility of the living, as well as curing sicknesses, affecting the weather and mediating between humans and the spirit world. A core component was control of

White conch shell

the spirits, to ensure the safe passage of the soul into the next world. For centuries Bönpo priests controlled the complex burial rites of the Yarlung kings. Bön was the state religion of Tibet until the reign of Songtsen Gampo (r 629–49).

Bön is thought to have its geographical roots in the kingdom of Shangshung, which is located in western Tibet, and its capital at Kyunglung (Valley of the Garuda). Bön's founding father was Shenrab Miwoche, also known as Tonpa Shenrab, the Teacher of Knowledge, who was born in the second millennium BC in the mystical land of Olma Lungring in Tajik (thought to be possibly the Mt Kailash area or even Persia). Buddhists often claim that Shenrab is merely a carbon copy of Sakyamuni (Sakya Thukpa), and certainly there are similarities to be found. Biographies state that he was born a royal prince and ruled for 30 years before becoming an ascetic. His 10 wives bore him 10 children who formed the core of his religious disciples. Many of the tales of Shenrab Miwoche deal with his protracted struggles with the demon king Khyabpa Lagring.

Bön was first suppressed by the eighth Yarlung king, Drigum Tsenpo, and subsequently by King Trisong Detsen. The Bön master Gyerpung Drenpa Namkha (a *gyerpung* is the Bön equivalent of a lama or guru) struggled with Trisong Detsen to protect the Bön faith until the king finally broke Shangshung's political power. Following the founding of Samye Monastery, many Bön priests went into exile or converted to Buddhism, and many of the Bön texts were hidden.

The modern Bön religion is known as Yungdrung (Eternal Bön). A *yungdrung* is a swastika, Bön's most important symbol. (Yungdrungling means 'swastika park' and is a common name for Bön monasteries.) The Nine Ways of Bön is the religion's major text. Bönpos still refer to Mt Kailash as Yungdrung Gutseg (Nine-Stacked-Swastika Mountain).

The Bön order, as it survives today, is to all intents and purposes the fifth school of Tibetan Buddhism. There are estimated to be as many as 400,000 followers of Bön across the plateau, mainly in the Changtang region of northern Tibet and the Ngaba (Aba) region of northern Sìchuān (Kham).

The lotus (*padma* in Sanskrit, *metok* in Tibetan) is an important Buddhist symbol and the thrones of many deities are made from a lotus leaf. The leaf symbolises purity and transcendence, in the world but not of it, rising as it does from muddy waters to become a flower of great beauty.

Important Figures of Tibetan Buddhism

This is a brief iconographical guide to some of the gods and goddesses of the vast Tibetan Buddhist pantheon, as well as to important historical figures. It is neither exhaustive nor scholarly, but it may help you to recognise a few of the statues and murals you encounter during your trip. Tibetan names are given first, with Sanskrit names provided in parentheses. (The exception is Sakya Thukpa, who is generally known by his Sanskrit name, Sakyamuni.)

Buddhas

Sakyamuni (Sakya Thukpa)

Sakyamuni (Sakya Thukpa)

Sakyamuni is the Historical Buddha (the Buddha of the Present Age), whose teachings set in motion the Buddhist faith. In Tibetan-style representations he is always pictured sitting cross-legged on a lotus-flower throne. His tight curled hair is dark blue and there is a halo of enlightenment around his head. The Buddha is recognised by 32 marks on his body, including a dot between his eyes, a bump on the top of his head, three folds of skin on his neck and the Wheel of Law on the soles of his feet. In his left hand he holds a begging bowl, and his right hand touches the earth in the 'witness' *mudra* (hand gesture). He is often flanked by his two principal disciples Sariputra and Maudgalyana.

Marmedze (Dipamkara)

The Past Buddha, Marmedze, came immediately before Sakyamuni and spent 100,000 years on earth. His hands are shown in the 'protection' *mudra* and he is often depicted in a trinity with the Present and Future Buddhas, known as the *dusum sangay*.

Öpagme (Amitabha)

The Buddha of Infinite Light resides in the 'pure land of the west' (Dewachen in Tibetan, or Sukhavati in Sanskrit). The Panchen Lama is considered a reincarnation of this buddha. He is red, his hands are held together in his lap in a 'meditation' *mudra* and he holds a begging bowl.

Tsepame
(Amitayus)

Tsepame (Amitayus)

The Buddha of Longevity, like Öpagme, is red and holds his hands in a meditation gesture, but he holds a vase containing the nectar of immortality. He is often seen in groups of nine.

Medicine Buddhas (Menlha)

The medicine buddha holds a medicine bowl in his left hand and herbs in his right, while rays of healing light emanate from his blue body. He is often depicted in a group of eight.

Dhyani Buddhas (Gyalwa Ri Nga)

Each of the five Dhyani buddhas is a different colour, and each of them has different *mudras,* symbols and attributes. They are Öpagme, Nampar Namse (Vairocana), Mikyöba (or Mitrukpa; Akhshobya), Rinchen Jungne (Ratnasambhava) and Donyo Drupa (Amoghasiddhi).

Jampa (Maitreya)

Jampa, the Future Buddha, is passing the life of a bodhisattva until it is time to return to earth in human form 4000 years after the disappearance of Sakyamuni. He is normally seated in European fashion, with a scarf around his waist, often with a white stupa in his hair and his hands by his chest in the *mudra* of turning the Wheel of Law. Jampa is much larger than the average human and so statues of Jampa are often several storeys high.

Jampa (Maitreya)

Bodhisattvas

These are beings who have reached the state of enlightenment but work for the salvation of other beings before they themselves enter nirvana. Unlike buddhas, they are often shown decorated with crowns and princely jewels.

Chenresig (Avalokiteshvara)

The 'glorious gentle one', Chenresig (Guānyīn to the Chinese) is the Bodhisattva of Compassion. His name means 'he who gazes upon the world with suffering in his eyes'. The Dalai Lamas are considered to be reincarnations of Chenresig (as is King Songtsen Gampo), and pictures of the Dalai Lama and Chenresig are interchangeable, depending on the political climate.

In the four-armed version (known more specifically in Tibetan as Tonje Chenpo), his body is white and he sits on a lotus blossom. He holds crystal rosary beads and a lotus, and clutches to his heart a jewel that fulfils all wishes. A deer skin is draped over his left shoulder.

There is also a powerful 11-headed, 1000-armed version, known as Chaktong Chentong. The head of this version is said to have exploded when confronted with the myriad problems of the world. One of his

Chenresig
(Avalokiteshvara)

heads is that of wrathful Chana Dorje (Vajrapani), and another (the top one) is that of Öpagme (Amitabha), who is said to have reassembled Chenresig's body after it exploded. Each of the 1000 arms has an eye in the palm. His eight main arms hold a bow and arrow, lotus, rosary, vase, wheel, staff and a wish-fulfilling jewel.

Jampelyang (Manjushri)

Jampelyang
(Manjushri)

The Bodhisattva of Wisdom, Jampelyang is regarded as the first divine teacher of Buddhist doctrine. He is connected to science and agriculture and school children; architects and astrologers often offer prayers to him. His right hand holds the flaming sword of awareness, which cuts through delusion. His left arm cradles a scripture on a half-opened lotus blossom and his left hand is in the 'teaching' *mudra*. He is often yellow and may have blue hair or an elaborate crown. He is sometimes called Manjughosa.

Drölma (Tara)

Drölma (Tara)

A female bodhisattva with 21 different manifestations or aspects, Drölma is also known as the saviouress. She was born from a tear of compassion that fell from the eyes of Chenresig and is thus considered the female version of Chenresig and a protector of the Tibetan people. She also symbolises purity and fertility and is believed to be able to fulfil wishes. Images usually represent Dröljang (Green Tara), who is associated with night, or Drölkar (White Tara), who is associated with day (and also Songtsen Gampo's Chinese wife). She is often seen as part of the Tsela Nam Sum longevity triad, along with red Tsepame (Amitayus) and three-faced, eight-armed female Namgyelma (Vijaya).

Protector Deities

Protectors are easily recognised by their fierce expressions, bulging eyes, warrior stance (with one leg outstretched in a fencer's pose), halo of flames and Tantric implements. They either stand trampling on the human ego or sit astride an animal mount, dressed in military regalia and flayed animal or human skins. They represent on various levels the transformed original demons of Tibet, the wrathful aspects of other deities and, on one level at least, humankind's inner psychological demons.

Four Guardian Kings (Chökyong)

The four Chökyong (Lokapalas in Sanskrit) are normally seen at the entrance hallway of monasteries and are possibly of Mongol origin. They are the protectors of the four cardinal directions: the eastern chief is white with a lute; the southern is green with a red beard and holds a sword; and the western is red and holds a green *naga*. Namtöse (Vaishravana), the protector of the north, doubles as the god of wealth (Zhambhala or Jambhala) and can be seen with an orange body (the colour of 100,000 suns) and clumpy beard, riding a snow lion and holding a banner of victory, a jewel-spitting mongoose and a lemon.

Since the 1959 departure of the Dalai Lama, Tibet has been largely cut off from its Buddhist teachers and lineage masters, most of whom remain in exile.

Dorje Jigje (Yamantaka)

Dorje Jigje is a favourite protector of the Gelugpa order. A wrathful form of Jampelyang, he is also known as the destroyer of Yama (the Lord of Death). He is blue with eight heads, the main one of which is the head of a bull. He wears a garland of skulls around his neck and a belt of skulls around his waist, and holds a skull cup, butchers' chopper and a flaying knife in his 34 arms. He tramples on eight Hindu gods, eight mammals and eight birds with his 16 feet.

Nagpo Chenpo (Mahakala)

A wrathful Tantric deity and manifestation of Chenresig, Nagpo Chenpo (Great Black One) has connections to the Hindu god Shiva. He can be seen in many varieties with anything from two to six arms. He is black ('as a water-laden cloud') with fanged teeth, wears a cloak of elephant skin and a tiara of skulls, carries a trident and skull cup, and has flaming hair. In a form known as Gompo (or Yeshe Gompo), he is believed by nomads to be the guardian of the tent.

Tamdrin
(Hayagriva)

Tamdrin (Hayagriva)

Another wrathful manifestation of Chenresig, Tamdrin (the 'horse necked') has a red body. His right face is white, his left face is green and he has a horse's head in his hair. He wears a tiara of skulls, a garland of 52 severed heads and a tiger skin around his waist. His six hands hold a skull cup, a lotus, a sword, a snare, an axe and a club, and his four legs stand on a sun disc, trampling corpses. On his back are the outspread wings of Garuda and the skins of a human and an elephant. He has close connections to the Hindu god Vishnu and is popular among herders and nomads.

Chana Dorje
(Vajrapani)

Chana Dorje (Vajrapani)

The name of the wrathful Bodhisattva of Energy means 'thunderbolt in hand'. In his right hand Chana Dorje holds a thunderbolt (*dorje* or *vajra*), and so is often prayed to during times of droughts or floods. He is blue with a tiger skin around his waist and a snake around his neck. Together with Chenresig and Jampelyang, he forms part of the trinity known as the Rigsum Gonpo.

Palden Lhamo (Shri Devi)

The special protector of Lhasa, the Dalai Lama and the Gelugpa order, Palden Lhamo is a female counterpart of Nagpo Chenpo and closely connected with divination. Her origins probably lie in the Hindu goddess Kali. She is blue, wears clothes of tiger skin, rides on a saddle of human skin, and has earrings made of a snake. She uses the black and white dice around her waist (tied to a bag of diseases) to determine people's fates. She holds the moon in her hair, the sun in her belly and a corpse in her mouth, and rides a wild ass with reins of poisonous snakes and an eye in its rump.

Palden Lhamo
(Shri Devi)

Historical Figures

Guru Rinpoche (Padmasambhava)

The 'lotus-born' 8th-century Tantric master and magician from modern-day Swat in Pakistan, Guru Rinpoche subdued Tibet's evil spirits and helped to establish Buddhism in Tibet. He is regarded by followers of Nyingmapa Buddhism as the 'second Buddha'. His domain is the copper-coloured mountain called Zangdok Pelri. He has bug eyes and a curly moustache and holds a thunderbolt in his right hand, a skull cup in his left hand and a *katvanga* (staff) topped with three heads – one shrunken, one severed and one skull – in the crook of his left arm. He has a *phurbu* (ritual dagger) in his belt. Guru Rinpoche has eight manifestations, known collectively as the Guru Tsengye, which correspond to different stages of his life. He is often flanked by his consorts Mandarava (Indian) and Yeshe Tsogyel (Tibetan).

Guru Rinpoche
(Padmasambhava)

Tsongkhapa

Tsongkhapa

Founder of the Gelugpa order and a manifestation of Jampelyang, Tsongkhapa (1357–1419) wears the yellow hat of the Gelugpas. Also known as Je Rinpoche, he is normally portrayed in the *yab-se sum* trinity with his two main disciples, Kedrub Je (later recognised as the first Panchen Lama) and Gyaltsab Je. His hands are in the 'teaching' *mudra* and he holds two lotuses.

Fifth Dalai Lama

Fifth Dalai Lama

The greatest of all the Dalai Lamas, the fifth (Ngawang Lobsang Gyatso; 1617–82) unified Tibet and built the bulk of the Potala. He was born at Chongye (in the Yarlung Valley) and was the first Dalai Lama to exercise temporal power. He wears the Gelugpa yellow hat and holds a flower or thunderbolt in his right hand and a bell *(drilbu)* in his left. He may also be depicted holding the Wheel of Law (symbolising the beginning of political control of the Dalai Lamas) and a lotus flower or other sacred objects.

King Songtsen Gampo

King Songtsen Gampo

Tibet was unified under Songtsen Gampo (r 629–49). Together with his two wives, he is credited with introducing Buddhism to the country early in the 7th century. He has a moustache and wears a white turban with a tiny red Öpagme poking out of the top. He is flanked by Princess Wencheng Konjo, his Chinese wife, on the left, and Princess Bhrikuti, his Nepali wife, on his right.

King Trisong Detsen

The founder of Samye Monastery (r 755–97) is normally seen in a trio of kings with Songtsen Gampo and King Ralpachen (r 817–35). He is regarded as a manifestation of Jampelyang and so holds a scripture on a lotus in the crook of his left arm and a sword of wisdom in his right. He resembles Songtsen Gampo but without the buddha in his turban.

Milarepa

Milarepa

A great 11th-century Tibetan magician and poet, Milarepa (c 1040–1123) is believed to have attained enlightenment in the course of one lifetime. He became an alchemist in order to poison an uncle who had stolen his family's lands and then spent six years meditating in a cave in repentance. During this time he wore nothing but a cotton robe and so became known as Milarepa (Cotton-Clad Mila). Most images of Milarepa depict him smiling and holding his hand to his ear as he sings.

Tibetan Art

It is Buddhism that inspires almost all Tibetan art. Paintings, architecture, literature, even dance, all in some way or another attest to its influence. Perhaps more unexpected is that, despite the harshness of their surroundings, Tibetans have great aesthetic taste, from stylish traditional carpets and painted furniture to jewellery and traditional dress. In Tibet's often austere landscape the colours of Tibetan murals and traditional dress take on an almost rebellious vibrancy.

Art & History

The arts of Tibet represent the synthesis of many influences. The Buddhist art and architecture of the Pala and Newari kingdoms of India and Nepal were an important early influence in central Tibet, and the Buddhist cultures of Khotan and Kashmir spilled over the mountains into western Tibet. Newari influence is clearly visible in the early woodcarvings of the Jokhang, and Kashmiri influence is particularly strong in the murals of Tsaparang in western Tibet. Chinese influences, too, were assimilated, as is clear at Shalu Monastery near Shigatse and in the Karma Gadri style prevalent in eastern Kham. A later, clearly Tibetan style known as Menri was perfected in the monasteries of Drepung, Ganden and Sera.

Tibetan art is deeply conservative and conventional. Personal expression and innovation are not greatly valued, indeed individual interpretation is actually seen as an obstacle to Tibetan art's main purpose, which is to represent the path to enlightenment. The creation of religious art is seen primarily as an act of merit and the artist generally remains anonymous.

Much of Tibet's artistic heritage fell victim to the Cultural Revolution. What was not destroyed was, in many cases, ferreted away to China or onto the Hong Kong art market. Over 13,500 images have since been returned to Tibet but this is still just a fraction of the number stolen. Many of Tibet's traditional artisans were persecuted or fled Tibet. It is only in recent years that remaining artists have again been able to return to their work and start to train young Tibetans in skills that faced the threat of extinction. New but traditional handicraft workshops are popping up all the time in Lhasa's old town.

Art of Tibet by Robert Fisher is a portable colour guide to all the arts of Tibet, from the iconography of thangkas to statuary.

Dance & Drama

Anyone who is lucky enough to attend a Tibetan festival should have the opportunity to see performances of *cham,* a ritual masked dance performed over several days by monks and lamas. Although every movement and gesture of *cham* has significance, it is no doubt the spectacle of the colourful masked dancers that awes the average pilgrim.

Cham is all about the suppression of malevolent spirits and is a clear throwback to the pre-Buddhist Bön faith. The chief officiant is an unmasked Black Hat lama who is surrounded by a mandalic grouping of masked monks representing manifestations of various protective deities. The act of exorcism – it might be considered as such – is focused on a human effigy made of dough or perhaps wax or paper, through which the evil spirits are channelled.

The proceedings of *cham* can be interpreted on a number of levels. The Black Hat lama is sometimes identified with the monk who slew Langdharma, the anti-Buddhist king of the Yarlung era, and the dance is seen as echoing the suppression of malevolent forces inimical to the establishment of Buddhism in Tibet. Some anthropologists, on the other hand, have also seen in *cham* a metaphor for the gradual conquering of the ego, which is the ultimate aim of Buddhism. The ultimate destruction of the effigy that ends the dance might represent the destruction of the ego itself. Whatever the case, *cham* is a splendid, dramatic performance that marks the cultural highlight of the year for most Tibetans.

Lhamo Opera

Lighter forms of entertainment usually accompany performances of *cham. Lhamo,* not to be confused with *cham,* is Tibetan opera. A largely secular art form, it portrays the heroics of kings and the villainy of demons, and recounts events in the lives of historical figures. *Lhamo* was developed in the 14th century by Thangtong Gyalpo, known as Tibet's Leonardo da Vinci because he was also an engineer, a major bridge builder and a physician. Authentic performances still include a statue of Thangtong on the otherwise bare stage. After the stage has been purified, the narrator gives a plot summary in verse and the performers enter, each with his or her distinct step and dressed in the bright and colourful silks of the aristocracy.

Music

Music is one aspect of Tibetan cultural life in which there is a strong secular heritage. In the urban centres, songs were an important vent for social criticism, news and political lampooning. In Tibetan social life, both work and play are seen as occasions for singing. Even today it is not uncommon to see the monastery reconstruction squads pounding on the roofs of buildings and singing in unison. Where there are groups of men and women, the singing alternates between the two groups in the form of rhythmic refrains.

The ultimate night out in Lhasa is to a *nangma* venue, where house dancers and singers perform traditional songs and dances as part of a stage show, with members of the audience often joining in at smaller venues.

Tibet also has a secular tradition of wandering minstrels. It's still possible to see minstrels performing in Lhasa and Shigatse, where they play on the streets and occasionally (when they are not chased out by the owners) in restaurants. Generally, groups of two or three singers perform heroic epics and short songs to the accompaniment of a four-stringed guitar and a nifty little shuffle, before moving around tables soliciting donations with a grin. In times past, groups of such performers travelled around Tibet, providing entertainment for villagers who had few distractions from the constant round of daily chores.

While the secular music of Tibet has an instant appeal for foreign listeners, the liturgical chants of Buddhist monks and the music that accompanies *cham* dances is a lot less accessible. Buddhist chanting creates an eerie haunting effect, but can soon become very monotonous. The music of *cham* is a discordant cacophony of trumpet blasts and boom-crash drums – atmospheric as an accompaniment to the dancing but not necessarily the kind of thing you would want to add to a playlist.

Tibetan religious rituals use *rolmo* and *silnyen* (cymbals), *nga* (suspended drums), *damaru* (hand drums), *drilbu* (bells), *drungchen* (long trumpets), *kangling* (conical oboes; formerly made from human

Tibetan Art Websites

www.asianart. com – general

www.himalayan art.org – online collections

www.treasury oflices.org – excellent resource on Tibet, with art sections

thighbones) and *dungkhar* (conch shells). Secular instruments include the *dramnyen* (a six-stringed lute), *piwang* (two-stringed fiddle), *ling-bu* (flute) and *gyumang* (Chinese-style zither).

The country's biggest musical export (or rather exile) is Yungchen Lhamo, who fled Tibet in 1989 and has since released several excellent world-music recordings, including a duet with Annie Lennox. She also appeared on Natalie Merchant's *Ophelia* album.

Literature

The development of a Tibetan written script is credited to a monk by the name of Tonmi Sambhota and corresponded with the early introduction of Buddhism during the reign of King Songtsen Gampo. Before this, pre-Buddhist traditions were passed down as oral histories that told of the exploits of early kings, the spirits and the origins of the Tibetan people. Some of these oral traditions were later recorded using the Tibetan script.

The Tibetan epic *Gesar of Ling* is the world's longest epic poem, 25 times as long as *The Iliad*, and takes years to recite in full!

But for the most part, literature in Tibet was dominated by Buddhism, first as a means of translating Buddhist scriptures from Sanskrit into Tibetan and second, as time went by, in association with the development of Tibetan Buddhist thought. There is nothing in the nature of a secular literary tradition – least of all novels – such as can be found in China or Japan.

One of the great achievements of Tibetan culture was the development of a literary language that could, with remarkable faithfulness, reproduce the concepts of Sanskrit Buddhist texts. The compilation of Tibetan-Sanskrit dictionaries in the early 9th century ensured consistency in all subsequent translations.

Through the 12th and 13th centuries, Tibetan literary endeavour was almost entirely consumed by the monumental task of translating the complete Buddhist canon into Tibetan. The result was the 108 volumes of canonical texts (Kangyur), which record the words of the Historical Buddha, Sakyamuni, and 208 volumes of commentary (Tengyur) by Indian masters that make up the basic Buddhist scriptures shared by all Tibetan religious orders. What time remained was used in the compilation of biographies and the collection of songs of revered lamas. Perhaps most famous among these is the *Hundred Thousand Songs of Milarepa*. Milarepa was an ascetic to whom many songs and poems concerning the quest for buddhahood are attributed.

Alongside Buddhist scriptures exists an ancient tradition of storytelling, usually concerning the taming of Tibet's malevolent spirits to allow the introduction of Buddhism. Many of these stories were passed from generation to generation orally, but some were recorded. Examples include the epic *Gesar of Ling* and the biography of Guru Rinpoche, whose countless tales of miracles and battles with demons are known to peoples across the entire Himalayan region. The oral poetry of the Gesar epic is particularly popular in eastern Tibet, where a tiny number of ageing bards manage to keep alive a tradition that dates back to the 10th century.

Tales of Tibet: Sky Burials, Prayer Wheels & Wind Horses, edited by Herbert J Batt, gathers contemporary fiction by Tibetan and Chinese writers. The scholarly introduction explains how the nationality of the authors influences this sometimes elegiac, sometimes confronting collection.

Wood-block printing has been in use for centuries and is still the most common form of printing in monasteries. Blocks are carved in mirror image; printers then work in pairs putting strips of paper over the inky block and shuttling an ink roll over it. The pages of the text are kept loose, wrapped in cloth and stored along the walls of monasteries. Tibet's most famous printing presses were in Derge in modern-day Sìchuān, at Nartang Monastery and at the Potala. You can see traditional block printing at Drepung, Ganden and Sera monasteries outside Lhasa. Sakya Monastery has a particularly impressive Tibetan library.

Very little of the Tibetan literary tradition has been translated into English. Translations that may be of interest include the *Bardo Thödol,* or *Tibetan Book of the Dead,* a mysterious but fascinating account of the stages and visions that occur between death and rebirth. The book gained a certain cult status in the late 1960s thanks to the interest of such luminaries as Carl Jung and Timothy Leary.

Architecture

For an in-depth look at Lhasa's traditional Tibetan architecture and interactive maps of Lhasa, check out www.tibet heritagefund.org.

Most early religious architecture – the Jokhang in Lhasa for example – owed much to Pala (Indian) and especially Newari (Nepali) influences. A distinctively Tibetan style of architectural design gradually emerged, and found its expression in huge chörtens (stupas), hilltop *dzong*s (forts) and the great Gelugpa monastic complexes, as well as the lesser-known stone towers of Kongpo and the Qiang regions of western Sìchuān. The great American architect Frank Lloyd Wright is said to have had a picture of the Potala on the wall of his office.

Monastery Layout

Tibetan monasteries are based on a conservative design and share a remarkable continuity of layout. Many are built in spectacular high locations above villages. Most were originally surrounded by an outer wall, built to defend the treasures of the monastery from bands of brigands, Mongolian hordes or even attacks from rival monasteries. Most monasteries have a kora (pilgrimage path) around the complex, replete with holy rocks and meditation retreats high on the hillside behind. A few monasteries have a sky-burial site and most are still surrounded by ruins dating from the Cultural Revolution.

Main Buildings Inside the gates there is usually a central courtyard used for special ceremonies and festivals and a *darchen* (flag pole). Surrounding buildings usually include a *dukhang* (main assembly or prayer hall) with *gönkhang* (protector chapels) and *lhakhang* (subsidiary chapels), as well as monks' quarters, a *kangyur lhakhang* (library) and, in the case of larger monasteries, *tratsang* (colleges), *kangtsang* (halls of residence), kitchens and a *barkhang* (printing press). At the entrance to most buildings are murals of the Four Guardian Kings and perhaps a Wheel of Life or a mandala mural.

Two years after killing off his main character, Arthur Conan Doyle explained the resurrection of Sherlock Holmes by saying that he had spent two years wandering in Tibet. Tibetan writer Jamyang Norbu cleverly conjectures on what Holmes may have been up to in his 2003 novel *The Mandala of Sherlock Holmes.*

Main Prayer Hall The *dukhang* consists of rows of low seats and tables, often strewn with cloaks, hats, ritual instruments, drums and huge telescopic horns. There is a small altar with seven bowls of water, butter lamps and offerings of mandalas made from seeds. The main altar houses the most significant statues, often Sakyamuni (Sakya Thukpa), Jampa (Maitreya) or a trinity of the Past, Present and Future Buddhas and perhaps the founder of the monastery or past lamas. Larger monasteries contain funeral chörtens of important lamas, as well as special relics such as 'self-arising' (ie not human-made) footprints or handprints made from stone. There may be a *tsangkhang* (inner sanctum) behind the main hall, the entrance of which is flanked by protector gods, often one blue, Chana Dorje (Vajrapani) and the other red, Tamdrin (Hayagriva). There may well be an inner kora (*korlam*) of prayer wheels. Back at the entrance, side stairs lead to higher floors.

Protector Chapels *Gönkhang* are dark and spooky protector chapels that hold wrathful manifestations of deities, frequently covered with a cloth because of their terrible appearance. Murals here are often traced against a black background and walls are decorated with Tantric deities, grinning skeletons or even dismembered bodies. The altars often have grain, dice or mirrors, used for divination, and the pillars are decorated with festival masks, antique weapons and sometimes stuffed snakes and wolves. Deep Tantric drumming often pulsates through the room. Women are often not allowed into protector chapels.

Roof Stairs lead up to subsidiary chapels and monk accommodation. The roof usually has excellent views as well as vases of immortality, victory banners, dragons and copper symbols of the Wheel of Law flanked by two deer, recalling the Buddha's first sermon at the deer park of Sarnath.

Chörtens

Probably the most prominent Tibetan architectural motif is the chörten. Chörtens were originally built to house the cremated relics of the Historical Buddha and as such have become a powerful symbol of the Buddha and his teachings. Later, chörtens also served as reliquaries for lamas and holy men and monumental versions would often encase whole mummified bodies, as is the case with the tombs of the Dalai Lamas in the Potala. The tradition is very much alive: a stunning gold reliquary chörten was constructed in 1989 at Tashilhunpo Monastery to hold the body of the 10th Panchen Lama.

In the early stages of Buddhism, images of the Buddha did not exist and chörtens served as the major symbol of the new faith. Over the next two millennia, chörtens took many different forms across the Buddhist world, from the sensuous stupas of Burma to the pagodas of China and Japan. Most elaborate of all are the *kumbums* (100,000 Buddha images), of which the best remaining example in Tibet is at Gyantse. Many chörtens were built to hold ancient relics and sacred texts and have been plundered over the years by treasure seekers and vandals.

Chörtens are highly symbolic. The five levels represent the four elements, plus eternal space: the square base symbolises earth, the dome is water, the spire is fire, and the top moon and sun are air and space. The 13 discs of the ceremonial umbrella can represent the branches of the tree of life or the 10 powers and three mindfulnesses of the Buddha. The top seed-shaped pinnacle symbolises enlightenment. The chörten as a whole can therefore be seen as a representation of the path to enlightenment. The construction can also physically represent the Buddha, with the base as his seat and the dome as his body.

Houses & Homes

Typical features of Tibetan secular architecture, which are also used to a certain extent in religious architecture, are buildings with inward-sloping walls made of large, tightly fitting stones or sun-baked bricks. Below the roof is a layer of twigs, squashed tight by the roof and painted to give Tibetan houses their characteristic brown band. Roofs are flat, as there is little rain or snow, made from pounded earth and edged with walls. You may well see singing bands of men and women pounding a new roof with sticks weighted with large stones. In the larger structures wooden pillars support the roof inside. The exteriors are generally whitewashed brick, although in some areas, such as Sakya in Tsang, other colours may be used. In rural Tibet homes are often surrounded by walled compounds, and in some areas entrances are protected by painted scorpions and swastikas.

Nomads, who take their homes with them, live in *bar* (yak-hair tents), which are normally roomy and can accommodate a whole family. An opening at the top of the tent lets out smoke from the fire.

Painting

As with other types of Tibetan art, painting is very symbolic and can be interpreted on many different levels. It is almost exclusively devotional in nature.

Tibetan mural painting was strongly influenced by Indian, Newari and, in the far west, Kashmiri painting styles, with later influence coming from China. Paintings usually followed stereotypical forms with a central Buddhist deity surrounded by smaller, lesser deities and emanations. The use of colour and proportion is decided purely by convention

See traditional craftsmen at the Ancient Art Restoration Centre (AARC) in Lhasa, next to Dropenling. The AARC managed the restoration of the Potala and Sera and Drepung Monasteries; craftsmen here include thangka painters, metal workers, wood-carvers and dye makers.

MANDALAS

The mandala (*kyilkhor,* literally 'circle') is more than a beautiful artistic creation, it's also a three-dimensional meditational map. What on the surface appears to be a plain two-dimensional design emerges, with the right visual approach, as a three-dimensional picture. Mandalas can take the form of paintings, patterns of sand, three-dimensional models or even whole monastic structures, as at Samye. In the case of the two-dimensional mandala, the correct visual approach can be achieved only through meditation. The painstakingly created sand mandalas also perform the duty of illustrating the impermanence of life (they are generally swept away after a few days).

and rigid symbolism. Later came depictions of revered Tibetan lamas or Indian spiritual teachers, often surrounded by lineage lines or incidents from the lama's life.

Chinese influence began to manifest itself more frequently in Tibetan painting from around the 15th century. The freer approach of Chinese landscape painting allowed some Tibetan artists to break free from some of the more formalised aspects of Tibetan religious art and employ landscape as a decorative motif. Painting in Tibet was passed on from artisan to apprentice in much the same way that monastic communities maintained lineages of teaching.

Thangkas

Religious paintings mounted on brocade and rolled up between two sticks are called thangkas. Their eminent portability was essential in a land of nomads, as mendicant preachers and doctors often used them as a visual learning aid. Not so portable are the huge thangkas known as *gheku* or *koku,* the size of large buildings, that are unfurled every year during festivals.

The production of a thangka is an act of devotion and the process is carefully formalised. Linen (or now more commonly cotton) is stretched on a wooden frame, stiffened with glue and coated with a mix of chalk and lime called *gesso.* Iconography is bound by strict mathematical measurements. A grid is drawn onto the thangka before outlines are sketched in charcoal, starting with the main central deity and moving outwards.

Colours are added one at a time, starting with the background and ending with shading. Pigments were traditionally natural: blue from lapis, red from cinnabar and yellow from sulphur. Most thangkas are burnished with at least a little gold. The last part of the thangka to be painted is the eyes, which are filled in during a special 'opening the eyes' ceremony. Finally a brocade backing of three colours and a protective 'curtain' are added, the latter to protect the thangka.

Best Monastic Murals

Shalu, near Shigatse

Gongkar Chöde, Yarlung Valley

Thöling, Zanda

Statuary & Sculpture

Tibetan statuary, like Tibetan painting, is almost exclusively religious in nature. Ranging in height from several centimetres to several metres, statues usually depict deities and revered lamas. Most of the smaller statues are hollow and are stuffed with paper texts, prayers, amulets and juniper when consecrated. Very few clay or metal sculptures remaining in Tibet date from before 1959.

Metal statues are traditionally sculpted in wax and then covered in clay. When the clay is dry it is heated. The wax melts and is removed, leaving a mould that can be filled with molten metal. Statues are generally then gilded and painted.

Sculptures are most commonly made from bronze or stucco mixed with straw, but can even be made out of butter and *tsampa* (roasted-barley flour), mounted on a wooden frame.

Handicrafts

A burgeoning economy in Lhasa has fuelled a real growth in traditional crafts in recent years, though these are partially for the Chinese tourist market.

Tibet has a 1000-year history of carpet making; the carpets are mostly used as seat covers, bed covers and saddle blankets. Knots are double tied (the best carpets have 100 knots per square inch), which results in a particularly thick pile. Tibet's secret carpet ingredient is its particularly high-quality sheep wool, which is hand spun and coloured with natural dyes such as indigo, walnut, madder and rhubarb. Tibetan cashmere goat's wool and antelope wool are also in great demand. Gyantse and Shigatse were the traditional centres of carpet production, although the modern industry is based almost exclusively in Tibetan exile communities in Nepal.

Inlaid handicrafts are common, particularly in the form of prayer wheels, daggers, butter lamps and bowls, although most of what you see these days in Lhasa is made by Tibetan communities in Nepal. Nomads in particular wear stunning silver jewellery; you may also see silver flints, horse tack, amulets known as *gau,* and ornate chopstick and knife sets.

Tibetan singing bowls, made from a secret mix of seven different metals, are a meditation device that originated from pre-Buddhist Bön practices. The bowls produce a 'disassociated' mystic hum when a playing stick is rotated around the outer edge of the bowl.

Woodcarving is another valued handicraft, used in the production of brightly coloured Tibetan furniture and window panels, not to mention blocks used in printing.

Food & Drink

Though you won't starve, food will probably not be a highlight of your trip to Tibet. A few restaurants in Lhasa and some guesthouses in the countryside have begun to elevate a subsistence diet into the beginnings of a cuisine, but Tibetan food is usually more about survival than pleasure. On the plus side, fresh vegetables and packaged goods are now widely available and you are never far away from a good Chinese *fànguǎn* (饭馆) or *cāntīng* (餐厅) restaurant.

Staples & Specialities

Tibetan

The basic Tibetan meal is *tsampa*, a kind of dough made with roasted-barley flour and yak butter mixed with water, tea or beer – something wet. Tibetans skilfully knead and mix the paste by hand into dough-like balls, which is not as easy as it looks! *Tsampa* with milk powder and sugar makes a pretty good porridge and is a fine trekking staple, but only a Tibetan can eat it every day and still look forward to the next meal.

Some common Tibetan dishes include *momos* and *thugpa*. Momos are small dumplings filled with yak meat or vegetables or both. They are normally steamed but can be fried and a few places serve cheese or potato versions. More common is *thugpa*, a noodle soup with meat or vegetables or both. Variations on the theme include *hipthuk* (squares of noodles and yak meat in a soup) and *thenthuk* (flat noodles). Glass noodles known as *phing* are also sometimes used.

The other main option is *shemdre* (sometimes called curried beef), a stew of potatoes and yak meat on a bed of rice. In smarter restaurants in Lhasa or Shigatse you can try dishes such as *damje* or *shomday* (butter-fried rice with raisins and yogurt), *droma desi* (wild ginseng with raisins, sugar, butter and rice) and *shya vale* (fried pancake-style pasties with a yak-meat filling). Formal Tibetan restaurants (*sarkhang* in Tibetan) in particular are very big on yak offal, with large sections of menus sumptuously detailing the various ways of serving up yak tongues, stomachs and lungs.

In rural areas and markets you might see strings of little white lumps drying in the sun that even the flies leave alone – this is dried yak cheese and it's eaten like a boiled sweet. For the first half-hour it is like having a small rock in your mouth, but eventually it starts to soften up and taste like old, dried yak cheese.

Also popular among nomads is *yak sha* (dried yak jerky). It is normally cut into strips and left to dry on tent lines and is pretty chewy stuff.

Chinese

Chinese restaurants can be found in every settlement in Tibet these days, but they're around 50% more expensive than elsewhere in China.

Chinese food in Tibet is almost exclusively Sichuanese, the spiciest of China's regional cuisines. One popular Sichuanese sauce is *yúxiāng* (鱼香), a spicy, piquant sauce of garlic, vinegar and chilli that is supposed to resemble the taste of fish (though it's more like a sweet and tangy marinade). You'll also taste *huājiāo* (花椒; Sichuan pepper), a curious mouth-numbing spice popular in Sichuanese food.

Outside Lhasa, few Chinese restaurants have menus in English, and when they do the prices are often marked up. We indicate restaurants with English menus by the English-menu icon. In most restaurants you can simply wander out into the kitchen and point to the vegetables and meats you want fried up, but you'll miss out on many of the most interesting sauces and styles this way.

Chinese snacks are excellent and make for a fine light meal. The most common are *shuǐjiǎo* (ravioli-style dumplings), ordered by the bowl or weight (half a *jīn,* or 250g, is enough for one person), and *bāozi* (thicker steamed dumplings), which are similar to *momos* and are normally ordered by the steamer – they're a common breakfast food. Both are dipped in soy sauce, vinegar or chilli (or a mix of all). You can normally get a bowl of noodles anywhere for around ¥15; *shāguō mǐxiàn* is a particularly tasty form of rice noodles cooked in a clay pot. *Chǎomiàn* (fried noodles) and *dàn chǎofàn* (egg fried rice) are not as popular as in the West, but you can get them in many Chinese and backpacker restaurants.

You can get decent breakfasts of yogurt, muesli and toast at top-end hotels or Nepali restaurants in Lhasa, Gyantse and Shigatse, but elsewhere you are more likely to see Chinese-style dumplings, fried bread sticks (油条; *yóutiáo*) and tasteless rice porridge (稀饭; *xīfàn*). One good breakfast-type food that is widely available is scrambled eggs and tomato (*fānqié chǎodàn*).

Muslim

The Muslim restaurants found in almost all urban centres in Tibet offer an interesting alternative to Chinese or Tibetan food. They are normally recognisable by a green flag hanging outside or Arabic script on the restaurant sign. Most chefs come from the Línxià area of Gānsù. The food is based on noodles, and, of course, there's no pork.

Dishes worth trying include *gānbànmiàn,* a kind of stir-fried spaghetti bolognaise made with beef (or yak) and sometimes green peppers; and *chǎomiànpiàn,* fried noodle squares with meat and vegetables. *Xīnjiāng bànmiàn* (Xīnjiāng noodles) are similar, but the sauce comes in a separate bowl, to be poured over the noodles. It's fun to go into the kitchen and see your noodles being handmade on the spot.

Muslim restaurants also offer good breads and excellent *bā bǎo chá* (eight treasure tea), which is made with dried raisins, plums and rock sugar, and only releases its true flavour after several cups.

Nepali

Food in Nepali restaurants is a mixture of western and Indian-influenced tastes. Curries are generally the best option, from the various vegetable curries to creamy chicken butter masala or boneless chicken tikka. A 'thali' or 'set' generally comes with two curries, rice, dal (lentil curry),

Best Cookbooks

Tibetan Cooking: Recipes for Daily Living, Celebration, and Ceremony by Elizabeth Kelly

The Lhasa Moon Tibetan Cookbook by Tsering Wangmo

FOOD & DRINK STAPLES & SPECIALITIES

SELF-CATERING

There will likely be a time somewhere on your trip when you'll need to be self-sufficient, whether you're staying overnight at a monastery or are caught between towns on an overland trip. Unless you have a stove, your main saviour will be instant noodles. Vegetables such as onions, carrots and bok choy (even seaweed and pickled vegetables) can save even the cheapest pack of noodles from culinary oblivion, as can a packet of mixed spices brought from home.

It's a good idea to stock up on instant coffee, tea, oats, hot chocolate and dried soups, as flasks of boiling water are offered in every hotel and restaurant.

pickles and possibly yogurt. Yak steaks are popular, as are chicken sizzlers (chicken breast, potatoes and other vegetables and gravy served on a sizzling iron plate). The ever-popular lassi is a yogurt drink, either salty or sweet, often flavoured with mango or other fruit.

Drinks

The local beverage that every traveller ends up trying at least once is yak-butter tea.

The more palatable alternative to yak-butter tea is sweet, milky tea. It is similar to the tea drunk in neighbouring Nepal or Pakistan and is generally served a thermos at a time. Soft drinks and mineral water are available everywhere.

Yak-Butter Tea

Bö cha, literally 'Tibetan tea', is unlikely to be a highlight of your trip to Tibet. Made from yak butter mixed with salt, milk, soda, tea leaves and hot water all churned up in a wooden tube, the soupy mixture has more the consistency of bouillon than of tea (one traveller described it as 'a cross between brewed old socks and sump oil'). When mixed with *tsampa* (roasted-barley flour) and yak butter it becomes the staple meal of most Tibetans, and you may well be offered it at monasteries, at people's houses and even while waiting for a bus by the side of the road.

At most restaurants you mercifully have the option of drinking *cha ngamo* (sweet, milky tea), but there will be times when you just have to be polite and down a cupful of *bö cha* (without gagging). Most nomads think nothing of drinking up to 40 cups of the stuff a day. On the plus side it does replenish your body's lost salts and prevents your lips from cracking. As one reader told us, 'Personally, we like yak-butter tea, not so much for the taste as the view from the cup'.

Most distressing for those not sold on the delights of yak-butter tea is the fact that your cup will be refilled every time you take even the smallest sip, as a mark of the host's respect. There's a pragmatic reason for this as well: there's only one thing worse than hot yak-butter tea – cold yak-butter tea.

Alcoholic Drinks

The Tibetan home brew is known as *chang* (青稞酒; *qingkējiǔ*), a fermented-barley beer. It has a rich, fruity taste and most people seem to like it. Tibetan connoisseurs serve it out of a jerrycan, the dirtier the better. Sharing *chang* is a good way to get to know local people, if drunk in small quantities.

Those trekking in the Everest region should try the local variety (similar to Nepali *tongba*), which is served in a big pot. Hot water is poured into the fermenting barley and the liquid is drunk through a wooden straw – it is very good.

On our research trips we have never suffered any adverse effects from drinking copious amounts of *chang*. However, you should be aware that it is often made with contaminated water, and there is always some risk in drinking it.

The main brand of local beer is Lhasa Beer, now brewed in Lhasa in a joint venture with Carlsberg at the world's highest brewery.

Supermarkets in Lhasa stock several types of Chinese red wine, including Shangri-La, produced in the Tibetan areas of northeastern Yúnnán using methods handed down by French missionaries at the beginning of the 19th century.

The Future of Tibet

China is playing the long game in Tibet. It is betting that over time economic advancement will win over Tibetan hearts and minds and compensate for the lack of religious and political freedoms. Yet as Tibetans struggle with the perceived lack of control over their land, religion and resources, many reply that they are not so easily bought. As the rest of the world turns away, alienation and tension looks set to remain high on the plateau.

Full Speed Ahead

As ground is broken on a never-ending series of airports, highways and rail links, China's future policy in Tibet is clear: invest billions on massive economic development to improve the lives of hundreds of thousands of Tibetans.

Unfortunately the modernisation is squarely on China's terms. Questions over the suitability and sustainability of hydroelectric projects, mining and mass tourism look set to dominate the next decade, as environmental problems intensify alongside exploitation. Moreover, with a transient migrant Chinese population spearheading the economic growth, the bulk of the profits from mining, tourism and other industries in Tibet are flowing straight out of the plateau back into China. It's a bittersweet boom that looks set only to accelerate.

Encouragingly, Tibet is now seriously cool among Chinese backpackers from Běijīng to Guǎngzhōu, many of whom are as enamoured with Tibet as their Western counterparts.

The International Arena

The more things change in Tibet, the more they stay the same outside. Talks between the Chinese and the Dharamsala-based Tibetan government in exile remain stalled, with the Chinese taking every opportunity to denounce the Nobel Peace Prize–winning Dalai Lama for being a 'wolf in sheep's clothing' or trying to 'split the motherland'. The Dalai Lama himself has abandoned any hope of nationhood, opting to push for cultural, religious and linguistic autonomy within the Chinese state, yet even this 'middle path' of conciliation has yielded nothing. Fearful of upsetting their trade balance with China, foreign governments, corporations and even cultural organisations meekly avoid mentioning Tibet in any way that China could construe as critical.

In an age of terrorism, intolerance and rising religious extremism it is perhaps surprising how little attention the Dalai Lama's remarkable insistence on non-violence gets from the world community. As years pass with no discernible progress, tensions inside the Tibetan community are intensifying, with younger Tibetans increasingly pushing for direct, perhaps even violent, action.

For its part China seems incapable of seeing Tibetan dissent in any terms other than 'separatism' and 'splittism'. The fear in Běijīng is that continued unrest or concessions made to the Tibetans will cause a domino effect with other restive nationalities like the Uyghur of Xīnjiāng, a stand largely backed by an increasingly nationalist Chinese public. Until that changes, a political settlement will remain elusive. The political reality is that Tibet is firmly a part of China. No one expects that to change any time soon.

'The empire long divided, must unite; long united it must divide. Thus has it ever been.' *Romance of the Three Kingdoms*, 14th century

As modern Tibet teeters on the edge of losing its cultural identity, some observers look to the cyclical nature of Chinese history. Over the centuries China has grown, cracked and collapsed. If that happens again, or if fundamental changes occur in Chinese domestic politics, Tibet may perhaps once again have a say in its own affairs.

The Politics of Reincarnation

Only in Tibet could the 13th-century practice of reincarnation become a 21st-century political hot potato. Disputes between Dharamsala and Běijīng over the selection of various lamas, most notably the Panchen Lama, have spotlighted how religious decisions are becoming increasingly politicised, a trend that will doubtless only intensify as the Dalai Lama advances in his 80s.

In 2018 the Dharamsala-backed 11th Panchen Lama turned 29 in his 23rd year of house arrest.

Both sides have their eyes firmly on the future here, for it is the Panchen Lama who traditionally assists in choosing the next Dalai Lama. The Chinese government knows that the struggle to control future reincarnations is fundamental to controlling Tibet; the rather bizarre result being that the avowedly atheist Chinese Communist Party is now in charge of choosing incarnate lamas for a religion it doesn't believe in. For his part, the Dalai Lama has made it clear that he will only be reborn in Tibet if he is allowed to return there as part of a political settlement.

The spectre of the death of the Dalai Lama haunts the entire Tibetan world. More than just 'a simple monk' or even a god-king, the Dalai Lama has become a shining symbol of Tibetan identity. When he dies, Tibet will have lost something essential to its modern identity. Some commentators even believe that the death of the Dalai Lama may herald the death of the Tibetan cause, one reason why both sides are laying the ground for future rebirth.

Cultural Survival

The greatest threat to Tibetan cultural life comes from indiscriminate economic change and Chinese migration, as government subsidies and huge infrastructure projects change the face and ethnic make-up of cities across the breadth of Tibet. As Tibetan culture becomes diluted, there is a fear that Tibetans will become a minority in their own country, a situation the Dalai Lama has described as 'cultural genocide'. Tibetans point to Amdo in Qīnghǎi, once a Tibetan-dominated area that now has three Han Chinese to every Tibetan.

Tragedy in Crimson: How the Dalai Lama Conquered the World but Lost the Battle with China, by former Běijīng-based journalist Tim Johnson, examines the current state of Tibet, its political status and possible future.

Education is another sore point that has long-term cultural consequences. An education system that exclusively uses the (Mandarin) Chinese language reinforces the fact that only Sinicised Tibetans are able to actively participate in Tibet's economic advances. Parents face the unenviable balancing act of preserving Tibetan language and tradition (often sending their children to Dharamsala for a Tibetan education), while preparing the coming generation for the realities of life in a Chinese-language-dominated economy.

And yet for all the new supermarkets, karaoke joints, brothels and mobile phones, Tibet's traditional and religious values remain at the core of most Tibetans' identities, and the quintessence of rural Tibet remains remarkably intact. Some 60 years of political indoctrination and religious control has failed to dull the devotion of most Tibetans to either Buddhism or the Dalai Lama and there's little sign of this changing.

It's hard to separate myth from reality in Tibet. The half-truths and propaganda from all sides can be so enticing, so pervasive and so entrenched that it's hard to see the place through balanced eyes. The reality is that Tibet is no fragile Shangri-la but a resilient land underpinned by a unique culture and a deep faith, and it is perhaps this above all that offers Tibet's best hope for its future.

Survival Guide

Directory A-Z

Accessible Travel

High altitudes, rough roads and lack of access make Tibet a difficult place for people with mobility challenges. Getting to monasteries in particular often involves a hike up a hillside or navigating steep, very narrow steps. Few hotels offer any facilities for guests with disabilities.

Download Lonely Planet's free *Accessible Travel* guide from http://lptravel.to/AccessibleTravel.

Navyo Nepal (www.navyonepal.com) A Nepal-based, Italian-owned company that has experience in running tours to Tibet and Nepal for travellers with disabilities.

Accommodation

Booking Services

You can sometimes get good deals on midrange and top-end hotels in Tibet at Chinese booking sites, though many of the Lhasa hotels listed on these sites are dull places with poor locations or places that don't accept foreigners. Chinese booking agencies are generally more reliable than international agencies when it comes to local hotels honouring your reservations.

You can also ask your tour agency to book for you as they are often able to get deals on the types of hotels and guesthouses foreign travellers like to stay in.

Trip (www.trip.com) Reliable Chinese agency, part of Ctrip.

Elong (www.elong.net) Affiliated with Expedia.com.

Lonely Planet (www.lonelyplanet.com/china/tibet/hotels) Recommendations and bookings.

Camping

Camping out is well understood by Tibetans, many of whom still spend their summers herding livestock in mountain valleys. Always ask permission if camping near a settlement or encampment, watch out for the dogs and expect an audience.

The question of whether you need a sleeping bag depends entirely on where you plan to go and how you plan to travel. Those who aim to spend time in Lhasa and then head down to Nepal via the sights of Tsang, or who are doing a short loop around Eastern Tibet, could easily do without one. If you're heading out to more remote areas such as Everest or Mt Kailash, a sleeping bag isn't essential but is always a nice comfort, especially in budget hotels. Anyone trekking should definitely bring one along, even if your agency has one you can borrow.

Guesthouses & Hotels

Lhasa is full of clean, well-run Tibetan-style guesthouses and hostels, many of which are aimed at Chinese backpackers.

Monasteries such as Samye, Tsurphu, Drigung Til, Dorje Drak, Mindroling, Tidrum and Reting have their own pilgrim guesthouses – normally a bank of carpeted seats that double as beds, but sometimes also proper hotels – and a night here can be a magical experience. You'll have to check whether foreigners are allowed to stay in the monastery guesthouses as regulations change frequently.

Hotels are divided into *bīnguǎn* (宾馆), *fàndiàn* (饭店) and *dàjiǔdiàn* (大酒店; hotels), and cheaper places are known as *zhāodàisuǒ* (招待所; guesthouses) and *lǚguǎn* (旅馆; simple hostels). The Tibetan terms are *drukhang* (hotel) and *dronkhang* (guesthouse).

Most of the larger hotels are anonymous Chinese-style places that share several traits: the plumbing is often dodgy, the toilets stinky, the carpets dotted with a mosaic of cigarette burns and the light bulbs too dim to read by. The one thing that will always work is the TV. Top-end hotels are limited to the main cities. Lhasa now boasts several luxury and boutique hotels.

Budget accommodation generally means a room without a bathroom, or at the top end of the scale a simple room with a hot-water bathroom. Midrange hotels generally have rooms with a private bathroom and (at least for part of the day) hot-water showers.

Most midrange hotels provide a kettle, while budget places provide a thermos of boiling water. Bedding is provided, but in the cheapest places it's often not that clean and it's nice to have your own sleeping bag or liner.

In some towns (such as Tsetang, Ali and Purang), and in most of eastern Tibet, the local Public Security Bureau (PSB) keeps a frustratingly tight lid on which places can and cannot accept foreigners, and budget hotels are often not permitted to accept foreigners.

If you are arranging your own accommodation, bear in mind that your driver and guide will want to stay in a hotel that gives them a free room (not many Chinese-run places will do this). You're not obliged to stay where they want but bear in mind that it's a smart idea to do what you can to keep your driver and guide happy and on your side.

BATHHOUSES

Cheap hotels often don't have hot showers, but the staff can normally direct you to a simple bathhouse (淋浴; *línyù; sugpo truya* in

Tibetan), where you can get a hot shower for around ¥25. These are purely functional places, and sometimes they're a bit grotty, but after a trek or a few days off the beaten track you'll be glad for the chance to wash. Bring your own towel and flip-flops.

DISCOUNTS

In some areas of Tibet, notably in Lhasa, accommodation prices vary seasonally. Midrange and top-end hotels in particular almost always discount their rooms from the largely fictitious rack rates. We list full high-season (May to early October) rates throughout, but you'll normally get a discount of 20% to 30% outside of July and August. Prices are even more deeply discounted in winter.

ROOM TYPES

Rooms are generally divided into *biāozhǔn* (标准; standard), which come with a bathroom, and *pǔtōng* (普通; ordinary), which don't. Standard rooms are often divided into *jīngjì* (经济; economy) and *hǎohuá* (豪华; deluxe) rooms. Both standard and ordinary rooms can be either twins (two beds) or doubles (one large bed), though twins are far more common. Sometimes each twin bed is large enough for two (so couples don't always have to search for a double room), but in a triple room the beds are always just large enough for a single person.

Some hotels (generally the cheaper ones) also price their *pǔtōng* accommodation per bed rather than

per room, which can work out well for solo travellers. To guarantee that you have the room to yourself, you would theoretically have to pay for all beds (and a few hotel owners will try to force you to do so), but usually that's not necessary. Groups are sometimes expected to share rooms at remote truck-stop places, since many only have four- or five-bed rooms.

Single rooms are normally the same price (or even more expensive!) as a double room. Where they are cheaper they are generally much smaller than a twin/double. Twins and doubles are usually priced the same.

Activities

Tibet offers the type of topography to delight horse riders, mountaineers, white-water rafters and others, though the problem, as always, is the confusing travel-permit system.

Cycling

Tibet offers some of the most extreme and exhilarating mountain biking in the world. Unfortunately, the current permit system means that independent tours on bikes are effectively impossible, or at least much more expensive than they were a few years ago, since cyclists require a guide and vehicle support like other tourists.

The most popular route is the two-week, paved roller-coaster ride along the Friendship Hwy from Lhasa down to Kyirong and Kathmandu. Riders with a Tibetan tour company need to bring their own bikes, though you can often rent bikes when opting for a foreign tour company.

For a double shot of inspiration, check out the home page of Martin Adserballe (www.adserballe.com). **Bike China Adventures** (www.bikechina.com) is a US-run company that runs organised supported bike rides in Tibetan areas of Sìchuān and may be able to offer help on cycling to Lhasa.

Other specialised companies that operate cycling trips from Lhasa to Kathmandu include **Redspokes Adventure Tours** (www.redspokes.co.uk) and **Bike Adventures** (www.bikeadventures.co.uk) in the UK, or **Global Cycling Adventures** (www.global cyclingadventures.com) in the US.

If you are travelling via Kathmandu, Nepali mountain-bike agencies such as **Dawn Till Dusk** (www.nepal biking.com) can offer tips, equipment and organised biking tours in Tibet.

Many of Nepal's established trekking companies also run Tibet bike tours, notably **Makalu Adventure** (www.makaluadventure.com) and the foreign-run **Kamzang Journeys** (www.kamzang.com).

Horse Riding

There's something romantic about travelling across Tibet on horseback. The easiest place to arrange this is in the Kham region of western Sìchuān, where it's just a matter of coming to an agreement with local herdsmen. A kora of Lake Manasarovar on horseback is a great idea and a few travellers have managed to arrange this. You may also be able to arrange day horse rental in villages in Eastern Tibet.

Tibet Wind Horse Adventure (Map p70; ☑0891-683 3009; www.windhorsetibet.com; B32 Shenzheng Huayuan, Sera Beilu) offers a one-day trip on horseback in the Dechen Valley

near Lhasa, as well as an adventurous five-day ride from Tidrum Nunnery to Reting Monastery.

Mountaineering

There are some huge peaks in Tibet, including the 8000m-plus giants of Cho Oyu, Shishapangma and, of course, Everest, which are enough to send a quiver of excitement through vertically inclined explorers. Unfortunately, the Chinese government charges high fees for mountaineering permits, which puts mountaineering in Tibet out of the range of most individuals or groups devoid of commercial sponsorship.

Foreign travel companies such as **Alpine Ascents** (www.alpineascents.com) and **Jagged Globe** (www.jagged-globe.co.uk) can arrange mountaineering ascents of Cho Oyu, the world's most frequently climbed 8000m peak.

Rafting

Tibet Wind Horse Adventure (Map p70; ☑0891-683 3009; www.windhorsetibet.com; B32 Shenzheng Huayuan, Sera Beilu) offers rafting trips between June and October: a half-day on the Tolung-chu, one or two days on the Drigung-chu, or ambitious five-day trips on the Reting Tsangpo or longer multi-location trips. Prices depend on group size.

Children

Children can be a great icebreaker in Tibet and generally generate a lot of interest. Many hotels have family rooms, which normally have three or four beds, sometimes arranged in two connected rooms.

Most foreign-orientated restaurants, and especially Nepali-run ones, have dishes like pizza and pancakes. Crisps (chips) and sweets are available in supermarkets everywhere; healthier options are hard to find.

You should bring your own car seat if travelling overland with small children. You need to be particularly careful with children and altitude sickness; children are not more susceptible to altitude than adults, but they are often less able to describe their symptoms. In general Tibet is a physically tough destination for adults, let alone younger children.

A fun book to get kids in the mood for a Tibetan adventure is *Tintin in Tibet*. If entering via Kathmandu, several bookshops sell colouring books featuring mandala and Tibetan *thangka* (Buddhist painting) designs.

Check out Lonely Planet's *Travel With Children* for handy hints and advice about the pros and cons of travelling with kids.

Practicalities

➡ Tibet is probably not a great place to bring a very small child.

➡ You should bring all supplies (including nappies and medicines) with you.

➡ Small spoons can be useful, as most places have only chopsticks.

➡ There's plenty of boiling water to sterilise bottles etc. It's possible to make a cot from the copious duvets supplied with most hotel rooms.

➡ Be especially careful with children and altitude sickness, as they won't be on the lookout for signs.

➡ Children under 1.5m (5ft) or under a certain age (the definition depends on the site) get in free at most sights in Tibet.

Climate

Most of Tibet is a high-altitude desert plateau at more than 4000m. Days in summer (June to September) are warm, sunny and generally dry, but temperatures drop quickly after dark. It's always cool above

Climate
Lhasa

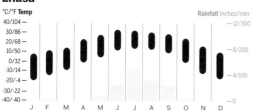

4000m and often freezing at night, though thanks to the Himalayan rain shadow there is surprisingly little snow in the Land of Snows. Sunlight is very strong at these altitudes, so bring plenty of high-factor sunscreen and lip balm.

Customs Regulations

Chinese border crossings have gone from being severely traumatic to exceedingly easy for travellers. You are unlikely to be checked even when flying into or out of the country.

➡ You can legally bring in or take out ¥20,000 in Chinese currency and must declare any cash amount exceeding US$5000 or its equivalent.

➡ It is illegal to import any printed material, film, tapes etc 'detrimental to China's politics, economy, culture and ethics'. This is a particularly sensitive subject in Tibet, but even here it is highly unusual to have Chinese customs officials grilling travellers about their reading matter. Maps and political books printed in Dharamsala, India, could cause a problem.

➡ It is currently illegal to bring into China pictures, books, videos or speeches of/about or by the Dalai Lama. Moreover, you may be placing a recipient of these in danger of a fine or jail sentence. Images of the Tibetan national flag are even 'more' illegal.

➡ If travelling from Nepal to Tibet by air or overland, it's a good idea to bury your guidebook deep in your pack or sleeping bag (and to have a backup on your tablet or mobile phone), as customs officials have been known to confiscate Lonely Planet *Tibet* guides.

➡ Be very circumspect if you are asked to take any packages, letters or photos out of Tibet for anyone else, including monks. If caught, you'll most likely be detained, interrogated and then expelled.

➡ Anything made in China before 1949 is considered an antique; you will need a certificate to take it out of the country. If it was made before 1795, it cannot legally be taken out of the country.

Electricity

Electricity is 220V, 50 cycles AC. Note that electronics such as laptops and iPods (anything with a hard drive) are occasionally affected by altitudes above 4500m.

Plugs have at least five designs: three-pronged angled pins (as in Australia), three-pronged round pins (as in Hong Kong), two flat pins (US style but without the ground wire), two narrow round pins (European style) and three rectangular pins (British style). US plugs work in Tibet without the need for an adapter.

Embassies & Consulates

The only diplomatic representation in Tibet is the **Nepali Consulate-General** (尼泊尔领事馆, Níbó'ěr Lǐngshìguǎn; Map p54; ☑0891-681 5744; www.nepalembassy.org.cn; 13 Luobulingka Beilu; ☺10am-noon Mon-Fri) in Lhasa. Visas are generally issued the next day at 4pm. It's located on a side street between the Lhasa Hotel and the Norbulingka.

Visa fees change frequently, but at the time of research 15-/30-/90-day multiple-entry visas cost ¥175/280/700. Bring one visa photo.

Chinese tourists have to get their visas here and these are currently free. Foreigners will generally find it easier to obtain tourist visas on the spot at the Nepalese border (bring two passport photos and cash in US dollars).

For Chinese embassies abroad, consult the Chinese Foreign Ministry website at www.fmprc.gov.cn/mfa_eng.

Consulates in Chéngdū

French Consulate (法国驻成都总领事馆; Fǎguózhù Chéngdūzǒng Lǐngshìguǎn; Map p240; ☑028 6666 6060, emergency 138 8031 3831; www.cn.ambafrance.org/-Chengdu-Consulat-; 30th fl, Times Plaza, 2 Zongfu Lu; 总府路2号时代广场30楼; ◎9am-12.30pm & 2.15-6pm Mon-Thu, to 4.30pm Fri; Ⓜ Chunxi Rd)

US Consulate (美国领事; Měiguó Lǐngshìguǎn; Map p240; ☑028 8558 3992; https://china.usembassy-china.org.

cn; 4 Lingshiguan Lu; 领事馆路4号; ◎1-4pm Tue, Thu & Fri; Ⓜ Nijiaqiao)

Embassies in Běijīng

In case of emergency in Tibet, your nearest embassy is most likely in Běijīng.

Australian Embassy (澳大利亚大使馆; Àodàlìyà Dàshǐguǎn; ☑010 5140 4111; www.china.embassy.gov.au; 21 Dongzhimenwai Dajie; 东直门外大街21号; ◎9am-noon & 2-3.30pm Mon-Fri; Ⓢ Line 2 to Dongzhimen, exit B)

Canadian Embassy (加拿大大使馆; Jiānádà Dàshǐguǎn; ☑010 5139 4000; www.china.gc.ca; 19 Dongzhimenwai Dajie; 东直门外大街19号; ◎8.30-11am Mon-Fri & 1.30-3pm Tue & Thu; Ⓢ Line 2 to Dongzhimen, exit B)

French Embassy (法国驻华大使馆; Fǎguó Zhùhuá Dàshǐguǎn; ☑010 8531 2000; www.ambafrance-cn.org; 60 Tianze Lu; 天泽路60号; ◎8.30am-noon Mon-Fri; 9am-noon last Sat of month; Ⓢ Line 10 to Liangmaqiao, exit B)

German Embassy (德国大使馆; Déguó Dàshǐguǎn; ☑010 8532 9000; www.china.diplo.de; 17 Dongzhimenwai Dajie; 东直门

外大街17号; ◎8am-noon & 1-5pm Mon, to 5.30pm Tue-Thu, 8am-noon & 12.30-3pm Fri; Ⓢ Line 2 to Dongzhimen, exit B)

Irish Embassy (爱尔兰大使馆; Ài'ěrlán Dàshǐguǎn; ☑010 8531 6200; www.irishembassy.cn; 3 Ritan Donglu; 日坛东路3号; ◎9am-12.30pm & 2-5pm Mon-Fri; Ⓢ Line 1 to Yonganli, exit A1)

Netherlands Embassy (荷兰大使馆; Hélán Dàshǐguǎn; ☑010 8532 0200; www.netherlandsworldwide.nl/countries/china/; 4 Liangmahe Nanlu; 亮马河南路4号; ◎9am-12.30pm & 2-5.30pm Mon-Fri; Ⓢ Line 10 to Liangmaqiao, exit B)

New Zealand Embassy (新西兰大使馆; Xīnxīlán Dàshǐguǎn; ☑010 8532 7000; www.mfat.govt.nz; 3 Sanlitun Dongsanjie; 三里屯东三街3号; ◎8.30am-noon & 1-5pm Mon-Fri; Ⓢ Line 10 to Agricultural Exhibition Center, exit D2)

UK Embassy (联合王国大使馆; Liánhé Wángguó Dàshǐguǎn; ☑010 5192 4000; www.gov.uk; 11 Guanghua Lu; 光华路11号; ◎9am-noon Mon, Tue, Thu & Fri; Ⓢ Line 1 to Yonganli, exit A1)

US Embassy (美国大使馆; Měiguó Dàshǐguǎn; ☑010 8531 3300; https://china.usembassy-china.org.cn/; 55 Anjialou Lu, off Liangmaqiao Lu; 亮马桥安家楼路55号; ◎by appointment; Ⓢ Line 10 to Liangmaqiao, exit B)

Insurance

Travel insurance is particularly recommended in a remote and wild region like Tibet. Check especially that the policy covers ambulances or an emergency flight home, which is essential in the case of altitude sickness. Some policies specifically exclude 'dangerous activities' such as rafting and even trekking.

You may prefer a policy that pays doctors or hospitals directly rather than your having to pay on the spot and claim later. If you have to claim later, make sure you keep all documentation.

ETIQUETTE

Tibetans are some of the most easygoing people you will meet, but will particularly appreciate you following etiquette in temples and monasteries.

Clothing Don't wear short skirts or shorts, especially at religious sites.

Pointing Don't point at people or statues with your finger; use your full upturned hand.

Touching Don't pat children on the head, as the head is considered sacred.

Direction Always circle a Buddhist monastery building or chörten clockwise.

Guests Tibetans show respect to an honoured guest or a lama by placing a *kathak* (prayer scarf) around their neck. When reciprocating, hold the scarf out in both hands with palms turned upwards.

Saving Face In general negotiations ensure that the person you are dealing with does not lose face and is not forced to back down in front of others. Outright confrontation is a last resort, especially with officialdom.

Some policies ask you to call a centre in your home country where an immediate assessment of your problem is made. Note that reverse-charge (collect) calls are not possible in Tibet.

It is very useful to have trip- and flight-cancellation insurance for Tibet. Many travellers only pick up their Tibet Tourism Bureau (TTB) permits a day or two before flying to Tibet and if the agency can't get the permits in time or the permit gets lost or delayed in the post then you will not be allowed to board your flight to Tibet. Insurance is especially useful if you are heading to western or eastern Tibet as these regions are frequently closed with little to no warning. The announcement for opening is made in March or April each year, but some years the region closes again suddenly after a brief opening, or opens later in the season after a prolonged closure.

Worldwide travel insurance is available at www.lonelyplanet.com/travel-insurance. You can buy, extend and claim online any time – even if you're already on the road.

Internet Access

Most hotels, cafes and even restaurants now offer free wi-fi access (无线网; *wúxiàn wǎng*). Sometimes hotels will only offer it in the lobby. Connecting to the internet through a smartphone's 3G or 4G service is often more reliable and coverage is good in central Tibet.

Internet cafes (网吧; *wǎngbā*) are in almost every town in Tibet, but few allow foreigners to use the computers.

Some social-networking sites (such as Facebook) and websites (eg those of the Dalai Lama, but also Google) as well as apps like WhatsApp have been blacklisted by the Chinese government and are unavailable inside China

EATING PRICE RANGES

The following price ranges refer to a standard dish in Chinese restaurants or a main course in western restaurants. There are no additional taxes, though some higher-end places may add a service charge.

$ less than ¥30

$$ ¥30–80

$$$ more than ¥80

unless you use a VPN (virtual private network), which is essentially an easy-to-use piece of software for a laptop computer or an app for a smartphone. Make sure you install this before departing for China.

Gmail is also spotty but again usually works well with a VPN.

Language Courses

Most urban Tibetans speak Mandarin in addition to Tibetan. Even in the countryside you can get by with basic Mandarin in most restaurants and hotels, since they are normally run by Mandarin-speaking Han or Hui Chinese. That said, Tibetans are extremely pleased when foreign visitors at least greet them in Tibetan, so it's well worth learning a few phrases. Very few Tibetans outside of the tourism industry speak English.

It is possible to enrol in a Tibetan language course at Lhasa's Tibet University. International students can only begin studies in autumn and must register by 31 March. Beginner- to advanced-level language classes are available, as well as cultural classes on such topics as calligraphy, history and painting. For an application form contact the **Foreign Affairs Office** (Map p54; ✆0891-634 3254; www.utibet.edu.cn; Jiangsu Lù). If you are accepted, the university will help arrange a student ('X') visa and, after three months, residency status in Lhasa. Students have to stay in campus accommodation.

It should also be possible to hire a private tutor from the university.

Many travellers find it more convenient to study in Dharamsala or Kathmandu, although students say that the mix of dialects and high levels of English make them less effective places to study. Courses offered there include Tibetan Buddhist philosophy, Tibetan language and Tibetan performing arts.

Many universities in the West also have Tibetan language courses and it's also possible to take classes just about anywhere with a private teacher via Skype.

Legal Matters

Most crimes are handled administratively by the Public Security Bureau (PSB; 公安局; Gōng'ānjú), which acts as police, judge and executioner.

China takes a particularly dim view of opium and all its derivatives. Foreigners have been executed for drug offences (trafficking in more than 50g of heroin can result in the death penalty). It's difficult to say what attitude the Chinese police will take towards foreigners caught using marijuana – they often don't care what foreigners do if it's not political, and if Chinese or Tibetans aren't involved. Then again the Chinese are fond of making examples of wrongdoings and you don't want to be the example. If arrested you should immediately contact your nearest embassy, which is probably in Běijīng.

In general, as you must travel throughout Tibet with guides, refrain from doing anything that would get them into trouble, such as visiting off-limits monasteries, photographing riot police or military installations, arguing with police or officials, talking politics openly or even visiting private Tibetan homes without special permission.

Public Security Bureau (PSB)

The PSB is the name given to China's police, both uniformed and plain clothed. The foreign-affairs branch of the PSB deals with foreigners. This branch (also known as the 'entry-exit branch') is responsible for issuing visa extensions and Alien Travel Permits.

In Tibet it is fairly unusual for foreigners to have problems with the PSB, though making an obvious display of pro-Tibetan political sympathies is guaranteed to lead to problems. Photographing Tibetan protests or military sites will lead to the confiscation of your camera or memory card and possibly a brief detention.

Attempting to travel into, through or out of Tibet without a travel permit, or to a destination not listed on your travel permit, is likely to end in an encounter with the PSB, most likely when checking into a hotel in a closed area. If you are caught in a closed area without a permit, you face a fine. Make sure you are friendly and repentant: the only times things get nasty is if you (or the police) lose your cool. Get a receipt to make sure you don't get fined a second time during your return to where you came from.

If you do have a serious run-in with the PSB, you may have to write a confession of guilt. In the most serious cases, you can be expelled from China (at your own expense).

LGBT+ Travellers

Homosexuality has historical precedents in Tibet, especially in Tibetan monasteries, where male lovers were known as *trap'i kedmen,* or 'monk's wife'. The Dalai Lama has sent mixed signals about homosexuality, stating in his book *Beyond Dogma* (1996) that, for practicing Buddhists, gay sex is 'sexual misconduct', 'improper' and 'inappropriate', but also openly supporting gay sex and marriage from the point of view of wider society.

The official attitude to gays and lesbians in China is also ambiguous, with responses ranging from draconian penalties to tacit acceptance. Travellers are advised to act with discretion. Chinese men routinely hold hands and drape their arms around each other without anyone inferring any sexual overtones.

HE Travel (☏800-825 9766; www.hetravel.com; 1325 West Indiana Ave, Salt Lake City) This US-based company has organised gay and lesbian group trips to Tibet in the past.

Out Adventures (☏866-360 1152; www.out-adventures.com; 579 Richmond St West, Suite 402, Toronto) A Canada-based company that can organise tailor-made tours to Tibet.

Utopia (www.utopia-asia.com/tipschin.htm) Has a good website and publishes a guide to gay travel in China, though with little specific to Tibet.

Maps

Good mapping for Tibet is not easy to come by, especially inside China, so stock up on maps before you leave. Good online map shops include Stanfords (www.stanfords.co.uk) and the Map Shop (www.themapshop.co.uk).

Maps of Tibet

Chinese provincial atlases to Tibet are available in bookshops throughout China.

They show the most detail but are of little use if you or the person you are asking doesn't read Chinese characters. Most locals know place names in Tibetan only, not Chinese.

Road maps available in Kathmandu include *Tibet – South-Central* by Nepa Maps, *Latest Map of Kathmandu to Tibet* by Mandala Maps, and the *Namaste Trekking Map* and *Lhasa to Kathmandu* (a mountain-biking map) by Himalayan Map House. They are marginally better than Chinese-produced maps but still aren't up to scratch.

Amnye Machen Institute in Dharamsala (www.amnyemachen.org) The *Tibet and Adjacent Areas under Chinese Communist Occupation* is an unusual map that covers the entire Tibetan world. It uses traditional Tibetan place names, which not everyone in Tibet (certainly not the many Chinese immigrants) will know.

Gecko Maps (www.geckomaps.com, in German, formerly Karto Atelier) Produces an excellent general *Himalaya-Tibet* map, as well as trekking and panoramic maps of Mt Kailash. Gecko also has a 1:50,000 *Kailash Tibet* map and a 1:600,000 *East Tibet* map covering Lhasa to Chéngdū.

Google Earth (www.google.com/earth) Offers fascinating detail on Tibet, including many monasteries and several treks. However, road names and even town names are often incorrect.

ITMB (www.itmb.com) Publishes a good and (usefully) waterproof *Tibet* map (1:1,850,000; 2006).

Reise Know-How (www.reise-know-how.de, in German) Perhaps the best overview is this 1:1,500,000 *Tibet* map.

TerraQuest (www.terraquest.eu/en/Maps) TerraQuest does a useful laminated 1:400,000 *Tibet* map, with insets covering the Friendship Hwy, Nam-tso and Central Tibet.

Tibet Map Institute (www.tibetmap.com) Try this website for detailed and downloadable online maps of Tibet.

Maps of Lhasa

Gecko Maps produces *The Lhasa Map*. The map has architectural detail of the old town, which helps identify which buildings are genuinely old and which are merely facades, but it's getting a bit dated. More offbeat, and also dated these days (published in 1995), is the Amnye Machen Institute's *Lhasa City* (1:12,500).

On This Spot – Lhasa, published by the International Campaign for Tibet (www.savetibet.org) in 2001, is a unique political map of the Lhasa region, pinpointing the locations of prisons, demonstrations, human-rights abuses and more. It's a really fascinating read but is too politically subversive to take into Tibet.

Money

The Chinese currency is known as rénmínbì (RMB) or 'people's money'. The basic unit of this currency is the yuán, designated by a '¥'. In spoken Chinese, the word 'kuài' is almost always substituted for the yuán. Ten jiǎo (commonly known as máo) make up one yuán.

Basic bargaining skills are essential for travel in Tibet. You can bargain in shops, hotels and travel agencies, at street stalls, and with pedicab drivers, but there is one important rule to follow: be polite. Aggressive bargaining will usually only serve to firm the conviction of both Tibetans and Chinese that the original asking price is the one they want.

Although big hotels may add a tax or 'service charge' of 10% to 15%, all other taxes are included in prices, including airline departure tax.

ATMs

Several ATMs (自动取款机; *zìdòng qǔkuǎnjī*) in Lhasa and Shigatse and even as far afield as Ali accept foreign cards. The Bank of China accepts Visa, MasterCard,

American Express, Maestro, Cirrus and Plus. Check before trying your card, as many ATMs can only be used by domestic account holders.

ATMs have a ¥2400 transaction limit but no daily limit, unless set by your bank. ATMs at ICBC banks also sometimes take foreign cards. Cards are occasionally eaten by machines, so try to make your transaction during bank hours.

Credit Cards

You'll get very few opportunities to splurge on the plastic in Tibet, unless you spend a few nights in a top-end hotel. Most local tours, train tickets and even flights out of Lhasa still can't be paid for using a credit card (unless purchased online). The few shops that do accept credit cards often have a 4% surcharge.

The Lhasa central branch of the Bank of China is the only place in Tibet that provides cash advances on a credit card. A 3% commission is deducted.

Exchanging Money

In Tibet, the main place to change foreign currency is the Bank of China. Top-end hotels in Lhasa have exchange services, but only for guests. Outside Lhasa the only places to change money are in Shigatse, Purang (cash only), and Ali in far-western Tibet.

The currencies of Australia, Canada, the US, the UK, Hong Kong, Japan and the eurozone are acceptable at the Lhasa Bank of China. ATM currency-exchange machines accept the currencies of the US, the UK, the eurozone, Hong Kong and Japan but have a maximum of US$700 per transaction (no daily limit).

The official rate is given at all banks and most hotels, so there is no need to shop around for the best deal. There's no commission to change cash.

The only places in Tibet to officially change yuán back into foreign currency are the central Lhasa branch and (less reliably) the Kyirong branch of the Bank of China. You will need your original exchange receipts.

Moneychangers at the Nepal border will change yuán into Nepali rupees and vice versa. Yuán can also easily be reconverted in Hong Kong and, increasingly, in many Southeast Asian countries.

China has a problem with counterfeit notes. Very few Tibetans or Chinese will accept a ¥100 note without first subjecting it to intense scrutiny, and many will not accept old, tattered notes or coins. Check the watermark when receiving any ¥100 note.

International Transfers

Getting money sent to you in Lhasa is possible, but it can be a drag. One option is to use the Bank of China's central office in Lhasa.

The second option is via Western Union (www.westernunion.com), which can wire money to one of several Postal Savings Bank of China outlets in Lhasa.

Tipping

Restaurants Tipping is not expected in restaurants or hotels in Tibet.

Guides Approximately ¥35 to ¥50 per day per person.

Drivers Approximately ¥25 to ¥30 per day per person.

Travellers Cheques

Travellers cheques are rarely used these days but can be useful in Tibet. Besides the advantage of safety, travellers cheques actually get you a slightly higher exchange rate than cash. US dollar cheques from the major companies such as Thomas Cook, Visa and American Express are your best bet.

Opening Hours

Opening hours listed are for summer; winter hours generally start half an hour later and finish half an hour earlier.

Government Offices & PSB
9.30am to 1pm and 3pm to 6.30pm Monday to Friday, sometimes 10am to 1pm Saturday

Banks 9.30am to 5.30pm Monday to Friday, 10.30am to 4pm Saturday and Sunday

Restaurants 10am to 10pm

Shops 10am to 9pm

Bars May close at 8pm or 2am, depending on their location and clientele

Many smaller monasteries have no set opening hours and will open up chapels once you've tracked down the right monk. Others, such as Sakya, are notorious for only opening certain rooms at certain times. Your best bet is to tag along with pilgrims or a tour group.

Photography

Lonely Planet's *Guide to Travel Photography* is full of helpful tips for photography while on the road.

Shops in Lhasa stock a decent range of memory cards and rechargeable batteries (though don't expect to find every camera model's type).

Battery life plummets at Tibet's higher elevations and lower temperatures. Keep your batteries warm and separate from your camera overnight and during cold weather. Just heating up batteries in your pocket or the sun can draw some extra juice from them.

Photographs of airports and military installations are prohibited, and bridges are also a touchy subject. Don't take any photos or especially video footage of civil unrest or public demonstrations. Chinese authorities are very wary about foreign TV crews filming unauthorised documentaries on Tibet.

Restrictions on photography are also imposed at most monasteries and museums. This is partly an attempt to stop the trade of antiquities out of Tibet (statues are often stolen to order from photos taken by seemingly innocuous 'tourists'). In the case of flash photography, such restrictions protect wall murals from damage. Inside the larger monasteries, a fee of ¥20 to ¥50 is often imposed in each chapel for taking a photograph. Video fees can be up to ¥800 (US$100) in some monasteries. You are free, however, to take any photos of the exteriors of monasteries.

Post

China's postal service is generally inexpensive and efficient: airmail letters and postcards take around a week to 10 days to reach most destinations. Writing the country of destination in Chinese can speed up the delivery. Domestic post is very swift, often reaching the destination in one or two days. Lhasa is the only place in Tibet from which it's possible to send international parcels by air or surface mail.

Post offices are very picky about how you pack things; do not finalise your packing until the parcel has its last customs clearance. If you have a receipt for the goods, then put it in the box when you are mailing it, since it may be opened again by customs further down the line.

China Post operates an express mail service (EMS) – a worldwide priority mail service – that is fast and reliable. Documents to most foreign countries arrive in around five days.

Public Holidays

Chinese New Year, otherwise known as the Spring Festival, is definitely not the time to travel around China, cross borders (especially the Hong Kong one) or be caught short of money.

Serf Emancipation Day was introduced as a public holiday in Tibet in 2009 to commemorate 50 years of Communist Chinese control in Tibet and what China says was the freeing of one million Tibetan 'serfs'. Don't expect much in the way of celebration among the ex-serfs.

Many Tibetan businesses, restaurants, shops and travel agencies are closed on the days of **Losar** (⊘Feb) and **Saga Dawa** (⊘May/Jun). Tibetan festivals like these are held according to the Tibetan lunar calendar, which usually runs at least a month behind the Gregorian calendar. Ask around for the exact dates of religious festivals because monasteries often only fix these a few months in advance. Check Tibetan lunar dates against Gregorian dates at www.shambhala.com/tibetan-lunar-calendar.

China has several traditional and modern national holidays. They mean little to many Tibetans, but government offices and banks will be closed on many of these dates. Note that the length of holidays is subject to change.

New Year's Day 1 January

Chinese New Year 5 February 2019; a week's holiday for most

Serf Emancipation Day 28 March

Qing Ming Jie (Tomb Sweeping Festival) First weekend in April; a three-day holiday; not really observed in Tibet

Labour Day 1 May; a three-day holiday

International Children's Day 1 June

Dragon Boat Festival 7 June 2019

Mid-Autumn Festival 13 September 2019

National Day 1 October; a week-long holiday

The following are politically sensitive dates, as are 5 March, 27 September, 1 October and 10 December, which mark past political protests. It may be difficult for travellers to fly into Tibet for a few days before these dates. Tibet generally closes to foreign travellers for the entire month of March.

10 March Anniversary of the 1959 Tibetan uprising and flight of the Dalai Lama

23 May Anniversary of the signing of the Agreement on Measures for the Peaceful Liberation of Tibet

1 September Anniversary of the founding of the Tibet Autonomous Region (TAR)

Safe Travel

Tibet is a safe place to travel and crime rates are low.

➡ Most dangers come from the physical environment, notably the altitude.

➡ Frequent checkposts, mind-numbing speed restrictions and entrenched officialdom can become wearing, especially to independent-minded travellers.

➡ Travel regulations are liable to change on a whim. You'll likely face a battle visiting a little-known temple or making even a small detour off your itinerary if it's not pre-arranged. Permission to visit a site may be denied at any moment.

Dogs

If you are exploring remote monasteries or villages on foot, keep an eye open for dogs, especially at remote homesteads or nomad encampments, where the powerful and aggressive mastiffs should be given a very wide berth. Travel with a walking pole or stick if possible and try not to walk alone.

Political Disturbances

Tourists can be caught up in Tibet's political violence and backpackers have even been injured in crossfire in the past. If a demonstration or full-blown riot breaks out (as it did in 2008), it's safest to stay in your hotel. If things get really bad, local authorities or your embassy may organise emergency flights out of Lhasa.

Tourists sometimes forget that Tibet is a very tightly controlled place. Do not bring into Tibet pictures of the Dalai Lama, publications by the Dalai Lama, Tibetan flags or anything that could be construed by the Chinese authorities as pro-Tibetan political activity.

Plain-clothes police officers are everywhere in Tibet, and even some monks and monastery officials work for the security services (every monastery has government security personnel posted there), so be very circumspect about political conversations with anyone you don't personally know.

Theft

Theft is rare in Tibet, which is generally safer than other provinces of China. Trekkers in the Everest region have reported problems in the past with petty theft, and pickpockets work parts of Lhasa.

Small padlocks are useful for backpacks and dodgy hotel rooms. Bicycle chain locks come in handy not only for hired bikes but also for attaching backpacks to railings or luggage racks.

If something of yours is stolen, you should report it immediately to the nearest foreign-affairs branch of the Public Security Bureau (PSB). They will ask you to fill in a loss report, which you will also need to claim the loss on your travel insurance.

On the Road

Simply travelling through Tibet brings its own frustrations these days. High-priced admission tickets for monasteries and even some lakes (and passes!) can be a source of irritation, especially when coupled with locked monastery chapels and ever-increasing travel restrictions.

Driving on Tibet's roads entails stopping at dozens of checkpoints; some check passports and permits, others check the driver's papers, and still others act as speed controls. On many sections of road your driver will be given a fixed time before which he cannot arrive at the next checkpoint, leading to dozens of cars parked by the side of the road just before the second checkpost as they wait out the remaining 10 minutes on their time chit. The 250km section of road between Lhasa and Shigatse currently has at least 20 separate checkposts. Try to have patience with your driver, who probably doesn't like the restrictions any more than you do but will face fines if caught speeding.

GOVERNMENT TRAVEL ADVICE

The following government websites offer travel advisories and information on current hot spots.

Australian Department of Foreign Affairs (www.smartraveller.gov.au)

UK Foreign & Commonwealth Office (www.gov.uk/foreign-travel-advice)

Canadian Department of Foreign Affairs (www.voyage.gc.ca)

New Zealand Department of Foreign Affairs & Trade (www.safetravel.govt.nz)

US State Department (http://travel.state.gov)

Telephone

Mobile-phone coverage is generally good, even in far-western Tibet and at Everest Base Camp!

Public telephones can be found in small shops but are increasingly hard to find.

Most hotels in Lhasa have International Direct Dial (IDD) telephones but levy a hefty surcharge on calls.

WhatsApp is blocked in China unless you have a VPN, though Skype seems to work. Most Chinese and Tibetans use the messaging app WeChat.

Mobile Phones

Purchasing a local phone or data SIM card in Lhasa can be complicated, as you normally need to show a local residency card. It's much easier to buy your SIM card elsewhere in China (Chéngdū is a good option) and in fact many hostels sell them at reception.

A SIM card from China Telecom or China Unicom costs ¥120, which gives you around 200 minutes of local calls plus enough data for two weeks of emails and internet usage for most. You can add credit with a credit-charging card (充值卡; *chōngzhí ka*) for ¥50 or ¥100 of credit. It's best to take your guide with you to purchase a card as there are many options.

Time

Time throughout China – including Tibet – is set to Běijīng time, which is eight hours ahead of GMT/UTC. When it is noon in Běijīng it is also noon in far-off Lhasa, even if the sun only indicates around 9am or 10am.

Toilets

Chinese toilets might be dismal, but Tibetan toilets make them look like little bowers of heaven. The standard model is a deep hole in the ground, often without partitions, with faeces littered all over the floor and sometimes even the walls (!?). Many Tibetans (including women with long skirts) prefer to urinate in the street.

On the plus side, there are some fabulous 'toilets with a view'. Honours go to the Samding Monastery Guesthouse and the public toilets in the Potala Palace.

With the exception of midrange and top-end places, hotel and restaurant toilets in Tibet are of the squat variety – as the cliché goes, good for the digestion and character building, too. *Always* carry an emergency stash of toilet paper or tissues with you.

Tourist Information

Tibet is officially a province of China and does not have tourist offices as such. Similarly, the Tibetan government-in-exile does not provide information specifically relating to travel in Tibet. Several of the pro-Tibet organisations abroad offer travel advice.

Visas

Visa regulations for China are subject to change, so treat the following as general guidelines. In 2013 the visa system had a major overhaul and there are now 13 categories of visa.

Apart from citizens of Brunei, Japan and Singapore (for stays of less than 15 days), all visitors to Tibet require a valid China visa. Visas for individual travel in China involve jumping through some hoops but are usually routine to get from most Chinese embassies or their associated visa centres.

Most visa offices will issue a standard 30-day (sometimes 60- or 90-day) single-entry tourist ('L' category) visa in three to five working days. The 'L' means *lǚxíng* (travel). Fees vary, as do durations: UK citizens pay £85 for a multiple-entry L visa, normally valid for one or even two years, Americans pay US$140 for a multiple-entry visa (often valid for up to 10 years), while most other countries' citizens pay US$40.

In many countries the visa service has been outsourced to a **China Visa Application Service Centre** (www.visaforchina.org), which levies additional charges that can effectively double the price.

The visa application form asks you a lot of questions (your entry and exit points, travel itinerary, means of transport etc), but once in China you can deviate from this as much as you like. When listing your itinerary, pick the obvious contenders: Běijīng, Shànghǎi and so on. Don't mention Tibet and don't list your occupation as 'journalist'. You may need to show proof of a return air ticket, hotel bookings and photocopies of previous Chinese visas. You must also have one entire blank page in your passport for the visa, as well as a passport valid for at least six months.

Most visas take four working days to be issued, assuming all your documentation is in order. Express services are normally available for an extra fee.

Note that you must be physically present in the country you apply in (ie you cannot send your passport back to your home country if you are staying somewhere else).

Some embassies and visa services offer a postal service (for an additional fee), which takes around three weeks. In the US and Canada mailed visa applications have to go via a visa agent, at extra cost. In the US many people use **China Visa Service Center** (www.mychinavisa. com). Express services are available for a premium.

A standard single-entry visa must be used within three months from the date of issue and is activated on the date you enter China. There is some confusion over the validity of Chinese visas. Most Chinese officials look at the 'valid until' date, but on most 30-day visas this is actually the date by which you must have *entered* the country, not the visa's expiry date. Longer-stay visas are often activated on the day of issue, not the day you enter the country, so there's no point in getting one too far in advance of your planned entry date. Check with the embassy if you are unsure.

It's possible to travel in Tibet with a tourist ('L'), student ('X'), resident ('D') or business ('M', 'F' or 'Z') visa, but not on a journalist ('J') visa. For an M, F or Z visa the agency handling your TTB permit may ask you to provide documentation showing your place of work in China, or a letter of invitation.

Arranging Visas in Hong Kong

Hong Kong is usually a reliable place to pick up visas, often with next-day service, but confirm with the companies listed here before you decide this is the route you will take to obtain a visa.

Single-entry, double-entry, multiple-entry and business visas are usually available at the following places in Hong Kong. For reference, a single-entry L visa costs HK$200 for three-day service, HK$500 for next-day service, but varies according to nationality.

China Travel Service (中國旅行社, CTS; ☑customer service 852 2998 7888, tour hotline 852 2998 7333; www.ctshk.com) With several locations.

Forever Bright Trading Limited (☑852 2369 3188; www.fbt-chinavisa.com.hk; Room 916-917, Tower B, New Mandarin Plaza, 14 Science Museum Rd, Tsim Sha Tsui East, Kowloon; ⊙8.30am-6.30pm Mon-Fri, to

1.30pm Sat; Ⓜ East Tsim Sha Tsui, exit P2)

Arranging Visas in Kathmandu

The Chinese embassy in Kathmandu does not issue visas to individual travellers, only to those booked on a tour and then only paper group visas (not a stamp in your passport). If you turn up with a Chinese visa in your passport, it will be cancelled.

Nepali agencies currently charge around US$85 per person for a group visa. US/Canadian citizens pay US$177/135. Allow at least three working days for processing; faster service is sometimes available for a premium but not at the time of research. The embassy needs your actual passport, so you need to budget four or five days in Kathmandu before your Tibet trip. You will need to have a visa invitation letter issued from your Tibetan agency before you can apply for a Chinese visa.

Group visas are issued for the duration of your tour. If you are continuing on to China after your tour you can request your own individual 30-day group visa.

The visa office at Nepal's **Chinese Embassy** (Map p232; ☑01-4440286; http://np.china-embassy.org; Hattisar, Kathmandu; ⊙9.45-11am Mon-Fri) accepts applications from 9.45am to 11am Monday to Friday. Note that the main embassy is in Baluwatar, but the separate visa office is in Hattisar. Your Nepali agent (or the agent of your Tibet tour company) will make the application for you.

If you are flying from Kathmandu directly to Chinese cities outside Tibet (ie Chéngdū or Shànghǎi), you can enter China on an individual tourist visa issued from abroad. Thus if you want to continue travelling in China after your Tibet trip for a trip longer than 30 days, the easiest thing is to fly

from Kathmandu to Chéngdū and then on to Lhasa with your TTB permit and on your normal Chinese visa.

Visa Extensions

The *wàishìkē* (foreign affairs) section of the local PSB handles visa extensions. Extensions are very difficult to get in Tibet, so don't count on one. It is far easier to extend your visa in other areas of China such as Chéngdū, Xīníng or Xī'ān, where a 30-day extension is commonplace.

Volunteering

There are very limited opportunities for volunteer work in the TAR. There are considerably more opportunities outside the TAR, in Tibetan areas of Sìchuān and Qīnghǎi, and especially in Dharamsala (see www.volunteertibet.org.in).

Conscious Journeys (www.consciousjourneys.org) Runs medical 'voluntourism' trips to Tibetan areas of Sìchuān, as well as responsibly run tours in Tibet.

Rokpa (www.rokpauk.org/volunteering.html) Volunteer teaching positions in the Jyekundo (Yùshù) region of Qīnghǎi.

Weights & Measures

The metric system is used, though traders measure fruit and vegetables by the *jin* (500g).

Women Travellers

Women are generally not permitted to enter the *gönkhang* (protector chapel) in a monastery, ostensibly for fear of upsetting the powerful protector deities inside.

Several women have written of the favourable reactions they have received from Tibetan women when wearing Tibetan dress; you can get one made in Lhasa.

Transport

GETTING THERE & AWAY

For most international travellers, getting to Tibet will involve at least two legs: first to a gateway city such as Kathmandu (Nepal) or Chéngdū (China), and then into Tibet.

The most popular options from the gateway towns into Tibet are as follows:

➡ International flight from Kathmandu to Lhasa

➡ Domestic Chinese flight to Lhasa from Chéngdū, Kūnmíng, Xīníng, Běijīng or many others

➡ Train via Qīnghǎi to Lhasa, starting in Xīníng, Lánzhōu, Běijīng or other Chinese cities

➡ The overland drive from Kathmandu to Lhasa via the new crossing at Kyirong, along the Friendship Hwy. At the time of writing, bureaucratic obstacles to entering Tibet from China were many and involved signing up for a preplanned and prepaid tour. The situation from Nepal is even trickier because of group-visa requirements. Political events, both domestic and international, can mean that regulations for entry into Tibet change overnight. Nerves of steel are definitely useful when arranging flights and permits. Always check on the latest developments before booking flights.

Note that it can be very hard to get hold of air and train tickets to Lhasa around the Chinese New Year and the week-long holidays around 1 May and 1 October.

Flights, hotels and tours can be booked online at www.lonelyplanet.com/bookings.

Entering Tibet

Arriving in China is pretty painless these days. All travellers fill in a customs and health declaration form on arrival in the country. Expect closer scrutiny of your group documents and luggage when crossing into Tibet from Nepal, where some travellers have on occasion had Tibet-related books and images confiscated.

Passport

Chinese embassies will not issue a visa if your passport has less than six months' validity remaining.

Air

There are no direct long-haul flights to Tibet. You will almost certainly have to stop for at least a night in Chéngdū, Guǎngzhōu or Běijīng, as you need to to pick up your permit or meet your group in your chosen gateway city before heading to Lhasa.

If routing via Kathmandu, budget at least four working days there in order to secure your Chinese group visa.

Airports & Airlines

For China, you generally have the choice of flying first to **Běijīng** (http://en.bcia.com.cn), **Shànghǎi** (www.shanghai-airport.com), **Guǎngzhōu** (www.guangzhouairport

---

CLIMATE CHANGE & TRAVEL

Every form of transport that relies on carbon-based fuel generates CO_2, the main cause of human-induced climate change. Modern travel is dependent on aeroplanes, which might use less fuel per kilometre per person than most cars but travel much greater distances. The altitude at which aircraft emit gases (including CO_2) and particles also contributes to their climate change impact. Many websites offer 'carbon calculators' that allow people to estimate the carbon emissions generated by their journey and, for those who wish to do so, to offset the impact of the greenhouse gases emitted with contributions to portfolios of climate-friendly initiatives throughout the world. Lonely Planet offsets the carbon footprint of all staff and author travel.

online.com) or **Hong Kong** (www.hongkongairport.com); there is also a small but growing number of international flights direct to **Chéngdū** (www.cdairport.com/en). There's little difference in fares to these airports,

There are direct flights from Běijīng and Shànghǎi to Lhasa, so it is no longer necessary to first fly into Chéngdū.

TO & FROM CHÉNGDŪ

Chéngdū's Shuangliu International Airport is well connected to other cities in China, with daily flights arriving from Běijīng, Shànghǎi, Guǎngzhōu, Kūnmíng and Hong Kong among others. There is also a growing number of international carriers making nonstop flights into Chéngdū, mainly from Asian hubs like Bangkok, Kuala Lumpur, Seoul, Tokyo and Singapore. From Europe it's possible to reach Chéngdū nonstop from Amsterdam and Frankfurt, and from the USA there are direct flights from Los Angeles and San Francisco. Arriving from other international destinations will likely require you to change planes and possibly make a layover in a mainland Chinese hub.

International airlines flying into Chéngdū include the following.

Air Asia (www.airasia.com) From Kuala Lumpur.

Air China (www.airchina.com) From Frankfurt, Hong Kong, Bangkok, Kathmandu, Paris, Rome, Singapore, Sydney, Seoul and Tokyo.

Asiana (www.flyasiana.com) From Seoul.

China Eastern (http://ph.ceair.com/en/) From Bangkok and Osaka.

China Southern (www.csair.com/en/) From Amsterdam and many cities via Guǎngzhōu.

Etihad (www.etihad.com) Via Abu Dhabi.

Hainan Airlines (www.hainanairlines.com) From Los Angeles and New York

KLM (www.klm.com) From Amsterdam.

Qatar Airways (www.qatarairways.com) Via Doha.

Sichuan Airlines (https://global.sichuanair.com/US-EN) From Auckland, Bangkok, Chiang Rai, Kathmandu, Melbourne, Seoul, Singapore, Tokyo and Vancouver.

United Airlines (www.united.com) From San Francisco.

Chéngdū has long been the main gateway to Lhasa for travellers coming by air, and multiple flights a day go to Lhasa in the height of summer. Flights cost ¥1680 one way but are often discounted down to ¥1200.

Flights into Lhasa are operated by **Air China** (CA; www.airchina.com.cn), **Sichuan Airlines** (3U; www.scal.com.cn), **Tibet Airlines** (TV; wwwtibetairlines.com) and **China Eastern** (MU; http://ph.ceair.com/en/, www.ceair.com). Note that on many online booking sites you need to spell Lhasa as 'Lasa'.

Try to book the first flight of the day because weather conditions and visibility will be optimal in the morning. On a clear day the views from the plane are stupendous, so try to get a window seat. In general the best views are from the left side of the plane from Chéngdū to Lhasa and the right side from Lhasa to Chéngdū. Getting into Lhasa early also gives you a little more time to acclimatise if you are on a short tour.

If you are coming to Tibet from somewhere outside China, have your agency mail your permit to a hotel in Chéngdū, where you can pick it up and fly out the next day. Make sure the permit is sent a few days before you arrive and preferably let the hotel know it's coming.

There are also daily flights (¥1530) from Chéngdū to Nyingtri (Nyingchi; Línzhī) in eastern Tibet, which might be an offbeat option if you plan to visit the Kongpo region. At around 3000m elevation, the region is lower than Lhasa and so helps with acclimatisation.

TO & FROM KATHMANDU

Generally, long-haul flights to/from Kathmandu are relatively expensive, as a limited number of carriers operate out of the Nepali capital. The national carrier, Nepal Airlines (www.nepalairlines.com.np), is notoriously unreliable and is to be avoided if possible.

One option is to buy separate discounted flights to Delhi and from Delhi on to Kathmandu, but note that without a single through ticket you will likely have to arrange an Indian transit or tourist visa in order to pick up your baggage and transfer between flights at Delhi airport.

International airlines flying into and out of Kathmandu include the following.

Air India (www.airindia.in) Good connections via New Delhi.

China Southern (www.csair.com/en/) Good option from Australia via Guǎngzhōu.

Etihad (www.etihad.com) Quality airline with fast connections through the Middle East, but pricier than most.

Jet Airways (www.jetairways.com) Good service and connections via New Delhi.

Thai Airways (www.thaiairways.com) Flights from Bangkok.

Turkish Airlines (www.turkishairlines.com) Fast connections from Europe via Istanbul.

Air China and Sichuan Airlines operate flights between Kathmandu and Lhasa daily in high season. Fares vary wildly between US$200 and US$400 one way, depending on the month.

Individual travellers can't buy air tickets from the Air China office in Kathmandu without a TTB permit, but it doesn't seem a problem to buy them online. To board the plane you'll have to show your group China visa, which you'll only get through booking a tour with a Lhasa- or Kathmandu-based agency.

It is possible to buy air tickets from Kathmandu to other destinations in China, such as Chéngdū (from US$280 one way); you don't need a Tibet

DEPARTURE TAX

Departure tax in China is worked into the price of both domestic and international tickets, so there's nothing additional to pay at the airport.

Tourism Bureau (TTB) permit to take these flights.

TO & FROM YÚNNÁN

There are some useful daily flight connections between Lhasa and the popular traveller centres of Lìjiāng, Kūnmíng and Déqīn (the main airport for Zhōngdiàn, also known as Gyeltang or Shangri-la). As with other flights to Lhasa, foreigners won't be allowed on board without a TTB permit.

ONWARD CONNECTIONS TO TIBET

Within China there are flight connections to Lhasa from a dozen cities (and growing), including direct flights from Běijīng, Guǎngzhōu, Lánzhōu, Xi'an, Xīníng and Kūnmíng.

There are also some interesting daily flights within the Tibetan world, namely from Lhasa to Yùshù (Jyekundo; ¥1060) in Qīnghǎi, Xiàhé (¥1950) in Gānsù, Kàngdìng (¥1500) in Sìchuān and Déqīn (also known as Zhōngdiàn, Gyeltang or Shangri-la) in Yúnnán. Some of the more obscure routes are with the Chinese budget airline **Lucky Air** (Xiángpéng Hángkōng; www.luckyair.net).

That said, most travellers still fly in to Lhasa from Chéngdū, as there are more flights, cheaper fares and more tour agencies there. There are also flights from Chéngdū to Nyingtri (Línzhī).

Your Tibet permit will be checked when checking in for your flight to Lhasa, as well as on arrival at Lhasa's Gongkar airport.

Note that flights to and from Lhasa are sometimes cancelled or delayed in the winter months, so if you are flying at this time give yourself a couple of days' leeway if you have a connecting flight.

Baggage allowance on flights to Lhasa is 20kg in economy class and 40kg in 1st class, so you'll have to limit your gear to avoid penalties, regardless of what you are allowed to bring on your international flight into China.

Tickets

There are essentially two ways to buy an air ticket to Tibet's gateway cities: buy a single international ticket to a city like Chéngdū or buy an international ticket to Běijīng, Shànghǎi or Guǎngzhōu and then buy a discounted domestic Chinese air ticket online.

Note that if transiting through a city like Běijīng en route to a domestic Chinese destination you will need to clear immigration and customs in Běijīng, so allow plenty of time for your domestic connection.

The cheapest tickets to China are generally available on price-comparison websites such as Kayak (www.kayak.com) and Skyscanner (www.skyscanner.net).

You can buy discounted domestic tickets within China (except Lhasa) from online Chinese ticket agencies such as Elong (www.elong.net) and Trip (www.trip.com). These sites can sell you tickets to gateway cities but will not sell you a ticket from Chéngdū to Tibet without Chinese ID, though international online ticket sites such as One Travel (www.onetravel.com) and Expedia (www.expedia.com) will. If this sounds too complicated, you can always ask your Tibetan tour agency to handle domestic tickets to Lhasa.

Airfares to China peak between June and September.

Land

Some individual travellers make their way to Tibet as part of a grand overland trip through China, Nepal, India and onwards. In many ways, land travel to Tibet is the best way to go, not only for the scenery en route but also because it can help spread the altitude gain over a few days.

Overland trips inside the Tibet Autonomous Region have to be organised tours with vehicle rental and a guide.

Several travel agencies in Nepal organise overland budget group tours (p43) to Lhasa.

Road

In theory there are several land routes into Tibet. The bulk of overland travellers take the Friendship Hwy between Kathmandu and Lhasa.

The Qīnghǎi–Tibet Hwy and the very remote Xīnjiāng–Tibet Hwy are possible on a tour with all the proper permits. The Qīnghǎi–Tibet Hwy is also possible on an organised cycling tour but there's a lot of truck traffic en route.

The spectacular overland routes into Tibet along the Sìchuān–Tibet Hwy and the Yúnnán–Tibet Hwy are popular with Chinese travellers but have been closed to foreign travellers for years now due to the closure of Chamdo prefecture on the Tibet side. At the time of writing the road from northwest Yúnnán to Lhasa was open to a limited number of groups, so check with Lhasa agencies to see if this route is fully open.

In the current climate it's most unwise to try any route without being part of an organised tour – you have a very high chance of being caught and fined and of dragging any Tibetan who has helped you into your troubles.

OTHER ROUTES INTO TIBET

A little-travelled route into Tibet, for trekking groups only, passes through Purang

(Taklakot in Nepali). Special visas are required for this trip. Trekkers start by travelling by road or flying from Kathmandu to Nepalganj, then flying from there to Simikot in the far west of Nepal. From Simikot it's a five- or six-day walk to the Tibetan border at Sher, up the Humla Karnali valley. The Nepali government is building a road from the border to Simikot along this route, so consider the alternative trek route via the neighbouring Limi Valley. Some Indian groups travel this section by chartered helicopter. From the border you can then drive the 28km to Purang and the further 107km to the Mt Kailash area via Lake Manasarovar.

Tibetan, Chinese and Indian travellers can cross into Tibet's Yadong region from Gangtok in Sikkim via the 4310m Nathu-la, tracing the former trading routes between Lhasa, Kalimpong and Calcutta, and the path taken by Younghusband's invasion of Tibet in 1903. The route is not open to foreign travellers.

Indian pilgrims on a quota system travel to Purang via the Lipu Lekh pass from Pithoragarh.

Train

The world's highest train, the Qīnghǎi–Tibet Railway (p34), connects mainland China with Lhasa over the Tibetan plateau. Trains leave from Běijīng, Chéngdū, Shànghǎi, Xīníng and Guǎngzhōu daily, and every other day from Chóngqìng (via Xī'ān) and Lánzhōu, to link with the Chéngdū and Xīníng trains, respectively. Xīníng is probably the most popular place to start a train ride to Lhasa, though getting tickets can prove a challenge.

A twice-daily train service from Lhasa to Shigatse started in late 2014. Future extensions will include lines from Lhasa to Tsetang and the eastern region of Kongpo, to the Nepal border at Kyirong and from Golmud to Dūnhuáng in Gānsù province.

China and Nepal recently agreed to build a rail line from Kyirong to Kathmandu, with India pledging to continue the line to the Indian border. Were this to happen it would make for an epic trans-Himalayan crossing by rail.

GETTING AROUND

Air

Tibet is one of China's biggest provinces, but flights within the Tibet Autonomous Region (TAR) are few and far between and tickets can be hard to secure. There are airports at Lhasa (Gongkar), Nyingtri (Nyingchi), Chamdo (Bangda), Ali and Shigatse. Apart from Lhasa, these are of limited use to tourists.

Shigatse's Peace Airport has flights to Chéngdū (¥1880) with **Tibet Airlines** (www.tibetairlines.com.cn) and to Shànghǎi and Xī'ān with **China Eastern** (www.ceair.com).

Tibet Airlines also has flights between Lhasa and Ali's Ngari Gunsa Airport, but these are expensive at ¥2690 one way. **Lucky Air** (www.luckyair.net) currently operates an intriguing twice-weekly Ali to Kashgar flight (¥2040).

A sixth airport is under construction in Nagchu (Dagring). When finished it will be the highest civilian airport in the world. Three more airports are planned at Lhoka (Longzi), Tingri and Purang (in Ngari), with construction due to start in 2019.

Bicycle

Long-distance cyclists, the majority of whom are Chinese, are an increasingly frequent sight on the roads of Tibet, especially along the Friendship Hwy and Hwy 318 in eastern Tibet. For foreign travellers, cycling in Tibet is no longer a cheap or easy adventure; like everyone else, you'll need to

arrange a tour (p309) with a guide, who will likely follow you in a support vehicle.

Most long-distance cyclists bring their own bikes to Tibet, though it is possible to buy a decent Chinese-made or (better) Taiwanese-made mountain bike in Lhasa. Do not expect the quality of these bikes to be equal to that of those you might buy at home – bring plenty of spare parts. Bikes have a relatively high resale value in Kathmandu and you might even make a profit if the bike is in good shape (unlikely after a trip across Tibet!).

Tibet poses unique challenges to individual cyclists. The good news is that the main roads are all paved and in excellent condition and the traffic is fairly light. The main challenges come from the climate, terrain and altitude: wind squalls and dust storms can make your work particularly arduous; the warm summer months can bring flash flooding; and then there is the question of your fitness in the face of Tibet's high-altitude mountainous terrain.

A full bicycle-repair kit, several spare inner tubes, and a spare tyre and chain are essential. Preferably bring an extra rim and some spare spokes. Extra brake wire and brake pads are useful (you'll be descending 3000m from Lhasa to Kathmandu!). Other useful equipment includes reflective clothing, a helmet, a dust mask, goggles, gloves and padded trousers.

Most long-distance cyclists will probably find formal accommodation and restaurants only available at two- or three-day intervals, so you will also need to bring camping equipment.

The Trailblazer guidebook *Himalaya by Bike*, by Laura Stone, has a small section on cycling the Friendship Hwy. The website www.bikechina.com is another good resource.

Obviously, you need to be physically fit to undertake road touring in Tibet. Spend time acclimatising to the altitude and taking leisurely rides around Lhasa before setting off on a long trip.

On the plus side, although Tibet has some of the highest roads in the world (be aware that official pass altitudes are often off by hundreds of metres), gradients are usually manageable. The Tibetan roads are designed for low-powered Chinese trucks, which tackle the many passes of the region via low-gradient switchback roads. Apart from the military convoys, which can include a hundred or more trucks, you rarely have to put up with much traffic.

Touring Routes

The most popular touring route at present is Lhasa to Kathmandu along the Friendship Hwy. It is an ideal route in that it takes in most of Tibet's main sights, offers superb scenery and (for those leaving from Lhasa) features a spectacular roller-coaster ride down from the heights of the La Lung-la into the Langtang region of Nepal. The trip will take a minimum of two weeks, although to do it justice and include stopovers at Gyantse, Shigatse and Sakya, budget 20 days. The entire trip is just over 940km, though most people start from Shigatse. The roadside kilometre markers are a useful way of knowing exactly how far you have gone and how far you still have to go.

Keen cyclists with good mountain bikes might want to consider the paved detour to Everest Base Camp as a side trip on the Lhasa–Kathmandu route. The 108km one-way trip starts from the Shegar turn-off, and it takes around two days to get to Rongphu Monastery.

Other possibilities are endless. Tsurphu, Ganden and Drigung Til Monasteries are relatively easy trips and good for acclimatisation (though the road to Tsurphu is rough and Ganden has a fierce final 10km uphill section). The Gyama Valley is an easy detour on a bike if you are headed to Ganden. Cycling in the Yarlung Valley region is another fine option. Some cyclists even tackle the paved road to Nam-tso, although the nomads' dogs can be a problem here.

Permits

It's currently not possible to cycle anywhere in Tibet independently. You must sign up for a 'tour', which means being followed by a support vehicle and guide. There are no specific permits for cycling, but you will need all the usual permits as if you were travelling in a rented vehicle.

Hazards

Cycling in Tibet is not to be taken lightly. Dogs are a major problem, especially in more remote areas. Children have been known to throw stones at cyclists. Erratic driving is another serious concern.

Wear a cycling helmet and lightweight leather gloves and, weather permitting, try to keep as much of your body covered with protective clothing as possible. It goes without saying that cyclists should also be prepared with a comprehensive medical kit.

Boat

The charming ferry boats that used to cross the Yarlung Tsangpo river to places like Samye and Dorje Drak monasteries have been consigned to history with the spread of new roads, so there is no longer a way to get around Tibet by boat.

Bus

Most places visited by travellers are connected to some sort of public transport. Unfortunately, foreign travellers have not been permitted to take public buses for many years now and the situation is not expected to change.

TRAIN SCHEDULES TO LHASA

TRAIN NUMBER	FROM	DEPARTURE	DISTANCE (KM)	DURATION (HR)	HARD/SOFT SLEEPER
Z21	Běijīng (west)	8pm	3753	40	¥720/1144
Z322	Chéngdū	9.37pm every other day	3360	37	¥668/1062
Z223	Chóngqìng	10.25pm every other day	3654	36	¥707/1125
Z264	Guǎngzhōu	11.45am	4980	55	¥865/1468
Z164	Shànghǎi	8.10pm	4373	52	¥794/1263
**	Xīníng	various	1960	22	¥484/768
Z917	Lánzhōu	11.16am	2188	24	¥522/823
**	Xī'ān	various	2864	32	¥612/970

NB Sleeper fares listed are the cheapest berth. Unless noted, services run every day.

** Multiple train options

FRIENDSHIP HIGHWAY (NEPAL TO TIBET)

The 1000km-or-so stretch of road between Kathmandu and Lhasa is without a doubt one of the most spectacular in the world.

The old route via the border crossing at Kodari (1873m) and Zhāngmù (2250m) was badly affected by Nepal's 2015 earthquake and remains closed to international traffic.

The main Nepal–Tibet border crossing has shifted to Rasuwagadhi at the meeting of Nepal's Langtang region and Tibet's Kyirong Valley. Chinese travellers have been using the border for a few years now, but it was only opened to foreigners in 2017. It's a spectacular and little-explored route that allows you to combine a trek in Nepal's Langtang region with a visit to lovely Peiku-tso on the Tibetan side.

The section of road on the Tibetan side is paved, but the Nepali road is slow going, especially during the monsoon months from June to September. Figure on an entire day from Rasuwagadhi to Kathmandu and consider hiring a 4WD for the trip (Rs 16,000).

The new Kyirong route joins the former Kodari route just north of the La Lung-la (4845m) on the Friendship Hwy and continues to Tingri.

It is essential to watch out for the effects of altitude sickness during the early stages of this trip. If you intend to head up to Everest Base Camp (5150m), you really need to slip in a rest day at Tingri or Kyirong. In terms of acclimatisation it is better to fly to Lhasa and then travel back to Kathmandu, rather than the other way around.

Car & Motorcycle

Hiring a vehicle, driver and guide through a local Tibetan agency is currently the only way to get around the majority of destinations in Tibet. Tourist vehicles used to be almost all 4WD Toyota Land Cruisers, but the improvement of paved roads across Tibet, even to Everest Base Camp and western Tibet, means that eight-seater minivans are now the most common form of vehicle hire.

In 2016 the Tibet government centralised vehicle hire into just a couple of large transportation companies and made it illegal for other drivers or vehicle owners to work with tourists.

Cost are relatively high. Your tour agency will quote you a price based on the number of kilometres in your itinerary, and you can figure on around US$150 to US$200 per day for vehicle hire, driver and petrol. This can be shared by up to six passengers.

You'll need to agree with the agencies on the details of vehicle hire (p44), from the cost of extra days to who pays vehicle entry fees to places like Everest Base Camp.

A couple of agencies such as **Himalayan Offroad** (Map p232; ☏01-4700770; www.himalayanoffroad.com; Chaksibari Marg, Thamel) in Kathmandu offer all-inclusive motorbike tours of Tibet. A 12-day motorbike ride from Kathmandu to Lhasa and back, via Everest Base Camp, riding Honda 250cc dirt bikes or Enfield Bullets, costs around US$3000 per person in a group of five, including bikes, petrol, accommodation, support vehicle and permits. Bring your own jackets, trousers and gloves. They also run a 14-day trip to Mt Kailash costing around US$560 more per person.

Local Transport

Local city transport only really operates in Lhasa and Shigatse. Buses run on set routes and charge a fixed fare of ¥1. Note that at the time of writing, foreigners were not allowed to access public transport outside Lhasa.

Pedicabs (pedal-operated tricycles transporting passengers) are available in Lhasa, Gyantse, Shigatse and Bāyī, but they require extensive haggling and are often as expensive, if not more expensive, than a taxi.

One result of China's economic infusion into Tibet is the large number of taxis now available in most towns, even Ali in western Tibet. In Lhasa most taxi fares are between ¥10 and ¥15.

City transport only really operates in Lhasa and Shigatse. Buses run on set routes and charge a fixed fare of ¥1.

Pedicabs (pedal-operated tricycles transporting passengers) are available in Lhasa, Gyantse, Shigatse and Bāyī, but they require extensive haggling and are often as expensive, if not more expensive, than a taxi.

One result of China's economic infusion into Tibet is the large number of taxis now available in most towns, even Ali in western Tibet. In Lhasa most taxi fares are between ¥10 and ¥15.

Train

It's possible for travellers to take the twice-daily train between Lhasa and Shigatse, meaning budget travellers could visit Lhasa and Shigatse on a guided tour without having to shell out for vehicle hire.

Health

Tibet poses some unique and particular risks to your health, mostly associated with altitude. There is no need to be overly worried: very few travellers are adversely affected by altitude for very long, and greater risks are present in the form of road accidents and dog bites.

Make sure you're healthy before you start travelling. If you are going on a long trip, make sure your teeth are OK. If you wear glasses, take a spare pair and your prescription.

Experienced travellers will rely on their own medical knowledge and supplies. Outside Lhasa and Shigatse there is very little in the way of expert medical care. Make sure you travel with a well-stocked medical kit and knowledge of how to use it.

BEFORE YOU GO

Health Insurance

Tibet is a remote location, and if you become seriously injured or very sick, you may need to be evacuated by air. Under these circumstances, you don't want to be without adequate health insurance. Be sure your policy covers evacuation.

Medical Checklist

Carry a good supply of all medications and prescriptions with you, including a note of their active ingredients rather than the brand names. It can be useful to have a legible prescription or letter from your doctor to show that you legally use the medication.

It's a good idea to carry a well-supplied first-aid kit to Tibet. If you plan on trekking, be sure your kit includes comprehensive supplies.

You may find it useful to bring the following:

➡ Antibiotics

➡ Diamox – to aid with the prevention of altitude sickness

➡ Homeopathic medicines like gentiana for altitude sickness

➡ Diarrhoea and dysentery medicines

➡ Pain relievers

➡ Cold and flu tablets, throat lozenges and nasal decongestant

➡ Water-purification tablets or iodine

Further Reading

Medicine for Mountaineering & Other Wilderness Activities by James Wilkerson is still the classic text for trekking first aid and medical advice.

Pocket First Aid and Wilderness Medicine by Jim Duff and Ross Anderson is a great pocket-size guide that's easily carried on a trek or climb.

The High Altitude Medicine Handbook by Andrew J Pollard and David R Murdoch is a small-format guide full of valuable information on prevention and emergency care.

Travellers' Health by Richard Dawood is comprehensive, easy to read, authoritative and highly recommended, although it's rather large so consider the ebook version.

IN TIBET

Availability & Cost of Health Care

Outside Lhasa and Shigatse health-care advice is patchy at best and nonexistent at worst. Self-diagnosis and treatment can be risky, so you should always seek medical help where possible.

Standards of medical attention are so low in most places in Tibet that, for the worst ailments, the best advice is to go straight to Lhasa, or in extreme cases, Kathmandu or Chéngdū.

CIWEC Clinic Travel Medicine Center (Map p232; ☑01-4424111, 01-4435232; www.ciwec-clinic.com; Kapurdhara Marg, Lazimpat; ⊗emergency 24hr, clinic 9am-noon & 1-4pm Mon-Fri) Kathmandu-based clinic in operation since 1982. Staff members are mostly foreigners and a doctor is on call around the clock. Credit cards are accepted and the centre is used to dealing with insurance claims.

Global Doctor Chéngdū Clinic (环球医生; Huánqiú Yīshēng; Map p240;☑028 8528 3660, 24hr emergency 139 8225 6966; www.globaldoctor.asia; 2nd fl, 9-11 Lippo Tower, 62 Kehua Beilu; 科华北路62号 力宝大厦2层9-11号; ⊘9am-6pm Mon-Sat; Ⓜ Nijiaqiao) In Chéngdū. Offers pre-Tibet medical examinations and a Tibet Travellers Assist Package that can be useful if you are worried about an existing medical condition.

Infectious Diseases

Rabies

Rabies is a fatal viral infection found in Tibet, carried in the saliva of animals (such as dogs, cats, bats and monkeys). Any bite, scratch or even lick from an animal should be cleaned immediately and thoroughly. Scrub gently with soap and running water, and then apply alcohol or iodine solution. Prompt medical help should be sought to receive a course of injections to prevent the onset of symptoms and save the patient from death.

If you have any potential exposure to rabies, seek medical advice in Lhasa (or ideally Kathmandu, Chéngdū or Běijīng) as soon as possible. If you need treatment you will likely have to travel to Bangkok or Hong Kong.

Dysentery & Diarrhoea

Dysentery, cholera and giardiasis are common ailments in Tibet that cause diarrhoea. Ask your doctor for a course of antibiotics to take with you in the event of infection (especially if travelling in high mountain areas or trekking). You should seek medical advice if you think you have giardiasis or amoebic dysentery, but where this is not possible, tinidazole or metronidazole are often-recommended drugs.

Respiratory Infections

Upper respiratory tract infections (like the common cold) are very frequent ailments all over China, including Tibet, where the high altitude aggravates symptoms. High pollution levels in Kathmandu and China can cause complications at the beginning or end of your trip.

Any upper respiratory tract infection, including influenza, can lead to complications, such as bronchitis and pneumonia, which may be treated with antibiotics.

Environmental Hazards

High Altitude

Acute mountain sickness (AMS; also known as altitude sickness) is common at high elevations; relevant factors are the rate of ascent and individual susceptibility. The former is the major risk factor. On average, one tourist a year dies in Tibet from AMS.

Any traveller who flies to where the elevation is around 3600m is likely to experience some symptoms of AMS.

AMS is a notoriously fickle affliction and can also affect trekkers and walkers accustomed to walking at high altitudes. It has been fatal at 3000m, although 3500m to 4500m is the usual range. High altitude can also aggravate upper respiratory tract infections (like the common cold).

It's very easy to get sunburnt at high altitudes, so bring a wide-brimmed hat and bring high-SPF sunblock with you.

ACCLIMITISATION

AMS is linked to low atmospheric pressure. Those who travel up to Everest Base Camp, for instance, reach an altitude where atmospheric pressure is about half of that at sea level.

With an increase in altitude, the human body needs time to develop physiological mechanisms to cope with the decreased oxygen. This process of acclimatisation is still not fully understood, but

RECOMMENDED VACCINATIONS

China doesn't officially require any immunisations for entry into the country (apart from a yellow fever vaccination certificate for travellers arriving from countries with risk of yellow fever transmission); however, the further off the beaten track you go, the more necessary it is to take all precautions.

Plan well ahead (at least eight weeks before travel), as some vaccinations require more than one injection. Discuss requirements with your doctor and check with your national health provider for up-to-date recommendations before departure.

A rabies vaccination is recommended for those spending more than a month in Tibet. The vaccine requires three injections spread over one month. If you are prevaccinated and then bitten, you need only get two further shots of vaccine, as soon as possible, three days apart. If not prevaccinated, you require a Rabies Immuno Globulin (RIG) injection, plus five shots of vaccine over the course of 28 days.

The influenza vaccine is recommended for travellers to China and Tibet, and is good for up to one year.

it is known to involve modifications to breathing patterns and heart rate induced by the autonomic nervous system, and an increase in the blood's oxygen-carrying capabilities. These compensatory mechanisms usually take one to three days to develop at a particular altitude. You are unlikely to get AMS once you are acclimatised to a given height, but you can still get ill when you travel higher. If the ascent is too high and too fast, these compensatory reactions may not kick into gear fast enough.

SYMPTOMS

Mild symptoms of AMS usually develop during the first 24 hours at altitude. These will generally disappear through acclimatisation in several hours to several days.

Symptoms tend to be worse at night and include headache, dizziness, lethargy, loss of appetite, nausea, breathlessness and irritability. Difficulty sleeping is another common symptom, and many travellers have trouble for the first few days after arriving in Lhasa.

AMS may become more serious without warning and can be fatal. Symptoms are caused by the accumulation of fluid in the lungs and brain, and include breathlessness at rest, a dry, irritative cough (which may progress to the production of pink, frothy sputum), severe headache, lack of coordination (typically leading to a 'drunken walk'), confusion, irrational behaviour, vomiting and eventually unconsciousness.

The symptoms of AMS, however mild, are a warning: be sure to take them seriously! Travellers and trekkers should keep an eye on each other, as those experiencing symptoms, especially severe symptoms, may not be in a position to recognise them. One thing to note is that while the symptoms of mild AMS often precede those of severe AMS, this is not always the case. Severe AMS

can strike with little or no warning.

PREVENTION

The best way to prevent AMS is to avoid rapid ascents to high altitudes. If you are travelling by car to Tibet from Nepal, or by train from China, you will experience rapid altitude gain. An itinerary that takes you straight up to Everest Base Camp is unwise; plan to see it well after you've acclimatised. If you fly into Lhasa, take it easy for at least three days; this is enough for most travellers to get over any initial ill effects.

To prevent AMS:

➡ Ascend slowly. Have frequent rest days, spending two to three nights at each rise of 1000m. If you reach a high altitude by trekking, acclimatisation takes place gradually and you are less likely to be affected than if you fly or drive directly to high altitude.

➡ Trekkers should bear in mind the climber's adage of 'climb high, sleep low'. It is always wise to sleep at a lower altitude than the greatest height that's reached during the day.

➡ Once above 3000m, care should be taken not to increase the sleeping altitude by more than 400m per day.

➡ Drink extra fluids. Tibet's mountain air is cold and dry, and moisture is lost as you breathe. Evaporation of sweat may occur unnoticed and result in dehydration.

➡ Avoid alcohol, as it may increase the risk of dehydration, and don't smoke.

➡ Avoid sedatives.

➡ When trekking, take a day off to rest and acclimatise if feeling overtired. If you or anyone else in your party is having a tough time, make allowances for unscheduled stops.

➡ Don't push yourself when climbing up to passes; rather, take plenty of breaks. You

can usually get over the pass as easily tomorrow as you can today. Try to plan your itinerary so that long ascents can be divided into two or more days. Given the complexity and unknown variables involved with AMS and acclimatisation, trekkers should always err on the side of caution and ascend mountains slowly.

TREATMENT

Treat mild symptoms by resting at the same altitude until recovery, which usually takes a day or two. Take paracetamol or acetaminophen for headaches. If symptoms persist or become worse, however, *immediate* descent is necessary. Even 500m can help.

The most effective treatment for severe AMS is to get down to a lower altitude as quickly as possible. In less severe cases the victim will be able to stagger down with some support; in other cases they may need to be carried down. Whatever the case, any delay could be fatal.

AMS victims may need to be flown out of Tibet as quickly as possible, so make sure you have adequate travel insurance.

The drug acetazolamide (Diamox) is recommended for the prevention of AMS – take 125mg twice a day as a preventive dose. Be aware that even when you are on Diamox, you should not ignore any symptoms of AMS. Diamox should be avoided in those with a sulphur allergy.

Drug treatments should never be used to avoid descent or to enable further ascent (although they can help get people well enough to descend).

Several hotels in Lhasa sell a Tibetan herbal remedy that locals use to ease the symptoms of mild altitude sickness. The remedy is known as *solomano* in Tibetan and *hóngjǐngtiān* (红景天) in Chinese. Locals also recommend a Chinese herbal medicine called *gāoyuánníng* (高原宁)

and the drug *gāoyuánkāng* (高原康; dexamethasone). A box of vials costs ¥35 to ¥50. Always consult with your doctor before taking any remedy or medication.

HYPOTHERMIA & FROSTBITE

Tibet's extreme climate must be treated with respect. Sub-freezing temperatures mean there is a risk of hypothermia or frostbite, even during the summer season, when high areas around western Tibet and the northern Changtang can be hit without warning by sudden snow storms. Exposed plains and ridges are prone to extremely high winds and this significantly adds to the cold. Always be prepared for cold, wet or windy conditions if you're out walking at high altitudes.

Hypothermia occurs when the body loses heat faster than it can produce it and the core temperature of the body falls. It is surprisingly easy to progress from very cold to dangerously cold through a combination of wind, wet clothing, fatigue and hunger, even if the air temperature is above freezing.

Symptoms of hypothermia are exhaustion, numb skin (particularly toes and fingers), shivering, slurred speech, irrational or violent behaviour, lethargy, stumbling, dizzy spells, muscle cramps and violent bursts of energy. Irrationality may take the form of sufferers claiming they are warm and trying to take off their clothes.

To treat mild hypothermia, first get the person out of the wind and rain, remove their clothing if it's wet and replace it with dry, warm clothing. Give them hot liquids (not alcohol) and some high-energy, easily digestible food. Do not rub victims; instead, allow them to slowly warm themselves. This should be enough to treat the early stages of

hypothermia. The early recognition and treatment of mild hypothermia is the only way to prevent severe hypothermia, which is a critical condition.

Signs and symptoms of frostbite include a whitish or waxy cast to the skin, or even crystals on the surface, plus itching, numbness and pain. Temporary precautions include warming the affected areas by immersing them in warm (not hot) water or with blankets or clothes, only until the skin becomes flushed. Note: frostbitten areas should only be rewarmed if there is not a likelihood they will be frostbitten again prior to reaching medical care. Frostbitten parts should not be rubbed. Pain and swelling are inevitable. Blisters should not be broken.

Tap Water

The number-one rule is don't drink the tap water, including ice. Most hotels provide a kettle or thermos of boiling water, which is safe to drink. While trekking you should boil your own water or treat it with water-purification tablets, as livestock contaminate many of the water sources. Tea is always safe to drink. In rural areas, locally brewed beer (*chang*) is sometimes made with contaminated water and there is always some risk in drinking it. Large 5L bottles of drinking water are available in most supermarkets. Vegetables and fruit should be washed with purified or bottled water or peeled where possible.

Tibetan Medicine

The basic teachings of Tibetan medicine share much with those of other Asian medical traditions, which, according to some scholars, made their way to the East via India from ancient Greece. These traditions look at symptoms as

indications of an imbalance in the body and seek to restore that balance.

The theory of Tibetan medicine is based on an extremely complex system of checks and balances between what can be broadly described as three 'humours' (related to state of mind), seven 'bodily sustainers' (related to the digestive tract) and three 'eliminators' (related to the elimination of bodily wastes). There is also the influence of harmful spirits to consider: 360 harmful female influences, 360 harmful male influences, 360 malevolent *naga* (water spirits) influences and, finally, 360 influences stemming from past karma. All these combine to produce 404 basic disorders and 84,000 illnesses!

How does a Tibetan doctor assess the condition of a patient? The most important skill is pulse diagnosis. A Tibetan doctor is attuned to 360 'subtle channels' of energy that run through the body's skin and muscle, internal organs, and bone and marrow. The condition of these channels can be ascertained through six of the doctor's fingers (the first three fingers of each hand). Tibetan medicine also relies on urine analysis as an important diagnostic tool.

Yuthok Yongten Gonpo (1182–1251), the physician of King Trisong Detsen, who was born near Ralung Monastery, is credited as the founder of the Tibetan medical system. For more on Tibetan medicine, see www.tibetan-medicine.org.

If you get sick, you can get a diagnosis from Lhasa's **Mentsikhang** (Traditional Tibetan Hospital, 藏医院, Zàngyīyuàn; Map p56; Yuthok Lam; ☉9.30am-12.30pm & 3.30-6pm), opposite the Barkhor. Two English-speaking doctors attend to foreigners on the 3rd floor.

Language

The two principal languages of Tibet are Tibetan and Mandarin Chinese. In urban Tibet (the countryside is another matter) almost all Tibetans speak Tibetan and Mandarin, and all Tibetans undertaking higher studies do so in Chinese. Linguistically, Chinese and Tibetan have little in common. They use different sentence structures, and the tones are far less crucial in Tibetan than in Chinese. Also, unlike the dialects of China, Tibetan has never used Chinese characters for its written language.

TIBETAN

Tibetan belongs to the Tibeto-Burman group of languages, and is spoken by around six million people, mainly in Tibet but also within Tibetan communities in Nepal, India, Bhutan and Pakistan. The Lhasa dialect is the standard form of Tibetan.

Most sounds in Tibetan are similar to those in English, so if you read our coloured pronunciation guides as if they were English, you'll be understood. Note that the symbol å is pronounced as the 'a' in 'ago', ö as the 'er' in 'her', and ü as the 'u' in 'flute' but with a raised tongue.

When a vowel is followed by n, m or ng, this indicates a nasalised sound (pronounced with air escaping through the nose). When a consonant is followed by h, the consonant is aspirated (ie accompanied by a puff of air).

Basics

There are no words in Tibetan that are the direct equivalents of the English 'yes' and 'no'. You'll be understood if you use la ong for 'yes' and la men for 'no'.

Hello.	བཀྲ་ཤིས་བདེ་ལེགས།	ta·shi de·lek
Goodbye.	ག་ལེར་ཕེབས།	ka·lee pay
	(said when staying)	
	ག་ལེར་བཞུགས།	ka·lee shu
	(said when leaving)	

Sorry.	དགོངས་དག	gong·da
Excuse me.	དགོངས་དག	gong·da
Please.	ཐུགས་རྗེ་གནང་བ།	tu·jay·sig
Thank you.	ཐུགས་རྗེ་ཆེ།	tu·jay·chay

How are you?
ཁྱེད་རང་སྐུ་གཟུགས་   kay·râng ku·su
བདེ་པོ་ཡིན་པས།   de·po yin·bay

Fine, and you?
བདེ་པོ་ཡིན། ཁྱེད་རང་ཡང་   de·bo·yin kay·râng·yång
སྐུ་གཟུགས་བདེ་པོ་ཡིན་པས།   ku·su de·po yin·bay

What's your name?
ཁྱེད་རང་གི་མཚན་ལ་   kay·râng·gi tsen·lâ
ག་རེ་རེད།   kâ·ray·ray

My name is ...
ངའི་མིང་ལ་ ... རེད།   ngay·ming·la ... ray

Do you speak English?
ཁྱེད་རང་དབྱིན་ཇི་སྐད་   kay·râng in·ji·kay
ཤེས་ཀྱི་ཡོད་པས།   shing·gi yö·bay

I don't understand.
ཧ་གོ་མ་སོང་།   ha ko ma·song

WANT MORE?

For in-depth language information and handy phrases, check out Lonely Planet's *Tibet Phrasebook* and *China Phrasebook*. You'll find them at **shop. lonelyplanet.com**, or you can buy Lonely Planet's iPhone phrasebooks at the Apple App Store.

Accommodation

I'm looking ... གཅིག་མིག་ ...·chig mig

for a ... བཙལ་གྱི་ཡོད། ta·gi·yö

campsite གུར་བརྒྱབ་ནས་ gur gyâb·nay

  སྡོད་སའི་ས་ཆ dö·say sa·cha

guesthouse མགྲོན་ཁང་ drön·khâng

hotel འགྲུལ་ཁང་ drü·khâng

I'd like to book a room.

ཁང་མི་གཅིག་ལ་སྒྲ་དགོས་ཡོད། khâng·mi·chig la gö·yö

How much for one night?

མཚན་གཅིག་ལ་ལ་གོང་ tsen chig·la gong

ག་ཚོད་རེད། kâ·tsay ray

I'd like to stay with a Tibetan family.

ངས་བོད་པའི་མི་ཚང་ nga bö·pay mi·tsâng

མཉམ་དུ་བསྡད་འདོད་ཡོད། nyâm·do den·dö yö

I need some hot water.

ང་ལ་ཆུ་ཚ་པོ་དགོས། nga·la chu tsa·po gö

Numbers – Tibetan

1	༡	chig
2	༢	nyi
3	༣	soom
4	༤	shi
5	༥	nga
6	༦	doog
7	༧	dün
8	༨	gye
9	༩	gu
10	༡༠	chu
20	༢༠	nyi·shu
30	༣༠	soom·chu
40	༤༠	shib·chu
50	༥༠	ngâb·chu
60	༦༠	doog·chu
70	༧༠	dün·chu
80	༨༠	gyay·chu
90	༩༠	goob·chu
100	༡༠༠	gya
1000	༡༠༠༠	chig·tong

Directions

Where is ...?

... ག་བར་ཡོད་རེད། ... ka·bah yö·ray

Can you show me (on the map)?

(ས་བཀྲ་འདི་ནང་) (sâp·ta di·nâng)

སྟོན་གནང་དང་། tön nâng·da

Turn left/right.

གཡོན་ལ་/གཡས་ལ་ yön·la/yeh·la

སྐྱོག་གནང་། kyog·nâng

straight ahead ཁ་ཐུག་འགྲོ། ka·toog·do

behind ... ... རྒྱབ་ལ་ ... gyâb·lâ

in front of ... ... མདུན་ལ་ ... dün·lâ

near (to) ... ... འཁྲིས་ལ་ ... tee·lâ

opposite ... ... ཕར་ཕྱོགས་ལ་ ... pha·chog·lâ

Eating & Drinking

What do you recommend?

ཁྱེད་རང་བྱེད་ན་ག་རེ་ kay·râng chay·na kâ·ray

ཡག་གི་རེད། yâ·gi·ray

What's in that dish?

ཁ་ལག་ལ་གི་ནེ་ནང་ག་རེ་ kha·la pha·gi·nâng kâ·ray

ཡོད་རེད། yö·ray

I'm vegetarian.

ང་ཤ་མི་ཟ་མཁན་ཡིན། nga sha mi·sa·ken yin

That meal was delicious.

ཁ་ལག་ཞིམ་པོ་ཞེ་དྲགས་ kha·la shim·bu shay·ta

བྱུང་། choong

breakfast ཞོགས་ཁའི་ཁ་ལག shog·kay kha·la

coffee ཇ་ཀོ་ཕི་ cha ka·bi

dinner དགོང་དག་ཁ་ལག gong·da kha·la

fish ཉ་ཤ་ nya·sha

food ཁ་ལག kha·la

fruit ཤིང་ཏོག་ shing·tog

juice ཁུ་བ་ khu·wa

lunch ཉིན་གུང་ nyin·goong

  ཁ་ལག kha·la

meat ཤ་ sha

milk   འོ་མ་ oh·ma

Tibetan Trekking Essentials

How many hours to ...?
... བར་དུ་ཆུ་ཚོད་ག་ཚོད་འགོར་གྱི་རེད།
... bah·tu chu·tsö kâ·tsay go·gi·ray

I want to rent a yak/horse.
ང་གཡག/རྟ་གཅིག་གླ་དགོས་ཡོད།
nga yâk/ta·chig la·gö·yö

I need a porter.
ང་དོ་པོ་ཁུར་མཁན་གཅིག་དགོས།
nga doh·bo khu·khen·chig gö

I need a guide.
ང་ལམ་རྒྱུས་ཁྱེད་མཁན་གཅིག་དགོས།
nga lâm·gyü chay·khen·chig gö

How much does it cost per day?
ཉིན་མ་རེ་རེ་ལ་གླ་ཇ་ག་ཚོད་རེད།
nyi·ma ray·ray·la la·ja kâ·tsay ray

Which way to ...?
... འགྲོ་ཡག་གི་ལམ་ག་ག་གི་རེད།
... doh·ya·gi lâm·ga ka·gi·ray

Is this the trail to ...?
འདི་ ... འགྲོ་ཡག་གི་ལམ་ག་རེད་པས།
di ... doh·ya·gi lâm·ga re·bay

What is the next village on the trail?
ལམ་ག་ནེས་ཕྱིན་ན་དང་པོ་ལུང་པ་ག་རེ་སླེབས་ཀྱི་རེད།
lâm·ga te·nay chin·na dâng·po loong·pa ka·ray leb·ki·ray

I have altitude sickness.
ང་ལ་དུག་ན་གིས།
nga lâ·du na·gi

I must get to low ground as quickly as possible.
ང་ས་དམའ་སར་གང་མགྱོགས་མགྱོགས་འགྲོ་དགོས་ཀྱི་འདུག
nga sa mah·sa gâng gyok·gyok joh go·ki·du

Slowly, slowly!	ག་ལེ་ག་ལེ།	ka·lee ka·lee
Let's go!	ད་འགྲོ།	ta doh
north	བྱང་	châng
south	ལྷོ་	lho
east	ཤར་	shâr
west	ནུབ་	noob
cave	བྲག་ཕུག	dâg·phuk
hot spring	ཆུ་ཚན་	chu·tsen
lake	མཚོ་	tso
mountain	རི་	ri
pass	ལ་	la
river	གཙང་པོ་	tsâng·po
road/trail	ལམ་	lam
sleeping bag	ཉལ་ཁུག	nye·koog
tent	གུར་	gur
valley	ལུང་གཤོང་	loong shong

restaurant	ཟ་ཁང་	sa·khâng
tea	ཇ་	cha
vegetable	སྔོ་ཚལ་	ngo·tsay
(boiled) water	ཆུ་ (འཁོལ་མ་)	chu (khö·ma)

For more food terms, see the Glossary.

Emergencies

Help!	རོགས་གནང་དང་།	rog nâng·da
Go away!	ཕར་རྒྱུགས།	phâh gyook
Call ...	... སྐད།	... kay
	གཏོང་དང་།	tong·da
a doctor	ཨེམ་ཆི	ahm·chi
the police	སྐོར་སྲུང་བ	kor·soong·wa

I'm lost.
ངལམ་ག་བརླགས་ས་འག
nga lâm·ga la·sha

I'm allergic to ...
ངར་ ... ཕོགས་ཀྱི་ཡོད།
ngah ... pho·gi·yö

Shopping & Services

Do you have any ... ?
ཁྱེད་རང་ལ་ ...
kay·râng·la ...
བཙོང་ཡག་ཡོད་པས།
tsong·ya yö·bay

How much is it?
གོང་ག་ཚོད་རེད།
gong kâ·tsay ray

It's too expensive.
གོང་ཆེ་དྲགས་ས་འག
gong chay·ta·sha

Signs – Tibetan

འཛུལ་ས་	Entrance
དོན་ས་	Exit
སྒོ་ཕྱེ་	Open
སྒོ་བརྒྱབ་	Closed
པར་བརྒྱབ་མི་ཆོག	No Photographs
གསང་སྤྱོད་	Toilets

I'll give you ...

	ངས་ ... སྤྲད་དགོས།	ngay ... tay go
bank	དངུལ་ཁང་	ngü·khâng
post office	སྦྲག་ཁང་	da·khâng
tourist office	ཡུལ་སྐོར་	yu·kor
	སྟོ་འཚམས་པའི་	to·châm·pay
	ལས་ཁུངས་	lay·khoong

Time & Dates

What time it is?

ད་ལྟ་ཆུ་ཚོད་ག་ཚོད་རེད།	tân·da chu·tsö kâ·tsay·ray

It's half past (two).

ཆུ་ཚོད་ (གཉིས་) དང་ ཕྱེད་ཀ་རེད།	chu·tsö (nyi)·dâng chay·ka ray

It's (two) o'clock.

ཆུ་ཚོད་ (གཉིས་) པ་རེད།	chu·tsö (nyi)·pa ray

yesterday	ཁ་ས་	kay·sa
today	དེ་རིང་	te·ring
tomorrow	སང་ཉིན་	sa·nyin
Monday	གཟའ་ཟླ་བ་	sa da·wa
Tuesday	གཟའ་མིག་དམར་	sa mig·ma
Wednesday	གཟའ་ལྷག་པ་	sa lhâg·bâ
Thursday	གཟའ་ཕུར་བུ་	sa phu·bu
Friday	གཟའ་པ་སངས་	sa pa·sâng
Saturday	གཟའ་སྤེན་པ་	sa pem·pa
Sunday	གཟའ་ཉི་མ་	sa nyi·mâ

Transport

Where is this	... འདི་ག་པར་	... ka·bah
... going?	འགྲོ་གི་རེད།	doh·gi ray
boat	གྲུ་གཟིངས་	dru·zing
bus	སྤྱི་སྤྱོད་	chi·chö
	ལང་ཁོར་འཁོར་	lâng·kho
plane	གནམ་གྲུ་	nâm·du
I'd like to	ང་ ... གཅིག	nga ...·chig
hire a ...	གཡར་འདོད་ཡོད།	yar dhö·yö
car	མོ་ཊ་	mo·ta
donkey	བོང་གུ་	boong·gu
landcruiser	ལེན་ཀུ་རུ་ས་	len ku·ru·sa
pack animals	ཁལ་སེམས་ཅན་/	kel sem·chen/
	ཁལ་མ་	kel·ma
porter	དོ་པོ་ཁུར་མཁན་	doh·po khu·khen
yak	གཡག་	yak

How much is it daily/weekly?

ཉིན་/བདུན་ཕྲག་རེ་རེར་	nyin/dun·tâg ray·ray
གོང་ག་ཚོ་རེད།	gong kâ·tsay ray

Does this road lead to ...?

ལམ་ག་འདི་ ...	lâm·ga·di ...
འགྲོ་ཡག་རེད་པས།	doh·ya re·bay

Can I get there on foot?

ཕ་གིར་གོམ་པ་བརྒྱབ་ནས་	pha·gay gom·pa gyâb·nay
སླེབས་ཐུབ་ཀྱི་རེད་པས།	leb thoob·ki re·bay

MANDARIN

Pronunciation

In this section we've provided Pinyin (a system of writing Chinese using the Roman alphabet) alongside the Mandarin script.

Vowels

a	as in 'father'
ai	as in 'aisle'
ao	as the 'ow' in 'cow'
e	as in 'her', with no 'r' sound
ei	as in 'weigh'
i	as the 'ee' in 'meet' (or like a light 'r' as in 'Grrr!' after c, ch, r, s, sh, z or zh)
ian	as the word 'yen'

ie	as the English word 'yeah'
o	as in 'or', with no 'r' sound
ou	as the 'oa' in 'boat'
u	as in 'flute'
ui	as the word 'way'
uo	like a 'w' followed by 'o'
yu/ü	like 'ee' with lips pursed

Consonants

Note that in Pinyin apostrophes are some-times used to separate syllables in order to avoid mispronunciation, eg píng'ān.

c	as the 'ts' in 'bits'
ch	as in 'chop', but with the tongue curled up and back
h	as in 'hay', but articulated from farther back in the throat
q	as the 'ch' in 'cheese'
r	as the 's' in 'pleasure'
sh	as in 'ship', but with the tongue curled up and back
x	as in 'ship'
z	as the 'dz' in 'suds'
zh	as the 'j' in 'judge' but with the tongue curled up and back

Tones

Mandarin has many words with the same pronunciation but a different meaning. What distinguishes these words is their 'tonal' quality – the raising and the lowering of pitch on certain syllables. For example, the word ma has four different meanings according to tone, as shown below. Tones are indicated in Pinyin by the following accent marks on vowels:

high tone	mā (mother)
rising tone	má (hemp, numb)
falling-rising tone	mǎ (horse)
falling tone	mà (scold, swear)

Basics

Hello.	你好。	Nǐhǎo.
Goodbye.	再见。	Zàijiàn.
How are you?	你好吗？	Nǐhǎo ma?
Fine. And you?	好。你呢？	Hǎo. Nǐ ne?
Yes./No.	是。/不是。	Shì./Bùshì.
Please ...	请……	Qǐng ...
Thank you.	谢谢你。	Xièxie nǐ.
You're welcome.	不客气。	Bù kèqi.
Excuse me.	劳驾。	Láojià.
Sorry.	对不起。	Duìbùqǐ.

What's your name?
你叫什么名字？　Nǐ jiào shénme míngzi?

My name is ...
我叫……　　　　　Wǒ jiào ...

Do you speak English?
你会说英文吗？　Nǐ huìshuō Yīngwén ma?

I don't understand.
我不明白。　　　Wǒ bù míngbai.

Accommodation

Do you have a single/double room?
有没有(单人/套)房？　Yǒuméiyǒu (dānrén/tào) fáng?

How much is it per night/person?
每天/人多少钱？　Měi tiān/rén duōshǎo qián?

campsite	露营地	lùyíngdì
guesthouse	宾馆	bīnguǎn
hostel	招待所	zhāodàisuǒ
hotel	酒店	jiǔdiàn
air-con	空调	kōngtiáo
bathroom	浴室	yùshì
bed	床	chuáng
window	窗	chuāng

Numbers – Mandarin

1	一	yī
2	二/两	èr/liǎng
3	三	sān
4	四	sì
5	五	wǔ
6	六	liù
7	七	qī
8	八	bā
9	九	jiǔ
10	十	shí
20	二十	èrshí
30	三十	sānshí
40	四十	sìshí
50	五十	wǔshí
60	六十	liùshí
70	七十	qīshí
80	八十	bāshí
90	九十	jiǔshí
100	一百	yībǎi
1000	一千	yīqiān

Signs – Mandarin		
入口	Rùkǒu	**Entrance**
出口	Chūkǒu	**Exit**
问讯处	Wènxùnchù	**Information**
开	Kāi	**Open**
关	Guān	**Closed**
禁止	Jìnzhǐ	**Prohibited**
厕所	Cèsuǒ	**Toilets**
男	Nán	**Men**
女	Nǚ	**Women**

Directions

Where's (a bank)?
(银行)在哪儿?   (Yínháng) zài nǎr?

What is the address?
地址在哪儿?   Dìzhǐ zài nǎr?

Could you write the address, please?
能不能请你   Néngbunéng qǐng nǐ
把地址写下来?   bǎ dìzhǐ xiě xiàlái?

Can you show me where it is on the map?
请帮我找它在   Qǐng bāngwǒ zhǎo tā zài
地图上的位置。   dìtú shàng de wèizhi.

Go straight ahead.
一直走。   Yìzhí zǒu.

at the next corner
在下一个拐角   zài xià yīge guǎijiǎo

at the traffic lights
在红绿灯   zài hónglǜdēng

behind	背面	bèimiàn
far	远	yuǎn
in front of ...	……的前面	... de qiánmian
near	近	jìn
next to	旁边	pángbiān
on the corner	拐角	guǎijiǎo
opposite	对面	duìmiàn
Turn left/right.	左/右转。	Zuǒ/Yòu zhuǎn.

Eating & Drinking

What would you recommend?
有什么菜可以   Yǒu shénme cài kěyǐ
推荐的?   tuījiàn de?

What's in that dish?
这道菜用什么   Zhèdào cài yòng shénme
东西做的?   dōngxi zuòde?

That was delicious!
真好吃!   Zhēn hǎochī!

The bill, please!   买单!   Mǎidān!
Cheers!   干杯!   Gānbēi!

I don't eat ...   我不吃……   Wǒ bùchī ...
  fish   鱼   yú
  nuts   果仁   guǒrén
  poultry   家禽   jiāqín
  red meat   牛羊肉   niúyángròu

Emergencies

Help!   救命!   Jiùmìng!
I'm lost.   我迷路了。   Wǒ mílù le.
Go away!   走开!   Zǒukāi!

There's been an accident!
出事了!   Chūshì le!

Call a doctor!
请叫医生来!   Qǐng jiào yīshēng lái!

Call the police!
请叫警察!   Qǐng jiào jǐngchá!

I'm ill.
我生病了。   Wǒ shēngbìng le.

I'm allergic to (antibiotics).
我对(抗菌素)   Wǒ duì (kàngjūnsù)
过敏。   guòmǐn.

Shopping & Services

I'd like to buy ...
我想买……   Wǒ xiǎng mǎi ...

Can I look at it?
我能看看吗?   Wǒ néng kànkan ma?

How much is it?
多少钱?   Duōshǎo qián?

That's too expensive!
太贵了!   Tàiguì le!

Can you lower the price?
能便宜一点吗?   Néng piányi yīdiǎn ma?

There's a mistake in the bill.
帐单上   Zhàngdān shàng
有问题。   yǒu wèntí.

internet cafe	网吧	wǎngbā
post office	邮局	yóujú
tourist office	旅行店	lǚxíng diàn

Time & Dates

What time is it?
现在几点钟?   Xiànzài jǐdiǎn zhōng?

It's (10) o'clock.
(十)点钟。   (Shí)diǎn zhōng.

Half past (10).
(十)点三十分。   (Shí)diǎn sānshífēn.

morning	早上	zǎoshang
afternoon	下午	xiàwǔ
evening	晚上	wǎnshàng
yesterday	昨天	zuótiān
today	今天	jīntiān
tomorrow	明天	míngtiān
Monday	星期一	xīngqī yī
Tuesday	星期二	xīngqī èr
Wednesday	星期三	xīngqī sān
Thursday	星期四	xīngqī sì
Friday	星期五	xīngqī wǔ
Saturday	星期六	xīngqī liù
Sunday	星期天	xīngqī tiān

Transport

boat	船	chuán
bus	长途车	chángtú chē
plane	飞机	fēijī
taxi	出租车	chūzū chē
train	火车	huǒchē

I want to go to ...
我要去······   Wǒ yào qù ...

What time does it leave?
几点钟出发?   Jǐdiǎnzhōng chūfā?

What time does it get to ...?
几点钟到······?   Jǐdiǎnzhōng dào ...?

I want to get off here.
我想这儿下车。   Wǒ xiǎng zhèr xiàchē.

When's the ...	······ (车)	... (chē)
(bus)?	几点走?	jǐdiǎn zǒu?
first	首趟	Shǒutàng
last	末趟	Mòtàng
next	下一趟	Xià yītàng
A ... ticket	一张到	Yīzhāng dào
to (Dalian).	(大连)的	(Dàlián) de
	······票。	... piào.
1st-class	头等	tóuděng
2nd-class	二等	èrděng

Question Words – Mandarin

How?	怎么?	Zěnme?
What?	什么?	Shénme?
When?	什么时候	Shénme shíhòu?
Where?	哪儿	Nǎr?
Which?	哪个	Nǎge?
Who?	谁?	Shuí?
Why?	为什么?	Wèishénme?

one-way	单程	dānchéng
return	双程	shuāngchéng
cancelled	取消	qǔxiāo
delayed	晚点	wǎndiǎn
ticket office	售票处	shòupiàochù
timetable	时刻表	shíkè biǎo
I'd like to	我要租	Wǒ yào zū
hire a ...	一辆······	yīliàng ...
4WD	四轮驱动	sìlún qūdòng
bicycle	自行车	zìxíngchē
car	汽车	qìchē
motorcycle	摩托车	mótuochē

Does this road lead to ...?
这条路到······吗?   Zhè tiáo lù dào ... ma?

How long can I park here?
这儿可以停多久?   Zhèr kěyǐ tíng duōjiǔ?

The car has broken down (at ...).
汽车是(在······)坏的。   Qìchē shì (zài ...) huài de.

I have a flat tyre.
轮胎瘪了。   Lúntāi biě le.

I've run out of petrol.
没有汽油了。   Méiyou qìyóu le.

bicycle pump	打气筒	dǎqìtóng
child seat	婴儿座	yīng'érzuò
diesel	柴油	cháiyóu
helmet	头盔	tóukuī
gas/petrol	汽油	qìyóu
mechanic	机修工	jīxiūgōng
service station	加油站	jiāyóu zhàn

GLOSSARY

The main entries in this chapter are the Tibetan terms, unless otherwise indicated. (S) denotes Sanskrit and (M) stands for Mandarin.

Who's Who

This section presents some of the deities, historical figures and other people mentioned in this book. Many terms are of Sanskrit origin.

Akshobhya (S) – see *Mikyöba*

Amitabha (S) – see *Öpagme*

Amitayus (S) – see *Tsepame*

Atisha (S) – see *Jowo-je*

Avalokiteshvara (S) – see *Chenresig*

Bhrikuti – the Nepali consort of King Songtsen Gampo (Tibetan: Pesa Chitsun)

Büton Rinchen Drup – compiler of the Tibetan Buddhist canon; established a sub-school of Tibetan Buddhism, based in Shalu Monastery

Chana Dorje (S: Vajrapani) – the wrathful Bodhisattva of Energy whose name means 'thunderbolt in hand'

Chenresig (S: Avalokiteshvara) – an embodiment of compassionate bodhisattvahood and the patron saint of Tibet; the Dalai Lamas are considered to be manifestations of this deity

Chögyel (S: Dharmaraja) – Gelugpa protector deity; blue, with the head of a bull

Chökyong (S: Lokapalas) – the Four Guardian Kings

Citipati – dancing skeletons, often seen in protector chapels

Dalai Lama – spiritual head of the Gelugpa order, which ruled over Tibet from 1642 until 1959; the term is an honorific that means 'ocean of wisdom' and was bestowed by the Mongolian Altyn Khan; also believed to be the manifestation of Chenresig (Avalokiteshvara)

Dharmaraja (S) – see *Chögyel*

Dorje Chang (S: Vajradhara) – one of the five Dhyani buddhas, recognisable by his crossed arms holding a bell and thunderbolt

Dorje Drolo – wrathful form of Guru Rinpoche, seated on a tiger

Dorje Jigje (S: Yamantaka) – a meditational deity who comes in various aspects; the Red and Black aspects are probably the most common

Dorje Lekpa – Dzogchen deity, recognisable by his round green hat and goat mount

Dorje Shugden – controversial protector deity outlawed by the Dalai Lama

Drölma (S: Tara) – a female meditational deity who is a manifestation of the enlightened mind of all buddhas; she is sometimes referred to as the mother of all buddhas, and has many aspects, but is most often seen as Green Tara or as Drölkar (White Tara)

Dromtönpa – 11th-century disciple of Jowo-je *(Atisha)* who founded the Kadampa order and Reting Monastery

Ekajati (S) – see *Tsechigma*

Gar Tsongtsen – Prime Minister of King Songtsen Gampo who travelled to Chang'an in 641, returning with Princess Wencheng

Gesar – a legendary king and also the name of an epic concerning his fabulous exploits; the king's empire is known as Ling, and thus the stories, which are usually sung and told by professional bards, are known as the *Stories of Ling*

Gompo Gur – a form of Nagpo Chenpo (Mahakala) and protector of the Sakyapa school

Guru Rinpoche – credited with having suppressed demons and other malevolent forces in order to introduce Buddhism into Tibet during the 8th century; in the Nyingmapa order he is revered as the Second Buddha

Hayagriva (S) – see *Tamdrin*

Jamchen Chöje – disciple of Tsongkhapa and founder of Sera Monastery; also known as Sakya Yeshe

Jampa (S: Maitreya) – the Buddha of Loving Kindness; also the Future Buddha, the fifth of the 1000 buddhas who will descend to earth (Sakyamuni or Sakya Thukpa was the fourth)

Jampelyang (S: Manjushri) – the Bodhisattva of Insight; usually depicted holding a sword (which symbolises discriminative awareness) in one hand and a book (which symbolises his mastery of all knowledge) in the other

Jamyang Chöje – founder of Drepung Monastery

Je Rinpoche – see *Tsongkhapa*

Jowo Sakyamuni – the most revered image of Sakyamuni (Sakya Thukpa) in Tibet, it depicts the Historical Buddha at the age of 12 and is kept in the Jokhang in Lhasa

Jowo-je (S: Atisha) – 11th-century Buddhist scholar from contemporary Bengal whose arrival in Tibet at the invitation of the king of Guge was a catalyst for the revival of Buddhism on the high plateau

Karmapa – a lineage (17 so far) of spiritual leaders of the Karma Kagyupa; also known as the Black Hats

Khenlop Chösum – Trinity of Guru Rinpoche, Trisong Detsen and Shantarakshita, found at Samye Monastery

Kunga Gyaltsen – see *Sakya Pandita*

Langdharma – the 9th-century Tibetan king accused of having persecuted Buddhists

Lokapalas (S) – see *Chökyong*

Longchen Rabjampa – (1308–63) *Nyingmapa* and *Dzogchen* teacher and writer, revered as a manifestation of Jampelyang; also known as Longchenpa

Machik Labdronma – (1031–1129) female yogini connected to Shugsheb Nunnery

Mahakala (S) – see *Nagpo Chenpo*

Maitreya (S) – see *Jampa*

Manjushri (S) – see *Jampelyang*

Marpa – 11th-century ascetic whose disciple, Milarepa, founded the Kagyupa order

Mikyöba (S: Akshobhya) – the Buddha of the State of Perfected Consciousness, or Perfect Cognition; literally 'unchanging', 'the immutable one'

Milarepa – (1040–1123) disciple of Marpa and founder of the Kagyupa order; renowned for his songs

Nagpo Chenpo – The Great Black One, wrathful manifestation of Chenresig that carries echoes of the Indian god Shiva; see *Mahakala*.

Namgyelma – three-faced, eight-armed female deity and one of the three deities of longevity

Namse (S: Vairocana) – Buddha of Enlightened Consciousness, generally white; also a renowned Tibetan translator

Namtöse (S: Vaishravana) – the Guardian of the North, one of the Chökyong or Four Guardian Kings

Nechung – protector deity of Tibet and the Dalai Lamas; manifested in the State Oracle, who is traditionally installed at Nechung Monastery

Nyenchen Tanglha – mountain spirit and protector deity that has its roots in Bön

Nyentri Tsenpo – legendary first king of Tibet

Öpagme (S: Amitabha) – the Buddha of Perfected Perception; literally 'infinite light'

Palden Lhamo (S: Shri Devi) – special protector of Lhasa, the Dalai Lama and the Gelugpa order; the female counterpart of Nagpo Chenpo (Mahakala)

Panchen Lama – literally 'guru and great teacher'; the lineage is associated with Tashilhunpo Monastery, Shigatse, and goes back to the 17th century; the Panchen Lama is a manifestation of Öpagme (Amitabha)

Pehar – oracle and protector of the Buddhist state, depicted with six arms, wearing a round hat and riding a snow lion

Rahulla – Dzogchen deity with nine heads, eyes all over his body, a mouth in his belly and the lower half of a serpent (coiled on the dead body of ego)

Ralpachen – 9th-century king whose assassination marked the end of the Yarlung Valley dynasty

Rigsum Gonpo – trinity of bodhisattvas consisting of Chenresig (Avalokiteshvara), Jampelyang (Manjushri) and Chana Dorje (Vajrapani)

Rinchen Zangpo – (958–1055) the Great Translator, who travelled to India for 17 years and established monasteries across Ladakh, Spiti and western Tibet

Sakya Pandita (S) – literally 'scholar from Sakya'; former abbot of Sakya Monastery who established the priest-patron system with the Mongols; also known as Kunga Gyaltsen

Sakya Thukpa – see *Sakyamuni*

Sakyamuni (S) – literally the 'sage of Sakya'; the founder of Buddhism, the Historical Buddha; known in Tibetan as Sakya Thukpa; see also *Siddhartha Gautama* and *buddha*

Samvara (S) – a wrathful multi-armed deity and manifestation of Sakyamuni (Demchok in Tibetan)

Shantarakshita – Indian scholar of the 8th century and first abbot of Samye Monastery; Kende Shewa in Tibetan

Shenrab – founder of the Bön faith

Shiromo – Bönpo deity, the equivalent of Sakyamuni

Shri Devi (S) – see *Palden Lhamo*

Siddhartha Gautama (S) – the personal name of the Historical Buddha; see also *Sakyamuni* (Sakya Thukpa)

Songtsen Gampo – the 7th-century king associated with the introduction of Buddhism to Tibet

Tamdrin (S: Hayagriva) – literally 'horse necked'; a wrathful meditational deity and manifestation of Chenresig, usually associated with the Nyingmapa order

Tangtong Gyelpo – (1385–1464) Tibetan yogi, treasure finder *(terton)*, bridge builder, medic and developer of Tibetan opera; often depicted holding a chain link in his hands

Tara (S) – see *Drölma*

Tenzin Gyatso – the 14th and current Dalai Lama

Terdak Lingpa – founder of Mindroling Monastery

Trisong Detsen – 8th-century Tibetan king; founder of Samye Monastery

Tsechigma (S: Ekajati) – protectress with one eye, one tooth and one breast, associated with the Dzogchen movement

Tsepame (S: Amitayus) – a meditational deity associated with longevity; literally 'limitless life'; often featured in a trinity with Drölma (Tara) and Namgyelma (Vijaya)

Tseringma – protector goddess of Mt Everest, depicted riding a snow lion

Tsongkhapa – 14th-century founder of the Gelugpa order and Ganden Monastery, also known as 'Je Rinpoche'

Vairocana (S) – see *Namse*

Vaishravana (S) – see *Namtöse*

Vajradhara (S) – see *Dorje Chang*

Vajrapani (S) – see *Chana Dorje*

Vijaya (S) – Sanskrit name for Namgyelma

Wencheng – Chinese wife of King Songtsen Gampo; called Wencheng Konjo in Tibetan

Yama (S) – Lord of Death, who resides in sky-burial sites

Yamantaka (S) – see *Dorje Jigje*

Yeshe Tsogyel – female consort of Guru Rinpoche and one-time wife of King Trisong Detsen

General Terms

Amdo – a traditional province of Tibet, now Qīnghǎi province

AMS – acute mountain sickness; often referred to as altitude sickness

ani – Tibetan for 'nun', as in ani gompa (nunnery)

arhat (S) – literally 'worthy one'; a person who has achieved nirvana; the Tibetan term is 'neten'

Bardo – as detailed in the *Tibetan Book of the Dead*, this term refers to the intermediate stages between death and rebirth

Barkhor – an intermediate circumambulation circuit, or kora, but most often specifically the intermediate circuit around the Jokhang temple of Lhasa

bīnguǎn (M) – guesthouse or hotel

Black Hat – strictly speaking, this refers to the black hat embellished with gold that was presented to the second Karmapa of the Karma Kagyupa order of Tsurphu Monastery by a Mongol prince, and worn ceremoniously by all subsequent incarnations of the Karmapa; by extension the black hat represents the Karma Kagyupa order

Bö – Tibetans' name for their own land, sometimes written 'Bod' or 'Po'

Bodhgaya – the place in contemporary Bihar, India, where Sakyamuni, the Historical Buddha, attained enlightenment

bodhisattva (S) – literally 'enlightenment hero'; the bodhisattva chooses not to take the step to nirvana, being motivated to stay within the Wheel of Life by compassion for all sentient beings

Bön – the indigenous religion of Tibet and the Himalayan borderlands; in its ancient form its main components were royal burial rites, the cult of indigenous deities and magical practices; in the 11th century, Bön was systematised along Buddhist lines and it is this form that survives today

Bönpo – a practitioner of Bön

buddha (S) – literally 'awakened one'; a being who through spiritual training has broken free of all illusion and karmic consequences and is 'enlightened'; most often specifically the Historical Buddha, Sakyamuni

Büton – suborder of Tibetan Buddhism based on the teachings of Büton Rinchen Drup, the 14th-century compiler of the major Buddhist texts; associated with Shalu Monastery, near Shigatse

CAAC – Civil Aviation Authority of China

chakje – handprint of a deity or a religious figure made in rock

chaktsal – ritual prostration

chaktsal gang – prostration point

cham – a ritual dance carried out by monks and lamas, usually at festivals; all participants except the central lama are masked

chang – Tibetan barley beer

Changtang – vast plains of north Tibet extending into Xīnjiāng and Qīnghǎi; the world's largest and highest plateau

chö – see *dharma*

chömay – butter lamp

chörten – Tibetan for stupa; usually used as reliquary for the cremated remains of important lamas

chu – river, stream, brook etc

chuba – long-sleeved sheepskin cloak

CITS – China International Travel Service

CTS – China Travel Service

cūn (M) – village; 'tson' in Tibetan

dakini (S) – see *khandroma*

dharma (S) – 'chö' in Tibetan, and sometimes translated as 'law', this very broad term covers the truths expounded by Sakyamuni, the Buddhist teachings, the path and goal of nirvana; in effect it is the 'law' that must be understood, followed and achieved in order for one to be a Buddhist

doring – stele; carved obelisk commemorating a historic event or edict

dorje – literally 'diamond' or 'thunderbolt'; a metaphor for the indestructible, indivisible nature of buddhahood; also a Tantric hand-held sceptre symbolising 'skilful means'

drokpa – nomad

drubkhang – meditation chamber

dukhang – assembly hall

dukkha (S) – suffering, the essential condition of all life

dungkhar – conch shell

dürtro – sky-burial site

dzo – domesticated cross between a bull and a female yak

Dzogchen – the Great Perfection teachings associated with the Nyingmapa order

dzong – fort

Eightfold Path – one of the Four Noble Truths taught by Sakyamuni; the path that must be taken to achieve enlightenment and liberation from the Wheel of Life

FIT office – Family (or Foreign) and Independent Traveller office

Four Noble Truths – as stated in the first speech given by Sakyamuni after he achieved enlightenment, the Four Noble Truths are: the truth that all life is suffering; the truth that suffering originates in desire; the truth that desire may be extinguished; and the truth that there is a path to this end

Ganden (S) – the pure land of Jampa (Maitreya) and the seat of the Gelugpa order; 'Tushita' in Tibetan

garuda (S: khyung) – mythological bird associated with Hinduism; in Tibetan Tantric Buddhism it is seen as a wrathful force that transforms malevolent influences

gau – an amulet or 'portable shrine' worn around the neck, containing the image of an important spiritual figure, usually the Dalai Lama

Gelugpa – major order of Tibetan Buddhism, associated with the Dalai Lamas, the Panchen Lamas, and the Drepung, Sera,

Ganden and Tashilhunpo Monasteries; founded by Tsongkhapa in the 14th century and sometimes known as the Yellow Hats

geshe – title awarded on completion of the highest level of study (something like a doctorate) that monks may undertake after completing their full indoctrinal vows; usually associated with the Gelugpa order

gompa – monastery

gönkhang – protector chapel

Guge – a 9th-century kingdom of western Tibet

guru (S) – spiritual teacher; literally 'heavy'; the Tibetan equivalent is lama

Hinayana (S) – also called Theravada, this is a major school of Buddhism that follows the original teachings of the Historical Buddha, Sakyamuni, and places less importance on the compassionate bodhisattva ideal and more on individual enlightenment; see also *Mahayana*

Jokhang – situated in Lhasa, this is the most sacred and one of the most ancient of Tibet's temples; also known as the Tsuglhakhang

Kadampa – order of Tibetan Buddhism based on the teachings of the Indian scholar Atisha (Jowo-je); the school was a major influence on the Gelugpa order

Kagyupa – order of Tibetan Buddhism that traces its lineage back through Milarepa and Marpa and eventually to the Indian mahasiddhas; divided into numerous suborders, the most famous of which is the Karma Kagyupa, or the Karmapa; also known as Kagyud

kangtsang – monastic residential quarters

Kangyur – the Tibetan Buddhist canon; its complement is the *Tengyur*

karma (S) – action and its consequences, the psychic 'imprint' that action leaves on the mind and that continues into further rebirths; the term is found in both Hinduism and Buddhism,

and may be likened to the law of cause and effect

Karma Kagyupa – suborder of the Kagyupa order, established by Gampopa and Dusum Khyenpa in the 12th century; represented by the Black Hat

kathak – prayer scarf; used as a ritual offering or as a gift

Kham – traditional eastern Tibetan province; much of it is now part of western Sichuān and northwestern Yúnnán

Khampa – a person from Kham

khandroma (S: dakini) – literally 'sky dancer' or 'sky walker'; a flying angel-like astral being that communicates between the worlds of buddhas, humans and demons

khenpo – abbot

kora – ritual circumambulation circuit; pilgrimage circuit

kumbum – literally '100,000 images', this is a chörten that contains statuary and paintings; the most famous in Tibet is the Gyantse Kumbum in Tsang

la – mountain pass

lama – literally 'unsurpassed'; Tibetan equivalent of Sanskrit word 'guru'; a title bestowed on monks of particularly high spiritual attainment

lamaism – term used by early Western writers on the subject of Tibet to describe Tibetan Buddhism; also used by the Chinese in the term 'lamajiao', literally 'lama religion'

lamrim – the stages on the path to enlightenment; a graduated approach to enlightenment as expounded by Tsongkhapa; associated with the Gelugpa order

lapse – a cairn

lha – life spirit; it may also be present in inanimate objects such as lakes, mountains and trees

lhakhang – chapel

ling – Tibetan term meaning 'royal', usually associated with lesser, outlying temples

lingkhor – an outer pilgrimage circuit; famously, the outer pilgrimage of Lhasa

Losar – Tibetan New Year

lu (M) – road; see also *naga*

mahasiddha – literally 'of great spiritual accomplishment'; a Tantric practitioner who has reached a high level of awareness; there are 84 famous mahasiddhas; the Tibetan term is 'drubchen'

Mahayana (S) – the other major school of Buddhism along with Hinayana; this school emphasises compassion and the altruism of the bodhisattva who remains on the Wheel of Life for the sake of all sentient beings

mandala – a circular representation of the three- dimensional world of a meditational deity; used as a meditation device; the Tibetan term is 'kyilkhor'

mani – prayer

mani lhakhang – small chapel housing a single large prayer wheel

mani stone – a stone with the mantra 'Om mani padme hum' ('hail to the jewel in the lotus') carved on it

mani wall – a wall made with mani stones

mantra (S) – literally 'protection of the mind'; one of the Tantric devices used to achieve identity with a meditational deity and break through the world of illusion; a series of syllables recited as the pure sound made by an enlightened being

meditational deity – a deified manifestation of the enlightened mind with which, according to Tantric ritual, the adept seeks union and thus experience of enlightenment

momo – Tibetan dumpling

Mönlam – a major Lhasa festival established by Tsongkhapa

Mt Meru – the sacred mountain at the centre of the universe; also known as Sumeru

naga (S) – water spirits that may take the form of serpents or semi-humans; the latter can be seen in images of the *naga* kings; the Tibetan term is 'lu'

nangkhor – inner circumambulation circuit, usually within the

CHINESE MENU READER

Snacks

beef noodles in a soup	*niúròu miàn*	牛肉面
boiled dumplings	*shuǐjiǎo*	水饺
fried Muslim noodles and beef	*gānbàn miàn*	干拌面
fried noodle squares	*chǎo miànpian*	炒面片
fried noodles with vegetables	*shūcài chǎomiàn*	蔬菜炒面
fried rice with egg	*jīdàn chǎofàn*	鸡蛋炒饭
fried rice with vegetables	*shūcài chǎofàn*	蔬菜炒饭
Muslim noodles	*lāmiàn*	拉面
steamed meat buns	*bāozi*	包子
steamed white rice	*mǐfàn*	米饭
vermicelli noodles in casserole pot	*shāguō mǐxiàn*	沙锅米线
wonton (soup)	*húndùn (tāng)*	馄饨(汤)
Xīnjiāng noodles	*Xīnjiāng lāmiàn*	新疆拉面

Top Chinese Dishes

double-cooked fatty pork	*huíguō ròu*	回锅肉
dry-fried runner beans	*gānbiān sìjìdòu*	干煸四季豆
egg and tomato	*fānqié chǎodàn*	番茄炒蛋
eggplant with garlic, ginger, vinegar and scallions	*yúxiāng qiézi*	鱼香茄子
fried green beans	*sùchǎo biǎndòu*	素炒扁豆
fried vegetables	*sùchǎo sùcài*	素炒素菜
pork and green peppers	*qīngjiāo ròupiàn*	青椒肉片
pork and sizzling rice crust	*guōbā ròupiàn*	锅巴肉片
pork in soy sauce	*jīngjiàng ròusī*	京酱肉丝
braised eggplant	*hóngshāo qiézi*	红烧茄子
spicy chicken with peanuts	*gōngbào jīdīng*	宫爆鸡丁
spicy tofu	*málà dòufu*	麻辣豆腐
stir-fried baby bok choy	*sùchǎo xiǎo báicài*	素炒小白菜
stir-fried broccoli	*sùchǎo xīlánhuā*	素炒西兰花
stir-fried greens	*sùchǎo yóucài /kòngxīncài*	素炒油菜/空心菜
stir-fried spinach	*sùchǎo bōcài*	素炒菠菜
sweet and sour pork fillets	*tángcù lǐjí*	糖醋里脊
wood mushrooms and pork	*mù'ěr ròu*	木耳肉

Drinks

beer	*píjiǔ*	啤酒
boiled water	*kāi shuǐ*	开水
hot	*rède*	热的
ice cold	*bīngde*	冰的
mineral water	*kuàngquán shuǐ*	矿泉水
Muslim tea	*bābǎo wǎnzi*	八宝豌子
tea	*chá*	茶

EATING TIBETAN

ENGLISH	TIBETAN PRONUNCIATION	TIBETAN SCRIPT	CHINESE PRONUNCIATION	CHINESE SCRIPT
Butter tea	*bo-cha*	བོད་ཇ།	*sūyóu chá*	酥油茶
Noodles	*thuk-pa*	ཐུག་པ།	*zàngmiàn*	藏面
Rice, potato and yak-meat stew	*shemdre*	ཤ་འབྲས།	*gālí niúròu fàn*	咖喱牛肉饭
Roasted barley flour	*tsampa*	རྩམ་པ།	*zānbā*	糌粑
Tibetan yoghurt	*sho*	ཞོ།	*suānnǎi*	酸奶
Vegetable dumplings	*tse-momo*	ཚལ་མོག་མོག	*sùcài bāozi*	素菜包子
Yak-meat dumplings	*sha-momo*	ཤ་མོག་མོག	*niúròu bāozi*	牛肉包子

interior of a temple or monastic assembly hall, and taking in various chapels en route

neten – see *arhat*

Newari – the people of the Nepali Buddhist kingdoms in the Kathmandu Valley

Ngari – ancient name for the province of western Tibet; later incorporated into Ütsang

Ngorpa – sub-school of the Sakyapa school of Tibetan Buddhism founded by Ngorchen Kunga Sangpo and based at Ngor Monastery in Tsang

nirvana (S) – literally 'beyond sorrow'; an end to desire and suffering, and an end to the cycle of rebirth

Norbulingka – the summer palace of the Dalai Lamas in Lhasa

Nyingmapa – the earliest order of Tibetan Buddhism, based largely on the Buddhism brought to Tibet by Guru Rinpoche

Om mani padme hum – this mantra means 'hail to the jewel in the lotus' and is associated with Chenresig, patron deity of Tibet

oracle – in Tibetan Buddhism an oracle serves as a medium for protector deities, as in the State Oracle of Nechung Monastery near Drepung, Lhasa; the State Oracle was consulted on all important matters of state

Pandita – a title conferred on great scholars of Buddhism, as in Sakya Pandita

parikrama – the Hindu equivalent of a kora

PLA – People's Liberation Army (Chinese army)

PRC – People's Republic of China

protector deities – deities who can manifest themselves in either male or female forms and serve to protect Buddhist teachings and followers; they may be either wrathful aspects of enlightened beings or worldly powers who have been tamed by *Tantric* masters; the Tibetan term is 'chojung'

PSB – Public Security Bureau

puk – cave

pure lands – otherworldly realms that are the domains of buddhas; realms completely free of suffering, and in the popular Buddhist imagination are probably something like the Christian heaven

Qiang – proto-Tibetan tribes that troubled the borders of the Chinese empire

Qomolangma – Tibetan name for Mt Everest as transliterated by the Chinese; also spelt 'Chomolangma'

Qu (M) – administrative district

rangjung – self-manifesting or self-arising; for example, a rock spire could be a rangjung chörten

rebirth – a condition of the Wheel of Life; all beings experience limitless rebirths until they achieve enlightenment

regent – a representative of an incarnate lama who presides over a monastic community during the lama's minority; regents came to play an important political role in the Gelugpa lamaist government

ri – mountain

Rinpoche – literally 'high in esteem', a title bestowed on highly revered lamas; such lamas are usually incarnate but this is not a requirement

ritrö – hermitage

RMB – acronym for Renminbi or 'people's money', the currency of China

rogyapas – the 'body breakers' who prepare bodies for sky burial

sadhu – an Indian ascetic who has renounced all attachments

Saga Dawa – festival held at the full moon of the fourth lunar month to celebrate the enlightenment of Sakyamuni

Sakyapa – Tibetan Buddhist order associated with Sakya Monastery and founded in the 11th century; also known as the Red Hats

samsara (S) – 'kyor dumi' in Tibetan; the cycle of birth, death and rebirth

Samye – the first Buddhist monastery in Tibet, founded by King Trisong Detsen in the 8th century

sang – incense

sangha (S) – community of Buddhist monks or nuns

sangkang – pot-bellied incense burners

Sanskrit – ancient language of India; a classical mode of expression with the status that Latin had in earlier Western society

self-arising – thought to have been created naturally (ie not by humans); often applied to rock carvings; see also *rangjung*

serdung – golden funeral stupa

Shambhala – the mythical great northern paradise, believed to be near the Kunlun mountains

Shangshung – ancient kingdom of western Tibet and place of origin of the Bön faith

shedra – Buddhist college

sky burial – funerary practice of chopping up the corpses of the dead in designated high places (dürtro) and leaving them for the birds

spirit trap – collection of coloured threads wrapped around a wooden frame, used to trap evil spirits

stupa – see *chörten*

sutra (S) – Buddhist scriptures that record the teachings of the Historical Buddha, Sakyamuni

suzerainty – system whereby a dominant power controls a region or country's foreign relations but allows it sovereignty in its internal affairs

Tantra – scriptures and oral lineages associated with Tantric Buddhism

Tantric – of Tantric Buddhism, a movement combining mysticism with Buddhist scripture

TAR – Tibetan Autonomous Region

Tengyur – a Tibetan Buddhist canonical text of collected commentaries on the teachings of Sakyamuni

terma – 'discovered' or 'revealed' teachings; teachings that have been hidden until the world is ready to receive them; one of the most famous *termas* is the *Tibetan Book of the Dead*

terton – discoverer of *terma*, sometimes referred to as a 'treasure finder'

thamzing (M) – 'struggle sessions', a misconceived Chinese tool for changing the ideological orientation of individuals; ultimately a coercive tool that encouraged deceit under the threat of torture

thangka – a Tibetan religious painting usually framed by a silk brocade

Theravada – see *Hinayana*

thugpa – traditional Tibetan noodle dish

torana – halo-like garland that surrounds Buddhist statues

torma – offerings of sculptured *tsampa*

trapa – Tibetan for 'monk'

tratsang – monastic college

Tripa – the post of abbot at Ganden Monastery; head of the Gelugpa order

trulku – incarnate lama, sometimes inaccurately called a 'Living Buddha' by the Chinese

tsampa – roasted-barley flour, traditional staple of the Tibetan people

tsangkhang – inner chapel

tsangpo – large river

tsatsa – stamped clay religious icons

tsenyi lhakhang – debating hall

tso – 'lake'

tsogchen – cathedral or great chapel, also an assembly hall

tsuglhakhang – literally 'grand temple', but often specifically the Jokhang of Lhasa

TTB – Tibet Tourism Bureau

Ütsang – the area comprising the provinces of Ü and Tsang, also incorporating Ngari, or western Tibet; effectively central Tibet, the political, historical and agricultural heartland of Tibet

Vajrayana (S) – literally the 'diamond vehicle', a branch of Mahayana Buddhism that finds a more direct route to bodhisattva-hood through identification with meditational deities; vajrayana is the Sanskrit term for the form of Buddhism found in Tibet, known in the West as Tantrism

Wheel of Life – this term refers to the cyclical nature of existence and the six realms where rebirth takes place; often depicted in monasteries

xian (M) – country town

xiang (M) – village

yabyum – Tantric sexual union, symbolising the mental union of female insight and male compassion; fierce deities are often depicted in yabyum with their consorts

yidam – see *meditational deity*; may also have the function of being a personal protector deity that looks over an individual or family

yogin (S: yoga) – an adept of Tibetan Buddhist techniques for achieving a union with the fundamental nature of reality; the techniques include meditation and identification with a meditational deity

yuan (M) – unit of Chinese currency

zhāodàisuŏ (M) – guesthouse, usually a basic hostel

Behind the Scenes

SEND US YOUR FEEDBACK

We love to hear from travellers – your comments keep us on our toes and help make our books better. Our well-travelled team reads every word on what you loved or loathed about this book. Although we cannot reply individually to postal submissions, we always guarantee that your feedback goes straight to the appropriate authors, in time for the next edition. Each person who sends us information is thanked in the next edition – the most useful submissions are rewarded with a selection of digital PDF chapters.

Visit **lonelyplanet.com/contact** to submit your updates and suggestions or to ask for help. Our award-winning website also features inspirational travel stories, news and discussions.

Note: We may edit, reproduce and incorporate your comments in Lonely Planet products such as guidebooks, websites and digital products, so let us know if you don't want your comments reproduced or your name acknowledged. For a copy of our privacy policy visit lonelyplanet.com/privacy.

OUR READERS

Many thanks to the travellers who used the last edition and wrote to us with helpful hints, useful advice and interesting anecdotes: Albert Horváth, Alfonso Para, Annebeth Muntinga, Dania Hasberg & Robert Rauer, Jason Whyte, Jim Brennan, Martin Kesting, Melissa Catelli, Patrick Bruyere, Pierre Laffont, Tanja Nijhoff

AUTHOR THANKS

Megan Eaves

My sincere thanks to my fellow Tibet writers: Bradley, for the considerable expertise and advice; Stephen, for sharing beers on a Lhasa rooftop and taking everything in your stride. Thanks also to my guide Palmo, who showed me the kindness and compassion of the Tibetan people. I also owe thanks, as always, to Jennifer Carey and Tom Hall at Lonely Planet, who have given me my dream job and trust me to run off and do it. And to my family, who unfailingly support my wild wanderlust. To Bill, for getting me to this part of my life. And finally, my truest gratitude to the many nuns and monks across Tsang who welcomed me into their sacred spaces and taught me to see the oneness of all things.

Stephen Lioy

Many people deserve a སྒུལ་རྗེ་ཆེ།. Megan, for trusting me with a complicated, rewarding destination and for our research on the best craft beers in Lhasa and Chéngdū. Major thanks to Tashi and our tireless driver, both of whom helped to find the beauty in every last Tibetan town. Chéngdū is always better with Alina, and doubly so for the introductions to Jordan and Yereth.

Bradley Mayhew

Thanks to Tibet Highland Tours, especially Dechen and small Tenzin, and to guide Tashi and driver Tsering for yet another excellent trip to western Tibet. Thanks to Sandra Braunfels for being a great travel companion. Sonam Jamphel of Explore Tibet and Jamin York of Himalaya Journeys were both generous with their expertise. Cheers to Tenzin Dhondup and to Pasang at the Gesar Hotel.

ACKNOWLEDGMENTS

Climate map data adapted from Peel MC, Finlayson BL & McMahon TA (2007) 'Updated World Map of the Köppen-Geiger Climate Classification', Hydrology and Earth System Sciences, 11, 1633-44.

Cover photograph: Monk with prayer beads, Reinhard Goldmann/Getty ©

THIS BOOK

This 10th edition of Lonely Planet's *Tibet* guidebook was curated by Stephen Lioy, and researched and written by Stephen, Megan Eaves and Bradley Mayhew. The previous edition was written by Bradley Mayhew and Robert Kelly. This guidebook was produced by the following:

Destination Editors Megan Eaves, Joe Bindloss
Senior Product Editor Kate Chapman
Regional Senior Cartographer Valentina Kremenchutskaya
Product Editor Joel Cotterell
Cartographer Julie Dodkins
Book Designer Wibowo Rusli

Assisting Editors Katie Connolly, Kate Daly, Andrea Dobbin, Victoria Harrison, Kristin Odijk
Cover Researcher Naomi Parker
Thanks to Ewa Dziarnowska, Paul Harding, Andi Jones, Anne Mason, Jamin York, Guan Yuanyuan

Index

Map Legend

Sights

- Beach
- Bird Sanctuary
- Buddhist
- Castle/Palace
- Christian
- Confucian
- Hindu
- Islamic
- Jain
- Jewish
- Monument
- Museum/Gallery/Historic Building
- Ruin
- Sento Hot Baths/Onsen
- Shinto
- Sikh
- Taoist
- Winery/Vineyard
- Zoo/Wildlife Sanctuary
- Other Sight

Activities, Courses & Tours

- Bodysurfing
- Diving/Snorkelling
- Canoeing/Kayaking
- Course/Tour
- Skiing
- Snorkelling
- Surfing
- Swimming/Pool
- Walking
- Windsurfing
- Other Activity

Sleeping

- Sleeping
- Camping

Eating

- Eating

Drinking & Nightlife

- Drinking & Nightlife
- Cafe

Entertainment

- Entertainment

Shopping

- Shopping

Information

- Bank
- Embassy/Consulate
- Hospital/Medical
- Internet
- Police
- Post Office
- Telephone
- Toilet
- Tourist Information
- Other Information

Geographic

- Beach
- Hut/Shelter
- Lighthouse
- Lookout
- Mountain/Volcano
- Oasis
- Park
- Pass
- Picnic Area
- Waterfall

Population

- Capital (National)
- Capital (State/Province)
- City/Large Town
- Town/Village

Transport

- Airport
- Border crossing
- Bus
- Cable car/Funicular
- Cycling
- Ferry
- Metro station
- Monorail
- Parking
- Petrol station
- Subway station
- Taxi
- Train station/Railway
- Tram
- Underground station
- Other Transport

Note: Not all symbols displayed above appear on the maps in this book

Routes

- Tollway
- Freeway
- Primary
- Secondary
- Tertiary
- Lane
- Unsealed road
- Road under construction
- Plaza/Mall
- Steps
- Tunnel
- Pedestrian overpass
- Walking Tour
- Walking Tour detour
- Path/Walking Trail

Boundaries

- International
- State/Province
- Disputed
- Regional/Suburb
- Marine Park
- Cliff
- Wall

Hydrography

- River, Creek
- Intermittent River
- Canal
- Water
- Dry/Salt/Intermittent Lake
- Reef

Areas

- Airport/Runway
- Beach/Desert
- Cemetery (Christian)
- Cemetery (Other)
- Glacier
- Mudflat
- Park/Forest
- Sight (Building)
- Sportsground
- Swamp/Mangrove

OUR STORY

A beat-up old car, a few dollars in the pocket and a sense of adventure. In 1972 that's all Tony and Maureen Wheeler needed for the trip of a lifetime – across Europe and Asia overland to Australia. It took several months, and at the end – broke but inspired – they sat at their kitchen table writing and stapling together their first travel guide, *Across Asia on the Cheap*. Within a week they'd sold 1500 copies. Lonely Planet was born.

Today, Lonely Planet has offices in Franklin, London, Melbourne, Oakland, Beijing and Delhi, with more than 600 staff and writers. We share Tony's belief that 'a great guidebook should do three things: inform, educate and amuse'.

OUR WRITERS

Stephen Lioy

Ü, Eastern Tibet, Chengdu Stephen is a photographer, writer, hiker, and travel blogger based in Central Asia. A 'once in a lifetime' Eurotrip and post-university move to China set the stage for what would eventually become a semi-nomadic lifestyle based on sharing his experiences with would-be travellers and helping provide that initial push out of comfort zones and into all that the planet has to offer. Follow Stephen's travels at www.monkboughtlunch.com or see his photography at www.stephenlioy.com.

Megan Eaves

Tsang, Xining, Qinghai–Tibet Railway Megan is Lonely Planet's North Asia Destination Editor and her writing has appeared in Lonely Planet's guidebooks to China and South Korea. Having lived everywhere from her home state of New Mexico to eastern China and Prague, she's now based in Lonely Planet's London office, where she's the resident beer nerd and dumpling addict. If lost, she is likely to be found stargazing in a desert somewhere.

Bradley Mayhew

Lhasa, Ngari, Tibetan Treks, Kathmandu Bradley has been writing guidebooks for 20 years now. He started travelling while studying Chinese at Oxford University, and has since focused his expertise on China, Tibet, the Himalayas and Central Asia. He is the co-author of Lonely Planet guides to *Tibet, Nepal, Trekking in the Nepal Himalaya, Bhutan, Central Asia* and many others. Bradley has also fronted two TV series for Arte and SWR, one retracing the route of Marco Polo via Turkey, Iran, Afghanistan, Central Asia and China, and the other trekking Europe's ten most scenic long-distance trails. Bradley also wrote the Plan, Understand and Survival Guide chapters.

Published by Lonely Planet Publications Pty Ltd
ABN 36 005 607 983
10th edition – May 2019
ISBN 978 1 78657 375 9
© Lonely Planet 2019   Photographs © as indicated 2019
10 9 8 7 6 5 4 3 2 1
Printed in Singapore

Although the authors and Lonely Planet have taken all reasonable care in preparing this book, we make no warranty about the accuracy or completeness of its content and, to the maximum extent permitted, disclaim all liability arising from its use.